CLOSED·END FUNDS

THE COMPLETE GUIDE TO

5TH EDITION

CLOSED END FUNDS

FINDING VALUE IN TODAY'S STOCK MARKET

JON CHATFIELD

EDITOR

International Publishing Corporation
Chicago, Illinois

Library of Congress Catalog Number: 93-78543

ISBN Number: 0-942641-52-3

The data in this *Guide* were gathered from company releases. This publication is designed to provide accurate and authoritative information in regard to the subject matter covered. However, it is sold with the understanding that the publisher is not engaged in rendering legal or professional investment services. If legal advice or other expert assistance is required, a competent professional should be retained.

Table of Contents

Preface

Misconception Number One: Because a fund is selling at a substantial discount to net asset value, something must be wrong. It's as if they were damaged merchandise and must be sold off cheap. Not so!

Misconception Number Two: The discount isn't really all that relevant because you buy at a discount and sell at a discount and so you aren't any better off as a result. As the song goes, "It ain't necessarily so. . . ."

Why pay full price for a stock or bond portfolio when you can get one at a discount? When offered top-of-the-line merchandise at discounts of up to 10 percent or better, do you still insist on paying full retail prices?

Most investors do just that when they pass over closed-end funds in order to buy the more familiar open-end variety. Why are the closed-ends neglected? First, closed-end funds don't advertise as much as their open-ended cousins. Second, brokers don't promote them. Closed-end funds are not as profitable, commission-wise, as other financial products. Brokers are paid attractive commissions only when the closed-end fund is initially offered. After the Initial Public Offering (IPO), the broker receives a standard commission to buy or sell shares of closed-end funds. As a result, many investors don't know closed-end funds exist, or that they provide a discount-store approach to investing.

The closed-end funds covered in this book include nearly all closed-end funds traded on the New York Stock Exchange (NYSE), American Stock Exchange (AMEX), and Over-The-Counter (OTC) markets. Approximately 30 percent of these funds are equity; 70 percent bond. Of the 373 funds covered in this *Guide,* 8 trade on the OTC, 27 on the AMEX, and 338 on the NYSE.

This *Guide* will simplify working with this large and dynamic market. It begins in Chapter 1 with a definition of closed-end funds including their major attractions, methods of tracking the discount or premium, and a list of sources that supply regular net asset value and share prices. Chapter 2 discusses recent developments and how these new changes are affecting the closed-end fund market. Chapter 3 provides a description of various fund characteristics, including investment objectives, dividend distributions and tax considerations, services, costs, and fees, shareholder reports, and other special considerations. Chapter 4 elaborates on the various fund categories with a discussion of the assorted bond and equity funds.

Chapter 5 presents guidelines for creating model portfolios, risk tolerance considerations, and a discussion of how to select specific closed-end funds. Chapter 6 will assist you in reading the fund summaries contained in the book.

Once you have become familiar with closed-end funds, their characteristics, and how to structure a portfolio with them, review the fund performance rankings in Chapter 7. Chapters 8 and 9 contain the fund summaries, and Chapter 10 lists those funds with less than one year of operating history.

For more information about any fund, write or call the fund to obtain a copy of its prospectus and latest annual report. Carefully review this information, keeping in mind what you have learned in this *Guide*, before making investment decisions. Finally, the Appendix offers additional sources of information.

1

Closed-End Funds:
An Overview

DEFINITION

Closed-end investment company, publicly traded fund, investment trust, and publicly traded investment fund are all terms applied to the closed-end fund. Similar to open-end mutual funds, a closed-end fund is created when investors pool their money for a shared investment goal. Collective buying power affords an opportunity to participate in a well-diversified professionally managed investment portfolio.

Closed-end funds differ from open-end funds in one very distinct way. While the shares of an open-end mutual fund can be continually issued or redeemed on demand at net asset value (NAV), shares of a closed-end fund cannot. For the most part, the capitalization of a closed-end fund is fixed. New shares may be created to satisfy capital gains distributions, and occasionally rights offerings for additional shares are issued to shareholders, but unlike open-ends, there is no continuing offering of new shares. Sometimes a closed-end fund may choose to repurchase some of its outstanding shares on the open market. But this is not a regular requirement for the benefit of shareholders wishing to sell. Usually, the only way a closed-end fund can redeem its shares at NAV is when it open-ends, is liquidated, or when a tender offer is made.

Investors who wish to sell their shares must find a buyer. This transaction is facilitated by listing the shares on one of the major stock exchanges. Share price is determined independently of NAV by factors of supply and demand, general market sentiment, portfolio composition, yield, fees, liquidity, and extraneous factors such as year-end tax selling or unrealized capital gains.

MAJOR ATTRACTIONS

Closed-end funds are an attractive investment alternative because they offer professional investment management, a portfolio of diversified securities, and the opportunity to purchase these assets at a discount.

Professional Investment Management

Most of us lack the time, temperament, or training necessary to manage our investments on a full-time basis, but neither can we afford to hire a full-time professional investment manager. Pooling our investment dollars in a closed-end fund allows us to hire a professional manager and spread the cost of the management fee. The manager decides what and when to buy or sell, what and when to hold, and when it may be more advisable to own dollars instead of stocks or bonds.

This is also true of open-end mutual funds, but there is one important difference. Because of the fixed capitalization structure of closed-end funds, managers are not hampered by continuous buying and selling of fund shares in order to accommodate new investors and redemptions. This responsibility of open-end funds frequently conflicts with ideal market timing. A well-managed closed-end fund can generally buy and sell on more favorable terms and thus maintain a consistent investment philosophy.

Diversification

Diversification reduces risk by spreading investments over a broad spectrum of holdings. A closed-end fund can take pooled assets to the market and make not a few but many purchases. The combined buying power allows diversification in many different companies, industries, and countries. The closed-end fund arena includes aggressive, balanced, and conservative stock funds, taxable and tax-free income funds, precious metals, bullion, global, and international funds.

There are two basic types of closed-end fund: diversified and non-diversified. Diversified funds generally offer greater stability and lower risk because of the broader base and resulting higher liquidity of holdings. Non-diversified funds only invest in one type of security although they can own many different issues. An example of a non-diversified fund would be a precious metal fund or a single state municipal bond fund. The opening statement of every fund prospectus discloses the degree of portfolio diversification. (This information is also available in the fund summaries in this *Guide*.)

Marketability

Shares of closed-end funds are afforded a high degree of liquidity because they are traded on the major exchanges. Shares may be purchased from either a full-service securities broker or dealer, or a discount broker.

Closed-end funds may be purchased either in an Initial Public Offering (IPO) or in the aftermarket. As a rule of thumb, unless a fund offers something unique, such as an opportunity to invest in closed or restricted markets (Chile, Mexico, Korea), it should be bought in the aftermarket when the chance exists for purchase at a discount to NAV.

Regulation

Closed-end funds are regulated by the Securities and Exchange Commission (SEC), the Securities Act of 1933, the Securities Exchange Act of 1934, and the Investment Company Act of 1940. The statutes require that full disclosure of all relevant fund characteristics be made available to potential investors through the issuance of a prospectus. They also mandate that shareholders be kept informed of fund activities and developments through quarterly, semiannual, or annual reports. Normally, the reports contain a message from management regarding fund performance, the outlook for the economy, portfolio composition, expenses incurred to operate the fund, and other information specific to the operation and performance of the fund.

Discounts

The Efficient Market Theory holds that at any given time stocks are accurately priced because they always reflect all the current market information. The major implication of this theory is that no one, except by sheer luck, can consistently beat the market. Closed-end funds could still present an exception to this theory.

Shares of equity closed-end funds have historically traded at discounts to their underlying NAV. (For a more complete discussion of the discount see Chapter 2, Recent Developments.) Discounts generally deepen during uncertain economic times and shrink, or move to a premium, during upward-moving markets. Actual trends can be determined by reviewing various closed-end fund resources listed in Appendix B of this book.

In the past, this characteristic of closed-end funds presented some rather interesting possibilities for both profit and loss. For example, assume that unfavorable and depressed market conditions have forced the shares of the ABC closed-end fund with a $10 per share NAV to sell for only $8, i.e., at a 20 percent discount. But then the clouds of pessimism are dispersed and a bull rally doubles the fund's NAV to $20 per share. Investor elation then propels the shares up from a 20 percent discount to a 20 percent premium above the new $20 price, or to $24. The providential result: While the fund's NAV increased just 100 percent (from $10 to $20), the share price increased 200 percent (from $8 to $24). This not-so-imaginary example illustrates how closed-end funds could easily double the performance of the market averages in both directions. However, recent increasing investor involvement in the closed-end market has resulted in a considerable narrowing of both average discounts and discount swings.

Despite increasing investor awareness, it is still possible to profit by buying closed-end funds at a discount and then selling them when the discount shrinks. Such a strategy is not merely theoretical but has actually been shown to work.

As an Assistant Professor at the University of Alabama, Seth Copeland Anderson studied eight different closed-end fund trading strategies and then compared their investment results. Each of the trading systems required purchasing funds at specific discounts from NAV and later selling the shares when the discounts narrowed to a predetermined and smaller percentage. The study, published in the Fall 1986 issue of the *The Journal of Portfolio Management*, used the weekly stock price, NAV, and distribution data for 17 diversified and specialized closed-end funds over three independent time periods:

- July 1965 to December 1969
- January 1970 to December 1976
- January 1977 to August 1984

At the time of the study, the selected funds represented approximately 85 percent of the total assets of all the closed-end funds.

Each portfolio consisted of $100,000, equally divided among those funds that met the criteria for each of the eight investment strategies. If four funds under Strategy 2 were selling at discounts of more than 10 percent, equal dollar amounts of $25,000 were invested in each. The funds were then held until the discount dropped to 5 percent. As shares were sold, or if a new fund met the criteria for inclusion in the portfolio, the dollar amounts were readjusted to always allow an equal amount to be invested in each fund.

The results produced a perfect record with every one of the trading systems tested, over all three periods, beating the performance of the Standard & Poor's Index of 500 common stocks (S&P 500). The most successful strategy was to buy those funds selling at a 20 percent discount and to sell them when the discount narrowed to 15 percent. On a compounded basis, this purely mechanical technique produced an astounding return of nearly 3,000 percent over the combined 20-year test period. Professor Anderson found that investors beat the market as well over each of the three time periods even without active trading: funds were simply bought at the beginning of each period and sold at the end.

The study results provide possible trading strategies that could enable investors to earn excess rates of return and demonstrate that the inefficiencies of the market for closed-end fund shares do offer potential for profit. Table 1.1 presents the results of this study.

The evolutionary changes that have taken place in the closed-end fund market since the original Anderson study have greatly affected overall discounts. For a number of reasons, specified in the Recent Developments Chapter (Chapter 2) of this book, discounts for nearly all closed-end funds have considerably narrowed. Recent studies have shown that the strategy and methods utilized by the Anderson study remain valid, however, the discount ranges must be adjusted to reflect the new environment. In addition, new strategies for trading closed-end funds are emerging with the changing market.

The case for closed-end funds remains compelling. With their discounts, low fees, and coherent management, they particularly lend themselves to asset allocation and multifund investing.

TRACKING THE DISCOUNT OR PREMIUM

Closed-end fund share discounts or premiums are determined by comparing NAV with the market price. NAV is calculated by totaling the market value of all securities in the fund portfolio, adding all other assets such as cash or equivalents, deducting all liabilities, and then dividing by the number of shares outstanding. When the market value of a share is above its NAV, it is said to be selling at a premium. When market price is below the NAV, it is selling at a discount. The formula used to determine the actual premium or discount is:

$$\frac{(\text{Stock Price} - \text{NAV})}{\text{NAV}}$$

Table 1.1 Study Results of Eight Trading Strategies (Seth Copeland Anderson)

| Strategies | | Average Performance (%) | | |
| Disc. From NAV for: | | July 1965 to | Jan. 1970 to | Jan. 1977 to |
Buy (%)	Sell (%)	Dec. 1969	Dec. 1976	Aug. 1984
5	0	+114	+105	+260
10	5	+129	+110	+262
15	10	+147	+104	+334
20	10	+136	+ 83	+387
20	15	+135	+126	+448
25	10	+171	+ 61	+404
25	15	+123	+ 86	+387
30	15	+ 49	+ 98	+344
Buy and Hold (No Trading)		+86	+51	+273
Standard & Poor's 500 Index		+24	+49	+126

Adapted from The Journal of Portfolio Management, *Fall 1986, with permission.*

A number of publications report the share premium or discount of closed-end funds in addition to other information. Equity fund figures for Friday are supplied by the Monday edition of *The Wall Street Journal* under the heading "Publicly Traded Funds". The table gives NAV, market price, and premium/discount for the preceding Friday. Figure 1.1 is an example of a Journal listing for a closed-end fund.

In this example, February 8, 1993, the Journal reported that the Adams Express diversified common stock fund, which is traded on the New York Stock Exchange, had a NAV of $21.05 per share, a market price of 20-7/8 per share ($20.88), and was selling at a 0.83 percent discount to NAV. Any footnotes regarding the reporting date, currency exchange rates, and whether the prices reflect dividend or tax payments are shown at the bottom of each chart. The same information can be found every Monday in *Barron's*. The *Barron's* tables also include the bond funds, but these figures are based on closing figures from the previous Friday. The identical bond figures also appear in the Wednesday edition of the *Journal.*

A moving average of individual fund premum/discount figures is available in the monthly newsletter, *The Closed-End Fund Digest* (see Figure 1.2). Value Line and Morningstar also publish summations for selected closed-end funds.

Annual premium/discount figures, along with pertinent information found only in a fund's annual report, are supplied in the tables of each fund summary included in this *Guide*. Investors who are familiar with closed-end fund investing can go directly to Chapter 7, where fund performance rankings for 1992 are listed by category, followed by the fund summaries. Individuals who require more information about closed-end fund characteristics, how categories are defined, and how to interpret the fund summaries should review Chapters 2-5.

Figure 1.1 An Example of a Closed-End Fund Quotation

Fund Name	Stock Exch.	N.A. Value	Stock Price	% Diff.
Diversified Common Stock Funds				
Adams Express	NYSE	21.05	20-7/8	-0.83

Source: The Wall Street Journal, *February 8, 1993*

Figure 1.2 Equity Fund Statistics

Fund	Sym.	-As of 1/29/93-			Cur 12 Mo.	12 Mo.	-1/31/92-		-12 Mo. TR-	
		Stk Pr	NAV	Pr/Dsc	Avg p/d	Dist	Stk Pr	NAV	Stk Pr	NAV
Adams Express	ADX	20.000	20.48	(2.34%)	(4.61%)	1.62	19.000	20.21	13.79%	9.35%
Baker Fentress	BKF	17.000	20.83	(18.39%)	(15.23%)	1.52	17.625	21.42	5.08%	4.34%
Bergstrom Cap	BEM	132.125	102.63	28.74%	16.97%	2.00	126.500	99.78	6.03%	4.86%
Blue Chip Value	BLU	7.750	7.63	1.57%	0.72%	0.58	7.625	8.36	9.25%	(1.79%)
CenFd Canada	CEF	3.625	3.99	(9.15%)	(7.90%)	0.00	3.875	4.28	(6.45%)	(6.78%)
Central Sec	CET	11.625	13.85	(16.06%)	(17.79%)	0.86	9.250	11.61	34.97%	26.70%
Allmon Trust	GSO	10.000	10.28	(2.72%)	(5.96%)	0.50	10.000	10.40	5.03%	3.68%
Couns Tandem	CTF	14.125	16.54	(14.60%)	(13.89%)	0.91	14.125	16.88	6.42%	3.35%
Dover Reg Finl	DVRFS	6.000	7.41	(19.03%)	n/a	0.00	n/a	n/a	n/a	n/a
Engex Inc	EGX	9.125	11.98	(23.83%)	(21.06%)	0.00	8.750	11.03	4.29%	8.61%
Gabelli Trust	GAB	10.250	10.58	(3.12%)	0.13%	1.06	10.125	10.61	11.70%	9.71%
Gen'l Am Inv	GAM	30.000	28.56	5.04%	0.97%	2.00	29.000	30.60	10.34%	(0.13%)
Inefficient Mkt Fd	IMF	9.875	11.49	(14.06%)	(12.18%)	0.05	8.875	10.34	11.83%	11.61%
Jundt Growth Fund	JF	14.875	15.57	(4.46%)	(4.27%)	0.00	16.000	15.46	(7.03%)	0.71%
Liberty All-Star	USA	11.125	10.78	3.20%	0.98%	1.07	10.750	11.20	13.44%	5.80%
MG Sm Cap	MGC	12.250	11.95	2.51%	(1.02%)	0.80	12.875	12.30	1.36%	3.66%
Patriot Prem Div	PDF	10.375	10.46	(0.81%)	(0.89%)	0.80	9.375	10.22	19.21%	10.19%
Patriot Prem Div II	PDT	11.750	12.56	(6.45%)	(3.97%)	0.90	11.625	12.47	8.82%	7.94%
Patriot Sel Div Tr	DIV	17.750	16.22	9.43%	7.21%	1.64	16.750	16.71	15.78%	6.90%
Pfd Income Fd	PFD	18.375	17.11	7.39%	2.90%	2.94	18.000	16.15	18.42%	24.15%
Pfd Inc Opp Fd	PFO	13.000	12.24	6.21%	n/a	1.14	n/a	n/a	n/a	n/a
Putnam Div Inc	PDI	12.250	11.53	6.24%	5.57%	1.16	10.875	11.35	23.26%	11.76%
Royce Value Tr	RVT	12.250	12.51	(2.08%)	(5.18%)	0.90	10.375	11.22	26.75%	19.52%
Salomon Bros Fd	SBF	13.750	15.16	(9.30%)	(7.98%)	0.90	13.875	15.66	5.59%	2.55%
Source Cap	SOR	47.750	42.87	11.38%	9.61%	3.60	44.250	41.23	16.05%	12.71%
Tri-Continental	TY	25.500	28.03	(9.03%)	(4.11%)	0.78	27.750	28.61	(5.30%)	0.70%
Zweig Fund	ZF	13.000	11.36	14.44%	13.70%	1.14	13.750	12.40	2.84%	0.81%
Group Average				(2.20%)	(2.69%)				10.06%	7.24%

Reprinted with Permission, The Closed-End Fund Digest, *February 1993, Madent Publishing Co., Inc.*

2

Recent Developments

In less than ten years closed-end mutual funds have emerged as vibrant and viable investment vehicles. Since 1986, the number of closed-end funds has more than quadrupled to over 380 funds.

Once relegated to the investment scrap heap after the Crash of 1929, another Crash, that of 1987, saw them rise from the ashes to reach extraordinary heights of attention. A plethora of new funds came to market. Capital flooded into new issue single country funds and, most notably, tax-free municipal funds. In fact, John Nuveen & Co. is the current reigning king of closed-end funds, with nearly a fifth of the $92 billion market under management.

The rapid expansion of the closed-end fund realm should continue to accelerate now that topics unique to the vehicle have drawn the attention of industry groups and the SEC. At the top of the list are two items: 1. the question of the discount to net asset value and 2. how to bring more flexibility to the funds. In mid-1991, SEC and industry responses to these questions resulted in revolutionary change, aspects of which are discussed below.

SOARING ASSETS, NARROWING DISCOUNTS

1993 was a banner year for closed-end funds. But it was much more than capital influx, rising NAVs, and soaring share prices. It was also a year of profound change in the market. The most significant occurrence, separate from any influence from policy issues, was the continued shrinkage of the discount. Since 1979, the average discount for domestic equity funds has narrowed from around 29 percent to about 4 percent. While it is true that the field for this group is relatively small, there are only about a dozen truly diversified domestic funds, and many of those have either high payout policies or provisions to open-end at some future point. Year-end discounts on all categories of closed-end funds were indicative of the changing environment. On the equity side, where larger discounts were the historic norm, Dual-Purpose funds traded at near parity, Multi Country funds at a negative 6.9 percent, Single Country funds at a negative 7.9 percent, and Convertible funds traded at a 7.6 percent discount. The Bond Income funds saw their discounts move to premiums. Most prominent were the Tax-Free group trading at a 6.4 percent premium, Investment Grade Corporates traded at 3.3 percent premiums, U.S. Government funds at a 3.1 percent premium, International funds (really currency plays) at practically NAV, Multi-Sector, minus 1.1 percent, and Junk at a 3.8 percent discount.

This appears to present a problem for value hunters because it is difficult to justify the payment of a premium for a fund. One of the historical appeals of closed-end fund investing has been the ability to trade the discount spectrum. (See Seth Anderson's Study on page 5.) While it is still prudent to avoid significant overvaluations, it is even more important to recognize that narrow discounts are no longer reasons to avoid specific funds. Gone are the days when investors could move to the sidelines to wait out shrinking discount cycles.

It is still possible to find bargains by comparing average discounts to NAV. Recent studies continue to support the strategy of buying a fund when it trades at a discount that is 5 percentage points lower than its own average discount. But now, that fund must also trade at a wider discount than that of similar funds to rate as a buy.

As an example, if a fund that normally trades with a 10 percent discount to NAV can be purchased at a 15 percent discount, it is a buy only if similar funds are not trading at a 20 percent or wider discount.

WHY THE DISCOUNT?

Historically, closed-end funds have traded at discounts to their NAV. The question of why is multi-faceted. Primarily discounts exist because investors have not been able to redeem their shares on demand at NAV. Unlike open-end mutual funds that continually issue and redeem shares at NAV, closed-end funds have a fixed number of shares that trade on a stock exchange. The result is that supply and demand determine share price.

Another cause for discount has been the lack of promotion for closed-end funds by the brokerage community. It's ironic that the only time such promotion occurs is when a new fund is being pushed to market. But that's the very worst time to purchase a closed-end fund because offering fees and commissions are built into the price and constitute premiums. After the fund is floated, the once hot sales topic all but disappears.

High expense ratios are another reason closed-end funds can trade at a discount. Sometimes it's just not worth a 2 or 3 percent management fee to assemble a portfolio.

Tax liability can also lead to discounts. For instance, suppose a mature fund had purchased shares of Apple computer and Xerox during their formative stages at very low prices. Further, suppose that the fund now has a NAV of $12, of which $5 is unrealized gain on the value of those judiciously purchased shares. When the fund sells out those positions they will have $12 in cash and will distribute the $5 as a capital gains distribution. The investor will have to pay a tax on that $5 gain even if his or her funds did not earn it. But just because a fund can be identified as trading at a wide discount as a result of unrealized capital gains, don't pass it by. It's still an excellent candidate for IRA and pension accounts where the tax liability is nullified.

Discounts can also be the result of illiquidity. This can be a problem with funds that have restricted securities or invest in small or low capitalized or specific foreign markets. Poor performance can be another factor. Some funds have stringent anti-takeover provisions that can protect poor management. Currency risks can also cause discounts in funds that invest abroad. Any one or a combination of these issues can result in a closed-end fund that trades at a discount to NAV.

THE INDUSTRY TACKLES THE DISCOUNT

1991 will be remembered as the year the industry began to seriously address several of these discount factors. The end result has been that we have now entered the era of narrow discounts. This is not to be viewed as a brief occurrence, it is an evolutionary event. There are a handful of basic reasons behind this phenomenon. The easiest explanation lies in the recognition of the rapid growth of the industry and the resultant increase in investor awareness. More and more brokerage firms, investment advisers, and individuals are trading closed-ends. Many newsletters are springing up to track the market. The consequence has been an increase in the general knowledge and activity in the market, and the shrinkage of the discount.

Secondly, many new funds have introduced innovative mechanisms in their charters specifically designed to narrow the discount. Among the first devices to occur several years ago was the pay-out policies adopted by many equity funds. Share tender option features were also introduced, and some funds inaugurated open-ending provisions. As the trend extended, discounts continued to narrow.

Once it is understood, on a broader scale, that these devices are now in place and expanding, new opportunities will be found to trade closed-end funds with small discounts. It is safe to say that from now on, certain closed-end funds can be purchased at discounts that are narrower than historical averages.

THE FRANKENSTEIN FUNDS (HYBRIDS)

By far the most important change affecting the shrinking of the discount has been the recognition of the traditional bane of all closed-end fund investors, the inability to exit a fund at NAV. In response to this curse, a new product looms on the horizon. The concept, first introduced by the SEC in late May of 1991 at an industry conference sponsored by the Investment Company Institute, promotes the creation of a hybrid mutual fund that would combine the features of both open-end and closed-end funds. SEC chairman Richard C. Breeden told leaders of the conference that the SEC is considering "increasing flexibility of choice" for investors by the creation of a third category of mutual fund, the Hybrid fund. These funds will be similar in all aspects to closed-end funds, but investors will be able to redeem shares periodically at NAV.

Shareholders of existing closed-end funds will be able to vote to adopt this new format. While exact details describing the nature of the proposed fund have yet to be determined, the key feature of hybrid funds is this redemption right. Such a right would allow the shareholder to redeem shares at NAV as often as once a month or perhaps every quarter.

Even if the right occurred only once a quarter it could effectively eliminate the tendency of equity funds to trade at discounts yet still allow managers to go about the business of investing without undue worry about skittish investors. Plus, once it's possible to get out of a fund at, or even near NAV, it becomes prudent to buy funds previously considered to be trading at too narrow a discount.

A word of caution. While these proposed SEC changes will permit funds to make periodic redemptions at NAV, there is no certainty that existing fund management will bring the issue to a shareholder vote. Don't forget, there is a basic conflict of interest between fund management and shareholders that is tied to the question of compensation. The threat of a shrinking asset pool due to redemptions or buybacks leads to a shrinking management fee.

NEW WAYS TO ANALYZE A FUND

When trying to determine the merits of a particular closed-end fund the investor should run through the following checklist:

1. What is the discount/premium? Discount analysis still remains the most important consideration for an investor.

2. Is the fund's discount wider than average? Is it wider than other funds in its category? Is the fund at a premium?

3. Should the fund be a candidate for shorting? Many municipal funds fall into this camp if one can borrow the shares and is willing to take on the responsibility for paying the dividend.

4. What is the expense ratio? Is it higher or lower than other funds in the same category?

5. What is the dividend ratio? Look in the latest quarterly reports. Is it comparable to other similar funds?

6. What has been the historical performance for the fund? While important, performance can be the most misleading of all the variables. Most investors will pay more for a fund or manager with a good performance history. But remember the line, "past performance is not an indication of future results." The Gabelli Equity Fund is a case in point. For many years Mario Gabelli was a top-performing asset manager. When he brought out his Gabelli Equity Fund investors rushed to pay a premium for his historic results and justifiable reputation. However, the fund languished and underperformed the market. Another problem with buying performance can arise when a stellar performing fund may have had its portfolio concentrated in an industry with strong relative strength. When the cycle changes the fund will underperform the market. Of course, a good reverse indicator may be to buy closed-end funds that are invested in areas of weak relative strength, at a wide discount, and when the leadership rotates into that segment the discount will narrow and the fund will have strong performance.

7. How large is the fund? The larger funds can usually afford greater liquidity.

WHERE ARE THE BARGAINS NOW?

In the current market, most of the truly attractive discounts reside in the country funds. When Americans began to look for investment opportunities outside our own borders, a new category of closed-end funds arose to fill the demand. These Single and Multi Country funds allow investment in, say, Chile, where investors can participate in the rapid growth of the region, through a vehicle which trades on the NYSE. These funds chose closed-end status precisely because of the lack of a requirement for shareholder redemption at NAV within seven days. In many less-liquid foreign markets managers are not always able to liquidate their shares within the time frame required by law for open-end funds.

Premiums in the foreign funds generally occur when investors stampede into a fund at the same time on the same news. Because there are very few plays on many foreign markets these funds are easily pushed to premiums. But bad news such as assasinations, coups, earthquakes, floods, volcanic eruptions, currency devaluations, or even U.S. Supreme Court decisions can cause everyone to panic and flee the funds without regard to the actual NAV. Depressing news generally presents the best buying opportunities for these funds. New rules being considered by the SEC will soon present more opportunities for U.S. investors looking overseas.

CHANGES FOR FOREIGN INVESTING

Closed- and open-end mutual fund investors have all been laboring under rules and regulations dating back to 1940. In a world of global economic reality and the potential for 24-hour trading, old ways of doing business are unravelling under the strain.

U.S. markets are not the only places to invest any longer. Opportunities exist on markets all over the world. The American investor is faced with a uniquely modern problem. How can one invest in these foreign markets? American Depositary Receipts (ADRs) have been the traditional method whereby, instead of buying shares of foreign-based companies in overseas markets, Americans can buy shares in the U.S. in the form of an ADR. These receipts for the shares of foreign-based corporations are held in the vault of a U.S. bank. The holder of an ADR is entitled to all dividends and captial gains. ADRs are available for hundreds of stocks from numerous countries.

For the small investor desiring broad overseas diversification, ADRs are not a good choice. Diversity would be possible for U.S. investors if they were allowed to purchase shares of foreign mutual funds. But none are available. Current SEC regulations stipulate that foreign investment companies be governed by the same standards and provide the same safeguards as U.S. mutual funds. The former absence of U.S. demand for foreign mutual funds negated any need for these assurances to be provided.

As a result, no foreign mutual fund has ever been cleared for sale in the U.S. and won't until the SEC standards are changed and/or updated. That's exactly what the SEC is now trying to accomplish. Officials are attempting to develop guidelines that will continue to protect American investors while allowing them to buy overseas funds. Whether current SEC regulations will be relaxed, or if those foreign funds desiring entrance to U.S. markets will provide comparable safeguards remains to be seen.

Publicly traded investment funds will transform and remain as excellent vehicles for participating in international market sectors. One important development will be the continuing expansion into other market spheres, most notably international real estate. As economic perceptions change so will the potential for new profits both here and abroad. Good fortune to all and stay tuned.

RIGHTS OFFERINGS

Rights offerings are a form of corporate financing whereby a company offers to sell to existing stockholders additional shares of the companies stock on a pro-rata basis at a price usually below the current market. Each shareholder is issued rights evidenced by a certificate known as a subscription warrant, which can be exercised before the expiration date. The right may or may not be transferable. If non-transferable, the rights may only be exercised by the shareholder to whom they have been issued. If transferable the rights if not exercised by the shareholder to whom they where issued may be sold prior to their expiration. During the period when the rights are issued and outstanding, the transferable rights will trade separately, while the shares of the original security will trade "ex-rights". The number of shares to be sold will determine the ratio at which shareholders may subscribe. If a corporation has an existing capitalization of 1 million shares and wishes to sell an additional 500,000 shares, the ratio of the number of rights required to purchase one share of stock would be two for one. Two rights are necessary to subscribe for each additional share. The price at which the shareholder purchases the additional share is the "subscription price". The subscription period is limited. When transferable, the value of the right is determined by subtracting the subscription price from the market value and dividing by the number of rights required to purchase one share.

$$\text{Value of 1 right} = \frac{\text{Market Price - Subscription Price}}{\text{Number of rights to subscribe to one share}}$$

Rights offerings are a way of increasing capital available for investment, without disturbing existing stock positions and incurring any capital gains or losses, in order to take advantages of any new perceived investment opportunities. Rights offerings are advantages to the investor from the standpoint that they are able to increase their equity position in the fund, on a pro-rata basis, directly through the corporation, without incurring any commission expense, and usually at favorable prices or a discount . If the stock is already trading at a discount, the rights offering would permit the investor to acquire shares at an extremely favorable price.

Rights offerings increase the number of shares outstanding and thus the fund's liquidity. If the shareholder is unable or unwilling to exercise his rights, and the shares are transferable, the sale of the rights will reduce the investor's overall interest in the fund. However the sale of the rights will result in additional income to the investors, and will result in a capital gain or loss. Usually rights offerings are conducted during periods of market strength, at a time when investor enthusiasm is high. Therefore investors are making additional purchases and the fund manager is investing in new funds during periods of excessive valuations. The sale of rights may result in dilution. For example, suppose a 10 million share fund with total assets of $150,000 million (NAV $15.00) wishes to sell an additional 5 million shares at $14.00 per share, a 7 percent discount to the NAV. After the rights offering, the fund has $220 million in assets which, when divided by 15 million shares outstanding, has a NAV after the rights offering of $14.66, resulting in a dilution of 2.3 percent.

Stockholders Rights Issued in 1992

Bergstrom Capital issued nontransferable rights to stockholders of record January 3. Ten rights were required to subscribe to one share at $103.17. Rights expired January 30.

Duff & Phelps Utilities Income issued one-fifth of a right for each common share to stockholders of record October 2. One whole right entitled shareholders to buy one share at NAV at the close of business October 30. Rights expired October 29 and were nontransferable.

First Australia Prime Income issued to stockholders of record September 9 one-sixth of a right for each common share. One whole right entitled shareholders to purchase one common share. Rights were nontransferable and expired October 9.

Gabelli Equity Trust issued one right for each share of record September 28. Six rights required to purchase one share at $8.00 per share. Rights expired October 28. Rights were transferable.

Jundt Growth Fund, Inc. issued one right for each seven common shares held of record November 26. Each right entitled stockholders to buy one share of common stock at the lower of the NAV or closing price on the Friday preceding the exercise date. Rights were nontransferable and expired on March 19.

Kleinwort Benson Australian Income Fund issued nontransferable rights to stockholders of record August 24. Ten rights were required to buy one share of common at 90 percent of the average of the last sale price on the three trading days after October 5, the date the rights expired.

Liberty All Star Equity Fund issued nontransferable rights to shareholders of record February 27. Ten rights were required to purchase one share of beneficial interest at the lower of 95 percent of the NAV on April 1. Rights expired March 31.

Mexico Fund issued transferable rights to shareholders of record March 20. Three rights were required to purchase one share at $20.00. Rights expired April 8.

Pilgrim Regional Bank Shares issued nontransferable rights to stockholders of record August 14. Three rights were required to purchase one share at $10.50 per share. Rights expired September 17.

RAC Income Fund issued nontransferable rights to stockholders of record December 19. Five rights were required to purchase one share at $11.47. Rights expired January 31.

Royce Value Trust issued nontransferable rights to stockholders of record August 26. Twenty rights were required to purchase one share at the closing price on September 25 less $0.375. Rights expired September 25.

Swiss Helvetia Fund issued nontransferable rights to stockholders of record May 14. Ten rights were required to purchase one share at 90 percent of average closing price for five days beginning June 17. Rights expired June 16.

Transamerica Income Shares issued nontransferable rights to stockholders of record October 30. Five rights were required to purchase one share of stock at 10 percent below the NAV per share on December 4 and the preceding four business days.

3
Closed-End Fund Characteristics

All closed-end funds are registered investment companies and, as such, share several characteristics. All have stated investment objectives, dividend distribution policies, shareholder services, costs and fees, a Board of Directors, and all must provide shareholder reports.

INVESTMENT OBJECTIVE

Each investor is unique, possessing a singular attitude toward investments and specific financial needs. There are many different financial goals.

Though investors may be willing to pool dollar resources to start an investment program, it is not likely that all investors will continue to share the same risk tolerance or have the same constant objectives. Fortunately, there are numerous types of closed-end funds through which investors can pool dollars with other investors sharing the same objectives.

Basically, all closed-end funds fall into one of the following general categories: income, growth, balanced (income and growth), convertible, and specialty. There are numerous alternatives and variations within these categories. Specialty funds, for example, may include international funds, emerging growth funds, single country funds, and specific sector funds. The large number of fund types and objectives allows for a great degree of flexibility. As investment needs change and grow it is helpful to have a wide variety of cost-effective, liquid investment options.

The specific objectives of each fund are disclosed in the prospectus. This *Guide* also presents brief outlines of the investment objectives for each of the funds.

DISTRIBUTIONS AND DIVIDENDS

Investment companies allow more flexibility for the payment of spendable funds than any other investment medium. Although the choices available are wide-ranging, the typical investment company makes only two kinds of payments to its shareholders: income dividends and distributions from capital gains.

Suppose you have decided to begin receiving a check each month. Your monthly checks will result from one or more of four sources. These are:

1. Dividends
2. Realized capital gains
3. Unrealized capital gains
4. Return of principal

If the amount you requested the fund to send each month is more than the dividends the fund is earning, the second source of funds would be your realized capital gains, the profits the fund has made buying and selling stocks. If your withdrawal is more than these two, they will need to use some of your unrealized gains. (This occurs when the fund has bought a stock, and it has increased in value, but they have not yet sold it. Thus the gain is unrealized.) If the amount per month you have requested is greater than these three, you will then start using a portion of your original investment which amounts to a return of principal. This isn't all bad. After all, you have saved it for this purpose. Your primary concern should be to make your savings last as long as you want them to.

The check a month can be an excellent way to use your accumulation in an orderly fashion while keeping the remainder at work in a diversified, continuously managed portfolio of common stocks.

Dividends

As a company prospers, profits are periodically apportioned to shareholders. The amount of these earnings distributions, called dividends, is determined by the company's board of directors and is usually paid quarterly. Dividends paid by closed-end funds represent the net earnings of the fund's investment portfolio after operating expenses are deducted. Unlike other dividend paying companies, such as utilities or mature industrial companies, tax law compels closed-end funds to pay out essentially all net income to their shareholders. They do not hold back or retain earnings.

Investment company dividend payments can be made monthly, quarterly, semi-annually, or annually and are taxable to the shareholder as ordinary income. Typically, the investment company is not subject to any federal tax on investment income. Any tax liability is passed directly through to the shareholder in direct ratio to his or her proportionate share of the securities owned by the fund.

Naturally, fund income dividends can be expected to fluctuate from year to year. This results from variations in prevalent corporate dividend payments and changes in fund investment policy. However, the broad diversity that underlies investment company dividends may result in a higher and more stable income stream than is obtainable from individual corporations.

The relationship between the dividend and the market price of a share is the dividend yield. To find the approximate yield, total all dividend payments made by the investment company for the preceding 12 months, then divide that number by the current offering price (ask price) of the share. The resulting percentage is the dividend yield "estimated return" per share. Do not include any capital gains distributions made during that period, and you may have to adjust the share price by the amount of any reinvested capital gain. Average yields for all the closed-end funds are available in the data pages.

Capital Gains

The difference between the purchase and sale price of an asset is known as the capital gain (or loss). In the course of normal operations, investment companies sell securities. Capital gains distributions occur when the profit from these sales is distributed to the shareholders. Capital gains distributions are naturally irregular. In fact, there is no guarantee that there will be any at all. But many companies have managed to continuously pay out capital gains in varying amounts for many years.

Under our present tax law, all capital gains, whether short-term or long-term, are treated as ordinary income and are taxable to the shareholder at ordinary tax rates which may not exceed 28 percent. Even if you are in a 33 percent bracket, the rate on capital gains cannot exceed 28 percent.

Most investment companies follow a policy of paying out all capital gains to the shareholders. This greatly simplifies tax reporting for the investor, and most investment companies follow this policy. However, sometimes an investment company will retain the realized gains and pay the applicable tax on behalf of the shareholder. Dual-purpose funds normally fall into this category. In this case, the shareholder will take his or her proportionate share of the tax paid on his or her behalf as a credit. The per-share amount of the gain is included on Schedule D of the individual's personal tax return. The investor will have to report the original cost of the shares in order to reveal the percentage of retained capital gains remaining after the tax paid by the company.

Capital gains distributions can distort the dividend yield computation, particularly if the distribution is substantial. Therefore, it is necessary to compensate for the fact that the price of the share will reflect the distribution, but the dividend will not.

For the previous 12 months, a $10 per share fund paid out a total of $0.85 in dividends. If it then paid out a year-end $1 capital gain distribution (10 percent) a justifiable yield figure would be obtained by relating only 90 percent of the previous 12 months' income dividends ($ 0.85) to the year-end price.

Price-per-share of the fund	$10
less $1 capital gains distribution	$9
12 months' dividend	0.85
x 90 percent	0.765
Dividend Yield (0.765 ÷ $9)	8.5%

However, it's more convenient to adjust the price instead of the dividend and merely add back the capital gains distribution.

Price-per-share of the fund	$10
less $1 capital gains distribution	$9
12 months' dividend	0.85
Dividend Yield [0.85 ÷ ($9 + $1)]	8.5%

If price or NAV performance figures are to be determined then adjustments for capital gains distributions are also necessary. A general rule of thumb is to consider the distribution was reinvested if the period in question is over a year. If the performance figures for less than a year are being computed, it is sufficient to add the amount of the distribution to the price or NAV at the end of the period.

Since shareholders usually have the option of receiving capital gains distributions in either additional shares (at NAV) or in cash, it's helpful to explore the benefits and drawbacks of both alternatives.

TO REINVEST OR NOT TO REINVEST

If an investor chooses to spend a portion of his or her principal and recognizes that in so doing the earning capabilities of the assets will decline, then capital gains should be taken in shares. Since principal is being diminished, the receipt of additional shares is essentially a return of capital.

The payment of a capital gains distribution by an investment company automatically causes the per-share NAV to decline by the same amount. If the NAV of a share of XYZ Fund is $9.50 and a 50¢ capital gain is paid out, then the new share price will fall 50¢ to $9.00. Because the value of the earning assets have been decreased, future per-share income will be less than if the distribution had not been made. Further, all future gains or losses in per-share NAV will be less than if the fund had not paid out the capital gains.

Depending upon the choice either to take the capital gains distribution in additional shares or in cash, the long-term effects on investment income can be substantial. Figure 3.1 compares the results. The white ribbon shows the actual dividends paid over a ten year period when all capital gains distributions were taken in cash. The dark ribbon shows the adjusted dividends obtained as a result of reinvesting all capital gains distributions over the same period.

Nothing is simple in our relative world. Despite the previous argument, some investors prefer to take all distributions in cash and then reinvest in other funds for

Figure 3.1 Long-Term Effects of Reinvested Capital Gains

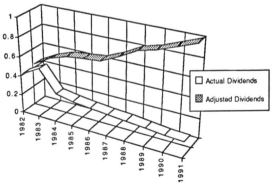

greater diversity. This is a good strategy when the shares are held in a tax sheltered account such as an IRA. And, there are circumstances when spending a portion or even all the capital gains may be the judicious choice. Investor needs vary and so do the demands for spendable cash. There is nothing sacred about principal. There is no law that states you must leave an estate to your heirs. Periodic withdrawals can be an excellent way to utilize accumulated resources in an orderly fashion while maintaining the balance at work in a diversified, professionally managed portfolio. The key concern is how long the assets will last. Figure 3.2 will help determine just how long principal will last when capital is used at a higher rate than it earns.

Figure 3.2 How Long Will Your Money Last?

		1%	2%	3%	4%	5%	6%	7%	8%	9%
		Percent Earnings of Investment								
	1%									
	2%	69								
	3%	40	55							
Payout	4%	28	35	46						
Rate	5%	22	25	30	41					
Percent	6%	18	20	23	28	36				
	7%	15	16	18	21	25	33			
	8%	13	14	15	17	20	23	30		
	9%	11	12	13	14	16	18	22	28	
	10%	10	11	12	13	14	15	17	20	26

Number of Years Money Will Last

Based upon the table, if you are using capital at the rate of 8 percent each year, but the investment is earning 7 percent, it will take 30 years to deplete the account. If you start at age 65, you will be 95 when the funds are exhausted.

TAXES

There are no tax benefits for an investor who chooses to invest in a closed-end fund rather than directly in individual securities. Fund investing does offer the benefit of simplifying tax reporting. It's much easier to determine income, gains, and losses held in a pooled investment vehicle than it is to list and compute data from an extended list of stocks and bonds.

In the first quarter of each year, all closed-end funds are required to send their shareholders detailed copies of the returns it supplied to the I.R.S. If the securities are held in street name then the brokerage house must consolidate and forward the data to the investor. The returns show the total of all distributions, whether qualified or non-qualified, including capital gains, and any distributions which may have been non-taxable. If the fund retained capital gains and paid the tax for the shareholder, all necessary information is supplied. The figures can then be transferred to the investor's tax form.

As previously described, all distributions of ordinary income and capital gains are taxable and are reported by the funds to the I.R.S. It doesn't matter whether the investor received the amounts in cash or in additional shares. If the investor reinvested all ordinary income and capital gains he or she must pay any required taxes from other sources.

"BACKUP WITHHOLDING"

All investment companies are subject to I.R.S. backup withholding provisions. This means that every time the company makes a dividend or interest payment to a shareholder it must deduct and withhold 20 percent of the payment if:

1. the investor failed to furnish his or her taxpayer identification number to the investment company; or

2. the I.R.S. has notified the fund that the taxpayer identification number furnished by the shareholder is incorrect; or

3. the investor under-reports interest and dividends received; or

4. the shareholder fails to report if he or she is subject to backup withholding.

REINVESTMENT AND TAXES

Over time the taxes that are paid on reinvested dollars (dividends and capital gains distributions) increase the tax cost of the investor's holdings. When the fund shares are redeemed, capital gains or losses must be computed. The tax cost utilized for this determination is the original purchase price paid for the shares plus all the dividends and capital gains distributions used to obtain additional shares.

For instance, an investor purchased $10,000 worth of Big Income Growth Fund (BIG) 8 years ago. All dividends ($4,250) and distributions ($7,500) were reinvested in additional shares. Today the total account is worth $28,500 and the investor redeems all shares. Despite the fact that the account has increased by $18,500 the investor is only liable for taxes on $6,750.

Original cost of investment	$10,000
Income dividends reinvested	$4,250
Capital gains in additional shares	$7,500
Total tax cost	$21,750
Proceeds from liquidation	$28,500
Taxable long-term gain	$6,750

Be sure to keep careful records of all costs. Even though many funds do provide complete computerized records of all transactions, as do the brokerage firms where trades initiate, investors should maintain their own.

COMPLICATIONS

Tax cost computations become much more complicated when partial share redemption takes place, such as when an automatic withdrawal strategy is utilized. This is particularly true if the shares were accumulated over a period of time.

Under a partial redemption, I.R.S. rules present the investor with two choices for determining the tax cost of his or her shares: 1. the price paid for the earliest shares purchased; or 2. using shares specifically "identified" and acquired at different times. Consult with a tax specialist for the best option.

HOW TO BUY A TAX

If the investment strategy of a fund has been successful and there has been a terrific advance in overall stock prices held in the portfolio, the fund will show a substantial unrealized appreciation. Because closed-end funds are allowed to engage a consistent management strategy without the intrusion of untimely calls for redemption, they usually exhibit the highest proportion of unrealized profits.

The possibility does exist whereby this considerable unrealized appreciation in the fund's portfolio will obligate a new purchaser to be held responsible for payment of a capital gains tax on profits that were earned before he became a shareholder.

The real question, however, is whether or not the new investor believes that the fund will suddenly liquidate all, or a large portion, of its entire portfolio. This has rarely ever happened. Even during periods of rapidly rising stock prices, capital gains distributions rarely exceed 9 to 10 percent of the fund's NAV.

Don't think of taxes on capital gains as an additional burden. It all works out in the end. Because tax payments are paid periodically, there will be less taxes due, or greater losses to use elsewhere, when the shares are finally sold. In fact, the tax liability will usually be about the same as if no gains had ever been paid out by the fund.

MINIMIZING THE TAX BITE

The easiest way to avoid unnecessary taxes on fund investments is to avoid purchasing shares of any fund just before the record date of a large distribution. Up until the record date, the amount of the distribution is included in the share price. Wait until after the record date and avoid paying tax on income or capital gains which your funds did not earn. Better yet, purchase the shares immediately after the pay date after the cost of the shares has fallen back.

Another easy way to minimize taxes on investment income is to invest in funds whose primary objective is long-term growth. These funds invest for maximum growth, not income, and it is very possible that fund expenses will exceed any income obtained. For example, Engex (EGX) is an equity closed-end fund that invests for maximum growth, not income. Over the past several years it has not paid any distributions (0 percent yield) and charges a 1 percent management fee. The equity shares of a dual-purpose fund will also generally have a higher management fee than distribution yield.

NON-TAXABLE DIVIDENDS

Closed-end municipal bond funds present an excellent avenue for obtaining current income that is exempt from federal income taxes. A number of municipal bond funds are also exempt from individual state taxes. Chapter 4 has a description of municipal bond funds.

COSTS AND FEES

Closed-end funds charge management and administrative fees before any income is distributed to shareholders. These fees generally run from one-half of one percent to one and one-half of one percent of the net assets of the fund. Plus, there is a normal brokerage commission to buy or sell fund shares.

UNDERSTANDING SHAREHOLDER REPORTS

All of the funds are required by law to supply shareholders with accurate, up-to-date reports. The fund will send quarterly, semi-annual, and annual reports describing the fund's performance, holdings, and expenses. Essentially, annual reports are audited financial statements. Quarterly reports are interim bulletins that update shareholders about any material changes in the portfolio or the affairs of the company. Since they are required to present comparative data, they are often more informative than the annual reports.

The annual report typically begins with a letter to the shareholders that chronicles the fund's performance for the year, followed by an economic review, and ending with a projection of what management sees for the future. Next is the Statement of Assets and Liabilities which also shows the current portfolio (see Figure 3.3). This is followed by the Statement of Operations, which breaks down all the expenses incurred by the fund. Naturally, the largest expense is normally the investment management fee, followed by the custodial, directors, and professional fees.

Closed-end funds differ from other companies listed on the open market in that their assets are almost exclusively in the form of cash, receivables, and securities. Therefore, most investors should be looking at where and in what percentages the fund assets are allocated and invested. What percentage of assets are in bonds, convertibles, straight equity, or cash? Actual holdings are not as important because they often change between reports. But the percentages allocated to particular industry groups may indicate how the fund will perform in differing market environments.

Subsequently, a determination of the relative accomplishment of the fund management can be learned by studying the data in Table 2 of the fund summaries (see Figure 3.4 for an example).

Figure 3.3 Statement of Assets and Liabilities: An Example

December 31, 1992

ASSETS

Investments, at value (note 1a)

General portfolio securities (cost $290,769,669) $564,914,201
Corporate discount notes (cost $18,503,637) 18,503,637
                                                                    583,417,838

Investment in controlled affiliate (note 1b) 228,129

Cash, Receivables and other assets

Cash $204,222
Receivable for securities sold 2,012,744
Dividends, interest and other receivables 2,347,159
Other 121,031
                                                                      4,685,156

Total Assets 588,331,123

LIABILITIES

Payable for securities purchased 23,576
Accrued expenses and other liabilities.......................................1,818,707

Total Liabilities 1,842,283

NET ASSETS $586,488,840

NET ASSET VALUE PER SHARE $28.56

Source: General American Investors, 1992 Annual Report. Statement of Assets and Liabilities

Figure 3.4 General American Investors Five-Year Statistical History

Fiscal Year Ending 12/31	1992	1991	1990	1989	1988
Net Assets ($mil):	586.50	587.20	382.20	381.90	301.80
Net Income Dist ($):	0.03	0.10	0.21	0.25	0.25
Cap Gains Dist ($):	3.06	2.04	1.70	1.48	1.90
Total Dist ($)	3.09	2.14	1.91	1.73	2.15
Yield from Dist (%)	10.66	12.59	10.54	12.93	16.86
Expense Ratio (%)	1.16	1.02	1.07	1.04	1.14
Portfolio Turnover (%)	14.42	21.30	18.77	26.91	19.37
NAV per share ($)	28.56	30.60	20.60	21.41	17.03
Market Price per share	30.00	29.00	17.00	18.13	13.3f
Premium (Discount) (%)	5.04	(5.23)	(17.48)	(15.37)	(21.49)
Total Return, Stk Price (%)	14.10	83.18	4.30	48.43	21.80

For example, from this chart (previous page) the following can be extracted:

Net Asset Value 12/31/91 ....$30.60
Net Asset Value 12/31/92 ....$28.56
Capital Gains Distribution. $3.06
Dividend, Net Income...0.03
Total Return (NAV) 1992 (%) 3.43
Net Asset Value 12/31/88 ....$17.03
Net Asset Value 12/31/92 ....$28.56
Capital Gains Distribution, 5-Years $10.18
Dividend Income Distribution, 5-Years $0.84
Total Return (NAV), 5-Years (%)...........................132.4

These results may be compared with unmanaged indexes, such as the S&P 500 or the Dow Jones Industrial Average (DJIA) to determine how the fund has performed. "Special Considerations" included in the annual report, should be read carefully to discern if any restrictions would prevent a fund from being open-ended or taken over. Many funds now offer provisions to convert to open-end status, or to liquidate the fund after a predetermined number of years or if the discount becomes excessive. These provisions offer a degree of protection for shareholders since any discount will be regained after the fund open-ends or liquidates.

BOARD OF DIRECTORS

Each fund has a Board of Directors elected by the shareholders and empowered to carry out certain tasks determined by the fund's "Articles of Incorporation". These powers include the appointment of fund management and the declaration of dividends.

Before investing it is important that you read the prospectus and recent annual and quarterly reports to assure that the fund meets your investment objectives.

4
Closed-End Fund Categories

OVERVIEW

There are two basic classifications of closed-end funds: Bond income funds and Equity funds. In order to clarify the characteristics of the bond and equity funds, this *Guide* has separated them into several categories. There are eight categories of bond funds and five categories of equity funds listed below.

Bond Funds

1. Corporate, Investment Grade
2. Flexible Portfolio
3. Government (U.S.)
4. High Yield Corporate (Junk)
5. International
6. Multi-Sector/Strategic
7. Single State Tax-Free
8. Federal Tax-Free

Equity Funds

1. Convertible (Bond and Equity)
2. Domestic and Specialized
3. Dual Purpose
4. Global and Multi Country
5. Single Country

BOND FUNDS

Five to ten years ago, all closed-end bond funds were basically the same. They would invest primarily in high-grade corporate and some Government securities. Modern bond portfolios have expanded to include tax-free, international, high-yield, and convertible securities. As fund managers strive for higher current yields and better returns, portfolio strategies have become more complex.

Fund managers are now able to use financial futures and options on U.S. Government bonds. This, coupled with the growth and accessibility of foreign markets, has allowed managers to increase portfolio returns by 2 to 3 percent over the older, "pure vanilla" variety. To simplify the review process, the 259 bond funds covered in the full and half-page summaries have been grouped by common characteristics. The following discussions highlight the common elements found within the groups of funds. Look for consistent or increasing current yield along with a stable NAV. Also, remember that as interest rates rise, bond prices decline and vice versa. Any portfolio principally invested in fixed income securities tends to increase in asset value when interest rates decline and decrease when interest rates rise. Prices of longer-term securities generally increase or decrease more sharply than those of shorter-term securities in response to interest changes. Global funds and those funds that invest in foreign bonds, have the added risk of exposure to currency fluctuations, which can also affect the NAV of the fund.

Corporate Bond Funds—Investment Grade

Most of the funds in this group have been in operation for years and therefore have long-term track records. The portfolios consist primarily of investment grade bonds, those rated BBB/Baa or better by Standard and Poor's or Moody's rating services. Quite a few of the fund managers are actually insurance companies or banks, with long histories of managing corporate bonds.

The returns on these funds may not be as high as the newer U.S. Government and high-yield (junk) bond funds, but their safety factor may make them more appealing to the conservative investor. The majority of these funds pay quarterly rather than monthly dividends, which lowers costs. However, this may not be as appealing to investors who are accustomed to receiving monthly payments.

The NAVs of corporate high-grade bond funds tend to fluctuate more widely because they don't use enhancements and hedging strategies as extensively as the government, international, multi-sector, and high-yield (junk) funds do. These funds are the "pure vanilla" variety. What you see is what you get!

Flexible Portfolio Bond Funds

The objective of flexible or total return bond funds is to produce total return comprised of current income along with capital appreciation. Under normal circumstances, a high percentage of these portfolios will be invested in fixed income securities. However, total return funds do have the ability to invest varying degrees in income producing common stocks or convertible securities. Some of the flexible funds can invest up to 75 percent in common stock when market conditions warrant it. These funds offer the flexibility similar to the open-end growth and income mutual funds.

The fund summaries should be read carefully, along with a recent fund prospectus. Total return funds perform well under most market conditions due to their flexibility. However, the manager's ability and experience are very important.

U.S. Government Bond Funds

The portfolios of this group are predominantly invested in U.S. Government bonds. Most are able to invest a limited percentage of their assets in foreign and corporate bonds. Many of the funds use the options and futures markets to enhance income and to hedge the portfolio. By using the options and futures markets, managers are able to moderate fluctuations normally affecting bonds during unstable interest rate periods. Most of this sector is now selling at high premiums which makes them unattractive investments. Many of them have or will be cutting their distributions to reflect the lower interest rates on U.S. Government bonds.

Government bond funds are actively managed by some of the country's most experienced management companies. For additional information, contact your broker or obtain a copy of the prospectus or a recent report directly from the fund.

High Yield Corporate (Junk) Bond Funds

Also known as junk bond funds, the assets of this category are invested primarily in corporate debt of domestic corporations that are rated BBB, Baa, or lower. The significant credit risk involved for investors in this sector was evidenced by dismal performance figures from 1989 through 1990. Most of the fund managers reduced payouts and upgraded portfolio holdings as much as possible to better weather the storm. Total returns for 1992 averaged 25.7 percent on stock price and 19.1 percent on NAV.

These are still high-risk investments and should be closely monitored. The performance of junk bond funds rests with the economic recovery. If the recovery continues, the deeper discounted funds may still have more upside potential.

International Bond Funds

This group of funds requires great expertise and astuteness on the part of the manager. Not only are fund managers required to seek high current yield, but they also must work diligently to protect the portfolios from the adverse effects of currency fluctuations. The long-term potential of this group of funds, if managed well, could prove to be the best of all the bond funds. Currency and bond trading can produce substantial short-term profits, or losses.

A few of the funds may be invested in the markets of a single country. This strategy makes these funds less flexible, and investors should monitor the country's currency on an ongoing basis. Verify the portfolio holdings in the data pages of this *Guide*. Most of the funds in this group can and will shift assets between various foreign and U.S. markets to reflect long-term currency trends. They will also use investment hedges such as options, futures, and foreign currency transactions to protect the portfolio. These hedging strategies can enhance distributions.

The diversity available through these funds makes them much less risky than investing in foreign markets directly.

Multi-Sector/Strategic Bond Funds

This group of funds invests for high current income with capital appreciation secondary. Volatility is controlled by diversification into three basic bond market sectors: U.S. Government bonds, corporate bonds (usually high yield), and foreign Government bonds. The percent exposure to each sector is determined by the fund managers who are also free to employ almost any of the hedging and enhancement strategies available with options and futures.

Most of these bond funds are aggressively managed to maximize returns, with frequent shifts of assets between the various sectors. The greater flexibility afforded by these funds allows higher current yields with less risk.

When determining whether or not to invest in a multi-sector fund, be sure to monitor the NAV of the selected fund in order to compare how it performs relative to its peers. The potential for this very flexible type of fund should be superior to those that are more limited; but remember, the manager's expertise is crucial.

Single State Tax-Free Bond Funds

As states raised taxes in an attempt to offset deficits, many new Single State funds came to market in 1992. Look at the portfolio information carefully before investing. Choose only those funds with 100 percent investment-grade bonds.

Federal Tax-Free Bond Funds

This remains the fastest growing category in the closed-end fund universe. From only 6 funds in early 1986, the field grew to 150 funds at the end of 1992. For greater clarity, this *Guide* divides the municipal bond funds into two categories, Federal Tax-Free, comprising 78 funds, and Single State Tax-Free with 72 funds.

In their quest for tax-free income from a managed portfolio, investors in 1992 drove up the prices of muni bond funds to premiums. Most of them have leveraged capital structures, which, given the current yield curve, has enabled them to increase their net income per share above what a non-leveraged mutual fund or unit trust would provide. Beware.

Don't consider these funds to be safe havens. Many of the portfolios are leveraged with auction-rate preferreds, which allows the fund to borrow at current low short-term rates and invest in the long end of the market where the returns are higher. Given the current yield curve, current returns have ranged between 7 and 8 percent, which is well above what a mutual fund or unit trust pays. As long as an investor feels that short-term rates will remain low and that the covered municipalities are fiscally sound, then all would appear well. But if the yield curve flattens or if interest rates rise or if defaults start becoming a factor, one can expect a very adverse effect on net income per share. Be cautious with this group. The premiums are high, and there is more to sound investing than high yield.

Term Trust Bond Funds

Initially introduced to the investment community in 1989, this type of closed-end fund did not receive popular acceptance until recently. There are currently 21 such funds outstanding, with the majority having been offered in 1992.

The stated objective of the Term Trust is to provide a high level of current income consistent with the investment objectives of the particular trust and to terminate the trust at a pre-determined time, distributing to shareholders all of the assets. The goal is generally to return the original offering price of shares of the trust to investors on or about the termination date. There is, of course, no guarantee that this objective will be accomplished.

Most of the Term Trusts use leverage to offer an attractive high yield in order to compete with bond funds that have longer term objectives. Leverage is also used by

Term Trusts to pay management fees and the initial offering expenses. The use of leverage may have an adverse effect upon the fund's NAV under certain circumstances.

EQUITY FUNDS

This section is divided into five groups: Convertible, Domestic and Specialized, Dual Purpose, Global and Multi Country, and Single Country. In all equity funds, with the exception of the Dual Purpose funds, yield from distributions, the yield an investor would receive if shares were purchased at the beginning of the period January 1, 1992, is included in Table 1 of the fund summaries.

Domestic and Specialized equity funds are quite diverse. Some emphasize investments in highly capitalized (blue chip) stocks, while others invest primarily in smaller capitalized or emerging growth stocks.

Global and Multi Country and Single Country equity funds are exposed to currency risks present in foreign markets, such as changes in the foreign currency exchange rates. Exchange rates will affect the U.S. dollar value of the fund's assets and yield. The managers of these funds, some of the nation's and the world's top money managers, will often use hedging techniques to minimize the risk. Global and Multi Country equity funds offer a more flexible portfolio, as they can invest just about anywhere in the world. The summaries for both of these groups of funds, especially the single country equity funds, should be read carefully, and a prospectus should be obtained from the fund before investing. With all of the new single country funds that have recently come to market, closed-end equity funds truly offer "a world of investment choice."

Convertible (Bond and Equity) Funds

This is one of the smallest categories with only eight funds, but in 1992 it had the biggest average discount at more than 5 percent with three funds selling at double digit discounts. Convertible funds offer an investment opportunity of current income with an equity kicker. The portfolios consist of bonds and preferred stocks that are convertible into the common stock of corporations.

Although current yields from this group are usually 2 to 3 percent less than straight bond funds, total returns make them extremely attractive, particularly near the latter part of bull markets. Current discounts to NAV may offer an attractive buying opportunity.

Domestic and Specialized Equity Funds

There are two classification of Domestic Equity funds: non-diversified and diversified.

At the time of the fund's initial public offering, a non-diversified fund will state in its prospectus that its investment objective is to have the ability to limit the scope of investment choices both as to industry and as to a particular investment. The primary characteristic of these funds is their concentration in specific areas such as financial services, health care, precious metals, petroleum/natural resources, and utilities. Non-diversified funds are best used as part of a diversified or limited-term portfolio because of their very specialized nature. Within this group, specialized or sector equity funds are included.

A diversified equity closed-end fund has as its stated investment objective (defined in its prospectus) limitations as to the quality of securities held, the percentage of securities that may be held in each sector as well as a percentage limitation on individual issues. Diversified funds by definition fulfill one of the basic investment objectives of "spreading" investment risk and were initially the norm. Some funds have been in existence since 1929. Others have been around for only a few years. The investment objectives range from investment in small capitalized or emerging growth stocks to emphasis on highly capitalized blue chip portfolios. The fund managers' objectives should correspond with each investor's goals.

Dual Purpose Equity Funds

The Dual Purpose concept was originally conceived to serve two types of investors: the income investor and the growth oriented investor. It is during the early life of this type of fund that the income investor is best served.

A Dual Purpose equity fund has two classes of shares: capital shares and preferred or income shares. The capital shares are entitled to all the capital gains and growth over the life of the fund, usually 10 to 12 years. The preferred or income shares are entitled to all the income from the entire portfolio in addition to a guaranteed repayment of the original investment, less the underwriting fees. The preferred shares also have a cumulative dividend, set at the time of the original offer, that is guaranteed to be paid from the total assets of the fund.

If the portfolio underperforms, the NAV of the capital shares diminishes in order to pay the preferred shares' principal and any unpaid cumulative dividends.

Dual Purpose funds make a very attractive short- or long- term trading vehicle if bought at the right time. The best time to buy the capital shares is when the discounts are steep and a bull market is in its early stage. Though it is not easy to tell when a bull market begins, it is obvious when a big discount is available. Often these events will coincide. The income shares should be bought on the initial public offering or in the early life of the fund when the shares are selling at or near the NAV. The distributions usually will increase as the fund matures, which will often cause the income shares to sell at a substantial premium. As the income shares approach the maturity date of the fund, the premium will disappear. Check the prospectus and the following summaries to determine the number of years left before the fund is open-ended. The capital shares are appropriate for cost averaging in an aggressive investment portfolio.

Global and Multi Country Equity Funds

On the logo of *The Closed-End Fund Digest* is the motto, "a world of investment choice." This group of funds exemplifies that slogan. A small troop, it offers worldwide investing on a more diversified basis than the single country funds. That's because Multi Country funds may invest regionally as well as in the securities of specific countries. The Pacific Basin region is covered by such funds as the Asia Pacific and Scudder New-Asia funds. Other funds in this group are more versatile.

The fast pace of global economic and social change has focused a lot of interest on this group. Most of the truly attractive discounts reside in the country funds.

These funds can be volatile and many of the markets are relatively illiquid. Country funds, both Multi and Single, are best used as trading vehicles. Their share prices can be affected by natural disasters, political upheavals, rumors, court decisions, and press releases. It's often best to buy these funds on bad news and exit on good news. Study this arena carefully before taking the plunge. Check Appendix B, "Sources of Additional Information," at the end of this *Guide.*

Single Country Equity Funds

Most of the world's stock markets are represented by Single Country equity funds. During 1992, attention was focused on emerging markets. Five country funds were introduced; three from China, one from Korea, and one from Japan.

There are many discount-driven bargains in this group. Because political and economic conditions can create more volatility than exists in domestic markets, it is best to include these funds as part of a diversified portfolio of five or six different countries. In addition, currency fluctuations can have a powerful effect on investment results.

Although Single Country equity funds offer the astute investor interesting and potentially rewarding investment opportunities, tread lightly.

5
Closed-End Fund
Portfolios

BEFORE YOU INVEST

An investor should answer three basic questions before making an investment decision:

- What is the required real rate of return?
- What is the anticipated inflation factor?
- What is the risk premium?

Upon resolving these questions, you will be better prepared to decide whether an investment should be made in equity funds, bond funds, or both.

The real rate of return consists of what investors require for passing up immediate consumption and allowing others to use their savings for a given period. It is called a real rate because it is determined before the inclusion of any value for inflation or risk. Historically, the real rate of return in the U.S. economy has been approximately 3 percent. Therefore, let's use this figure for our computations.

To obtain a real rate of 3 percent we must add on the anticipated inflation factor. The current consensus would put that figure at about 4 percent through the rest of the decade: 3% + 4% = 7%.

We combine the two to arrive at an approximate 7 percent required return factor. This is our required return on an investment before any explicit consideration of risk. For this reason, it is often called the risk free rate. This risk free rate is the minimum rate of return required of any investment (equities, bonds, real estate, etc.) to have a 3 percent real rate of return. If the risk free rate of return is less than the inflation rate, it would be better to spend the money now rather than invest it.

Finally, a third component must be considered, the risk premium. The risk premium is different for each type of investment. The higher the risk, the higher the risk premium. For example, U.S. Government Treasury bills or Federally insured certificates of deposit have risk premiums of nearly zero. All returns to the investor will be at the risk free rate of return. Corporate bonds fall between short-term Government obligations and common stock. Historically, the risk premium for these issues has run about 2 to 4 percent. For common stock, the investor's required return should be augmented with a 4 or 5 percent risk premium. Here are some required rates of return for three types of investments.

Short-Term Government Securities, CDs

Real Rate	3%
Anticipated Inflation	+4%
Risk Free Rate	7%

Corporate Bonds

Real Rate	3%
Anticipated Inflation	+4%
Risk Free Rate	7%
Risk Premium	+2% to 4%
Required Rate of Return	9% to 11%

Common Stocks

Real Rate	3%
Anticipated Inflation	+ 4%
Risk Free Rate	7%
Risk Premium	+ 4% or 5%
Required Rate of Return	11% or 12%

BETA

Not all risk is compensated for by proportionally higher returns. Risk can also be tempered through diversification. For instance, the risk of investing in U.S. stock funds can be partially eliminated by investments in foreign or global funds. However, each investment carries risk that cannot be moderated through diversification. This is called systematic risk and can be determined by observing the correlation between the movement of a security and the market in general. This relationship is called the beta coefficient. If a fund moves in step with the market, it has a beta coefficient of 1. If a fund is 50 percent more volatile than the market, the beta coefficient is 1.5, meaning it will rise or fall about 15 percent when the market moves by 10 percent.

Conservative investors interested in preserving capital should focus on funds with low betas. Those willing to assume higher risk in an effort to earn greater rewards should look for high beta funds.

The market is defined as the Standard & Poor's Index of 500 common stocks. The beta of the market is always 1. Money market funds have a beta coefficient of 0.

Betas are not meaningful with bond funds, funds with a preponderance of bonds, or precious metals funds. For bond funds, the weighted average maturity of the portfolio holdings has been reported in this *Guide*. The market risk of a fixed-income security is determined primarily by maturity. The longer the maturity, the greater the risk of price change with interest rate fluctuations. These funds usually move independently of the S&P 500. In this *Guide*, the Beta computations are based upon 36-month data whenever possible. Betas are helpful when used to estimate the market risk of an investment portfolio. This is figured by determining the weighted sum of the betas of the individual funds in the portfolio. If a portfolio is made up of four funds, with an equal market value for each, then the portfolio beta would be:

(0.25 x beta Fund 1) + (0.25 x beta Fund 2) + (0.25 x beta Fund 3)
+ (0.25 x beta Fund 4) = Portfolio Beta

A highly liquid, low-risk, short-term portfolio for an individual with a lower tax exposure might be made up of:

	% of Portfolio	Average Beta
Growth Stock Funds	35	0.90
Growth & Income Funds	45	0.68
Money Market Fund	20	0.00
	100	

Portfolio Beta [(0.35 x 0.90) + (0.45 x 0.68) + (0.20 x 0.00)] = 0.62

A higher risk, longer term, less liquid portfolio for an individual with high-tax exposure might be:

	% of Portfolio	Average Beta
Aggressive Common Stock Funds	85	1.10
Money Market Fund	15	0.00
	100	

Portfolio Beta [(0.85 x 1.10) + (0.15 x 0)] = 0.94

Of course it's not necessary to wade through all these calculations to arrive at your own portfolio makeup. It is very important to determine your level of risk tolerance and the individual risk levels of each fund you consider.

AVERAGE MATURITIES

A maturity date is the date on which the principal amount of a note, bond, bill, or other debt instrument is due and payable. The fund data pages found in this book contain average maturity figures for the bond income funds. This is an important analytical tool for determining interest rate exposure for the portfolio. The figures utilized in this book are the result of a weighted arithmetic mean for each portfolio examined.

Basically, with this information, an investor can select those portfolios that correspond to his or her perception of what long- and short-term interest rates will do. If it is determined that long-term rates will decline, for instance, then a portfolio with a higher average maturity would be desirable.

The following is a generalized list of closed-end funds ranked according to the level of risk. As the level of risk increases, so does the potential for capital gains.

PORTFOLIO RISK LEVELS

Low Risk

Prime Rate Funds, U.S. Government Bond Funds, and Total Return Funds that invest in:

- Certificates of Deposit
- Commercial short-term paper
- Treasury securities

Maturities in this group range from 90 days up to several years.

Medium Risk

Corporate, Multi-Sector, Convertible, International, and Municipal Bond Funds that invest in:

- Bonds and debentures, with maturities ranging up to 25 years

Medium to High Risk

Domestic Equity Funds, Single Country Funds, Global and Multi Country Equity Funds that invest in:

- Common stocks

The danger associated with long-term, fixed-income securities is that inflation may outstrip the interest paid by the security, resulting in a loss of purchasing power when the capital is returned. Also, if the security is sold before maturity and interest rates rise higher than they were when the bond was purchased, a capital loss will result.

Convertible bonds, convertible debentures, and convertible preferreds all fall into the medium risk category. They offer investors a combination. Essentially, these are securities with a fixed interest or dividend rate. They differ from bonds in that they can be converted into the common shares of the issuing companies at the rate of a given number of shares per $100 of bonds. Convertible issues should offer a higher yield than common stocks and slightly lower yields than bonds, because the conversion privilege has a value as well. Preferred shares offer income but no fixed maturity date. Non-convertible preferreds must be sold on the open market in order to recover the investor's capital.

International bond funds can offer political, interest rate, and currency dangers.

Common stocks provide only one guarantee, the right to participate in the growth or demise of a company. Dividends are not fixed but they can increase as profits rise. There is no promise of return of principal, but market values can rise handsomely. Or, the company could go bankrupt, leaving the common shares worthless.

Single country and foreign equity funds also present inherent risks in investing overseas. These include currency fluctuations, political interference, and labor disputes.

After you have estimated your tax exposure, liquidity needs, appropriate holding period, and level of risk, you are ready to select the individual funds and assemble your portfolio.

MODEL PORTFOLIO FRAMEWORKS

There are three basic types of investment portfolios:

1. Bond/Income Portfolios for investors seeking income
2. Equity Portfolios for investors seeking growth
3. Balanced Portfolios for investors looking for both growth and income.

Each of these groups can be further divided into more specialized portfolios. For instance, a bond/income portfolio can be tax-free, taxable, or international.

Your actual portfolio will, in all likelihood, be determined by your position in life. However imprecise, Table 5.1 does indicate general investment settings.

Aggressive investors, early in their careers, have a high risk tolerance, a long investment horizon, and a low tax liability. They would prefer a low dividend paying growth equity portfolio. Conservative investors, later in the cycle, primarily concerned with safeguarding principal and minimizing risk, would be more likely to assemble a bond/income portfolio. Investors should consider personal preferences, current market conditions, and individual investment requirements when structuring personal investment portfolios.

Table 5.1 Career Status and Investment Portfolios

Career Status	Risk Tolerance	Investment Horizon	Tax Liability
Early	High	Long	Low
Mid	High	Long	High
Late	Medium	Intermediate	Intermediate
Retired	Low	Intermediate	Low

The following sample model portfolios illustrate how closed-end funds can be used to structure an investment portfolio. They should be viewed only as guidelines and not be used as actual personal portfolios. They are fully invested portfolios.

Bond Income Portfolios

Taxable Portfolio

50%	Government Funds
30%	Multi-Sector Funds
5%	Corporate and High-Yield Funds
10%	Flexible and International Funds
5%	Convertible Funds

Under current market conditions, this portfolio will produce an estimated annual return from distributions of 9 percent. The yield could be maximized by putting a larger percentage in the higher yielding total return and international funds. If capital preservation or appreciation is required, a larger percentage could be put in total return funds.

Income Tax-Free Portfolio

100%   Municipal Funds

Since there is only one group to select from, assembling this portfolio might appear to be a simple task; it really is not. The funds in this group are quite divergent. There are insured, investment grade, high-yield or low-rated, leveraged funds, and funds that are Federal and State tax-free. With such a broad choice, careful selection is necessary to minimize risk.

With municipal bond funds there are two basic risk factors to consider: interest rate risk and credit risk. Generally, the longer the maturity of a bond, the higher the interest it pays. Therefore, unless the fund objective states otherwise, muni fund managers will always invest in longer maturity bonds in order to maximize yields. As interest rates rise and fall, the NAV of the fund will move inversely, to a greater degree, than shorter maturity portfolios.

Credit risk is always a factor to consider. The lower the rating, the higher the yield, and the greater the risk of default. You are relying on the expertise of the manager to correctly determine the actual risk involved with higher yielding muni bonds. Also, non-rated bonds are not necessarily low quality bonds. Many municipalities do not bother with the expense of having their issues rated because they are known to be highly credit worthy communities.

With careful evaluation, it is possible to construct a portfolio with a tax-free return of between 6 and 7 percent. (Remember, Uncle Sam gets none of it.) If a consistent tax-free yield is of primary importance, then any interest rate induced fluctuation of NAV is of minimal significance.

Equity Fund Portfolios

Domestic Portfolio		*Average Beta*
60%	Domestic Funds	$0.60 \times 0.63 = 0.38$
20%	Specialized/Sector Funds	$0.20 \times 0.51 = 0.10$
20%	Dual Purpose Funds	$0.20 \times 1.19 = 0.24$
Portfolio Beta		0.72

This portfolio offers fund groups that invest primarily in the U.S. securities markets. Domestic equity funds offer portfolios that concentrate on both large and small capitalized companies. As with all mutual funds that are dedicated to equities, underlying economic cycles will affect the stock markets which in turn will be reflected in portfolio NAV performance. Check the domestic equity fund summaries to determine which fund will perform best under existing market conditions.

Sector funds specialize in specific industries and allow investors to pinpoint an investment in precious metals, oil, health services, financial services, etc. Some of these, such as the precious metals and petroleum resources funds, can be good inflation hedges. Keep in mind, convertible funds generally offer higher current yields with growth potential.

Aggressive Growth Portfolio		*Average Beta*
30%	Domestic Funds	0.30 x 0.63 = 0.19
20%	Sector Funds	0.20 x 0.51 = 0.10
25%	Global/Single Country Funds	0.25 x 0.89 = 0.22
25%	Dual Purpose Funds (Capital Shares)	0.25 x 1.19 = 0.30
Portfolio Beta		0.81

A portfolio structured from these four groups of equity funds should perform very well in a strong bull market. When selecting from domestic and international equity funds, locate the ones that have performed the best in uptrending markets. Because of the non-domestic sector, this type of portfolio requires careful monitoring. Foreign investments present added risks of currency fluctuations and potential political instability.

Balanced Portfolio (Growth and Income)		*Average Beta*
20%	Government or Municipal Bond Funds	na
5%	High-Yield Funds	na
20%	Total Return Bond Funds	na
30%	Domestic Equity Funds	0.30 x 0.63 = 0.19
10%	Specialized/Sector Equity Funds	0.10 x 0.51 = 0.05
15%	International Equity Funds	0.15 x 0.92 = 0.14
Portfolio Beta		0.38

This type of portfolio dilutes risk by spreading it among several sectors. Several equity funds pay distributions equal to 10 percent of the NAV of the fund; these are particularly attractive for a balanced portfolio. Selecting from these fund groups with a mind toward high distributions, an investor can structure a portfolio with an annual return of 10 percent in cash, along with growth potential. This type of portfolio may not win a sprint race, but should finish very well in a marathon. The conservative, long-term investor should find this portfolio particularly appealing.

TRADING IN THE CLOSED-END FUND MARKET

Although closed-end funds are very attractive long-term investment vehicles, they also offer exceptional trading opportunities. It is still possible for a closed-end fund to trade at substantial discounts to their actual NAV, due to market conditions and the law of supply and demand. These discounts usually occur when overall stock market sentiment is bearish and investors and speculators are selling. The decreased demand causes the price of the funds to drop even further than the NAV of the underlying securities held in the fund.

For example, assume that during a bearish market the ABC Growth Fund is selling at $8 per share and that its NAV is $10 per share. The discount to the value of the underlying securities in the fund is 20 percent. When market sentiment begins to turn more positive, 500 shares are purchased at $8 per share or $4,000. The market rallies, increasing the NAV to $12 per share and the stock price rises accordingly to $12 per share, eliminating the bear market discount of 20 percent. The 500 shares purchased at $8 per share, or $4,000, will then be worth $6,000. This is a $2,000, or 50 percent, profit on the investment.

On the other hand, if $4,000 worth of open-end fund shares had been purchased at the same time, they would only be worth $5,000, a $1,000, or 25 percent, profit on the investment. This happened because the closed-end fund was purchased at a 20 percent discount, while the open-end fund was purchased at NAV. Simply put, the profit potential in a bull market is twice as good for closed-end funds as it is for open-end funds.

But take warning, this can be a double-edged sword. For example, assume 500 shares had been purchased at $12, or $6,000, when the NAV was $12. If market sentiment turned bearish and caused the NAV to drop to $10 per share and a discount of 20 percent developed, making the shares sell at $8, a $2,000 loss would result. This is twice the loss than if the same amount of money had been invested in an open-end fund.

One might think that to become a wealthy and successful trader one only needs to buy shares when the discount is substantial, or approximately 20 percent, and sell when the discount shrinks or goes to parity. This is certainly possible for the astute or fortunate individual who knows what funds to buy (and when to buy them) and what funds to sell (and when to sell them). However, these senses of judgment and timing are precisely the problem.

Determining when and what to buy and/or sell is not easy and requires some sophistication and monitoring of the investment portfolio. This *Guide* should help increase an investor's knowledge and henceforth his/her ability to trade. The explosive growth in closed-end funds has made investing in them much more complex than it used to be. Fortunately, there is much more information available now than in the past, and it may be necessary to subscribe to a newsletter or market timer to increase the chances for success. The financial press and several investment advisors have increased their coverage of closed-end funds. See Appendix B for examples.

TRADING OPPORTUNITIES

Trading opportunities exist when funds are trading at discounts historically deeper than average for the particular fund or on the short side at especially high premiums. The best trading opportunities exist in funds that may be takeover targets. This occurs when a fund is selling at a deep discount of 20 percent or more and an individual or group buys sufficient stock to have holdings beyond 5 percent of the outstanding shares. When this occurs, it becomes necessary for the group or individual to file a 13D form. A 13D filing is usually accompanied by a Statement of Purpose, which requires the individual or group to state whether holdings are for investment purposes only, or to seek control of the fund. These 13D filings are published weekly in *The Wall Street Journal* and *Barron's*. Sometimes these incursions are only made for a quick profit. An investor or group will accumulate a substantial position in order to create the impression of a takeover only to sell at a profit as the stock price moves up. Other times, it may be a serious, concerted effort to open-end the fund so that the full NAV is realized.

It is difficult to determine what an investor's motives are. There will often be a volume buildup prior to and shortly after an announcement in the press. It may be announced that an investor or group has taken a substantial position in the stock of the fund or has filed a 13D form. If the buildup in the stock has been substantial during this period and a good profit has been obtained, a trader usually considers selling into the strength. The ensuing pullback in price offers the trader a good reentry level. Because possible buyouts take a long time to be resolved, many holders lose patience and sell.

Criteria for trading in closed-end funds are changing in the new environment of narrow discounts. Currently the Country funds offer opportunities, as do Dual Purpose funds. For example, if the capital shares of a Dual Purpose fund are trading at a substantial discount, you make an automatic gain when it winds up and goes to NAV. While you are waiting, market risk can be hedged by selling options when the discounts widen. One strategy is to buy the fund and sell calls on the OEX Index. Stock index options can be a conservative way to increase income or insure your portfolio against losses, but it can also be a highly speculative way to buy or sell the dollar value of a basket of stocks.

MARKET TIMING

Short-term investment cycles, which reflect the state of the economy, have recently shortened, and investors and short-term traders can enhance returns by moving in and out of the equity and bond markets in a timely and propitious manner. Closed-end funds, with their vast number of equity and bond funds, could prove to be an excellent vehicle for these short-term traders.

Switching services have used mostly no-load families of funds for short-term trading because switching transactions from fund to fund within the fund family required no transaction charges. Many fund families have found constant switching costly and detrimental to long-term investors and have begun to invoke transaction charges. These charges have made many open-end funds less attractive to the timing services and their short-term trading-oriented clients. Some market timers have increased their use of closed-end funds.

As market timers increase use of closed-end funds, volume will also increase. This added activity will help increase the liquidity but also adds to the volatility of the closed-end fund arena. Active traders or those who desire to trade may subscribe to a timing service that tells them when to be in the equity market and when to be in cash.

SOME POINTERS

Short-term trading is not for everyone. And no one can be told how to be a successful trader. But there are some things to keep in mind.

• Avoid buying dividends. When buying shares of a fund, buy a few days after the ex-dividend date. When selling, sell just before the ex-dividend date. Usually, the stock price will raise by the amount of the dividend during the week prior to the ex-dividend date. And, it typically falls by the amount of the dividend after the ex-dividend date.

For example, if the XYZ Bond Fund is marked ex-dividend on April 10th, and the dividend is $0.10 per share during the week prior to April 10th, the stock will more than likely be selling at 9-7/8. On April 10th, and for a few days after, the stock will more than likely trade at 9-3/4. Waiting to purchase shares until April 10th or later will save $12.50, or $25 per 100 share purchase. A dividend of $10 per 100 shares would be missed, but $15 would be saved on the transaction.

• Make sure the fund you buy has a history of substantial daily volume. Illiquidity can increase the cost of trading. The spread between the bid and ask price is narrower when a stock normally trades at a substantial volume, usually 5,000 shares or more, than when it is traded infrequently. In volume trades, a few thousand shares can move the stock significantly, even if the number of shares bid or offered is small.

• Buy in multiple round lots. Commissions are substantially lower per 100 shares when trading in higher multiples.

• Ask for a discount. Active traders are good clients and should be entitled to a break on commissions.

• Use limit orders when buying or selling in size. It is important to ask the broker how many shares are offered or bid for.

• When buying in a somewhat soft market, try to buy on the bid side. Conversely, if selling in a relatively strong market, limit the price to the offered side of the market.

• Limit the downside of a losing trade to about 10 percent. Remember, they who fight and run away live to fight another day.

• Make sure your broker is working hard for you. A good broker should help with executions and should save the client money in the long run.

Whether investing for the long term, actively trading, or using the services of a market timer, always be familiar with the investment product. Individual investors desiring to invest or trade in the closed-end fund market should seek the advice of their brokers.

KEEPING UP

The active investor or trader should keep up with worldwide economic and business news by reading the business section of local newspapers or *The Wall Street Journal* and *Barron's* on a regular basis. *Forbes* and *Business Week* are also good sources of information. Hiring a professional money manager is an additional choice. Another alternative is to subscribe to an advisory newsletter, preferably one that specializes in closed-end funds. Many investors find *The Closed-End Fund Digest*, published monthly, to be a valuable resource. The Appendix also lists a number of other publications.

Remember, closed-end funds are pools of managed money. When you buy them, you are hiring the manager; when you sell, you are firing him or her.

6
Reading the Fund Summaries

SHAREHOLDER REPORT INFORMATION

The information contained in the fund summaries was obtained from company quarterly and annual reports. The significance of each category and the reason for its inclusion in the summaries are enumerated below.

Fund Name. The fund name, address, and telephone number is included for ease in contacting the fund directly. A toll-free number is given whenever possible.

Exchange. The exchange tells in what organized market the fund shares are traded. There are two main stock and bond exchanges in the U.S.: the New York Stock Exchange (NYSE) and the American Stock Exchange (AMEX). At both exchanges brokers and dealers execute orders from institutional and individual investors to buy and sell securities. An additional market, the Over-The-Counter market (OTC), does not have a physical location. Rather, it is a market linked by telephone and computer networks allowing stock and bond dealers to buy and sell electronically, rather than on the floor of an exchange.

Symbol. The letters of the ticker symbol identify a security for trading purposes both on an exchange and over-the-counter.

Transfer Agent. The transfer agent is usually a commercial bank appointed by the fund to maintain a record of fund shareholders, to issue or cancel certificates, and to resolve problems arising from lost, destroyed, or stolen certificates.

Background. Here, the date, number of shares, stock price, and NAV for the fund's initial public offering is listed when available. This is important in order to see where the fund started and how it has performed since its inception.

Objective. The investment objectives and parameters of each fund are briefly enumerated in this paragraph. (The primary objective is briefly listed under the fund's address and phone number.)

Portfolio. This category should be taken with a grain of salt since the portfolios are actively managed and subject to rapid change. However, the date given in this *Guide* is the latest available from the fund's 1992 annual or quarterly reports and can give an indication of how management works by showing the quality, selection, and allocation of issues in the portfolio at that time. To obtain the latest portfolio allocations contact the fund and request the most current report. Negative figures under "cash & other" or "liabilities", result from accrued fund expenses and/or outstanding share purchases that had not been settled at reporting time.

Fund Manager and Fee. The investment advisor and the fee charged can be useful when comparing costs versus results.

Distributions. When the fund pays out distributions from both income and capital gains. This is particularly important information for investors seeking consistent income.

Reinvestment Plan. Most funds have reinvestment plans allowing shareholders to reinvest distributions at the lower of either share price or NAV. Many funds also offer IRA, Keogh, Pension, and Profit Sharing as well as automatic withdrawal programs. Check with the fund regarding these services.

Shareholder Reports. The frequency of shareholder reports is noted.

Capitalization. The number and class of shares outstanding plus the amount of debt, if any, are listed. This is important to determine the size of the fund, the amount of any leverage used, and the level of debt management must meet before paying out distributions to the shareholders.

STATISTICS

There are two data tables for each fund with operating histories of one year or more. To allow for performance comparisons over the same period, Table 1, at the top of the page, tabulates data for the calendar year ending December 31 (see Table 6.1 for an example). Table 2 (see the example in Table 6.2) reports the fund's 5-year statistical history based on its Fiscal Year End (FYE). Newer funds without a full year of operation are depicted in Chapter 10 with an abbreviated data page containing basic fund information.

Table 6.1 12/31/92 Results (General American Investors)

| | – Period – | | | Yield | Total |
	End	Begin	Distributions	Distrib (%)	Return (%)
Share Price ($)	30.00	29.00	3.09	10.66	14.10
NAV per share ($)	28.56	30.60		10.10	3.43

Stock Price

Period. Beginning (January 1, 1992) and ending (December 31, 1992) period stock prices are shown for comparative purposes.

Distributions. Total of all distributions made during the 12-month period, as determined by the record date. This figure accounts for a change in the fund's NAV.

Yield from Distributions (%). Current yield from regular distributions (not counting extras) based upon stock price had fund shares been purchased on beginning date. The figure is calculated by dividing total distributions by period beginning stock price.

Total Return (%). The percentage increase (or decrease) in stock price from beginning period to ending period with all distributions reinvested.

Average Maturity. Shown for all bond funds. Determined as a weighted arithmetic mean, it is an indication of interest rate risk.

Beta. Shown for all equity funds except precious metals. It compares a fund's share price movement with that of the S&P 500 over the last 36 months. Funds without a 36 month history use at least a 12 month calculation.

NAV

Period. Beginning (January 1, 1992) and ending (December 31, 1992) period NAVs are shown for comparitive purposes.

Yield from Distributions (%). Current yield from regular distributions (not counting extras) calculated by dividing total distributions by period beginning NAV.

Total Return (%). The percentage increase (or decrease) in NAV from beginning period to ending period with all distributions reinvested.

Table 6.2 Statistical History (General American Investors)

Fiscal Year Ending 12/31	1992	1991	1990	1989	1988
Net Assets ($mil):	586.50	587.20	382.20	381.90	301.80
Net Income Dist ($):	0.03	0.10	0.21	0.25	0.25
Cap Gains Dist ($):	3.06	2.04	1.70	1.48	1.90
Total Dist ($)	3.09	2.14	1.91	1.73	2.15
Yield from Dist (%)	10.66	12.59	10.54	12.93	16.86
Expense Ratio (%)	1.16	1.02	1.07	1.04	1.14
Portfolio Turnover (%)	14.42	21.30	18.77	26.91	19.37
NAV per share ($)	28.56	30.60	20.60	21.41	17.03
Market Price per share	30.00	29.00	17.00	18.13	13.38
Premium (Discount) (%)	5.04	(5.23)	(17.48)	(15.37)	(21.49)
Total Return, Stk Price (%)	14.10	83.18	4.30	48.43	21.80

Fiscal Year Ending. The fiscal year of the fund.

Net Assets ($ mil.). The total aggregate value of the fund portfolio in millions of dollars.

Distributions: Net Income ($). The per share income distributions paid during the fiscal year.

Distributions: Capital Gains ($). Per share net distributions from realized capital gains paid during the fiscal year.

Total Distributions ($). The sum of Net Income and Capital Gains.

Yield From Distributions (%). Calculated by dividing total distributions by the beginning of year share price.

Expense Ratio (%). The ratio of the sum of all fund fees and expenses, divided by the average NAV, and stated as a percentage.

Portfolio Turnover Rate (%). A measure of fund trading activity. Expressed as a percentage, this is computed by dividing the lesser of fiscal year purchases or sales by the monthly average value of the securities owned by the fund. A figure of 100 percent implies complete portfolio turnover within one year.

NAV Per Share ($). The fiscal year end per share NAV.

Market Price Per Share ($). The fiscal year end per share market price.

Premium (Discount) (%). The percent difference between the fund NAV and the market price.

Total Return, Share Price ($). Calculated using the following formula:

$$\frac{\text{(Ending Value - Beginning Value)} + \text{Income} + \text{Capital Gains}}{\text{Beginning Value}}$$

Example: General American Investors
Ending Value $30.00
Beginning Value $29.00
Dividends, Net Income $0.03
Distributions, Capital Gains $3.06

$$\frac{(30.00 - 29.00) + 0.03 + 3.06}{29.00} = 14.10\%$$

7
Performance Rankings

Top 25 Bond Funds—1992
(by Share Price)

Rank	Fund Name	Symbol	1992 Total Return Shr Pr(%)	1992 Total Return NAV (%)	Avg. Mat. (Yrs.)
1	Prospect Street High Income Portfolio, Inc. ....PHY	PHY	44.62	21.04	9.2
2	Van Kampen Merritt Limited Term High Income Trust ....VLT	VLT	38.13	16.80	7.7
3	New America High Income Fund ....HYB	HYB	28.93	28.50	11.2
4	High Income Advantage Trust ....YLD	YLD	28.80	15.31	9.0
5	High Income Advantage Trust II ....YLT	YLT	28.19	16.81	8.6
6	High Yield Plus Fund, Inc. ....HYP	HYP	26.29	17.68	11.3
7	CIM High Yield Securities ....CIM	CIM	25.34	18.17	7.1
8	ACM Managed Income Fund, Inc. ....AMF	AMF	25.33	15.78	11.2
9	USF&G Pacholder Fund, Inc. ....PHF	PHF	24.41	18.60	5.6
10	High Yield Income Fund, Inc. ....HYI	HYI	22.67	17.43	8.3
11	CIGNA High Income Shares ....HIS	HIS	22.62	20.85	9.1
12	USLife Income Fund, Inc. ....UIF	UIF	22.34	13.53	16.8
13	High Income Advantage Trust III ....YLH	YLH	21.21	15.34	8.8
14	Franklin Universal Trust ....FT	FT	21.07	20.93	9.6
15	American Opportunity Income Fund, Inc. ....OIF	OIF	20.84	7.69	13.7
16	Van Kampen Merritt Municipal Income Trust ....VMT	VMT	20.74	13.57	23.0
17	American Government Income Fund, Inc. ....AGF	AGF	20.54	12.23	15.6
18	Kemper High Income Trust ....KHI	KHI	19.81	18.17	9.0
19	State Mutual Securities Trust ....SMS	SMS	19.66	10.74	12.4
20	Zenix Income ....ZIF	ZIF	19.58	18.68	10.1
21	Colonial Intermediate High Income Securities ....CIF	CIF	19.39	17.34	7.7
22	Kemper Multi-Market Income Trust ....KMM	KMM	19.26	15.94	6.0
23	Taurus Municipal New York Holdings, Inc. ....MNY	MNY	19.08	13.14	23.1
24	Van Kampen Merritt Intermediate Term High Income Trust ....VIT	VIT	18.60	20.61	5.6
25	Putnam Master Income Trust ....PMT	PMT	17.94	11.52	8.1

Top 25 Equity Funds—1992
(by Share Price)

Rank	Fund Name	Symbol	1992 Total Return		Beta
			Shr Pr(%)	NAV (%)	
1	Southeastern Thrift & Bank Fund, Inc. ...... STBF		83.31	76.13	0.55
2	First Financial Fund, Inc. .... FF		82.29	66.41	0.76
3	Dover Regional Financial .... DVRFS		55.93	34.30	0.44
4	Chile Fund, Inc. (The) .... CH		52.18	15.63	0.77
5	Malaysia Fund, Inc. (The) .... MF		38.30	20.15	1.00
6	Quest for Value Dual Purpose Fund, Inc.Capital Shares .... KFV		37.78	22.09	0.63
7	Convertible Holdings, Inc. Capital Shares .... CNV		36.19	19.07	0.86
8	Central Securities Corporation .... CET		35.03	27.97	0.59
9	Asia Pacific Fund, Inc. (The) .... APB		31.29	16.01	0.93
10	European Warrant Fund, Inc. (The) .... EWF		31.13	13.11	0.58
11	Pilgrim Regional BankShares .... PBS		30.95	31.13	0.80
12	Thai Fund, Inc. (The) .... TTF		28.66	40.10	1.01
13	Mexico Equity and Income Fund, Inc. .... MXE		28.34	19.06	0.79
14	Putnam High Income Convertible & Bond Fund .... PCF		27.23	26.36	0.38
15	Royce Value Trust, Inc. .... RVT		26.69	19.32	0.80
16	Jakarta Growth Fund, Inc. .... JGF		25.39	2.75	0.81
17	First Philippine Fund, Inc. .... FPF		25.38	21.47	0.48
18	Morgan Stanley Emerging Markets Fund .. MSF		25.17	13.94	0.61
19	Thai Capital Fund .... TC		24.64	34.98	2.49
20	Latin America Investment Fund, Inc. (The) .... LAM		24.15	30.06	1.20
21	Putnam Dividend Income Fund .... PDI		23.25	11.81	0.50
22	Castle Convertible Fund, Inc. .... CVF		23.23	16.08	0.89
23	Emerging Mexico Fund .... MEF		23.06	19.96	1.25
24	Bancroft Convertible Fund, Inc. .... BCV		21.95	21.50	0.68
25	Real Estate Securities Income Fund, Inc. .... RIF		21.74	13.06	0.54

1992 Bond Fund Rankings by Category
(by Share Price)

Rank	Fund Name	Symbol	1992 Total Return Shr Pr(%)	NAV (%)	Avg. Mat. (Yrs.)
	Corporate Bond Funds				
1	USLife Income Fund, Inc. ....UIF		22.34	13.53	16.8
2	State Mutual Securities Trust ....SMS		19.66	10.74	12.4
3	CNA Income Shares, Inc. ....CNN		16.35	9.09	14.8
4	Montgomery Street Income Securities............MTS		14.88	9.39	9.0
5	1838 Bond-Debenture Trading Fund. ....BDF		12.22	13.31	18.1
6	Mutual of Omaha Interest Shares, Inc............MUO		11.58	7.70	22.8
7	Hatteras Income Securities, Inc. ....HAT		11.43	9.67	14.4
8	American Capital Bond Fund, Inc....................ACB		9.59	9.25	20.1
9	Pacific American Income Shares, Inc. ....PAI		8.13	7.97	14.5
10	Independence Square Income Securities ....ISIS		6.90	10.91	19.6
11	John Hancock Income Securities Trust ....JHS		6.65	8.86	17.2
12	Bunker Hill Income Securities, Inc. ....BHL		5.84	10.61	13.8
13	John Hancock Investors Trust ....JHI		5.71	8.70	18.0
14	Transamerica Income Shares, Inc. ....TAI		5.00	7.15	23.1
15	Vestaur Securities, Inc. ....VES		4.44	7.64	18.5
16	Current Income Shares, Inc. ....CUR		3.09	9.12	22.7
17	Intercapital Income Securities, Inc. ....ICB		0.33	10.65	15.2
18	Circle Income Shares, Inc................................CINS		(3.23)	8.48	16.7
	Federal Tax-Free Bond Funds				
1	Van Kampen Merritt				
	Municipal Income Trust..............................VMT		20.74	13.57	23.0
2	Municipal Premium Income Trust ....PIA		15.28	11.21	24.0
3	Dreyfus Municipal Income, Inc......................DMF		15.28	18.52	24.5
4	InterCapital Insured				
	Municipal Bond Trust ....IMB		14.48	12.20	25.5
5	Putnam High Yield Municipal Trust..............PYM		13.44	12.17	23.7
6	InterCapital Quality				
	Municipal Investment Trust ....IQT		13.40	12.67	26.4
7	Putnam Investment Grade				
	Municipal Trust ....PGM		13.36	13.54	24.7
8	Putnam Managed Municipal				
	Income Trust...PMM		13.23	12.80	24.8
9	Dreyfus Strategic				
	Municipal Bond Fund, Inc. ....DSM		12.41	8.93	23.9
10	Municipal Income Trust II................................TFB		12.00	7.93	23.6
11	Municipal High Income Fund..........................MHF		11.61	8.54	22.2

Rank	Fund Name	Symbol	1992 Total Return Shr Pr(%)	1992 Total Return NAV (%)	Avg. Mat. (Yrs.)

Federal Tax-Free Bond Funds continued

Rank	Fund Name	Symbol	Shr Pr(%)	NAV (%)	(Yrs.)
12	American Municipal Term Trust II	BXT	11.34	11.95	7.7
13	Van Kampen Merritt Municipal Trust	VKQ	11.24	12.86	24.2
14	Seligman Select Municipal Fund	SEL	11.10	11.38	25.5
15	Nuveen Investment Quality Municipal Fund	NQM	10.60	10.65	22.4
16	Nuveen Municipal Advantage Fund	NMA	10.56	10.74	24.0
17	BlackRock Municipal Target Term Trust	BMN	10.18	12.11	14.6
18	American Municipal Term Trust, Inc.	AXT	10.07	12.21	20.3
19	Kemper Municipal Income Trust	KTF	10.02	10.66	24.0
20	Nuveen Municipal Value Fund, Inc.	NUV	10.00	8.87	21.4
21	MuniVest Fund, Inc.	MVF	9.86	10.24	22.6
22	MuniEnhanced Fund, Inc.	MEN	9.86	11.95	22.3
23	Nuveen Municipal Market Opportunity Fund	NMO	9.75	10.70	23.1
24	Nuveen Performance Plus Municipal Fund, Inc.	NPP	9.72	10.27	22.6
25	Duff & Phelps Utility Tax Free Income Fund	DTF	9.27	9.59	23.5
26	Van Kampen Merritt Investment Grade Municipal Trust	VIG	8.65	6.46	24.5
27	Nuveen Insured Quality Municipal Fund	NQI	8.63	11.16	24.2
28	Kemper Strategic Municipal Income Trust	KSM	8.57	8.92	22.0
29	Nuveen Premium Income Municipal Fund	NPI	7.29	9.73	22.7
30	Colonial Investment Grade Municipal Fund	CXH	7.23	6.49	23.1
31	MuniYield Fund	MYD	7.23	13.43	25.8
32	Nuveen Quality Income Municipal Fund	NQU	7.05	11.27	22.8
33	Colonial Municipal Income Trust	CMU	6.68	5.45	22.3
34	Municipal Income Trust	TFA	6.62	7.86	22.5
35	Nuveen Municipal Income Fund, Inc.	NMI	6.60	8.18	22.6
36	Nuveen Insured Municipal Opportunity Fund	NIO	4.97	10.78	24.4
37	Dreyfus Strategic Municipals, Inc.	LEO	4.89	7.76	23.2
38	MuniInsured Fund, Inc.	MIF	4.43	8.45	21.0

Rank	Fund Name	Symbol	1992 Total Return Shr Pr(%)	NAV (%)	Avg. Mat. (Yrs.)
	Federal Tax-Free Bond Funds continued				
39	Municipal Income Trust III ....TFC		4.26	6.88	25.0
40	Municipal Income				
	Opportunities Trust III ....OIC		4.00	5.61	N/A
41	MFS Municipal Income Trust ....MFM		3.72	7.37	20.8
42	Colonial High Income				
	Municipal Trust ....CXE		3.48	6.17	23.6
43	Seligman Quality Municipal Fund ....SQF		2.58	9.96	25.7
44	Nuveen Premier				
	Municipal Income Fund ....NPF		(0.33)	9.86	21.5
45	Nuveen Premier				
	Insured Municipal Fund..............................NIF		(2.67)	8.55	22.9
46	Municipal Income				
	Opportunities Trust ....OIA		(7.03)	1.92	21.0
47	Municipal Income				
	Opportunities Trust II ....OIB		(7.64)	2.11	N/A
48	Apex Municipal Fund, Inc. ....APX		(8.70)	2.51	23.5
	Flexible Bond Funds				
1	Franklin Universal Trust ....FT		21.07	20.93	9.6
2	Lincoln National Income Fund, Inc. ....LND		15.78	6.80	12.6
3	MFS Special Value Trust ....MFV		14.38	12.74	7.2
4	Franklin Multi Income Trust ....FMI		13.89	15.87	9.5
5	Zweig Total Return Fund, Inc. (The) ....ZTR		3.10	2.35	8.0
	High Yield Bond Funds				
1	Prospect Street				
	High Income Portfolio, Inc. ....PHY		44.62	21.04	9.2
2	Van Kampen Merritt				
	Limited Term High Income Trust ....VLT		38.13	16.80	7.7
3	New America High Income Fund ....HYB		28.93	28.50	11.2
4	High Income Advantage Trust ....YLD		28.80	15.31	9.0
5	High Income Advantage Trust II ....YLT		28.19	16.81	8.6
6	High Yield Plus Fund, Inc. ....HYP		26.29	17.68	11.3
7	CIM High Yield Securities ....CIM		25.34	18.17	7.1
8	USF&G Pacholder Fund, Inc. ....PHF		24.41	18.60	5.6
9	High Yield Income Fund, Inc. ....HYI		22.67	17.43	8.3
10	CIGNA High Income Shares ....HIS		22.62	20.85	9.1
11	High Income Advantage Trust III ....YLH		21.21	15.34	8.8
12	Kemper High Income Trust..............................KHI		19.81	18.17	9.0
13	Zenix Income ....ZIF		19.58	18.68	10.1

Rank	Fund Name	Symbol	1992 Total Return Shr Pr(%)	NAV (%)	Avg. Mat. (Yrs.)
	High Yield Bond Funds *continued*				
14	Colonial Intermediate High Income Securities .... CIF		19.39	17.34	7.7
15	Van Kampen Merritt Intermediate Term High Income .... VIT		18.60	20.61	5.6
	International Bond Funds				
1	Templeton Global Income Fund, Inc. .... GIM		10.81	1.58	11.7
2	Global Yield Fund, Inc. (The) .... PGY		2.09	(1.00)	5.8
3	Global Governments Plus Fund, Inc. .... GOV		1.55	(0.36)	10.7
4	First Australia Prime Income Fund .... FAX		1.44	(5.78)	5.9
5	Templeton Global Governments Income Trust .... TGG		1.37	0.33	6.6
6	Kleinwort Benson Australian Income Fund, Inc. .... KBA		(2.94)	(1.91)	5.4
7	Global Income Plus Fund, Inc. .... GLI		(6.15)	1.93	8.2
8	BlackRock North American Government Income Trust .... BNA		(8.67)	(1.63)	11.8
9	ACM Managed Multi-Market Trust .... MMF		(21.93)	(3.11)	2.8
	Multi Sector Bond Funds				
1	ACM Managed Income Fund, Inc. .... AMF		25.33	15.78	11.2
2	Kemper Multi-Market Income Trust .... KMM		19.26	15.94	6.0
3	Putnam Master Income Trust .... PMT		17.94	11.52	8.1
4	American Capital Income Trust .... ACD		15.04	13.12	12.1
5	Putnam Master Intermediate Income Trust .... PIM		14.06	11.56	6.5
6	Putnam Premier Income Trust .... PPT		14.06	11.15	8.3
7	Colonial Intermarket Income Trust I .... CMK		11.40	10.08	10.8
8	ACM Government Opportunity Fund .... AOF		10.80	6.35	9.3
9	Dreyfus Strategic Governments Income, Inc. .... DSI		10.61	5.29	6.7
10	American Strategic Income Portfolio, Inc. .... ASP		9.93	15.09	13.1
11	First Boston Income Fund, Inc. .... FBF		9.90	11.71	10.8
12	ACM Government Securities Fund .... GSF		9.78	9.10	9.9
13	Hyperion Total Return Fund .... HTR		9.23	5.46	12.3
14	ACM Government Income Fund .... ACG		7.73	8.59	12.1

Rank	Fund Name	Symbol	1992 Total Return Shr Pr(%)	NAV (%)	Avg. Mat. (Yrs.)

Multi Sector Bond Funds *continued*

Rank	Fund Name	Symbol	Shr Pr(%)	NAV (%)	(Yrs.)
15	Oppenheimer Multi-Sector Income Trust	OMS	7.09	7.66	10.9
16	MFS Multimarket Income Trust	MMT	7.07	5.20	12.9
17	Fortis Securities	FOR	6.94	8.70	11.3
18	Excelsior Income Shares	EIS	6.50	6.51	19.7
19	INA Investment Securities, Inc.	IIS	5.52	7.32	13.4
20	Fort Dearborn Income Securities	FTD	3.82	8.26	17.1
21	Oppenheimer Multi-Government Trust	OGT	3.14	4.10	10.9
22	First Boston Strategic Income Fund	FBI	2.89	12.79	7.5
23	MFS Charter Income Trust	MCR	2.31	6.63	11.8
24	MFS Intermediate Income Trust	MIN	2.16	3.20	6.3
25	Franklin Principal Maturity Trust	FPT	1.75	7.89	9.6
26	MFS Government Markets Income Trust	MGF	1.40	3.15	12.5

Single State Tax Free Bond Funds

Rank	Fund Name	Symbol	Shr Pr(%)	NAV (%)	(Yrs.)
1	Taurus Municipal New York Holdings, Inc.	MNY	19.08	13.14	23.1
2	New York Tax Exempt Income Fund, Inc.	XTX	17.28	8.83	17.2
3	Taurus MuniCalifornia Holdings, Inc.	MCF	14.59	8.95	22.8
4	Dreyfus New York Municipal Income, Inc.	DNM	14.15	10.02	22.4
5	Van Kampen Merritt New York Quality Municipal Trust	VNM	14.15	13.85	24.4
6	Nuveen New York Municipal Market Opportunity Fund	NNO	13.95	12.23	25.5
7	Van Kampen Merritt California Municipal Trust	VKC	13.03	11.03	23.7
8	Nuveen New York Municipal Income Fund	NNM	12.35	4.90	23.5
9	Nuveen New York Municipal Value Fund	NNY	12.04	8.97	24.0
10	Nuveen New York Performance Plus Municipal Fund	NNP	11.87	12.14	26.2
11	Nuveen California Investment Quality Municipal Fund	NQC	11.74	11.04	23.6
12	Van Kampen Merritt Pennsylvania Quality Municipal	VPQ	11.13	14.72	23.2
13	Nuveen New Jersey Quality Income Municipal Fund	NUJ	10.76	9.75	21.5
14	Nuveen California Select Quality Municipal Fund	NVC	10.55	10.56	24.7

Rank	Fund Name	Symbol	1992 Total Return Shr Pr(%)	NAV (%)	Avg. Mat. (Yrs.)

Single State Tax-Free Bond Funds continued

Rank	Fund Name	Symbol	1992 Total Return Shr Pr(%)	NAV (%)	Avg. Mat. (Yrs.)
15	Van Kampen Merritt Florida Quality Municipal Trust	VFM	10.38	12.48	23.8
16	Nuveen California Municipal Market Opportunity Fund	NCO	10.23	10.52	23.8
17	Nuveen Florida Quality Income Municipal Fund	NUF	10.00	10.83	24.4
18	Van Kampen Merritt California Quality Municipal Trust	VQC	9.87	10.75	25.1
19	Nuveen New York Investment Quality Municipal Fund	NQN	9.81	12.24	25.9
20	Nuveen Florida Investment Quality Municipal Fund	NQF	9.81	10.38	22.9
21	Nuveen New Jersey Investment Quality Municipal Fund	NQJ	9.49	9.76	21.6
22	Nuveen California Performance Plus Municipal Income Fund	NCP	9.36	11.30	22.9
23	Nuveen Pennsylvania Quality Income Municipal Fund	NUP	9.07	10.86	22.6
24	Nuveen Michigan Quality Income Municipal Fund	NUM	8.59	10.81	24.7
25	Nuveen New York Select Quality Municipal Fund	NVN	8.40	12.23	24.0
26	Dreyfus California Municipal Income Inc	DCM	8.11	7.27	24.3
27	Van Kampen Merritt Ohio Quality Muni	VOQ	7.61	12.34	20.7
28	Nuveen Ohio Quality Income Municipal Fund	NUO	6.89	10.04	22.4
29	Nuveen Texas Quality Income Municipal Fund	NTX	6.16	9.70	22.2
30	Nuveen California Municipal Value Fund	NCA	6.09	7.70	21.7
31	Nuveen California Quality Income Municipal Fund	NUC	6.05	8.95	22.6
32	Nuveen Pennsylvania Investment Quality Municipal Fund	NQP	4.86	11.53	21.3
33	Nuveen New York Quality Income Municipal Fund	NUN	3.83	10.08	24.3
34	Minnesota Municipal Term Trust	MNA	3.39	11.16	7.3
35	Nuveen California Municipal Income Fund	NCM	3.31	8.18	21.6

Rank	Fund Name	Symbol	1992 Total Return		Avg. Mat.
			Shr Pr(%)	NAV (%)	(Yrs.)
	Term Trust Bond Funds				
1	American Government Term Trust, Inc. ....AGT		13.55	3.47	11.3
2	American Adjustable Rate Term Trust, Inc. -1997 ....CDJ		6.30	5.91	18.3
3	American Adjustable Rate Term Trust, Inc. -1996 ....BDJ		6.02	5.28	16.0
4	American Adjustable Rate Term Trust, Inc. -1995 ....ADJ		5.78	5.14	11.3
5	BlackRock 1998 Term Trust, Inc. ....BBT		4.00	8.27	10.0
6	BlackRock Strategic Term Trust, Inc. ....BGT		3.85	7.24	12.0
7	BlackRock Advantage Term Trust, Inc. ....BAT		2.49	3.38	10.5
8	BlackRock Target Term Trust, Inc. ....BTT		1.12	9.96	9.4
	U.S. Government Bond Funds				
1	American Opportunity Income Fund, Inc. .....OIF		20.84	7.69	13.7
2	American Government Income Fund, Inc. ......AGF		20.54	12.23	15.6
3	American Government Income Portfolio ....AAF		17.03	10.89	15.2
4	ACM Government Spectrum Fund ....SI		9.56	6.56	10.5
5	Kemper Intermediate Government Trust ....KGT		6.98	4.49	5.8
6	RAC Income Fund, Inc. ....RMF		6.08	4.80	23.2
7	Putnam Intermediate Government Income Trust ....PGT		5.73	6.53	7.0
8	Dean Witter Government Income Trust ....GVT		2.53	5.00	8.9
9	BlackRock Income Trust, Inc. ....BKT		(11.57)	1.33	13.9

1992 Equity Fund Rankings by Category
(by Share Price)

Rank	Fund Name	Symbol	1992 Total Return Shr Pr(%)	NAV (%)	Beta
	Convertible (Bond & Equity) Funds				
1	Putnam High Income Convertible & Bond Fund	PCF	27.23	26.36	0.38
2	Castle Convertible Fund, Inc.	CVF	23.23	16.08	0.89
3	Bancroft Convertible Fund, Inc.	BCV	21.95	21.50	0.68
4	Lincoln National Convertible Securities Fund, Inc.	LNV	20.26	9.53	1.42
5	Ellsworth Convertible Growth & Income Fund	ECF	20.19	15.94	0.72
6	AIM Strategic Income Fund, Inc.	AST	16.59	10.05	0.65
7	TCW Convertible Securities Fund, Inc.	CVT	13.94	13.72	1.17
8	American Capital Convertible Securities, Inc.	ACS	12.00	11.65	1.24
	Non-Diversified Domestic Equity Funds				
1	Southeastern Thrift & Bank Fund, Inc.	STBF	83.31	76.13	0.55
2	First Financial Fund, Inc.	FF	82.29	66.41	0.76
3	Pilgrim Regional BankShares	PBS	30.95	31.13	0.80
4	Real Estate Securities Income Fund, Inc.	RIF	21.74	13.06	0.54
5	Duff & Phelps Utilities Income, Inc.	DNP	12.80	9.42	0.70
6	BGR Precious Metals, Inc.	BPTT	11.40	23.08	0.56
7	Hampton Utilities Trust	HU	9.12	7.32	0.59
8	Petroleum & Resources Corporation	PEO	4.81	5.66	0.55
9	H&Q Healthcare Investors	HQH	(26.21)	(11.16)	1.35
10	ASA Limited	ASA	(27.73)	(26.31)	0.82
	Diversified Domestic Equity Funds				
1	Dover Regional Financial	DVRFS	55.93	34.30	0.44
2	Central Securities Corporation	CET	35.03	27.97	0.59
3	Royce Value Trust, Inc.	RVT	26.69	19.32	0.80
4	Putnam Dividend Income Fund	PDI	23.25	11.81	0.50
5	Patriot Premium Dividend Fund I	PDF	19.19	11.05	0.61
6	Preferred Income Fund	PFD	18.44	24.15	0.36
7	Source Capital, Inc.	SOR	16.05	12.71	0.68
8	Patriot Select Dividend Trust	DIV	15.82	7.85	0.42
9	General American Investors Co., Inc.	GAM	14.10	3.43	0.49
10	Adams Express Company	ADX	13.79	9.35	0.36
11	Liberty All-Star Equity Fund	USA	13.49	5.80	0.92

Rank	Fund Name	Symbol	1992 Total Return		Beta
			Shr Pr(%)	NAV (%)	
	Diversified Domestic Equity Funds *continued*				
12	Inefficient Market Fund (The) ....IMF		11.82	11.61	0.28
13	Blue Chip Value Fund, Inc. ....BLU		11.66	0.48	1.16
14	Gabelli Equity Trust, Inc. (The) ....GAB		11.65	9.71	0.90
15	Bergstrom Capital Corporation ....BEM		9.38	(0.20)	1.08
16	Patriot Premium Dividend Fund II ....PDT		8.77	7.94	0.61
17	Baker, Fentress & Company ....BKF		6.69	5.30	0.38
18	Salomon Brothers Fund ....SBF		6.27	3.19	0.86
19	Charles Allmon Trust, Inc. ....GSO		4.40	3.08	0.22
20	Engex, Inc. ....EGX		4.34	5.34	0.28
21	Zweig Fund (The) ....ZF		2.84	0.81	0.69
22	Morgan Grenfell SMALLCap Fund, Inc. ....MGC		1.48	3.98	1.54
23	Counsellors Tandem Securities Fund, Inc. .....CTF		0.00	(2.01)	0.32
24	Tri-Continental Corporation............................TY		(2.77)	3.29	0.83
25	Jundt Growth Fund ....JF		(7.00)	(0.84)	1.46
26	Central Fund of Canada Limited.....................CEF		(9.79)	(6.78)	0.18
27	NAIC Growth ....GROW		(9.95)	9.44	N/A
	Dual Purpose Equity Funds				
1	Quest for Value Dual				
	Purpose Fund, Inc. Capital Shares.............KFV		37.78	22.09	0.63
2	Convertible Holdings, Inc. Capital Shares......CNV		36.19	19.07	0.86
3	Gemini II Inc. Capital Shares ....GMI		12.91	15.42	0.65
4	Quest for Value Dual				
	Purpose Fund, Inc. Income Shares ....KFV+		7.17	11.64	0.02
5	Gemini II Inc. Income Shares.........................GMI+		2.17	17.77	0.18
6	Convertible Holdings, Inc. Income Shares.....CNV+		(0.16)	14.50	(0.02)
	Multi Country Equity Funds				
1	Asia Pacific Fund, Inc. (The) ....APB		31.29	16.01	0.93
2	European Warrant Fund, Inc. (The) ....EWF		31.13	13.11	0.58
3	Morgan Stanley Emerging Markets Fund ......MSF		25.17	13.94	0.61
4	Latin America Investment Fund, Inc. (The) ...LAM		24.15	30.06	1.20
5	Templeton Global Utilities, Inc. ....TGU		19.54	8.30	0.98
6	Latin America Equity Fund, Inc. (The) ....LAQ		16.37	4.15	0.78
7	America's All Season Fund...............................FUND		(1.78)	(7.99)	0.44
8	Scudder New Asia Fund, Inc. ....SAF		(2.45)	2.01	0.67
9	Clemente Global Growth Fund, Inc................CLM		(3.61)	(3.14)	0.52
10	Worldwide Value Fund, Inc..............................VLU		(3.68)	(7.19)	0.77
11	G.T. Greater Europe Fund ....GTF		(5.26)	(6.63)	0.48
12	Europe Fund, Inc. (The) ....EF		(6.43)	(7.70)	0.64

Rank	Fund Name	Symbol	Shr Pr(%)	NAV (%)	Beta
	Multi Country Equity Funds continued				
13	Templeton Emerging Markets Fund, Inc. ......EMF		(7.78)	8.26	1.04
14	Scudder New Europe Fund, Inc. ....NEF		(7.88)	(10.43)	0.66
15	Alliance Global Environment Fund ....AEF		(15.65)	(13.41)	0.22
16	Z-Seven Fund, Inc. ....ZSEV		(20.93)	(14.33)	0.33
	Single Country Equity Funds				
1	Chile Fund, Inc. (The) ....CH		52.18	15.63	0.77
2	Malaysia Fund, Inc. (The) ....MF		38.30	20.15	1.00
3	Thai Fund, Inc. (The) ....TTF		28.66	40.10	1.01
4	Mexico Equity and Income Fund, Inc............MXE		28.34	19.06	0.79
5	Jakarta Growth Fund, Inc. ....JGF		25.39	2.75	0.81
6	First Philippine Fund, Inc................................FPF		25.38	21.47	0.48
7	Thai Capital Fund..TC		24.64	34.98	2.49
8	Emerging Mexico Fund ....MEF		23.06	19.96	1.25
9	Mexico Fund, Inc...MXF		17.80	11.65	0.71
10	India Growth Fund, Inc. ....IGF		8.92	(4.34)	1.18
11	Indonesia Fund, Inc. (The) ....IF		7.40	(1.17)	0.99
12	United Kingdom Fund, Inc. ....UKM		7.34	2.27	0.67
13	Swiss Helvetia Fund, Inc..................................SWZ		4.98	6.16	0.58
14	France Growth Fund, Inc. (The) ....FRF		4.62	(1.67)	0.67
15	Singapore Fund, Inc. ....SGF		(1.66)	(6.03)	0.83
16	Brazil Fund, Inc. (The) ....BZF		(3.12)	7.10	1.39
17	Future Germany Fund, Inc. (The) ....FGF		(7.45)	(8.92)	1.20
18	Irish Investment Fund, Inc. (The) ....IRL		(7.60)	(15.20)	0.55
19	Korea Fund, Inc. ....KF		(8.89)	2.94	0.81
20	New Germany Fund, Inc. (The) ....GF		(11.07)	(11.48)	1.27
21	Argentina Fund ....AF		(13.05)	(11.93)	1.09
22	First Australia Fund ....IAF		(13.14)	(16.37)	0.96
23	Germany Fund ....GER		(13.36)	(7.21)	0.78
24	ROC Taiwan Fund, Inc. ....ROC		(14.44)	(10.49)	0.77
25	Italy Fund, Inc. (The) ....ITA		(15.54)	(28.84)	0.98
26	Emerging Germany Fund, Inc. ....FRG		(16.26)	(14.67)	0.68
27	Portugal Fund, Inc. ....PGF		(17.33)	(16.81)	0.79
28	Growth Fund of Spain ....GSP		(18.66)	(23.48)	0.83
29	First Iberian Fund, Inc......................................IBF		(18.97)	(20.70)	0.88
30	Austria Fund (The) ....OST		(20.72)	(20.27)	0.84
31	Taiwan Fund, Inc. ....TWN		(23.39)	(8.33)	0.64
32	Japan OTC Equity Fund, Inc. ....JOF		(26.49)	(31.76)	0.92
33	Turkish Investment Fund, Inc. (The) ....TKF		(30.67)	(38.13)	1.02
34	Spain Fund, Inc. ....SNF		(35.15)	(30.10)	0.62

8
Bond Fund Summaries

Investment-Grade Corporate Bond Funds

1838 Bond-Debenture Trading Fund

1 Penn Square W., 17th Floor
Philadelphia, PA 19102
(215) 293-4300

NYSE : BDF
Transfer Agent
The Bank of New York
48 Wall St.
New York, NY 10015
(800) 524-4458

Income

12 Months Ending 12/31/92 Results

	Period End	Period Begin	Distributions	Yield Dist (%)	Total Return (%)
Share Price ($)	22.63	22.50	2.62	11.64	12.22
NAV per share ($)	21.38	21.18		12.37	13.31

Background: Formerly named Drexel Burnham Bond-Debenture Trading Fund. Began operations in October of 1971 with net assets of about $55 million.

Objective: Seeks high rate of return primarily from investment income and appreciation. At least 75% of assets are in debt securities rated within the highest four grades by Moody's or S&P, or obligations of the U.S. Government, or banks. Balance may consist of lower-grade debt securities and preferred stock with equity features.

Portfolio: (12/31/92) Corporate Bonds & Notes 64.7%, Commercial Paper 21.2%, U.S. Government & Agencies 16.9%, CMOs 10.2%. Sector Weightings: Industrial 29.9%, U.S. Government 16.9%, Electric Utilities 16.2%, CMOs 10.2%, Telephone Utilities 6.0%. Leveraged 13%.

Capitalization: (12/31/92) Common stock outstanding 3,294,716. No long-term debt.

Average Maturity (years): 18.1
Fund Manager: 1838 Investment Advisors, L.P.
Income Dist: Quarterly
Reinvestment Plan: Yes

Fee: 0.63%
Capital Gains Dist: Annually
Shareholder Reports: Quarterly

5 Year Performance

Fiscal Year Ending 3/31	1992	1991	1990	1989	1988
Net Assets ($mil):	56.20	52.80	51.90	50.90	—
Net Income Dist ($):	1.67	1.87	1.82	1.86	1.86
Cap Gains Dist ($):	0.48	0.00	0.00	0.00	0.00
Total Dist ($)	2.15	1.87	1.82	1.86	1.86
Yield from Dist (%)	10.55	9.59	9.58	8.86	8.36
Expense Ratio (%)	0.93	1.05	0.95	1.11	0.99
Portfolio Turnover (%)	52.89	88.26	135.34	76.67	95.71
NAV per share ($)	21.34	20.27	20.04	19.75	20.18
Market Price per share	22.63	20.38	19.50	19.00	21.00
Premium (Discount) (%)	6.04	0.54	(2.69)	(3.80)	4.06
Total Return, Stk Price (%)	21.59	14.10	12.21	(0.67)	2.74

American Capital Bond Fund, Inc.

c/o BFDS
P.O. Box 366
Boston, MA 02101
(800) 421-9696 / (713) 993-0500

NYSE : ACB
Transfer Agent
Boston Financial Data Services, Inc.
P.O. Box 366
Boston, MA 02101
(800) 821-1238 / (617) 328-5000

Income

12 Months Ending 12/31/92 Results

	Period End	Period Begin	Distributions	Yield Dist (%)	Total Return (%)
Share Price ($)	20.38	20.13	1.68	8.35	9.59
NAV per share ($)	20.05	19.89		8.45	9.25

Background: Originally called the American General Bond Fund. Initial public offering July 9, 1970 with net assets of approximately $45 million. Two additional offerings in 1971 and 1973 increased net assets by $177 million.

Objective: Seeks interest income with conservation of capital. Invests in a diversified portfolio of investment-grade U.S. corporate debt securities, with call protection, and U.S. Government securities.

Portfolio: (12/22/92) Long Term Bonds 93.4%, Cash & Equivalents 6.6%. Sector Weightings: Utilities 49.97%, Energy 15.68%, Raw Materials/Processing Industries 10.59%, Transportation 7.92%, Producer Manufacturing 5.11%, Finance 4.89%, Consumer Services 4.59%, Consumer Non-Durables 2.86%. Portfolio Ratings: AAA 2.05%, AA 6.24%, A 19.52%, BBB 65.47%, Lower or Non-Rated 0.12%.

Capitalization: (6/30/92) Common stock outstanding 11,010,623 . No long-term debt.

Average Maturity (years): 20.1

Fund Manager: American Capital Asset Management, Inc. **Fee:** 0.50%
Income Dist: Quarterly **Capital Gains Dist:** Annually
Reinvestment Plan: Yes **Shareholder Reports:** Semi-Annually

5 Year Performance

Fiscal Year Ending 6/30	1992	1991	1990	1989	1988
Net Assets ($mil):	218.50	204.40	204.80	220.80	232.00
Net Income Dist ($):	1.68	1.77	2.08	2.20	2.20
Cap Gains Dist ($):	0.00	0.00	0.00	0.00	0.00
Total Dist ($)	1.68	1.77	2.08	2.20	2.20
Yield from Dist (%)	9.21	10.73	9.73	10.41	10.29
Expense Ratio (%)	0.71	0.72	0.71	0.71	0.70
Portfolio Turnover (%)	39.00	18.00	14.00	13.00	41.00
NAV per share ($)	19.85	18.68	18.72	20.34	21.49
Market Price per share	20.00	18.25	16.50	21.38	21.13
Premium (Discount) (%)	0.76	(2.30)	(11.86)	5.06	(1.72)
Total Return, Stk Price (%)	18.79	21.33	(13.10)	11.59	9.12

Bunker Hill Income Securities, Inc.

156 W. 56th St.
New York, NY 10019
(800) 332-3863

NYSE : BHL

Transfer Agent
The Bank of New York
101 Barclay St., 11th Floor East
New York, NY 10286
(800) 524-4458

Income

12 Months Ending 12/31/92 Results

	Period End	Period Begin	Distributions	Yield Dist (%)	Total Return (%)
Share Price ($)	15.25	15.75	1.42	9.02	5.84
NAV per share ($)	15.67	15.45		9.19	10.61

Background: Initial public offering October 1973 of 1,900,000 shares at $25 per share. Initial NAV was $22.90 per share.

Objective: Seeks a high level of current income consistent with prudent risk. The fund invests at least 75% of its assets in investment-grade securities. May leverage up to 15%.

Portfolio: (9/30/92) Corporate Bonds 93.1%, U.S. Treasuries 6.2%, Commercial Paper 0.6%, Open-Ended Investment Company 0.2%. Sector Weightings: Air Transportation 21.6%, Utilities 21.2%, Finance 15.0%, Oil & Gas 11.6%, Municipal Bonds 4.8%. Portfolio Ratings: AAA 3.4%, AA 5.3%, A 2.5%, BBB 72.7%, Lower or Non-Rated 9.9%.

Capitalization: (9/30/92) Common stock outstanding 2,770,000. No long-term debt.

Average Maturity (years): 13.8

Fund Manager: Security Pacific Investment Managers
Income Dist: Quarterly
Reinvestment Plan: Yes

Fee: 0.50%
Capital Gains Dist: Annually
Shareholder Reports: Semi-Annually

5 Year Performance

Fiscal Year Ending 9/30	1992	1991	1990	1989	1988
Net Assets ($mil):	44.60	41.80	40.50	46.40	47.90
Net Income Dist ($):	1.53	1.77	1.93	1.87	2.01
Cap Gains Dist ($):	0.00	0.00	0.00	0.00	0.00
Total Dist ($)	1.53	1.77	1.93	1.87	2.01
Yield from Dist (%)	9.63	14.30	11.10	10.46	10.51
Expense Ratio (%)	1.09	1.09	1.06	1.05	1.02
Portfolio Turnover (%)	251.97	54.79	83.92	88.48	133.29
NAV per share ($)	16.12	15.22	14.79	17.02	17.56
Market Price per share	16.25	15.88	12.38	17.38	17.88
Premium (Discount) (%)	0.81	4.27	(16.36)	2.12	1.77
Total Return, Stk Price (%)	11.96	42.57	(17.66)	7.66	3.97

Circle Income Shares, Inc.
111 Monument Circle
Indianapolis, IN 46277-1611
(317) 321-8110

Transfer Agent
Bank One, Indianapolis, NA
111 Monument Circle
Indianapolis, IN 46277-1611
(317) 321-8110

Income

12 Months Ending 12/31/92 Results

	Period End	Period Begin	Distributions	Yield Dist (%)	Total Return (%)
Share Price ($)	11.00	12.38	0.98	7.92	(3.23)
NAV per share ($)	11.94	11.91		8.23	8.48

Background: Initial public offering June 21, 1973 of 1,000,000 shares. Net proceeds were $13,162,500. Subsequent offering November 20, 1975, raised an equal amount.

Objective: Seeks high current income consistent with prudent investment risk through investment principally in debt securities. Capital appreciation is secondary. The fund may leverage up to 25%.

Portfolio: (12/31/92) Corporate Bonds 65.3%, U.S. Government Instrumentality Obligations 29.8%, Short Term & Other 2.0%.

Capitalization: (6/30/92) Common stock outstanding 2,790,269. No long-term debt.

Average Maturity (years): 16.7
Fund Manager: Bank One, Indianapolis, NA **Fee:** 0.50%
Income Dist: Monthly **Capital Gains Dist:** Annually
Reinvestment Plan: Yes **Shareholder Reports:** Quarterly

5 Year Performance

Fiscal Year Ending 6/30	1992	1991	1990	1989	1988
Net Assets ($mil):	33.40	32.10	32.30	33.40	33.60
Net Income Dist ($):	1.08	1.20	1.17	1.32	1.32
Cap Gains Dist ($):	0.00	0.00	0.00	0.00	0.00
Total Dist ($)	1.08	1.20	1.17	1.32	1.32
Yield from Dist (%)	8.82	10.91	9.96	10.25	9.78
Expense Ratio (%)	0.44	0.48	0.48	0.49	0.44
Portfolio Turnover (%)	50.23	15.30	12.01	44.51	42.43
NAV per share ($)	11.95	11.75	11.84	12.25	12.32
Market Price per share	12.25	12.25	11.00	11.75	12.88
Premium (Discount) (%)	2.51	4.26	(7.09)	(4.08)	4.46
Total Return, Stk Price (%)	8.82	22.27	3.57	1.48	5.19

Investment-Grade Corporate Bond Funds 67

CNA Income Shares, Inc.

CNA Plaza
Chicago, IL 60685
(312) 822-4181

NYSE : CNN
Transfer Agent
The Bank of New York
Church Street Station
New York, NY 10277-0702
(800) 524-4458

Income

12 Months Ending 12/31/92 Results

	Period End	Period Begin	Distributions	Yield Dist (%)	Total Return (%)
Share Price ($)	11.75	11.13	1.20	10.78	16.35
NAV per share ($)	10.32	10.56		11.36	9.09

Background: Initial public offering May 1973. After deductions for underwriting and commissions, net proceeds totaled $66.5 million. In May of 1987 the fund issued $30 million five-year 9.125% convertible extendible notes for leverage.

Objective: Seeks high current income. Capital appreciation is secondary. At least 75% of assets must be invested in straight debt securities of the four highest ratings, and in U.S. and Canadian Government securities, bank debt, and cash or equivalents. Up to 25% of total assets may be invested in other debt securities, preferred and common stocks and convertible issues.

Portfolio: (12/31/92) Debt Securities 131.9%, Short Term Notes 2.6%. Sector Weightings: Utilities 23.8%, Government Debt 17.4%, Mortgage-Backed 15.9%, Transportation 12.6%, Energy 9.8%.

Capitalization: (12/31/92) Common stock outstanding 7,908,449. Leveraged $28,800,000 with convertible notes.

Average Maturity (years): 14.8
Fund Manager: Continental Assurance Co.
Income Dist: Quarterly
Reinvestment Plan: Yes

Fee: 0.50%
Capital Gains Dist: Annually
Shareholder Reports: Quarterly

5 Year Performance

Fiscal Year Ending 12/31	1992	1991	1990	1989	1988
Net Assets ($mil):	81.60	81.20	69.60	77.00	80.40
Net Income Dist ($):	1.20	1.16	1.20	1.24	1.29
Cap Gains Dist ($):	0.00	0.00	0.00	0.00	0.00
Total Dist ($)	1.20	1.16	1.20	1.24	1.29
Yield from Dist (%)	10.78	13.44	10.21	11.14	11.86
Expense Ratio (%)	0.84	1.05	0.97	0.88	0.88
Portfolio Turnover (%)	54.06	39.77	35.16	39.12	33.95
NAV per share ($)	10.32	10.56	9.16	10.29	11.12
Market Price per share	11.75	11.13	8.63	11.75	11.13
Premium (Discount) (%)	13.86	5.30	(5.90)	14.19	0.00
Total Return, Stk Price (%)	16.35	42.41	(16.34)	16.71	14.15

Current Income Shares, Inc.

P.O. Box 30151
Terminal Annex
Los Angeles, CA 90030
(213) 236-4056

NYSE : CUR

Transfer Agent
Harris Trust Co. of California
707 Wilshire Blvd., Suite 4840
Los Angeles, CA 90017
(213) 239-0670

Income

12 Months Ending 12/31/92 Results

	Period End	Period Begin	Distributions	Yield Dist (%)	Total Return (%)
Share Price ($)	12.63	13.25	1.03	7.77	3.09
NAV per share ($)	13.33	13.16		7.83	9.12

Background: Organized under sponsorship of Unionamerica, Inc., a financial services company. Initial public offering March 27, 1973 at $15 per share. Initial NAV was $13.80 per share.

Objective: Seeks high current income. Invests at least 75% of total assets in high-quality straight-debt securities; obligations of or guaranteed by the governments of the U.S. or Canada; commercial paper with an A-1 or A-2 Standard & Poor's rating, and cash equivalents. May employ leverage by borrowing up to 50% of total assets.

Portfolio: (12/31/92) Long-Term Bonds 97.8%. Sector Weightings: Utilities 39.8%, Industrial 30.2%, Canadian 17.6%, U.S. Government 4.3%, Transportation 4.3%. Portfolio Ratings: AAA 12.0%, AA 13.1%, A 26.5%, BBB 41.2%, Lower or Non-Rated 7.2%.

Capitalization: (12/31/92) Common stock outstanding 3,673,334. No long-term debt.

Average Maturity (years): 22.7
Fund Manager: Union Bank
Income Dist: Quarterly
Reinvestment Plan: Yes

Fee: 0.50%
Capital Gains Dist: Annually
Shareholder Reports: Semi-Annually

5 Year Performance

Fiscal Year Ending 12/31	1992	1991	1990	1989	1988
Net Assets ($mil):	49.00	48.40	43.40	45.20	43.80
Net Income Dist ($):	1.03	1.09	1.10	1.12	1.12
Cap Gains Dist ($):	0.00	0.00	0.00	0.00	0.00
Total Dist ($)	1.03	1.09	1.10	1.12	1.12
Yield from Dist (%)	7.77	9.08	8.98	10.18	9.53
Expense Ratio (%)	0.90	0.90	0.90	0.90	0.90
Portfolio Turnover (%)	87.06	82.38	106.20	84.50	129.00
NAV per share ($)	13.33	13.16	11.80	12.30	11.92
Market Price per share	12.63	13.25	12.00	12.25	11.00
Premium (Discount) (%)	(5.25)	0.68	1.69	(0.41)	(7.72)
Total Return, Stk Price (%)	3.09	19.50	6.94	21.55	3.15

Hatteras Income Securities, Inc.

One NCNB Plaza
Charlotte, NC 28255
(704) 386-5000

Income

NYSE : HAT

Transfer Agent
NationsBank Trust Co., NA
Stock Transfer Department
P.O. Box 105555
Atlanta, GA 30348-5555
(800) 442-3817 / (704) 386-5000

12 Months Ending 12/31/92 Results

	Period End	Period Begin	Distributions	Yield Dist (%)	Total Return (%)
Share Price ($)	18.00	17.50	1.50	8.57	11.43
NAV per share ($)	16.08	16.03		9.36	9.67

Background: Initial public offering April 17, 1973 of 2,750,000 shares at $20 per share. Initial NAV was $18.50 per share.

Objective: Seeks high current income. Capital appreciation is secondary. Invests at least 70% of assets in debt securities rated within the four highest categories of either S&P or Moody's. May invest up to 30% in other debt securities, convertible issues, and obligations of foreign governments. May also invest up to 30% in privately placed fixed-income securities.

Portfolio: Long-Term Debt Securities 95.0%, Government Obligations 16.0%, Short-Term 2.5%. Leveraged 13.5%.

Capitalization: Common stock outstanding 3,165,000. No long-term debt.

Average Maturity (years): 14.4
Fund Manager: NationsBank of North Carolina NA   **Fee:** 0.45%
Income Dist: Monthly   **Capital Gains Dist:** Annually
Reinvestment Plan: Yes   **Shareholder Reports:** Quarterly

5 Year Performance

Fiscal Year Ending 12/31	1992	1991	1990	1989	1988
Net Assets ($mil):	51.90	51.00	46.40	49.70	49.50
Net Income Dist ($):	1.50	1.56	1.57	1.63	1.62
Cap Gains Dist ($):	0.00	0.00	0.00	0.00	0.00
Total Dist ($)	1.50	1.56	1.57	1.63	1.62
Yield from Dist (%)	8.57	10.66	10.30	10.87	9.53
Expense Ratio (%)	N/A	0.99	1.01	0.97	1.01
Portfolio Turnover (%)	N/A	27.17	24.58	33.49	58.57
NAV per share ($)	16.08	16.03	14.88	15.99	15.99
Market Price per share	18.00	17.50	14.63	15.25	15.00
Premium (Discount) (%)	11.94	9.17	(1.75)	(4.63)	(6.19)
Total Return, Stk Price (%)	11.43	30.28	6.23	12.53	(2.24)

Independence Square Income Securities

One Aldwyn Center
Villanova, PA 19085
(215) 964-8882

OTC : ISIS

Transfer Agent
PNC Bank, N.A.
c/o PFPC Inc.
P.O. Box 8950
Wilmington, DE 19899
(302) 791-1072

Income

12 Months Ending 12/31/92 Results

	Period End	Period Begin	Distributions	Yield Dist (%)	Total Return (%)
Share Price ($)	17.13	17.38	1.45	8.34	6.90
NAV per share ($)	17.76	17.32		8.37	10.91

Background: Initial public offering February 1972 of 1,000,000 shares at $25 per share. Initial NAV was $23.08 per share.

Objective: Seeks high current income consistent with prudent investment. At least 60% of total assets are invested in debt securities rated in the top four categories by S&P's, Moody's or Fitch Investor Service. May invest up to 40% in preferred stocks and debt securities not included in top four categories. Up to 25% of total assets may be invested in private placements.

Portfolio: (12/31/92) Bonds & Debt Obligations 98.11%, U.S. Government Securities 0.96%, Short-Term 0.93%. Largest Holdings: Detroit Edison 9-7/8% (matures) 2019, American Airlines 14-3/8% (matures 2005), Arizona Public Service Co. 10-1/4% (matures 2020), Oglethorpe Power Fac GA 9.70% (matures 2011), Chase Manhattan CP Sub Notes 10% (matures 1999).

Capitalization: (12/31/92) Common stock outstanding 1,820,511. No long-term debt.

Average Maturity (years): 19.6
Fund Manager: PNC Institutional Mgt Corp.　　　　**Fee:** 0.20%
Income Dist: Monthly　　　　**Capital Gains Dist:** None
Reinvestment Plan: Yes　　　　**Shareholder Reports:** Quarterly

5 Year Performance

Fiscal Year Ending 12/31	1992	1991	1990	1989	1988
Net Assets ($mil):	32.30	31.40	29.10	30.90	29.90
Net Income Dist ($):	1.45	1.50	1.51	1.56	1.62
Cap Gains Dist ($):	0.00	0.00	0.00	0.00	0.00
Total Dist ($)	1.45	1.50	1.51	1.56	1.62
Yield from Dist (%)	8.34	10.00	9.15	9.75	9.97
Expense Ratio (%)	0.85	0.90	1.00	0.90	0.91
Portfolio Turnover (%)	18.00	6.00	25.00	57.00	45.00
NAV per share ($)	17.76	17.32	16.06	17.05	16.49
Market Price per share	17.13	17.38	15.00	16.50	16.00
Premium (Discount) (%)	(3.55)	0.29	(6.60)	(3.23)	(2.97)
Total Return, Stk Price (%)	6.90	25.87	0.06	12.88	8.43

Intercapital Income Securities, Inc.

Two World Trade Center
New York, NY 10048
(800) 869-3863 / (212) 392-2550

NYSE : ICB
Transfer Agent
Dean Witter Trust Co.
2 Montgomery St.
Jersey City, NJ 07302
(800) 896-3883

Income

12 Months Ending 12/31/92 Results

	Period End	Period Begin	Distributions	Yield Dist (%)	Total Return (%)
Share Price ($)	19.38	21.13	1.82	8.61	0.33
NAV per share ($)	18.33	18.21		9.99	10.65

Background: Initial public offering April 6, 1973 of 10,000,000 shares at $25 per share.

Objective: Seeks high current income consistent with prudent risk. Capital appreciation is secondary. Invests at least 50% in straight-debt securities rated in the top four categories by S&P or Moody's; in obligations of or guaranteed by the U.S. and Canadian Governments.

Portfolio: (9/30/92) Corporate Bonds 80.0%, U.S. Government & Agencies 17.2%, Short Term 2.8%.

Capitalization: (9/30/92) Common stock outstanding 12,200,518. No long-term debt.

Average Maturity (years): 15.2
Fund Manager: Dean Witter Reynolds InterCapital Division   **Fee:** 0.50%
Income Dist: Monthly   **Capital Gains Dist:** Annually
Reinvestment Plan: Yes   **Shareholder Reports:** Quarterly

5 Year Performance

Fiscal Year Ending 9/30	1992	1991	1990	1989	1988
Net Assets ($mil):	228.40	218.50	199.50	215.10	213.70
Net Income Dist ($):	1.89	1.84	2.10	2.10	2.10
Cap Gains Dist ($):	0.00	0.00	0.00	0.00	0.00
Total Dist ($)	1.89	1.84	2.10	2.10	2.10
Yield from Dist (%)	9.22	9.20	9.94	9.77	10.00
Expense Ratio (%)	0.69	0.72	0.72	0.67	0.72
Portfolio Turnover (%)	61.00	56.00	61.00	88.00	75.00
NAV per share ($)	18.72	18.03	16.97	18.83	19.28
Market Price per share	22.25	20.50	20.00	21.13	21.50
Premium (Discount) (%)	18.86	13.70	17.86	12.21	11.51
Total Return, Stk Price (%)	17.76	11.70	4.59	8.05	12.38

John Hancock Income Securities Trust

101 Huntington Ave.
Boston, MA 02199-7603
(800) 843-0090 / (617) 375-1500

Transfer Agent
Bank of Boston
P.O. Box 644
Boston, MA 02102
(617) 575-2900

Income

12 Months Ending 12/31/92 Results

	Period End	Period Begin	Distributions	Yield Dist (%)	Total Return (%)
Share Price ($)	16.75	17.00	1.38	8.12	6.65
NAV per share ($)	16.31	16.25		8.49	8.86

Background: Initial public offering February 14, 1973. Net proceeds were $176.7 million.

Objective: Seeks high current income consistent with prudent risk. Invests at least 75% of total assets in debt securities rated within the four highest categories by S&P or Moody's. Up to 20% of fund's assets may consist of income-producing preferred and common stocks.

Portfolio: (11/30/92) U.S. Treasuries 24.72%, Corporate Bonds 53.46%, Yankee Bonds 19.55%, Cash & Equivalents 2.27%. Largest Holdings: International Bank Reconstruction, Barclay's Bank, American Airlines.

Capitalization: Common stock outstanding 9,846,422. No long-term debt.

Average Maturity (years): 17.2
Fund Manager: John Hancock Advisors, Inc.
Income Dist: Quarterly
Reinvestment Plan: Yes

Fee: 0.50%
Capital Gains Dist: Annually
Shareholder Reports: Quarterly

5 Year Performance

Fiscal Year Ending 12/31	1992	1991	1990	1989	1988
Net Assets ($mil):	162.50	160.00	147.70	149.70	144.20
Net Income Dist ($):	1.38	1.46	1.47	1.47	1.47
Cap Gains Dist ($):	0.00	0.00	0.00	0.00	0.00
Total Dist ($)	1.38	1.46	1.47	1.47	1.47
Yield from Dist (%)	8.12	9.73	9.48	10.14	10.40
Expense Ratio (%)	0.81	0.74	0.70	0.71	0.71
Portfolio Turnover (%)	110.78	91.97	84.67	61.79	23.95
NAV per share ($)	16.31	16.25	15.19	15.61	15.24
Market Price per share	16.75	17.00	15.00	15.50	14.50
Premium (Discount) (%)	2.70	4.62	(1.25)	(0.70)	(4.86)
Total Return, Stk Price (%)	6.65	23.07	6.26	17.03	13.02

Investment-Grade Corporate Bond Funds 73

John Hancock Investors Trust

101 Huntington Ave.
Boston, MA 02199
(800) 843-0090 / (617) 375-1500

NYSE : JHI

Transfer Agent
Bank of Boston
P.O. Box 644
Boston, MA 02102
(617) 575-2900

Income

12 Months Ending 12/31/92 Results

	Period End	Period Begin	Distributions	Yield Dist (%)	Total Return (%)
Share Price ($)	23.50	24.00	1.87	7.79	5.71
NAV per share ($)	21.62	21.61		8.65	8.70

Background: Initial public offering January 29, 1971 of 5,120,000 shares at $25 per share. Initial NAV was $23.25 per share.

Objective: Seeks current income. Capital appreciation is secondary. Up to 50% of the fund's assets may be invested in private placements.

Portfolio: (11/30/92) Sector Weightings: U.S. Treasuries 13.0%, U.S. Agencies 11.0%, Banks 16.0%, Utilities 13.0%.

Capitalization: (12/31/92) Shares of beneficial interest outstanding 7,297,037. No long-term debt.

Average Maturity (years): 18.0
Fund Manager: John Hancock Advisors, Inc.   **Fee:** 0.50%
Income Dist: Quarterly   **Capital Gains Dist:** Annually
Reinvestment Plan: Yes   **Shareholder Reports:** Quarterly

5 Year Performance

Fiscal Year Ending 12/31	1992	1991	1990	1989	1988
Net Assets ($mil):	157.80	156.00	143.30	147.00	142.30
Net Income Dist ($):	1.87	1.93	1.98	1.99	1.99
Cap Gains Dist ($):	0.00	0.00	0.00	0.00	0.00
Total Dist ($)	1.87	1.93	1.98	1.99	1.99
Yield from Dist (%)	7.79	9.90	9.43	10.08	9.59
Expense Ratio (%)	0.82	0.74	0.71	0.71	0.70
Portfolio Turnover (%)	103.89	81.47	95.17	49.61	15.64
NAV per share ($)	21.62	21.61	20.08	20.87	20.46
Market Price per share	23.50	24.00	19.50	21.00	19.75
Premium (Discount) (%)	8.70	11.06	(2.89)	0.62	(3.47)
Total Return, Stk Price (%)	5.71	32.97	2.29	16.41	4.77

Montgomery Street Income Securities

101 California St., Suite 4100
San Francisco, CA 94111
(415) 981-8191

NYSE : MTS

Transfer Agent
First National Bank of Boston
P.O. Box 644
Boston, MA 02102
(617) 575-2900

Income

12 Months Ending 12/31/92 Results

	Period End	Period Begin	Distributions	Yield Dist (%)	Total Return (%)
Share Price ($)	20.88	19.63	1.67	8.51	14.88
NAV per share ($)	19.30	19.17		8.71	9.39

Background: Initial public offering February 14, 1973 of 8,000,000 shares at $25 per share. Initial NAV was $23.11 per share.

Objective: Seeks high income consistent with prudent risk. Capital appreciation is secondary. Invests 70% in straight debt securities rated in the top four categories by S&P or Moody's; obligations of, or debt guaranteed by, the U.S. or Canadian Governments not to exceed 25% of total assets; provincial or municipal securities; commercial paper; and cash. May invest up to 30% in lower quality bonds, debt issues with equity features, preferred stock, and dividend-paying utility common stocks.

Portfolio: (12/31/92) U.S. Government Agency Obligations 35.4%, Corporate Bonds & Notes 60.6%. Sector Weightings: Utilities 14.4%, Financial 12.3%, Energy 9.7%, Consumer Nondurable 7.3%, Consumer Cyclical 7.0%.

Capitalization: (12/31/92) Common stock outstanding 9,896,796. No long-term debt.

Average Maturity (years): 9.0
Fund Manager: Scudder, Stevens & Clark, Inc.   **Fee:** 0.50%
Income Dist: Quarterly   **Capital Gains Dist:** Annually
Reinvestment Plan: Yes   **Shareholder Reports:** Semi-Annually

5 Year Performance

Fiscal Year Ending 12/31	1992	1991	1990	1989	1988
Net Assets ($mil):	191.00	157.10	139.80	144.80	145.80
Net Income Dist ($):	1.67	1.76	1.78	1.85	1.84
Cap Gains Dist ($):	0.00	0.00	0.00	0.00	0.00
Total Dist ($)	1.67	1.76	1.78	1.85	1.84
Yield from Dist (%)	8.51	10.06	9.49	10.35	9.88
Expense Ratio (%)	0.75	0.69	0.57	0.52	0.86
Portfolio Turnover (%)	137.60	72.00	69.10	97.10	160.00
NAV per share ($)	19.30	19.17	17.21	17.97	18.21
Market Price per share	20.88	19.63	17.50	18.75	17.88
Premium (Discount) (%)	8.19	2.35	1.69	4.34	(1.81)
Total Return, Stk Price (%)	14.88	22.23	2.83	15.21	5.85

Mutual of Omaha Interest Shares, Inc.

10235 Regency Circle
Omaha, NE 68114
(800) 228-9596 / (402) 397-8555

Income

NYSE : MUO

Transfer Agent
Mellon Securities Trust Co.
85 Challenger Rd.
Overpeck Centre
Ridgfield Park, NJ 07660
(800) 526-0801

12 Months Ending 12/31/92 Results

	Period End	Period Begin	Distributions	Yield Dist (%)	Total Return (%)
Share Price ($)	14.75	14.25	1.15	8.07	11.58
NAV per share ($)	14.09	14.15		8.13	7.70

Background: Initial public offering January 1972 of 5,200,000 shares at $20 per share. Initial NAV was $18.40 per share.

Objective: Seeks current income. 80% of assets are invested in securities rated in the four highest categories by S&P or Moody's. The remaining 20% may be invested in private placements and non-rated securities.

Portfolio: (12/31/92) Bonds 94.7%, Short Term 5.0%, Cash & Other 0.3%.

Capitalization: (12/31/92) Common stock outstanding 7,141,052. No long-term debt.

Average Maturity (years): 22.8
Fund Manager: Mutual of Omaha Fund Management Co.   **Fee:** 0.63%
Income Dist: Quarterly   **Capital Gains Dist:** Annually
Reinvestment Plan: Yes   **Shareholder Reports:** Semi-Annually

5 Year Performance

Fiscal Year Ending 12/31	1992	1991	1990	1989	1988
Net Assets ($mil):	100.60	99.80	93.40	95.40	92.20
Net Income Dist ($):	1.15	1.17	1.22	1.26	1.57
Cap Gains Dist ($):	0.00	0.00	0.00	0.00	0.18
Total Dist ($)	1.15	1.17	1.22	1.26	1.75
Yield from Dist (%)	8.07	9.26	8.87	9.33	12.38
Expense Ratio (%)	0.82	0.82	0.84	0.85	0.85
Portfolio Turnover (%)	44.20	39.50	32.30	62.00	82.10
NAV per share ($)	14.09	14.15	13.34	13.73	13.53
Market Price per share	14.75	14.25	12.63	13.75	13.50
Premium (Discount) (%)	4.68	0.71	(5.40)	0.15	(0.22)
Total Return, Stk Price (%)	11.58	22.09	0.73	11.19	7.93

Pacific American Income Shares, Inc.

P.O. Box 983
Pasadena, CA 91102
(818) 584-4300

NYSE : PAI

Transfer Agent
First Interstate Bank of California
707 Wilshire Blvd.
Los Angeles, CA 90017
(213) 614-2408

Income

12 Months Ending 12/31/92 Results

	Period End	Period Begin	Distributions	Yield Dist (%)	Total Return (%)
Share Price ($)	15.63	15.75	1.40	8.89	8.13
NAV per share ($)	15.94	16.06		8.72	7.97

Background: Initial public offering March 1973. Initial share price $17.50. Initial NAV was $16.04.

Objective: Seeks a high level of current income. Capital appreciation is secondary. At least 75% must be invested in debt securities rated within the four highest categories by S&P or Moody's, government securities, commercial paper, and cash or equivalents. Not more than 25% of assets may be in private placements.

Portfolio: (12/31/92) Bonds 94.5%, Short-Term 4.53%, Convertibles 0.95%. Sector Weightings: Industrial & Misc. 27.1%, U.S. Government Agencies 23.4%, Utilities 14.2%, Mortgage Pass-Throughs 7.72%. Portfolio Ratings: Aaa 30.11%, Aa 2.18%, A 7.76%, Baa 25.4%, Lower or Non-Rated 12.41%.

Capitalization: (12/31/92) Common stock outstanding 8,929,806. Long-term debt $5,000,000 9-1/4% notes convertible into common at $13.73 per share in October 1993.

Average Maturity (years): 14.5
Fund Manager: Western Asset Management Co. **Fee:** 0.70%
Income Dist: Quarterly **Capital Gains Dist:** Annually
Reinvestment Plan: Yes **Shareholder Reports:** Quarterly

5 Year Performance

Fiscal Year Ending 12/31	1992	1991	1990	1989	1988
Net Assets ($mil):	142.30	107.70	98.10	102.20	101.70
Net Income Dist ($):	1.40	1.46	1.46	1.53	1.54
Cap Gains Dist ($):	0.00	0.00	0.00	0.00	0.00
Total Dist ($)	1.40	1.46	1.46	1.53	1.54
Yield from Dist (%)	8.89	10.62	9.49	10.20	10.35
Expense Ratio (%)	0.79	0.84	0.89	0.88	0.94
Portfolio Turnover (%)	83.51	41.52	48.48	60.01	35.85
NAV per share ($)	15.94	16.06	14.62	15.24	15.16
Market Price per share	15.63	15.75	13.75	15.38	15.00
Premium (Discount) (%)	(1.94)	(1.93)	(5.95)	0.85	(1.06)
Total Return, Stk Price (%)	8.13	25.16	(1.11)	12.73	11.16

State Mutual Securities Trust

440 Lincoln St.
Worchester, MA 01653
(508) 855-1000

Income

NYSE : SMS

Transfer Agent
The Bank of New York
P.O. Box 11002
Church Street Station
New York, NY 10249
(800) 524-4458

12 Months Ending 12/31/92 Results

	Period End	Period Begin	Distributions	Yield Dist (%)	Total Return (%)
Share Price ($)	11.75	10.63	0.97	9.13	19.66
NAV per share ($)	11.30	11.08		8.75	10.74

Background: Initial public offering February 20, 1973 of 7,700,000 shares at $15 per share. Initial NAV was $13.80 per share.

Objective: Seeks high current income. Capital appreciation is secondary. Invests primarily in fixed-income securities. Invests at least 40% of total assets in securities rated in the top four categories by S&P or Moody's, obligations issued or guaranteed by United States or Canadian Governments, high grade commercial paper, and cash and equivalents. May invest up to 50% of net assets in private placements. May borrow short-term up to 25%.

Portfolio: (12/31/92) Corporate Bonds 78.75%, U.S. Government & Agencies 18.46%, Foreign 2.3%. Sector Weightings: Electric, Gas & Sanitary 12.77%, Communication 11.46%, Banking 7.02%, Air Transportation 6.09%.

Capitalization: (21/31/92) Common stock outstanding 8,442,388. No long-term debt.

Average Maturity (years): 12.4
Fund Manager: State Mutual Life Assurance Co. of America   **Fee:** 0.30%
Income Dist: Quarterly   **Capital Gains Dist:** Annually
Reinvestment Plan: Yes   **Shareholder Reports:** Semi-Annually

5 Year Performance

Fiscal Year Ending 12/31	1992	1991	1990	1989	1988
Net Assets ($mil):	95.40	93.60	85.40	89.60	89.50
Net Income Dist ($):	0.97	0.97	1.04	1.09	1.13
Cap Gains Dist ($):	0.00	0.00	0.00	0.00	0.00
Total Dist ($)	0.97	0.97	1.04	1.09	1.13
Yield from Dist (%)	9.13	10.07	9.56	10.02	10.15
Expense Ratio (%)	0.76	0.77	0.82	0.84	0.81
Portfolio Turnover (%)	55.00	43.00	39.00	31.00	10.00
NAV per share ($)	11.30	11.08	10.11	10.68	10.67
Market Price per share	11.75	10.63	9.63	10.88	10.88
Premium (Discount) (%)	3.96	(4.10)	(4.85)	1.87	1.87
Total Return, Stk Price (%)	19.66	20.46	(1.93)	10.02	7.91

Transamerica Income Shares, Inc.

1150 S. Olive St.
Los Angeles, CA 90015
(213) 742-4141

NYSE : TAI
Transfer Agent
Mellon Securities Trust Co.
111 Founders Plaza, Suite 1100
East Hartford, CT 06108
(800) 288-9541

Income

12 Months Ending 12/31/92 Results

	Period End	Period Begin	Distributions	Yield Dist (%)	Total Return (%)
Share Price ($)	25.25	26.00	2.05	7.88	5.00
NAV per share ($)	24.18	24.48		8.37	7.15

Background: Initial public offering November 1972. Total net assets were approximately $121.5 million.

Objective: Seeks high current income consistent with prudent investing. Capital appreciation is secondary. May invest up to 20% of assets in convertible debt securities, preferred stock or other securities with equity features to achieve capital appreciation.

Portfolio: (9/30/92) Corporate Bonds & Notes 92.6%. Sector Weightings: Electric & Gas Utilities 22.7%, Industrials 21.2%, Financial 14.4%, Petroleum 9.2%, Telephones 6.6%. Portfolio Ratings: AAA 1.4%, AA 9.3%, A 30.4%, BBB 53.0%, Lower or Non-Rated 5.9%.

Capitalization: (12/31/92) Common stock outstanding 6,318,771. No long-term debt.

Average Maturity (years): 23.1
Fund Manager: Transamerica Investment Services, Inc.   **Fee:** 0.50%
Income Dist: Monthly   **Capital Gains Dist:** Annually
Reinvestment Plan: Yes   **Shareholder Reports:** Quarterly

5 Year Performance

Fiscal Year Ending 3/31	1992	1991	1990	1989	1988
Net Assets ($mil):	126.40	121.80	117.40	116.10	—
Net Income Dist ($):	2.16	2.16	2.16	2.23	2.48
Cap Gains Dist ($):	0.00	0.00	0.00	0.00	0.00
Total Dist ($)	2.16	2.16	2.16	2.23	2.48
Yield from Dist (%)	9.24	9.65	9.09	10.31	9.97
Expense Ratio (%)	0.68	0.69	0.71	0.68	0.6.
Portfolio Turnover (%)	30.00	17.00	30.00	15.00	38.00
NAV per share ($)	24.00	23.13	22.30	22.05	22.37
Market Price per share	25.50	23.38	22.38	23.75	21.63
Premium (Discount) (%)	6.25	1.08	0.31	7.71	(3.35)
Total Return, Stk Price (%)	18.31	14.12	3.33	20.11	(3.09)

USLife Income Fund, Inc.
125 Maiden Ln.
New York, NY 10038
(212) 709-6000

NYSE : UIF
Transfer Agent
Chemical Bank
450 W. 33rd St.
New York, NY 10001
(212) 270-6000

Income

12 Months Ending 12/31/92 Results

	Period End	Period Begin	Distributions	Yield Dist (%)	Total Return (%)
Share Price ($)	10.25	9.13	0.92	10.08	22.34
NAV per share ($)	9.74	9.39		9.80	13.53

Background: Initial public offering December 7, 1972 of 4,400,000 shares at $15 per share. Initial NAV was $13.80 per share.

Objective: Seeks high current income. Invests 50% in straight debt securities of the four highest grades determined by S&P, obligations guaranteed by the U.S. or Canadian Governments, and investment-grade commercial paper. May invest the balance in lower-rated fixed income debt securities, convertible bonds and preferred shares. May hold 10% in common shares, with a limit of 30% in private placements. The fund may borrow up to 25% of total assets.

Portfolio: (6/30/92) Corporate Obligations 95.4%, Common Stocks 0.4%.

Capitalization: (6/30/92) Common stock outstanding 5,414,072. No long-term debt.

Average Maturity (years): 16.8
Fund Manager: USLife Advisors, Inc.   **Fee:** 0.04%
Income Dist: Quarterly   **Capital Gains Dist:** Annually
Reinvestment Plan: Yes   **Shareholder Reports:** Semi-Annually

5 Year Performance

Fiscal Year Ending 6/30	1992	1991	1990	1989	1988
Net Assets ($mil):	52.40	50.60	46.70	52.30	51.00
Net Income Dist ($):	0.92	0.93	0.93	0.92	0.94
Cap Gains Dist ($):	0.00	0.00	0.00	0.00	0.00
Total Dist ($)	0.92	0.93	0.93	0.92	0.94
Yield from Dist (%)	10.08	12.40	10.05	10.51	10.89
Expense Ratio (%)	1.29	1.38	1.37	1.32	1.35
Portfolio Turnover (%)	36.55	59.73	36.53	41.97	72.72
NAV per share ($)	9.67	8.71	8.73	9.76	9.52
Market Price per share	10.25	9.13	7.50	9.25	8.75
Premium (Discount) (%)	6.00	4.82	(14.09)	(5.23)	(8.09)
Total Return, Stk Price (%)	22.34	34.13	(8.86)	16.23	12.28

Vestaur Securities, Inc.

Centre Square West, 11th Floor
P.O. Box 7558
Philadelphia, PA 19101-7558
(215) 567-3969

Income

NYSE : VES

Transfer Agent
First Chicago Trust Co. of New York
P.O. Box 3981
Church Street Station
New York, NY 10008-3981
(212) 791-6422

12 Months Ending 12/31/92 Results

	Period End	Period Begin	Distributions	Yield Dist (%)	Total Return (%)
Share Price ($)	14.38	14.88	1.16	7.80	4.44
NAV per share ($)	14.91	14.93		7.77	7.64

Background: Was organized under the sponsorship of First Pennsylvania Corp. Began operations in November 1972 with net assets of approximately $84 million.

Objective: Seeks high current income. Capital appreciation is secondary. Invests 75% in marketable or privately placed debt securities rated BBB or better, direct or guaranteed obligations of the U.S. or Canadian Governments, and commercial paper. May invest balance in low or unrated corporate obligations, debt securities with equity features, and preferred stocks. May leverage up to 20%.

Portfolio: (11/30/92) Industrial & Conglomerate 38.4%, Public Utilities 32.4%, U.S. Government 17.0%, Canadian & Provincial 6.0%, Financial & Insurance 3.2%.

Capitalization: (11/30/92) Common stock outstanding 6,541,816. No long-term debt.

Average Maturity (years): 18.5
Fund Manager: Core States Investment Advisors, Inc.   **Fee:** 0.50%
Income Dist: Quarterly   **Capital Gains Dist:** Annually
Reinvestment Plan: Yes   **Shareholder Reports:** Semi-Annually

5 Year Performance

Fiscal Year Ending 11/30	1992	1991	1990	1989	1988
Net Assets ($mil):	97.70	95.50	87.90	91.60	87.50
Net Income Dist ($):	1.17	1.21	1.21	1.22	1.23
Cap Gains Dist ($):	0.00	0.00	0.00	0.00	0.00
Total Dist ($)	1.17	1.21	1.21	1.22	1.23
Yield from Dist (%)	8.07	9.13	8.96	9.85	9.94
Expense Ratio (%)	0.90	0.90	1.00	1.00	1.00
Portfolio Turnover (%)	40.60	43.00	25.50	26.00	11.80
NAV per share ($)	14.93	14.78	13.75	14.32	13.68
Market Price per share	14.13	14.50	13.25	13.50	12.38
Premium (Discount) (%)	(5.36)	(1.89)	(3.64)	(5.73)	(9.58)
Total Return, Stk Price (%)	5.52	18.57	7.11	18.90	9.94

Flexible Portfolio Bond Funds

Franklin Multi Income Trust
P.O. Box 7777
San Mateo, CA 94403-7777
(800) 342-5236

NYSE : FMI
Transfer Agent
Shareholders Services Group
One Exchange Place
Boston, MA 02109
(800) 331-1710

Income

12 Months Ending 12/31/92 Results

	Period End	Period Begin	Distributions	Yield Dist (%)	Total Return (%)
Share Price ($)	9.88	9.50	0.94	9.89	13.89
NAV per share ($)	10.67	10.02		9.38	15.87

Background: Initial public offering October 24, 1989 of 5,750,000 shares at $10 per share. Initial NAV was $9.30 per share.

Objective: Seeks high current income and growth of income. The fund will invest up to 50% of its assets in dividend-paying public utilities and the balance in lower-rated corporate bonds.

Portfolio: (9/30/92) Corporate Bonds 76.1%, Common Stocks & Warrants 37.1%, Preferred Stocks 7.1%. Sector Weightings: Cable Television 7.1%, Health Care/Drugs/Hospital Supplies 6.4%, Automobile/Auto Parts/Truck Manufacturing 6.4%, Grocery/Convenience Chains 6.3%.

Capitalization: (9/30/92) Shares of beneficial interest outstanding 5,857,600. Long-term debt $15.9 million fixed-rate notes due October 1994.

Average Maturity (years): 9.5
Fund Manager: Franklin Advisers, Inc.   **Fee:** 0.85%
Income Dist: Monthly   **Capital Gains Dist:** Annually
Reinvestment Plan: Yes   **Shareholder Reports:** Semi-Annually

5 Year Performance

Fiscal Year Ending 3/31	1992	1991	1990 (5 mos.)	1989	1988
Net Assets ($mil):	59.50	50.40	50.40	—	—
Net Income Dist ($):	0.99	1.06	0.41	—	—
Cap Gains Dist ($):	0.00	0.01	0.00	—	—
Total Dist ($)	0.99	1.07	0.41	—	—
Yield from Dist (%)	12.38	12.97	—	—	—
Expense Ratio (%)	3.21	3.43	3.40	—	—
Portfolio Turnover (%)	22.19	26.07	4.66	—	—
NAV per share ($)	10.15	8.60	8.61	—	—
Market Price per share	9.75	8.00	8.25	—	—
Premium (Discount) (%)	(3.94)	(6.98)	(4.18)	—	—
Total Return, Stk Price (%)	34.25	9.94	—	—	—

Franklin Universal Trust

P.O. Box 7777
San Mateo, CA 94403-7777
(800) 342-5236

NYSE : FT

Transfer Agent
Provident National Bank
17th & Chestnut St.
Philadelphia, PA 19103
(800) 553-8080

Income

12 Months Ending 12/31/92 Results

	Period End	Period Begin	Distributions	Yield Dist (%)	Total Return (%)
Share Price ($)	8.25	7.50	0.83	11.07	21.07
NAV per share ($)	8.82	7.98		10.40	20.93

Background: Initial public offering September 23, 1988 of 26,000,000 shares at $10 per share. Initial NAV was $9.55 per share. Concurrently offered $90 million in Senior Fixed-Rate Notes at 9.5% per annum for a period of five years.

Objective: Seeks high current income and capital preservation from a diversified portfolio of bonds, high-dividend paying equities, precious metals and natural resource equity securities. On or about October 1993 the board will submit a proposal to shareholders to open-end the fund.

Portfolio: (1/31/93) Corporate Bonds 59.64%, Utility Stocks 19.1%, Misc. Equity & Preferred Stocks 9.98%, Convertible Bonds 6.37%, Cash & Equivalents 3.42%. Top Holdings: RJR Holdings, Ft. Howard, Pacific Gas & Electric Co., Southern Company, Texas Utilities.

Capitalization: (8/31/92) Shares of beneficial interest outstanding 26,779,333. Long-term debt $71,400,000 due October 1, 1993.

Average Maturity (years): 9.6
Fund Manager: Franklin Advisers, Inc.
Income Dist: Monthly
Reinvestment Plan: Yes

Fee: 0.75%
Capital Gains Dist: Annually
Shareholder Reports: Quarterly

5 Year Performance

Fiscal Year Ending 8/31	1992	1991	1990	1989 (11 mos.)	1988
Net Assets ($mil):	239.50	200.90	186.30	250.00	—
Net Income Dist ($):	0.80	0.93	1.15	0.93	—
Cap Gains Dist ($):	0.00	0.00	0.00	0.00	—
Total Dist ($)	0.80	0.93	1.15	0.93	—
Yield from Dist (%)	11.03	14.03	11.79	—	—
Expense Ratio (%)	3.36	4.01	5.47	4.94	—
Portfolio Turnover (%)	30.44	38.57	34.29	36.56	—
NAV per share ($)	8.94	7.50	7.01	9.44	—
Market Price per share	8.50	7.25	6.63	9.75	—
Premium (Discount) (%)	(4.92)	(3.33)	(5.42)	3.28	—
Total Return, Stk Price (%)	28.28	23.38	(20.21)	—	—

Lincoln National Income Fund, Inc.

1300 S. Clinton St.
Fort Wayne, IN 46801
(219) 455-2210

NYSE : LND

Transfer Agent
First National Bank of Boston
P.O. Box 644
Boston, MA 02102
(800) 442-2001/(617) 575-2900

Income

12 Months Ending 12/31/92 Results

	Period End	Period Begin	Distributions	Yield Dist (%)	Total Return (%)
Share Price ($)	28.63	27.63	3.36	12.16	15.78
NAV per share ($)	28.36	29.70		11.31	6.80

Background: Initial public offering November 1972. Initial NAV was $23.01 per share. Name changed to Lincoln National Income Fund from Lincoln National Direct Placement Fund on October 6, 1989.

Objective: Seeks a high level of current income from interest on fixed-income securities with secondary objective to obtain additional income through capital appreciation. Invests in securities bought directly from the issuer. A significant component of the portfolio is direct placement investments, some of which have equity features such as conversion privileges or warrants.

Portfolio: (12/31/92) Public Debt Securities 85.9%, Direct Placement Securities 10.1%, Short Term Investments 3.0%, Common Stocks & Warrants 2.6%.

Capitalization: (12/31/92) Common stock outstanding 2,449,853.

Average Maturity (years): 12.6
Fund Manager: Lincoln National Investment Management Co.   **Fee:** 0.50%
Income Dist: Quarterly   **Capital Gains Dist:** Annually
Reinvestment Plan: Yes   **Shareholder Reports:** Quarterly

5 Year Performance

Fiscal Year Ending 12/31	1992	1991	1990	1989	1988
Net Assets ($mil):	109.50	72.80	65.70	70.70	65.40
Net Income Dist ($):	2.62	2.29	2.35	2.32	2.31
Cap Gains Dist ($):	0.74	0.00	0.00	0.02	0.15
Total Dist ($)	3.36	2.29	2.35	2.34	2.46
Yield from Dist (%)	12.16	9.64	9.08	9.85	10.70
Expense Ratio (%)	1.00	0.97	0.97	0.96	0.97
Portfolio Turnover (%)	97.63	15.07	28.85	44.46	63.39
NAV per share ($)	28.36	29.70	26.80	28.88	26.69
Market Price per share	28.63	27.63	23.75	25.88	23.75
Premium (Discount) (%)	0.95	(7.00)	(11.38)	(10.42)	(11.02)
Total Return, Stk Price (%)	15.78	25.98	0.85	18.82	13.96

MFS Special Value Trust

500 Boylston St.
Boston, MA 02116-3741
(617) 954-5000

NYSE : MFV
Transfer Agent
State Street Bank & Trust Co.
P.O. Box 8200
Boston, MA 02266-8200
(800) 637-2304

Income

12 Months Ending 12/31/92 Results

	Period End	Period Begin	Distributions	Yield Dist (%)	Total Return (%)
Share Price ($)	14.75	14.88	2.27	15.26	14.38
NAV per share ($)	14.46	14.84		15.30	12.74

Background: Initial public offering November 24, 1989 of 60,000,000 shares at $15 per share. Initial NAV was $13.95 per share.

Objective: Seeks capital appreciation and to maintain an annual distribution rate of 11% based on the original offering price. The fund will invest 50% of its assets in U.S. Government securities and the remainder in equity securities involving above-average risk.

Portfolio: (10/31/92): Bonds 71.4%, Common Stocks 20.7%, Other 7.9%. Sector Weightings: U.S. Treasuries 52.6%, Industrials 15.7%, Banks 2.4%.

Capitalization: (10/31/92) Shares of beneficial interest outstanding 5,820,000. No long-term debt.

Average Maturity (years): 7.2

Fund Manager: Massachusetts Financial Services Co. **Fee:** 0.68%

Income Dist: Monthly **Capital Gains Dist:** Annually

Reinvestment Plan: Yes **Shareholder Reports:** Quarterly

5 Year Performance

Fiscal Year Ending 10/31	1992	1991	1990 (11 mos.)	1989	1988
Net Assets ($mil):	86.30	86.00	69.40	—	—
Net Income Dist ($):	0.77	0.90	1.04	—	—
Cap Gains Dist ($):	1.17	0.75	0.00	—	—
Total Dist ($)	1.94	1.65	1.04	—	—
Yield from Dist (%)	13.61	16.29	—	—	—
Expense Ratio (%)	1.35	1.37	1.40	—	—
Portfolio Turnover (%)	175.00	327.00	237.00	—	—
NAV per share ($)	14.82	14.90	11.66	—	—
Market Price per share	14.75	14.25	10.13	—	—
Premium (Discount) (%)	(0.47)	(4.36)	(13.21)	—	—
Total Return, Stk Price (%)	17.12	56.96	—	—	—

Zweig Total Return Fund, Inc. (The)

900 Third Ave.
New York, NY 10022
(212) 755-9860

Transfer Agent
Shareholders Services Group, Inc.
P.O. Box 1376
Boston, MA 02104
(800) 331-1710

Growth & Income

12 Months Ending 12/31/92 Results

	Period End	Period Begin	Distributions	Yield Dist (%)	Total Return (%)
Share Price ($)	10.00	10.63	0.96*	5.83	3.10
NAV per share ($)	9.06	9.79		6.33	2.35

Background: Initial public offering September 1988 of 60,000,000 shares at $10 per share. Initial NAV was $9.35 per share.

Objective: Seeks high total return consistent with preservation of capital by investing 50% to 60% of total assets in U.S. Government securities, investment-grade debt securities of domestic issuers, and certain Foreign Government securities. Also, 25% to 35% may be in equity securities. The fund intends to make monthly distributions equaling 10% of net assets on an annual basis, either from income or principal.

Portfolio: (12/31/92): U.S. Government Bonds 44.8%, Stocks 23.2%, Corporate Bonds 3.1%, Cash & Equivalents 29.9%. Top Holdings: Bank of Boston, Amgen, Sun Microsystems, Pfizer, Medco Containment.

Capitalization: (12/31/92) Common stock outstanding 68,886,660. No long-term debt.

Average Maturity (years): 8.0
Fund Manager: Zweig Advisors, Inc.   **Fee:** 0.70%
Income Dist: Monthly   **Capital Gains Dist:** Annually
Reinvestment Plan: Yes   **Shareholder Reports:** Quarterly

5 Year Performance

Fiscal Year Ending 12/31	1992	1991	1990	1989	1988 (3 mos.)
Net Assets ($mil):	624.10	648.10	573.80	596.50	564.3
Net Income Dist ($):	0.32	0.43	0.60	0.73	0.16
Cap Gains Dist ($):	0.30	0.53	0.04	0.23	0.00
Total Dist ($)	0.96*	0.96	0.64	0.96	0.16
Yield from Dist (%)	5.83	11.12	6.56	10.51	—
Expense Ratio (%)	1.13	1.11	1.09	1.14	1.19
Portfolio Turnover (%)	123.19	148.60	145.16	192.73	112.56
NAV per share ($)	9.06	9.79	9.02	9.59	9.24
Market Price per share	10.00	10.63	8.63	9.75	9.13
Premium (Discount) (%)	10.38	8.58	(4.43)	1.67	(1.30)
Total Return, Stk Price (%)	3.10	34.30	(4.92)	17.31	—

* Includes $0.34 return of capital.

U.S. Government Bond Funds

ACM Government Spectrum Fund

1345 Avenue of the Americas
New York, NY 10105
(800) 247-4154 / (212) 969-1000

NYSE : SI
Transfer Agent
State Street Bank & Trust Co.
225 Franklin St.
Boston, MA 02110
(800) 426-5523

Income

12 Months Ending 12/31/92 Results

	Period End	Period Begin	Distributions	Yield Dist (%)	Total Return (%)
Share Price ($)	9.00	9.00	0.86	9.56	9.56
NAV per share ($)	8.89	9.15		9.40	6.56

Background: Initial public offering May 19, 1988 of 20,000,000 shares at $10 per share. Initial NAV was $9.26 per share.

Objective: Seeks high current income consistent with preservation of capital. Invests at least 65% of total assets in U.S. Government obligations. Up to 35% of assets can be placed in debt obligations issued or guaranteed by selected foreign governments. May invest up to 20% in direct placements.

Portfolio: (12/31/92) U.S. Government & Agency Obligations 90.3%, Foreign 11.9%, Short Term 0.5%, Short Term Liabilities (2.7%).

Capitalization: (12/31/92) Common stock outstanding 31,747,194. No long-term debt.

Average Maturity (years): 10.5
Fund Manager: Alliance Capital Management L.P.   **Fee:** 0.30%
Income Dist: Monthly   **Capital Gains Dist:** Annually
Reinvestment Plan: Yes   **Shareholder Reports:** Semi-Annually

5 Year Performance

Fiscal Year Ending 12/31	1992	1991	1990	1989	1988 (7 mos.)
Net Assets ($mil):	282.30	288.70	274.30	285.40	277.80
Net Income Dist ($):	0.86	1.01	1.10	0.97	0.55
Cap Gains Dist ($):	0.00	0.00	0.00	0.00	0.01
Total Dist ($)	0.86	1.01	1.10	0.97	0.56
Yield from Dist (%)	9.56	12.05	12.05	10.92	—
Expense Ratio (%)	1.27	1.35	1.42	1.34	1.32
Portfolio Turnover (%)	471.00	442.00	419.00	353.00	171.00
NAV per share ($)	8.89	9.15	8.76	9.13	8.93
Market Price per share	9.00	9.00	8.38	9.13	8.88
Premium (Discount) (%)	1.24	(1.64)	(4.45)	0.05	(0.67)
Total Return, Stk Price (%)	9.56	19.45	3.83	13.74	—

American Government Income Fund, Inc.

NYSE : AGF

Piper Jaffray Tower
222 S. Ninth St.
Minneapolis, MN 55402
(800) 333-6000 / (612) 342-6223

Transfer Agent
Investors Fiduciary Trust Co.
127 W. 10th St.
Kansas City, MO 64105-1716
(800) 543-1627

Income

12 Months Ending 12/31/92 Results

	Period End	Period Begin	Distributions	Yield Dist (%)	Total Return (%)
Share Price ($)	8.88	8.13	0.92	11.32	20.54
NAV per share ($)	8.07	8.01		11.49	12.23

Background: Initial public offering April 29, 1988 of 16,500,000 shares at $8 per share. Initial NAV was $7.44 per share.

Objective: Seeks high current income consistent with preservation of capital and to return $10 per share to investors on or about August 31, 2001. Invests in obligations issued or guaranteed by the U.S. Government, its Agencies or Instrumentalities and repurchase agreements pertaining to U.S. Government securities. May invest 35% in other debt securities issued by non-governmental issuers in the U.S. and U.S. dollar- denominated and Canadian Government securities. All debt securities will be rated AA or better.

Portfolio: (10/31/92) Mortgage-backed Securities 40.0%, U.S. Government & Agencies 18.9%, Inverse Floaters 17.0%, Interest Only 7.5%, Principal Only 7.2%, Zero-Coupon Bonds 6.9%. Sector Weightings: FNMA CMOs 78.8%, FHLMC CMOs 53.9%, FNMA 36.8%, GNMA 18.3%.

Capitalization: (11/30/92) Common stock outstanding 20,809,080. No long-term debt.

Average Maturity (years): 15.6

Fund Manager: Piper Capital Management, Inc.

Fee: 0.60%

Income Dist: Monthly

Capital Gains Dist: Annually

Reinvestment Plan: Yes

Shareholder Reports: Semi-Annually

5 Year Performance

Fiscal Year Ending 10/31	1992	1991	1990	1989	1988 (6 mos.)
Net Assets ($mil):	174.50	159.10	139.20	141.10	140.70
Net Income Dist ($):	0.82	0.80	0.78	0.85	0.45
Cap Gains Dist ($):	0.00	0.00	0.00	0.03	0.00
Total Dist ($)	0.82	0.80	0.78	0.88	0.45
Yield from Dist (%)	10.09	11.03	9.90	11.17	—
Expense Ratio (%)	1.25	2.56	3.13	2.63	2.04
Portfolio Turnover (%)	123.00	111.00	61.00	46.00	55.00
NAV per share ($)	8.39	7.68	6.76	7.09	7.33
Market Price per share	8.75	8.13	7.25	7.88	7.88
Premium (Discount) (%)	4.29	5.73	7.25	11.00	7.37
Total Return, Stk Price (%)	17.71	23.17	1.90	11.17	—

American Government Income Portfolio

Piper Jaffray Tower
222 S. Ninth St.
Minneapolis, MN 55402
(800) 333-6000 / (612) 342-6223

NYSE : AAF

Transfer Agent
Investors Fiduciary Trust Co.
127 W. 10th St.
Kansas City, MO 64105-1716
(800) 543-1627

Income

12 Months Ending 12/31/92 Results

	Period End	Period Begin	Distributions	Yield Dist (%)	Total Return (%)
Share Price ($)	11.25	10.63	1.19	11.19	17.03
NAV per share ($)	10.32	10.38		11.46	10.89

Background: Initial public offering September 22, 1988 of 18,800,000 shares at $10 per share. Initial NAV was $9.30 per share.

Objective: Seeks high current income consistent with preservation of capital.

Portfolio: (10/31/92) U.S. Mortgage Securities 35.2%, Inverse Floaters 17.8%, U.S. Government Securities 13.7%, Other Mortgage-Backed Securities 9.6%.

Capitalization: (10/31/92) Common Stock outstanding 23,412,054. No long-term debt.

Average Maturity (years): 15.2
Fund Manager: Piper Capital Management, Inc.
Income Dist: Monthly
Reinvestment Plan: Yes

Fee: 0.60%
Capital Gains Dist: Annually
Shareholder Reports: Semi-Annually

5 Year Performance

Fiscal Year Ending 10/31	1992	1991	1990	1989	1988 (1 mo.)
Net Assets ($mil):	257.50	234.50	203.70	205.60	202.10
Net Income Dist ($):	1.04	1.00	0.79	0.75	0.06
Cap Gains Dist ($):	0.06	0.00	0.03	0.03	0.00
Total Dist ($)	1.10	1.00	0.82	0.78	0.06
Yield from Dist (%)	10.86	11.26	8.30	7.70	—
Expense Ratio (%)	1.25	1.01	1.03	1.12	1.13
Portfolio Turnover (%)	100.00	94.00	49.00	66.00	0.02
NAV per share ($)	11.00	10.02	8.73	9.16	9.37
Market Price per share	11.00	10.13	8.88	9.88	10.13
Premium (Discount) (%)	0.00	1.00	1.60	7.75	8.00
Total Return, Stk Price (%)	19.45	25.34	(1.82)	5.23	—

American Opportunity Income Fund, Inc.

Piper Jaffray Tower
222 S. Ninth St.
Minneapolis, MN 55402
(800) 333-6000

NYSE : OIF

Transfer Agent
Investors Fiduciary Trust Co.
127 W. 10th St.
Kansas City, MO 64105-1716
(816) 474-8786

Income

12 Months Ending 12/31/92 Results

	Period End	Period Begin	Distributions	Yield Dist (%)	Total Return (%)
Share Price ($)	11.75	10.75	1.24	11.53	20.84
NAV per share ($)	10.10	10.53		11.78	7.69

Background: Initial public offering September 1990 of 18,000,000 shares at $10 per share. Initial NAV was $9.30 per share.

Objective: Seeks a high level of current income from a portfolio of high-quality mortgage-backed securities. Capital appreciation is secondary. The fund will invest at least 65% of its total assets in U.S. Government mortgage-backed or agency securities, or issued by private issuers and rated AA or higher by S&P. Up to 15% of assets may be invested in foreign debt securities.

Portfolio: (8/31/92) U.S. Treasuries 32.3%, Mortgage-Backed 72.1%. Sector Weightings: Treasury Bonds 32.3%, FNMA 43.7%, GNMA 16.1%, FHLMC 12.3%.

Capitalization: (8/31/92) Common stock outstanding 21,080,363. No long-term debt.

Average Maturity (years): 13.7
Fund Manager: Piper Capital Management, Inc. **Fee:** 0.73%
Income Dist: Monthly **Capital Gains Dist:** Annually
Reinvestment Plan: Yes **Shareholder Reports:** Semi-Annually

5 Year Performance

Fiscal Year Ending 8/31	1992	1991	1990 (11 mos.)	1989	1988
Net Assets ($mil):	238.90	206.50	191.10	—	—
Net Income Dist ($):	1.08	1.05	0.80	—	—
Cap Gains Dist ($):	0.24	0.08	0.07	—	—
Total Dist ($)	1.32	1.13	0.87	—	—
Yield from Dist (%)	12.88	12.38	—	—	—
Expense Ratio (%)	1.15	1.15	1.05	—	—
Portfolio Turnover (%)	92.00	115.00	124.00	—	—
NAV per share ($)	11.33	9.81	9.13	—	—
Market Price per share	11.50	10.25	9.13	—	—
Premium (Discount) (%)	1.50	4.49	(0.11)	—	—
Total Return, Stk Price (%)	25.07	24.64	—	—	—

BlackRock Income Trust, Inc.

One Seaport Plaza
New York, NY 10292
(800) 227-7236 / (212) 214-3334

NYSE : BKT

Transfer Agent
State Street Bank & Trust Co.
One Heritage Dr.
North Quincy, MA 02171
(800) 451-6788

Income

12 Months Ending 12/31/92 Results

	Period End	Period Begin	Distributions	Yield Dist (%)	Total Return (%)
Share Price ($)	8.50	10.63	0.90	8.47	(11.57)
NAV per share ($)	8.99	9.76		9.22	1.33

Background: Initial public offering July 29, 1988 of 58,511,000 common shares at $10 per share. Initial NAV was $9.30 per share.

Objective: Seeks high monthly income consistent with preservation of capital. Invests in mortgage-backed securities and, to a lesser extent, in asset-backed securities, 80% rated AAA by S&P, or issued or guaranteed by the U.S. Government or its agencies. May invest up to 20% in other securities determined to be of comparable credit quality.

Portfolio: (10/31/92) Mortgage-Backed Securities 76.0%, Asset-Backed 3.0%, U.S. Treasuries 21.0%.

Capitalization: (10/31/92) Common stock outstanding 62,459,317. No long-term debt.

Average Maturity (years): 13.9
Fund Manager: BlackRock Financial Management L.P.   **Fee:** 0.65%
Income Dist: Monthly   **Capital Gains Dist:** Annually
Reinvestment Plan: Yes   **Shareholder Reports:** Semi-Annually

5 Year Performance

Fiscal Year Ending 10/31	1992	1991	1990	1989	1988 (3 mos.)
Net Assets ($mil):	555.70	582.80	519.40	511.10	567.40
Net Income Dist ($):	0.88	1.03	1.06	1.10	0.18
Cap Gains Dist ($):	0.00	0.00	0.00	0.00	0.00
Total Dist ($)	0.88	1.03	1.06	1.10	0.18
Yield from Dist (%)	8.69	12.67	12.11	11.00	—
Expense Ratio (%)	1.02	1.07	1.10	1.12	1.18
Portfolio Turnover (%)	131.00	261.00	77.00	69.00	74.00
NAV per share ($)	8.90	9.43	8.49	8.42	9.44
Market Price per share	9.13	10.13	8.13	8.75	10.00
Premium (Discount) (%)	2.47	7.32	(4.36)	3.92	5.93
Total Return, Stk Price (%)	(1.18)	37.27	5.03	(1.50)	—

Dean Witter Government Income Trust

Two World Trade Center
New York, NY 10048
(800) 869-3863 / (212) 392-2550

NYSE : GVT

Transfer Agent
Dean Witter Trust Co.
Two Montgomery St.
Jersey City, NJ 07302
(800) 526-3143

Income

12 Months Ending 12/31/92 Results

	Period End	Period Begin	Distributions	Yield Dist (%)	Total Return (%)
Share Price ($)	9.00	9.50	0.74	7.79	2.53
NAV per share ($)	9.55	9.80		7.55	5.00

Background: Initial public offering February 29, 1988 of 70,173,901 shares of beneficial interest at $10 per share. Initial NAV was $9.50 per share.

Objective: Seeks high current income consistent with preservation of capital. Invests 65% in U.S. Government securities; up to 35% in other debt securities, non-governmental issuers in the U.S., and foreign governments. The fund may be leveraged up to 25%.

Portfolio: (9/30/92) U.S. Government Agencies 73.7%, U.S. Treasuries 27.9%, Short Term Investment 0.1%.

Capitalization: (9/30/92) Shares of beneficial interest outstanding 57,818,800. No long-term debt.

Average Maturity (years): 8.9
Fund Manager: Dean Witter Reynolds, InterCapital Division　　　　　**Fee:** 0.60%
Income Dist: Monthly　　　　　**Capital Gains Dist:** Annually
Reinvestment Plan: Yes　　　　　**Shareholder Reports:** Quarterly

5 Year Performance

Fiscal Year Ending 9/30	1992	1991	1990	1989	1988 (7 mos.)
Net Assets ($mil):	561.70	561.30	538.90	538.80	603.70
Net Income Dist ($):	0.76	0.84	0.87	0.98	0.40
Cap Gains Dist ($):	0.00	0.00	0.00	0.00	0.00
Total Dist ($)	0.76	0.84	0.87	0.98	0.40
Yield from Dist (%)	8.10	9.60	9.80	10.59	—
Expense Ratio (%)	0.72	0.72	0.75	0.74	0.73
Portfolio Turnover (%)	70.00	10.00	20.00	64.00	252.00
NAV per share ($)	9.72	9.70	9.32	9.31	9.43
Market Price per share	9.38	9.38	8.75	8.88	9.25
Premium (Discount) (%)	(3.50)	(3.40)	(6.12)	(4.62)	(1.91)
Total Return, Stk Price (%)	8.10	16.80	8.33	6.59	—

Kemper Intermediate Government Trust

120 S. LaSalle St.
Chicago, IL 60603
(800) 537-6006 / (800) 422-2848

Transfer Agent
Investors Fiduciary Trust Co.
127 W. 10th St.
Kansas City, MO 64105
(816) 474-8786

Income

12 Months Ending 12/31/92 Results

	Period End	Period Begin	Distributions	Yield Dist (%)	Total Return (%)
Share Price ($)	8.75	8.88	0.75	8.45	6.98
NAV per share ($)	8.80	9.14		8.21	4.49

Background: Initial public offering July 2, 1988 of 28,000,000 shares at $10 per share. Initial NAV was $9.30 per share.

Objective: Seeks high current income consistent with preservation of capital. Invests at least 65% of assets in obligations issued or guaranteed by the U.S. Government and its agencies. Average maturity of between three and ten years is maintained. May use hedging strategies including options on U.S. and Foreign Government securities.

Portfolio: (11/30/92) U.S. Government Obligations 75.3%, Repurchase Agreements 51.5%, Liabilities, less Cash, Other (26.8%).

Capitalization: (11/30/92) Common stock outstanding 33,928,000. No long-term debt.

Average Maturity (years): 5.8
Fund Manager: Kemper Financial Services, Inc.
Income Dist: Monthly
Reinvestment Plan: Yes

Fee: 0.80%
Capital Gains Dist: Annually
Shareholder Reports: Quarterly

5 Year Performance

Fiscal Year Ending 11/30	1992	1991	1990	1989	1988 (5 mos.)
Net Assets ($mil):	298.90	301.20	288.40	302.10	300.50
Net Income Dist ($):	0.75	0.88	0.91	0.99	0.25
Cap Gains Dist ($):	0.00	0.00	0.00	0.01	0.00
Total Dist ($)	0.75	0.88	0.91	1.00	0.25
Yield from Dist (%)	8.33	10.06	9.33	10.95	—
Expense Ratio (%)	0.93	0.93	0.95	0.95	0.87
Portfolio Turnover (%)	494.00	368.00	253.00	115.00	0.00
NAV per share ($)	8.81	8.97	8.70	9.16	9.30
Market Price per share	9.00	9.00	8.75	9.75	9.13
Premium (Discount) (%)	2.16	0.33	0.57	6.44	(1.94)
Total Return, Stk Price (%)	8.33	12.91	(0.92)	17.74	—

Putnam Intermediate Government Income Trust

NYSE : PGT
Transfer Agent
Putnam Investor Services, Inc.
P.O. Box 41203
Providence, RI 02940
(800) 634-1587

One Post Office Square
Boston, MA 02109
(617) 292-1000

Income

12 Months Ending 12/31/92 Results

	Period End	Period Begin	Distributions	Yield Dist (%)	Total Return (%)
Share Price ($)	8.63	9.25	1.15	12.43	5.73
NAV per share ($)	8.97	9.50		12.11	6.53

Background: Initial public offering June 17, 1988 of 60,000,000 shares at $10 per share. Initial NAV was $9.30 per share.

Objective: Seeks current income and stable NAV primarily by investing in U.S. or Foreign Government and Government agency bonds with average maturities between three and ten years. At least 65% of assets are invested in U.S. Government and agency securities, options, futures and repurchase agreements. Up to 35% may be invested in Foreign Government securities.

Portfolio: (11/30/92) U.S. Government & Agencies 68.6%, Foreign Bonds & Notes 28.5%.

Capitalization: (11/30/92) Shares of beneficial interest outstanding 64,528,505. No long-term debt.

Average Maturity (years): 7.0
Fund Manager: Putnam Management Company, Inc.   **Fee:** 0.75%
Income Dist: Monthly   **Capital Gains Dist:** Annually
Reinvestment Plan: Yes   **Shareholder Reports:** Quarterly

5 Year Performance

Fiscal Year Ending 11/30	1992	1991	1990	1989	1988 (5 mos.)
Net Assets ($mil):	601.60	585.60	567.10	562.10	570.00
Net Income Dist ($):	0.60	0.68	0.73	0.79	0.34
Cap Gains Dist ($):	0.17	0.05	0.08	0.22	0.00
Total Dist ($)	0.77	0.73	0.81	1.01	0.34
Yield from Dist (%)	8.43	8.11	9.00	11.54	—
Expense Ratio (%)	0.92	1.01	1.02	1.00	0.42
Portfolio Turnover (%)	216.24	255.49	268.42	174.57	34.74
NAV per share ($)	9.32	9.21	9.08	9.11	9.38
Market Price per share	9.13	9.13	9.00	9.00	8.75
Premium (Discount) (%)	(2.04)	(0.87)	(0.88)	(1.21)	(6.72)
Total Return, Stk Price (%)	8.43	9.56	9.00	14.40	—

RAC Income Fund, Inc.

7202 Glen Forest Drive
Richmond, VA 23226
(804) 673-6118

NYSE : RMF
Transfer Agent
State Street Bank & Trust Co.
P.O. Box 366
Boston, MA 02101
(800) 426-5523

Income

12 Months Ending 12/31/92 Results

	Period End	Period Begin	Distributions	Yield Dist (%)	Total Return (%)
Share Price ($)	11.50	12.00	1.23	10.25	6.08
NAV per share ($)	10.99	11.66		10.55	4.80

Background: Initial public offering December 23, 1988 of 9,600,000 shares at $12 per share. Initial NAV was $11.16 per share.

Objective: Seeks high monthly income consistent with capital preservation. Invests primarily in fixed-income mortgage-backed securities with 80% in highest-rated categories or issued and guaranteed by the U.S. Government and its agencies or instrumentalities. The fund's goal is to distribute monthly income that is 150 to 200 basis points greater than the rate obtainable from U.S. Treasury securities, having the same maturity as the expected average life of the fund's investments.

Portfolio: (10/31/92) U.S. Government Agencies 53.2%, Corporate Bonds 44.4%, Residual Interests 16.9%, Options 0.1%, Other Assets, Less Liabilities (14.6%).

Capitalization: (10/31/92) Common stock outstanding 11,477,589. No long-term debt.

Average Maturity (years): 23.2
Fund Manager: Capital Management, Inc.
Income Dist: Monthly
Reinvestment Plan: Yes

Fee: 0.65%
Capital Gains Dist: Annually
Shareholder Reports: Semi-Annually

5 Year Performance

Fiscal Year Ending 10/31	1992	1991	1990	1989 (10 mos.)	1988
Net Assets ($mil):	126.90	120.10	112.40	112.10	—
Net Income Dist ($):	1.26	1.26	1.27	0.85	—
Cap Gains Dist ($):	0.00	0.00	0.00	0.00	—
Total Dist ($)	1.26	1.26	1.27	0.85	—
Yield from Dist (%)	10.50	11.72	12.10	—	—
Expense Ratio (%)	2.04	2.90	4.42	2.22	—
Portfolio Turnover (%)	219.43	132.44	155.40	241.80	—
NAV per share ($)	11.06	11.57	11.12	11.09	—
Market Price per share	12.38	12.00	10.75	10.50	—
Premium (Discount) (%)	11.93	3.72	(3.33)	(5.32)	—
Total Return, Stk Price (%)	13.67	23.35	14.48	—	—

High Yield Corporate (Junk) Bond Funds

CIGNA High Income Shares

One Financial Plaza
Springfield, MA 01103
(413) 784-0100

Transfer Agent
State Street Bank & Trust Co.
225 Franklin St.
Boston, MA 02110
(800) 426-5523

Income

12 Months Ending 12/31/92 Results

	Period End	Period Begin	Distributions	Yield Dist (%)	Total Return (%)
Share Price ($)	7.88	7.25	1.01	13.93	22.62
NAV per share ($)	6.99	6.62		15.26	20.85

Background: Initial public offering August 10, 1988 of 24,725,000 shares at $10 per share.

Objective: Seeks high current income and preservation of capital through investment in a diversified portfolio of high-yield, fixed-income securities. The fund may use leverage.

Portfolio: (12/31/92) High Yield Bonds & Notes 99.2%, Cash 2.1%, Other Assets; Less Liabilities (1.3%).

Capitalization: (12/31/92) Common stock outstanding 24,657,000. No long-term debt.

Average Maturity (years): 9.1
Fund Manager: Cigna Investments, Inc.   **Fee:** 0.75%
Income Dist: Monthly   **Capital Gains Dist:** Annually
Reinvestment Plan: Yes   **Shareholder Reports:** Quarterly

5 Year Performance

Fiscal Year Ending 12/31	1992	1991	1990	1989	1988 (5 mos.)
Net Assets ($mil):	177.00	163.20	127.30	194.10	228.50
Net Income Dist ($):	1.01	0.96	1.04	1.22	0.45
Cap Gains Dist ($):	0.00	0.00	0.02	0.00	0.00
Total Dist ($)	1.01	0.96	1.06	1.22	0.45
Yield from Dist (%)	13.93	25.60	13.68	13.01	—
Expense Ratio (%)	3.18	4.50	5.34	4.51	3.09
Portfolio Turnover (%)	n/a	35.00	14.00	32.00	9.00
NAV per share ($)	6.99	6.62	4.73	7.41	9.11
Market Price per share	7.88	7.25	3.75	7.75	9.38
Premium (Discount) (%)	12.73	9.52	(20.72)	4.59	2.85
Total Return, Stk Price (%)	22.62	118.93	(37.94)	(4.37)	—

High Yield Corporate (Junk) Bond Funds   99

CIM High Yield Securities

AMEX : CIM

One Exchange Place
53 State St., 4th Floor
Boston, MA 02109
(617) 573-1035

Transfer Agent
Shareholders Services Group, Inc.
P.O. Box 1376
Boston, MA 02105
(800) 331-3120

Income

12 Months Ending 12/31/92 Results

	Period End	Period Begin	Distributions	Yield Dist (%)	Total Return (%)
Share Price ($)	7.50	6.63	0.81	12.22	25.34
NAV per share ($)	7.58	7.10		11.41	18.17

Background: Initial public offering November 11, 1987 of 3,650,000 shares at $10 per share. Initial NAV was $9.33 per share.

Objective: Seeks high current income through investments in fixed-income securities of domestic corporate issuers, preferably growing companies with reasonable prospects for improving credit characteristics. The fund may leverage up to 15%. The fund will invest at least 80% of assets in lower-quality or non-rated fixed-income corporate securities.

Portfolio: (12/31/92) Corporate Bonds & Notes 124.8%, U.S. Government Securities 3.7%, Common Stocks 1.4%, Short Term Liabilities (32.1%).

Capitalization: (12/31/92) Shares of beneficial interest outstanding 3,960,019. No long-term debt.

Average Maturity (years): 7.1
Fund Manager: Chancellor Trust Co. **Fee:** 0.50%
Income Dist: Monthly **Capital Gains Dist:** Annually
Reinvestment Plan: Yes **Shareholder Reports:** Semi-Annually

5 Year Performance

Fiscal Year Ending 12/31	1992	1991	1990	1989	1988
Net Assets ($mil):	30.00	28.00	22.30	29.10	36.40
Net Income Dist ($):	0.81	0.83	0.87	1.15	1.13
Cap Gains Dist ($):	0.00	0.00	0.00	0.05	0.09
Total Dist ($)	0.81	0.83	0.87	1.20	1.22
Yield from Dist (%)	12.22	17.47	12.43	12.63	12.67
Expense Ratio (%)	1.65	2.46	2.35	2.28	2.36
Portfolio Turnover (%)	40.60	51.20	34.90	77.40	209.60
NAV per share ($)	7.58	7.10	5.65	7.38	9.41
Market Price per share	7.50	6.63	4.75	7.00	9.50
Premium (Discount) (%)	(1.06)	(6.62)	(15.93)	(5.15)	0.96
Total Return, Stk Price (%)	25.34	57.05	(19.71)	(13.68)	11.32

Colonial Intermediate High Income Securities

One Financial Center, 12th Floor
Boston, MA 02111
(800) 426-3750

NYSE : CIF

Transfer Agent
Shareholder Services Group
P.O. Box 1376
Boston, MA 02104
(800) 331-1710

Income

12 Months Ending 12/31/92 Results

	Period End	Period Begin	Distributions	Yield Dist (%)	Total Return (%)
Share Price ($)	6.25	5.88	0.77	13.10	19.39
NAV per share ($)	6.47	6.17		12.48	17.34

Background: Initial public offering July 21, 1988 of 11,000,000 shares at $10 per share. Net proceeds were approximately $102.3 million. Concurrently, the fund offered $33 million aggregate principal of Senior Extendible Notes for leveraging purposes.

Objective: Seeks high current income. Will invest at least 80% of total assets in high-yield fixed-income securities rated in the lower categories and unrated fixed-income securities regarded as comparable in quality. If the shares are selling at a 10% discount 12 weeks prior to November 1, 1993, the fund will submit a proposal to shareholders to open-end.

Portfolio: (10/31/92)) Corporate Bonds & Notes 89.2%, Government Bonds & Notes 10.2%. Sector Weightings: Consumer Non-Durables 35.5%, Manufacturing 27.5%, Transportation 10.9%, Energy 6.1%, Banking & Financial Services 5.1%. Largest Holdings: U.S. Treasury Note 8/15/95, U.S. Treasury Bond 5/15/95, RJR Nabisco, R.P. Scherer Corp., Texas Industries, Inc.

Capitalization: (10/31/92) Common stock outstanding 13,562,000. $27,400,000 in Senior Extendible Notes.

Average Maturity (years): 7.7
Fund Manager: Colonial Management Association, Inc.　　　　　**Fee:** 0.65%
Income Dist: Monthly　　　　　**Capital Gains Dist:** Annually
Reinvestment Plan: Yes　　　　　**Shareholder Reports:** Semi-Annually

5 Year Performance

Fiscal Year Ending 10/31	1992	1991	1990	1989	1988 (3 mos.)
Net Assets ($mil):	87.10	83.60	64.90	107.80	116.60
Net Income Dist ($):	0.78	0.78	1.11	1.20	0.25
Cap Gains Dist ($):	0.00	0.00	0.00	0.00	0.00
Total Dist ($)	0.78	0.78	1.11	1.20	0.25
Yield from Dist (%)	13.00	17.81	15.04	12.63	—
Expense Ratio (%)	4.24	5.18	5.50	4.50	4.30
Portfolio Turnover (%)	78.00	30.00	12.00	23.00	34.00
NAV per share ($)	6.43	6.29	4.88	8.26	9.22
Market Price per share	6.25	6.00	4.38	7.38	9.50
Premium (Discount) (%)	(2.80)	(4.61)	(10.45)	(10.77)	3.04
Total Return, Stk Price (%)	17.17	54.79	(25.61)	(9.68)	—

High Income Advantage Trust

Two World Trade Center
New York, NY 10048
(800) 869-3863 / (212) 392-2550

NYSE : YLD
Transfer Agent
Dean Witter Trust Co.
2 Montgomery St.
Jersey City, NJ 07302
(800) 526-3143

Income

12 Months Ending 12/31/92 Results

	Period End	Period Begin	Distributions	Yield Dist (%)	Total Return (%)
Share Price ($)	5.63	5.00	0.81	16.20	28.80
NAV per share ($)	5.29	5.29		15.31	15.31

Background: Initial public offering October 23, 1987 of 25,000,000 shares at $10 per share. Initial NAV was $9.25 per share.

Objective: Seeks high current income; capital appreciation is secondary. Invests principally in lower-rated or unrated fixed-income securities of domestic corporations.

Portfolio: (9/30/92) Corporate Bonds 93.8%, Common Stock 1.8%, Short-Term 4.7%, Warrants 0.1%. Sector Weightings: Entertainment, Gaming & Lodging 14.7%, Retail Food Chains 12.8%, Manufacturing-Diversified 8.7%, Health Care 8.3%, Forest & Paper Products 6.7%. Largest Holdings: Supermarkets General Holdings Corp., Kroger Co., Coltec Holdings, Inc., SPI Holdings, Inc., Thermadyne Industries, Inc.

Capitalization: (9/30/92) Shares of beneficial interest outstanding 30,069,252. No long-term debt.

Average Maturity (years): 9.0
Fund Manager: Dean Witter Reynolds InterCapital Division **Fee:** 0.75%
Income Dist: Monthly **Capital Gains Dist:** Annually
Reinvestment Plan: Yes **Shareholder Reports:** Quarterly

5 Year Performance

Fiscal Year Ending 9/30	1992	1991	1990	1989	1988 (11 mos.)
Net Assets ($mil):	174.70	162.00	158.50	247.90	—
Net Income Dist ($):	0.59	0.69	1.13	1.20	1.00
Cap Gains Dist ($):	0.00	0.00	0.00	0.05	0.00
Total Dist ($)	0.59	0.69	1.13	1.25	1.00
Yield from Dist (%)	12.74	15.33	14.34	12.65	—
Expense Ratio (%)	1.00	1.07	1.01	0.90	0.90
Portfolio Turnover (%)	108.00	149.00	20.00	44.00	126.00
NAV per share ($)	5.81	5.23	4.96	7.68	9.19
Market Price per share	5.75	4.63	4.50	7.88	9.88
Premium (Discount) (%)	(1.03)	(11.66)	(9.27)	2.47	7.40
Total Return, Stk Price (%)	36.93	18.22	(28.55)	(7.59)	—

High Income Advantage Trust II

Two World Trade Center
New York, NY 10048
(800) 869-3863 / (212) 938-4500

Transfer Agent
Dean Witter Trust Co.
2 Montgomery St.
Jersey City, NJ 07302
(800) 526-3143

Income

12 Months Ending 12/31/92 Results

	Period End	Period Begin	Distributions	Yield Dist (%)	Total Return (%)
Share Price ($)	5.88	5.25	0.85	16.19	28.19
NAV per share ($)	5.82	5.71		14.89	16.81

Background: Initial public offering October 4, 1988 of 40,000,000 shares at $10 per share. Initial NAV was $9.30 per share.

Objective: Seeks high current income; capital appreciation is secondary. Invests primarily in lower-rated or unrated bonds of domestic corporations. May invest up to 10% in private placements. May also invest in common stocks and securities of foreign issuers and enter into repurchase agreements.

Portfolio: (7/31/92) Corporate Bonds 94.8%, Common Stocks 0.5%, Cash & Other 4.2%. Sector Weightings: Entertainment 10.5%, Food/Beverage 9.1%, Retail/Food 9.1%, Cable 7.0%, Health Care 6.6%. Largest Holdings: Auburn Hills Trust, Fort Howard Corp., Unisys Corp., SCI Holdings Inc., Dr. Pepper/7-Up.

Capitalization: (7/31/92) Shares of beneficial interest outstanding 35,641,307. No long-term debt.

Average Maturity (years): 8.6
Fund Manager: Dean Witter Reynolds InterCapital Division   **Fee:** 0.75%
Income Dist: Monthly   **Capital Gains Dist:** Annually
Reinvestment Plan: Yes   **Shareholder Reports:** Quarterly

5 Year Performance

Fiscal Year Ending 7/31	1992	1991	1990	1989 (10 mos.)	1988
Net Assets ($mil):	229.30	210.60	251.80	343.60	—
Net Income Dist ($):	0.66	0.77	1.19	0.92	—
Cap Gains Dist ($):	0.00	0.00	0.00	0.00	—
Total Dist ($)	0.66	0.77	1.19	0.92	—
Yield from Dist (%)	12.87	13.10	14.64	—	—
Expense Ratio (%)	0.98	1.07	0.93	0.85	—
Portfolio Turnover (%)	99.00	129.00	31.00	101.00	—
NAV per share ($)	6.43	5.68	6.44	8.76	—
Market Price per share	6.50	5.13	5.88	8.13	—
Premium (Discount) (%)	1.09	(9.68)	(8.70)	(7.19)	—
Total Return, Stk Price (%)	39.57	0.34	(13.04)	—	—

High Yield Corporate (Junk) Bond Funds 103

High Income Advantage Trust III

Two World Trade Center
New York, NY 10048
(800) 869-3863 / (212) 938-9500

Transfer Agent
Dean Witter Trust Co.
2 Montgomery St.
Jersey City, NJ 07302
(800) 869-3863

Income

12 Months Ending 12/31/92 Results

	Period End	Period Begin	Distributions	Yield Dist (%)	Total Return (%)
Share Price ($)	6.50	6.13	0.93	15.17	21.21
NAV per share ($)	6.44	6.39		14.55	15.34

Background: Initial public offering February 8, 1989 of 10,760,000 shares at $10 per share. Initial NAV was $9.30 per share.

Objective: Seeks high current income from a portfolio of lower-rated or unrated bonds. The fund also invests in common stocks and securities of foreign issuers. The fund may also enter into repurchase agreements.

Portfolio: (7/31/92) Corporate Bonds 93.8%, Common Stock 0.6%, Short Term 3.9%. Sector Weightings: Consumer Products 5.3%, Retail/Food 7.1%, Cable 9.4%, Manufacturing 6.1%, Health Care 5.3%. Largest Holdings: Auburn Hills Trust, SCI Holdings Inc., Unisys Corp., Supermarkets General Holdings Corp., SPI Holdings, Inc.

Capitalization: (7/31/92) Shares of beneficial interest outstanding 13,046,000. No long-term debt.

Average Maturity (years): 8.8
Fund Manager: Dean Witter Reynolds InterCapital Division   **Fee:** 0.75%
Income Dist: Monthly   **Capital Gains Dist:** Annually
Reinvestment Plan: Yes   **Shareholder Reports:** Semi-Annually

5 Year Performance

Fiscal Year Ending 1/31	1992	1991	1990 (11 mos.)	1989	1988
Net Assets ($mil):	89.10	68.50	101.10	—	—
Net Income Dist ($):	0.77	1.15	0.95	—	—
Cap Gains Dist ($):	0.00	0.00	0.00	—	—
Total Dist ($)	0.77	1.15	0.95	—	—
Yield from Dist (%)	17.11	15.58	—	—	—
Expense Ratio (%)	1.17	1.05	0.93	—	—
Portfolio Turnover (%)	137.00	44.00	59.00	—	—
NAV per share ($)	6.83	5.18	7.59	—	—
Market Price per share	6.50	4.50	7.38	—	—
Premium (Discount) (%)	(4.83)	(13.13)	(2.90)	—	—
Total Return, Stk Price (%)	61.56	(23.44)	—	—	—

High Yield Income Fund, Inc.

One Seaport Plaza
New York, NY 10292
(212) 214-3332

NYSE : HYI

Transfer Agent
State Street Bank & Trust Co.
One Heritage Dr.
North Quincy, MA 02171
(800) 426-5523

Income

12 Months Ending 12/31/92 Results

	Period End	Period Begin	Distributions	Yield Dist (%)	Total Return (%)
Share Price ($)	7.38	6.75	0.90	13.33	22.67
NAV per share ($)	7.32	7.00		12.86	17.43

Background: Initial public offering October 30, 1987 of 9,500,000 shares at $10 per share. Net proceeds were approximately $88,350,000.

Objective: Seeks maximum current income; capital appreciation is secondary. Primary investments include high-yield debt instruments rated in the medium to lower categories (BBB or lower by S&P, or Baa or lower by Moody's), or unrated securities of comparable quality. At least 65% will be invested in securities with average maturities of between ten and twenty years.

Portfolio: (8/31/92) High-Yield Corporate Bonds 121.5%, Preferred Stock 1.2%, Warrants 0.1%, Short Term 1.4%, Liabilities (24.2%).

Capitalization: (8/31/92) Common stock outstanding 10,731,993. No long-term debt.

Average Maturity (years): 8.3
Fund Manager: Prudential Mutual Fund Management, Inc.   **Fee: 0.70%**
Income Dist: Monthly   **Capital Gains Dist:** Annually
Reinvestment Plan: Yes   **Shareholder Reports:** Quarterly

5 Year Performance

Fiscal Year Ending 8/31	1992	1991	1990	1989	1988 (9 mos.)
Net Assets ($mil):	80.00	73.10	72.50	91.80	97.80
Net Income Dist ($):	0.90	0.90	0.97	1.17	0.87
Cap Gains Dist ($):	0.00	0.00	0.00	0.09	0.04
Total Dist ($)	0.90	0.90	0.97	1.26	0.91
Yield from Dist (%)	13.57	16.36	11.41	13.08	—
Expense Ratio (%)	1.55	1.39	1.43	2.10	1.79
Portfolio Turnover (%)	74.00	72.00	27.00	105.00	50.00
NAV per share ($)	7.46	6.84	6.79	8.60	9.28
Market Price per share	7.63	6.63	5.50	8.50	9.63
Premium (Discount) (%)	2.28	(3.07)	(19.00)	(1.16)	3.66
Total Return, Stk Price (%)	28.66	36.91	(23.88)	1.35	—

High Yield Plus Fund, Inc.

One Seaport Plaza
New York, NY 10292
(212) 214-3332

Transfer Agent
State Street Bank & Trust Co.
One Heritage Dr.
North Quincy, MA 02171
(800) 426-5523

Income

12 Months Ending 12/31/92 Results

	Period End	Period Begin	Distributions	Yield Dist (%)	Total Return (%)
Share Price ($)	8.00	7.00	0.84	12.00	26.29
NAV per share ($)	8.08	7.58		11.08	17.68

Background: Initial public offering April 15, 1988 of 10,500,000 shares at $10 per share. Initial NAV was $9.30 per share.

Objective: Seeks high current income. Capital appreciation is secondary. Invests 65% in high-yield debt securities. May invest in hybrid securities offering both debt and equity features. May invest up to 25% in private placements. May borrow up to one-third of its total assets.

Portfolio: (12/31/92) High-Yield Corporate Bonds 113.9%, Short-Term 1.5%, Preferred Stocks 0.4%, Common Stocks 0.8%, Warrants 0.2%, Foreign Government Obligations 2.1%, Liabilities (18.9%).

Capitalization: (12/31/92) Common stock outstanding 10,880,016. No long-term debt.

Average Maturity (years): 11.3
Fund Manager: Prudential Mutual Fund Management, Inc.　　　　　**Fee:** 0.70%
Income Dist: Monthly　　　　　**Capital Gains Dist:** Annually
Reinvestment Plan: Yes　　　　　**Shareholder Reports:** Quarterly

5 Year Performance

Fiscal Year Ending 3/31	1992	1991	1990	1989 (11 mos.)	1988
Net Assets ($mil):	85.70	73.10	78.10	96.30	—
Net Income Dist ($):	0.87	0.99	1.12	0.93	—
Cap Gains Dist ($):	0.00	0.00	0.00	0.00	—
Total Dist ($)	0.87	0.99	1.12	0.93	—
Yield from Dist (%)	13.38	14.93	12.98	—	—
Expense Ratio (%)	2.26	2.21	2.57	1.44	—
Portfolio Turnover (%)	46.00	38.00	32.00	33.00	—
NAV per share ($)	7.91	6.80	7.22	8.90	—
Market Price per share	7.75	6.50	6.63	8.63	—
Premium (Discount) (%)	(2.02)	(4.41)	(8.31)	(3.15)	—
Total Return, Stk Price (%)	32.62	12.97	(10.20)	—	—

Kemper High Income Trust

120 S. LaSalle St.
Chicago, IL 60603
(800) 537-6006

NYSE : KHI

Transfer Agent
Investors Fiduciary Trust Co.
127 W. 10th St.
Kansas City, MO 64105
(816) 474-8786

Income

12 Months Ending 12/31/92 Results

	Period End	Period Begin	Distributions	Yield Dist (%)	Total Return (%)
Share Price ($)	9.38	8.63	0.96	11.12	19.81
NAV per share ($)	8.73	8.20		11.71	18.17

Background: Initial public offering April 21, 1988 of 19,550,000 shares of beneficial interest at $12 per share. Initial NAV was $11.11 per share.

Objective: Seeks high current income consistent with reasonable risk; capital appreciation is secondary. Invests in a range of income-producing securities, including U.S. Corporate, U.S. Government & Agencies, and Foreign Government debt obligations. The fund may engage in options and hedging transactions for leverage.

Portfolio: (12/1/92) High Yield Corporate Bonds 97%, Cash & Equivalents 3%. Sector Weightings: Manufacturing & Metals 23%, Consumer Products 15%, Communications & Entertainment 11%, Cable System & Broadcasting 9%, Restaurants 4%. Largest Holdings: K & F Industries, Owens—Illinois, Quantum Chemical, RJR Holdings, Starer Communications. Portfolio Ratings: Ba 15%, B 65%, Lower or Non-Rated 21%.

Capitalization: Shares of beneficial interest outstanding 21,957,000. No long-term debt.

Average Maturity (years): 9.0
Fund Manager: Kemper Financial Services, Inc.
Income Dist: Monthly
Reinvestment Plan: Yes

Fee: 0.85%
Capital Gains Dist: Annually
Shareholder Reports: Semi-Annually

5 Year Performance

Fiscal Year Ending 11/30	1992	1991	1990	1989	1988 (7 mos.)
Net Assets ($mil):	191.00	178.10	131.60	181.00	214.50
Net Income Dist ($):	0.97	0.94	1.20	1.30	0.69
Cap Gains Dist ($):	0.00	0.00	0.00	0.00	0.00
Total Dist ($)	0.97	0.94	1.20	1.30	0.69
Yield from Dist (%)	11.24	15.67	13.14	11.18	—
Expense Ratio (%)	2.03	2.20	2.25	1.93	1.28
Portfolio Turnover (%)	47.00	27.00	29.00	45.00	101.00
NAV per share ($)	8.70	8.28	6.25	8.86	10.84
Market Price per share	9.13	8.63	6.00	9.13	11.63
Premium (Discount) (%)	4.94	4.11	(4.00)	2.93	7.20
Total Return, Stk Price (%)	17.03	59.50	(21.14)	(10.32)	—

New America High Income Fund

NYSE : HYB
Transfer Agent
State Street Bank & Trust Co.
P.O. Box 8200
Boston, MA 02266-8200
(800) 426-5523

1 Seaport Plaza
New York, NY 10292
(800) 415-6788 / (212) 214-3332

Income

12 Months Ending 12/31/92 Results

	Period End	Period Begin	Distributions	Yield Dist (%)	Total Return (%)
Share Price ($)	4.13	3.63	0.55	15.15	28.93
NAV per share ($)	4.32	3.79		14.51	28.50

Background: Initial public offering February 19, 1988 of 23,000,000 common shares at $10 per share. Initial NAV was $9.35 per share.

Objective: Seeks high current income. Invests in high-yielding, lower-rated bonds (BB or lower). Up to 20% may be in securities not readily marketable; 20% may be in zero-coupon bonds; up to 10% in foreign securities.

Portfolio: (12/31/92) High-Yield Corporate Bonds 88.32%, Foreign Government Securities 2.3%, Short Term 2.2%, Common & Preferred Stock 2.4%.

Capitalization: (12/31/92) Common stock outstanding 24,973,953. Long-term debt of $45.5 million in Senior Extendible Notes. Leveraged with 790 shares preferred stock, stated value $100,000 per share.

Average Maturity (years): 11.2
Fund Manager: Wellington Management Company **Fee:** 0.50%
Income Dist: Monthly **Capital Gains Dist:** Annually
Reinvestment Plan: Yes **Shareholder Reports:** Semi-Annually

5 Year Performance

Fiscal Year Ending 12/31	1992	1991	1990	1989	1988 (10 mos.)
Net Assets ($mil):	142.90	128.20	118.80	210.70	281.40
Net Income Dist ($):	0.55	0.56	0.75	1.25	1.18
Cap Gains Dist ($):	0.00	0.00	0.00	0.10	0.00
Total Dist ($)	0.55	0.56	0.75	1.35	1.18
Yield from Dist (%)	15.15	22.40	12.76	13.50	—
Expense Ratio (%)	4.82	5.22	5.89	4.49	4.22
Portfolio Turnover (%)	129.86	121.15	49.98	65.40	149.00
NAV per share ($)	4.32	3.79	3.42	6.23	8.60
Market Price per share	4.13	3.63	2.50	5.88	10.00
Premium (Discount) (%)	(4.40)	(4.49)	(26.90)	(5.62)	16.28
Total Return, Stk Price (%)	28.93	67.60	(44.73)	(27.70)	—

Prospect Street High Income Portfolio, Inc.

One Exchange Place, 37th Floor
Boston, MA 02109
(617) 742-3800

Income

NYSE : PHY

Transfer Agent
Bank of New York
P.O. Box 11258
Church Street Station
New York, NY 10277
(800) 524-4458

12 Months Ending 12/31/92 Results

	Period End	Period Begin	Distributions	Yield Dist (%)	Total Return (%)
Share Price ($)	4.13	3.25	0.57	17.54	44.62
NAV per share ($)	4.09	3.85		14.81	21.04

Background: Initial public offering December 5, 1988 of 13,000,000 shares at $10 per share. Initial NAV was $9.30 per share.

Objective: Seeks high current income from a leveraged portfolio of high-yield and speculative securities.

Portfolio: (10/31/92) Fixed Income 86.6%, Common Stocks & Warrants 1.8%, Short Term & Other 11.6%. Sector Weightings: Health Care 8.2%, Insurance Cos. 6.93%, Financial Services 6.6%, Oil Related 5.8%, Broadcasting 5.8%.

Capitalization: (10/31/92) Common stock outstanding 13,707,582. Leveraged with 300 shares preferred stock, stated value $100,000 per share.

Average Maturity (years): 9.2
Fund Manager: Prospect Street Investment Management Co.   **Fee:** 0.50%
Income Dist: Monthly   **Capital Gains Dist:** Annually
Reinvestment Plan: Yes   **Shareholder Reports:** Quarterly

5 Year Performance

Fiscal Year Ending 10/31	1992	1991	1990	1989 (11 mos.)	1988
Net Assets ($mil):	85.20	83.00	75.00	—	—
Net Income Dist ($):	0.45	0.36	0.76	1.12	—
Cap Gains Dist ($):	0.00	0.00	0.09	0.01	—
Total Dist ($)	0.45	0.36	0.85	1.13	—
Yield from Dist (%)	12.86	15.13	13.08	—	—
Expense Ratio (%)	2.28	2.93	6.15	4.89	—
Portfolio Turnover (%)	97.86	114.00	63.50	89.70	—
NAV per share ($)	4.03	3.89	3.30	6.82	—
Market Price per share	4.00	3.50	2.38	6.50	—
Premium (Discount) (%)	(0.74)	(10.03)	(28.18)	(4.69)	—
Total Return, Stk Price (%)	27.14	62.18	(50.31)	—	—

USF&G Pacholder Fund, Inc.

Towers of Kenwood
8044 Montgomery Rd., Suite 382
Cincinnatti, OH 45236
(513) 985-3200

AMEX : PHF
Transfer Agent
State Street Bank & Trust Co.
225 Franklin St.
Boston, MA 02110
(800) 426-5523

Income

12 Months Ending 12/31/92 Results

	Period End	Period Begin	Distributions	Yield Dist (%)	Total Return (%)
Share Price ($)	19.38	17.25	2.08	12.06	24.41
NAV per share ($)	18.52	17.37		11.97	18.60

Background: Initial public offering November 17, 1988 of 1,800,000 shares at $20 per share. Initial NAV was $18.60 per share.

Objective: Seeks high total return by investing in high-yielding, lower-rated or unrated fixed-income securities.

Portfolio: (12/31/92) Corporate Debt Securities 86.8%, Commercial Paper 12.2%, Common Stock 0.5%. Sector Weightings: Food/Drug Retailers 7.1%, Chemicals 5.4%, Oil & Gas 5.3%, Conglomerate 5.3%, Leisure & Amusement 5.4%.

Capitalization: (12/31/92) Common stock outstanding 1,823,850. Leveraged with 10,000 shares preferred stock, stated value $1,000 per share.

Average Maturity (years): 5.6
Fund Manager: Pacholder & Company
Income Dist: Quarterly
Reinvestment Plan: Yes

Fee: 0.40%
Capital Gains Dist: Annually
Shareholder Reports: Quarterly

5 Year Performance

Fiscal Year Ending 12/31	1992	1991	1990	1989	1988 (1 mo.)
Net Assets ($mil):	44.00	31.70	26.40	30.20	33.00
Net Income Dist ($):	2.08	2.14	1.80	2.10	0.18
Cap Gains Dist ($):	0.00	0.00	0.00	0.00	0.00
Total Dist ($)	2.08	2.14	1.80	2.10	0.18
Yield from Dist (%)	12.06	17.29	11.61	12.08	—
Expense Ratio (%)	1.90	1.37	2.34	2.15	2.10
Portfolio Turnover (%)	121.29	48.34	33.08	101.71	—
NAV per share ($)	18.52	17.37	14.49	16.58	18.21
Market Price per share	19.38	17.25	12.38	15.50	17.38
Premium (Discount) (%)	4.64	(0.69)	(14.56)	(6.51)	(4.61)
Total Return, Stk Price (%)	24.41	56.62	(8.52)	1.27	—

Van Kampen Merritt Intermediate Term High Income Trust

One Parkview Plaza
Oakbrook Terrace, IL 60181
(800) 225-2222

NYSE : VIT
Transfer Agent
State Street Bank & Trust Co.
225 Franklin St.
Boston, MA 02101
(800) 426-5523

Income

12 Months Ending 12/31/92 Results

	Period End	Period Begin	Distributions	Yield Dist (%)	Total Return (%)
Share Price ($)	7.25	6.88	0.91	13.23	18.60
NAV per share ($)	6.23	5.92		15.37	20.61

Background: Initial public offering January 19, 1989 of 10,000,000 shares at $10 per share. Initial NAV was $9.10 per share.

Objective: Seeks high current income consistent with preservation of capital. May invest up to 65% in high-yield securities rated BB or lower by S&P.

Portfolio: (12/31/92) High-Yield Corporate Bonds 94.9%, Cash & Other 5.2%. Sector Weightings: Chemicals & Plastics 9.9%, Automotive 9.3%, Electronics 7.6%, Publishing/Broadcasting 7.2%, Oil & Gas 6.9%.

Capitalization: (12/31/92) Common stock outstanding 13,711,000. Leveraged with 588 shares preferred stock, stated value $100,000 per share.

Average Maturity (years): 5.6
Fund Manager: Van Kampen Merritt Investment Advisory Corp.   **Fee:** 0.75%
Income Dist: Monthly   **Capital Gains Dist:** Annually
Reinvestment Plan: Yes   **Shareholder Reports:** Semi-Annually

5 Year Performance

Fiscal Year Ending 12/31	1992	1991	1990	1989 (11 mos.)	1988
Net Assets ($mil):	144.20	140.00	121.90	—	—
Net Income Dist ($):	0.91	0.84	1.08	1.02	—
Cap Gains Dist ($):	0.00	0.00	0.00	0.00	—
Total Dist ($)	0.91	0.84	1.08	1.02	—
Yield from Dist (%)	13.23	20.34	14.63	—	—
Expense Ratio (%)	1.11	1.42	1.90	—	—
Portfolio Turnover (%)	109.38	78.37	57.49	33.12	—
NAV per share ($)	6.23	5.92	4.60	7.49	—
Market Price per share	7.25	6.88	4.13	7.38	—
Premium (Discount) (%)	16.41	16.05	(10.22)	(1.47)	—
Total Return, Stk Price (%)	18.60	86.92	(29.40)	—	—

Van Kampen Merritt Limited Term High Income Trust

One Parkview Plaza
Oakbrook Terrace, IL 60181
(800) 225-2222

NYSE : VLT
Transfer Agent
State Street Bank & Trust Co.
225 Franklin St.
Boston, MA 02101
(800) 426-5523

Income

12 Months Ending 12/31/92 Results

	Period End	Period Begin	Distributions	Yield Dist (%)	Total Return (%)
Share Price ($)	9.38	7.50	0.98	13.07	38.13
NAV per share ($)	7.92	7.62		12.86	16.80

Background: Initial public offering April 28, 1989 of 8,000,000 shares at $12 per share. Initial NAV was $11.16 per share.

Objective: Seeks high current income consistent with preservation of capital. Invests primarily in lower-grade or unrated securities.

Portfolio: (12/31/92) High-Yield Corporate Bonds 96.7%, Other 3.4%. Sector Weightings: Electronics 9.3%, Chemicals & Plastics 8.7%, Containers & Packaging 8.1%, Publishing/ Broadcasting 6.8%, Health Care & Education 6.6%.

Capitalization: (12/31/92) Common stock outstanding 8,109,000. Leveraged with 900 shares preferred stock, stated value $50,000 per share.

Average Maturity (years): 7.7
Fund Manager: Van Kampen Merritt Investment Advisory Corp.   **Fee:** 0.75%
Income Dist: Monthly   **Capital Gains Dist:** Annually
Reinvestment Plan: Yes   **Shareholder Reports:** Quarterly

5 Year Performance

Fiscal Year Ending 12/31	1992	1991	1990	1989 (8 mos.)	1988
Net Assets ($mil):	109.20	108.20	94.10	135.50	—
Net Income Dist ($):	0.98	0.92	1.24	0.91	—
Cap Gains Dist ($):	0.00	0.00	0.00	0.00	—
Total Dist ($)	0.98	0.92	1.24	0.91	—
Yield from Dist (%)	13.07	17.52	13.78	—	—
Expense Ratio (%)	1.89	2.73	2.12	1.57	—
Portfolio Turnover (%)	145.05	96.79	64.64	31.04	—
NAV per share ($)	7.92	7.62	5.88	9.31	—
Market Price per share	9.38	7.50	5.25	9.00	—
Premium (Discount) (%)	18.49	(1.57)	(10.71)	(3.33)	—
Total Return, Stk Price (%)	38.13	60.38	(27.89)	—	—

Zenix Income

Two World Trade Center
New York, NY 10048
(212) 298-7350

NYSE : ZIF

Transfer Agent
The Shareholder Services Group
P.O. Box 1376
Boston, MA 02109
(800) 331-1710

Income

12 Months Ending 12/31/92 Results

	Period End	Period Begin	Distributions	Yield Dist (%)	Total Return (%)
Share Price ($)	6.50	6.13	0.83	13.54	19.58
NAV per share ($)	6.35	6.05		13.72	18.68

Background: Initial public offering April 20, 1988 of 9,775,000 shares at $10 per share. Initial NAV was $9.23 per share.

Objective: Seeks high current income. Invests in fixed income securities, including preferred stock, bonds, debentures, notes, and mortgage-backed or other asset-backed securities. Invests 65% in high-yield fixed-income securities rated BB/Ba to C. May invest up to 20% in illiquid securities. May invest up to 20% in non-rated securities. May invest up to 20% in zero-coupon securities.

Portfolio: (12/31/92) Corporate Bonds & Notes 119.3%, Commercial Paper 8.5%, Other Assets, Less Liabilities (29.4%). Sector Weightings: Health Care 9.4%, Packaging/Containers 8.8%, Broadcasting 7.1%, Construction 7.0%, Chemicals 5.8%.

Capitalization: (3/31/92) Common stock outstanding 11,856,000. Long-term debt $25,818,000 due 1995. Leveraged with preferred stock.

Average Maturity (years): 10.1
Fund Manager: Shearson Lehman Advisors
Income Dist: Monthly
Reinvestment Plan: Yes

Fee: 0.50%
Capital Gains Dist: Annually
Shareholder Reports: Quarterly

5 Year Performance

Fiscal Year Ending 3/31	1992	1991	1990	1989 (11 mos.)	1988
Net Assets ($mil):	105.80	92.50	99.30	120.10	—
Net Income Dist ($):	0.85	0.90	1.20	1.01	—
Cap Gains Dist ($):	0.00	0.00	0.00	0.00	—
Total Dist ($)	0.85	0.90	1.20	1.01	—
Yield from Dist (%)	15.45	15.00	13.14	—	—
Expense Ratio (%)	2.15	2.47	2.32	2.04	—
Portfolio Turnover (%)	86.00	68.00	81.00	105.00	—
NAV per share ($)	6.39	5.58	6.30	8.71	—
Market Price per share	6.63	5.50	6.00	9.13	—
Premium (Discount) (%)	3.76	(1.43)	(4.76)	4.71	—
Total Return, Stk Price (%)	36.00	6.67	(21.14)	—	—

International Bond Funds

ACM Managed Multi-Market Trust

1345 Avenue of the Americas
New York, NY 10105
(800) 247-4154 / (212) 969-1000

NYSE : MMF
Transfer Agent
State Street Bank & Trust Co.
225 Franklin St.
Boston, MA 02110
(800) 426-5523

Income

12 Months Ending 12/31/92 Results

	Period End	Period Begin	Distributions	Yield Dist (%)	Total Return (%)
Share Price ($)	8.75	12.63	1.11	8.79	(21.93)
NAV per share ($)	9.50	10.95		10.14	(3.11)

Background: Initial public offering January 21, 1990. Initial NAV was $11.16 per share.

Objective: Seeks high current income. Invests in high-quality debt securities with maturities under five years.

Portfolio: (11/30/92) Short & Medium Term Notes 100%. Country Exposure: U.S. 26.4%, Canada 21.3%, New Zealand 18.9%, Mexico 16.1%, Spain 14.2%, Australia 9.6%, Italy 7.5%, Denmark 3.7%.

Capitalization: (11/30/92) Common stock outstanding 9,974,000. Bank borrowing $28,750,000.

Average Maturity (years): 2.8
Fund Manager: Alliance Capital Management, Inc. **Fee:** 0.65%
Income Dist: Monthly **Capital Gains Dist:** Annually
Reinvestment Plan: Yes **Shareholder Reports:** Semi-Annually

5 Year Performance

Fiscal Year Ending 11/30	1992	1991	1990 (9 mos.)	1989	1988
Net Assets ($mil):	95.80	111.10	113.30	—	—
Net Income Dist ($):	1.09	1.34	1.18	—	—
Cap Gains Dist ($):	0.00	0.17	0.00	—	—
Total Dist ($)	1.09	1.51	1.18	—	—
Yield from Dist (%)	8.90	13.13	—	—	—
Expense Ratio (%)	3.06	3.37	2.90	—	—
Portfolio Turnover (%)	176.00	95.00	101.00	—	—
NAV per share ($)	9.61	11.22	11.53	—	—
Market Price per share	9.25	12.25	11.50	—	—
Premium (Discount) (%)	(3.75)	9.18	(0.26)	—	—
Total Return, Stk Price (%)	(15.59)	19.65	—	—	—

BlackRock North American Government Income Trust, Inc.

One Seaport Plaza
New York, NY 10292
(800) 227-7236 / (212) 214-3334

NYSE : BNA
Transfer Agent
State Street Bank & Trust Co.
One Heritage Dr.
North Quincy, MA 02171
(800) 451-6788

Income

12 Months Ending 12/31/92 Results

	Period End	Period Begin	Distributions	Yield Dist (%)	Total Return (%)
Share Price ($)	12.50	15.00	1.20	8.00	(8.67)
NAV per share ($)	12.72	14.15		8.48	(1.63)

Background: Initial public offering December 20, 1991 of 32,000,000 shares at $15 per share. Initial NAV was $14.10 per share.

Objective: Seeks high monthly income consistent with the preservation of capital. The trust will invest in a portfolio of high quality Canadian and U.S. dollar-denominated securities. At least 65% of the trust's assets will be invested in securities of the U.S. and Canadian governments or their agencies or instrumentalities. The fund may enter into repurchase agreements.

Portfolio: (10/31/92) Foreign 64%, Mortgage-Backed 29%, U.S. Government & Agencies 6%, Zeros 1%. Country Exposure: Canada 64%, U.S. 36%.

Capitalization: (10/31/92) Common stock outstanding 36,207,000. No long-term debt.

Average Maturity (years): 11.8
Fund Manager: BlackRock Financial Management L.P.
Income Dist: Monthly
Reinvestment Plan: Yes

Fee: 0.60%
Capital Gains Dist: Annually
Shareholder Reports: Semi-Annually

5 Year Performance

Fiscal Year Ending 10/31	1992 (10 mos.)	1991	1990	1989	1988
Net Assets ($mil):	475.20	—	—	—	—
Net Income Dist ($):	0.98	—	—	—	—
Cap Gains Dist ($):	0.00	—	—	—	—
Total Dist ($)	0.98	—	—	—	—
Yield from Dist (%)	—	—	—	—	—
Expense Ratio (%)	0.90	—	—	—	—
Portfolio Turnover (%)	314.00	—	—	—	—
NAV per share ($)	13.13	—	—	—	—
Market Price per share	13.50	—	—	—	—
Premium (Discount) (%)	2.82	—	—	—	—
Total Return, Stk Price (%)	—	—	—	—	—

First Australia Prime Income Fund

One Seaport Plaza
New York, NY 10292
(800) 323-9995

Transfer Agent
State Street Bank & Trust Co.
One Heritage Drive
North Quincy, MA 02171
(800) 451-6788

Income

12 Months Ending 12/31/92 Results

	Period End	Period Begin	Distributions	Yield Dist (%)	Total Return (%)
Share Price ($)	10.13	11.13	1.16	10.42	1.44
NAV per share ($)	9.43	11.24		10.32	(5.78)

Background: Initial public offering April 1986 of 75,000,000 shares at $10 per share. Initial NAV was $9.16 per share.

Objective: Seeks current income. Invests primarily in Australian debt securities. May also invest in New Zealand and U.S. Treasury securities.

Portfolio: (12/31/92) Australian Long Term Government & Corporate Bonds 124.2%, Short Term & Other 6.5%, Liabilities (30.7%).

Capitalization: (12/31/92) Common stock outstanding 101,804,406. Leveraged with 3,000 preferred shares, stated value $100,000 per share.

Average Maturity (years): 5.9
Fund Manager: EquitiLink International Management Limited   **Fee:** 0.65%
Income Dist: Monthly   **Capital Gains Dist:** Annually
Reinvestment Plan: Yes   **Shareholder Reports:** Quarterly

5 Year Performance

Fiscal Year Ending 10/31	1992	1991	1990	1989	1988
Net Assets ($mil):	1,277.90	1,272.60	1,161.40	1,100.20	928.70
Net Income Dist ($):	1.10	1.24	1.13	1.08	1.40
Cap Gains Dist ($):	0.29	0.00	0.08	0.23	0.00
Total Dist ($)	1.39	1.24	1.21	1.31	1.40
Yield from Dist (%)	12.49	13.58	13.63	14.35	18.35
Expense Ratio (%)	1.43	1.59	1.54	1.35	1.04
Portfolio Turnover (%)	17.00	83.00	80.00	46.00	60.00
NAV per share ($)	9.61	11.31	10.02	9.31	10.81
Market Price per share	10.13	11.13	9.13	8.88	9.13
Premium (Discount) (%)	5.41	(1.59)	(8.88)	(4.73)	(15.63)
Total Return, Stk Price (%)	3.50	35.49	16.44	11.61	38.01

Global Governments Plus Fund, Inc.

One Seaport Plaza
New York, NY 10292
(212) 214-3334

Transfer Agent
State Street Bank & Trust Co.
One Heritage Dr.
North Quincy, MA 02171
(800) 426-5523

Income

12 Months Ending 12/31/92 Results

	Period End	Period Begin	Distributions	Yield Dist (%)	Total Return (%)
Share Price ($)	7.00	7.75	0.87	11.23	1.55
NAV per share ($)	7.38	8.28		10.51	(0.36)

Background: Initial public offering July 24, 1987, of 52,011,000 shares at $10 per share. Initial NAV was $9.30 per share.

Objective: Seeks high income through interest and capital appreciation. Invests in longer-term U.S. Government securities and Foreign Government securities. The fund will invest 35% of assets in securities with average maturities less than 1 year. All investments are rated AA or higher.

Portfolio: (12/31/92) Long Term Bonds 90.9%, Short Term & Other 9.1%. Country Exposure: U.S. 61.6%, Canada 7.6%, Sweden 6.9%, U.K. 5.1%, Italy 5.0%.

Capitalization: (12/31/92) Common stock outstanding 45,642,508. No long-term debt.

Average Maturity (years): 10.7
Fund Manager: Prudential Mutual Fund Management, Inc. **Fee:** 0.75%
Income Dist: Quarterly **Capital Gains Dist:** Annually
Reinvestment Plan: Yes **Shareholder Reports:** Semi-Annually

5 Year Performance

Fiscal Year Ending 12/31	1992	1991	1990	1989	1988
Net Assets ($mil):	336.80	377.90	376.70	434.20	469.10
Net Income Dist ($):	0.67	0.66	0.59	0.59	0.64
Cap Gains Dist ($):	0.20	0.00	0.00	0.00	0.32
Total Dist ($)	0.87	0.66	0.59	0.59	0.96
Yield from Dist (%)	11.23	9.10	7.87	6.46	9.60
Expense Ratio (%)	1.15	1.29	1.47	1.59	1.59
Portfolio Turnover (%)	346.00	267.00	503.00	477.00	452.00
NAV per share ($)	7.38	8.28	8.25	8.25	8.95
Market Price per share	7.00	7.75	7.25	7.50	9.13
Premium (Discount) (%)	(5.15)	(6.40)	(12.12)	(9.09)	1.90
Total Return, Stk Price (%)	1.55	16.00	4.53	(11.39)	0.90

Global Income Plus Fund, Inc.

1285 Avenue of the Americas
New York, NY 10019
(212) 713-3678

NYSE : GLI

Transfer Agent
Provident National Bank
P.O. Box 8950
Wilmington, DE 19899
(800) 553-8080

Income

12 Months Ending 12/31/92 Results

	Period End	Period Begin	Distributions	Yield Dist (%)	Total Return (%)
Share Price ($)	8.75	10.25	0.87	8.49	(6.15)
NAV per share ($)	9.18	9.86		8.82	1.93

Background: Initial public offering August 25, 1988, of 24,150,000 shares at $10 per share. Initial NAV was $9.30 per share.

Objective: Seeks high current income, capital appreciation is secondary. Invests 65% in debt securities of Foreign Governments and Agencies, instrumentalities, political subdivisions; U.S. Government securities and debt securities of U.S. and foreign issuers rated AAA or AA at purchase. May invest up to 35% in lower-rated debt securities.

Portfolio: (10/31/92) Long Term Debt 60.39%, Short Term 34.41%, Cash & Other 5.0%. Country Exposure: U.S. 20.4%, Spain 8.4%, Australia 6.1%, Canada 7.0%.

Capitalization: (10/31/92) Common stock outstanding 26,096,318. No long-term debt.

Average Maturity (years): 8.2
Fund Manager: Mitchell Hutchins Asset Management   **Fee:** 0.85%
Income Dist: Quarterly   **Capital Gains Dist:** Annually
Reinvestment Plan: Yes   **Shareholder Reports:** Quarterly

5 Year Performance

Fiscal Year Ending 10/31	1992	1991	1990	1989	1988 (2 mos.)
Net Assets ($mil):	245.60	242.20	243.20	226.00	229.50
Net Income Dist ($):	0.72	1.17	0.97	0.99	0.00
Cap Gains Dist ($):	0.14	0.00	0.00	0.00	0.00
Total Dist ($)	0.86	1.17	0.97	0.99	0.00
Yield from Dist (%)	8.82	12.47	11.76	9.90	—
Expense Ratio (%)	1.12	1.13	1.27	1.17	1.40
Portfolio Turnover (%)	85.60	53.80	127.84	179.70	30.00
NAV per share ($)	9.41	9.62	9.86	9.16	9.50
Market Price per share	9.75	9.75	9.38	8.25	10.00
Premium (Discount) (%)	3.61	1.35	(4.97)	(9.93)	5.26
Total Return, Stk Price (%)	8.82	16.42	25.45	(7.60)	—

Global Yield Fund, Inc. (The)

One Seaport Plaza
New York, NY 10292
(800) 451-6788 / (212) 214-3332

NYSE : PGY

Transfer Agent
State Street Bank & Trust Co.
One Heritage Dr.
North Quincy, MA 02171
(800) 426-5523

Income

12 Months Ending 12/31/92 Results

	Period End	Period Begin	Distributions	Yield Dist (%)	Total Return (%)
Share Price ($)	7.50	8.13	0.80	9.84	2.09
NAV per share ($)	8.10	8.99		8.90	(1.00)

Background: Initial public offering June 30, 1986 of 65,550,000 shares at $10 per share. Initial NAV was $9.29 per share.

Objective: Seeks high current income. Capital appreciation is secondary. Invests 65% in government and agencies, semi-government, short-term bank securities or deposits. Balance invested in other corporate or bank securities. May invest in debt securities of Canada, United States, Australia, Hong Kong, Japan, New Zealand, Singapore, and 14 European countries. Not more than 40% will be in any one currency, except for U.S. dollars when the fund is in a temporary defensive posture.

Portfolio: (12/31/92) Long Term Bonds 81.4%, Short Term 13.8%. Country Exposure: Spain 8.1%, Sweden 9.8%, Australia 9.9%, U.S. 15.6%, Canada 8.4%.

Capitalization: (12/31/92) Common stock outstanding 66,109,411. No long-term debt.

Average Maturity (years): 5.8
Fund Manager: Prudential Mutual Fund Management, Inc.   **Fee:** 0.75%
Income Dist: Quarterly   **Capital Gains Dist:** Annually
Reinvestment Plan: Yes   **Shareholder Reports:** Semi-Annually

5 Year Performance

Fiscal Year Ending 12/31	1992	1991	1990	1989	1988
Net Assets ($mil):	535.60	593.40	591.30	595.80	638.20
Net Income Dist ($):	0.75	0.62	0.88	0.94	0.99
Cap Gains Dist ($):	0.05	0.00	0.00	0.00	0.59
Total Dist ($)	0.80	0.62	0.88	0.94	1.58
Yield from Dist (%)	9.84	7.75	11.17	10.02	16.21
Expense Ratio (%)	1.01	0.99	1.03	1.07	1.01
Portfolio Turnover (%)	192.00	141.00	221.00	734.00	371.00
NAV per share ($)	8.10	8.99	8.96	8.57	9.41
Market Price per share	7.50	8.13	8.00	7.88	9.38
Premium (Discount) (%)	(7.41)	(9.68)	(10.71)	(8.05)	(0.43)
Total Return, Stk Price (%)	2.09	9.38	12.69	(5.97)	12.41

Kleinwort Benson Australian Income Fund, Inc.

200 Park Ave.
New York, NY 10166
(800) 237-4218 / (212) 687-2515

Income

NYSE : KBA

Transfer Agent
U.S. Trust Co. of New York
c/o Mutual Funds Service Co.
126 High St.
Boston, MA 02110
(800) 292-4224 / (617) 482-9300

12 Months Ending 12/31/92 Results

	Period End	Period Begin	Distributions	Yield Dist (%)	Total Return (%)
Share Price ($)	9.13	10.88	1.43	13.14	(2.94)
NAV per share ($)	9.84	11.49		12.45	(1.91)

Background: Initial public offering November 20, 1986 of 5,500,000 shares at $10 per share. Initial NAV was $9.35 per share.

Objective: Seeks high current income by investing primarily in high-quality Australian dollar-denominated debt securities of Australian issuers. Long-term capital appreciation is secondary. The fund may invest up to 25% of assets in New Zealand government debt.

Portfolio: (10/31/92) Australian Government Bonds 21.3%, Other Semi-Government Bonds 23.9%, New South Wales Treasury Bonds 20.5%, Eurobonds 15.9%, Australian Corporate Bonds 4.4%, New Zealand Government Bonds 4.7%.

Capitalization: (10/31/92) Common stock outstanding 6,979,231. No long-term debt.

Average Maturity (years): 5.4
Fund Manager: Kleinwort Benson Int'l Investment Ltd.   **Fee:** 0.70%
Income Dist: Monthly   **Capital Gains Dist:** Annually
Reinvestment Plan: Yes   **Shareholder Reports:** Quarterly

5 Year Performance

Fiscal Year Ending 10/31	1992	1991	1990	1989	1988
Net Assets ($mil):	69.60	74.70	65.30	62.70	73.30
Net Income Dist ($):	1.02	1.01	1.06	0.97	1.26
Cap Gains Dist ($):	0.57	0.00	0.00	0.58	0.44
Total Dist ($)	1.59	1.01	1.06	1.55	1.70
Yield from Dist (%)	14.45	11.88	11.01	13.78	20.61
Expense Ratio (%)	1.48	1.62	1.61	1.75	1.48
Portfolio Turnover (%)	53.66	11.39	23.78	11.87	26.63
NAV per share ($)	9.97	11.77	10.29	9.88	11.57
Market Price per share	9.63	11.00	8.50	9.63	11.25
Premium (Discount) (%)	(3.51)	(6.54)	(17.40)	(2.63)	(2.77)
Total Return, Stk Price (%)	2.00	41.29	(0.73)	(0.62)	56.97

Templeton Global Governments Income Trust

NYSE : TGG

700 Central Ave.
St. Petersburg, FL 33701
(800) 237-0738 / (813) 823-8712

Transfer Agent
Dean Witter Trust Co.
2 Montgomery St.
Jersey City, NJ 07302
(800) 526-3143

Income

12 Months Ending 12/31/92 Results

	Period End	Period Begin	Distributions	Yield Dist (%)	Total Return (%)
Share Price ($)	8.63	9.50	1.00	10.53	1.37
NAV per share ($)	8.19	9.16		10.92	0.33

Background: Initial public offering November 22, 1988 of 17,500,000 shares at $10 per share. Initial NAV was $9.30 per share.

Objective: Seeks high current income consistent with preservation of capital. Invests at least 65% in debt securities issued and guaranteed by governments, government agencies, supranational entities, political subdivisions and other government entities. Remaining assets are invested in U.S. and Foreign corporate debt and preferred equity. May hedge against interest rate and currency risks through the use of options, futures, and foreign currency transactions.

Portfolio: (11/30/92) U.S. Government & Agency Bonds 86.4%, Corporate Bonds 8.9%, Short Term & Other 4.7%. Country Exposure: U.S. 14.5%, France 14.1%, Australia 13.3%, Denmark 11.5%, Canada 10.9%.

Capitalization: (8/31/92) Common stock outstanding 22,215,285. No long-term debt.

Average Maturity (years): 6.6

Fund Manager: Templeton, Galbraith and Hansberger Ltd. **Fee:** 0.55%

Income Dist: Monthly **Capital Gains Dist:** Annually

Reinvestment Plan: Yes **Shareholder Reports:** Quarterly

5 Year Performance

Fiscal Year Ending 8/31	1992	1991	1990	1989 (9 mos.)	1988
Net Assets ($mil):	200.80	184.70	188.60	179.90	—
Net Income Dist ($):	0.84	0.86	0.93	0.70	—
Cap Gains Dist ($):	0.00	0.04	0.00	0.00	—
Total Dist ($)	0.84	0.90	0.93	0.70	—
Yield from Dist (%)	9.08	11.07	10.33	—	—
Expense Ratio (%)	1.08	1.11	1.14	1.18	—
Portfolio Turnover (%)	306.92	135.10	112.55	91.60	—
NAV per share ($)	9.04	8.54	8.92	8.67	—
Market Price per share	9.75	9.25	8.13	9.00	—
Premium (Discount) (%)	7.85	8.31	(8.97)	3.81	—
Total Return, Stk Price (%)	14.49	24.85	0.67	—	—

Templeton Global Income Fund, Inc.

700 Central Ave.
St. Petersburg, FL 33701
(800) 237-0738 / (813) 823-8712

Income

NYSE : GIM

Transfer Agent
Mellon Financial Services
85 Challenger Road
Overpark Center
Ridgefield Park, NJ 07660
(800) 526-0801

12 Months Ending 12/31/92 Results

	Period End	Period Begin	Distributions	Yield Dist (%)	Total Return (%)
Share Price ($)	9.00	8.88	0.84	9.46	10.81
NAV per share ($)	8.17	8.87		9.47	1.58

Background: Initial public offering March 17, 1988 of 110,000,000 shares at $10 per share. Initial NAV was $9.35 per share.

Objective: Seeks high current income. Capital appreciation is secondary. Invests 85% of its assets in a portfolio of fixed-income securities rated AA or AAA, including debt securities and preferred stock of U.S. and Foreign issuers. May borrow against its portfolio and invest 35% in dividend-paying common stocks of U.S. and Foreign corporations.

Portfolio: (8/31/92) Government Bonds 64.1%, Corporate Bonds 25.3%, Other 10.2%. Country Exposure: U.S. 13.9%, Australia 17.2%, Canada 13.1%, New Zealand 7.8%, Denmark 7.2%, Spain 7.1%, Sweden 6.0%, France 5.7%.

Capitalization: (8/31/92) Common stock outstanding 119,085,832. No long-term debt.

Average Maturity (years): 11.7
Fund Manager: Templeton, Galbraith, and Hansberger Ltd.   **Fee:** 0.55%
Income Dist: Monthly   **Capital Gains Dist:** Annually
Reinvestment Plan: Yes   **Shareholder Reports:** Quarterly

5 Year Performance

Fiscal Year Ending 8/31	1992	1991	1990	1989	1988 (5 mos.)
Net Assets ($mil):	1,055.50	991.00	992.60	994.90	993.30
Net Income Dist ($):	0.84	0.86	0.96	0.98	0.34
Cap Gains Dist ($):	0.00	0.09	0.00	0.00	0.00
Total Dist ($)	0.84	0.95	0.96	0.98	0.34
Yield from Dist (%)	10.02	12.87	10.51	9.92	—
Expense Ratio (%)	0.81	0.82	0.81	0.81	0.78
Portfolio Turnover (%)	189.94	257.11	130.40	78.73	20.08
NAV per share ($)	8.86	8.48	8.51	8.62	8.92
Market Price per share	9.25	8.38	7.38	9.13	9.88
Premium (Discount) (%)	4.40	(1.30)	(13.40)	5.80	10.65
Total Return, Stk Price (%)	20.41	26.42	(8.65)	2.33	—

Multi-Sector/Strategic Bond Funds

ACM Government Income Fund

1345 Avenue of the Americas
New York, NY 10105
(800) 247-4154 / (212) 969-1000

Transfer Agent
State Street Bank & Trust Co.
225 Franklin St.
Boston, MA 02110
(800) 426-5523

Income

12 Months Ending 12/31/92 Results

	Period End	Period Begin	Distributions	Yield Dist (%)	Total Return (%)
Share Price ($)	11.00	11.13	0.99	8.89	7.73
NAV per share ($)	10.51	10.59		9.35	8.59

Background: Initial public offering August 21, 1987 of 43,500,000 shares at $12 per share. Initial NAV was $11.16 per share.

Objective: Seeks high current income with capital preservation through obligations issued or guaranteed by the U.S. Government, its agencies or instrumentalities, and in repurchase agreements. May use options, repurchase agreements, and futures to enhance income. May invest 35% in securities issued by non- and foreign-government issuers.

Portfolio: (12/31/92) U.S. Treasuries 52.2%, Corporate Bonds & Notes 26.3%, Foreign 12.7%, U.S. Government & Agencies 19.7%.

Capitalization: (12/31/92) Common stock outstanding 48,456,639. No long-term debt.

Average Maturity (years): 12.1
Fund Manager: Alliance Capital Management L.P.   **Fee:** 0.30%
Income Dist: Monthly   **Capital Gains Dist:** Annually
Reinvestment Plan: Yes   **Shareholder Reports:** Semi-Annually

5 Year Performance

Fiscal Year Ending 12/31	1992	1991	1990	1989	1988
Net Assets ($mil):	509.20	509.20	483.00	504.10	493.50
Net Income Dist ($):	0.99	1.25	1.32	1.24	1.23
Cap Gains Dist ($):	0.00	0.00	0.00	0.00	0.22
Total Dist ($)	0.99	1.25	1.32	1.24	1.45
Yield from Dist (%)	8.89	11.76	12.13	11.81	12.89
Expense Ratio (%)	1.57	1.93	2.21	1.79	1.99
Portfolio Turnover (%)	521.00	516.00	348.00	310.00	288.00
NAV per share ($)	10.51	10.59	10.15	10.66	10.55
Market Price per share	11.00	11.13	10.63	10.88	10.50
Premium (Discount) (%)	4.66	5.10	4.63	1.97	(0.47)
Total Return, Stk Price (%)	7.73	16.46	9.83	15.43	6.22

ACM Government Opportunity Fund

1345 Avenue of the Americas
New York, NY 10105
(800) 247-4154 / (212) 969-1000

NYSE : AOF
Transfer Agent
Shareholder Services Group, Inc.
One Exchange Pl.
Boston, MA 02109
(800) 331-1710

Income

12 Months Ending 12/31/92 Results

	Period End	Period Begin	Distributions	Yield Dist (%)	Total Return (%)
Share Price ($)	9.38	9.63	1.29	13.40	10.80
NAV per share ($)	9.10	9.77		13.20	6.35

Background: Initial public offering August 19, 1988 of 11,500,000 shares at $10 per share. Initial NAV was $9.30 per share.

Objective: Seeks high current income consistent with prudent risk. Capital appreciation is secondary. Invests at least 65% of assets in U.S. Government securities and related repurchase agreements. May invest up to 35% in Foreign Government securities and dividend-paying equity securities. May use options and futures.

Portfolio: (11/30/92) U.S. Treasuries 62.4%, U.S. Government & Agencies 13.8%, Foreign Securities 8.6%, Equity 13.1%, Cash 2.1%.

Capitalization: (7/31/92) Common stock outstanding 11,991,439. No long-term debt.

Average Maturity (years): 9.3
Fund Manager: Alliance Capital Management L.P.　　　　　　**Fee:** 0.75%
Income Dist: Monthly　　　　　　**Capital Gains Dist:** Annually
Reinvestment Plan: Yes　　　　　　**Shareholder Reports:** Semi-Annually

5 Year Performance

Fiscal Year Ending 7/31	1992	1991	1990	1989 (11 mos.)	1988
Net Assets ($mil):	115.80	105.9	104.10	110.40	—
Net Income Dist ($):	0.90	1.06	1.01	0.84	—
Cap Gains Dist ($):	0.04	0.00	0.03	0.11	—
Total Dist ($)	0.94	1.06	1.04	0.95	—
Yield from Dist (%)	10.02	12.47	10.95	—	—
Expense Ratio (%)	1.22	1.22	1.24	1.23	—
Portfolio Turnover (%)	505.00	365.00	287.00	123.00	—
NAV per share ($)	9.66	9.02	9.01	9.59	—
Market Price per share	9.75	9.38	8.50	9.50	—
Premium (Discount) (%)	0.93	3.99	(5.66)	(0.94)	—
Total Return, Stk Price (%)	13.97	22.82	0.42	—	—

ACM Government Securities Fund

1345 Avenue of the Americas
New York, NY 10105
(800) 247-4154 / (212) 969-1000

NYSE : GSF
Transfer Agent
State Street Bank & Trust Co.
225 Franklin St.
Boston, MA 02110
(800) 426-5523

Income

12 Months Ending 12/31/92 Results

	Period End	Period Begin	Distributions	Yield Dist (%)	Total Return (%)
Share Price ($)	10.63	10.63	1.04	9.78	9.78
NAV per share ($)	10.47	10.55		9.86	9.10

Background: Initial public offering January 21, 1988 of 56,000,000 shares at $12 per share. Initial NAV was $11.16 per share.

Objective: Seeks high current income consistent with preservation of capital. Invests primarily in securities issued or guaranteed by the U.S. Government, its agencies or instrumentalities, or in repurchase agreements. May invest 35% in fixed-income securities including stable Foreign Government issues.

Portfolio: (12/31/92) U.S. Treasuries 57.0%, Corporate Bonds & Notes 25.5%, Foreign 13.0%, U.S. Government Agencies 15.3%, Other Assets, Less Liabilities (11.7%).

Capitalization: (12/31/92) Common stock outstanding 67,628,312. No long-term debt.

Average Maturity (years): 9.9
Fund Manager: Alliance Capital Management L.P.   **Fee:** 0.30%
Income Dist: Monthly   **Capital Gains Dist:** Annually
Reinvestment Plan: Yes   **Shareholder Reports:** Semi-Annually

5 Year Performance

Fiscal Year Ending 12/31	1992	1991	1990	1989	1988 (11 mos.)
Net Assets ($mil):	708.00	707.00	673.20	698.60	681.90
Net Income Dist ($):	1.04	1.26	1.28	1.26	1.10
Cap Gains Dist ($):	0.00	0.00	0.00	0.00	0.06
Total Dist ($)	1.04	1.26	1.28	1.26	1.16
Yield from Dist (%)	9.78	12.60	11.91	12.29	—
Expense Ratio (%)	1.52	1.83	2.05	1.65	1.77
Portfolio Turnover (%)	497.00	480.00	360.00	303.00	267.00
NAV per share ($)	10.47	10.55	10.16	10.60	10.48
Market Price per share	10.63	10.63	10.00	10.75	10.25
Premium (Discount) (%)	1.53	0.76	(1.57)	1.42	(2.19)
Total Return, Stk Price (%)	9.78	18.90	4.93	17.17	—

ACM Managed Income Fund, Inc.

1345 Avenue of the Americas
New York, NY 10105
(800) 247-4154 / (212) 969-1000

NYSE : AMF
Transfer Agent
State Street Bank & Trust Co.
225 Franklin St.
Boston, MA 02110
(800) 426-5523

Income

12 Months Ending 12/31/92 Results

	Period End	Period Begin	Distributions	Yield Dist (%)	Total Return (%)
Share Price ($)	10.13	9.00	1.15	12.78	25.33
NAV per share ($)	9.05	8.81		13.05	15.78

Background: Initial public offering October 27, 1988 of 19,100,000 shares at $10 per share. Initial NAV was $9.26 per share.

Objective: Seeks high current income and capital appreciation. Invests primarily in obligations issued or guaranteed by the U.S. government and its agencies or instrumentalities. Remainder of assets may be invested in corporate fixed income.

Portfolio: (11/30/92) U.S. Government Agencies 48.9%, Corporate Bonds 48.9%, Short-Term 2.2%.

Capitalization: (12/31/92) Common stock outstanding 18,719,649. Leveraged with 950 shares preferred stock, stated value $100,000 per share.

Average Maturity (years): 11.2
Fund Manager: Alliance Capital Management L.P.   **Fee:** 0.65%
Income Dist: Monthly   **Capital Gains Dist:** Annually
Reinvestment Plan: Yes   **Shareholder Reports:** Semi-Annually

5 Year Performance

Fiscal Year Ending 8/31	1992	1991	1990	1989 (10 mos.)	1988
Net Assets ($mil):	267.60	257.9	248.60	182.10	—
Net Income Dist ($):	0.98	1.01	1.01	0.76	—
Cap Gains Dist ($):	0.00	0.00	0.13	0.00	—
Total Dist ($)	0.98	1.01	1.14	0.76	—
Yield from Dist (%)	11.36	14.17	12.49	—	—
Expense Ratio (%)	1.09	1.11	1.09	1.06	—
Portfolio Turnover (%)	630.00	293.00	310.00	129.00	—
NAV per share ($)	9.32	8.39	7.93	9.40	—
Market Price per share	10.25	8.63	7.13	9.13	—
Premium (Discount) (%)	9.98	2.74	(10.21)	(2.98)	—
Total Return, Stk Price (%)	30.13	35.20	(9.42)	—	—

American Capital Income Trust

2800 Post Oak Blvd.
P.O. Box 1411
Houston, TX 77251-1411
(800) 421-9696 / (713) 993-0500

NYSE : ACD

Transfer Agent
Boston Financial Services, Inc.
P.O. Box 366
Boston, MA 02101
(800) 421-9696

Income

12 Months Ending 12/31/92 Results

	Period End	Period Begin	Distributions	Yield Dist (%)	Total Return (%)
Share Price ($)	7.63	7.38	0.86	11.65	15.04
NAV per share ($)	7.85	7.70		11.17	13.12

Background: Initial public offering April 22, 1988 of 13,000,000 shares of beneficial interest at $10 per share. Initial NAV was $9.30 per share.

Objective: Seeks high current income. Invests in fixed-income securities issued by the U.S. Government and domestic corporations, including high-yield securities.

Portfolio: (12/31/92) Corporate Bonds & Notes 39.3%, U.S. Government & Agency Obligations 47.2%, Preferred Stocks 8.1%, Repurchase Agreements 4.7%.

Capitalization: (12/31/92) Shares of beneficial interest outstanding 15,224,113. No long-term debt.

Average Maturity (years): 12.1
Fund Manager: American Capital Asset Management, Inc.   **Fee:** 0.65%
Income Dist: Monthly   **Capital Gains Dist:** Annually
Reinvestment Plan: Yes   **Shareholder Reports:** Semi-Annually

5 Year Performance

Fiscal Year Ending 12/31	1992	1991	1990	1989	1988 (8 mos.)
Net Assets ($mil):	119.60	116.30	100.60	119.40	134.30
Net Income Dist ($):	0.86	0.89	0.97	1.08	0.67
Cap Gains Dist ($):	0.00	0.00	0.00	0.03	0.00
Total Dist ($)	0.86	0.89	0.97	1.10	0.67
Yield from Dist (%)	11.65	15.81	12.93	12.05	—
Expense Ratio (%)	0.08	1.03	1.00	0.97	0.93
Portfolio Turnover (%)	54.00	50.00	29.00	20.00	46.00
NAV per share ($)	7.85	7.70	6.66	7.90	9.06
Market Price per share	7.63	7.38	5.63	7.50	9.13
Premium (Discount) (%)	(2.80)	(4.29)	(15.47)	(5.06)	0.77
Total Return, Stk Price (%)	15.04	46.89	(12.00)	(5.81)	—

American Strategic Income Portfolio, Inc.

Piper Jaffray Tower
222 S. Ninth St.
Minneapolis, MN 55402
(800) 333-6000 / (612) 342-6426

Transfer Agent
Investors Fiduciary Trust Co.
P. O. Box 419432
Kansas City, MO 64105
(800) 543-1627

Income

12 Months Ending 12/31/92 Results

	Period End	Period Begin	Distributions	Yield Dist (%)	Total Return (%)
Share Price ($)	15.25	15.00	1.24	8.27	9.93
NAV per share ($)	14.85	13.98		8.87	15.09

Background: Initial public offering December 27, 1991 of 1,400,000 shares at $15 per share. Initial NAV was $13.98 per share.

Objective: Seeks high current income. Capital appreciation is secondary. Investment strategy emphasizes investments in mortgage-backed securities. Fund will also invest in asset-backed securities, U.S. Government securities, Corporate Debt securities, Municipal Obligations, Unregistered securities, and Derivative Mortgage-Backed securities.

Portfolio: (12/22/92) Whole Loan and Participation Mortgages 35.3%, U.S. Government 24.9%, Agency-Backed CMOs 11.1%, Non-Agency CMOs 5.5%, Short Term 5.5%, Other 1.2%.

Capitalization: (11/30/92) Common stock outstanding 5,285,373 shares. No long-term debt.

Average Maturity (years): 13.1
Fund Manager: Piper Capital Management, Inc.   **Fee:** 0.20%
Income Dist: Monthly   **Capital Gains Dist:** Annually
Reinvestment Plan: Yes   **Shareholder Reports:** Semi-Annually

5 Year Performance

Fiscal Year Ending 11/30	1992 (11 mos.)	1991	1990	1989	1988
Net Assets ($mil):	78.70	—	—	—	—
Net Income Dist ($):	1.13	—	—	—	—
Cap Gains Dist ($):	0.00	—	—	—	—
Total Dist ($)	1.13	—	—	—	—
Yield from Dist (%)	—	—	—	—	—
Expense Ratio (%)	1.45	—	—	—	—
Portfolio Turnover (%)	72.00	—	—	—	—
NAV per share ($)	14.89	—	—	—	—
Market Price per share	16.25	—	—	—	—
Premium (Discount) (%)	9.13	—	—	—	—
Total Return, Stk Price (%)	—	—	—	—	—

Colonial Intermarket Income Trust I

One Financial Center, 12th Floor
Boston, MA 02111
(800) 426-3750

NYSE : CMK
Transfer Agent
State Street Bank & Trust Co.
225 Franklin St.
Boston, MA 02110
(800) 426-5523

Income

12 Months Ending 12/31/92 Results

	Period End	Period Begin	Distributions	Yield Dist (%)	Total Return (%)
Share Price ($)	11.00	10.88	1.12	10.29	11.40
NAV per share ($)	11.33	11.31		9.90	10.08

Background: Initial public offering September 22, 1989 of 10,000,000 shares at $12 per share. Initial NAV was $11.16 per share.

Objective: Seeks high current income. Invests in securities issued or guaranteed by the U.S. Government, its agencies or instrumentalities; debt secured by foreign governments; high-yield securities, some of which may be convertible. The percentage of assets in any one sector is limited to 50%. The fund may engage in hedging transactions for leverage.

Portfolio: (12/22/92) Corporate 46.5%, Foreign Government 31.5%, U.S. Agencies 9.8%, Cash & Equivalents 6.5%, U.S. Treasuries 5.6%, Common Stock 0.1%. Portfolio Ratings: AAA 30.1%, AA 23.3%, BB 9.1%, Lower or Non-Rated 37.5%.

Capitalization: (11/30/92) Common stock outstanding 11,009,000. No long-term debt.

Average Maturity (years): 10.8
Fund Manager: Colonial Management Associates, Inc.   **Fee:** 0.75%
Income Dist: Monthly   **Capital Gains Dist:** Annually
Reinvestment Plan: Yes   **Shareholder Reports:** Semi-Annually

5 Year Performance

Fiscal Year Ending 11/30	1992	1991	1990	1989 (2 mos.)	1988
Net Assets ($mil):	123.60	124.80	117.10	123.9	—
Net Income Dist ($):	1.13	1.23	1.35	0.12	—
Cap Gains Dist ($):	0.00	0.01	0.00	0.00	—
Total Dist ($)	1.13	1.24	1.35	0.12	—
Yield from Dist (%)	10.27	12.88	11.61	—	—
Expense Ratio (%)	1.04	1.07	1.11	0.90	—
Portfolio Turnover (%)	129.00	109.00	153.00	0.00	—
NAV per share ($)	11.22	11.33	10.64	11.26	—
Market Price per share	11.13	11.00	9.63	11.63	—
Premium (Discount) (%)	(0.89)	(2.91)	(9.59)	3.20	—
Total Return, Stk Price (%)	11.45	27.10	(5.59)	—	—

Dreyfus Strategic Governments Income, Inc.

144 Glenn Curtiss Blvd.
Uniondale, NY 11556
(800) 334-6899

NYSE : DSI
Transfer Agent
Mellon Bank, N.A.
One Mellon Bank Center
Pittsburgh, PA 15258
(412) 236-8000

Income

12 Months Ending 12/31/92 Results

	Period End	Period Begin	Distributions	Yield Dist (%)	Total Return (%)
Share Price ($)	11.63	11.50	1.09	9.48	10.61
NAV per share ($)	10.86	11.35		9.60	5.29

Background: Initial public offering June 23, 1988 of 13,000,000 shares at $12 per share. Initial NAV was $11.15 per share.

Objective: Seeks current income consistent with capital preservation. Invests at least 65% in securities issued by the U.S. Government and its agencies and Foreign Governments. May invest up to 35% in non-government securities. May use options.

Portfolio: (11/30/92) U.S. Government & Agencies 54.7%, Foreign Government Bonds & Notes 20.4%, Foreign Corporate Bonds & Notes 6.9%, U.S. Corporate Bonds 3.7%, Other 9.7%, Short Term 3.2%.

Capitalization: (11/30/92) Common stock outstanding 14,830,505. No long-term debt.

Average Maturity (years): 6.7
Fund Manager: The Dreyfus Corporation
Income Dist: Monthly
Reinvestment Plan: Yes

Fee: 0.70%
Capital Gains Dist: Annually
Shareholder Reports: Semi-Annually

5 Year Performance

Fiscal Year Ending 5/31	1992	1991	1990	1989 (11 mos.)	1988
Net Assets ($mil):	163.20	159.80	156.20	157.00	—
Net Income Dist ($):	1.03	1.08	1.08	0.94	—
Cap Gains Dist ($):	0.03	0.00	0.00	0.03	—
Total Dist ($)	1.06	1.08	1.08	0.97	—
Yield from Dist (%)	9.52	10.93	9.93	—	—
Expense Ratio (%)	0.88	0.87	0.89	0.89	—
Portfolio Turnover (%)	56.29	26.38	16.34	83.78	—
NAV per share ($)	11.06	10.92	10.70	10.76	—
Market Price per share	11.50	11.13	9.88	10.88	—
Premium (Discount) (%)	3.98	1.83	(7.66)	1.02	—
Total Return, Stk Price (%)	12.85	23.58	0.74	—	—

Excelsior Income Shares
114 W. 47th St.
New York, NY 10036
(800) 428-8890 / (212) 852-3732

NYSE : EIS
Transfer Agent
U.S. Trust Co. of New York
770 Broadway, 6th Floor
New York, NY 10003
(800) 257-2356

Income

12 Months Ending 12/31/92 Results

	Period End	Period Begin	Distributions	Yield Dist (%)	Total Return (%)
Share Price ($)	17.75	18.00	1.42	7.89	6.50
NAV per share ($)	18.54	18.74		7.58	6.51

Background: Initial public offering May, 1973 of 2,202,797 shares of common stock at $25 per share. Initial NAV was $22.88 per share.

Objective: Seeks high current income consistent with prudent risk. Capital appreciation is secondary. Invests 75% in high-grade fixed-income securities, U.S. and Canadian Government obligations, commercial paper, and other cash equivalents. May invest 25% in lower-grade debt securities, securities with equity features, and preferred stocks. May not invest more than 20% in private placements.

Portfolio: (12/31/92) U.S. Government & Agencies 65.1%, Corporate Bonds & Notes 33.9%, Short-Term 1.0%. Portfolio Ratings: AAA 65.75%, Aa 17.66%, A 8.79%, Baa 3.72%.

Capitalization: (12/31/92) Common stock outstanding 2,220,891. No long-term debt.

Average Maturity (years): 19.7
Fund Manager: U.S. Trust Co. of New York
Income Dist: Quarterly
Reinvestment Plan: Yes

Fee: 0.50%
Capital Gains Dist: Annually
Shareholder Reports: Quarterly

5 Year Performance

Fiscal Year Ending 12/31	1992	1991	1990	1989	1988
Net Assets ($mil):	41.20	41.60	38.9	38.9	37.00
Net Income Dist ($):	1.33	1.45	1.48	1.39	1.28
Cap Gains Dist ($):	0.09	0.00	0.00	0.00	0.00
Total Dist ($)	1.42	1.45	1.48	1.39	1.28
Yield from Dist (%)	7.89	8.92	9.18	9.27	8.46
Expense Ratio (%)	0.98	0.98	1.00	1.03	1.07
Portfolio Turnover (%)	155.60	65.49	175.30	260.45	469.40
NAV per share ($)	18.54	18.74	17.50	17.52	16.64
Market Price per share	17.75	18.00	16.25	16.13	15.00
Premium (Discount) (%)	(4.26)	(3.95)	(7.14)	(7.99)	(9.86)
Total Return, Stk Price (%)	6.50	19.69	9.92	16.80	7.60

First Boston Income Fund, Inc.

Tower 49, 12 E. 49th St.
New York, NY 10017
(800) 541-4905 / (800) 332-5577

NYSE : FBF
Transfer Agent
Chemical Bank
450 W. 33rd St., 8th Floor
New York, NY 10001
(800) 647-4273

Income

12 Months Ending 12/31/92 Results

	Period End	Period Begin	Distributions	Yield Dist (%)	Total Return (%)
Share Price ($)	8.38	8.38	0.83	9.90	9.90
NAV per share ($)	8.42	8.28		10.02	11.71

Background: Initial public offering April 8, 1987 of 24,000,000 shares at $10 per share. Initial NAV was $9.30 per share.

Objective: Seeks high level of current income consistent with preservation of capital. Invests two-thirds in securities rated in one of the four highest categories by S&P or Moody's. Unrated securities will be of comparable quality. Balance of investments will not be subject to a rating quality limitation.

Portfolio: (12/31/92) Corporate Bonds 73.4%, U.S. Government & Agency Securities 19.7%, Common Stock 1.0%, Preferred Stock 2.1%, Short Term & Other 3.8%. Sector Weightings: Manufacturing 23.5%, Services 18.3%, Consumer Products 8.2%, Retail Trade 7.4%.

Capitalization: (12/31/92) Common stock outstanding 24,214,473. No long-term debt.

Average Maturity (years): 10.8
Fund Manager: First Boston Asset Management Corp.
Income Dist: Monthly
Reinvestment Plan: Yes

Fee: 0.50%
Capital Gains Dist: Annually
Shareholder Reports: Quarterly

5 Year Performance

Fiscal Year Ending 12/31	1992	1991	1990	1989	1988
Net Assets ($mil):	203.80	199.9	175.40	201.30	207.30
Net Income Dist ($):	0.83	0.90	0.90	0.90	0.90
Cap Gains Dist ($):	0.00	0.00	0.00	0.00	0.00
Total Dist ($)	0.83	0.90	0.90	0.90	0.90
Yield from Dist (%)	9.90	14.11	11.42	11.42	10.91
Expense Ratio (%)	0.86	0.87	0.89	0.92	0.91
Portfolio Turnover (%)	115.20	53.30	61.40	95.80	113.50
NAV per share ($)	8.42	8.28	7.25	8.32	8.58
Market Price per share	8.38	8.38	6.38	7.88	7.88
Premium (Discount) (%)	(0.48)	1.09	(12.14)	(5.29)	(8.16)
Total Return, Stk Price (%)	9.90	45.45	(7.61)	11.42	6.42

First Boston Strategic Income Fund

Tower 49, 12 E. 49th St.
New York, New York 10017
(800) 541-4905 / (800) 332-5577

NYSE : FBI

Transfer Agent
Manufacturers Hanover Trust Co.
450 W. 33rd St., 8th Floor
New York, NY 10001
(800) 647-4273

Income

12 Months Ending 12/31/92 Results

	Period End	Period Begin	Distributions	Yield Dist (%)	Total Return (%)
Share Price ($)	9.63	10.38	1.05	10.12	2.89
NAV per share ($)	9.80	9.62		10.91	12.79

Background: Initial public offering April 22, 1988 of 7,250,000 shares at $12 per share. Initial NAV was $11.16 per share.

Objective: Seeks high current income consistent with preservation of capital. Allocates assets between three sectors of the fixed-income securities market: U.S. Government, High Yield and International.

Portfolio: (12/31/92) Corporate Bonds & Notes 79.4%, U.S. Government & Agencies 8.9%, Common Stock 0.8%, Preferred Stock 2.8%, Foreign Currency Denominated Securities 4.5%. Sector Weightings: Manufacturing 24.2%, Services 19.0%, Retail Trade 10.9%, Consumer Products 6.2%, Oil & Gas 5.4%.

Capitalization: (12/31/92) Common stock outstanding 8,395,566. No long-term debt.

Average Maturity (years): 7.5
Fund Manager: First Boston Asset Management   **Fee:** 0.47%
Income Dist: Monthly   **Capital Gains Dist:** Annually
Reinvestment Plan: Yes   **Shareholder Reports:** Quarterly

5 Year Performance

Fiscal Year Ending 12/31	1992	1991	1990	1989	1988 (9 mos.)
Net Assets ($mil):	82.50	80.60	73.10	84.40	90.80
Net Income Dist ($):	1.05	1.20	1.20	1.00	0.77
Cap Gains Dist ($):	0.00	0.00	0.00	0.31	0.00
Total Dist ($)	1.05	1.20	1.20	1.31	0.77
Yield from Dist (%)	10.12	15.23	12.97	11.91	—
Expense Ratio (%)	1.01	1.00	1.00	1.07	0.85
Portfolio Turnover (%)	107.70	48.00	81.00	105.50	112.10
NAV per share ($)	9.80	9.62	8.70	10.06	10.86
Market Price per share	9.63	10.38	7.88	9.25	11.00
Premium (Discount) (%)	(1.73)	7.80	(9.43)	(8.05)	1.29
Total Return, Stk Price (%)	2.89	46.95	(1.84)	(4.00)	—

Fort Dearborn Income Securities

209 S. LaSalle, 11th Floor
Chicago, IL 60604-1295
(312) 346-0676

NYSE : FTD
Transfer Agent
First Chicago Trust Co. of New York
30 W. Broadway
New York, NY 10007
(800) 446-2617

Income

12 Months Ending 12/31/92 Results

	Period End	Period Begin	Distributions	Yield Dist (%)	Total Return (%)
Share Price ($)	15.63	16.25	1.24	7.63	3.82
NAV per share ($)	16.33	16.23		7.64	8.26

Background: Initial public offering January, 1972 of 6,000,000 shares at $20 per share. Initial NAV was $18.75 per share.

Objective: Seeks current income. Capital appreciation is secondary. Invests at least 75% of total assets in investment-grade (BBB or higher) or equivalent debt obligations, obligations of the U.S. Government, prime commercial paper, and cash. May invest balance in private placements, preferred stocks, bonds with equity features, and Foreign Government, or corporate obligations. May use leverage through bank borrowings up to 20% of net assets.

Portfolio: (9/30/92) Corporate Bonds & Notes 72.5%, U.S. Government & Agency Securities 23.7%, Foreign 9.7%. Portfolio Ratings: AAA 36.5%, AA 14.4%, A 23.6%, BAA 25.5%.

Capitalization: (9/30/92) Common stock outstanding 7,067,184. No long-term debt.

Average Maturity (years): 17.1
Fund Manager: Brinson Partners, Inc.   **Fee:** 0.50%
Income Dist: Quarterly   **Capital Gains Dist:** Annually
Reinvestment Plan: Yes   **Shareholder Reports:** Quarterly

5 Year Performance

Fiscal Year Ending 9/30	1992	1991	1990	1989	1988
Net Assets ($mil):	117.60	109.50	100.00	104.60	102.20
Net Income Dist ($):	1.24	1.33	1.36	1.36	1.36
Cap Gains Dist ($):	0.00	0.00	0.00	0.00	0.00
Total Dist ($)	1.24	1.33	1.36	1.36	1.36
Yield from Dist (%)	7.87	9.85	9.54	9.30	9.89
Expense Ratio (%)	0.86	0.81	0.80	0.80	0.80
Portfolio Turnover (%)	32.50	180.50	190.80	213.80	202.40
NAV per share ($)	16.64	15.63	14.45	15.19	14.84
Market Price per share	16.33	15.75	13.50	14.25	14.63
Premium (Discount) (%)	(1.86)	0.77	(6.57)	(6.19)	(1.48)
Total Return, Stk Price (%)	11.56	26.52	4.28	6.70	16.29

Fortis Securities

P.O. Box 64284
St. Paul, MN 55164
(800) 800-2638

NYSE : FOR

Transfer Agent
Norwest Bank of Minnesota
P.O. Box 738
South St. Paul, MN 55075
(612) 450-4064 / (800) 468-9716

Income

12 Months Ending 12/31/92 Results

	Period End	Period Begin	Distributions	Yield Dist (%)	Total Return (%)
Share Price ($)	11.13	11.38	1.04	9.14	6.94
NAV per share ($)	9.95	10.11		10.29	8.70

Background: Initial public offering September 27, 1972 of 9,300,000 shares at $14.50 per share. Initial NAV was $13.80 per share. Originally St. Paul Securities, the name was changed to AMEV Securities on September 27, 1987. In February 1993, the name was again changed, to Fortis Securities.

Objective: Seeks high current income through a diversified portfolio of marketable debt securities and privately placed debt. Invests at least 75% in securities rated investment grade by S&P. May invest 25% in lower-rated or non-rated securities.

Portfolio: (9/30/92) U.S. Government Bonds 52.0%, Corporate Bonds 50.0%. Non-U.S. Government Bonds 48.0%.

Capitalization: (12/31/92) Common stock outstanding 11,884,133. No long-term debt.

Average Maturity (years): 11.3
Fund Manager: Fortis Advisers, Inc.
Income Dist: Monthly
Reinvestment Plan: Yes

Fee: 0.45%
Capital Gains Dist: Annually
Shareholder Reports: Quarterly

5 Year Performance

Fiscal Year Ending 7/31	1992	1991	1990	1989	1988
Net Assets ($mil):	118.20	113.40	107.20	113.00	109.30
Net Income Dist ($):	1.06	1.07	1.10	1.09	1.08
Cap Gains Dist ($):	0.00	0.00	0.00	0.00	0.00
Total Dist ($)	1.06	1.07	1.10	1.09	1.08
Yield from Dist (%)	0.00	11.89	10.23	10.25	9.82
Expense Ratio (%)	0.82	0.88	0.86	0.86	0.83
Portfolio Turnover (%)	49.00	67.00	117.00	100.00	120.00
NAV per share ($)	10.13	9.91	9.62	10.42	10.36
Market Price per share	11.50	10.88	9.00	10.75	10.63
Premium (Discount) (%)	13.52	9.69	(6.44)	3.17	2.51
Total Return, Stk Price (%)	12.92	32.78	(6.05)	11.38	6.45

Franklin Principal Maturity Trust

P.O. Box 7777
San Mateo, CA 94403-7777
(800) 342-5236

NYSE : FPT

Transfer Agent
The Shareholder Services Group
One Exchange Place
Boston, MA 02109
(800) 331-1710

Income

12 Months Ending 12/31/92 Results

	Period End	Period Begin	Distributions	Yield Dist (%)	Total Return (%)
Share Price ($)	7.50	8.00	0.64	8.00	1.75
NAV per share ($)	8.25	8.24		7.77	7.89

Background: Initial public offering January 19, 1989 of 17,700,000 shares at $10 per share. Initial NAV was $9.30 per share.

Objective: Seeks preservation of capital and high monthly dividends. Will invest 30% of assets in zero-coupon bonds to assure the return of $10 per share net asset value in 2001. Balance of portfolio will be invested in high-yield corporate and mortgage-backed bonds.

Portfolio: (11/30/92) Zero-Coupon Bonds 76.0%, Corporate Bonds 27.0%, Mortgage-Backed 20.3%, Municipal Bonds 11.4%, Preferred Stocks 1.6%, Common Stocks & Warrants 5.7%, Liabilities in Excess of Other Assets, Net (43.4%).

Capitalization: (11/30/92) Shares of beneficial interest outstanding 20,462,600. No long-term debt.

Average Maturity (years): 9.6
Fund Manager: Franklin Advisers, Inc.
Income Dist: Monthly
Reinvestment Plan: Yes

Fee: 0.75%
Capital Gains Dist: Annually
Shareholder Reports: Semi-Annually

5 Year Performance

Fiscal Year Ending 11/30	1992	1991	1990	1989 (10 mos.)	1988
Net Assets ($mil):	165.60	164.9	150.60	175.9	—
Net Income Dist ($):	0.46	0.73	1.00	0.79	—
Cap Gains Dist ($):	0.00	0.00	0.00	0.00	—
Total Dist ($)	0.46	0.73	1.00	0.79	—
Yield from Dist (%)	5.94	9.26	10.12	—	—
Expense Ratio (%)	3.27	4.06	4.49	3.60	—
Portfolio Turnover (%)	61.69	49.91	28.96	38.73	—
NAV per share ($)	8.09	8.06	7.36	8.60	—
Market Price per share	7.50	7.75	7.88	9.88	—
Premium (Discount) (%)	(7.29)	(3.85)	7.07	14.77	—
Total Return, Stk Price (%)	2.71	7.61	(10.12)	—	—

Hyperion Total Return Fund

520 Madison Ave., 10th Floor
New York, NY 10022
(212) 980-8400

NYSE : HTR
Transfer Agent
Boston Financial Data Services, Inc.
2 Heritage Dr.
North Quincy, MA 02171
(800) 426-5523

Income

12 Months Ending 12/31/92 Results

	Period End	Period Begin	Distributions	Yield Dist (%)	Total Return (%)
Share Price ($)	11.25	11.38	1.18	10.37	9.23
NAV per share ($)	10.79	11.35		10.40	5.46

Background: Initial public offering July 28, 1989 of 24,800,000 shares at $12 per share. Initial NAV was $11.16 per share.

Objective: Seeks high level of current income. Invests at least 60% of assets in high-quality mortgage-backed securities and the remainder in high-yield securities and mortgage-backed securities. The fund may utilize short-term borrowing and reverse repurchase agreements for leverage.

Portfolio: (11/30/92) U.S. Government & Agencies 83.5%, Corporate Obligations 22.5%, Mortgage-Related Securities 28.9%, Asset-Backed Securities 11.7%, Liabilities in excess of other assets (46.6%).

Capitalization: (12/31/92) Common stock outstanding 24,694,806. No long term-debt.

Average Maturity (years): 12.3
Fund Manager: Hyperion Capital Management , Inc.
Income Dist: Monthly
Reinvestment Plan: Yes

Fee: 0.65%
Capital Gains Dist: Annually
Shareholder Reports: Quarterly

5 Year Performance

Fiscal Year Ending 11/30	1992	1991	1990	1989	1988
Net Assets ($mil):	269.00	281.9	262.70	275.20	—
Net Income Dist ($):	1.23	1.10	1.11	0.32	—
Cap Gains Dist ($):	0.00	0.00	0.12	0.00	—
Total Dist ($)	1.23	1.10	1.23	0.32	—
Yield from Dist (%)	10.47	11.28	11.05	—	—
Expense Ratio (%)	1.06	1.10	1.16	1.09	—
Portfolio Turnover (%)	390.31	65.43	200.50	9.21	—
NAV per share ($)	10.87	11.50	10.75	11.09	—
Market Price per share	11.63	11.75	9.75	11.13	—
Premium (Discount) (%)	6.99	2.17	(9.30)	0.27	—
Total Return, Stk Price (%)	9.45	31.79	(1.35)	—	—

INA Investment Securities, Inc.

P.O. Box 13856
Philadelphia, PA 19101
(413) 784-0100

NYSE : IIS
Transfer Agent
State Street Bank & Trust Co.
P.O. Box 8200
Boston, MA 02266-8200
(800) 426-5523

Income

12 Months Ending 12/31/92 Results

	Period End	Period Begin	Distributions	Yield Dist (%)	Total Return (%)
Share Price ($)	17.25	17.75	1.48	8.34	5.52
NAV per share ($)	18.75	18.85		7.85	7.32

Background: Initial public offering January 24, 1973 of 4,230,000 shares at $25 per share. Initial NAV was $23 per share.

Objective: Seeks high level of current income. Invests at least 90% of net assets in debt securities and preferred stock with or without conversion or equity features. Securities must be rated in the four highest categories by S&P and Moody's.

Portfolio: (12/31/92) Long Term Bonds 68.4%, U.S. Government & Agency Securities 28.8%, Short Term Instruments 1.7%. Sector Weightings: Financial 18.9%, Industrial 12.1%, Transportation 11.7%, Oil & Gas 8.6%. Portfolio Ratings: AAA 37.3%, AA 10.9%, A 16.6%, BBB 17.4%, Lower or Non-Rated 17.8%.

Capitalization: (12/31/92) Common stock outstanding 4,792,215. No long-term debt.

Average Maturity (years): 13.4
Fund Manager: CIGNA Investments, Inc.
Income Dist: Quarterly
Reinvestment Plan: Yes

Fee: 0.55%
Capital Gains Dist: Annually
Shareholder Reports: Quarterly

5 Year Performance

Fiscal Year Ending 12/31	1992	1991	1990	1989	1988
Net Assets ($mil):	89.80	90.30	82.70	85.70	84.10
Net Income Dist ($):	1.48	1.52	1.63	1.68	1.75
Cap Gains Dist ($):	0.00	0.00	0.00	0.00	0.00
Total Dist ($)	1.48	1.52	1.63	1.68	1.75
Yield from Dist (%)	8.34	10.22	9.59	9.95	10.37
Expense Ratio (%)	0.90	0.93	0.96	1.03	0.95
Portfolio Turnover (%)	41.00	72.00	68.00	71.00	56.00
NAV per share ($)	18.75	18.85	17.25	17.89	17.62
Market Price per share	17.25	17.75	14.88	17.00	16.88
Premium (Discount) (%)	(8.00)	(5.84)	(13.74)	(4.97)	(4.26)
Total Return, Stk Price (%)	5.52	29.50	(2.88)	10.66	10.37

Kemper Multi-Market Income Trust

120 S. LaSalle St.
Chicago, IL 60603
(800) 537-6006

NYSE : KMM
Transfer Agent
Investors Fiduciary Trust Co.
127 W. 10th St.
Kansas City, MO 64105
(800) 422-2848

Income

12 Months Ending 12/31/92 Results

	Period End	Period Begin	Distributions	Yield Dist (%)	Total Return (%)
Share Price ($)	10.25	9.50	1.08	11.37	19.26
NAV per share ($)	10.85	10.29		10.50	15.94

Background: Initial public offering January 23, 1989 of 10,000,000 shares at $12 per share. Initial NAV was $11.16.

Objective: Seeks high income consistent with a prudent total return. Invests in a diversified portfolio of income-producing securities. The fund may invest in: U.S. Government and Agency paper, Foreign Government obligations, and Foreign corporate securities. No limitation on portfolio allocation percentages. The fund may leverage with preferreds.

Portfolio: (11/30/92) U.S. Government Obligations 33.1%, Foreign Government Obligations 6.5%, Corporate Obligations 59.2%, Common Stocks & Other 1.7%.

Capitalization: (11/30/92) Common shares outstanding 19,798,000. No long-term debt.

Average Maturity (years): 6.0
Fund Manager: Kemper Financial Services, Inc.
Income Dist: Monthly
Reinvestment Plan: Yes

Fee: 0.85%
Capital Gains Dist: Annually
Shareholder Reports: Quarterly

5 Year Performance

Fiscal Year Ending 11/30	1992	1991	1990	1989 (10 mos.)	1988
Net Assets ($mil):	215.40	204.50	155.40	203.20	—
Net Income Dist ($):	1.09	1.16	1.40	1.05	—
Cap Gains Dist ($):	0.00	0.00	0.00	0.00	—
Total Dist ($)	1.09	1.16	1.40	1.05	—
Yield from Dist (%)	11.03	15.72	13.49	—	—
Expense Ratio (%)	0.99	1.00	1.00	0.94	—
Portfolio Turnover (%)	101.00	24.00	32.00	38.00	—
NAV per share ($)	10.88	10.36	7.88	10.33	—
Market Price per share	10.38	9.88	7.38	10.38	—
Premium (Discount) (%)	(4.60)	(4.73)	(6.47)	(100.00)	—
Total Return, Stk Price (%)	16.09	49.59	(15.41)	—	—

MFS Charter Income Trust

500 Boylston St.
Boston, MA 02116-3741
(617) 954-5000

NYSE : MCR
Transfer Agent
State Street Bank & Trust Co.
P.O. Box 8200
Boston, MA 02266-8200
(800) 637-2304

Income

12 Months Ending 12/31/92 Results

	Period End	Period Begin	Distributions	Yield Dist (%)	Total Return (%)
Share Price ($)	9.50	10.38	1.12	10.79	2.31
NAV per share ($)	10.30	10.71		10.46	6.63

Background: Initial public offering July 21, 1989. Initial NAV was $11.16 per share.

Objective: Seeks current income by investing one third of its portfolio in each of the following sectors: U.S. Government securities, debt obligations of Foreign Governments and other foreign issuers, and high-yielding corporate fixed-income securities.

Portfolio: (12/1/92) Bonds 88.9%, Convertible Preferred Stocks 0.6%, Common Stocks 0.2%, Short Term & Other 12.3%.

Capitalization: (11/30/92) Common stock outstanding 87,852,839. No long-term debt.

Average Maturity (years): 11.8
Fund Manager: Massachusetts Financial Services Company **Fee:** 0.32%
Income Dist: Monthly **Capital Gains Dist:** Annually
Reinvestment Plan: Yes **Shareholder Reports:** Semi-Annually

5 Year Performance

Fiscal Year Ending 11/30	1992	1991	1990	1989 (4 mos.)	1988
Net Assets ($mil):	898.80	923.30	864.30	977.90	—
Net Income Dist ($):	0.90	1.06	1.22	0.38	—
Cap Gains Dist ($):	0.15	0.00	0.07	0.00	—
Total Dist ($)	1.05	1.06	1.29	0.38	—
Yield from Dist (%)	9.65	11.61	11.73	—	—
Expense Ratio (%)	0.98	1.02	1.08	0.74	—
Portfolio Turnover (%)	198.00	416.00	184.00	480.00	—
NAV per share ($)	10.23	10.59	9.93	11.00	—
Market Price per share	9.88	10.88	9.13	11.00	—
Premium (Discount) (%)	(3.42)	2.64	(8.01)	0.00	—
Total Return, Stk Price (%)	0.46	30.78	(5.27)	—	—

MFS Government Markets Income Trust

500 Boylston St.
Boston, MA 02116-3741
(617) 954-5000

NYSE : MGF
Transfer Agent
State Street Bank & Trust Co.
P.O. Box 8200
Boston, MA 02266-8200
(800) 637-2304

Income

12 Months Ending 12/31/92 Results

	Period End	Period Begin	Distributions	Yield Dist (%)	Total Return (%)
Share Price ($)	7.13	7.88	0.86	10.91	1.40
NAV per share ($)	7.65	8.25		10.42	3.15

Background: Initial public offering May 20, 1987 of 85,000,000 shares at $10 per share. Initial NAV was $9.40 per share.

Objective: Seeks high level of current income. Invests at least 65% in obligations issued or guaranteed by the U.S. Government and may engage in transactions involving related options. May invest up to 35% in obligations issued or guaranteed by Foreign Governments.

Portfolio: (11/30/92) U.S. Treasuries 66%, Foreign 26.5%, Repurchase Agreements 3.6%, Short Term 1.2%.

Capitalization: (11/30/92) Common stock outstanding 97,911,555. No long-term debt.

Average Maturity (years): 12.5
Fund Manager: Massachusetts Financial Services Company **Fee:** 0.32%
Income Dist: Monthly **Capital Gains Dist:** Annually
Reinvestment Plan: Yes **Shareholder Reports:** Semi-Annually

5 Year Performance

Fiscal Year Ending 11/30	1992	1991	1990	1989	1988
Net Assets ($mil):	743.10	786.00	814.00	857.20	873.50
Net Income Dist ($):	0.57	0.64	0.68	0.90	0.88
Cap Gains Dist ($):	0.00	0.00	0.00	0.00	0.17
Total Dist ($)	0.57	0.64	0.68	0.90	1.05
Yield from Dist (%)	7.13	7.87	6.80	8.88	10.63
Expense Ratio (%)	1.03	1.04	1.05	1.08	1.11
Portfolio Turnover (%)	245.00	805.00	535.00	640.00	307.00
NAV per share ($)	7.59	8.08	8.41	8.92	9.18
Market Price per share	7.25	8.00	8.13	10.00	10.13
Premium (Discount) (%)	(4.48)	(0.99)	(3.33)	12.11	10.24
Total Return, Stk Price (%)	(2.25)	6.27	(11.90)	7.60	13.16

MFS Intermediate Income Trust

500 Boylston St.
Boston, MA 02116-3741
(617) 954-5000

NYSE : MIN

Transfer Agent
State Street Bank & Trust Co.
P.O. Box 8200
Boston, MA 02266-8200
(800) 637-2304

Income

12 Months Ending 12/31/92 Results

	Period End	Period Begin	Distributions	Yield Dist (%)	Total Return (%)
Share Price ($)	7.25	7.88	0.80	10.15	2.16
NAV per share ($)	7.90	8.43		9.49	3.20

Background: Initial public offering March 11, 1988 of 200,000,000 shares at $10 per share.

Objective: Seeks to preserve capital and provide high current income from investments in shorter-term U.S. Government securities and stable Foreign Governments. Maintains an average maturity between three and seven years.

Portfolio: (10/31/92) U.S. Treasuries 57%, Foreign 39%, Short Term 4%. Country Exposure: Sweden 10%, Spain 10%, Canada 7%, Australia 7%, Denmark 2%.

Capitalization: (10/31/92) Common stock outstanding 200,252,216. No long-term debt.

Average Maturity (years): 6.3
Fund Manager: Massachussetts Financial Services Company   **Fee:** 0.32%
Income Dist: Monthly   **Capital Gains Dist:** Annually
Reinvestment Plan: Yes   **Shareholder Reports:** Semi-Annually

5 Year Performance

Fiscal Year Ending 10/31	1992	1991	1990	1989	1988
Net Assets ($mil):	1,615.40	1,643.70	1,695.40	1,790.70	1,836.70
Net Income Dist ($):	0.60	0.62	0.63	0.92	0.39
Cap Gains Dist ($):	0.00	0.00	0.00	0.00	0.00
Total Dist ($)	0.60	0.62	0.63	0.92	0.39
Yield from Dist (%)	7.50	8.27	7.20	9.81	—
Expense Ratio (%)	1.01	1.00	1.01	1.10	0.99
Portfolio Turnover (%)	401.00	1,004.00	554.00	546.00	206.00
NAV per share ($)	8.07	8.24	8.45	8.87	9.16
Market Price per share	8.00	8.00	7.50	8.75	9.38
Premium (Discount) (%)	(0.87)	(2.91)	(11.24)	(1.35)	2.29
Total Return, Stk Price (%)	7.50	14.93	(7.09)	3.09	—

MFS Multimarket Income Trust

500 Boylston St.
Boston, MA 02116-3741
(617) 954-5000

NYSE : MMT
Transfer Agent
State Street Bank & Trust Co.
P.O. Box 8200
Boston, MA 02266-8300
(800) 637-2304

Income

12 Months Ending 12/31/92 Results

	Period End	Period Begin	Distributions	Yield Dist (%)	Total Return (%)
Share Price ($)	7.13	7.50	0.90	12.00	7.07
NAV per share ($)	7.59	8.07		11.15	5.20

Background: Initial public offering March 5, 1987 of 110,000,000 shares at $10 per share. Initial NAV was $9.40 per share.

Objective: Seeks high current income. Preservation of capital is secondary, while capital appreciation is incidental. May invest in U.S. Government securities, corporate bonds and notes, bank and municipal obligations. May invest up to 40% in each of the electricity and telephone industries. The Trust may enter into options and futures transactions and forward currency exchange contracts and purchase securities on a "when issued" basis.

Portfolio: (11/30/92) Treasuries 34%, Foreign 30%, High Yield 18%, GNMAs 9%, Short Term 9%. Country Exposure: Sweden 10%, Spain 9%, Canada 4%, Australia 4%, France 3%.

Capitalization: (10/31/92) Shares of beneficial interest outstanding 123,179,935. No long-term debt.

Average Maturity (years): 12.9
Fund Manager: Massachusetts Financial Services Company **Fee:** 0.34%
Income Dist: Monthly **Capital Gains Dist:** Annually
Reinvestment Plan: Yes **Shareholder Reports:** Quarterly

5 Year Performance

Fiscal Year Ending 10/31	1992	1991	1990	1989	1988
Net Assets ($mil):	947.30	929.40	917.50	1,056.50	—
Net Income Dist ($):	0.65	0.70	0.79	1.11	0.74
Cap Gains Dist ($):	0.00	0.00	0.00	0.00	0.00
Total Dist ($)	0.65	0.70	0.79	1.11	0.74
Yield from Dist (%)	8.39	10.77	8.65	11.10	8.11
Expense Ratio (%)	1.11	1.11	1.19	1.23	1.12
Portfolio Turnover (%)	425.00	740.00	365.00	423.00	159.00
NAV per share ($)	7.69	7.93	7.54	8.66	9.01
Market Price per share	7.63	7.75	6.50	9.13	10.00
Premium (Discount) (%)	(0.91)	(2.27)	(13.79)	5.31	10.99
Total Return, Stk Price (%)	6.84	30.00	(20.15)	2.40	17.63

Oppenheimer Multi-Government Trust

Two World Trade Center
New York, NY 10048
(800) 525-7048 / (212) 323-0200

NYSE : OGT

Transfer Agent
Shareholder Financial Services
P.O. Box 173673
Denver, CO 80217-3673
(800) 647-7374

Income

12 Months Ending 12/31/92 Results

	Period End	Period Begin	Distributions	Yield Dist (%)	Total Return (%)
Share Price ($)	8.63	9.25	0.91	9.84	3.14
NAV per share ($)	8.48	9.02		10.09	4.10

Background: Initial public offering November 23, 1988 of 5,500,000 shares at $10 per share. Initial NAV was $9.30 per share.

Objective: Seeks high current income consistent with preservation of capital. Capital appreciation is secondary. Invests at least 50% of total assets in U.S. Government securities. Not more than 25% of total assets will be invested in Foreign Government securities.

Portfolio: (10/31/92) Long-Term U.S. Government Obligations 52.2%, Corporate Bonds & Notes 30.4%, Long-Term Foreign Government Obligations 15.5%. Sector Weightings: Retail 6.0%, Manufacturing-Diversified 4.8%, Information Technology 2.8%, Oil & Gas 2.6%, Services 2.1%.

Capitalization: (10/31/92) Common stock outstanding 6,510,689. No long-term debt.

Average Maturity (years): 10.9
Fund Manager: Oppenheimer Management Corp.   **Fee:** 0.65%
Income Dist: Monthly   **Capital Gains Dist:** Annually
Reinvestment Plan: Yes   **Shareholder Reports:** Semi-Annually

5 Year Performance

Fiscal Year Ending 10/31	1992	1991	1990	1989 (11 mos.)	1988
Net Assets ($mil):	55.70	57.20	54.70	57.40	—
Net Income Dist ($):	0.92	0.99	0.94	0.80	—
Cap Gains Dist ($):	0.00	0.00	0.05	0.04	—
Total Dist ($)	0.92	0.99	0.99	0.84	—
Yield from Dist (%)	9.68	12.56	11.15	—	—
Expense Ratio (%)	1.32	1.21	1.22	1.34	—
Portfolio Turnover (%)	98.40	59.90	95.30	98.70	—
NAV per share ($)	8.55	8.97	8.66	9.12	—
Market Price per share	8.63	9.50	7.88	8.88	—
Premium (Discount) (%)	0.94	5.91	(9.12)	(2.74)	—
Total Return, Stk Price (%)	0.53	33.12	(0.11)	—	—

Oppenheimer Multi-Sector Income Trust

Two World Trade Center
New York, NY 10048
(800) 525-7048 / (212) 323-0200

NYSE : OMS

Transfer Agent
Shareholder Financial Services
P.O. Box 173673
Denver, CO 80217-3673
(800) 647-7374

Income

12 Months Ending 12/31/92 Results

	Period End	Period Begin	Distributions	Yield Dist (%)	Total Return (%)
Share Price ($)	10.63	11.00	1.15	10.45	7.09
NAV per share ($)	10.38	10.71		10.74	7.66

Background: Initial public offering March 31, 1988 of 28,000,000 shares at $12 per share. Initial NAV was $11.16 per share.

Objective: Seeks high current income consistent with preservation of capital. Capital appreciation is secondary. Seven sector asset allocation of the fixed income securities: U.S. Government, corporate, international, mortgage-backed, municipal, convertible, and money market. Maximum allocation: U.S. Government 100%, corporate and money markets 50%, all others 25%.

Portfolio: (10/31/92) Corporate Bonds & Notes 35.1%, Mortgage-Backed Securities 25.4%, Foreign Fixed-Income Securities 21.2%, Convertible Securities 8.3%, Municipal Securities 5.1%, U.S. Government Securities 4.4%, Money Market Instruments 0.5%. Sector Weightings: Retail 7.2%, Oil & Gas 4.1%, Manufacturing-Diverfied 3.7%, Containers-Paper 1.8%, Automobiles, Trucks and Parts 1.7%.

Capitalization: (10/31/92) Common stock outstanding 28,624,670. No long-term debt.

Average Maturity (years): 10.9
Fund Manager: Oppenheimer Management Corp.   **Fee:** 0.65%
Income Dist: Monthly   **Capital Gains Dist:** Annually
Reinvestment Plan: Yes   **Shareholder Reports:** Semi-Annually

5 Year Performance

Fiscal Year Ending 10/31	1992	1991	1990	1989	1988 (7 mos.)
Net Assets ($mil):	299.40	301.60	278.50	299.70	314.70
Net Income Dist ($):	1.16	1.07	1.10	1.13	0.59
Cap Gains Dist ($):	0.00	0.10	0.02	0.01	0.06
Total Dist ($)	1.16	1.17	1.12	1.14	0.65
Yield from Dist (%)	10.42	12.47	11.34	10.24	—
Expense Ratio (%)	1.11	1.16	1.03	1.03	1.01
Portfolio Turnover (%)	95.90	59.70	85.70	162.00	60.10
NAV per share ($)	10.46	10.64	9.88	10.63	11.17
Market Price per share	11.00	11.13	9.38	9.88	11.13
Premium (Discount) (%)	5.16	4.61	(5.16)	(7.15)	(0.45)
Total Return, Stk Price (%)	9.25	31.13	6.28	(0.99)	—

Putnam Master Income Trust

One Post Office Square
Boston, MA 02109
(800) 225-1581

NYSE : PMT

Transfer Agent
Putnam Investor Services, Inc.
P.O. Box 41203
Providence, RI 02940-1203
(800) 634-1587

Income

12 Months Ending 12/31/92 Results

	Period End	Period Begin	Distributions	Yield Dist (%)	Total Return (%)
Share Price ($)	8.75	8.25	0.98	11.88	17.94
NAV per share ($)	9.09	9.03		10.85	11.52

Background: Initial public offering December 18, 1987 of 50,247,000 shares at $10 per share. Initial NAV was $9.30 per share.

Objective: Seeks high current income consistent with preservation of capital. Intends to diversify investments among three sectors of the fixed-income securities markets: U.S. Government and agencies, high-yield corporate, and Foreign issues. Debt securities will be rated A or better at the time of purchase.

Portfolio: (12/31/92) High Yield 41%, Foreign 31%, U.S. Government Securities 28%. Sector Weightings: Manufacturing/Industrial 11%, Retail/Container 8%, Hotel/Recreation 5%, Health Care 4%, Chemical/Paper/Auto 3%.

Capitalization: (10/31/92) Common stock outstanding 53,375,649. No long-term debt.

Average Maturity (years): 8.1
Fund Manager: Putnam Management Company, Inc.   **Fee:** 0.75%
Income Dist: Monthly   **Capital Gains Dist:** Annually
Reinvestment Plan: Yes   **Shareholder Reports:** Quarterly

5 Year Performance

Fiscal Year Ending 10/31	1992	1991	1990	1989	1988 (10 mos.)
Net Assets ($mil):	488.30	468.20	429.00	482.50	515.30
Net Income Dist ($):	0.77	0.82	0.84	0.96	0.80
Cap Gains Dist ($):	0.10	0.00	0.01	0.19	0.03
Total Dist ($)	0.87	0.82	0.85	1.15	0.83
Yield from Dist (%)	10.38	11.71	10.14	12.78	—
Expense Ratio (%)	0.95	1.08	1.08	1.06	0.85
Portfolio Turnover (%)	221.30	323.27	125.33	323.44	117.10
NAV per share ($)	9.15	8.80	8.01	8.86	9.50
Market Price per share	8.38	8.38	7.00	8.38	9.00
Premium (Discount) (%)	(8.42)	(4.77)	(12.61)	(5.53)	(5.26)
Total Return, Stk Price (%)	10.38	31.43	(6.32)	5.89	—

Putnam Master Intermediate Income Trust
One Post Office Square
Boston, MA 02109
(800) 225-1581

NYSE : PIM
Transfer Agent
Putnam Investors Services, Inc.
P.O. Box 41203
Providence, RI 02940-1203
(800) 634-1587

Income

12 Months Ending 12/31/92 Results

	Period End	Period Begin	Distributions	Yield Dist (%)	Total Return (%)
Share Price ($)	8.00	7.75	0.84	10.84	14.06
NAV per share ($)	8.52	8.39		10.01	11.56

Background: Initial public offering April 29, 1988 of 40,000,000 shares at $10 per share. Initial NAV was $9.30 per share.

Objective: Seeks high current income with relative stability of NAV. Invests in U.S. Government securities, high-yield and international fixed-income securities having a dollar-weighted average maturity of more than five years but not more than ten years.

Portfolio: (11/30/92) High Yield 41%, Foreign 31%, U.S. Government & Agencies 28%. Country Exposure: Netherlands 6%, Japan 5%, Canada 3%, Germany 3%, Great Britain 3%.

Capitalization: (9/30/92) Common stock outstanding 39,005,338. No long-term debt.

Average Maturity (years): 6.5
Fund Manager: Putnam Management Company, Inc.
Income Dist: Monthly
Reinvestment Plan: Yes

Fee: 0.75%
Capital Gains Dist: Annually
Shareholder Reports: Quarterly

5 Year Performance

Fiscal Year Ending 9/30	1992	1991	1990	1989	1988 (6 mos.)
Net Assets ($mil):	339.9	317.70	301.60	301.60	345.90
Net Income Dist ($):	0.74	0.76	0.85	0.99	0.34
Cap Gains Dist ($):	0.00	0.00	0.08	0.08	0.00
Total Dist ($)	0.74	0.76	0.93	1.07	0.34
Yield from Dist (%)	9.55	11.69	11.10	10.83	—
Expense Ratio (%)	0.98	1.08	1.04	1.04	0.39
Portfolio Turnover (%)	134.43	204.31	211.22	202.47	33.18
NAV per share ($)	8.71	8.16	7.60	8.62	9.27
Market Price per share	8.50	7.75	6.50	8.38	9.88
Premium (Discount) (%)	(2.41)	(5.02)	(14.47)	(2.90)	6.47
Total Return, Stk Price (%)	19.23	30.92	(11.34)	(4.35)	—

Multi Sector/Strategic Bond Funds   149

Putnam Premier Income Trust

One Post Office Square
Boston, MA 02109
(800) 225-1581

NYSE : PPT

Transfer Agent
Putnam Investor Services, Inc.
P.O. Box 2107
Boston, MA 02208
(800) 648-7410

Income

12 Months Ending 12/31/92 Results

	Period End	Period Begin	Distributions	Yield Dist (%)	Total Return (%)
Share Price ($)	8.00	7.75	0.84	10.84	14.06
NAV per share ($)	8.53	8.43		9.96	11.15

Background: Initial public offering February 26, 1988 of 140,000,000 shares at $10 per share. Initial NAV was $9.30 per share.

Objective: Seeks high current income. Investments are allocated among three sectors of the fixed-income securities market: U.S. Government, high-yield, and International. Capital appreciation is incidental. Generally, the fund invests a portion of its assets in each sector, but at times it may only be in one sector.

Portfolio: (11/30/92) Corporate Bonds & Notes 42%, U.S. Government & Agencies 31%, Foreign 27%. Country Exposure: France 5%, Netherlands 5%, Japan 5%, Germany 4%, Great Britian 3%, Canada 3%.

Capitalization: (7/31/92) Shares of beneficial interest outstanding 140,475,959. No long-term debt.

Average Maturity (years): 8.3
Fund Manager: Putnam Management Company, Inc.   **Fee:** 0.75%
Income Dist: Monthly   **Capital Gains Dist:** Annually
Reinvestment Plan: Yes   **Shareholder Reports:** Quarterly

5 Year Performance

Fiscal Year Ending 7/31	1992	1991	1990	1989	1988
Net Assets ($mil):	1,195.00	1,106.80	1,169.00	1,279.00	1,255.50
Net Income Dist ($):	0.75	0.75	0.75	0.88	0.33
Cap Gains Dist ($):	0.00	0.00	0.02	0.27	0.05
Total Dist ($)	0.75	0.75	0.77	1.15	0.38
Yield from Dist (%)	9.68	10.52	8.11	11.94	—
Expense Ratio (%)	0.88	1.06	1.02	0.99	0.40
Portfolio Turnover (%)	203.27	350.45	165.97	249.07	41.74
NAV per share ($)	8.51	7.90	8.20	8.98	8.95
Market Price per share	8.88	7.75	7.13	9.50	9.63
Premium (Discount) (%)	4.23	(1.90)	(13.17)	5.79	7.49
Total Return, Stk Price (%)	24.26	19.21	(16.84)	10.59	—

Single State Tax-Free Bond Funds

Dreyfus California Municipal Income Inc

144 Glenn Curtiss Blvd.
Uniondale, NY 11556
(800) 334-6899 / (516) 794-5210

AMEX : DCM
Transfer Agent
Mellon Bank, N.A.
P.O. Box 444
Pittsburgh, PA 15230
(412) 236-8000

Tax-Free Income

12 Months Ending 12/31/92 Results

	Period End	Period Begin	Distributions	Yield Dist (%)	Total Return (%)
Share Price ($)	9.00	8.88	0.60	6.76	8.11
NAV per share ($)	9.43	9.35		6.42	7.27

Background: Initial public offering October 21, 1988 of 4,255,000 shares at $10 per share. Initial NAV was $9.22 per share.

Objective: Seeks high current income exempt from Federal and California personal income taxes consistent with the preservation of capital. Under normal conditions the fund will invest 100% of its assets in investment-grade California municipals. Fund may use leverage.

Portfolio: (9/30/92) Municipal Bonds 100%. Portfolio Ratings: AAA 35.9%, AA 4.2%, A 26.2%, BBB 11.8%, Non-Rated 21.9%.

Capitalization: (9/30/92) Common stock outstanding 4,439,679. No long-term debt. Fund may use leverage.

Average Maturity (years): 24.3
Fund Manager: The Dreyfus Corporation   **Fee:** 0.70%
Income Dist: Monthly   **Capital Gains Dist:** Annually
Reinvestment Plan: Yes   **Shareholder Reports:** Semi-Annually

5 Year Performance

Fiscal Year Ending 9/30	1992	1991	1990	1989 (11 mos.)	1988
Net Assets ($mil):	41.70	40.70	40.50	40.30	—
Net Income Dist ($):	0.60	0.63	0.64	0.48	—
Cap Gains Dist ($):	0.00	0.03	0.02	0.00	—
Total Dist ($)	0.60	0.66	0.66	0.48	—
Yield from Dist (%)	6.07	7.04	6.85	—	—
Expense Ratio (%)	1.11	1.04	1.00	1.07	—
Portfolio Turnover (%)	27.77	15.43	29.53	14.33	—
NAV per share ($)	9.40	9.22	9.30	9.38	—
Market Price per share	9.38	9.88	9.38	9.63	—
Premium (Discount) (%)	(0.32)	7.05	0.86	2.56	—
Total Return, Stk Price (%)	1.01	12.37	4.26	—	—

Dreyfus New York Municipal Income, Inc.

144 Glenn Curtiss Blvd.
Uniondale, NY 11556
(800) 334-6899 / (516) 794-5210

AMEX : DNM

Transfer Agent
Mellon Bank, N.A.
P.O. Box 444
Pittsburgh, PA 15230
(412) 236-8000

Tax-Free Income

12 Months Ending 12/31/92 Results

	Period End	Period Begin	Distributions	Yield Dist (%)	Total Return (%)
Share Price ($)	10.50	9.75	0.63	6.46	14.15
NAV per share ($)	10.13	9.78		6.44	10.02

Background: Initial public offering October 21, 1988 of 3,000,000 shares at $10 per share. Initial NAV was $9.21 per share.

Objective: Seeks high current income exempt from Federal, New York State and City income taxes consistent with the preservation of capital. Invests only in those municipal obligations considered investment-grade by S&P or Moody's.

Portfolio: (12/22/92) Revenue Bonds 81.93%, General Obligation Bonds 4.22%, Special Tax Bonds 4.2%, Other 9.65%. Portfolio Ratings: AAA 3.3%, AA 17.07%, A 23.58%, BBB 45.27%, Non-Rated 10.78%.

Capitalization: (9/30/92) Common stock outstanding 3,649,355. No long-term debt.

Average Maturity (years): 22.4
Fund Manager: The Dreyfus Corporation   **Fee:** 0.70%
Income Dist: Monthly   **Capital Gains Dist:** Annually
Reinvestment Plan: Yes   **Shareholder Reports:** Semi-Annually

5 Year Performance

Fiscal Year Ending 9/30	1992	1991	1990	1989 (1 mo.)	1988
Net Assets ($mil):	36.90	34.90	32.80	33.00	—
Net Income Dist ($):	0.61	0.63	0.66	0.48	—
Cap Gains Dist ($):	0.02	0.01	0.00	0.00	—
Total Dist ($)	0.63	0.64	0.66	0.48	—
Yield from Dist (%)	6.54	6.92	6.85	—	—
Expense Ratio (%)	1.11	1.10	1.07	1.15	—
Portfolio Turnover (%)	15.23	15.53	11.76	38.28	—
NAV per share ($)	10.13	9.67	9.20	9.41	—
Market Price per share	10.13	9.63	9.25	9.63	—
Premium (Discount) (%)	0.00	(0.52)	0.54	2.34	—
Total Return, Stk Price (%)	11.73	11.03	2.91	—	—

Minnesota Municipal Term Trust

NYSE : MNA
Piper Jaffray Tower
Transfer Agent
222 S. Ninth St.
Investors Fiduciary Trust Co.
Minneapolis, MN 55402
127 W. 10th St.
(800) 333-6000 / (612) 342-6426
Kansas City, MO 64105-1716
(816) 474-8786

Tax-Free Income

12 Months Ending 12/31/92 Results

	Period End	Period Begin	Distributions	Yield Dist (%)	Total Return (%)
Share Price ($)	10.38	10.63	0.61	5.74	3.39
NAV per share ($)	10.15	9.68		6.30	11.16

Background: Initial public offering September 19, 1991 of 5,727,000 shares at $10 per share. Initial NAV was $9.45 per share.

Objective: Seeks high current income exempt from Federal and Minnesota State income taxes. The fund will terminate and distribute all of its assets to shareholders on or shortly before April 15, 2002. Termination may be extended to April 15, 2007. At least 65% of the fund's assets will be invested in municipal securities rated A or higher. The fund will not invest in any obligations rated below BB or non-rated.

Portfolio: (12/31/92) Minnesota Municipal Coupons 92.5%, Minnesota Municipal Zeros 7.5%. Portfolio Ratings: AAA 40.0%, AA 30.0%, A 29.0%, BBB 1.0%.

Capitalization: (12/31/92) Common stock outstanding 5,732,710. Leveraged with 576 shares preferred stock with $50,000 per share liquidation preference. No long-term debt.

Average Maturity (years): 7.3
Fund Manager: Piper Capital Management, Inc.　　　　　**Fee:** 0.25%
Income Dist: Monthly　　　　　**Capital Gains Dist:** Annually
Reinvestment Plan: Yes　　　　　**Shareholder Reports:** Semi-Annually

5 Year Performance

Fiscal Year Ending 12/31	1992	1991 (3 mos.)	1990	1989	1988
Net Assets ($mil):	87.00	84.30	—	—	—
Net Income Dist ($):	0.60	0.10	—	—	—
Cap Gains Dist ($):	0.01	0.00	—	—	—
Total Dist ($)	0.61	0.10	—	—	—
Yield from Dist (%)	5.74	—	—	—	—
Expense Ratio (%)	0.66	0.55	—	—	—
Portfolio Turnover (%)	17.00	23.00	—	—	—
NAV per share ($)	10.15	9.68	—	—	—
Market Price per share	10.38	10.63	—	—	—
Premium (Discount) (%)	2.27	9.71	—	—	—
Total Return, Stk Price (%)	3.39	—	—	—	—

New York Tax Exempt Income Fund, Inc.

500 W. Madison St.
Chicago, IL 60606
(312) 559-3000

Transfer Agent
Shareholders Financial Services Inc.
P.O. Box 173673
Denver, CO 80217-3673
(800) 647-7374

Tax-Free Income

12 Months Ending 12/31/92 Results

	Period End	Period Begin	Distributions	Yield Dist (%)	Total Return (%)
Share Price ($)	11.13	10.13	0.75	7.40	17.28
NAV per share ($)	10.46	10.30		7.28	8.83

Background: Initial public offering October, 1987 of 2,000,000 shares at $10.00 per share. Initial NAV was $9.35 per share.

Objective: Seeks high current income exempt from Federal, New York State, and New York City income taxes. Invests primarily in a diversified portfolio of tax-exempt New York municipal obligations, 80% of which are rated BBB or better. May invest up to 20% in unrated New York municipal securities.

Portfolio: (10/31/92) Municipal Bonds & Notes 98.2%, Other 1.8%. Portfolio Ratings: AAA 44.9%, AA 17.8%, A 24.8%, BBB 12.5%.

Capitalization: (10/31/92) Common stock outstanding 2,339,927. No long-term debt.

Average Maturity (years): 17.2
Fund Manager: Shareholders Financial Services, Inc. **Fee:** 0.50%
Income Dist: Monthly **Capital Gains Dist:** Annually
Reinvestment Plan: Yes **Shareholder Reports:** Quarterly

5 Year Performance

Fiscal Year Ending 10/31	1992	1991	1990	1989	1988
Net Assets ($mil):	24.30	23.70	22.70	23.20	23.00
Net Income Dist ($):	0.64	0.64	0.56	0.63	0.59
Cap Gains Dist ($):	0.04	0.03	0.11	0.06	0.08
Total Dist ($)	0.68	0.67	0.67	0.69	0.67
Yield from Dist (%)	6.80	7.24	7.14	7.36	6.54
Expense Ratio (%)	0.97	0.97	1.12	1.34	1.53
Portfolio Turnover (%)	9.00	2.00	4.00	24.00	45.00
NAV per share ($)	10.37	10.22	9.78	10.00	9.92
Market Price per share	10.88	10.00	9.25	9.38	9.38
Premium (Discount) (%)	4.92	(2.15)	(5.42)	(6.30)	(5.54)
Total Return, Stk Price (%)	15.60	15.35	5.76	7.36	(1.95)

Nuveen California Investment Quality Municipal Fund

NYSE : NQC

John Nuveen & Co. Inc.
Investment Bankers
333 West Wacker Dr.
Chicago, IL 60606
(800) 252-4630 / (312) 917-7700
Tax-Free Income

Transfer Agent
U.S. Trust
Nuveen Exchange-Traded Fund Investor Services
770 Broadway
New York, NY 10003
(800) 257-8787

12 Months Ending 12/31/92 Results

	Period End	Period Begin	Distributions	Yield Dist (%)	Total Return (%)
Share Price ($)	16.00	15.25	1.04	6.82	11.74
NAV per share ($)	15.46	14.86		7.00	11.04

Background: Initial public offering November 20, 1990 of 11,500,000 shares at $15 per share. Initial NAV was $14.05 per share.

Objective: Seeks high current income exempt from Federal and California State income taxes and enhancement of portfolio value. At least 80% of the fund's assets will be invested in California municipal obligations rated in the top four categories by S&P or Moody's. May not invest more than 20% in unrated California municipal obligations.

Portfolio: (10/31/92) Municipal Bonds 100%. Portfolio Ratings: AAA 43.0%, AA 32%, A 17%, BBB 8%.

Capitalization: (10/31/92) Common stock outstanding 12,773,908. Fund is leveraged with 1,800 shares preferred stock, stated value $50,000 per share.

Average Maturity (years): 23.6
Fund Manager: Nuveen Advisory Corporation **Fee:** 0.60%
Income Dist: Monthly **Capital Gains Dist:** Annually
Reinvestment Plan: Yes **Shareholder Reports:** Semi-Annually

5 Year Performance

Fiscal Year Ending 10/31*	1992 (10 mos.)	1991 (11 mos.)	1990	1989	1988
Net Assets ($mil):	287.619	276.60	—	—	—
Net Income Dist ($):	0.85	0.76	—	—	—
Cap Gains Dist ($):	0.00	0.00	—	—	—
Total Dist ($)	0.85	0.76	—	—	—
Yield from Dist (%)	5.44	—	—	—	—
Expense Ratio (%)	0.76	0.78	—	—	—
Portfolio Turnover (%)	0.00	19.00	—	—	—
NAV per share ($)	15.47	14.70	—	—	—
Market Price per share	16.00	15.63	—	—	—
Premium (Discount) (%)	3.43	6.33	—	—	—
Total Return, Stk Price (%)	7.81	—	—	—	—

*Prior to 1992, the fund's fiscal year end was 8/31.

Nuveen California Municipal Income Fund

John Nuveen & Co. Inc.
Investment Bankers
333 West Wacker Dr.
Chicago, IL 60606
(800) 252-4630 / (312) 917-7700
Tax-Free Income

Transfer Agent
U.S. Trust
Nuveen Exchange-Traded Fund Investor Services
770 Broadway
New York, NY 10003
(800) 257-8787

12 Months Ending 12/31/92 Results

	Period End	Period Begin	Distributions	Yield Dist (%)	Total Return (%)
Share Price ($)	12.63	13.00	0.80	6.15	3.31
NAV per share ($)	12.16	11.98		6.68	8.18

Background: Initial public offering April 27, 1988, of 5,000,000 common shares at $12 per share. Initial NAV was $11.21 per share.

Objective: Seeks high current income exempt from regular Federal and California State income taxes. Invests 100% of net assets in tax-exempt California municipal bonds, at least 75% of which are rated BBB or higher at time of purchase.

Portfolio: (8/31/92) Municipal Bonds 98.9%, Other 1.1%. Portfolio Ratings: AAA 13.0%, AA 40.0%, A 31.8%, BBB 9.0%, Non-Rated 16.0%.

Capitalization: (8/31/92) Common stock outstanding 5,118,000. No long-term debt.

Average Maturity (years): 21.6
Fund Manager: Nuveen Advisory Corporation
Income Dist: Monthly
Reinvestment Plan: Yes

Fee: 0.65%
Capital Gains Dist: Annually
Shareholder Reports: Semi-Annually

5 Year Performance

Fiscal Year Ending 8/31*	1992 (9 mos.)	1991 (12 mos.)	1990 (12 mos.)	1989 (12 mos.)	1988 (6 mos.)
Net Assets ($mil):	61.927	61.413	59.10	59.40	58.30
Net Income Dist ($):	0.60	0.79	0.80	0.81	0.28
Cap Gains Dist ($):	0.10	0.00	0.08	0.01	0.00
Total Dist ($)	0.69	0.79	0.88	0.82	0.28
Yield from Dist (%)	5.52	6.72	7.18	7.05	—
Expense Ratio (%)	0.82	0.73	0.76	0.72	0.74
Portfolio Turnover (%)	14.00	9.00	7.00	23.00	21.00
NAV per share ($)	12.10	12.00	11.71	11.81	11.64
Market Price per share	13.13	12.50	11.75	12.25	11.63
Premium (Discount) (%)	8.51	4.17	0.34	3.73	(0.17)
Total Return, Stk Price (%)	10.56	13.11	3.10	12.38	—

Prior to 1991, the fund's fiscal year end was 10/31. In 1992 the fiscal year changed to 8/31.

156   Closed-End Funds

Nuveen California Municipal Market Opportunity Fund

NYSE : NCO

John Nuveen & Co. Inc.
Investment Bankers
333 West Wacker Dr.
Chicago, IL 60606
(800) 252-4630 / (312) 917-7700
Tax-Free Income

Transfer Agent
U.S. Trust
Nuveen Exchange-Traded Fund Investor Services
770 Broadway
New York, NY 10003
(800) 257-8787

12 Months Ending 12/31/92 Results

	Period End	Period Begin	Distributions	Yield Dist (%)	Total Return (%)
Share Price ($)	15.75	15.25	1.06	6.95	10.23
NAV per share ($)	15.65	15.12		7.01	10.52

Background: Initial public offering May 18, 1990 of 7,600,000 shares at $15 per share. Initial NAV was $14.05 per share.

Objective: Seeks high current tax-free income and enhancement of portfolio value relative to the California municipal bond market through investment in undervalued California bonds and municipal securities. The fund will invest substantially all of its assets in municipal obligations rated within the top four categories by S&P or Moody's. Up to 20% may be invested in unrated municipal obligations the adviser deems to be investment-grade quality.

Portfolio: (8/31/92) Municipal Bonds 97.8%, Short Term & Other 2.2%. PortfolioRatings: AAA 38.0%, AA 25.0%, A 29.0%, BBB 8.0%.

Capitalization: (8/31/92) Common stock outstanding 7,722,000. Leveraged with 1,000 shares auction-rate preferred stock, stated value $50,000 per share. No long-term debt.

Average Maturity (years): 23.8
Fund Manager: Nuveen Advisory Corporation
Income Dist: Monthly
Reinvestment Plan: Yes

Fee: 0.60%
Capital Gains Dist: Annually
Shareholder Reports: Semi-Annually

5 Year Performance

Fiscal Year Ending 8/31 *	1992 (10 mos.)	1991	1990 (5 mos.)	1989	1988
Net Assets ($mil):	175.30	169.60	159.80	—	—
Net Income Dist ($):	0.87	1.02	0.26	—	—
Cap Gains Dist ($):	0.00	0.00	0.00	—	—
Total Dist ($)	0.87	1.02	0.26	—	—
Yield from Dist (%)	5.61	7.03	—	—	—
Expense Ratio (%)	0.79	0.80	0.83	—	—
Portfolio Turnover (%)	3.00	0.00	38.00	—	—
NAV per share ($)	15.58	14.95	13.76	—	—
Market Price per share	16.13	15.50	14.50	—	—
Premium (Discount) (%)	3.53	3.68	5.38	—	—
Total Return, Stk Price (%)	9.68	13.93	—	—	—

* Prior to 1992, the fund's fiscal year end was 10/31.

Nuveen California Municipal Value Fund

NYSE : NCA

John Nuveen & Co. Inc.
Investment Bankers
333 West Wacker Dr.
Chicago, IL 60606
(800) 252-4630 / (312) 917-7700
Tax-Free Income

Transfer Agent
U.S. Trust
Nuveen Exchange-Traded Fund Investor Services
770 Broadway
New York, NY 10003
(800) 257-8787

12 Months Ending 12/31/92 Results

	Period End	Period Begin	Distributions	Yield Dist (%)	Total Return (%)
Share Price ($)	11.00	11.00	0.67	6.09	6.09
NAV per share ($)	10.52	10.39		6.45	7.70

Background: Initial public offering October 7, 1987 of 18,000,000 shares at $10.00 per share. Initial NAV was $9.35 per share.

Objective: Seeks capital appreciation and current income exempt from regular Federal and California State income tax. Invests in a diversified portfolio of California municipal bonds of which not less than 80% are rated BBB or higher. May invest 20% in lower-grade or non-rated municipal obligations, but no more than 10% will be invested in such lower-rated California municipal obligations.

Portfolio: (8/31/92) Municipal Bonds 98.9%, Other 1.1%. Portfolio Ratings: AAA 35.0%, AA 23.0%, A 18.0%, BBB 6.0%, Non-Rated 18.0%.

Capitalization: (8/31/92) Common stock outstanding 18,544,000. No long-term debt.

Average Maturity (years): 21.7
Fund Manager: Nuveen Advisory Corporation   **Fee:** 0.35%
Income Dist: Monthly   **Capital Gains Dist:** Annually
Reinvestment Plan: Yes   **Shareholder Reports:** Semi-Annually

5 Year Performance

Fiscal Year Ending 7/31	1992	1991	1990	1989	1988 (10 mos.)
Net Assets ($mil):	194.40	195.63	184.90	185.10	174.60
Net Income Dist ($):	0.66	0.66	0.67	0.67	0.42
Cap Gains Dist ($):	0.02	0.00	0.03	0.08	0.00
Total Dist ($)	0.69	0.66	0.70	0.75	0.42
Yield from Dist (%)	6.57	6.36	5.71	6.98	—
Expense Ratio (%)	0.83	0.88	0.91	0.94	—
Portfolio Turnover (%)	0.06	5.00	2.00	27.00	35.00
NAV per share ($)	10.61	10.25	10.12	10.19	9.67
Market Price per share	11.25	10.50	10.38	12.25	10.75
Premium (Discount) (%)	6.03	2.44	2.47	20.22	11.17
Total Return, Stk Price (%)	13.71	7.51	(9.55)	20.93	—

Nuveen California Performance Plus Municipal Income Fund

NYSE : NCP

John Nuveen & Co. Inc.
Investment Bankers
333 West Wacker Dr.
Chicago, IL 60606
(800) 252-4630 / (312) 917-7700
Tax-Free Income

Transfer Agent
U.S. Trust
Nuveen Exchange-Traded Fund Investor Services
770 Broadway
New York, NY 10003
(800) 257-8787

12 Months Ending 12/31/92 Results

	Period End	Period Begin	Distributions	Yield Dist (%)	Total Return (%)
Share Price ($)	15.75	15.38	1.07	6.96	9.36
NAV per share ($)	15.67	15.04		7.11	11.30

Background: Initial public offering November 17, 1989 of 10,500,000 shares at $15.00 per share. Initial NAV was $14.05 per share.

Objective: Seeks current income exempt from regular Federal and California State income taxes. The fund may be leveraged to one-third of capital. Of the fund's net assets, 80% are invested in municipal obligations rated in the top four categories by S&P or Moody's. No more than 20% may be invested in municipal obligations rated BBB or lower.

Portfolio: (8/31/92) Municipal Bonds 97.9%, Short Term & Other 2.1%. Portfolio Ratings: AAA 39.0%, AA 27.1%, A 27.0%, BBB 5.0%, Non-Rated 2.0%.

Capitalization: (8/31/92) Common stock outstanding 12,182,000. Leveraged with 2,000 shares preferred stock, stated value $50,000 per share. No long-term debt.

Average Maturity (years): 22.9
Fund Manager: Nuveen Advisory Corporation
Income Dist: Monthly
Reinvestment Plan: Yes

Fee: 0.60%
Capital Gains Dist: Annually
Shareholder Reports: Semi-Annually

5 Year Performance

Fiscal Year Ending 8/31*	1992	1991	1990 (11 mos.)	1989	1988
Net Assets ($mil):	279.80	269.90	255.90	—	—
Net Income Dist ($):	0.87	1.02	0.77	—	—
Cap Gains Dist ($):	0.00	0.00	0.00	—	—
Total Dist ($)	0.87	1.02	0.77	—	—
Yield from Dist (%)	5.48	7.09	—	—	—
Expense Ratio (%)	0.79	0.78	0.79	—	—
Portfolio Turnover (%)	7.00	6.28	30.00	—	—
NAV per share ($)	15.58	14.88	13.82	—	—
Market Price per share	15.88	15.88	14.38	—	—
Premium (Discount) (%)	1.93	6.72	4.05	—	—
Total Return, Stk Price (%)	5.48	17.52	—	—	—

*Prior to 1992, the fund's fiscal year end was 10/31.

Nuveen California Quality Income Municipal Fund

NYSE : NUC

John Nuveen & Co. Inc.
Investmetn Bankers
333 West Wacker Dr.
Chicago, IL 60606
(800) 252-4630 / (312) 917-7700
Tax-Free Income

Transfer Agent
U.S. Trust
Nuveen Exchange-Traded Fund Investor Services
770 Broadway
New York, NY 10003
(800) 257-8787

12 Months Ending 12/31/92 Results

	Period End	Period Begin	Distributions	Yield Dist (%)	Total Return (%)
Share Price ($)	14.38	14.38	0.87	6.05	6.05
NAV per share ($)	14.59	14.19		6.13	8.95

Background: Initial public offering November 20, 1991 of 20,000,000 shares at $15 per share. Initial NAV was $14.05 per share.

Objective: Seeks current income exempt from regular Federal and California State income taxes.

Portfolio: (8/31/92) Municipal Bonds 99.4%, Short Term & Other 0.6%. Portfolio Ratings: AAA 32.0%, AA 26.0%, A 36.0%, BBB 6.0%.

Capitalization: (8/31/92) Common stock outstanding 21,243,000. Leveraged with 3,000 shares preferred stock, stated value $50,000 per share.

Average Maturity (years): 22.6
Fund Manager: Nuveen Advisory Corporation
Income Dist: Monthly
Reinvestment Plan: Yes

Fee: 0.65%
Capital Gains Dist: Annually
Shareholder Reports: Semi-Annually

5 Year Performance

Fiscal Year Ending 8/31	1992 (9 mos.)	1991	1990	1989	1988
Net Assets ($mil):	457.95	—	—	—	—
Net Income Dist ($):	0.53	—	—	—	—
Cap Gains Dist ($):	0.00	—	—	—	—
Total Dist ($)	0.53	—	—	—	—
Yield from Dist (%)	—	—	—	—	—
Expense Ratio (%)	0.76	—	—	—	—
Portfolio Turnover (%)	20.00	—	—	—	—
NAV per share ($)	14.50	—	—	—	—
Market Price per share	14.50	—	—	—	—
Premium (Discount) (%)	0.00	—	—	—	—
Total Return, Stk Price (%)	—	—	—	—	—

Nuveen California Select Quality Municipal Fund

NYSE : NVC

John Nuveen & Co. Inc.	*Transfer Agent*
Investment Bankers	U.S. Trust
333 West Wacker Dr.	Nuveen Exchange-Traded Fund Investors Services
Chicago, IL 60606	770 Broadway
(800) 252-4630 / (312) 917-7700	New York, NY 10003
Tax-Free Income	(800) 257-8787

12 Months Ending 12/31/92 Results

	Period End	Period Begin	Distributions	Yield Dist (%)	Total Return (%)
Share Price ($)	15.00	14.50	1.03	7.10	10.55
NAV per share ($)	15.10	14.59		7.06	10.56

Background: Initial public offering May 22, 1991 of 20,000,000 shares at $15 per share. Initial NAV was $14.05 per share.

Objective: Seeks current income exempt from Federal and California State income taxes.

Portfolio: (10/31/92) Municipal Bonds 98.4%, Other 1.6%. Portfolio Ratings: AAA 31.0%, AA 25.0%, A 39.0%, BBB 3.0%, Non-Rated 2.0%.

Capitalization: (10/31/92) Common stock outstanding 22,129,000. Leveraged with 3,000 shares preferred stock, stated value $50,000 per share.

Average Maturity (years): 24.7

Fund Manager: Nuveen Advisory Corporation	**Fee:** 0.65%
Income Dist: Monthly	**Capital Gains Dist:** Annually
Reinvestment Plan: Yes	**Shareholder Reports:** Semi-Annually

5 Year Performance

Fiscal Year Ending 8/31*	1992 (10 mos.)	1991 (5 mos.)	1990	1989	1988
Net Assets ($mil):	480.50	467.40	—	—	—
Net Income Dist ($):	0.82	0.24	—	—	—
Cap Gains Dist ($):	0.00	0.00	—	—	—
Total Dist ($)	0.82	0.24	—	—	—
Yield from Dist (%)	5.47	—	—	—	—
Expense Ratio (%)	0.79	0.75	—	—	—
Portfolio Turnover (%)	16.00	6.00	—	—	—
NAV per share ($)	14.93	14.41	—	—	—
Market Price per share	14.63	15.00	—	—	—
Premium (Discount) (%)	(2.08)	4.09	—	—	—
Total Return, Stk Price (%)	3.00	—	—	—	—

* Prior to 1992, the fund's fiscal year was 10/31.

Nuveen Florida Investment Quality Municipal Fund

John Nuveen & Co. Inc.
Investment Bankers
333 West Wacker Dr.
Chicago, IL 60606
(800) 252-4630 / (312) 917-7700
Tax-Free Income

NYSE : NQF
Transfer Agent
U.S. Trust
Nuveen Exchange-Traded Fund Investor Services
770 Broadway
New York, NY 10003
(800) 257-8787

12 Months Ending 12/31/92 Results

	Period End	Period Begin	Distributions	Yield Dist (%)	Total Return (%)
Share Price ($)	16.00	15.50	1.02	6.58	9.81
NAV per share ($)	15.25	14.74		6.92	10.38

Background: Initial public offering February 21, 1991 of 15,680,000 shares at $15 per share. Initial net asset value $14.05 per share.

Objective: Seeks current income exempt from Federal income tax. The fund will invest primarily in investment-grade quality municipal bonds.

Portfolio: (6/30/93) Municipal Bonds 97.0%, Short Term & Other 3.0%. Portfolio Ratings: AAA 60.0%, AA 29.0%, A 4.0%, BBB 7.0%.

Capitalization: (6/30/92) Common stock outstanding 15,789,732. Leveraged with 2,000 preferred shares, stated value $50,000 per share.

Average Maturity (years): 22.9
Fund Manager: Nuveen Advisory Corporation
Income Dist: Monthly
Reinvestment Plan: Yes

Fee: 0.60%
Capital Gains Dist: Annually
Shareholder Reports: Semi-Annually

5 Year Performance

Fiscal Year Ending 6/30*	1992 (8 mos.)	1991 (8 mos.)	1990	1989	1988
Net Assets ($mil):	346.60	337.80	—	—	—
Net Income Dist ($):	0.66	0.50	—	—	—
Cap Gains Dist ($):	0.00	0.00	—	—	—
Total Dist ($)	0.66	0.50	—	—	—
Yield from Dist (%)	4.29	—	—	—	—
Expense Ratio (%)	0.77	0.76	—	—	—
Portfolio Turnover (%)	4.00	0.00	—	—	—
NAV per share ($)	14.99	14.49	—	—	—
Market Price per share	16.00	15.38	—	—	—
Premium (Discount) (%)	6.74	6.14	—	—	—
Total Return, Stk Price (%)	8.32	—	—	—	—

Prior to 1992, the fund's fiscal year end was 10/31.

Nuveen Florida Quality Income Municipal Fund

NYSE : NUF

John Nuveen & Co. Incorpoorated
Investment Bankers
333 West Wacker Dr.
Chicago, IL 60606
(800) 252-4630 / (312) 917-7700
Tax-Free Income

Transfer Agent
U.S. Trust
Nuveen Exchange-Traded Fund Investor Services
770 Broadway
New York, NY 10003
(800) 257-8787

12 Months Ending 12/31/92 Results

	Period End	Period Begin	Distributions	Yield Dist (%)	Total Return (%)
Share Price ($)	15.00	14.50	0.95	6.55	10.00
NAV per share ($)	14.91	14.31		6.64	10.83

Background: Initial public offering October 17, 1991 of 11,744,972 shares at $15 per share. Initial NAV $14.05 per share.

Objective: Seeks high current income exempt from Federal income tax and enhancement of portfolio value. The fund will invest substantially all of its assets in investment-grade Florida municipal obligations or in unrated securities that the fund adviser believes to be of investment-grade quality.

Portfolio: (6/30/92) Municipal Bonds 101.7%, Short Term & Other (1.7%). Portfolio Ratings: AAA 57.0%, AA 27.0%, A 8.0%, BBB 8.0%.

Capitalization: (6/30/92) Common stock outstanding 11,787,079. Leveraged with 2,000 shares preferred stock, stated value $50,000 per share.

Average Maturity (years): 24.4
Fund Manager: Nuveen Advisory Corporation
Income Dist: Monthly
Reinvestment Plan: Yes

Fee: 0.65%
Capital Gains Dist: Annually
Shareholder Reports: Semi-Annually

5 Year Performance

Fiscal Year Ending 6/30	1992 (8 mos.)	1991	1990	1989	1988
Net Assets ($mil):	256.70	—	—	—	—
Net Income Dist ($):	0.46	—	—	—	—
Cap Gains Dist ($):	0.00	—	—	—	—
Total Dist ($)	0.46	—	—	—	—
Yield from Dist (%)	—	—	—	—	—
Expense Ratio (%)	0.81	—	—	—	—
Portfolio Turnover (%)	0.00	—	—	—	—
NAV per share ($)	14.57	—	—	—	—
Market Price per share	14.63	—	—	—	—
Premium (Discount) (%)	0.41	—	—	—	—
Total Return, Stk Price (%)	—	—	—	—	—

Nuveen Michigan Quality Income Municipal Fund

NYSE : NUM

John Nuveen & Co. Inc.
Investment Bankers
333 West Wacker Dr.
Chicago, IL 60606
(800) 252-4630 / (312) 917-7700
Tax-Free Income

Transfer Agent
U.S. Trust
Nuveen Exchange-Traded Fund Investor Services
770 Broadway
New York, NY 10003
(800) 257-8787

12 Months Ending 12/31/92 Results

	Period End	Period Begin	Distributions	Yield Dist (%)	Total Return (%)
Share Price ($)	15.50	15.13	0.93	6.15	8.59
NAV per share ($)	14.86	14.25		6.53	10.81

Background: Initial public offering October 17, 1991 of 10,763,316 shares at $15 per share. Initial NAV was $14.05 per share.

Objective: Seeks current income exempt from regular Federal and Michigan State income taxes. Capital appreciation is secondary. The fund will invest substantially all of its assets in investment-grade municipal bonds or unrated securities that the adviser believes to be of investment-grade quality.

Portfolio: (7/31/92) Sector Weightings: General Obligations 31%, Health Care 18%, Housing 14%, Water/Sewer 10%. Portfolio Ratings: AAA 43%, AA 44%, A 12%, BBB 1%.

Capitalization: (7/31/92) Common stock outstanding 10,830,751. Fund is leveraged with 1,600 shares preferred stock with a $50,000 per share liquidation preference.

Average Maturity (years): 24.7
Fund Manager: Nuveen Advisory Corporation
Income Dist: Monthly
Reinvestment Plan: Yes

Fee: 0.65%
Capital Gains Dist: Annually
Shareholder Reports: Semi-Annually

5 Year Performance

Fiscal Year Ending 7/31*	1992 (2 mos.)	1991 (7 mos.)	1990	1989	1988
Net Assets ($mil):	244.90	234.40	—	—	—
Net Income Dist ($):	0.15	0.38	—	—	—
Cap Gains Dist ($):	0.00	0.00	—	—	—
Total Dist ($)	0.15	0.38	—	—	—
Yield from Dist (%)	0.99	—	—	—	—
Expense Ratio (%)	0.85	0.82	—	—	—
Portfolio Turnover (%)	0.00	1.00	—	—	—
NAV per share ($)	15.23	14.29	—	—	—
Market Price per share	15.63	15.13	—	—	—
Premium (Discount) (%)	2.63	5.88	—	—	—
Total Return, Stk Price (%)	—	—	—	—	—

* The fund's first fiscal year ended 5/31/92. In 1992, the fiscal year changed to 7/31.

Nuveen New Jersey Investment Quality Municipal Fund

John Nuveen & Co. Inc.
Investment Bankers
333 West Wacker Dr.
Chicago, IL 60606
(800) 252-4630 / (312) 917-7700
Tax-Free Income

NYSE : NQJ
Transfer Agent
U.S. Trust
Nuveen Exchange-Traded Fund Investor Services
770 Broadway
New York, NY 10003
(800) 257-8787

12 Months Ending 12/31/92 Results

	Period End	Period Begin	Distributions	Yield Dist (%)	Total Return (%)
Share Price ($)	15.88	15.38	0.96	6.24	9.49
NAV per share ($)	15.01	14.55		6.60	9.76

Background: Initial public offering February 21, 1991 of 11,685,000 shares at $15 per share. Initial NAV was $14.05 per share.

Objective: Seeks current income exempt from Federal and New Jersey State income taxes. Capital appreciation is secondary. The fund will invest substantially all of its assets in investment-grade New Jersey municipal bonds or in unrated securities that the fund adviser believes to be of investment-grade quality.

Portfolio: (6/30/92) Municipal Bonds 97.9%, Short Term & Other 2.1%. Portfolio Ratings: AAA 58.0%, AA 21.0%, A 16.0%, BBB 2.0%.

Capitalization: (6/30/92) Common stock outstanding 11,846,786. Leveraged with 2,000 shares preferred stock, stated value $50,000 per share.

Average Maturity (years): 21.6
Fund Manager: Nuveen Advisory Corporation
Income Dist: Monthly
Reinvestment Plan: Yes

Fee: 0.60%
Capital Gains Dist: Annually
Shareholder Reports: Semi-Annually

5 Year Performance

Fiscal Year Ending 6/30 *	1992 (8 mos.)	1991 (8 mos.)	1990	1989	1988
Net Assets ($mil):	255.60	248.20	—	—	—
Net Income Dist ($):	0.62	0.49	—	—	—
Cap Gains Dist ($):	0.00	0.00	—	—	—
Total Dist ($)	0.62	0.49	—	—	—
Yield from Dist (%)	4.00	—	—	—	—
Expense Ratio (%)	0.76	0.76	—	—	—
Portfolio Turnover (%)	9.00	2.00	—	—	—
NAV per share ($)	14.82	14.32	—	—	—
Market Price per share	15.38	15.50	—	—	—
Premium (Discount) (%)	3.78	8.24	—	—	—
Total Return, Stk Price (%)	3.23	—	—	—	—

* The fund's first fiscal year ended 10/31/91.

Nuveen New Jersey Quality Income Municipal Fund

John Nuveen & Co. Inc.
Investment Bankers
333 West Wacker Dr.
Chicago, IL 60606
(800) 252-4630 / (312) 917-7700
Tax-Free Income

NYSE : NUJ

Transfer Agent
U.S. Trust
Nuveen Exchange-Traded Fund Investor Services
770 Broadway
New York, NY 10003
(800) 257-8787

12 Months Ending 12/31/92 Results

	Period End	Period Begin	Distributions	Yield Dist (%)	Total Return (%)
Share Price ($)	15.13	14.50	0.93	6.41	10.76
NAV per share ($)	14.71	14.25		6.53	9.75

Background: Initial public offering October 17, 1991 of 7,000,000 shares at $15 per share. Initial NAV was $14.05 per share.

Objective: Seeks current income exempt from Federal and New Jersey State income taxes. Capital appreciation is secondary. The fund will invest substantially all of its assets in New Jersey investment-grade municipal obligations.

Portfolio: (6/30/92) Municipal Bonds 97.8%, Short Term & Other 2.2%. Portfolio Ratings: AAA 35.0%, AA 26.0%, A 25.0%, BBB 11.0%, Non-Rated 3.0%.

Capitalization: (6/30/92) Common stock outstanding 7,035,776. Leveraged with 1,000 shares preferred stock, stated value $50,000 per share.

Average Maturity (years): 21.5
Fund Manager: Nuveen Advisory Corporation
Income Dist: Monthly
Reinvestment Plan: Yes

Fee: 0.65%
Capital Gains Dist: Annually
Shareholder Reports: Semi-Annually

5 Year Performance

Fiscal Year Ending 6/30	1992 (8 mos.)	1991	1990	1989	1988
Net Assets ($mil):	152.50	—	—	—	—
Net Income Dist ($):	0.44	—	—	—	—
Cap Gains Dist ($):	0.00	—	—	—	—
Total Dist ($)	0.44	—	—	—	—
Yield from Dist (%)	—	—	—	—	—
Expense Ratio (%)	0.87	—	—	—	—
Portfolio Turnover (%)	14.00	—	—	—	—
NAV per share ($)	14.56	—	—	—	—
Market Price per share	14.50	—	—	—	—
Premium (Discount) (%)	(0.41)	—	—	—	—
Total Return, Stk Price (%)	—	—	—	—	—

Nuveen New York Investment Quality Municipal Fund

NYSE : NQN

John Nuveen & Co. Inc.	*Transfer Agent*
Investment Bankers	U.S. Trust
333 West Wacker Dr.	Nuveen Exchange-Traded Fund Investor Services
Chicago, IL 60606	770 Broadway
(800) 252-4630 / (312) 917-7700	New York, NY 10003
Tax-Free Income	(800) 257-8787

12 Months Ending 12/31/92 Results

	Period End	Period Begin	Distributions	Yield Dist (%)	Total Return (%)
Share Price ($)	16.50	16.00	1.07	6.69	9.81
NAV per share ($)	15.98	15.19		7.04	12.24

Background: Initial public offering November 20, 1990 of 15,000,000 shares at $15 per share. Initial NAV was $14.05 per share.

Objective: Seeks high current income exempt from Federal, New York State and City income taxes. Enhancement of portfolio value relative to the New York municipal bond market is secondary. The fund will invest substantially all of its assets in New York municipal bonds whose timely payment of principal and interest is guaranteed by AAA-rated insurers or backed by escrow accounts containing U.S. Government or U.S. Government Agency securities.

Portfolio: (9/30/92) Portfolio Ratings: AAA 87.0%, AA 11.0%, A 1%, BBB 1%.

Capitalization: (9/30/92) Common stock outstanding 16,751,000. Leveraged with 2,000 shares auction-rate preferred stock, stated value $50,000 per share.

Average Maturity (years): 25.9
Fund Manager: Nuveen Advisory Corporation **Fee:** 0.60%
Income Dist: Monthly **Capital Gains Dist:** Annually
Reinvestment Plan: Yes **Shareholder Reports:** Semi-Annually

5 Year Performance

Fiscal Year Ending 9/30*	1992 (11 mos.)	1991 (11 mos.)	1990	1989	1988
Net Assets ($mil):	385.10	368.30	—	—	—
Net Income Dist ($):	0.97	0.77	—	—	—
Cap Gains Dist ($):	0.02	0.00	—	—	—
Total Dist ($)	0.99	0.77	—	—	—
Yield from Dist (%)	6.29	—	—	—	—
Expense Ratio (%)	0.79	0.80	—	—	—
Portfolio Turnover (%)	5.00	10.00	—	—	—
NAV per share ($)	15.83	14.98	—	—	—
Market Price per share	16.75	15.75	—	—	—
Premium (Discount) (%)	5.81	5.14	—	—	—
Total Return, Stk Price (%)	12.63	—	—	—	—

Prior to 1992, the fund's fiscal year end was 10/31.

Nuveen New York Municipal Income Fund

John Nuveen & Co. Inc.
Investment Bankers
333 West Wacker Dr.
Chicago, IL 60606
(800) 252-4630 / (312) 917-7700
Tax-Free Income

NYSE : NNM

Transfer Agent
U.S. Trust
Nuveen Exchange-Traded Fund Investor Services
770 Broadway
New York, NY 10003
(800) 257-8787

12 Months Ending 12/31/92 Results

	Period End	Period Begin	Distributions	Yield Dist (%)	Total Return (%)
Share Price ($)	12.63	11.98	0.83	6.93	12.35
NAV per share ($)	12.02	12.25		6.78	4.90

Background: Initial public offering April, 1988 of 2,300,000 shares at $12.00 per share. Initial NAV was $11.21 per share.

Objective: Seeks a high level of current income exempt from Federal, New York State and City income taxes. Invests 100% of net assets in a diversified portfolio of tax-exempt New York municipal obligations. Invests 75% of assets rated BBB or higher by S&P or Moody's.

Portfolio: (9/30/92) Municipal Bonds 96.8%, Other 3.2%. Portfolio Ratings: AAA 13.0%, AA 21.0%, A 12.0%, BBB 37.0%, BB 3.0%, Non-Rated 14.0%.

Capitalization: (9/30/92) Common stock outstanding 2,464,000. No long-term debt.

Average Maturity (years): 23.5
Fund Manager: Nuveen Advisory Corporation   **Fee:** 0.50%
Income Dist: Monthly   **Capital Gains Dist:** Annually
Reinvestment Plan: Yes   **Shareholder Reports:** Semi-Annually

5 Year Performance

Fiscal Year Ending 9/30*	1992 (10 mos.)	1991	1990	1989	1988 (8 mos.)
Net Assets ($mil):	30.10	29.70	27.60	28.20	27.70
Net Income Dist ($):	0.66	0.80	0.81	0.81	0.28
Cap Gains Dist ($):	0.07	0.00	0.07	0.03	0.00
Total Dist ($)	0.73	0.80	0.88	0.83	0.28
Yield from Dist (%)	5.90	6.67	7.49	7.14	—
Expense Ratio (%)	0.93	0.92	0.86	0.90	0.94
Portfolio Turnover (%)	3.00	14.00	11.00	36.00	39.00
NAV per share ($)	12.20	11.94	11.37	11.71	11.53
Market Price per share	12.50	12.38	12.00	11.75	11.63
Premium (Discount) (%)	2.46	3.69	5.54	0.34	0.78
Total Return, Stk Price (%)	6.87	9.83	9.62	8.17	—

* Prior to 1991, the fund's fiscal year end was 10/31. The 1991 fiscal year ended 11/30. In 1992, the fiscal year end was changed to 9/30.

Nuveen New York Municipal Market Opportunity Fund

John Nuveen & Co. Inc.
Investment Bankers
333 West Wacker Dr.
Chicago, IL 60606
(800) 252-4630 / (312) 917-7700
Tax-Free Income

NYSE : NNO
Transfer Agent
U.S. Trust
Nuveen Exchange-Traded Fund Investor Services
770 Broadway
New York, NY 10003
(800) 257-8787

12 Months Ending 12/31/92 Results

	Period End	Period Begin	Distributions	Yield Dist (%)	Total Return (%)
Share Price ($)	16.63	15.63	1.18	7.55	13.95
NAV per share ($)	16.07	15.37		7.68	12.23

Background: Initial public offering May 17, 1990 of 5,000,000 shares at $15 per share. Initial NAV was $14.05.

Objective: Seeks high current income exempt from Federal and New York State and City income taxes.

Portfolio: (9/30/92) Municipal Bonds 98.4%, Short Term & Other 1.6%. Portfolio Ratings: AAA 24.0, AA 26.0%, A 16.0%, BBB 34.0%.

Capitalization: (9/30/92) Common stock outstanding 5,711,000. Leveraged with 1,000 shares auction-rate preferred stock, stated value $50,000 per share.

Average Maturity (years): 25.5
Fund Manager: Nuveen Advisory Corporation
Income Dist: Monthly
Reinvestment Plan: Yes

Fee: 0.50%
Capital Gains Dist: Annually
Shareholder Reports: Semi-Annually

5 Year Performance

Fiscal Year Ending 9/30*	1992 (11 mos.)	1991	1990 (5 mos.)	1989	1988
Net Assets ($mil):	131.769	126.00	115.70	—	—
Net Income Dist ($):	1.01	1.06	0.26	—	—
Cap Gains Dist ($):	0.01	0.00	0.00	—	—
Total Dist ($)	1.03	1.06	0.26	—	—
Yield from Dist (%)	6.59	7.37	—	—	—
Expense Ratio (%)	0.84	0.84	0.87	—	—
Portfolio Turnover (%)	3.00	29.00	12.00	—	—
NAV per share ($)	16.07	15.23	13.54	—	—
Market Price per share	16.50	15.63	14.38	—	—
Premium (Discount) (%)	2.68	2.56	6.13	—	—
Total Return, Stk Price (%)	12.16	16.06	—	—	—

* Prior to 1992, the fund's fiscal year end was 10/31.

Nuveen New York Municipal Value Fund

John Nuveen & Co. Inc.
Investment Bankers
333 West Wacker Dr.
Chicago, IL 60606
(800) 252-4630 / (312) 917-7700
Tax-Free Income

NYSE : NNY
Transfer Agent
U.S. Trust Nuveen Exchange-Traded Fund
Investor Services
770 Broadway
New York, NY 10003
(800) 257-8787

12 Months Ending 12/31/92 Results

	Period End	Period Begin	Distributions	Yield Dist (%)	Total Return (%)
Share Price ($)	11.38	10.88	0.81	7.44	12.04
NAV per share ($)	10.61	10.48		7.73	8.97

Background: Initial public offering October 7, 1987 of 11,000,000 shares at $10 per share. Initial NAV was $9.35 per share.

Objective: Seeks current income exempt from Federal, New York State and City income taxes. Invests at least 80% of its assets in New York municipal obligations that are rated in the top four categories by S&P or Moody's. Remaining 20% may be invested in lower- or non-rated New York municipal obligations.

Portfolio: (9/30/92) Municipal Bonds 99.1%, Short Term & Other 0.9%. Portfolio Ratings: AAA 20.0%, AA 35.0%, A 16.0%, BBB 28.0%, Non-Rated 1.0%.

Capitalization: (7/31/92) Common stock outstanding 11,462,000. No long-term debt.

Average Maturity (years): 24.0
Fund Manager: Nuveen Advisory Corporation
Income Dist: Monthly
Reinvestment Plan: Yes

Fee: 0.35%
Capital Gains Dist: Annually
Shareholder Reports: Semi-Annually

5 Year Performance

Fiscal Year Ending 7/31	1992	1991	1990	1989	1988 (9 mos.)
Net Assets ($mil):	122.20	116.20	114.40	115.40	109.80
Net Income Dist ($):	0.68	0.68	0.68	0.68	0.46
Cap Gains Dist ($):	0.13	0.05	0.04	0.24	0.00
Total Dist ($)	0.80	0.72	0.72	0.91	0.46
Yield from Dist (%)	7.53	6.94	6.77	9.10	—
Expense Ratio (%)	0.90	0.96	0.98	1.03	0.99
Portfolio Turnover (%)	9.00	14.00	16.00	24.00	58.00
NAV per share ($)	10.27	10.20	10.37	9.95	9.35
Market Price per share	11.63	10.63	10.38	10.63	10.00
Premium (Discount) (%)	13.24	4.22	0.10	6.83	6.95
Total Return, Stk Price (%)	16.93	9.34	4.42	15.40	—

Nuveen New York Performance Plus Municipal Fund

John Nuveen & Co. Inc.	**NYSE : NNP**
Investment Bankers	*Transfer Agent*
333 West Wacker Dr.	U.S. Trust
Chicago, IL 60606	Nuveen Exchange-Traded Fund Investor Services
(800) 252-4630 / (312) 917-7700	770 Broadway
Tax-Free Income	New York, NY 10003
	(800) 257-8787

12 Months Ending 12/31/92 Results

	Period End	Period Begin	Distributions	Yield Dist (%)	Total Return (%)
Share Price ($)	16.50	15.75	1.12	7.11	11.87
NAV per share ($)	15.79	15.08		7.43	12.14

Background: Initial public offering November 17, 1989 of 6,800,000 shares at $15 per share. Initial NAV was $14.05 per share.

Objective: Seeks high current tax-free income from a leveraged portfolio of investment-grade long-term municipal bonds.

Portfolio: (9/30/92) Municipal Bonds 98.2%, Other 1.8%. Portfolio Ratings: AAA 18.0%, AA 30.0%, A 19.0%, BBB 33.0%.

Capitalization: (9/30/92) Common stock outstanding 6,994,873. Leveraged with 1,000 shares preferred stock, stated value $50,000 per share.

Average Maturity (years): 26.2
Fund Manager: Nuveen Advisory Corporation **Fee:** 0.60%
Income Dist: Monthly **Capital Gains Dist:** Annually
Reinvestment Plan: Yes **Shareholder Reports:** Semi-Annually

5 Year Performance

Fiscal Year Ending 9/30 *	1992 (11 mos.)	1991	1990 (11 mos.)	1989	1988
Net Assets ($mil):	160.10	153.30	142.20	—	—
Net Income Dist ($):	1.00	1.05	0.79	—	—
Cap Gains Dist ($):	0.00	0.00	0.00	—	—
Total Dist ($)	1.00	1.05	0.79	—	—
Yield from Dist (%)	6.56	7.37	—	—	—
Expense Ratio (%)	0.81	0.84	0.83	—	—
Portfolio Turnover (%)	1.00	46.00	72.00	—	—
NAV per share ($)	15.73	14.93	13.44	—	—
Market Price per share	16.75	15.25	14.25	—	—
Premium (Discount) (%)	6.48	2.14	6.03	—	—
Total Return, Stk Price (%)	16.39	14.39	—	—	—

*Prior to 1991, the fund's fiscal year ended 10/31. In 1992, the fund changed its fiscal year end to 9/30.

Nuveen New York Quality Income Municipal Fund

NYSE : NUN

John Nuveen & Co. Inc.	*Transfer Agent*
Investment Bankers	U.S. Trust
333 West Wacker Dr.	Nuveen Exchange-Traded Investor Services
Chicago, IL 60606	770 Broadway
(800) 252-4630 / (312) 917-7700	New York, NY 10003
Tax-Free Income	(800) 257-8787

12 Months Ending 12/31/92 Results

	Period End	Period Begin	Distributions	Yield Dist (%)	Total Return (%)
Share Price ($)	14.38	14.63	0.81	5.54	3.83
NAV per share ($)	14.81	14.19		5.71	10.08

Background: Initial public offering November 25, 1991 of 23,500,000 shares at $15 per share. Initial NAV was $14.05 per share.

Objective: Seeks high current income exempt from both regular Federal income taxes and New York State and City income taxes. All of the fund's assets are invested in a diversified portfolio of tax-exempt New York municipal obligations which are insured as to timely payment of principal and interest.

Portfolio: (9/30/92) Portfolio Ratings: AAA 97.0%, AA 3%.

Capitalization: (9/30/92) Common stock outstanding 23,359,000. Leveraged with 3,000 shares preferred stock, stated value $50,000 per share.

Average Maturity (years): 24.3

Fund Manager: Nuveen Advisory Corporation	**Fee:** 0.65%
Income Dist: Monthly	**Capital Gains Dist:** Annually
Reinvestment Plan: Yes	**Shareholder Reports:** Semi-Annually

5 Year Performance

Fiscal Year Ending 9/30	1992 (10 mos.)	1991	1990	1989	1988
Net Assets ($mil):	510.70	—	—	—	—
Net Income Dist ($):	0.59	—	—	—	—
Cap Gains Dist ($):	0.00	—	—	—	—
Total Dist ($)	0.59	—	—	—	—
Yield from Dist (%)	—	—	—	—	—
Expense Ratio (%)	0.79	—	—	—	—
Portfolio Turnover (%)	20.00	—	—	—	—
NAV per share ($)	14.58	—	—	—	—
Market Price per share	14.63	—	—	—	—
Premium (Discount) (%)	0.34	—	—	—	—
Total Return, Stk Price (%)	—	—	—	—	—

Nuveen New York Select Quality Municipal Fund

NYSE : NVN

John Nuveen & Co. Inc.
Investment Bankers
333 West Wacker Dr.
Chicago, IL 60606
(800) 252-4630 / (312) 917-7700
Tax-Free Income

Transfer Agent
U. S. Trust
Nuveen Exchange-Traded Fund Investor Services
770 Broadway
New York, NY 10003
(800) 257-8787

12 Months Ending 12/31/92 Results

	Period End	Period Begin	Distributions	Yield Dist (%)	Total Return (%)
Share Price ($)	15.13	14.88	1.00	6.72	8.40
NAV per share ($)	15.43	14.64		6.83	12.23

Background: Initial public offering May 22, 1991 of 20,000,000 shares at $15 per share. Initial NAV was $14.05 per share.

Objective: Seeks current income exempt from regular Federal, New York State and City income taxes, with a secondary objective of enhancement of portfolio value, relative to the New York Municipal bond market. Invests substantially all of its assets in high-grade New York municipal bonds.

Portfolio: (9/30/92) Municipal Bonds 98.7%, Short Term & Other 1.3%. Portfolio Ratings: AAA 89.0%, AA 10.0%, BBB 1%.

Capitalization: (9/30/92) Common stock outstanding 22,262,000. Leveraged with 3,000 shares of preferred stock, stated value $50,000 per share.

Average Maturity (years): 24.0
Fund Manager: Nuveen Advisory Corporation **Fee:** 0.65%
Income Dist: Quarterly **Capital Gains Dist:** Monthly
Reinvestment Plan: Yes **Shareholder Reports:** Semi-Annually

5 Year Performance

Fiscal Year Ending 9/30 *	1992	1991 (5 mos.)	1990	1989	1988
Net Assets ($mil):	489.90	467.20	—	—	—
Net Income Dist ($):	0.88	0.24	—	—	—
Cap Gains Dist ($):	0.00	0.00	—	—	—
Total Dist ($)	0.88	0.24	—	—	—
Yield from Dist (%)	5.77	—	—	—	—
Expense Ratio (%)	0.83	0.79	—	—	—
Portfolio Turnover (%)	16.00	5.00	—	—	—
NAV per share ($)	15.27	14.39	—	—	—
Market Price per share	15.25	15.25	—	—	—
Premium (Discount) (%)	(0.13)	5.98	—	—	—
Total Return, Stk Price (%)	5.77	—	—	—	—

* Prior to 1992, the fund's fiscal year ended 10/31. In 1992, the fund's fiscal year end was changed to 9/30.

Nuveen Ohio Quality Income Municipal Fund

John Nuveen & Co. Inc.
Investment Bankers
333 West Wacker Dr.
Chicago, IL 60606
(800) 252-4630 / (312) 917-7700
Tax-Free Income

NYSE : NUO

Transfer Agent
U.S. Trust
Nuveen Exchange-Traded Fund Investor Services
770 Broadway
New York, NY 10003
(800) 257-8787

12 Months Ending 12/31/92 Results

	Period End	Period Begin	Distributions	Yield Dist (%)	Total Return (%)
Share Price ($)	15.38	15.25	0.92	6.03	6.89
NAV per share ($)	14.64	14.14		6.51	10.04

Background: Initial public offering October 17, 1991 of 4,350,000 shares of common stock. Initial NAV was $14.05 per share.

Objective: Seeks current income exempt from Federal and Ohio State income taxes. Capital appreciation is secondary. The fund will invest at least 80% of its assets in municipal bonds rated in the top four categories by S&P or Moody's. Up to 20% may be invested in non-rated Ohio municipal obligations the adviser considers to be of investment-grade quality.

Portfolio: (7/31/92) Sector Weightings: General Obligations 29%, Health Care 21%, Water & Sewer 19%, Housing 10%. Portfolio Ratings: AAA 45, AA 24%, A 24%, BBB 7%.

Capitalization: (7/31/92) Common stock outstanding 4,374,721. Leveraged with 700 shares cumulative preferred stock with $50,000 per share liquidation preference.

Average Maturity (years): 22.4
Fund Manager: Nuveen Advisory Corporation
Income Dist: Monthly
Reinvestment Plan: Yes

Fee: 0.65%
Capital Gains Dist: Annually
Shareholder Reports: Semi-Annually

5 Year Performance

Fiscal Year Ending 7/31*	1992 (2 mos.)	1991 (thru 5/31/92)	1990	1989	1988
Net Assets ($mil):	100.70	—	—	—	—
Net Income Dist ($):	0.15	0.37	—	—	—
Cap Gains Dist ($):	0.00	0.00	—	—	—
Total Dist ($)	0.15	0.37	—	—	—
Yield from Dist (%)	1.00	—	—	—	—
Expense Ratio (%)	1.00	0.89	—	—	—
Portfolio Turnover (%)	30.00	6.00	—	—	—
NAV per share ($)	15.02	14.07	—	—	—
Market Price per share	15.25	15.00	—	—	—
Premium (Discount) (%)	1.53	6.61	—	—	—
Total Return, Stk Price (%)	2.67	—	—	—	—

* The fund's first fiscal year ended 5/31/92. The fiscal year was then changed to 7/31.

Nuveen Pennsylvania Investment Quality Municipal Fund

NYSE : NQP

John Nuveen & Co. Inc.	*Transfer Agent*
Investment Bankers	U.S. Trust
333 West Wacker Dr.	Nuveen Exchange-Traded Fund Investor Services
Chicago, IL 60606	770 Broadway
(800) 252-4630 / (312) 917-7700	New York, NY 10003
Tax-Free Income	(800) 257-8787

12 Months Ending 12/31/92 Results

	Period End	Period Begin	Distributions	Yield Dist (%)	Total Return (%)
Share Price ($)	16.00	16.25	1.04	6.40	4.86
NAV per share ($)	15.50	14.83		7.01	11.53

Background: Initial public offering February 21, 1991 of 8,200,000 shares at $15 per share. Initial NAV was $14.05 per share.

Objective: Seeks current income exempt from Federal and Pennsylvania State income taxes. Enhancement of portfolio value is secondary. The fund will invest at least 80% of its assets in Pennsylvania municipal obligations rated in the top four categories by S&P or Moody's. Up to 20% may be invested in non-rated Pennsylvania municipal obligations the adviser considers to be of investment-grade quality.

Portfolio: (6/30/92) Municipal Bonds 98.3%, Other 1.7%. Portfolio Rating: AAA 46.0%, AA 24.0%, A 10.0%, BBB 20.0%.

Capitalization: (6/30/92) Common stock outstanding 8,293,645. Leveraged with 1,000 shares preferred stock, stated value $50,000 per share.

Average Maturity (years): 21.3
Fund Manager: Nuveen Advisory Corporation **Fee:** 0.60%
Income Dist: Monthly **Capital Gains Dist:** Annually
Reinvestment Plan: Yes **Shareholder Reports:** Semi-Annually

5 Year Performance

Fiscal Year Ending 6/30[a]	1992 (8 mos)	1991 (8 mos.)	1990	1989	1988
Net Assets ($mil):	185.60	187.83	—	—	—
Net Income Dist ($):	0.66	0.50	—	—	—
Cap Gains Dist ($):	0.00	0.00	—	—	—
Total Dist ($)	0.66	0.50	—	—	—
Yield from Dist (%)	4.22	—	—	—	—
Expense Ratio (%)	0.78	0.81	—	—	—
Portfolio Turnover (%)	0.00	0.00	—	—	—
NAV per share ($)	15.14	14.60	—	—	—
Market Price per share	15.50	15.63	—	—	—
Premium (Discount) (%)	2.38	7.05	—	—	—
Total Return, Stk Price (%)	3.39	—	—	—	—

* Prior to 1992, the fund's first fiscal year end was 10/31.

Nuveen Pennsylvania Quality Income Municipal Fund

NYSE : NUP

John Nuveen & Co. Inc.
Investment Bankers
333 West Wacker Dr.
Chicago, IL 60606
(800) 252-4630 / (312) 917-7700
Tax-Free Income

Transfer Agent
U.S. Trust
Nuveen Exchange-Traded Fund Investor Services
770 Broadway
New York, NY 10003
(800) 257-8787

12 Months Ending 12/31/92 Results

	Period End	Period Begin	Distributions	Yield Dist (%)	Total Return (%)
Share Price ($)	15.38	15.00	0.98	6.53	9.07
NAV per share ($)	14.95	14.37		6.82	10.86

Background: Initial public offering October 17, 1991 of 6,978,171 shares at $15 per share. Initial NAV was $14.05 per share.

Objective: Seeks current income exempt from Federal and Pennsylvania State income taxes. Enhancement of portfolio value is secondary. The fund will invest at least 80% of its assets in Pennsylvania municipal obligations rated in the top four categories by S&P or Moody's. Up to 20% of assets may be in non-rated municipal obligations the adviser considers to be of investment-grade quality.

Portfolio: (12/1/92) Sector Weightings: Health Care 17.9%, Water & Sewer 17.5%, General Obligation 16.4%. Portfolio Ratings: AAA 45.1%, AA 19.0%, A 18.7%, BBB 17.2%.

Capitalization: (6/30/92) Common stock outstanding 7,012,914. Leveraged with 1,000 shares preferred stock, stated value $50,000 per share.

Average Maturity (years): 22.6
Fund Manager: Nuveen Advisory Corporation
Income Dist: Monthly
Reinvestment Plan: Yes

Fee: 0.65%
Capital Gains Dist: Annually
Shareholder Reports: Semi-Annually

5 Year Performance

Fiscal Year Ending 6/30	1992 (8 mos.)	1991	1990	1989	1988
Net Assets ($mil):	152.80	—	—	—	—
Net Income Dist ($):	0.46	—	—	—	—
Cap Gains Dist ($):	0.00	—	—	—	—
Total Dist ($)	0.46	—	—	—	—
Yield from Dist (%)	—	—	—	—	—
Expense Ratio (%)	0.87	—	—	—	—
Portfolio Turnover (%)	9.00	—	—	—	—
NAV per share ($)	14.66	—	—	—	—
Market Price per share	14.88	—	—	—	—
Premium (Discount) (%)	1.50	—	—	—	—
Total Return, Stk Price (%)	—	—	—	—	—

Nuveen Texas Quality Income Municipal Fund

NYSE : NTX

John Nuveen & Co. Inc.
Investment Bankers
333 West Wacker Dr.
Chicago, IL 60606
(800) 252-4630 / (312) 917-7700
Tax-Free Income

Transfer Agent
U.S. Trust
Nuveen Exchange-Traded Fund Investor Services
770 Broadway
New York, NY 10003
(800) 257-8787

12 Months Ending 12/31/92 Results

	Period End	Period Begin	Distributions	Yield Dist (%)	Total Return (%)
Share Price ($)	15.25	15.25	0.94	6.16	6.16
NAV per share ($)	14.66	14.22		6.61	9.70

Background: Initial public offering October 17, 1991 of 7,000,000 shares at $15 per share. Initial NAV was $14.05 per share.

Objective: Seeks high monthly income exempt from regular Federal income tax. The fund will invest at least 80% of its assets in Texas municipal obligations rated in the top four categories by S&P or Moody's. Up to 20% may be invested in non-rated securities the adviser considers to be of investment-grade quality.

Portfolio: (12/1/92) Municipal Bonds 100%. Sector Weightings: Pollution Control 24%, Housing 17%, Health Care 14%, Government Obligation 14%, Transportation 9%, Electric Utilities 9%. Portfolio Ratings: AAA 46%, AA 10%, A 37%, BBB 6%, Non-Rated 1%.

Capitalization: (7/31/92) Common stock outstanding 7,028,480. Leveraged with 1,000 shares preferred stock, stated value $50,000 per share.

Average Maturity (years): 22.2
Fund Manager: Nuveen Advisory Corporation
Income Dist: Monthly
Reinvestment Plan: Yes

Fee: 0.65%
Capital Gains Dist: Quarterly
Shareholder Reports: Semi-Annually

5 Year Performance

Fiscal Year Ending 7/31*	1992 (2 mos.)	1991 (thru 5/31/92)	1990	1989	1988
Net Assets ($mil):	156.00	—	—	—	—
Net Income Dist ($):	0.15	0.38	—	—	—
Cap Gains Dist ($):	0.00	0.00	—	—	—
Total Dist ($)	0.15	0.38	—	—	—
Yield from Dist (%)	1.01	—	—	—	—
Expense Ratio (%)	0.86	0.86	—	—	—
Portfolio Turnover (%)	25.00	0.01	—	—	—
NAV per share ($)	15.09	14.19	—	—	—
Market Price per share	15.38	14.88	—	—	—
Premium (Discount) (%)	1.92	4.86	—	—	—
Total Return, Stk Price (%)	—	—	—	—	—

* The fund's first fiscal year ended 5/31/92.

Taurus MuniCalifornia Holdings, Inc.
P.O. Box 9011
Princeton, NJ 08543
(800) 543-6217 / (609) 282-2800

Transfer Agent
Bank of New York
110 Washington St.
New York, NY 10286
(800) 524-4458

Tax-Free Income

12 Months Ending 12/31/92 Results

	Period End	Period Begin	Distributions	Yield Dist (%)	Total Return (%)
Share Price ($)	12.88	12.13	1.02	8.41	14.59
NAV per share ($)	11.76	11.73		8.70	8.95

Background: Initial public offering January 25, 1990 of 5,000,000 shares at $12 per share. Initial NAV was $11.16 per share.

Objective: Seeks current income exempt from Federal and California State income taxes. Of the fund's assets, 80% will be invested in long-term California municipal obligations rated in the top four categories by S&P or Moody's. The fund may invest in certain tax-exempt securities classified as "private activity" bonds, which may be subject to the Alternative Minimum Tax (AMT).

Portfolio: (10/31/92) Municipal Bonds 97.7%, Other 2.3%. State Weightings: California 95.5%, Puerto Rico 2.2%. Portfolio Ratings: Investment Grade 100%.

Capitalization: (10/31/92) Common stock outstanding 5,121,232. Leveraged with 400 shares auction-rate preferred stock with $50,000 per share liquidation preference.

Average Maturity (years): 22.8
Fund Manager: Fund Asset Management, Inc.
Income Dist: Monthly
Reinvestment Plan: Yes

Fee: 0.50%
Capital Gains Dist: Annually
Shareholder Reports: Quarterly

5 Year Performance

Fiscal Year Ending 10/31	1992	1991	1990 (9 mos.)	1989	1988
Net Assets ($mil):	79.00	78.50	74.50	—	—
Net Income Dist ($):	0.88	0.82	0.49	—	—
Cap Gains Dist ($):	0.06	0.01	0.00	—	—
Total Dist ($)	0.94	0.83	0.49	—	—
Yield from Dist (%)	7.67	7.46	—	—	—
Expense Ratio (%)	0.88	0.91	0.97	—	—
Portfolio Turnover (%)	50.50	27.89	85.91	—	—
NAV per share ($)	11.53	11.66	11.05	—	—
Market Price per share	12.50	12.25	11.13	—	—
Premium (Discount) (%)	8.41	5.06	0.72	—	—
Total Return, Stk Price (%)	9.71	17.52	—	—	—

Taurus Municipal New York Holdings, Inc.
P.O. Box 9011
Princeton, NJ 08543
(800) 543-6217 / (609) 282-5000

NYSE : MNY
Transfer Agent
Bank of New York
110 Washington St.
New York, NY 10286
(800) 524-4458

Tax-Free Income

12 Months Ending 12/31/92 Results

	Period End	Period Begin	Distributions	Yield Dist (%)	Total Return (%)
Share Price ($)	13.38	12.00	0.91	7.58	19.08
NAV per share ($)	12.26	11.64		7.82	13.14

Background: Initial public offering February, 1990 of 6,000,000 shares at $12 per share. Initial NAV was $11.16 per share.

Objective: Seeks current income exempt from regular Federal and New York State and City income taxes.

Portfolio: (10/31/92) Municipal Bonds 94.3%, Other 5.7%. State Weightings: New York 92.1%, Puerto Rico 2.2%. Portfolio Ratings: AAA 92.7%, AA 0.4%, A 2.6%, BBB 3.2%.

Capitalization: (10/31/92) Common stock outstanding 6,508,080. Leveraged with 600 shares preferred stock.

Average Maturity (years): 23.1
Fund Manager: Fund Asset Management, Inc.   **Fee:** 0.50%
Income Dist: Monthly   **Capital Gains Dist:** Annually
Reinvestment Plan: Yes   **Shareholder Reports:** Quarterly

5 Year Performance

Fiscal Year Ending 10/31	1992	1991	1990 (10 mos.)	1989	1988
Net Assets ($mil):	107.80	103.70	96.70	—	—
Net Income Dist ($):	0.90	0.83	0.52	—	—
Cap Gains Dist ($):	0.00	0.00	0.00	—	—
Total Dist ($)	0.90	0.83	0.52	—	—
Yield from Dist (%)	7.50	7.63	—	—	—
Expense Ratio (%)	0.82	0.86	0.88	—	—
Portfolio Turnover (%)	20.18	35.80	59.18	—	—
NAV per share ($)	11.95	11.64	10.76	—	—
Market Price per share	12.75	12.00	10.88	—	—
Premium (Discount) (%)	6.69	3.09	1.12	—	—
Total Return, Stk Price (%)	13.75	17.92	—	—	—

Van Kampen Merritt California Municipal Trust

One Parkview Plaza
Oakbrook Terrace, IL 60181
(800) 225-2222

AMEX : VKC
Transfer Agent
State Street Bank & Trust Co.
225 Franklin St.
P.O. Box 366
Boston, MA 02101
(800) 451-6788

Tax-Free Income

12 Months Ending 12/31/92 Results

	Period End	Period Begin	Distributions	Yield Dist (%)	Total Return (%)
Share Price ($)	10.25	9.75	0.77	7.90	13.03
NAV per share ($)	10.30	9.97		7.72	11.03

Background: Initial public offering October 25, 1988 of 3,000,000 shares at $10 per share. Initial NAV was $9.30 per share.

Objective: Seeks high current income exempt from Federal and California State income taxes by investing primarily in California municipals rated at least BBB or Baa.

Portfolio: (9/30/92) Municipal Bonds 97.4%, Cash & Other 2.6%. Sector Weightings: Single Family Housing 15.2%, Health Care 13.9%, Multi-Family Housing 9.2%, Retail Electric 8.8%, Public Building 8.5%. Portfolio Ratings: AAA 22.1%, AA 21.1%, A 45%, BBB 11.8%.

Capitalization: (6/30/92) Common stock outstanding 3,141,449. Leveraged with 400 shares preferred stock, stated value $50,000 per share.

Average Maturity (years): 23.7
Fund Manager: Van Kampen Merritt Investment Advisory Corp.   **Fee:** 0.60%
Income Dist: Monthly   **Capital Gains Dist:** Annually
Reinvestment Plan: Yes   **Shareholder Reports:** Semi-Annually

5 Year Performance

Fiscal Year Ending 6/30	1992	1991	1990	1989 (8 mos.)	1988
Net Assets ($mil):	51.90	49.50	48.40	29.30	—
Net Income Dist ($):	0.65	0.65	0.65	0.39	—
Cap Gains Dist ($):	0.03	0.00	0.00	0.00	—
Total Dist ($)	0.68	0.65	0.65	0.39	—
Yield from Dist (%)	6.97	7.12	6.50	—	—
Expense Ratio (%)	2.07	1.88	0.50	0.87	—
Portfolio Turnover (%)	40.60	99.43	99.54	57.06	—
NAV per share ($)	10.15	9.41	9.10	9.42	—
Market Price per share	9.88	9.75	10.00	10.00	—
Premium (Discount) (%)	(2.63)	3.64	0.27	6.20	—
Total Return, Stk Price (%)	8.31	13.91	(2.20)	—	—

Van Kampen Merritt California Quality Municipal Trust

One Parkview Plaza
Oakbrook Terrace, IL 60181
(800) 225-2222

Tax-Free Income

NYSE : VQC
Transfer Agent
State Street Bank & Trust Co.
225 Franklin St.
P.O. Box 366
Boston, MA 02101
(800) 426-5523

12 Months Ending 12/31/92 Results

	Period End	Period Begin	Distributions	Yield Dist (%)	Total Return (%)
Share Price ($)	14.75	14.38	1.05	7.30	9.87
NAV per share ($)	15.64	15.07		6.97	10.75

Background: Initial public offering September 20, 1991 of 15,546,204 shares at $15 per share. An additional $7,787,129 shares sold at NAV (approximately $15 per share) in a continuous offering ending November 5, 1991. In December 1992 the fund changed its symbol from "VKM" to "VQC."

Objective: Seeks a high level of current income exempt from regular Federal and California State income taxes, consistent with preservation of capital.

Portfolio: (9/30/92) Municipal Bonds 96.4%, Cash & Other 3.6%. Sector Weightings: Single Family Housing 17.7%, General Purpose 13.9%, Retail Electric 10%, Water & Sewer 10%, Public Education 9.6%, Public Building 8.3%. Portfolio Ratings: AAA 33.1%, AA 22.8%, A 30.9%, BBB 4.2%, Non-Rated 9%.

Capitalization: (8/31/92) Common stock outstanding 9,623,295 shares. Leveraged with 1,500 preferred shares, stated value $50,000 per share.

Average Maturity (years): 25.1
Fund Manager: Van Kampen Merritt Investment Advisory Corp. **Fee:** 0.70%
Income Dist: Monthly **Capital Gains Dist:** Annually
Reinvestment Plan: Yes **Shareholder Reports:** Semi-Annually

5 Year Performance

Fiscal Year Ending 8/31	1992 (11 mos.)	1991	1990	1989	1988
Net Assets ($mil):	227.20	—	—	—	—
Net Income Dist ($):	0.70	—	—	—	—
Cap Gains Dist ($):	0.00	—	—	—	—
Total Dist ($)	0.70	—	—	—	—
Yield from Dist (%)	—	—	—	—	—
Expense Ratio (%)	1.09	—	—	—	—
Portfolio Turnover (%)	93.29	—	—	—	—
NAV per share ($)	15.82	—	—	—	—
Market Price per share	15.13	—	—	—	—
Premium (Discount) (%)	(4.34)	—	—	—	—
Total Return, Stk Price (%)	—	—	—	—	—

Van Kampen Merritt Florida Quality Municipal Trust

One Parkview Plaza
Oakbrook Terrace, IL 60181
(800) 225-2222

NYSE : VFM

Transfer Agent
State Street Bank & Trust Co.
225 Franklin St.
P.O. Box 366
Boston, MA 02101

Tax-Free Income

(800) 426-5523

12 Months Ending 12/31/92 Results

	Period End	Period Begin	Distributions	Yield Dist (%)	Total Return (%)
Share Price ($)	15.63	15.13	1.07	7.07	10.38
NAV per share ($)	16.06	15.23		7.03	12.48

Background: Initial public offering September 20, 1991 of 2,827,665 shares at $15 per share.

Objective: Seeks a high level of current income exempt from Federal income tax, consistent with preservation of capital.

Portfolio: (9/30/92) Municipal Bonds 97.7%, Other Assets 2.3%. Portfolio Ratings: AAA 65.4%, AA 11.3%, A 4.6%, BBB 16.7%, Non-Rated 2.0%.

Capitalization: (8/31/92) Common stock outstanding 6,428,084. Leveraged with 1,000 shares preferred stock, stated value $50,000 per share.

Average Maturity (years): 23.8
Fund Manager: Van Kampen Merritt Investment Advisory Corp.   **Fee:** 0.70%
Income Dist: Monthly   **Capital Gains Dist:** Annually
Reinvestment Plan: Yes   **Shareholder Reports:** Semi-Annually

5 Year Performance

Fiscal Year Ending 8/31	1992 (11 mos.)	1991	1990	1989	1988
Net Assets ($mil):	152.90	—	—	—	—
Net Income Dist ($):	0.74	—	—	—	—
Cap Gains Dist ($):	0.00	—	—	—	—
Total Dist ($)	0.74	—	—	—	—
Yield from Dist (%)	—	—	—	—	—
Expense Ratio (%)	1.12	—	—	—	—
Portfolio Turnover (%)	36.60	—	—	—	—
NAV per share ($)	16.01	—	—	—	—
Market Price per share	15.63	—	—	—	—
Premium (Discount) (%)	(2.39)	—	—	—	—
Total Return, Stk Price (%)	—	—	—	—	—

Van Kampen Merritt New York Quality Municipal Trust

One Parkview Plaza
Oakbrook Terrace, IL 60181
(800) 225-2222

NYSE : VNM

Transfer Agent
State Street Bank & Trust Co.
P.O. Box 366
Boston, MA 02266
(800) 426-5523

Tax-Free Income

12 Months Ending 12/31/92 Results

	Period End	Period Begin	Distributions	Yield Dist (%)	Total Return (%)
Share Price ($)	15.63	14.63	1.07	7.31	14.15
NAV per share ($)	16.27	15.23		7.03	13.85

Background: Initial public offering September 20, 1991 of 3,033,763 shares at $15 per share. Net proceeds were $45,343,445.

Objective: Seeks a high level of current income exempt from Federal and New York State and City income taxes, consistent with preservation of capital.

Portfolio: (9/30/92) Municipal Bonds 98.1%, Other Assets 1.9%. Portfolio Ratings: AAA 11.2%, AA 21.6%, A 28.9%, BBB 31.2%, Non-Rated 7.1%.

Capitalization: (8/31/92) Common stock outstanding 5,643,496 shares. Leveraged with 900 shares preferred stock, stated value $50,000 per share.

Average Maturity (years): 24.4
Fund Manager: Van Kampen Merritt Investment Advisory Corp.　　**Fee:** 0.70%
Income Dist: Monthly　　**Capital Gains Dist:** Annually
Reinvestment Plan: Yes　　**Shareholder Reports:** Semi-Annually

5 Year Performance

Fiscal Year Ending 8/31	1992	1991	1990	1989	1988
	(11 mos.)				
Net Assets ($mil):	137.00	—	—	—	—
Net Income Dist ($):	0.74	—	—	—	—
Cap Gains Dist ($):	0.00	—	—	—	—
Total Dist ($)	0.74	—	—	—	—
Yield from Dist (%)	—	—	—	—	—
Expense Ratio (%)	1.17	—	—	—	—
Portfolio Turnover (%)	65.10	—	—	—	—
NAV per share ($)	16.30	—	—	—	—
Market Price per share	15.63	—	—	—	—
Premium (Discount) (%)	(4.13)	—	—	—	—
Total Return, Stk Price (%)	—	—	—	—	—

Van Kampen Merritt Ohio Quality Muni

One Parkview Plaza
Oakbrook Terrace IL 60181
(800) 225-2222

Tax-Free Income

NYSE : VOQ

Transfer Agent
State Street Bank & Trust Co.
225 Franklin St.
P.O. Box 366
Boston, MA 02101
(800) 426-5523

12 Months Ending 12/31/92 Results

	Period End	Period Begin	Distributions	Yield Dist (%)	Total Return (%)
Share Price ($)	15.63	15.50	1.05	6.77	7.61
NAV per share ($)	15.97	15.15		6.93	12.34

Background: Initial public offering September 20, 1991 of 2,113,741 shares at $15 per share. Net proceeds $31,577,115.

Objective: Seeks a high level of current income exempt from Federal and Ohio State income taxes, consistent with preservation of capital. Fund may use leverage.

Portfolio: (9/30/92) Municipal Bonds 97.1%, Cash & Other 2.9%. Sector Weightings: Health Care 22.3%, Retail Electric 17.1%, General Purpose 12.8%, Public Building 10.8%, Water & Sewer 9.8%.

Capitalization: (8/31/92) Common stock outstanding 4,175,210.

Average Maturity (years): 20.7
Fund Manager: Van Kampen Merritt Investment Advisory Corp.   **Fee:** 0.70%
Income Dist: Monthly   **Capital Gains Dist:** Annually
Reinvestment Plan: Yes   **Shareholder Reports:** Semi-Annually

5 Year Performance

Fiscal Year Ending 8/31	1992 (11 mos.)	1991	1990	1989	1988
Net Assets ($mil):	101.80	—	—	—	—
Net Income Dist ($):	0.73	—	—	—	—
Cap Gains Dist ($):	0.00	—	—	—	—
Total Dist ($)	0.73	—	—	—	—
Yield from Dist (%)	—	—	—	—	—
Expense Ratio (%)	1.22	—	—	—	—
Portfolio Turnover (%)	42.70	—	—	—	—
NAV per share ($)	15.99	—	—	—	—
Market Price per share	16.25	—	—	—	—
Premium (Discount) (%)	1.64	—	—	—	—
Total Return, Stk Price (%)	—	—	—	—	—

Van Kampen Merritt Pennsylvania Quality Municipal

One Parkview Plaza
Oakbrook Terrace IL 60181
(800) 225-2222

Tax-Free Income

NYSE : VPQ

Transfer Agent
State Street Bank & Trust Co.
225 Franklin St.
P.O. Box 366
Boston, MA 02101
(800) 426-5523

12 Months Ending 12/31/92 Results

	Period End	Period Begin	Distributions	Yield Dist (%)	Total Return (%)
Share Price ($)	15.50	15.00	1.17	7.80	11.13
NAV per share ($)	16.29	15.22		7.69	14.72

Background: Initial public offering September 20, 1991 of 5,798,057 shares at $15 per share. Initial NAV was $14.78 per share.

Objective: Seeks a high level of current income exempt from regular Federal and Pennsylvania State income taxes, consistent with the preservation of capital.

Portfolio: (9/30/92) Municipal Bonds 97.9%, Other Assets 2.1%. Portfolio Ratings: AAA 36.1%, AA 10.1%, A 14.3%, BBB 35.1%, Non-Rated 4.4%.

Capitalization: (8/31/92) Common stock outstanding 8,053,340. Fund is leveraged with 1,300 shares preferred stock, stated value $50,000 per share.

Average Maturity (years): 23.2
Fund Manager: Van Kampen Merritt Investment Advisory Corp.　　**Fee:** 0.70%
Income Dist: Monthly　　**Capital Gains Dist:** Annually
Reinvestment Plan: Yes　　**Shareholder Reports:** Semi-Annually

5 Year Performance

Fiscal Year Ending 8/31	1992 (11 mos.)	1991	1990	1989	1988
Net Assets ($mil):	197.00	—	—	—	—
Net Income Dist ($):	0.75	—	—	—	—
Cap Gains Dist ($):	0.00	—	—	—	—
Total Dist ($)	0.75	—	—	—	—
Yield from Dist (%)	—	—	—	—	—
Expense Ratio (%)	1.11	—	—	—	—
Portfolio Turnover (%)	55.37	—	—	—	—
NAV per share ($)	16.39	—	—	—	—
Market Price per share	15.75	—	—	—	—
Premium (Discount) (%)	(3.89)	—	—	—	—
Total Return, Stk Price (%)	—	—	—	—	—

Federal Tax-Free Bond Funds

American Municipal Term Trust, Inc.

Piper Jaffray Tower
222 S. Ninth St.
Minneapolis, MN 55402
(800) 333-6000 / (612) 342-6426

Tax-Free Income

NYSE : AXT
Transfer Agent
Investors Fiduciary Trust Co.
127 W. 10th St.
Kansas City, MO 64105-1716
(816) 474-8786

12 Months Ending 12/31/92 Results

	Period End	Period Begin	Distributions	Yield Dist (%)	Total Return (%)
Share Price ($)	10.50	10.13	0.65	6.42	10.07
NAV per share ($)	10.56	9.99		6.51	12.21

Background: Initial public offering March 1991 of 7,500,000 shares at $10 per share. Initial NAV was $9.44 per share.

Objective: Seeks high current income exempt from regular Federal income tax and to return $10 per share to investors on termination of the trust on or shortly before April 15, 2001.

Portfolio: (12/22/92) Municipal Coupons 92.9%, Municipal Zeros 7.1%. Portfolio Ratings: AAA 70.0%, AA 19.0%, A 8.0%, BBB 3.0%.

Capitalization: (12/31/92) Common stock outstanding 8,455,000. Fund is leveraged with auction-rate preferred stock.

Average Maturity (years): 20.3
Fund Manager: Piper Capital Management, Inc.
Income Dist: Monthly
Reinvestment Plan: Yes

Fee: 0.25%
Capital Gains Dist: Annually
Shareholder Reports: Quarterly

5 Year Performance

Fiscal Year Ending 12/31	1992	1991 (9 mos.)	1990	1989	1988
Net Assets ($mil):	131.80	127.00	—	—	—
Net Income Dist ($):	0.65	0.49	—	—	—
Cap Gains Dist ($):	0.00	0.00	—	—	—
Total Dist ($)	0.65	0.49	—	—	—
Yield from Dist (%)	6.42	—	—	—	—
Expense Ratio (%)	56.00	0.56	—	—	—
Portfolio Turnover (%)	24.00	0.00	—	—	—
NAV per share ($)	10.56	9.99	—	—	—
Market Price per share	10.50	10.13	—	—	—
Premium (Discount) (%)	(0.57)	1.30	—	—	—
Total Return, Stk Price (%)	10.07	—	—	—	—

American Municipal Term Trust II

Piper Jaffray Tower
222 S. Ninth St.
Minneapolis, MN 55402
(800) 333-6000 / (612) 342-6426

Transfer Agent
Investors Fiduciary Trust Co.
127 W. 10th St.
Kansas City, MO 64105-1716
(816) 474-8786

Tax-Free Income

12 Months Ending 12/31/92 Results

	Period End	Period Begin	Distributions	Yield Dist (%)	Total Return (%)
Share Price ($)	10.38	9.88	0.62	6.28	11.34
NAV per share ($)	10.25	9.71		6.39	11.95

Background: Initial public offering September 19, 1991 of 7,000,000 shares at $10 per share. Initial NAV was $9.45 per share.

Objective: Seeks high current income exempt from regular Federal income tax and to return $10 per share to investors on termination of the trust on or shortly before April 15, 2002.

Portfolio: (12/22/92) Municipal Coupon Securities 92.7%, Municipal Zeros 7.3%. Portfolio Ratings: AAA 68.0%, AA 13.0%, A 11.0%, BBB 8.0%.

Capitalization: (12/31/92) Shares of beneficial interest outstanding 7,356,000. Leveraged with auction-rate preferreds.

Average Maturity (years): 7.7
Fund Manager: Piper Capital Management, Inc. **Fee:** 0.25%
Income Dist: Monthly **Capital Gains Dist:** Annually
Reinvestment Plan: Yes **Shareholder Reports:** Quarterly

5 Year Performance

Fiscal Year Ending 12/31	1992	1991 (3 mos.)	1990	1989	1988
Net Assets ($mil):	112.50	108.40	—	—	—
Net Income Dist ($):	0.62	0.16	—	—	—
Cap Gains Dist ($):	0.00	0.00	—	—	—
Total Dist ($)	0.62	0.16	—	—	—
Yield from Dist (%)	6.28	—	—	—	—
Expense Ratio (%)	0.58	0.58	—	—	—
Portfolio Turnover (%)	18.00	0.00	—	—	—
NAV per share ($)	10.25	9.71	—	—	—
Market Price per share	10.38	9.88	—	—	—
Premium (Discount) (%)	1.27	1.65	—	—	—
Total Return, Stk Price (%)	11.34	—	—	—	—

P.O. Box 9011   *Transfer Agent*
Princeton, NJ 08543-9011   The Bank of New York
(609) 282-2800   101 Washington St.
                                                                    New York, NY 10286
                                                      (800) 524-4458 / (212) 495-1784

Tax-Free Income

12 Months Ending 12/31/92 Results

	Period End	Period Begin	Distributions	Yield Dist (%)	Total Return (%)
Share Price ($)	9.63	11.50	0.87	7.57	(8.70)
NAV per share ($)	10.14	10.74		8.10	2.51

Background: Initial public offering July 25, 1989 of approximately 18,000,000 shares at $12 per share. Initial NAV was $11.10 per share.

Objective: Seeks high current income exempt from regular Federal income taxes by investing primarily in a portfolio of medium- to lower-grade or unrated municipal bonds.

Portfolio: (12/31/92) Municipal Bonds 97.6% %, Short Term & Other 2.4%. Portfolio Ratings: AAA 2.1%, AA 1.1%, A 4.3%, BBB 7.3%, Non-Rated 85.2%.

Capitalization: (12/31/92) Common stock outstanding 19,258,000. No long-term debt.

Average Maturity (years): 23.5
Fund Manager: Fund Asset Management, Inc.   **Fee:** 0.65%
Income Dist: Monthly   **Capital Gains Dist:** Annually
Reinvestment Plan: Yes   **Shareholder Reports:** Quarterly

5 Year Performance

Fiscal Year Ending 6/30	1992	1991	1990 (11 mos.)	1989	1988
Net Assets ($mil):	198.00	206.70	208.90	—	—
Net Income Dist ($):	0.91	0.94	0.75	—	—
Cap Gains Dist ($):	0.00	0.00	0.00	—	—
Total Dist ($)	0.91	0.94	0.75	—	—
Yield from Dist (%)	7.91	8.17	—	—	—
Expense Ratio (%)	0.83	0.84	0.78	—	—
Portfolio Turnover (%)	3.00	31.00	122.00	—	—
NAV per share ($)	10.31	10.92	11.18	—	—
Market Price per share	11.00	11.50	11.50	—	—
Premium (Discount) (%)	6.69	5.31	2.86	—	—
Total Return, Stk Price (%)	3.57	8.17	—	—	—

BlackRock Municipal Target Term Trust

One Seaport Plaza
New York, NY 10292
((800) 451-6788 / (212) 214-3332

Transfer Agent
State Street Bank & Trust Co.
One Heritage Drive
North Quincy, MA 02171
(800) 451-6788

Tax-Free Income

12 Months Ending 12/31/92 Results

	Period End	Period Begin	Distributions	Yield Dist (%)	Total Return (%)
Share Price ($)	10.00	9.63	0.61	6.33	10.18
NAV per share ($)	10.04	9.50		6.42	12.11

Background: Initial public offering on September 20, 1991 of 40,000,000 shares at $10 per share. Initial NAV was $9.40 per share.

Objective: Seeks current income exempt from regular Federal income taxes and to return $10 per share to common shareholders on or about December 31, 2006.

Portfolio: (12/31/92) Municipal Bonds 145.1%, Short Term 1.6%, Other 2.7%. Average Quality AAA.

Capitalization: (12/31/92) Common stock outstanding 45,410,639. Leveraged with 4,500 shares preferred stock, stated value $50,000 per share.

Average Maturity (years): 14.6
Fund Manager: BlackRock Financial Management L.P.   **Fee:** 0.35%
Income Dist: Monthly   **Capital Gains Dist:** Annually
Reinvestment Plan: Yes   **Shareholder Reports:** Semi-Annually

5 Year Performance

Fiscal Year Ending 12/31	1992	1991 (3 mos.)	1990	1989	1988
Net Assets ($mil):	680.90	659.20	—	—	—
Net Income Dist ($):	0.61	0.05	—	—	—
Cap Gains Dist ($):	0.00	0.00	—	—	—
Total Dist ($)	0.61	0.05	—	—	—
Yield from Dist (%)	6.33	—	—	—	—
Expense Ratio (%)	0.91	0.81	—	—	—
Portfolio Turnover (%)	35.00	1.00	—	—	—
NAV per share ($)	10.04	9.50	—	—	—
Market Price per share	10.00	9.63	—	—	—
Premium (Discount) (%)	(0.40)	1.37	—	—	—
Total Return, Stk Price (%)	10.18	—	—	—	—

Colonial High Income Municipal Trust

One Financial Center, 12th Floor
Boston, MA 02111-2621
(800) 225-2365 / (617) 426-3750

NYSE : CXE
Transfer Agent
The First National Bank of Boston
100 Federal St.
Boston, MA 02110
(617) 929-5445

Tax-Free Income

12 Months Ending 12/31/92 Results

	Period End	Period Begin	Distributions	Yield Dist (%)	Total Return (%)
Share Price ($)	8.25	8.63	0.68	7.88	3.48
NAV per share ($)	8.78	8.91		7.63	6.17

Background: Initial public offering February 16, 1989 of 30,000,000 shares at $10 per share. Initial NAV was $9.30 per share.

Objective: Seeks high current income by investing primarily in medium- and lower-quality municipal bonds. Typically these bonds are smaller issues collateralized by real estate loans.

Portfolio: (12/31/92) Municipal Bonds 97.4%, Short Term 1.3%, Other 1.3%. Portfolio Ratings: AAA 14.4%, AA 3.9%, A 13.5%, BBB 10.5%, BB 2.0%, Non-Rated 55.9%.

Capitalization: (12/31/92) Common stock outstanding 30,718,000. No long-term debt.

Average Maturity (years): 23.6
Fund Manager: Colonial Management Associates, Inc.   **Fee:** 0.80%
Income Dist: Monthly   **Capital Gains Dist:** Annually
Reinvestment Plan: Yes   **Shareholder Reports:** Semi-Annually

5 Year Performance

Fiscal Year Ending 12/31	1992	1991	1990	1989 (10 mos.)	1988
Net Assets ($mil):	269.80	273.20	273.90	282.00	—
Net Income Dist ($):	0.68	0.76	0.83	0.57	—
Cap Gains Dist ($):	0.00	0.00	0.03	0.00	—
Total Dist ($)	0.68	0.76	0.86	0.57	—
Yield from Dist (%)	7.88	8.56	9.17	—	—
Expense Ratio (%)	0.96	0.97	0.96	0.90	—
Portfolio Turnover (%)	15.00	17.00	23.00	58.00	—
NAV per share ($)	8.78	8.91	9.00	9.35	—
Market Price per share	8.25	8.63	8.88	9.38	—
Premium (Discount) (%)	(6.04)	(3.25)	(1.33)	0.21	—
Total Return, Stk Price (%)	3.48	5.74	3.84	—	—

Colonial Investment Grade Municipal Fund

One Financial Center, 12th Floor
Boston, MA 02111
(800) 426-3750

Transfer Agent
The First National Bank of Boston
100 Federal St.
Boston, MA 02110
(800) 426-5523

Tax-Free Income

12 Months Ending 12/31/92 Results

	Period End	Period Begin	Distributions	Yield Dist (%)	Total Return (%)
Share Price ($)	11.75	11.75	0.85	7.23	7.23
NAV per share ($)	10.96	11.09		7.66	6.49

Background: Initial public offering May 26, 1989 of 11,500,000 shares at $12 per share. Initial NAV was $11.12 per share.

Objective: Seeks current income exempt from regular Federal income tax. The fund will invest at least 80% of its assets in investment-grade municipal bonds. The fund may borrow up to 10% of assets temporarily.

Portfolio: (12/31/92) Municipal Bonds 96.1%, Short Term & Other 3.9%. Portfolio Ratings: AAA 18.0%, AA 10.0%, A 25.0%, BBB 22.0%, BB 2.0%, Non-Rated 22.0%.

Capitalization: (12/31/92) Common stock outstanding 11,509,000. No long-term debt.

Average Maturity (years): 23.1
Fund Manager: Colonial Management Associates, Inc.
Income Dist: Monthly
Reinvestment Plan: Yes

Fee: 0.65%
Capital Gains Dist: Annually
Shareholder Reports: Semi-Annually

5 Year Performance

Fiscal Year Ending 12/31	1992	1991	1990	1989 (8 mos.)	1988
Net Assets ($mil):	126.20	127.60	124.90	126.90	—
Net Income Dist ($):	0.85	0.89	0.95	0.52	—
Cap Gains Dist ($):	0.00	0.00	0.00	0.00	—
Total Dist ($)	0.85	0.89	0.95	0.52	—
Yield from Dist (%)	7.23	7.91	7.92	—	—
Expense Ratio (%)	0.86	0.87	0.45	—	—
Portfolio Turnover (%)	18.00	15.00	22.00	32.00	—
NAV per share ($)	10.96	11.09	10.85	11.02	—
Market Price per share	11.75	11.75	11.25	12.00	—
Premium (Discount) (%)	7.21	5.95	3.69	8.89	—
Total Return, Stk Price (%)	7.23	12.36	1.67	—	—

Colonial Municipal Income Trust

One Financial Center, 12th Floor
Boston, MA 02111
(800) 426-3750

NYSE : CMU
Transfer Agent
State Street Bank & Trust Co.
225 Franklin St.
Boston, MA 02110
(800) 426-5523

Tax-Free Income

12 Months Ending 12/31/92 Results

	Period End	Period Begin	Distributions	Yield Dist (%)	Total Return (%)
Share Price ($)	7.50	7.63	0.64	8.39	6.68
NAV per share ($)	7.87	8.07		7.93	5.45

Background: Initial public offering March 19, 1987 of 26,000,000 shares of beneficial interest at $10 per share. Initial NAV was $9.40 per share.

Objective: Seeks high current income exempt from regular Federal income tax by investing in medium- and lower-quality municipal bonds and notes. Invests at least 80% in tax-exempt bonds rated BBB/Baa or lower by S&P or Moody's.

Portfolio: (11/30/92) Municipal Bonds 97.9%. Sector Weightings: Hospitals & Health Care 20.8%, Nursing Homes 20.7%, Housing 18.7%, Pollution Control 11.5%. Portfolio Ratings: AAA 3.0%, AA 2.0%, A 4.0%, BBB 17.0%, BB 2.0%, Non-Rated 69.0%.

Capitalization: (11/30/92) Shares of beneficial interest outstanding 27,043,000. No long-term debt.

Average Maturity (years): 22.3
Fund Manager: Colonial Management Associates, Inc.　　**Fee:** 0.65%
Income Dist: Monthly　　**Capital Gains Dist:** Annually
Reinvestment Plan: Yes　　**Shareholder Reports:** Semi-Annually

5 Year Performance

Fiscal Year Ending 11/30	1992	1991	1990	1989	1988
Net Assets ($mil):	213.40	216.40	223.10	229.20	235.9
Net Income Dist ($):	0.64	0.71	0.72	0.78	0.78
Cap Gains Dist ($):	0.00	0.00	0.00	0.00	0.00
Total Dist ($)	0.64	0.71	0.72	0.78	0.78
Yield from Dist (%)	7.64	9.01	7.48	8.00	9.18
Expense Ratio (%)	0.87	0.87	0.86	0.87	0.87
Portfolio Turnover (%)	10.00	12.00	20.00	18.00	52.00
NAV per share ($)	7.89	8.06	8.37	8.65	8.98
Market Price per share	7.88	8.38	7.88	9.63	9.75
Premium (Discount) (%)	(0.13)	3.85	(5.97)	11.21	8.57
Total Return, Stk Price (%)	1.67	15.36	(10.70)	6.77	23.88

Dreyfus Municipal Income, Inc.

144 Glenn Curtiss Blvd.
Uniondale, NY 11556
(800) 334-6899 / (516) 794-5210

NYSE : DMF

Transfer Agent
Mellon Bank, NA
P.O. Box 444
Pittsburgh, PA 15230
(412) 236-8000

Tax-Free Income

12 Months Ending 12/31/92 Results

	Period End	Period Begin	Distributions	Yield Dist (%)	Total Return (%)
Share Price ($)	10.63	9.88	0.76	7.69	15.28
NAV per share ($)	10.95	9.88		7.69	18.52

Background: Initial public offering October 24, 1988 of 16,000,000 shares at $10 per share. Initial NAV was $9.30 per share.

Objective: Seeks high current income exempt from regular Federal income tax consistent with preservation of capital. Invests primarily in investment-grade municipal obligations. May engage in options and futures transactions.

Portfolio: (9/30/92) Municipal Bonds 100%. State Weightings: Texas 17.4%, Illinois 15.6%, Pennsylvania 13.6%, Colorado 8.8%, Florida 8.1%. Portfolio Ratings: AAA 0%, AA 12.2%, A 26.0%, BBB 30.1%, BB 2.6%, Non-Rated 29.1%.

Capitalization: (9/30/92) Common stock outstanding 19,491,000. No long-term debt.

Average Maturity (years): 24.5
Fund Manager: The Dreyfus Corporation
Income Dist: Monthly
Reinvestment Plan: Yes

Fee: 0.70%
Capital Gains Dist: Annually
Shareholder Reports: Semi-Annually

5 Year Performance

Fiscal Year Ending 9/30	1992	1991	1990	1989 (11 mos.)	1988
Net Assets ($mil):	196.00	188.40	176.40	—	—
Net Income Dist ($):	0.70	0.68	0.70	0.52	—
Cap Gains Dist ($):	0.08	0.04	0.02	0.00	—
Total Dist ($)	0.78	0.72	0.72	0.52	—
Yield from Dist (%)	7.80	7.38	7.29	—	—
Expense Ratio (%)	0.86	0.88	0.85	0.88	—
Portfolio Turnover (%)	22.75	36.40	27.11	95.24	—
NAV per share ($)	10.06	9.83	9.34	9.52	—
Market Price per share	10.50	10.00	9.75	9.88	—
Premium (Discount) (%)	4.37	1.73	4.39	3.68	—
Total Return, Stk Price (%)	12.80	9.95	5.97	—	—

Dreyfus Strategic Municipal Bond Fund, Inc.

144 Glenn Curtiss Blvd.
Uniondale, NY 11556
(800) 334-6899 / (516) 794-5210

NYSE : DSM
Transfer Agent
The Shareholder Services Group, Inc.
Exchange Place
Boston, MA 02109
(617) 722-7000

Tax-Free Income

12 Months Ending 12/31/92 Results

	Period End	Period Begin	Distributions	Yield Dist (%)	Total Return (%)
Share Price ($)	10.25	9.75	0.71	7.28	12.41
NAV per share ($)	9.78	9.63		7.37	8.93

Background: Initial public offering in November 22, 1989 of 41,000,000 shares at $10 per share. Initial NAV was $9.32 per share.

Objective: Seeks tax-free income from a portfolio of investment-grade, tax-free bonds. The fund may issue preferred shares for leverage.

Portfolio: (11/30/92) Municipal Bonds 100%. State Weightings: Pennsylvania 12.4%, Texas 11.8%, New York 10.1%, Illinois 8.7%, Massachusetts 8.0%. Portfolio Ratings: AAA 7.6%, AA 13.4%, A 15.9%, BBB 22.4%, Non-Rated 39.8%.

Capitalization: (11/30/92) Common shares outstanding 43,838,576. No long-term debt.

Average Maturity (years): 23.9
Fund Manager: The Dreyfus Corporation
Income Dist: Monthly
Reinvestment Plan: Yes

Fee: 0.50%
Capital Gains Dist: Annually
Shareholder Reports: Semi-Annually

5 Year Performance

Fiscal Year Ending 11/30	1992	1991	1990	1989 (8 days)	1988
Net Assets ($mil):	428.80	408.30	389.30	326.40	—
Net Income Dist ($):	0.71	0.71	0.59	0.00	—
Cap Gains Dist ($):	0.00	0.00	0.00	0.00	—
Total Dist ($)	0.71	0.71	0.59	0.00	—
Yield from Dist (%)	7.19	7.47	6.13	—	—
Expense Ratio (%)	0.84	0.88	0.56	—	—
Portfolio Turnover (%)	8.58	22.41	16.51	—	—
NAV per share ($)	9.78	9.61	9.44	9.32	—
Market Price per share	10.25	9.88	9.50	9.63	—
Premium (Discount) (%)	4.81	2.71	0.64	3.22	—
Total Return, Stk Price (%)	10.93	11.47	4.78	—	—

Dreyfus Strategic Municipals, Inc.

144 Glenn Curtiss Blvd.
Uniondale, NY 11556
(800) 334-6899 / (516) 794-5210

Transfer Agent
The Bank of New York
110 Washington St.
New York, NY 10268
(800) 524-4458

Tax-Free Income

12 Months Ending 12/31/92 Results

	Period End	Period Begin	Distributions	Yield Dist (%)	Total Return (%)
Share Price ($)	10.38	10.63	0.77	7.24	4.89
NAV per share ($)	10.06	10.05		7.66	7.76

Background: Initial public offering September 23, 1987 of 45,000,000 shares at $10 per share.

Objective: Seeks current income exempt from regular Federal income tax, consistent with preservation of capital. Invests at least 80% of net assets in municipal obligations, of which at least 50% must be investment-grade.

Portfolio: (9/30/92) Municipal Bonds 99.7%, Short Term & Other 0.3%. Portfolio Ratings: AAA 10.0%, AA 8.0%, A 7.0%, BBB 30.1%, Non-Rated 37.0%.

Capitalization: (9/30/92) Common stock outstanding 52,808,538. No long-term debt.

Average Maturity (years): 23.2
Fund Manager: The Dreyfus Corporation   **Fee:** 0.75%
Income Dist: Monthly   **Capital Gains Dist:** Annually
Reinvestment Plan: Yes   **Shareholder Reports:** Semi-Annually

5 Year Performance

Fiscal Year Ending 9/30	1992	1991	1990	1989	1988
Net Assets ($mil):	533.20	510.10	482.50	478.60	452.50
Net Income Dist ($):	0.75	0.76	0.76	0.78	0.70
Cap Gains Dist ($):	0.03	0.12	0.05	0.15	0.00
Total Dist ($)	0.78	0.88	0.81	0.93	0.70
Yield from Dist (%)	7.43	8.80	7.71	9.30	7.00
Expense Ratio (%)	0.88	0.88	0.89	0.91	0.69
Portfolio Turnover (%)	21.80	6.43	10.51	11.43	55.55
NAV per share ($)	10.10	9.96	9.79	9.97	9.91
Market Price per share	10.75	10.50	10.00	10.50	10.00
Premium (Discount) (%)	6.44	5.42	2.15	5.32	0.91
Total Return, Stk Price (%)	9.81	13.80	2.95	14.30	7.00

Duff & Phelps Utility Tax Free Income Fund

55 E. Monroe St.
Chicago, IL 60603
(312) 368-5510

NYSE : DTF

Transfer Agent
State Street Bank & Trust Co.
One Heritage Drive
North Quincy, MA 02171
(800) 426-5523

Tax-Free Income

12 Months Ending 12/31/92 Results

	Period End	Period Begin	Distributions	Yield Dist (%)	Total Return (%)
Share Price ($)	15.38	14.88	0.88	5.91	9.27
NAV per share ($)	14.77	14.28		6.16	9.59

Background: Initial public offering November 22, 1991 of 7,300,000 shares of common stock at $15 per share. Initial NAV was $14.05 per share.

Objective: Seeks current income exempt from regular Federal income tax consistent with the preservation of capital. The fund will invest primarily in a diversified portfolio of investment-grade, tax-exempt utility obligations.

Portfolio: (10/31/92) Municipal Bonds 97.7%, Short Term & Other 2.3%. Portfolio Ratings: AAA 8.0%, AA 46.0%, A 38.0%, BBB 8%.

Capitalization: (10/31/92) Common stock outstanding 8,289,839. Leveraged with 1,300 shares preferred stock, stated value $50,000 per share.

Average Maturity (years): 23.5
Fund Manager: Duff & Phelps Investment Management   **Fee:** 0.50%
Income Dist: Monthly   **Capital Gains Dist:** Annually
Reinvestment Plan: Yes   **Shareholder Reports:** Quarterly

5 Year Performance

Fiscal Year Ending 10/31	1992 (11 mos.)	1991	1990	1989	1988
Net Assets ($mil):	182.20	—	—	—	—
Net Income Dist ($):	0.72	—	—	—	—
Cap Gains Dist ($):	0.00	—	—	—	—
Total Dist ($)	0.72	—	—	—	—
Yield from Dist (%)	—	—	—	—	—
Expense Ratio (%)	1.35	—	—	—	—
Portfolio Turnover (%)	35.00	—	—	—	—
NAV per share ($)	14.14	—	—	—	—
Market Price per share	14.75	—	—	—	—
Premium (Discount) (%)	4.31	—	—	—	—
Total Return, Stk Price (%)	—	—	—	—	—

InterCapital Insured Municipal Bond Trust

InterCapital Division
Two World Trade Center
New York, NY 10048
(800) 869-3863 / (212) 392-2550

NYSE : IMB

Transfer Agent
Dean Witter Trust Co.
Two Montgomery St.
Jersey City, NJ 07302
(800) 869-3863

Tax-Free Income

12 Months Ending 12/31/92 Results

	Period End	Period Begin	Distributions	Yield Dist (%)	Total Return (%)
Share Price ($)	16.75	15.75	1.28	8.13	14.48
NAV per share ($)	15.18	14.67		8.73	12.20

Background: Initial public offering February 28, 1991 of 4,600,000 shares at $15 per share. Initial NAV was $14.06 per share.

Objective: Seeks current income exempt from regular Federal income tax. Invests in a portfolio of securities covered by insurance guaranteeing timely payment of principal and interest.

Portfolio: (10/31/92) Municipal Bonds 95.5%, Short-Term Municipal Obligations 1.7%, Cash & Other 2.8%. Sector Weightings: Mortgage Revenue Single-Family 35.3%, Hospital Revenue 11.3%, Pollution Control Revenue 9.4%, Water & Sewer Revenue 9.3%, Transportation Facilities Revenue 9.3%. Portfolio Ratings: AAA 100%.

Capitalization: (10/31/92) Shares of beneficial interest outstanding 5,257,113. Leveraged with 800 shares auction-rate preferred stock with $40,000 per share liquidation preference.

Average Maturity (years): 25.5
Fund Manager: Dean Witter Reynolds InterCapital Division   **Fee:** 0.35%
Income Dist: Monthly   **Capital Gains Dist:** Annually
Reinvestment Plan: Yes   **Shareholder Reports:** Semi-Annually

5 Year Performance

Fiscal Year Ending 10/31	1992	1991 (8 mos.)	1990	1989	1988
Net Assets ($mil):	118.00	117.10	—	—	—
Net Income Dist ($):	1.08	0.52	—	—	—
Cap Gains Dist ($):	0.02	0.00	—	—	—
Total Dist ($)	1.10	0.52	—	—	—
Yield from Dist (%)	7.10	—	—	—	—
Expense Ratio (%)	0.99	1.00	—	—	—
Portfolio Turnover (%)	7.00	16.00	—	—	—
NAV per share ($)	14.84	14.66	—	—	—
Market Price per share	16.38	15.50	—	—	—
Premium (Discount) (%)	10.31	5.73	—	—	—
Total Return, Stk Price (%)	12.77	—	—	—	—

InterCapital Quality Municipal Investment Trust

InterCapital Division
Two World Trade Center
New York, NY 10048
(800) 869-3863 / (212) 392-2550

NYSE : IQT

Transfer Agent
Dean Witter Trust Co.
Two Montgomery St.
Jersey City, NJ 07302
(800) 869-3863

Tax-Free Income

12 Months Ending 12/31/92 Results

	Period End	Period Begin	Distributions	Yield Dist (%)	Total Return (%)
Share Price ($)	15.38	14.63	1.21	8.27	13.40
NAV per share ($)	14.97	14.36		8.43	12.67

Background: Initial public offering September 27, 1991 of 18,600,000 shares at $15 per share. Initial NAV was $14.06 per share.

Objective: Seeks current income exempt from regular Federal income tax through a diversified portfolio of tax-exempt municipal obligations rated in the top three categories by S&P or Moody's. Emphasis is on longer-term maturities that produce a higher yield, although the portfolio may be more susceptible to greater market fluctuation due to interest rate changes. The fund can be leveraged up to 35%.

Portfolio: (10/31/92) Municipal Bonds 95.3%, Short Term 4.7%. Portfolio Ratings: AAA 21.0%, AA 30.0%, A 41.0%, BBB 8.0%.

Capitalization: (10/31/92) Common stock outstanding 18,607,113. Leveraged with $140,000,000 in auction-rate preferred shares.

Average Maturity (years): 26.4
Fund Manager: Dean Witter Reynolds InterCapital Division   **Fee:** 0.35%
Income Dist: Monthly   **Capital Gains Dist:** Annually
Reinvestment Plan: Yes   **Shareholder Reports:** Semi-Annually

5 Year Performance

Fiscal Year Ending 10/31	1992	1991 (1 mo.)	1990	1989	1988
Net Assets ($mil):	409.90	262.10	—	—	—
Net Income Dist ($):	0.97	0.00	—	—	—
Cap Gains Dist ($):	0.00	0.00	—	—	—
Total Dist ($)	0.97	0.00	—	—	—
Yield from Dist (%)	6.36	—	—	—	—
Expense Ratio (%)	0.79	0.49	—	—	—
Portfolio Turnover (%)	9.00	0.00	—	—	—
NAV per share ($)	14.51	14.09	—	—	—
Market Price per share	15.00	15.25	—	—	—
Premium (Discount) (%)	3.38	8.23	—	—	—
Total Return, Stk Price (%)	4.72	—	—	—	—

Kemper Municipal Income Trust

120 S. LaSalle St.
Chicago, IL 60603
(800) 537-6006

NYSE : KTF
Transfer Agent
Investors Fiduciary Trust Co.
127 W. 10th St.
Kansas City, MO 64105
(800) 422-2848 / (816) 474-8786

Tax-Free Income

12 Months Ending 12/31/92 Results

	Period End	Period Begin	Distributions	Yield Dist (%)	Total Return (%)
Share Price ($)	12.75	12.38	0.87	7.03	10.02
NAV per share ($)	12.52	12.10		7.19	10.66

Background: Initial public offering October 20, 1988 of 35,000,000 shares at $12 per share. Initial NAV was $11.11 per share.

Objective: Seeks a high level of current income exempt from regular Federal income tax by investing in a diversified portfolio of investment-grade, tax-exempt municipal securities. Average maturity of securities within the portfolio is expected to range from 10 to 30 years. The fund may not invest more than 20% of net assets in unrated securities.

Portfolio: (11/30/92) Municipal Bonds 97.0%, Cash & Other 3.0%. Portfolio Ratings: AAA 20.0%, AA 37.0%, A 22.0%, BBB 18.0%, Non-Rated 3.0%.

Capitalization: (11/30/92) Common stock outstanding 37,040,000. Leveraged with 43,000 preferred shares, stated value $5,000 per share.

Average Maturity (years): 24.0
Fund Manager: Kemper Financial Services, Inc.   **Fee:** 0.55%
Income Dist: Monthly   **Capital Gains Dist:** Annually
Reinvestment Plan: Yes   **Shareholder Reports:** Semi-Annually

5 Year Performance

Fiscal Year Ending 11/30	1992	1991	1990	1989	1988 (1 mo.)
Net Assets ($mil):	676.10	649.90	623.70	622.90	392.10
Net Income Dist ($):	0.87	0.87	0.87	0.78	0.00
Cap Gains Dist ($):	0.00	0.00	0.00	0.00	0.00
Total Dist ($)	0.87	0.87	0.87	0.78	0.00
Yield from Dist (%)	7.25	7.73	7.48	6.50	—
Expense Ratio (%)	0.71	0.72	0.66	0.62	0.65
Portfolio Turnover (%)	5.00	4.00	15.00	38.00	13.00
NAV per share ($)	12.45	11.85	11.25	11.35	11.13
Market Price per share	12.63	12.00	11.25	11.63	12.00
Premium (Discount) (%)	1.45	1.27	0.00	2.38	7.82
Total Return, Stk Price (%)	12.50	14.40	4.21	3.42	—

Kemper Strategic Municipal Income Trust

120 S. LaSalle St.
Chicago, IL 60603
(800) 537-6006

NYSE : KSM

Transfer Agent
Investors Fiduciary Trust Co.
127 W. 10th St.
Kansas City, MO 64105
(800) 422-2848 / (816) 474-8786

Tax-Free Income

12 Months Ending 12/31/92 Results

	Period End	Period Begin	Distributions	Yield Dist (%)	Total Return (%)
Share Price ($)	12.38	12.25	0.92	7.51	8.57
NAV per share ($)	11.90	11.77		7.82	8.92

Background: Initial public offering March 22, 1989 of 10,000,000 shares at $12 per share. Initial NAV was $11.05 per share.

Objective: Seeks high current income exempt from regular Federal income tax by investing in municipal obligations, of which at least 50% are investment-grade. Up to 50% may be in lower-quality obligations. During temporary defensive periods, the fund may invest any percentage of its assets in taxable short term investments. May use leverage when appropriate.

Portfolio: (11/30/92) Municipal Obligations 96.6%, Cash & Other 3.4%. Sector Weightings: Health Care 27%, General Obligations 7.3%, Airports 7.2%. Portfolio Ratings: AAA 3%, AA 22%, A 11%, BBB 17%, Non-Rated 47%.

Capitalization: (11/30/92) Common stock outstanding 10,293,000. No long-term debt.

Average Maturity (years): 22.0
Fund Manager: Kemper Financial Services, Inc.   **Fee:** 0.60%
Income Dist: Monthly   **Capital Gains Dist:** Annually
Reinvestment Plan: Yes   **Shareholder Reports:** Quarterly

5 Year Performance

Fiscal Year Ending 11/30	1992	1991	1990	1989 (8 mos)	1988
Net Assets ($mil):	122.00	120.30	114.90	116.00	—
Net Income Dist ($):	0.83	0.81	0.85	0.45	—
Cap Gains Dist ($):	0.10	0.11	0.10	0.00	—
Total Dist ($)	0.93	0.92	0.95	0.45	—
Yield from Dist (%)	7.67	8.56	8.26	—	—
Expense Ratio (%)	0.77	0.77	0.76	0.77	—
Portfolio Turnover (%)	10.00	20.00	57.00	22.00	—
NAV per share ($)	11.86	11.65	11.37	11.55	—
Market Price per share	12.13	12.13	10.75	11.50	—
Premium (Discount) (%)	2.28	4.03	(5.45)	(0.43)	—
Total Return, Stk Price (%)	7.67	21.40	1.74	—	—

MFS Municipal Income Trust

500 Boylston St.
Boston, MA 02116
(617) 954-5000

NYSE : MFM

Transfer Agent
State Street Bank & Trust Co.
225 Franklin St.
Boston, MA 02110
(800) 637-2304

Tax-Free Income

12 Months Ending 12/31/92 Results

	Period End	Period Begin	Distributions	Yield Dist (%)	Total Return (%)
Share Price ($)	8.50	8.88	0.71	8.00	3.72
NAV per share ($)	8.91	8.96		7.92	7.37

Background: Initial public offering November 18, 1986 of 35,000,000 shares of beneficial interest at $10 per share. Initial NAV was $9.40 per share.

Objective: Seeks high current income exempt from Federal income tax. Invests 80% or more in tax-exempt securities issued by the states, territories, and possessions of the United States, at least 75% in tax-exempt securities rated BBB/Baa or lower, or unrated. The fund may not invest more than 25% of its assets in industrial revenue bonds.

Portfolio: (12/1/92) Municipal Bonds 97.4%, Other 2.6%. Sector Weightings: Health Care 32%, Housing 22%, Industrial Revenue 18.6%, Other 24.1%. Portfolio Ratings: AAA 10.29%, AA 6.32%, A 5.07%, BBB & Below 8.65%, Non-Rated 67.11%.

Capitalization: (10/31/92) Common shares outstanding 36,781,925. No long-term debt.

Average Maturity (years): 20.8
Fund Manager: Massachusetts Financial Services Co.   **Fee:** 0.40%
Income Dist: Monthly   **Capital Gains Dist:** Annually
Reinvestment Plan: Yes   **Shareholder Reports:** Quarterly

5 Year Performance

Fiscal Year Ending 10/31	1992	1991	1990	1989	1988
Net Assets ($mil):	323.10	325.10	325.80	338.50	327.20
Net Income Dist ($):	0.72	0.73	0.76	0.76	0.74
Cap Gains Dist ($):	0.00	0.00	0.00	0.00	0.00
Total Dist ($)	0.72	0.73	0.76	0.76	0.74
Yield from Dist (%)	7.89	8.59	7.69	7.79	8.71
Expense Ratio (%)	1.34	1.27	1.21	1.28	1.25
Portfolio Turnover (%)	17.00	21.00	19.00	16.00	37.00
NAV per share ($)	8.78	8.96	8.95	9.46	9.23
Market Price per share	9.00	9.13	8.50	9.88	9.75
Premium (Discount) (%)	2.51	1.90	(5.03)	4.44	5.63
Total Return, Stk Price (%)	6.46	16.00	(6.28)	9.13	23.41

Municipal High Income Fund

Two World Trade Center, 71st Floor
New York, NY 10048
(800) 869-3863 / (212) 392-2550

NYSE : MHF

Transfer Agent
The Shareholder Services Group
Exchange Place
Boston, MA 02104
(617) 722-7000

Tax-Free Income

12 Months Ending 12/31/92 Results

	Period End	Period Begin	Distributions	Yield Dist (%)	Total Return (%)
Share Price ($)	9.50	9.13	0.69	7.56	11.61
NAV per share ($)	9.60	9.48		7.28	8.54

Background: Initial public offering November 28, 1988 of 16,600,000 shares at $10.00 per share. Initial NAV was $9.35 per share.

Objective: Seeks high current tax-free income. Up to 100% of the portfolio may be invested in municipal obligations rated as low as BB. Because of this low rating, the portfolio is subject to greater volatility and risk. Up to 30% of the fund's assets may be invested in non-publicly traded municipal obligations, and up to 25% may be in municipal zeros.

Portfolio: (10/31/92) Municipal Bonds 96.6%, Short Term & Other 3.4%. Portfolio Ratings: AAA 0.9%, AA 7.6%, A 11.2%, BBB 39.9%, BB 5.7%, Non-Rated 34.7%.

Capitalization: (10/31/92) Common stock outstanding 18,869,000.

Average Maturity (years): 22.2
Fund Manager: Shearson Lehman Advisors
Income Dist: Monthly
Reinvestment Plan: Yes

Fee: 0.40%
Capital Gains Dist: Annually
Shareholder Reports: Quarterly

5 Year Performance

Fiscal Year Ending 10/31	1992	1991	1990	1989 (11 mos.)	1988
Net Assets ($mil):	179.10	173.30	164.50	164.20	—
Net Income Dist ($):	0.69	0.75	0.76	0.64	—
Cap Gains Dist ($):	0.00	0.00	0.00	0.00	—
Total Dist ($)	0.69	0.75	0.76	0.64	—
Yield from Dist (%)	7.26	8.21	8.00	—	—
Expense Ratio (%)	0.87	0.90	0.87	0.86	—
Portfolio Turnover (%)	12.00	22.00	11.00	16.00	—
NAV per share ($)	9.49	9.42	9.28	9.52	—
Market Price per share	9.13	9.50	9.13	9.50	—
Premium (Discount) (%)	(3.79)	0.85	(1.72)	(0.21)	—
Total Return, Stk Price (%)	3.37	12.27	4.11	—	—

Municipal Income Opportunities Trust

NYSE : OIA

Two World Trade Center, 71st Floor
New York, NY 10048
(800) 869-3863 / (212) 392-2550

Transfer Agent
Dean Witter Trust Co.
Two Montgomery St.
Jersey City, NJ 07302
(800) 869-3863

Tax-Free Income

12 Months Ending 12/31/92 Results

	Period End	Period Begin	Distributions	Yield Dist (%)	Total Return (%)
Share Price ($)	7.88	9.25	0.72	7.78	(7.03)
NAV per share ($)	8.84	9.38		7.68	1.92

Background: Initial public offering September 19, 1988 of 20,000,000 shares at $10 per share. Initial NAV was $9.40 per share. In 1993 the fund changed its name and symbol from Allstate Municipal Income Opportunities Trust (AMO).

Objective: Seeks high current income exempt from regular Federal income tax. Invests at least 80% of net assets in municipal obligations except during temporary defensive periods. Will invest at least 65% of total assets in a diversified portfolio of unrated municipal obligations which are deemed to be of medium quality.

Portfolio: (11/30/92) Municipal Bonds 95.8%, Short Term & Other 4.2%. Portfolio Ratings: AAA 3.0%, AA 12.0%, A 5.0%, BBB 10.0%, Non-Rated 75.0%.

Capitalization: (11/30/92) Common stock outstanding 21,506,172. No long-term debt.

Average Maturity (years): 21.0
Fund Manager: Dean Witter Reynolds InterCapital Division   **Fee:** 0.60%
Income Dist: Monthly   **Capital Gains Dist:** Annually
Reinvestment Plan: Yes   **Shareholder Reports:** Semi-Annually

5 Year Performance

Fiscal Year Ending 5/31	1992	1991	1990	1989 (8 mos.)	1988
Net Assets ($mil):	194.90	202.40	199.20	194.70	—
Net Income Dist ($):	0.73	0.82	0.84	0.37	—
Cap Gains Dist ($):	0.00	0.00	0.00	0.00	—
Total Dist ($)	0.73	0.82	0.84	0.37	—
Yield from Dist (%)	7.39	8.00	8.00	—	—
Expense Ratio (%)	1.08	1.10	1.10	1.11	—
Portfolio Turnover (%)	4.00	7.00	8.00	9.00	—
NAV per share ($)	8.97	9.39	9.44	9.56	—
Market Price per share	9.38	9.88	10.25	10.50	—
Premium (Discount) (%)	4.57	5.22	8.58	9.83	—
Total Return, Stk Price (%)	2.33	4.39	5.62	—	—

Municipal Income Opportunities Trust II

Two World Trade Center, 71st Floor
New York, NY 10048
(800) 869-3863 / (212) 392-2550

NYSE : OIB

Transfer Agent
Dean Witter Trust Co.
Two Montgomery St.
Jersey City, NJ 07302
(800) 869-3863

Tax-Free Income

12 Months Ending 12/31/92 Results

	Period End	Period Begin	Distributions	Yield Dist (%)	Total Return (%)
Share Price ($)	8.00	9.43	0.71	7.53	(7.64)
NAV per share ($)	8.99	9.50		7.47	2.11

Background: Initial public offering June 30, 1989 of 20,000,000 shares at $10.00 per share. Initial NAV was $9.50 per share. In 1993, the fund changed its name and symbol from Allstate Municipal Income Opportunities Trust II (AOT).

Objective: Seeks high current income exempt from regular Federal income taxes consistent with the preservation of capital.

Portfolio: (8/31/92) Municipal Bonds 97.1%, Short Term & Other 2.9%. **Portfolio Ratings:** Non-Rated 78.0%, Investment Grade 22.0%.

Capitalization: (8/31/92) Common stock outstanding 21,039,707. No long-term debt.

Average Maturity (years): N/A
Fund Manager: Dean Witter Reynolds InterCapital Division **Fee:** 0.60%
Income Dist: Monthly **Capital Gains Dist:** Annually
Reinvestment Plan: Yes **Shareholder Reports:** Quarterly

5 Year Performance

Fiscal Year Ending 2/28	1992	1991	1990 (8 mos.)	1989	1988
Net Assets ($mil):	194.30	190.40	190.00	—	—
Net Income Dist ($):	0.78	0.74	0.34	—	—
Cap Gains Dist ($):	0.00	0.01	0.00	—	—
Total Dist ($)	0.78	0.75	0.34	—	—
Yield from Dist (%)	8.32	8.11	—	—	—
Expense Ratio (%)	1.06	1.06	1.07	—	—
Portfolio Turnover (%)	5.00	34.00	0.00	—	—
NAV per share ($)	9.23	9.28	9.34	—	—
Market Price per share	9.88	9.38	9.25	—	—
Premium (Discount) (%)	6.93	1.08	(0.96)	—	—
Total Return, Stk Price (%)	13.65	9.51	—	—	—

Municipal Income Opportunities Trust III

2 World Trade Center, 71st Floor
New York, NY 10048
(800) 869-3863 / (212) 392-2550

NYSE : OIC

Transfer Agent
Dean Witter Trust Co.
2 Montgomery St.
Jersey City, NJ 07302
(800) 869-3863

Tax-Free Income

12 Months Ending 12/31/92 Results

	Period End	Period Begin	Distributions	Yield Dist (%)	Total Return (%)
Share Price ($)	9.13	9.50	0.75	7.89	4.00
NAV per share ($)	9.41	9.62		7.80	5.61

Background: Initial public offering April 30, 1990 of 10,000,000 shares at $10 per share. Initial NAV was $9.30 per share. In 1993 the fund changed its name and symbol from Allstate Municipal Income Opportunities Trust III (AIO).

Objective: Seeks high current income exempt from regular Federal income tax. Invests in medium-grade tax-exempt bonds and selected qualified issues.

Portfolio: (9/30/92) Municipal Bonds 95.8%, Short Term & Other 4.2%. Sector Weightings: Hospital Revenue 33.2%, Tax Allocation 15.1%, Transportation Facilities 11.7%, Mortgage Revenue (Single Family) 11.4%, Mortgage Revenue (Multi-Family) 11.3%. Portfolio Ratings: Non-Rated 59.0%, Higher 41.0%.

Capitalization: (9/30/92) Shares of beneficial interest outstanding 11,495,006. No long-term debt.

Average Maturity (years): N/A
Fund Manager: Dean Witter Reynolds InterCapital Division   **Fee:** 0.60%
Income Dist: Monthly   **Capital Gains Dist:** Annually
Reinvestment Plan: Yes   **Shareholder Reports:** Semi-Annually

5 Year Performance

Fiscal Year Ending 3/31	1992	1991 (11 mos.)	1990	1989	1988
Net Assets ($mil):	101.30	107.80	—	—	—
Net Income Dist ($):	0.72	0.50	—	—	—
Cap Gains Dist ($):	0.06	0.00	—	—	—
Total Dist ($)	0.78	0.50	—	—	—
Yield from Dist (%)	8.21	—	—	—	—
Expense Ratio (%)	1.14	1.12	—	—	—
Portfolio Turnover (%)	11.00	10.00	—	—	—
NAV per share ($)	9.51	9.44	—	—	—
Market Price per share	9.13	9.50	—	—	—
Premium (Discount) (%)	(4.00)	0.64	—	—	—
Total Return, Stk Price (%)	4.32	—	—	—	—

Municipal Income Trust

Two World Trade Center, 71st Floor
New York, NY 10048
(800) 869-3863 / (212) 392-2550

NYSE : TFA

Transfer Agent
Dean Witter Trust Co.
Two Montgomery St
Jersey City, NJ 07302
(800) 869-3863

Tax-Free Income

12 Months Ending 12/31/92 Results

	Period End	Period Begin	Distributions	Yield Dist (%)	Total Return (%)
Share Price ($)	10.88	10.88	0.72	6.62	6.62
NAV per share ($)	10.67	10.56		6.82	7.86

Background: Initial public offering September 29, 1987 of 30,000,000 shares at $10 per share. Initial NAV was $9.35 per share. In 1993, the fund changed its name and symbol from Allstate Municipal Income Trust (ALM).

Objective: Seeks current income exempt from regular Federal income tax. Invests at least 80% in municipal obligations except during temporary defensive periods. Invests at least 65% in a diversified portfolio of investment-grade long-term municipal obligations.

Portfolio: (8/31/92) Municipal Bonds 95.9%, Short Term & Other 4.1%. Porfolio Ratings: Average Quality A.

Capitalization: (8/31/92) Common stock outstanding 33,153,050. No long-term debt.

Average Maturity (years): 22.5
Fund Manager: Dean Witter Reynolds InterCapital Division   **Fee:** 0.45%
Income Dist: Monthly   **Capital Gains Dist:** Annually
Reinvestment Plan: Yes   **Shareholder Reports:** Quarterly

5 Year Performance

Fiscal Year Ending 8/31	1992	1991	1990	1989	1988 (11 mos.)
Net Assets ($mil):	354.50	343.70	329.70	328.40	—
Net Income Dist ($):	0.72	0.68	0.85	0.78	0.61
Cap Gains Dist ($):	0.00	0.00	0.06	0.23	0.02
Total Dist ($)	0.72	0.68	0.91	1.01	0.63
Yield from Dist (%)	7.02	6.63	8.77	10.36	—
Expense Ratio (%)	0.73	0.75	0.79	0.76	0.78
Portfolio Turnover (%)	11.00	5.00	10.00	18.00	149.00
NAV per share ($)	10.69	10.37	10.01	10.36	10.20
Market Price per share	10.75	10.25	10.25	10.38	9.75
Premium (Discount) (%)	0.56	(1.16)	2.40	0.19	(4.41)
Total Return, Stk Price (%)	11.90	6.63	7.51	16.82	—

Municipal Income Trust II

Two World Trade Center, 71st Floor
New York, NY 10048
(800) 869-3863 / (212) 392-2550

NYSE : TFB

Transfer Agent
Dean Witter Trust Co.
Two Montgomery St.
Jersey City, NJ 07302
(800) 869-3863

Tax-Free Income

12 Months Ending 12/31/92 Results

	Period End	Period Begin	Distributions	Yield Dist (%)	Total Return (%)
Share Price ($)	10.50	10.00	0.70	7.00	12.00
NAV per share ($)	10.46	10.34		6.77	7.93

Background: Initial offering April 1988 of 28,289,132 shares at $10 per share. Initial NAV was $9.50 per share. In 1993 the fund changed its name and symbol from Allstate Municipal Income Trust II (ALT).

Objective: Seeks current income exempt from regular Federal income tax. Invests at least 80% of net assets in municipal obligations, except during temporary defensive periods. Invests at least 65% in investment-grade securities, and up to 35% may be invested in non-investment grade securities considered to be speculative investments.

Portfolio: (6/30/92) Municipal Bonds 96.4%, Short Term 3.6%. State Weightings: Pennsylvania 14.18%, Colorado 12.78%, Florida 12.50%, Indiana 7.28%, Wisconsin 7.09%. Portfolio Ratings: AAA 13.4%, AA 15.3%, A 36.2%, BBB 22.4%, Non-Rated 7.8%.

Capitalization: (12/31/92) Common stock outstanding 28,587,930. No long-term debt.

Average Maturity (years): 23.6
Fund Manager: Dean Witter Reynolds InterCapital Division   **Fee:** 0.50%
Income Dist: Monthly   **Capital Gains Dist:** Annually
Reinvestment Plan: Yes   **Shareholder Reports:** Quarterly

5 Year Performance

Fiscal Year Ending 12/31	1992	1991	1990	1989	1988 (8 mos.)
Net Assets ($mil):	300.20	296.60	280.30	285.10	274.1
Net Income Dist ($):	0.69	0.67	0.73	0.73	0.37
Cap Gains Dist ($):	0.01	0.03	0.02	0.07	0.01
Total Dist ($)	0.70	0.70	0.75	0.80	0.38
Yield from Dist (%)	7.00	7.46	7.50	8.21	—
Expense Ratio (%)	87.00	0.86	0.88	0.87	0.86
Portfolio Turnover (%)	N/A	15.00	24.00	35.00	27.00
NAV per share ($)	10.46	10.34	9.79	9.90	9.71
Market Price per share	10.50	10.00	9.38	10.00	9.75
Premium (Discount) (%)	0.38	(3.29)	(4.29)	1.01	0.41
Total Return, Stk Price (%)	12.00	14.07	1.30	10.77	—

Municipal Income Trust III

Two World Trade Center, 71st Floor
New York, NY 10048
(800) 869-3863 / (212) 392-2550

Transfer Agent
Dean Witter Trust Co.
Two Montgomery St.
Jersey City, NJ 07302
(800) 869-3863

Tax-Free Income

12 Months Ending 12/31/92 Results

	Period End	Period Begin	Distributions	Yield Dist (%)	Total Return (%)
Share Price ($)	9.38	9.63	0.66	6.85	4.26
NAV per share ($)	9.75	9.74		6.78	6.88

Background: Initial public offering October 5, 1989 of 6,900,000 shares at $10 per share. Initial NAV was $9.30 per share. In 1993, the fund changed its name and symbol from Allstate Municipal Income Trust III (ALL).

Objective: Seeks current income exempt from regular Federal income tax.

Portfolio: (8/31/92) Municipal Bonds 96.9%, Short Term & Other 3.1%. Portfolio Ratings: Average Quality A.

Capitalization: (8/31/92) Common stock outstanding 6,632,086. No long-term debt.

Average Maturity (years): 25.0
Fund Manager: Dean Witter Reynolds InterCapital Division   **Fee:** 0.50%
Income Dist: Monthly   **Capital Gains Dist:** Annually
Reinvestment Plan: Yes   **Shareholder Reports:** Quarterly

5 Year Performance

Fiscal Year Ending 8/31	1992	1991	1990 (10 mos.)	1989	1988
Net Assets ($mil):	65.00	63.60	62.10	—	—
Net Income Dist ($):	0.64	0.66	0.55	—	—
Cap Gains Dist ($):	0.06	0.04	0.00	—	—
Total Dist ($)	0.70	0.70	0.55	—	—
Yield from Dist (%)	7.27	8.00	—	—	—
Expense Ratio (%)	1.00	1.02	1.10	—	—
Portfolio Turnover (%)	8.00	40.00	150.00	—	—
NAV per share ($)	9.80	9.60	9.32	—	—
Market Price per share	9.38	9.63	8.75	—	—
Premium (Discount) (%)	(4.29)	0.21	(6.12)	—	—
Total Return, Stk Price (%)	4.67	18.06	—	—	—

Federal Tax-Free Bond Funds   209

Municipal Premium Income Trust

Two World Trade Center, 71st Floor
New York, NY 10048
(800) 869-3863 / (212) 392-2550

NYSE : PIA

Transfer Agent
Dean Witter Trust Co.
Two Montgomery St.
Jersey City, NJ 07302
(800) 869-3863

Tax-Free Income

12 Months Ending 12/31/92 Results

	Period End	Period Begin	Distributions	Yield Dist (%)	Total Return (%)
Share Price ($)	10.63	9.88	0.76	7.69	15.28
NAV per share ($)	10.35	9.99		7.61	11.21

Background: Initial public offering February 1, 1989 of 6,900,000 shares at $10 per share. Initial NAV was $9.30 per share. In 1993, the fund changed its name and symbol from Allstate Municipal Premium Income Trust (ALI).

Objective: Seeks high current income exempt from regular Federal income tax. Invests in a leveraged portfolio of tax-free bonds.

Portfolio: (11/30/92) Municipal Bonds 94.6%, Short Term & Other 5.4%. Portfolio Ratings: AAA 33.0%, AA 20.0%, A 19.0%, BBB 28.0%.

Capitalization: (11/30/92) Common stock outstanding 26,243,024. Leveraged with 1,250 shares preferred stock, stated value $100,000 per share.

Average Maturity (years): 24.0
Fund Manager: Dean Witter Reynolds InterCapital Division   **Fee:** 0.50%
Income Dist: Monthly   **Capital Gains Dist:** Annually
Reinvestment Plan: Yes   **Shareholder Reports:** Quarterly

5 Year Performance

Fiscal Year Ending 5/31	1992	1991	1990	1989 (3 mos.)	1988
Net Assets ($mil):	388.00	373.20	368.10	249.60	—
Net Income Dist ($):	0.72	0.70	0.69	0.15	—
Cap Gains Dist ($):	0.05	0.07	0.11	0.00	—
Total Dist ($)	0.77	0.77	0.80	0.15	—
Yield from Dist (%)	8.00	8.56	8.42	—	—
Expense Ratio (%)	1.44	1.59	1.02	0.96	—
Portfolio Turnover (%)	16.00	56.00	150.00	106.00	—
NAV per share ($)	10.02	9.61	9.35	9.59	—
Market Price per share	10.38	9.63	9.00	9.50	—
Premium (Discount) (%)	3.49	0.10	(3.74)	(0.94)	—
Total Return, Stk Price (%)	15.78	15.56	3.16	—	—

MuniEnhanced Fund, Inc.

P.O. Box 9011
Princeton, NJ 08543-9011
(609) 282-2800

AMEX : MEN

Transfer Agent
State Street Bank & Trust Co.
225 Franklin Square
Boston, MA 02110
(800) 426-5523

Tax-Free Income

12 Months Ending 12/31/92 Results

	Period End	Period Begin	Distributions	Yield Dist (%)	Total Return (%)
Share Price ($)	12.88	12.88	1.27	9.86	9.86
NAV per share ($)	12.22	12.05		10.54	11.95

Background: Initial public offering February, 1989 of 25,000,000 shares at $12 per share. Initial NAV was $11.16 per share.

Objective: Seeks high current income from a portfolio of insured tax-exempt bonds of investment-grade quality. May use leverage.

Portfolio: (7/31/92) Sector Weightings: Water/Waste 15.5%, Health Care 15.0%, Transportation 10.0%, Utilities 8.2%, Government Obligations 9.0%. Quality Ratings: AAA & AA 99.3%, Other 0.7%.

Capitalization: (7/31/92) Common stock outstanding 28,032,318. Leveraged with auction-rate preferreds.

Average Maturity (years): 22.3
Fund Manager: Fund Asset Management, Inc. **Fee:** 0.50%
Income Dist: Monthly **Capital Gains Dist:** Annually
Reinvestment Plan: Yes **Shareholder Reports:** Quarterly

5 Year Performance

Fiscal Year Ending 1/31	1992	1991	1990 (11 mos.)	1989	1988
Net Assets ($mil):	485.30	485.20	455.60	—	—
Net Income Dist ($):	0.84	0.79	0.64	—	—
Cap Gains Dist ($):	0.20	0.00	0.00	—	—
Total Dist ($)	1.04	0.79	0.64	—	—
Yield from Dist (%)	9.24	7.35	—	—	—
Expense Ratio (%)	70.00	71.00	66.00	—	—
Portfolio Turnover (%)	70.17	116.42	30.44	—	—
NAV per share ($)	11.96	11.45	11.15	—	—
Market Price per share	12.63	11.25	10.75	—	—
Premium (Discount) (%)	5.52	(1.75)	(3.59)	—	—
Total Return, Stk Price (%)	21.51	12.00	—	—	—

Munilnsured Fund, Inc.

P.O. Box 9011
Princeton, NJ 08543-9011
(609) 282-2800

AMEX : MIF

Transfer Agent
State Street Bank & Trust Co.
225 Franklin St.
Boston, MA 02101
(617) 328-5000

Tax-Free Income

12 Months Ending 12/31/92 Results

	Period End	Period Begin	Distributions	Yield Dist (%)	Total Return (%)
Share Price ($)	10.00	10.38	0.84	8.09	4.43
NAV per share ($)	10.07	10.06		8.35	8.45

Background: Initial public offering October 19, 1987 of 7,475,000 shares at $10.00 per share. Initial NAV was $9.63 per share.

Objective: Seeks current income exempt from regular Federal income tax. Invests 80% in municipal obligations. Maturities are one year or more and are covered by insurance to guarantee the timely repayment of principal and interest. Will not invest more than 25% of total assets in municipal bonds whose issuers are located within the same state.

Portfolio: (12/31/92) Municipal Bonds 98.2%, Short Term & Other 1.8%. Portfolio Ratings: AAA 82.0%, AA 8.0%, A 4.0%, BBB 3.0%.

Capitalization: (9/30/92) Common stock outstanding 7,866,000.

Average Maturity (years): 21.0
Fund Manager: Fund Asset Management, Inc. **Fee:** 0.50%
Income Dist: Monthly **Capital Gains Dist:** Annually
Reinvestment Plan: Yes **Shareholder Reports:** Quarterly

5 Year Performance

Fiscal Year Ending 9/30	1992	1991	1990	1989	1988 (11 mos.)
Net Assets ($mil):	80.70	77.80	74.30	76.60	72.6
Net Income Dist ($):	0.62	0.63	0.64	0.66	0.68
Cap Gains Dist ($):	0.40	0.40	0.08	0.22	0.15
Total Dist ($)	1.02	1.03	0.72	0.88	0.83
Yield from Dist (%)	10.20	10.30	7.48	8.80	8.10
Expense Ratio (%)	0.85	0.89	0.91	0.88	0.76
Portfolio Turnover (%)	84.01	92.00	133.00	77.00	92.00
NAV per share ($)	10.26	10.21	9.68	10.00	9.87
Market Price per share	10.88	10.00	10.00	9.63	10.00
Premium (Discount) (%)	6.04	(2.06)	3.31	(3.70)	1.32
Total Return, Stk Price (%)	19.00	10.30	11.32	5.10	5.66

MuniVest Fund, Inc.
P.O. Box 9011
Princeton, NJ 08543-9011
(609) 282-2800

AMEX : MVF
Transfer Agent
The Bank of New York
110 Washington St.
New York, NY 10286
(800) 524-4458

Tax-Free Income

12 Months Ending 12/31/92 Results

	Period End	Period Begin	Distributions	Yield Dist (%)	Total Return (%)
Share Price ($)	10.75	10.75	1.06	9.86	9.86
NAV per share ($)	9.92	9.96		10.64	10.24

Background: Initial public offering September 23, 1988 of 48,000,000 shares at $10.00 per share. Initial NAV was $9.35 per share.

Objective: Seeks current income exempt from Federal income tax. Invests in a portfolio of investment-grade municipal bonds.

Portfolio: (12/31/92) Municipal Bonds 95.8%, Short Term & Other 4.2%. Portfolio Ratings: AAA 30.0%, AA 35.0%, A 19.0%, BBB 14.0%, Other 2%.

Capitalization: (12/31/92) Common stock outstanding 57,754,775. Leveraged with 2,750 shares preferred stock, stated value $100,000 per share.

Average Maturity (years): 22.6
Fund Manager: Fund Asset Management, Inc.   **Fee:** 0.50%
Income Dist: Monthly   **Capital Gains Dist:** Annually
Reinvestment Plan: Yes   **Shareholder Reports:** Quarterly

5 Year Performance

Fiscal Year Ending 8/31	1992	1991	1990	1989 (11 mos.)	1988
Net Assets ($mil):	876.00	838.90	802.60	812.00	—
Net Income Dist ($):	0.79	0.73	0.71	0.58	—
Cap Gains Dist ($):	0.16	0.00	0.05	0.00	—
Total Dist ($)	0.95	0.73	0.76	0.58	—
Yield from Dist (%)	9.27	7.78	7.89	—	—
Expense Ratio (%)	0.65	0.66	0.67	0.61	—
Portfolio Turnover (%)	112.10	129.73	112.81	52.63	—
NAV per share ($)	10.19	9.76	9.28	9.58	—
Market Price per share	11.25	10.25	9.38	9.63	—
Premium (Discount) (%)	10.40	5.02	1.08	0.52	—
Total Return, Stk Price (%)	19.02	17.06	5.30	—	—

MuniYield Fund

P.O. Box 9011
Princeton, NJ 08543-9011
(609) 282-2800

NYSE : MYD

Transfer Agent
The Bank of New York
110 Washington St.
New York, NY 10286
(800) 524-4458

Tax-Free Income

12 Months Ending 12/31/92 Results

	Period End	Period Begin	Distributions	Yield Dist (%)	Total Return (%)
Share Price ($)	15.38	15.50	1.24	8.00	7.23
NAV per share ($)	15.14	14.44		8.59	13.43

Background: Initial public offering November 29, 1991 at $15.00 per share. Initial NAV was $14.18 per share.

Objective: Seeks current income exempt from Federal income tax.

Portfolio: (10/31/92) Municipal Bonds 97.9%. State Weightings: Texas 15.0%, New York 14.9%, Illinois 5.6%, Washington 5.6%, Alaska 4.6%. Portfolio Ratings: AAA 10.0%, AA 38.0%, A 27.0%, BBB 17.0%, Lower& Non-Rated 8%.

Capitalization: (10/31/92) Common stock outstanding 35,823,165. Fund is leveraged with 5,000 shares auction market preferred stock with a $50,000 per share liquidation preference.

Average Maturity (years): 25.8
Fund Manager: Fund Asset Management, Inc.   **Fee:** 0.50%
Income Dist: Monthly   **Capital Gains Dist:** Annually
Reinvestment Plan: Yes   **Shareholder Reports:** Quarterly

5 Year Performance

Fiscal Year Ending 10/31	1992 (11 mos.)	1991	1990	1989	1988
Net Assets ($mil):	776.30	—	—	—	—
Net Income Dist ($):	0.89	—	—	—	—
Cap Gains Dist ($):	0.00	—	—	—	—
Total Dist ($)	0.89	—	—	—	—
Yield from Dist (%)	—	—	—	—	—
Expense Ratio (%)	0.65	—	—	—	—
Portfolio Turnover (%)	66.45	—	—	—	—
NAV per share ($)	14.69	—	—	—	—
Market Price per share	15.13	—	—	—	—
Premium (Discount) (%)	3.00	—	—	—	—
Total Return, Stk Price (%)	—	—	—	—	—

Nuveen Insured Municipal Opportunity Fund

NYSE : NIO

John Nuveen & Co. Inc.
Investment Bankers
333 West Wacker Dr.
Chicago, IL 60606
(800) 252-4630 / (312) 917-7700

Transfer Agent
U.S. Trust
Nuveen Exchange-Traded Fund Investor Services
770 Broadway
New York, NY 10003
(800) 257-8787

Tax-Free Income

12 Months Ending 12/31/92 Results

	Period End	Period Begin	Distributions	Yield Dist (%)	Total Return (%)
Share Price ($)	14.63	14.88	0.99	6.65	4.97
NAV per share ($)	14.94	14.38		6.88	10.78

Background: Initial public offering September 19, 1991 of 79,007,000 shares at $15 per share. Initial NAV was $14.05.

Objective: Seeks current income exempt from Federal income tax. Capital appreciation of the portfolio value relative to the municipal bond market is secondary. Fund will invest substantially all of its assets in investment-grade municipal bonds.

Portfolio: (1/1/93) Municipal Bonds 98.0%, Cash & Other 2.0%. Portfolio Ratings: AAA 86.0%, AA 7.0%, A 6.0%, BBB 1.0%.

Capitalization: (10/31/92) Common stock outstanding 79,506,000. Leveraged with $300,000,000 in municipal auction-rate preferred stock. No long-term debt.

Average Maturity (years): 24.4
Fund Manager: Nuveen Advisory Corporation
Income Dist: Monthly
Reinvestment Plan: Yes

Fee: 0.65%
Capital Gains Dist: Annually
Shareholder Reports: Semi-Annually

5 Year Performance

Fiscal Year Ending 10/31	1992	1991 (1 mo.)	1990	1989	1988
Net Assets ($mil):	1,787.60	1,436.30	—	—	—
Net Income Dist ($):	0.97	0.08	—	—	—
Cap Gains Dist ($):	0.00	0.00	—	—	—
Total Dist ($)	0.97	0.08	—	—	—
Yield from Dist (%)	6.52	—	—	—	—
Expense Ratio (%)	0.79	0.77	—	—	—
Portfolio Turnover (%)	13.00	0.00	—	—	—
NAV per share ($)	14.40	14.13	—	—	—
Market Price per share	14.00	14.88	—	—	—
Premium (Discount) (%)	(2.78)	5.24	—	—	—
Total Return, Stk Price (%)	0.60	—	—	—	—

Nuveen Insured Quality Municipal Fund

NYSE : NQI

John Nuveen & Co., Inc.
Investment Bankers
333 West Wacker Dr.
Chicago, IL 60606
(800) 252-4630 / (312) 917-7700

Transfer Agent
U.S. Trust
Nuveen Exchange-Traded Fund Investor Services
770 Broadway
New York, NY 10003
(800) 257-8787

Tax-Free Income

12 Months Ending 12/31/92 Results

	Period End	Period Begin	Distributions	Yield Dist (%)	Total Return (%)
Share Price ($)	16.13	15.88	1.12	7.05	8.63
NAV per share ($)	15.61	15.05		7.44	11.16

Background: Initial public offering December 19, 1990 of 33,000,000 shares at $15 per share. Initial NAV was $14.05 per share.

Objective: Seeks high current income exempt from Federal income tax. The portfolio is made up of insured municipal obligations, guaranteeing timely payment of principal and interest. The fund will obtain portfolio insurance for bonds rated below AAA.

Portfolio: (10/31/92) Municipal Bonds 98.0%, Cash & Other 2.0%. Portfolio Ratings: AAA 82%, AA 13%, A 4%, BBB 1%. All bonds are insured or backed by escrow account.

Capitalization: (10/31/92) Common stock outstanding 36,787,000. Leveraged with $260,000,000 in auction-rate preferred stock.

Average Maturity (years): 24.2
Fund Manager: Nuveen Advisory Corporation
Income Dist: Monthly
Reinvestment Plan: Yes

Fee: 0.60%
Capital Gains Dist: Annually
Shareholder Reports: Semi-Annually

5 Year Performance

Fiscal Year Ending 10/31	1992	1991 (11 mos.)	1990	1989	1988
Net Assets ($mil):	816.00	835.40	—	—	—
Net Income Dist ($):	1.07	0.68	—	—	—
Cap Gains Dist ($):	0.03	0.00	—	—	—
Total Dist ($)	1.09	0.68	—	—	—
Yield from Dist (%)	7.03	—	—	—	—
Expense Ratio (%)	0.78	0.77	—	—	—
Portfolio Turnover (%)	5.00	39.00	—	—	—
NAV per share ($)	15.11	14.85	—	—	—
Market Price per share	15.25	15.50	—	—	—
Premium (Discount) (%)	0.93	4.38	—	—	—
Total Return, Stk Price (%)	5.42	—	—	—	—

Nuveen Investment Quality Municipal Fund

NYSE : NQM

John Nuveen & Co., Inc.
Investment Bankers
333 West Wacker Dr.
Chicago, IL 60606
(800) 252-4630 / (312) 917-7700

Transfer Agent
U.S. Trust
Nuveen Exchange-Traded Fund Investor Services
770 Broadway
New York, NY 10003
(800) 257-8787

Tax-Free Income

12 Months Ending 12/31/92 Results

	Period End	Period Begin	Distributions	Yield Dist (%)	Total Return (%)
Share Price ($)	16.63	16.13	1.21	7.50	10.60
NAV per share ($)	15.73	15.31		7.90	10.65

Background: Initial public offering June 21, 1990 of 34,000,000 shares at $15 per share. Initial NAV was $14.05 per share.

Objective: Seeks to provide stable tax-free income from a high-quality portfolio of long-term, tax-free bonds.

Portfolio: (10/31/92) Municipal Bonds 95.1%, Short Term & Other 4.9%. Portfolio Ratings: AAA 30.0%, AA 24.0%, A 25.0%, BBB 20.0%, Non-Rated 1.0%.

Capitalization: (10/31/92) Common stock outstanding 34,752,000. Leveraged with 5,000 municipal auction-rate preferred shares, $50,000 per share liquidation preference.

Average Maturity (years): 22.4
Fund Manager: Nuveen Advisory Corporation
Income Dist: Monthly
Reinvestment Plan: Yes

Fee: 0.60%
Capital Gains Dist: Annually
Shareholder Reports: Semi-Annually

5 Year Performance

Fiscal Year Ending 10/31	1992	1991	1990 (4 mos.)	1989	1988
Net Assets ($mil):	783.20	797.90	—	—	—
Net Income Dist ($):	1.16	1.09	0.18	—	—
Cap Gains Dist ($):	0.00	0.00	0.00	—	—
Total Dist ($)	1.16	1.09	0.18	—	—
Yield from Dist (%)	7.25	7.71	—	—	—
Expense Ratio (%)	0.74	0.75	0.72	—	—
Portfolio Turnover (%)	5.00	3.00	0.00	—	—
NAV per share ($)	15.34	15.13	13.93	—	—
Market Price per share	15.75	16.00	14.13	—	—
Premium (Discount) (%)	2.67	5.75	1.36	—	—
Total Return, Stk Price (%)	5.69	20.95	—	—	—

Nuveen Municipal Advantage Fund

	NYSE : NMA
John Nuveen & Co., Inc.
Investment Bankers
333 West Wacker Dr.
Chicago, IL 60606
(800) 252-4630 / (312) 917-7700

Transfer Agent
U.S. Trust
Nuveen Exchange-Traded Fund Investor Services
770 Broadway
New York, NY 10003
(800) 257-8787

Tax-Free Income

12 Months Ending 12/31/92 Results

	Period End	Period Begin	Distributions	Yield Dist (%)	Total Return (%)
Share Price ($)	16.50	16.00	1.19	7.44	10.56
NAV per share ($)	15.52	15.09		7.89	10.74

Background: Initial public offering December 20, 1989 of 40,250,000 shares at $15 per share. Initial NAV was $14.05 per share.

Objective: Seeks high current income exempt from Federal income tax. Portfolio is at least 80% investment-grade, tax-free municipal securities. May invest 20% of assets in unrated securities which the adviser deems to be high-grade.

Portfolio: (10/31/92) Municipal Bonds: 100%. Portfolio Ratings: AAA 25.0%, AA 34.0%, A 15.0%, BBB 24.0%, Non-Rated 2.0%.

Capitalization: (12/31/92) Common stock outstanding 41,307,151. Fund is leveraged with $300,000,000 auction rate preferred stock.

Average Maturity (years): 24.0
Fund Manager: Nuveen Advisory Corporation
Income Dist: Monthly
Reinvestment Plan: Yes

Fee: 0.60%
Capital Gains Dist: Annually
Shareholder Reports: Semi-Annually

5 Year Performance

Fiscal Year Ending 10/31	1992	1991	1990 (10 mos.)	1989	1988
Net Assets ($mil):	923.40	941.015	859.50	—	—
Net Income Dist ($):	1.13	1.10	0.72	—	—
Cap Gains Dist ($):	0.02	0.00	0.00	—	—
Total Dist ($)	1.15	1.10	0.72	—	—
Yield from Dist (%)	7.30	7.93	—	—	—
Expense Ratio (%)	0.75	0.76	0.75	—	—
Portfolio Turnover (%)	7.00	5.00	3.00	—	—
NAV per share ($)	15.13	14.95	13.78	—	—
Market Price per share	15.25	15.75	13.88	—	—
Premium (Discount) (%)	0.79	5.35	0.65	—	—
Total Return, Stk Price (%)	4.13	21.40	—	—	—

Nuveen Municipal Income Fund, Inc.

John Nuveen & Co., Inc.
Investment Bankers
333 West Wacker Dr.
Chicago, IL 60606
(800) 252-4630 / (312) 917-7700

NYSE : NMI

Transfer Agent
U.S. Trust
Nuveen Exchange-Traded Fund Investor Services
770 Broadway
New York, NY 10003
(800) 257-8787

Tax-Free Income

12 Months Ending 12/31/92 Results

	Period End	Period Begin	Distributions	Yield Dist (%)	Total Return (%)
Share Price ($)	12.88	12.88	0.85	6.60	6.60
NAV per share ($)	12.24	12.10		7.02	8.18

Background: Initial public offering April 20, 1988 of 7,290,000 shares at $12 per share. Initial NAV was $11.21 per share.

Objective: Seeks high current income exempt from Federal income tax. At least 75% of the fund's assets will be invested in securities rated BBB or higher. The balance is invested in municipal obligations that may be unrated but have the credit characteristics of investment-grade municipal obligations. No more than 10% of net assets may be invested in municipal obligations rated B or lower.

Portfolio: (10/31/92) Municipal Bonds 96.5%, Short Term & Other 3.5%. Portfolio Rating: AAA 11.0%, AA 16.0%, A 22.0%, BBB 30.0%, Non-Rated 21.0%.

Capitalization: (10/31/92) Common stock outstanding 7,533,000. No long-term debt.

Average Maturity (years): 22.6
Fund Manager: Nuveen Advisory Corporation
Income Dist: Monthly
Reinvestment Plan: Yes

Fee: 0.65%
Capital Gains Dist: Annually
Shareholder Reports: Semi-Annually

5 Year Performance

Fiscal Year Ending 7/31	1992	1991	1990	1989	1988 (3 mos.)
Net Assets ($mil):	90.90	92.40	86.40	86.50	81.4
Net Income Dist ($):	0.85	0.84	0.84	0.82	0.10
Cap Gains Dist ($):	0.06	0.00	0.00	0.00	0.00
Total Dist ($)	0.91	0.84	0.84	0.82	0.10
Yield from Dist (%)	7.43	7.00	6.92	7.81	—
Expense Ratio (%)	0.76	0.69	0.72	0.73	0.73
Portfolio Turnover (%)	2.00	3.00	7.00	35.00	0.00
NAV per share ($)	12.41	11.90	11.71	11.81	11.15
Market Price per share	13.50	12.25	12.00	12.13	10.50
Premium (Discount) (%)	8.78	2.94	2.48	2.62	(5.83)
Total Return, Stk Price (%)	17.63	9.08	5.85	23.33	—

Nuveen Municipal Market Opportunity Fund

NYSE : NMO

John Nuveen & Co., Inc.	*Transfer Agent*
Investment Bankers	U.S. Trust
333 West Wacker Dr.	Nuveen Exchange-Traded Fund Investor Services
Chicago, IL 60606	770 Broadway
(800) 252-4630 / (312) 917-7700	New York, NY 10003
	(800) 257-8787

Tax-Free Income

12 Months Ending 12/31/92 Results

	Period End	Period Begin	Distributions	Yield Dist (%)	Total Return (%)
Share Price ($)	16.38	16.00	1.18	7.38	9.75
NAV per share ($)	15.79	15.33		7.70	10.70

Background: Initial public offering May 18, 1990 of 43,000,000 shares at $15 per share. Initial NAV was $14.05 per share.

Objective: Seeks current income exempt from Federal income tax from a leveraged portfolio of primarily long-term (20 to 30 year maturities) tax-free bonds rated BBB or better. Up to 20% may be invested in non-rated tax-free municipal obligations.

Portfolio: (10/31/92) Municipal Bonds 98.0%, Short Term & Other 2.0%. Portfolio Ratings: AAA 20.0%, AA 33.0%, A 27.0%, BBB 19.0%, Non-Rated 1.0%.

Capitalization: (10/31/92) Common stock outstanding 43,940,000. Leveraged with 6,000 shares preferred stock, stated value $50,000 per share.

Average Maturity (years): 23.1

Fund Manager: Nuveen Advisory Corporation	**Fee:** 0.60%
Income Dist: Monthly	**Capital Gains Dist:** Annually
Reinvestment Plan: Yes	**Shareholder Reports:** Semi-Annually

5 Year Performance

Fiscal Year Ending 10/31	1992	1991	1990 (5 mos.)	1989	1988
Net Assets ($mil):	975.40	958.80	901.80	—	—
Net Income Dist ($):	1.14	1.10	0.45	—	—
Cap Gains Dist ($):	0.01	0.00	0.00	—	—
Total Dist ($)	1.15	1.10	0.45	—	—
Yield from Dist (%)	7.42	7.93	—	—	—
Expense Ratio (%)	0.74	0.75	0.73	—	—
Portfolio Turnover (%)	5.00	7.00	3.00	—	—
NAV per share ($)	15.37	15.16	13.98	—	—
Market Price per share	15.38	15.50	13.88	—	—
Premium (Discount) (%)	0.07	2.24	(0.79)	—	—
Total Return, Stk Price (%)	6.65	19.60	—	—	—

Nuveen Municipal Value Fund, Inc.

NYSE : NUV

John Nuveen & Co., Inc.
Investment Bankers
333 West Wacker Dr.
Chicago, IL 60606
(800) 252-4630 / (312) 917-7700

Transfer Agent
U.S. Trust
Nuveen Exchange-Traded Fund Investor Services
770 Broadway
New York, NY 10003
(800) 257-8787

Tax-Free Income

12 Months Ending 12/31/92 Results

	Period End	Period Begin	Distributions	Yield Dist (%)	Total Return (%)
Share Price ($)	11.38	11.00	0.72	6.55	10.00
NAV per share ($)	10.69	10.48		6.87	8.87

Background: Initial public offering June 17, 1987 of 150,000,000 shares at $10 per share. Initial NAV was $9.35 per share.

Objective: Seeks current income exempt from Federal income tax. Capital appreciation is secondary and obtained through selection of municipal securities undervalued in the opinion of the investment adviser. 100% of net assets are invested in tax-exempt municipal obligations of which 80% are rated BBB or higher. The fund intends to invest in longer-term maturities depending upon market conditions.

Portfolio: (10/31/92) Municipal Bonds 98.1%, Short Term & Other 1.9%. Portfolio Ratings: AAA 17.0%, AA 24.0%, A 26.0%, BBB 26.0%, BB 2.0%, Lower & Non-Rated 5.0%.

Capitalization: (10/31/92) Common stock outstanding 164,230,000. No long-term debt.

Average Maturity (years): 21.4
Fund Manager: Nuveen Advisory Corporation
Income Dist: Monthly
Reinvestment Plan: Yes

Fee: 0.35%
Capital Gains Dist: Annually
Shareholder Reports: Semi-Annually

5 Year Performance

Fiscal Year Ending 10/31	1992	1991	1990	1989	1988
Net Assets ($mil):	1,726.31	1,759.30	1,595.20	1,613.40	1,572.10
Net Income Dist ($):	0.71	0.71	0.71	0.72	0.68
Cap Gains Dist ($):	0.05	0.01	0.03	0.03	0.00
Total Dist ($)	0.76	0.73	0.74	0.74	0.68
Yield from Dist (%)	6.99	7.30	7.31	7.49	7.77
Expense Ratio (%)	0.77	0.83	0.86	0.89	0.94
Portfolio Turnover (%)	8.00	7.00	5.00	7.00	42.00
NAV per share ($)	10.51	10.42	9.97	10.14	9.94
Market Price per share	11.00	10.88	10.00	10.13	9.88
Premium (Discount) (%)	4.66	4.41	0.30	(0.10)	(0.60)
Total Return, Stk Price (%)	8.09	16.10	6.02	10.02	20.69

Nuveen Performance Plus Municipal Fund, Inc.

NYSE : NPP

John Nuveen & Co., Inc.
Investment Bankers
333 West Wacker Dr.
Chicago, IL 60606
(800) 252-4630 / (312) 917-7700

Transfer Agent
U.S. Trust
Nuveen Exchange-Traded Fund Investor Services
770 Broadway
New York, NY 10003
(800) 257-8787

Tax-Free Income

12 Months Ending 12/31/92 Results

	Period End	Period Begin	Distributions	Yield Dist (%)	Total Return (%)
Share Price ($)	15.50	15.13	1.10	7.27	9.72
NAV per share ($)	15.33	14.90		7.38	10.27

Background: Initial public offering June 6, 1989 of 55,000,000 shares at $15 per share. Initial NAV was $14.05 per share.

Objective: Seeks a high level of current income exempt from Federal income tax from a portfolio of investment-grade municipal bonds or unrated bonds that are perceived to be of investment-grade quality.

Portfolio: (10/31/92) Municipal Bonds 97.8%, Short Term & Other 2.2%. Portfolio Ratings: AAA 31.0%, AA 35.0%, A 22.0%, BBB 11.0%, Non-Rated 1.0%.

Capitalization: (5/31/92) Common stock outstanding 572,393,000. Leveraged with 4,000 preferred shares, stated value $100,000 per share.

Average Maturity (years): 22.6
Fund Manager: Nuveen Advisory Corporation
Income Dist: Monthly
Reinvestment Plan: Yes

Fee: 0.60%
Capital Gains Dist: Annually
Shareholder Reports: Semi-Annually

5 Year Performance

Fiscal Year Ending 5/31	1992	1991	1990 (11 mos.)	1989	1988
Net Assets ($mil):	1,254.80	1,279.50	1,116.00	—	—
Net Income Dist ($):	1.04	1.03	0.70	—	—
Cap Gains Dist ($):	0.00	0.00	0.00	—	—
Total Dist ($)	1.04	1.03	0.70	—	—
Yield from Dist (%)	7.11	7.36	—	—	—
Expense Ratio (%)	0.74	0.75	0.71	—	—
Portfolio Turnover (%)	5.00	14.00	24.00	—	—
NAV per share ($)	14.96	14.28	13.68	—	—
Market Price per share	15.00	14.63	14.00	—	—
Premium (Discount) (%)	0.27	2.38	2.34	—	—
Total Return, Stk Price (%)	9.64	11.86	—	—	—

Nuveen Premier Insured Municipal Fund

John Nuveen & Co., Inc.
Investment Bankers
333 West Wacker Dr.
Chicago, IL 60606
(800) 252-4630 / (312) 917-7700

NYSE : NIF

Transfer Agent
U.S. Trust
Nuveen Exchange-Traded Fund Investor Services
770 Broadway
New York, NY 10003
(800) 257-8787

Tax-Free Income

12 Months Ending 12/31/92 Results

	Period End	Period Begin	Distributions	Yield Dist (%)	Total Return (%)
Share Price ($)	14.00	15.00	0.60	4.00	(2.67)
NAV per share ($)	14.64	14.04		4.27	8.55

Background: Initial public offering December 19, 1991 of 17,500,000 shares at $15 per share. Initial NAV was $14.04 per share.

Objective: Seeks current income exempt from Federal income tax.

Portfolio: (10/31/92) Municipal Bonds 100%. Portfolio Ratings: AAA 100%

Capitalization: (10/31/92) Common stock outstanding 19,091,000. Preferred shares outstanding 2,800, stated value $50,000 per share.

Average Maturity (years): 22.9
Fund Manager: Nuveen Advisory Corporation
Income Dist: Monthly
Reinvestment Plan: Yes

Fee: 0.65%
Capital Gains Dist: Annually
Shareholder Reports: Semi-Annually

5 Year Performance

Fiscal Year Ending 10/31	1992 (10 mos.)	1991	1990	1989	1988
Net Assets ($mil):	407.90	—	—	—	—
Net Income Dist ($):	0.60	—	—	—	—
Cap Gains Dist ($):	0.00	—	—	—	—
Total Dist ($)	0.60	—	—	—	—
Yield from Dist (%)	4.00	—	—	—	—
Expense Ratio (%)	0.81	—	—	—	—
Portfolio Turnover (%)	3.00	—	—	—	—
NAV per share ($)	14.64	—	—	—	—
Market Price per share	14.00	—	—	—	—
Premium (Discount) (%)	(4.37)	—	—	—	—
Total Return, Stk Price (%)	(2.67)	—	—	—	—

Nuveen Premier Municipal Income Fund

John Nuveen & Co., Inc.
Investment Bankers
333 West Wacker Dr.
Chicago, IL 60606
(800) 252-4630 / (312) 917-7700

NYSE : NPF
Transfer Agent
U.S. Trust
Nuveen Exchange-Traded Fund Investor Services
770 Broadway
New York, NY 10003
(800) 257-8787

Tax-Free Income

12 Months Ending 12/31/92 Results

	Period End	Period Begin	Distributions	Yield Dist (%)	Total Return (%)
Share Price ($)	14.25	15.13	0.83	5.49	(0.33)
NAV per share ($)	14.55	14.00		5.93	9.86

Background: Initial public offering on December 18, 1991 of 17,500,000 shares at $15 per share. Initial NAV was $14.05 per share.

Objective: Seeks current income exempt from Federal income taxes.

Portfolio: (10/31/92) Municipal Bonds 100%. Portfolio Ratings: AAA 11.0%, AA 33.0%, A 26.0%, BBB 22.0%, Non-Rated 8.0%.

Capitalization: (10/31/92) Common stock outstanding 19,594,000. Leveraged with 2,800 shares auction-rate preferred stock, stated value $50,000 per share.

Average Maturity (years): 21.5
Fund Manager: Nuveen Advisory Corporation **Fee:** 0.65%
Income Dist: Monthly **Capital Gains Dist:** Annually
Reinvestment Plan: Yes **Shareholder Reports:** Semi-Annually

5 Year Performance

Fiscal Year Ending 10/31	1992 (10 mos.)	1991	1990	1989	1988
Net Assets ($mil):	415.70	—	—	—	—
Net Income Dist ($):	0.64	—	—	—	—
Cap Gains Dist ($):	0.00	—	—	—	—
Total Dist ($):	0.64	—	—	—	—
Yield from Dist (%)	—	—	—	—	—
Expense Ratio (%)	0.79	—	—	—	—
Portfolio Turnover (%)	16.00	—	—	—	—
NAV per share ($)	14.07	—	—	—	—
Market Price per share	14.00	—	—	—	—
Premium (Discount) (%)	(0.50)	—	—	—	—
Total Return, Stk Price (%)	—	—	—	—	—

Nuveen Premium Income Municipal Fund

John Nuveen & Co., Inc.
Investment Bankers
333 West Wacker Dr.
Chicago, IL 60606
(800) 252-4630 / (312) 917-7700

NYSE : NPI
Transfer Agent
U.S. Trust
Nuveen Exchange-Traded Fund Investor Services
770 Broadway
New York, NY 10003
(800) 257-8787

Tax-Free Income

12 Months Ending 12/31/92 Results

	Period End	Period Begin	Distributions	Yield Dist (%)	Total Return (%)
Share Price ($)	16.88	16.88	1.23	7.29	7.29
NAV per share ($)	16.03	15.73		7.82	9.73

Background: Initial public offering July 21, 1988 of 50,000,000 shares at $15 per share. Initial NAV was $14.05 per share.

Objective: Seeks high current tax-free income from a diversified portfolio of investment-grade, tax-exempt municipal obligations rated BBB or better. Not more than 20% of assets may be invested in non-rated securities the adviser deems to be of investment-grade quality. During temporary defensive periods the fund may invest up to 100% of its assets in taxable securities. May use leverage.

Portfolio: (1/1/93) Municipal Bonds 100%. Portfolio Ratings: AAA 26.0%, AA 34.0%, A 24.0%, BBB 15.0%, Non-Rated 1.0%.

Capitalization: (10/31/92) Common stock outstanding 52,000,000. No long-term debt.

Average Maturity (years): 22.7
Fund Manager: Nuveen Advisory Corporation **Fee:** 0.65%
Income Dist: Monthly **Capital Gains Dist:** Annually
Reinvestment Plan: Yes **Shareholder Reports:** Semi-Annually

5 Year Performance

Fiscal Year Ending 5/31	1992	1991	1990	1989 (10 mos.)	1988
Net Assets ($mil):	1,173.30	1,188.00	1090.40	1089.20	—
Net Income Dist ($):	1.14	1.08	1.08	0.75	—
Cap Gains Dist ($):	0.00	0.00	0.00	0.00	—
Total Dist ($)	1.14	1.08	1.08	0.75	—
Yield from Dist (%)	7.41	7.20	7.45	—	—
Expense Ratio (%)	0.66	0.65	0.65	0.62	—
Portfolio Turnover (%)	2.00	1.00	4.00	9.00	—
NAV per share ($)	15.76	15.18	14.60	14.72	—
Market Price per share	16.25	15.38	15.00	14.50	—
Premium (Discount) (%)	3.11	1.25	2.74	(1.49)	—
Total Return, Stk Price (%)	13.07	9.73	10.90	—	—

Nuveen Quality Income Municipal Fund

NYSE : NQU

John Nuveen & Co., Inc.
Investment Bankers
333 West Wacker Dr.
Chicago, IL 60606
(800) 252-4630 / (312) 917-7700

Transfer Agent
U.S. Trust
Nuveen Exchange-Traded Fund Investor Services
770 Broadway
New York, NY 10003
(800) 257-8787

Tax-Free Income

12 Months Ending 12/31/92 Results

	Period End	Period Begin	Distributions	Yield Dist (%)	Total Return (%)
Share Price ($)	14.75	14.75	1.04	7.05	7.05
NAV per share ($)	15.15	14.55		7.15	11.27

Background: Initial public offering July 19, 1991 of 52,250,000 shares at $15 per share. Initial NAV was $14.05 per share.

Objective: Seeks current income exempt from Federal income taxes. Capital appreciation is secondary. The fund will invest in investment-grade municipal bonds or unrated securities that the fund advisor believes to be of investment-grade quality.

Portfolio: (1/1/93) Municipal Funds 97.8%, Short Term & Other 2.2%. Portfolio Ratings: AAA 32.0%, AA 21.0%, A 27.0%, BBB 16.0%, Non-Rated 4.0%.

Capitalization: (10/31/92) Common stock outstanding 52,717,000. Leveraged with 8,000 preferred shares, stated value $50,000 per share.

Average Maturity (years): 22.8
Fund Manager: Nuveen Advisory Corporation   **Fee:** 0.65%
Income Dist: Monthly   **Capital Gains Dist:** Annually
Reinvestment Plan: Yes   **Shareholder Reports:** Semi-Annually

5 Year Performance

Fiscal Year Ending 10/31	1992	1991 (3 mos.)	1990	1989	1988
Net Assets ($mil):	1,170.80	1,198.50	—	—	—
Net Income Dist ($):	1.02	0.17	—	—	—
Cap Gains Dist ($):	0.00	0.00	—	—	—
Total Dist ($)	1.02	0.17	—	—	—
Yield from Dist (%)	6.97	—	—	—	—
Expense Ratio (%)	0.78	0.74	—	—	—
Portfolio Turnover (%)	8.00	0.00	—	—	—
NAV per share ($)	14.62	14.29	—	—	—
Market Price per share	14.25	14.63	—	—	—
Premium (Discount) (%)	(2.53)	2.31	—	—	—
Total Return, Stk Price (%)	4.37	—	—	—	—

Putnam High Yield Municipal Trust
One Post Office Square
Boston, MA 02109
(800) 225-1000 / (617) 292-1000

NYSE : PYM
Transfer Agent
Putnam Investor Services
P.O. Box 2701
Boston, MA 02208
(800) 634-1587

Tax-Free Income

12 Months Ending 12/31/92 Results

	Period End	Period Begin	Distributions	Yield Dist (%)	Total Return (%)
Share Price ($)	10.25	9.75	0.81	8.31	13.44
NAV per share ($)	9.33	9.04		8.96	12.17

Background: Initial public offering May 18, 1989 of 18,500,000 shares at $10 per share. Initial NAV was $9.30 per share.

Objective: Seeks high current income through investments in BB or lower-rated municipal obligations.

Portfolio: (3/31/92) Municipal Bonds 100%. Sector Weightings: Health Care 25.3%, Pollution Control 17.9%, Ports/Airports 17.7%. State Weightings: Illinois 8.4%, Michigan 7.9%, Ohio 7.3%, Pennsylvania 7.1%, Georgia 7.1%. Portfolio Ratings: AAA 16.0%, AA 3.0%, A 10.0%, BBB 25.0%, BB 20.0%, B 21.0%, Non-Rated 2.0%.

Capitalization: (3/31/92) Shares of beneficial interest outstanding 20,436,551. Leveraged with 9,000 shares remarketed preferred stock with $50,000 per share liquidation preference.

Average Maturity (years): 23.7
Fund Manager: Putnam Management Company, Inc.   **Fee:** 0.70%
Income Dist: Monthly   **Capital Gains Dist:** Annually
Reinvestment Plan: Yes   **Shareholder Reports:** Quarterly

5 Year Performance

Fiscal Year Ending 3/31	1992	1991	1990 (10 mos.)	1989	1988
Net Assets ($mil):	228.70	178.90	186.50	—	—
Net Income Dist ($):	0.81	0.81	0.59	—	—
Cap Gains Dist ($):	0.00	0.00	0.00	—	—
Total Dist ($)	0.81	0.81	0.59	—	—
Yield from Dist (%)	8.87	8.76	—	—	—
Expense Ratio (%)	1.13	0.90	0.70	—	—
Portfolio Turnover (%)	62.28	19.69	48.90	—	—
NAV per share ($)	8.99	8.85	9.28	—	—
Market Price per share	9.88	9.13	9.25	—	—
Premium (Discount) (%)	9.79	3.16	(0.32)	—	—
Total Return, Stk Price (%)	17.09	7.46	—	—	—

Putnam Investment Grade Municipal Trust

One Post Office Square
Boston, MA 02109
(800) 225-1000 / (617) 292-1000

NYSE : PGM
Transfer Agent
Putnam Investors Services, Inc.
P.O. Box 41203
Providence, RI 02940
(800) 634-1587

Tax-Free Income

12 Months Ending 12/31/92 Results

	Period End	Period Begin	Distributions	Yield Dist (%)	Total Return (%)
Share Price ($)	13.25	12.50	0.92	7.36	13.36
NAV per share ($)	12.50	11.82		7.78	13.54

Background: Initial public offering October, 1989 of 17,000,000 shares at $12 per share. Initial NAV was $11.11 per share.

Objective: Seeks high current income exempt from regular Federal income taxes through investment in long-term, investment-grade municipal bonds.

Portfolio: (11/30/92) Municipal Bonds 100%. Sector Weightings: Utilities 33.8%, Transportation 16.7%, Housing 13.0%, Hospitals/Health Care 12.0%. State Weightings: Massachusetts 10.7%, New York 10.2%, Texas 9.4%, Washington 7.2%, Pennsylvania 6.5%.

Capitalization: (11/30/92) Common stock outstanding 19,560,916. Fund is leveraged with 1,400 remarketed preferred shares with $100,000 per share liquidation preference.

Average Maturity (years): 24.7
Fund Manager: Putnam Management Company, Inc.   **Fee:** 0.70%
Income Dist: Monthly   **Capital Gains Dist:** Annually
Reinvestment Plan: Yes   **Shareholder Reports:** Quarterly

5 Year Performance

Fiscal Year Ending 11/30	1992	1991	1990	1989 (1 mo.)	1988
Net Assets ($mil):	381.70	363.00	311.70	213.90	—
Net Income Dist ($):	0.91	0.89	0.87	0.00	—
Cap Gains Dist ($):	0.00	0.00	0.01	0.00	—
Total Dist ($)	0.91	0.89	0.88	0.00	—
Yield from Dist (%)	7.66	7.91	7.41	—	—
Expense Ratio (%)	1.45	1.46	1.21	0.12	—
Portfolio Turnover (%)	44.39	72.49	89.65	13.17	—
NAV per share ($)	12.36	11.51	11.03	11.19	—
Market Price per share	13.25	11.88	11.25	11.88	—
Premium (Discount) (%)	7.20	3.13	1.99	6.08	—
Total Return, Stk Price (%)	19.19	13.51	2.10	—	—

Putnam Managed Municipal Income Trust

One Post Office Square, 7th Floor
Boston, MA 02109
(800) 225-1000 / (617) 292-1000

NYSE : PMM
Transfer Agent
Putnam Investor Services
P.O. Box 41203
Providence, RI 02940
(800) 634-1587

Tax-Free Income

12 Months Ending 12/31/92 Results

	Period End	Period Begin	Distributions	Yield Dist (%)	Total Return (%)
Share Price ($)	10.63	10.13	0.84	8.29	13.23
NAV per share ($)	10.00	9.61		8.74	12.80

Background: Initial public offering February 16, 1989 of 40,000,000 shares at $10 per share. Initial NAV was $9.30 per share.

Objective: Seeks high current income exempt from Federal income tax. May invest up to 50% in municipal securities rated BB or lower.

Portfolio: (11/30/92) Sector Weightings: Utilities 20.1%, Health Care 18.2%. State Weightings: California 11.6%, Georgia 11.0%, Florida 9.4%, Texas 8.3%, New York 7.4%. Portfolio Ratings: AAA 22.0%, AA 12.0%, A 22.0%, BBB 21.0%, BB 10.0%, B 10.0%.

Capitalization: (10/31/92) Common stock outstanding 43,395,575. Leveraged with 1,750 shares remarketed preferred stock with $100,000 per share liquidation preference.

Average Maturity (years): 24.8
Fund Manager: Putnam Management Company, Inc.   **Fee:** 0.70%
Income Dist: Monthly   **Capital Gains Dist:** Annually
Reinvestment Plan: Yes   **Shareholder Reports:** Quarterly

5 Year Performance

Fiscal Year Ending 10/31	1992	1991	1990	1989 (7 mos.)	1988
Net Assets ($mil):	600.80	580.50	555.60	567.70	—
Net Income Dist ($):	0.76	0.76	0.76	0.47	—
Cap Gains Dist ($):	0.00	0.00	0.02	0.00	—
Total Dist ($)	0.76	0.76	0.78	0.47	—
Yield from Dist (%)	7.60	8.56	8.00	—	—
Expense Ratio (%)	1.24	1.33	1.29	0.62	—
Portfolio Turnover (%)	67.72	49.62	41.48	107.11	—
NAV per share ($)	9.81	9.44	8.94	9.31	—
Market Price per share	9.88	10.00	8.88	9.75	—
Premium (Discount) (%)	0.61	5.93	(0.78)	4.73	—
Total Return, Stk Price (%)	6.40	21.17	(0.92)	—	—

Seligman Quality Municipal Fund

130 Liberty St.
New York, NY 10006
(800) 221-2450 / (212) 488-0384

Transfer Agent
Union Data Service Center, Inc.
130 Liberty St.
New York, NY 10006
(800) 221-2450

Tax-Free Income

12 Months Ending 12/31/92 Results

	Period End	Period Begin	Distributions	Yield Dist (%)	Total Return (%)
Share Price ($)	14.25	14.75	0.88	5.97	2.58
NAV per share ($)	14.69	14.16		6.21	9.96

Background: Initial public offering November 22, 1991 of 4,600,000 shares at $15 per share. Initial NAV was $14.06 per share.

Objective: Seeks high current income exempt from Federal income taxes consistent with the preservation of capital. Will invest 80% of the portfolio in securities rated AAA.

Portfolio: (10/31/92) Municipal Bonds 95.5%, Variable Rate Demand Notes 1.9%, Short Term & Other 2.6%. Portfolio Ratings: A and above 100%.

Capitalization: (10/31/92) Common stock outstanding 4,007,000. Leveraged with 672 shares preferred stock, stated value $50,000 per share.

Average Maturity (years): 25.7
Fund Manager: J. & W. Seligman & Co., Inc.
Income Dist: Monthly
Reinvestment Plan: Yes

Fee: 0.60%
Capital Gains Dist: Annually
Shareholder Reports: Quarterly

5 Year Performance

Fiscal Year Ending 10/31	1992 (11 mos.)	1991	1990	1989	1988
Net Assets ($mil):	98.90	—	—	—	—
Net Income Dist ($):	0.70	—	—	—	—
Cap Gains Dist ($):	0.00	—	—	—	—
Total Dist ($)	0.70	—	—	—	—
Yield from Dist (%)	—	—	—	—	—
Expense Ratio (%)	0.94	—	—	—	—
Portfolio Turnover (%)	9.33	—	—	—	—
NAV per share ($)	14.05	—	—	—	—
Market Price per share	14.13	—	—	—	—
Premium (Discount) (%)	0.57	—	—	—	—
Total Return, Stk Price (%)	—	—	—	—	—

Seligman Select Municipal Fund

130 Liberty St.
New York, NY 10006
(800) 221-2450 / (212) 488-0384

NYSE : SEL
Transfer Agent
Union Data Service Center, Inc.
130 Liberty St.
New York, NY 10006
(800) 221-2450

Tax-Free Income

12 Months Ending 12/31/92 Results

	Period End	Period Begin	Distributions	Yield Dist (%)	Total Return (%)
Share Price ($)	12.75	12.25	0.86	7.02	11.10
NAV per share ($)	12.45	11.95		7.20	11.38

Background: Initial public offering February 15, 1990 of 12,750,000 shares at $12 per share. Initial NAV was $11.16 per share.

Objective: Seeks high current income exempt from regular Federal income tax. Capital appreciation is secondary. 80% of investments are rated AAA. The balance must be BBB or higher. All or a portion of the dividend may be subject to Federal Alternative Minimum Tax (AMT).

Portfolio: (12/31/92) Municipal Bonds 98.1%, Short Term & Other 1.9%. Portfolio Ratings: AAA 81.0%, AA 4.0%, A 6.0%, BBB 9.0%.

Capitalization: (12/31/92) Common stock outstanding 12,924,136. Leveraged with 750 shares preferred stock, stated value $100,000 per share.

Average Maturity (years): 25.5
Fund Manager: J. & W. Seligman & Co., Inc.
Income Dist: Monthly
Reinvestment Plan: Yes

Fee: 0.55%
Capital Gains Dist: Annually
Shareholder Reports: Quarterly

5 Year Performance

Fiscal Year Ending 12/31	1992	1991	1990 (10 mos.)	1989	1988
Net Assets ($mil):	235.80	228.50	217.40	—	—
Net Income Dist ($):	0.84	0.84	0.63	—	—
Cap Gains Dist ($):	0.02	0.00	0.00	—	—
Total Dist ($)	0.86	0.84	0.63	—	—
Yield from Dist (%)	7.02	7.47	—	—	—
Expense Ratio (%)	0.90	0.90	0.78	—	—
Portfolio Turnover (%)	3.90	7.36	10.75	—	—
NAV per share ($)	12.45	11.95	11.15	—	—
Market Price per share	12.75	12.25	11.25	—	—
Premium (Discount) (%)	2.41	2.51	0.90	—	—
Total Return, Stk Price (%)	11.10	16.36	—	—	—

Van Kampen Merritt Investment Grade Municipal Trust

NYSE : VIG

One Parkview Plaza
Oakbrook Terrace, IL 60181
(800) 225-2222 / (708) 684-6000

Transfer Agent
State Street Bank & Trust Co.
225 Franklin St.
P.O. Box 366
Boston MA 02101

Tax-Free Income
(800) 341-2929

12 Months Ending 12/31/92 Results

	Period End	Period Begin	Distributions	Yield Dist (%)	Total Return (%)
Share Price ($)	12.38	12.25	0.93	7.59	8.65
NAV per share ($)	11.43	11.61		8.01	6.46

Background: Initial public offering November 22, 1989 of 4,630,000 shares at $12 per share. Initial NAV was $11.16 per share.

Objective: Seeks high current income. At least 80% must be invested in securities rated BBB or higher. The remainder may be invested in lower-grade securities, but not lower than B-. The fund may invest a substantial portion in municipal securities subject to the Alternative Minimum Tax (AMT).

Portfolio: (10/31/92) Municipal Bonds 97.9%, Short Term & Other 2.1%. State Weightings: Illinois 28.7%, Colorado 9.2%, Florida 8.9%, Montana 5.2%, Idaho 4.7%. Portfolio Ratings: AAA 21.0%, AA 18.0%, A 12.0%, BBB 40.0%, BB 2.0%, Non-Rated 10.0%.

Capitalization: (10/31/92) Common stock outstanding 4,839,000 shares. Leveraged with 250 remarketable preferred shares with a par value of $100,000 per share.

Average Maturity (years): 24.5
Fund Manager: Van Kampen Merritt Investment Advisory Corp.   **Fee:** 0.60%
Income Dist: Monthly   **Capital Gains Dist:** Annually
Reinvestment Plan: Yes   **Shareholder Reports:** Quarterly

5 Year Performance

Fiscal Year Ending 10/31	1992	1991	1990 (11 mos.)	1989	1988
Net Assets ($mil):	79.00	80.70	77.40	—	—
Net Income Dist ($):	0.93	0.89	0.73	—	—
Cap Gains Dist ($):	0.00	0.00	0.00	—	—
Total Dist ($)	0.93	0.89	0.73	—	—
Yield from Dist (%)	7.59	8.48	—	—	—
Expense Ratio (%)	1.52	1.53	1.41	—	—
Portfolio Turnover (%)	20.87	52.20	133.73	—	—
NAV per share ($)	11.15	11.50	10.83	—	—
Market Price per share	11.75	12.25	10.50	—	—
Premium (Discount) (%)	5.37	6.50	(3.05)	—	—
Total Return, Stk Price (%)	3.51	25.14	—	—	—

Van Kampen Merritt Municipal Income Trust

One Parkview Plaza
Oakbrook Terrace, IL 60181
(800) 225-2222 / (708) 684-6000

Tax-Free Income

NYSE : VMT
Transfer Agent
State Street Bank & Trust Co.
225 Franklin St.
P.O. Box 366
Boston, MA 02101
(800) 451-6788

12 Months Ending 12/31/92 Results

	Period End	Period Begin	Distributions	Yield Dist (%)	Total Return (%)
Share Price ($)	12.00	10.75	0.98	9.12	20.74
NAV per share ($)	10.65	10.24		9.57	13.57

Background: Initial public offering August 26, 1988 of 24,000,000 shares at $10 per share. Initial NAV was $9.30 per share.

Objective: Seeks high current income exempt from Federal income tax with preservation of capital. The fund will invest 80% of its assets in investment-grade municipal obligations, including bonds, notes, and commercial paper. Options and futures contracts may be utilized for income enhancement.

Portfolio: (12/31/92) Municipal Bonds 99.8%, Cash & Short Term 0.2%. Sector Weightings: Health Care 19.5%, Single Family Housing 16.9%, Industrial Revenue 11.3%, General Purpose 8.0%. Portfolio Ratings: AAA 29.8%, AA 12.3%, A 25.6%, BBB 32.3%.

Capitalization: (9/30/92) Common stock outstanding 26,920,066. No long-term debt. Leveraged with 330 shares preferred stock, stated value $500,000 per share.

Average Maturity (years): 23.0
Fund Manager: Van Kampen Merritt Investment Advisory Corp.   **Fee:** 0.60%
Income Dist: Monthly   **Capital Gains Dist:** Annually
Reinvestment Plan: Yes   **Shareholder Reports:** Semi-Annually

5 Year Performance

Fiscal Year Ending 6/30	1992	1991	1990	1989 (10 mos.)	1988
Net Assets ($mil):	452.70	426.70	418.30	424.40	—
Net Income Dist ($):	0.79	0.73	0.69	0.50	—
Cap Gains Dist ($):	0.03	0.06	0.00	0.00	—
Total Dist ($)	0.82	0.78	0.69	0.50	—
Yield from Dist (%)	8.09	8.43	7.17	—	—
Expense Ratio (%)	0.84	0.89	0.87	0.92	—
Portfolio Turnover (%)	26.53	68.76	116.21	89.63	—
NAV per share ($)	10.69	9.81	9.53	9.77	—
Market Price per share	11.38	10.13	9.25	9.63	—
Premium (Discount) (%)	6.47	3.31	(2.98)	(1.51)	—
Total Return, Stk Price (%) ...	20.43	17.95	3.22	—	—

Van Kampen Merritt Municipal Trust

One Parkview Plaza
Oakbrook Terrace, IL 60181
(800) 225-2222 / (708) 684-6000

Tax-Free Income

NYSE : VKQ
Transfer Agent
State Street Bank & Trust Co.
225 Franklin St.
P.O. Box 366
Boston, MA 02101
(800) 426-5523

12 Months Ending 12/31/92 Results

	Period End	Period Begin	Distributions	Yield Dist (%)	Total Return (%)
Share Price ($)	15.63	15.13	1.20	7.93	11.24
NAV per share ($)	16.00	15.24		7.87	12.86

Background: Initial public offering October 17, 1991 of 30,577,325 shares at $15 per share. Initial net asset value was $15 per share.

Objective: Seeks a high level of current income exempt from Federal income tax, consistent with preservation of capital. The fund will invest at least 80% of its assets in investment-grade municipal securities.

Portfolio: (12/31/92) Municipal Bonds 98.0%. Sector Weightings: Industrial Revenue 22.4%, Single Family Housing 13.3%, General Purpose 10.5%, Health Care 7.2%, Waste Disposal 7.2%. Portfolio Ratings: AAA 12.1%, AA 10.5%, A 33.1%, BBB 36.2%, Non-Rated 8.1%.

Capitalization: (8/31/92) Common stock outstanding 36,235,976. Leveraged with 6,000 shares preferred stock, stated value $50,000 per share.

Average Maturity (years): 24.2

Fund Manager: Van Kampen Merritt Investment Advisory Corp.   **Fee:** 0.70%

Income Dist: Monthly   **Capital Gains Dist:** Annually

Reinvestment Plan: Yes   **Shareholder Reports:** Semi-Annually

5 Year Performance

Fiscal Year Ending 8/31	1992	1991	1990	1989	1988
	(10 mos.)				
Net Assets ($mil):	891.70	—	—	—	—
Net Income Dist ($):	0.81	—	—	—	—
Cap Gains Dist ($):	0.00	—	—	—	—
Total Dist ($)	0.81	—	—	—	—
Yield from Dist (%)	—	—	—	—	—
Expense Ratio (%)	1.03	—	—	—	—
Portfolio Turnover (%)	99.51	—	—	—	—
NAV per share ($)	16.33	—	—	—	—
Market Price per share	15.13	—	—	—	—
Premium (Discount) (%)	(7.40)	—	—	—	—
Total Return, Stk Price (%)	—	—	—	—	—

Term Trust Bond Funds

American Adjustable Rate Term Trust Inc. —1995
Piper Jaffray Tower
222 S. Ninth St.
Minneapolis, MN 55402
(800) 333-6000 / (612) 342-6426

NYSE : ADJ
Transfer Agent
Investors Fiduciary Trust Co.
127 W. 10th St.
Kansas City, MO 64105-1716
(816) 474-8786

Income

12 Months Ending 12/31/92 Results

	Period End	Period Begin	Distributions	Yield Dist (%)	Total Return (%)
Share Price ($)	10.25	10.38	0.73	7.03	5.78
NAV per share ($)	9.70	9.92		7.36	5.14

Background: Initial public offering March 29, 1990 of 11,000,000 shares at $10 per share. Initial NAV was $9.60 per share.

Objective: Seeks a high level of current income and to return $10 per share to common shareholders on or about April 15, 1995. Invests in adjustable-rate, mortgage-backed securities.

Portfolio: (12/22/92) Agency ARMs 38.9%, Private ARMs 29.4%, Other Agencies 18.7%, Tax-Exempt Zeros 8.2%, Canadian Government 2.1%, Other 0.5%.

Capitalization: (8/31/92) Common stock outstanding 11,110,000. No long-term debt.

Average Maturity (years): 11.3
Fund Manager: Piper Capital Management, Inc.   **Fee:** 0.35%
Income Dist: Monthly   **Capital Gains Dist:** Annually
Reinvestment Plan: Yes   **Shareholder Reports:** Semi-Annually

5 Year Performance

Fiscal Year Ending 8/31	1992	1991	1990 (5 mos.)	1989	1988
Net Assets ($mil):	111.00	708.40	707.40	—	—
Net Income Dist ($):	0.77	0.88	0.31	—	—
Cap Gains Dist ($):	0.01	0.01	0.00	—	—
Total Dist ($)	0.78	0.89	0.31	—	—
Yield from Dist (%)	7.70	9.13	—	—	—
Expense Ratio (%)	0.72	0.73	0.61	—	—
Portfolio Turnover (%)	55.00	66.00	33.00	—	—
NAV per share ($)	9.99	9.76	9.67	—	—
Market Price per share	10.50	10.13	9.75	—	—
Premium (Discount) (%)	5.11	3.69	0.83	—	—
Total Return, Stk Price (%)	11.35	13.03	—	—	—

American Adjustable Rate Term Trust Inc. —1996

Piper Jaffray Tower
222 S. Ninth St.
Minneapolis, MN 55402
(800) 333-6000 / (612) 342-6426

NYSE : BDJ

Transfer Agent
Investors Fiduciary Trust Co.
127 W. 10th St.
Kansas City, MO 64105-1716
(816) 474-8786

Income

12 Months Ending 12/31/92 Results

	Period End	Period Begin	Distributions	Yield Dist (%)	Total Return (%)
Share Price ($)	10.00	10.13	0.74	7.31	6.02
NAV per share ($)	9.43	9.66		7.66	5.28

Background: Initial public offering September 27, 1990 of 55,000,000 shares at $10 per share. Initial NAV was $9.60 per share.

Objective: Seeks high current income, and to distribute $10 per share to common shareholders on or about March 31, 1996. The fund will invest primarily in adjustable-rate, mortgage-backed securities. The fund may borrow up to 33-1/3% of the total value of its assets by entering into repurchase agreements.

Portfolio: (12/22/92) Agency ARMs 37.0%, Private ARMs 31.9%, Other Agencies 16.3%, Tax-Exempt Zeros 7.6%, Short-Term 4.4%, Canadian Government 2.5%, Other 0.3%.

Capitalization: (8/31/92) Common stock outstanding 26,930,000. No long-term debt.

Average Maturity (years): 16.0
Fund Manager: Piper Capital Management, Inc.   **Fee:** 0.35%
Income Dist: Monthly   **Capital Gains Dist:** Annually
Reinvestment Plan: Yes   **Shareholder Reports:** Semi-Annually

5 Year Performance

Fiscal Year Ending 8/31	1992	1991 (11 mos.)	1990	1989	1988
Net Assets ($mil):	262.30	259.50	—	—	—
Net Income Dist ($):	0.79	0.77	—	—	—
Cap Gains Dist ($):	0.00	0.00	—	—	—
Total Dist ($)	0.79	0.77	—	—	—
Yield from Dist (%)	7.80	—	—	—	—
Expense Ratio (%)	0.62	0.64	—	—	—
Portfolio Turnover (%)	26.00	60.00	—	—	—
NAV per share ($)	9.74	9.64	—	—	—
Market Price per share	10.25	10.13	—	—	—
Premium (Discount) (%)	5.24	4.98	—	—	—
Total Return, Stk Price (%)	8.98	—	—	—	—

American Adjustable Rate Term Trust, Inc. —1997

Piper Jaffray Tower
222 S. 9th St.
Minneapolis, MN 55402
(800) 333-6000 / (612) 342-6426

NYSE : CDJ

Transfer Agent
Investors Fiduciary Trust Co.
127 W. 10th St.
Kansas City, MO 64105
(816) 474-8786

Income

12 Months Ending 12/31/92 Results

	Period End	Period Begin	Distributions	Yield Dist (%)	Total Return (%)
Share Price ($)	9.88	10.00	0.75	7.50	6.30
NAV per share ($)	9.46	9.64		7.78	5.91

Background: Initial public offering July 24, 1991 of 21,856,590 shares of common stock at $10 per share. Initial NAV was $9.58 per share.

Objective: Seeks high current income and to return $10 per share to common shareholders on or about March 31, 1997. The fund will invest primarily in adjustable-rate, mortgage-backed securities.

Portfolio: (12/22/92) Agency ARMs 34.2%, Private ARMs 36.7%, Other Agencies 15.9%, Tax-Exempt Zeros 7.5%, Short Term 3.4%, Canadian Government 2.2%, Other 0.1%.

Capitalization: (8/31/92) Common stock outstanding 50,540,612. No long-term debt.

Average Maturity (years): 18.3
Fund Manager: Piper Capital Management, Inc.
Income Dist: Monthly
Reinvestment Plan: Yes

Fee: 0.35%
Capital Gains Dist: Annually
Shareholder Reports: Semi-Annually

5 Year Performance

Fiscal Year Ending 8/31	1992	1991 (1 mo.)	1990	1989	1988
Net Assets ($mil):	489.10	211.70	—	—	—
Net Income Dist ($):	0.80	0.00	—	—	—
Cap Gains Dist ($):	0.03	0.00	—	—	—
Total Dist ($)	0.83	0.00	—	—	—
Yield from Dist (%)	8.10	—	—	—	—
Expense Ratio (%)	0.60	0.60	—	—	—
Portfolio Turnover (%)	38.00	10.00	—	—	—
NAV per share ($)	9.68	9.68	—	—	—
Market Price per share	10.00	10.25	—	—	—
Premium (Discount) (%)	3.31	5.89	—	—	—
Total Return, Stk Price (%)	5.66	—	—	—	—

American Government Term Trust, Inc.

Piper Jaffray Tower
222 S. Ninth St.
Minneapolis, MN 55402
(800) 333-6000 / (612) 342-6223

NYSE : AGT

Transfer Agent
Investors Fiduciary Trust Co.
127 W. 10th St.
Kansas City, MO 64105-1716
(800) 543-1627

Income

12 Months Ending 12/31/92 Results

	Period End	Period Begin	Distributions	Yield Dist (%)	Total Return (%)
Share Price ($)	11.13	10.63	0.94	8.84	13.55
NAV per share ($)	9.49	10.08		9.33	3.47

Background: Initial public offering January 26, 1989 of 8,000,000 shares at $10 per share. Initial NAV was $9.35 per share.

Objective: Seeks high current income from a portfolio of mortgage-backed securities, other mortgage securities, and zero-coupon bonds. Will terminate operations and destribute net assets to shareholders on or shortly before August 31, 2001.

Portfolio: (11/30/92) U.S. Agency Mortgage Securities 47.8%, U.S. Government & Agency Zero-Coupon Bonds 30.7%, U.S. Agency & Other CMOs 10.4%, Residual Interests in CMOs 6.3%, Municipal Zero-Coupon Bonds 4.3%.

Capitalization: (11/30/92) Common stock outstanding 8,060,000. No long-term debt.

Average Maturity (years): 11.3
Fund Manager: Piper Capital Management, Inc.
Income Dist: Monthly
Reinvestment Plan: Yes

Fee: 0.45%
Capital Gains Dist: Annually
Shareholder Reports: Semi-Annually

5 Year Performance

Fiscal Year Ending 11/30	1992	1991	1990	1989 (10 mos.)	1988
Net Assets ($mil):	76.30	80.40	73.60	75.30	—
Net Income Dist ($):	0.85	0.95	0.90	0.81	—
Cap Gains Dist ($):	0.09	0.00	0.00	0.04	—
Total Dist ($)	0.94	0.95	0.90	0.85	—
Yield from Dist (%)	9.06	9.50	8.67	—	—
Expense Ratio (%)	1.04	1.11	1.05	0.99	—
Portfolio Turnover (%)	70.00	53.00	44.00	94.00	—
NAV per share ($)	9.47	9.97	9.13	9.34	—
Market Price per share	10.88	10.38	10.00	10.38	—
Premium (Discount) (%)	14.89	4.01	9.53	11.13	—
Total Return, Stk Price (%)	13.87	13.30	5.01	—	—

BlackRock 1998 Term Trust, Inc.

One Seaport Plaza
New York, NY 10292
(800) 227-7236 / (212) 214-3334

NYSE : BBT
Transfer Agent
State Street Bank & Trust Co.
One Heritage Drive
North Quincy, MA 02171
(800) 451-6788

Income

12 Months Ending 12/31/92 Results

	Period End	Period Begin	Distributions	Yield Dist (%)	Total Return (%)
Share Price ($)	9.88	10.25	0.78	7.61	4.00
NAV per share ($)	10.22	10.16		7.68	8.27

Background: Initial public offering April 19, 1991 of 51,000,000 shares of beneficial interest at $10 per share. Initial NAV was $9.50 per share.

Objective: Seeks high monthly income through a portfolio of high-quality mortgage-backed assets. The fund will liquidate on or shortly before December 31, 1998 when it will return all of its net assets to shareholders. The objective is to return at least $10 per share.

Portfolio: (12/31/92) Mortgage-Backed Securities 65%, U.S. Government & Agencies 11%, Zero-Coupon Bonds 13%, Asset-Backed Securities 11%.

Capitalization: (12/31/92) Common stock outstanding 58,660,527. No long-term debt.

Average Maturity (years): 10.0
Fund Manager: BlackRock Financial Management L.P.   **Fee:** 0.50%
Income Dist: Monthly   **Capital Gains Dist:** Annually
Reinvestment Plan: Yes   **Shareholder Reports:** Semi-Annually

5 Year Performance

Fiscal Year Ending 12/31	1992	1991 (8 mos.)	1990	1989	1988
Net Assets ($mil):	599.30	595.70	—	—	—
Net Income Dist ($):	0.78	0.42	—	—	—
Cap Gains Dist ($):	0.00	0.00	—	—	—
Total Dist ($)	0.78	0.42	—	—	—
Yield from Dist (%)	7.61	—	—	—	—
Expense Ratio (%)	0.82	0.78	—	—	—
Portfolio Turnover (%)	8.00	154.00	—	—	—
NAV per share ($)	10.22	10.16	—	—	—
Market Price per share	9.88	10.25	—	—	—
Premium (Discount) (%)	(3.33)	0.89	—	—	—
Total Return, Stk Price (%)	4.00	—	—	—	—

Term Trust Bond Funds   239

BlackRock Advantage Term Trust, Inc.

One Seaport Plaza
New York, NY 10292
(800) 227-7236 / (212) 214-3334

NYSE : BAT
Transfer Agent
State Street Bank & Trust Co.
One Heritage Drive
North Quincy, MA 02171
(800) 451-6788

Income

12 Months Ending 12/31/92 Results

	Period End	Period Begin	Distributions	Yield Dist (%)	Total Return (%)
Share Price ($)	10.63	11.25	0.90	8.00	2.49
NAV per share ($)	10.43	10.96		8.21	3.38

Background: Initial public offering April 17, 1990 of 9,375,000 shares at $10 per share. Initial NAV was $9.30 per share.

Objective: Seeks high monthly income and return of $10 per share on or shortly before December 31, 2005. At least 80% of the fund's assets are in mortgage-backed securities and zero-coupon securities rated AAA or guaranteed by the U.S. Government.

Portfolio: (12/31/92) Mortgage-Backed Securities 42.0%, U.S. Government & Agencies 24.1%, Taxable Zero-Coupon Bonds 25.0%, Municipal Zero-Coupon Bonds 8.0%, Asset-Backed Securities 1.0%.

Capitalization: (12/31/92) Common stock outstanding 9,510,667. No long-term debt.

Average Maturity (years): 10.5
Fund Manager: BlackRock Financial Management L.P.   **Fee:** 0.60%
Income Dist: Monthly   **Capital Gains Dist:** Annually
Reinvestment Plan: Yes   **Shareholder Reports:** Quarterly

5 Year Performance

Fiscal Year Ending 12/31	1992	1991	1990 (9 mos.)	1989	1988
Net Assets ($mil):	99.10	104.20	94.00	—	—
Net Income Dist ($):	0.90	1.06	0.51	—	—
Cap Gains Dist ($):	0.00	0.00	0.06	—	—
Total Dist ($)	0.90	1.06	0.57	—	—
Yield from Dist (%)	8.00	10.60	—	—	—
Expense Ratio (%)	1.37	1.30	1.17	—	—
Portfolio Turnover (%)	3.00	254.00	180.00	—	—
NAV per share ($)	10.43	10.96	9.89	—	—
Market Price per share	10.63	11.25	10.00	—	—
Premium (Discount) (%)	1.92	2.65	1.11	—	—
Total Return, Stk Price (%)	2.49	23.10	—	—	—

BlackRock Strategic Term Trust

One Seaport Plaza
New York, NY 10292
(800) 227-7236 / (212) 214-3334

NYSE : BGT
Transfer Agent
Dean Witter Trust Co.
2 Montgomery St.
Jersey City, NJ 07302
(800) 526-3134

Income

12 Months Ending 12/31/92 Results

	Period End	Period Begin	Distributions	Yield Dist (%)	Total Return (%)
Share Price ($)	9.88	10.38	0.90	8.67	3.85
NAV per share ($)	9.76	9.94		9.05	7.24

Background: Initial public offering December 20, 1990 of 50,000,000 shares at $10 per share. Initial NAV was $9.40 per share.

Objective: Seeks high current income from a portfolio of AAA- and AA-rated mortgage-backed securities. The fund seeks to return $10 per share in 2002.

Portfolio: (12/31/92) Mortgage-Backed 75.0%, Taxable Zero-Coupon Bonds 16.0%, Municipal Zero-Coupon Bonds 5.0%, Asset-Backed Securities 4.0%.

Capitalization: (12/31/92) Common stock outstanding 57,510,639. No long-term debt.

Average Maturity (years): 12.0
Fund Manager: BlackRock Financial Management L.P.   **Fee:** 0.60%
Income Dist: Monthly   **Capital Gains Dist:** Annually
Reinvestment Plan: Yes   **Shareholder Reports:** Semi-Annually

5 Year Performance

Fiscal Year Ending 12/31	1992	1991 (11 mos.)	1990	1989	1988
Net Assets ($mil):	561.40	571.60	—	—	—
Net Income Dist ($):	0.90	0.81	—	—	—
Cap Gains Dist ($):	0.00	0.00	—	—	—
Total Dist ($)	0.90	0.81	—	—	—
Yield from Dist (%)	8.67	—	—	—	—
Expense Ratio (%)	0.92	0.96	—	—	—
Portfolio Turnover (%)	18.00	199.00	—	—	—
NAV per share ($)	9.76	9.94	—	—	—
Market Price per share	9.88	10.38	—	—	—
Premium (Discount) (%)	1.23	4.33	—	—	—
Total Return, Stk Price (%)	3.85	—	—	—	—

BlackRock Target Term Trust, Inc.

One Seaport Plaza
New York, NY 10292
(800) 227-7236 / (212) 214-3334

NYSE : BTT

Transfer Agent
State Street Bank & Trust Co.
One Heritage Drive
North Quincy, MA 02171
(800) 451-6788

Income

12 Months Ending 12/31/92 Results

	Period End	Period Begin	Distributions	Yield Dist (%)	Total Return (%)
Share Price ($)	10.00	10.75	0.87	8.09	1.12
NAV per share ($)	10.28	10.14		8.58	9.96

Background: Initial public offering November 8, 1988 of 83,000,000 shares at $10 per share. Initial NAV was $9.39 per share.

Objective: Seeks high monthly income and to return $10 per share to common shareholders on or about December 31, 2001.

Portfolio: (12/31/92) Mortgage-Backed Securities 54.0%, Taxable Zero-Coupon Bonds 39.0%, Municipal Zero-Coupon Bonds 3.0%, Asset-Backed Securities 4.0%.

Capitalization: (12/31/92) Common stock outstanding 95,460,639. No long-term debt.

Average Maturity (years): 9.4

Fund Manager: BlackRock Financial Management L.P.   **Fee:** 0.60%

Income Dist: Monthly   **Capital Gains Dist:** Annually

Reinvestment Plan: Yes   **Shareholder Reports:** Semi-Annually

5 Year Performance

Fiscal Year Ending 12/31	1992	1991	1990	1989 (11 mos.)	1988
Net Assets ($mil):	981.30	967.70	882.40	902.10	—
Net Income Dist ($):	0.87	0.95	0.96	0.83	—
Cap Gains Dist ($):	0.00	0.00	0.00	0.00	—
Total Dist ($)	0.87	0.95	0.96	0.83	—
Yield from Dist (%)	8.09	9.50	9.85	—	—
Expense Ratio (%)	0.89	0.92	0.92	0.92	—
Portfolio Turnover (%)	30.00	279.00	114.00	177.00	—
NAV per share ($)	10.28	10.14	9.24	9.45	—
Market Price per share	10.00	10.75	10.00	9.75	—
Premium (Discount) (%)	(2.72)	6.02	8.23	3.17	—
Total Return, Stk Price (%)	1.12	17.00	12.41	—	—

9

Equity Fund Summaries

Convertible (Bond & Equity) Funds

AIM Strategic Income Fund, Inc.

11 Greenway Plaza, Suite 1919
Houston, TX 77046
(800) 347-1919

AMEX : AST
Transfer Agent
State Street Bank & Trust Co.
1776 Heritage Dr.
North Quincy, MA 02171
(800) 426-5523

Growth & Income

12 Months Ending 12/31/92 Results

	Period End	Period Begin	Distributions	Yield Dist (%)	Total Return (%)
Share Price ($)	9.13	8.50	0.78	9.18	16.59
NAV per share ($)	9.29	9.15		8.52	10.05

Background: Initial public offering March 23, 1989 of 5,700,000 shares at $10 per share. Initial NAV was $9.23 per share.

Objective: Seeks high current income consistent with stability of principal. Invests in convertible securities and employs short-selling to enhance income and to hedge against market risk.

Portfolio: (12/31/92) Convertible Bonds & Notes 85.9%, Convertible Preferred Stocks 18.1%. Sector Weightings: Capital Goods 25.6%, Retail 15.3%, Consumer Nondurables 10.2%, Consumer Durables 9.9%, Wholesale 8.9%. Largest Holdings: International Game Technology 3.9%, Home Depot 3.6%, Motorola, Inc. 3.4%, Clayton Homes, Inc. 3.2%, Office Depot, Inc. 3.2%.

Capitalization: (12/31/92) Common stock outstanding 6,966,568. No long-term debt.

Beta: 0.65
Fund Manager: AIM Advisors, Inc.   **Fee:** 0.80%
Income Dist: Monthly   **Capital Gains Dist:** Annually
Reinvestment Plan: Yes   **Shareholder Reports:** Semi-Annually

5 Year Performance

Fiscal Year Ending 12/31	1992	1991	1990	1989 (9 mos.)	1988
Net Assets ($mil):	64.70	63.10	59.60	62.10	—
Net Income Dist ($):	0.60	0.80	0.98	0.77	—
Cap Gains Dist ($):	0.18	0.05	0.04	0.00	—
Total Dist ($)	0.78	0.85	1.02	0.77	—
Yield from Dist (%)	9.18	10.79	10.46	—	—
Expense Ratio (%)	1.66	1.60	1.58	1.40	—
Portfolio Turnover (%)	89.70	89.40	91.73	161.82	—
NAV per share ($)	9.29	9.15	8.64	9.12	—
Market Price per share	9.13	8.50	7.88	9.75	—
Premium (Discount) (%)	(1.72)	(7.10)	(8.80)	6.91	—
Total Return, Stk Price (%)	16.59	18.65	(8.72)	—	—

American Capital Convertible Securities, Inc.

Boston Financial Data Services
P.O. Box 366
Boston, MA 02101
(800) 421-9696 / (713) 993-0500

Transfer Agent
Boston Financial Data Services
P.O. Box 366
Boston, MA 02101
(800) 821-1238

Growth & Income

12 Months Ending 12/31/92 Results

	Period End	Period Begin	Distributions	Yield Dist (%)	Total Return (%)
Share Price ($)	20.38	19.25	1.18	6.13	12.00
NAV per share ($)	23.64	22.23		5.31	11.65

Background: Formerly known as American General Convertible Securities. Initial public offering was June 1, 1972 at $25 per share. Beginning net assets approximately $69.5 million.

Objective: Seeks current income with potential for long-term capital appreciation. Invests at least 80% of total assets in convertible securities and debt securities which may be acquired with warrants.

Portfolio: (12/31/92) Convertible Corporate Bonds 51.0%, Convertible Preferred Stock 19.0%, Non-Convertible Corporate Bonds 6.0%, Common Stock 18.0%, Other 6.0%.

Capitalization: (12/31/92) Common stock outstanding 3,242,000. No long-term debt.

Beta: 1.24
Fund Manager: American Capital Asset Management, Inc. **Fee:** 0.50%
Income Dist: Quarterly **Capital Gains Dist:** Annually
Reinvestment Plan: Yes **Shareholder Reports:** Semi-Annually

5 Year Performance

Fiscal Year Ending 12/31	1992	1991	1990	1989	1988
Net Assets ($mil):	76.60	72.10	62.90	73.70	—
Net Income Dist ($):	1.18	1.40	1.40	1.57	1.47
Cap Gains Dist ($):	0.00	0.00	0.14	0.75	1.33
Total Dist ($)	1.18	1.40	1.54	2.32	2.80
Yield from Dist (%)	6.13	8.62	7.65	11.67	11.43
Expense Ratio (%)	0.88	0.89	0.86	0.84	0.82
Portfolio Turnover (%)	87.00	168.00	95.00	90.00	69.00
NAV per share ($)	23.64	22.23	19.41	22.73	21.94
Market Price per share	20.38	19.25	16.25	20.13	19.88
Premium (Discount) (%)	(13.79)	(13.41)	(16.28)	(11.48)	(9.43)
Total Return, Stk Price (%)	12.00	27.08	(11.62)	12.93	(7.43)

Bancroft Convertible Fund, Inc.

56 Pine St., Suite 310
New York, NY 10005
(212) 269-9236

Growth & Income

AMEX : BCV
Transfer Agent
Mellon Securities Trust Co.
P.O. Box 470
Washington Bridge Station
New York, NY 10033
(800) 526-0801

12 Months Ending 12/31/92 Results

	Period End	Period Begin	Distributions	Yield Dist (%)	Total Return (%)
Share Price ($)	20.38	18.50	2.18	11.78	21.95
NAV per share ($)	23.25	20.93		10.42	21.50

Background: Initial public offering October 4, 1971 of 2,000,000 shares at $25 per share. Initial NAV was $22.93 per share. On November 10, 1988 the fund increased its shares with a rights offering to stockholders of record. Subscription price was $17.32 per share.

Objective: Seeks income and potential for capital appreciation. Invests at least 80% of total assets in debt securities and preferred stocks convertible into (or having the right to purchase) common stock or other equity securities.

Portfolio: (10/31/92) Bonds & Notes 78.0%, Preferred Stock 18.4%, Common Stock 4.7%, Other Assets & Liabilities (1.1%). Sector Weightings: Energy 14.9%, Banking 13.6%, Financial/Insurance 12.9%, Broadcasting/Cable 6.9%, Automotive 5.3%.

Capitalization: (10/31/92) Common stock outstanding 2,612,954. No long-term debt.

Beta: 0.68
Fund Manager: Davis/Dinsmore Management Co.   **Fee:** 0.75%
Income Dist: Quarterly   **Capital Gains Dist:** Annually
Reinvestment Plan: Yes   **Shareholder Reports:** Quarterly

5 Year Performance

Fiscal Year Ending 10/31	1992	1991	1990	1989	1988 (7 mos.)
Net Assets ($mil):	59.40	54.90	46.70	54.70	—
Net Income Dist ($):	1.32	1.46	1.40	1.36	0.40
Cap Gains Dist ($):	0.00	0.00	0.39	0.25	0.91
Total Dist ($)	1.32	1.46	1.79	1.61	1.31
Yield from Dist (%)	7.18	9.49	9.68	7.80	6.55
Expense Ratio (%)	1.20	1.30	1.40	1.50	1.70
Portfolio Turnover (%)	71.30	38.80	18.00	51.40	29.10
NAV per share ($)	22.75	21.02	17.86	21.40	22.63
Market Price per share	20.63	18.38	15.38	18.50	20.63
Premium (Discount) (%)	(9.36)	(12.61)	(13.94)	(13.55)	(8.88)
Total Return, Stk Price (%)	19.42	29.00	(7.19)	(2.52)	9.70

Castle Convertible Fund, Inc.

75 Maiden Ln.
New York, NY 10038
(212) 806-8800

Growth & Income

AMEX : CVF

Transfer Agent
Alger Shareholder Services, Inc.
30 Montgomery St.
Box 2001
Jersey City, NJ 07302-9811
(201) 547-3621

12 Months Ending 12/31/92 Results

	Period End	Period Begin	Distributions	Yield Dist (%)	Total Return (%)
Share Price ($)	23.75	20.75	1.82	8.77	23.23
NAV per share ($)	25.54	23.57		7.72	16.08

Background: Began operations as C.I. Convertible Fund, Inc. Raised approximately $22.5 million in its initial public offering in November 1971. Offer price was $25 per share. Initial NAV was $23.13 per share. An offering of warrants in 1985 raised an additional $26,543,400.

Objective: Seeks current income and possible long-term capital appreciation. The fund will invest at least 65% of its assets in convertible bonds and convertible preferreds. Leverage may be used.

Portfolio: (6/30/92) Corporate Bonds & Notes 66.0%, Convertible Preferred Stock 24.0%, Common Stock 11%. Sector Weightings: Electronics 12.0%, Utilities 12.0%, Drugs & Health Care 8.0%, Insurance 8.0%, Computer & Business Equipment 7.0%.

Capitalization: (6/30/92) Common stock outstanding 2,211,863. No long-term debt.

Beta: 0.89
Fund Manager: Fred Alger Management, Inc.   **Fee:** 0.75%
Income Dist: Quarterly   **Capital Gains Dist:** Annually
Reinvestment Plan: Yes   **Shareholder Reports:** Semi-Annually

5 Year Performance

Fiscal Year Ending 6/30	1992	1991	1990	1989	1988
Net Assets ($mil):	53.50	49.10	47.90	47.80	49.70
Net Income Dist ($):	1.70	1.66	1.67	1.88	2.98
Cap Gains Dist ($):	0.00	0.00	0.00	0.00	1.17
Total Dist ($)	1.70	1.66	1.67	1.88	4.15
Yield from Dist (%)	9.13	8.79	8.96	8.40	15.51
Expense Ratio (%)	1.10	1.15	1.16	1.26	1.20
Portfolio Turnover (%)	68.69	48.37	64.93	71.29	68.29
NAV per share ($)	24.20	22.18	21.65	21.59	22.53
Market Price per share	21.25	18.63	18.88	18.63	22.38
Premium (Discount) (%)	(12.19)	(16.01)	(12.84)	(13.76)	(0.71)
Total Return, Stk Price (%)	23.19	7.47	10.31	(8.36)	(0.82)

Convertible (Bond & Equity) Funds   247

Ellsworth Convertible Growth & Income Fund

56 Pine St.
New York, NY 10005
(212) 269-9236

Transfer Agent
The Bank of New York
101 Barclay St.
New York, NY 10286
(800) 524-4458

Growth & Income

12 Months Ending 12/31/92 Results

	Period End	Period Begin	Distributions	Yield Dist (%)	Total Return (%)
Share Price ($)	8.25	7.38	0.62	8.40	20.19
NAV per share ($)	9.42	8.66		7.16	15.94

Background: Initial public offering June 30, 1986 of 5,725,000 shares at $10 per share. Initial NAV was $9.30 per share.

Objective: Seeks a high level of total return through current income and capital appreciation. Under normal conditions the fund will invest at least 65% of its assets in convertibles and common stock received from conversion. The fund may use arbitrage techniques and covered call writing to enhance distributions. Up to 10% of assets may be invested in foreign securities and restricted securities.

Portfolio: (12/31/92) Corporate Bonds & Notes 74.5%, Preferred Stock 20.7%, Common Stocks 3.4%. Sector Weightings: Banking 14.9%, Energy 12.6%, Financial & Insurance 13.0%, Broadcasting & Cable 7.3%, Automotive 6.8%.

Capitalization: (9/30/92) Common stock outstanding 6,118,443. No long-term debt.

Beta: 0.72

Fund Manager: Davis, Dinsmore Management Co. **Fee:** 0.75%

Income Dist: Quarterly **Capital Gains Dist:** Annually

Reinvestment Plan: Yes **Shareholder Reports:** Quarterly

5 Year Performance

Fiscal Year Ending 9/30	1992	1991	1990	1989	1988
Net Assets ($mil):	56.90	51.70	45.90	53.80	51.80
Net Income Dist ($):	0.50	0.58	0.65	0.56	0.55
Cap Gains Dist ($):	0.00	0.00	0.16	0.20	0.45
Total Dist ($)	0.50	0.58	0.81	0.76	1.00
Yield from Dist (%)	6.78	9.09	10.28	10.30	12.12
Expense Ratio (%)	1.20	1.40	1.30	1.40	1.40
Portfolio Turnover (%)	70.00	37.00	23.00	34.00	32.00
NAV per share ($)	9.31	8.45	7.50	9.00	8.66
Market Price per share	8.38	7.38	6.38	7.88	7.38
Premium (Discount) (%)	(9.99)	(12.66)	(15.07)	(12.56)	(14.90)
Total Return, Stk Price (%)	20.33	24.76	(8.76)	17.07	1.58

Lincoln National Convertible Securities Fund, Inc.

1300 S. Clinton St.
Fort Wayne, IN 46801
(219) 455-2210

NYSE : LNV
Transfer Agent
First National Bank of Boston
P.O. Box 644
Boston, MA 02102
(800) 442-2001

Income

12 Months Ending 12/31/92 Results

	Period End	Period Begin	Distributions	Yield Dist (%)	Total Return (%)
Share Price ($)	16.50	15.50	2.14	13.81	20.26
NAV per share ($)	17.62	18.04		11.86	9.53

Background: Initial public offering June 19, 1986 of 6,900,000 shares at $15 per share. Initial NAV was $13.96 per share.

Objective: Seeks a high level of total return through capital appreciation and current income. Invests at least 65% of assets in convertible securities, including direct placements.

Portfolio: (12/31/92) Public Debt Securities 52%, Direct Placement Securities 15%, Convertible Preferred Stocks/Public Issues 30%, Common Stock 2.0%, Short Term 1%.

Capitalization: (12/31/92) Common stock outstanding 6,286,361. No long-term debt.

Beta: 1.42
Fund Manager: Lincoln National Investment Management Co.　　　　**Fee:** 0.60%
Income Dist: Quarterly　　　　　　　　　　　　　　**Capital Gains Dist:** Annually
Reinvestment Plan: Yes　　　　　　　　　　　**Shareholder Reports:** Quarterly

5 Year Performance

Fiscal Year Ending 12/31	1992	1991	1990	1989	1988
Net Assets ($mil):	110.70	113.40	85.40	95.70	91.60
Net Income Dist ($):	0.97	1.02	1.02	1.07	0.95
Cap Gains Dist ($):	1.17	0.00	0.00	0.50	0.00
Total Dist ($)	2.14	1.02	1.02	1.57	0.95
Yield from Dist (%)	13.81	8.87	7.62	11.63	8.09
Expense Ratio (%)	0.83	0.89	0.97	0.94	0.96
Portfolio Turnover (%)	166.26	132.99	134.64	147.31	110.70
NAV per share ($)	17.62	18.04	13.59	15.21	13.41
Market Price per share	16.50	15.50	11.50	13.38	13.50
Premium (Discount) (%)	(6.36)	(14.08)	(15.38)	(12.10)	0.67
Total Return, Stk Price (%)	20.26	43.65	(6.43)	10.74	22.98

Putnam High Income Convertible & Bond Fund

One Post Office Square
Boston, MA 02109
(617) 292-1000

NYSE : PCF

Transfer Agent
Putnam Investor Services
P.O. Box 2701
Boston, MA 02208
(800) 634-1587

Growth & Income

12 Months Ending 12/31/92 Results

	Period End	Period Begin	Distributions	Yield Dist (%)	Total Return (%)
Share Price ($)	9.00	7.75	0.86	11.10	27.23
NAV per share ($)	8.68	7.55		11.39	26.36

Background: Initial public offering July 9, 1987 of 125,000,000 shares at $10 per share. Initial NAV was $9.30 per share.

Objective: Seeks high current income. Capital appreciation is secondary. The fund will invest in high-yielding convertible securities which at the time of purchase are trading principally on their current yield rather than on the value of the underlying equity securities. The fund will also invest in lower-rated, higher-yielding securities to augment income.

Portfolio: (10/31/92) Corporate Bonds & Notes 44.0%, Convertible Bonds 38.0%, Convertible Preferreds 11.0%, Preferreds 4.0%, Cash 3.0%. Sector Weightings: Recreation 8.1%, Conglomerates 7.5%, Computers 4.8%, Electronics 3.9%, Oils 3.5%.

Capitalization: (8/31/92) Common stock outstanding 12,821,159. No long-term debt.

Beta: 0.38
Fund Manager: Putnam Management Company, Inc.   **Fee:** 0.75%
Income Dist: Monthly   **Capital Gains Dist:** Annually
Reinvestment Plan: Yes   **Shareholder Reports:** Quarterly

5 Year Performance

Fiscal Year Ending 8/31	1992	1991	1990	1989	1988
Net Assets ($mil):	108.90	95.80	87.90	105.80	105.30
Net Income Dist ($):	0.94	0.85	0.92	0.85	0.85
Cap Gains Dist ($):	0.00	0.01	0.02	0.00	0.00
Total Dist ($)	0.94	0.86	0.94	0.85	0.85
Yield from Dist (%)	12.32	14.63	11.93	10.63	8.83
Expense Ratio (%)	1.13	1.31	1.26	1.15	1.18
Portfolio Turnover (%)	45.84	68.36	53.30	69.68	85.34
NAV per share ($)	8.49	7.56	6.94	8.37	8.32
Market Price per share	8.88	7.63	5.88	7.88	8.00
Premium (Discount) (%)	4.59	0.93	(15.42)	(5.97)	(3.85)
Total Return, Stk Price (%)	28.70	44.39	(13.45)	9.12	(8.10)

TCW Convertible Securities Fund, Inc.

865 S. Figueroa St.
Los Angeles, CA 90017
(213) 244-0662

Growth & Income

NYSE : CVT
Transfer Agent
The Bank of New York
Church Street Station
P.O. Box 11002
New York, NY 10277-0770
(800) 524-4458

12 Months Ending 12/31/92 Results

	Period End	Period Begin	Distributions	Yield Dist (%)	Total Return (%)
Share Price ($)	9.13	8.75	0.84	9.60	13.94
NAV per share ($)	8.36	8.09		10.38	13.72

Background: Initial public offering February 26, 1987 of 20,000,000 shares at $10 per share. Initial NAV was $9.27 per share.

Objective: Seeks a high rate of total return (both income and capital appreciation). Under normal market conditions, 65% of total assets will be in convertible securities. Securities may be BB or lower as rated by S&P. The balance of the portfolio may be in non-convertible equity and investment-grade debt securities issued or guaranteed by the U.S. Government.

Portfolio: (12/31/92) Convertible Securities: 100%. Sector Weightings: Leisure Time 14.6%, Banks/Financial 9.0%, Service-Business 8.1%, Pollution Control 6.4%, Health Care 5.4%.

Capitalization: (12/31/92) Common stock outstanding 25,731,000. No long-term debt.

Beta: 1.17
Fund Manager: TCW Funds Management, Inc.
Income Dist: Quarterly
Reinvestment Plan: Yes

Fee: 0.75%
Capital Gains Dist: Annually
Shareholder Reports: Semi-Annually

5 Year Performance

Fiscal Year Ending 12/31	1992	1991	1990	1989	1988
Net Assets ($mil):	215.20	172.30	144.60	175.70	167.80
Net Income Dist ($):	0.84	0.84	0.84	0.84	0.76
Cap Gains Dist ($):	0.00	0.00	0.00	0.00	0.00
Total Dist ($)	0.84	0.84	0.84	0.84	0.76
Yield from Dist (%)	9.60	12.21	10.50	11.38	11.69
Expense Ratio (%)	0.88	0.94	0.94	0.95	0.94
Portfolio Turnover (%)	139.39	114.13	99.53	84.17	70.62
NAV per share ($)	8.36	8.09	6.85	8.36	7.99
Market Price per share	9.13	8.75	6.88	8.00	7.38
Premium (Discount) (%)	9.21	8.16	0.44	(4.31)	(7.76)
Total Return, Stk Price (%)	13.94	39.39	(3.50)	19.78	25.23

Domestic Equity Funds—Diversified

Adams Express Company

Seven St. Paul St., Suite 1140
Baltimore, MD 21202
(800) 638-2479 / (410) 752-5900

NYSE : ADX
Transfer Agent
The Bank of New York
101 Barclay St.
New York, NY 10007
(800) 524-4458

Growth & Income

12 Months Ending 12/31/92 Results

	Period End	Period Begin	Distributions	Yield Dist (%)	Total Return (%)
Share Price ($)	20.00	19.00	1.62	8.53	13.79
NAV per share ($)	20.48	20.21		8.02	9.35

Background: Formed in 1858 as an express company. Shares have been publicly traded since 1873. Has a long term interest in Petroleum and Resources Co., an affiliated investment company.

Objective: Seeks growth and income consistent with preservation of capital primarily through investments in large-cap, blue chip common stocks. Options may be utilized.

Portfolio: (12/31/92) Stocks & Convertibles 92.3%, Short Term 7.7%. Sector Weightings: Health Care 14.7%, Oil & Natural Gas 10.3%, Distribution 10.3%, Telecommunications 9.2%, Consumer Staples 7.5%. Largest Holdings: Petroleum & Resources, Wal-Mart, International Flavors & Fragrances, American International Group, General Electric Co.

Capitalization: (12/31/92) Common stock outstanding 34,026,625. No long-term debt.

Beta: 0.36
Fund Manager: Adams Express Company
Income Dist: Quarterly
Reinvestment Plan: Yes

Fee: 0.00%
Capital Gains Dist: Annually
Shareholder Reports: Quarterly

5 Year Performance

Fiscal Year Ending 12/31	1992	1991	1990	1989	1988
Net Assets ($mil):	696.90	661.90	529.50	550.10	455.80
Net Income Dist ($):	0.46	0.54	0.66	0.70	0.50
Cap Gains Dist ($):	1.16	1.09	1.06	1.36	1.32
Total Dist ($)	1.62	1.63	1.72	2.06	1.82
Yield from Dist (%)	8.53	11.05	11.00	13.97	12.23
Expense Ratio (%)	0.49	0.58	0.50	0.51	0.55
Portfolio Turnover (%)	17.97	17.64	24.71	26.04	18.00
NAV per share ($)	20.48	20.21	16.82	18.35	16.11
Market Price per share	20.00	19.00	14.75	15.63	14.75
Premium (Discount) (%)	(2.34)	(5.99)	(12.31)	(14.88)	(8.44)
Total Return, Stk Price (%)	13.79	39.86	5.37	19.93	11.36

Baker, Fentress & Company

200 W. Madison St., Suite 3510
Chicago, IL 60606
(312) 236-9190

Growth

NYSE : BKF
Transfer Agent
Harris Trust & Savings Bank
Corporate Trust Operations
111 W. Monroe St.
Chicago, IL 60603
(312) 461-2545

12 Months Ending 12/31/92 Results

	Period End	Period Begin	Distributions	Yield Dist (%)	Total Return (%)
Share Price ($)	17.00	17.63	1.81	10.27	6.69
NAV per share ($)	20.82	21.49		8.42	5.30

Background: Formed in 1891 as an investment banker and broker-dealer in securities. Became a private investment company in 1960 and a registered investment company in 1970.

Objective: Seeks capital appreciation. Invests primarily in non-diversified, small-cap common stocks and other equity securities (preferred stocks, options to purchase equities, limited partnerships, business trusts, and convertible debt securities). The fund has a target distribution of 8% per annum, distributed semi-annually.

Portfolio: (12/31/92) Public Portfolio 69.5%, Controlled Affiliate 15.2%, Private Placement 14.6%, Cash & Other 0.7%. Sector Weightings: Technology 12.7%, Finance 14.6%, Basic Industry 8.7%, Health Care 7.8%. Largest Holdings: Gidding & Lewis, Abbott Laboratories, Aon Corporation, Great Lakes Chemical Corp., Hewlett Packard.

Capitalization: (12/31/92) Common stock outstanding 20,164,869. No long-term debt.

Beta: 0.38
Fund Manager: Internally Managed
Income Dist: Semi-Annually
Reinvestment Plan: Yes

Fee: 0.00%
Capital Gains Dist: Annually
Shareholder Reports: Quarterly

5 Year Performance

Fiscal Year Ending 12/31	1992	1991	1990	1989	1988
Net Assets ($mil):	419.80	417.40	350.20	456.20	406.30
Net Income Dist ($):	0.39	0.58	0.70	0.72	0.67
Cap Gains Dist ($):	1.42	1.15	1.25	2.72	1.59
Total Dist ($)	1.81	1.73	1.95	3.44	2.26
Yield from Dist (%)	10.27	11.93	9.07	17.30	13.10
Expense Ratio (%)	0.76	0.84	0.68	0.64	0.64
Portfolio Turnover (%)	28.36	50.70	26.19	35.47	53.23
NAV per share ($)	20.82	21.49	18.66	25.18	24.08
Market Price per share	17.00	17.63	14.50	21.50	19.88
Premium (Discount) (%)	(18.35)	(18.01)	(22.29)	(14.61)	(17.48)
Total Return, Stk Price (%)	6.69	33.52	(23.49)	25.45	28.35

Bergstrom Capital Corporation

505 Madison St., Suite 220
Seattle, WA 98104
(206) 623-7302

AMEX : BEM
Transfer Agent
State Street Bank & Trust Co.
P.O. Box 8200
Boston, MA 02266
(800) 426-5523

Growth

12 Months Ending 12/31/92 Results

	Period End	Period Begin	Distributions	Yield Dist (%)	Total Return (%)
Share Price ($)	132.13	122.63	2.00	1.63	9.38
NAV per share ($)	102.68	104.89		1.91	(0.20)

Background: Bergstrom Capital (formerly Claremont Capital) was originally formed in 1968 as Diebold Venture Capital. The name was changed to Bergstrom Capital in November 1988.

Objective: Seeks long-term capital appreciation. Invests in firms expected to derive maximum benefit from development and use of advanced technologies. Over 85% of investments are represented by marketable securities. The fund may leverage its assets and may engage in short sales.

Portfolio: (12/31/92) Common Stocks & Convertibles 85.5%, Short Term 14.5%. Sector Weightings: Biotechnology 33.6%, Telephone Systems 8.4%, Regulated Investment Companies 7.3%, Industrial & Commercial Services 6.1%, Medical Supplies 3.2%. Largest Holdings: Amgen, Inc., RCM Growth Equity Fund, Inc., Baxter International, Inc., GMAC 4.125% Notes Due 1/5/93, GMAC 4.15% Notes Due 1/22/93.

Capitalization: (12/31/92) Common stock outstanding 1,237,500. No long-term debt.

Beta: 1.08
Fund Manager: Bergstrom Advisers, Inc.   **Fee:** 0.75%
Income Dist: Annually   **Capital Gains Dist:** Annually
Reinvestment Plan: No   **Shareholder Reports:** Quarterly

5 Year Performance

Fiscal Year Ending 12/31	1992	1991	1990	1989	1988
Net Assets ($mil):	127.10	118.00	71.00	66.00	57.00
Net Income Dist ($):	1.05	1.07	1.46	1.47	1.14
Cap Gains Dist ($):	0.95	1.93	1.54	4.93	2.16
Total Dist ($)	2.00	3.00	3.00	6.40	3.30
Yield from Dist (%)	1.63	4.91	4.61	13.26	7.46
Expense Ratio (%)	0.79	0.88	0.99	0.97	1.06
Portfolio Turnover (%)	13.55	16.82	9.84	35.58	16.12
NAV per share ($)	102.68	104.89	62.98	58.95	50.74
Market Price per share	132.13	122.63	61.13	65.13	48.25
Premium (Discount) (%)	28.67	16.90	(2.95)	10.47	(4.91)
Total Return, Stk Price (%)	9.38	105.53	(1.54)	48.23	16.50

Blue Chip Value Fund, Inc.

633 17th St., Suite 1800
Denver, CO 80202
(303) 293-5999

Transfer Agent
Mellon Securities Trust Co.
c/o Mellon Securities Transfer Service
111 Founders Plaza, Suite 1100
East Hartford, CT 06108
(800) 288-9541

Growth & Income

12 Months Ending 12/31/92 Results

	Period End	Period Begin	Distributions	Yield Dist (%)	Total Return (%)
Share Price ($)	7.75	7.63	0.77	10.09	11.66
NAV per share ($)	7.63	8.36		9.21	0.48

Background: Initial public offering April 15, 1987 of 8,500,000 shares at $10.00 per share. Initial NAV was $9.30 per share.

Objective: Seeks capital appreciation and current income through a diversified portfolio selected from a proprietary screen of the 300 largest dividend-paying companies. Can borrow up to 10% for leverage.

Portfolio: (12/31/92) Common Stock 102.0%, Other Assets, Less Liabilities (2.0%). Sector Weightings: Credit Sensitive 31.8%, International Goods & Services 22.5%, Consumer Staples 31.3%, Consumer Cyclical 10.2%, Capital Goods 4.2%.

Capitalization: (12/31/92) Common stock outstanding 9,488,000. No long-term debt.

Beta: 1.16
Fund Manager: Denver Investment Advisors, Inc.
Income Dist: Quarterly
Reinvestment Plan: Yes

Fee: 0.65%
Capital Gains Dist: Quarterly
Shareholder Reports: Quarterly

5 Year Performance

Fiscal Year Ending 12/31	1992	1991	1990	1989	1988
Net Assets ($mil):	72.40	78.20	65.30	73.30	67.50
Net Income Dist ($):	0.12	0.13	0.14	0.30	0.19
Cap Gains Dist ($):	0.65	0.83	0.61	0.48	0.00
Total Dist ($)	0.77	0.96	0.75	0.78	0.19
Yield from Dist (%)	10.09	16.00	10.71	13.00	3.45
Expense Ratio (%)	1.42	1.63	1.96	1.98	2.22
Portfolio Turnover (%)	118.20	111.89	103.90	164.80	135.10
NAV per share ($)	7.63	8.36	6.97	7.83	7.13
Market Price per share	7.75	7.63	6.00	7.00	6.00
Premium (Discount) (%)	1.57	(8.85)	(13.92)	(10.60)	(15.85)
Total Return, Stk Price (%)	11.66	43.17	(3.57)	29.67	12.55

Central Fund of Canada Limited

AMEX : CEF

P.O. Box 7319
Ancaster, Ontario
L9G 3N6, Canada
(416) 648-7878

Transfer Agent
R-M Trust Co.
Chemical Bank
New York, NY 10001
(800) 647-4273

Business Man's Risk

12 Months Ending 12/31/92 Results

	Period End	Period Begin	Distributions	Yield Dist (%)	Total Return (%)
Share Price ($)	3.50	3.88	0.00	0.00	(9.79)
NAV per share ($)	3.99	4.28		0.00	(6.78)

Background: Incorporated in 1961. In 1983 the company changed to a holding company with its assets held through its wholly owned subsidiaries.

Objective: Acts as an inflation hedge. Under normal conditions, at least 90% of the fund's assets will be in gold and silver bullion. The bullion is stored on a segregated basis in the underground vaults of the Canadian Imperial Bank of Commerce and is insured by Lloyd's of London.

Portfolio: (1/31/93) Gold Bullion 64.4%, Silver Bullion 34.5%, Cash & Other Assets 1.1%.

Capitalization: (1/31/93) Class A shares outstanding 16,824,300. No long-term debt.

Beta: 0.18
Fund Manager: The Central Group Alberta Ltd.   **Fee:** 0.50%
Income Dist: Annually   **Capital Gains Dist:** None
Reinvestment Plan: No   **Shareholder Reports:** Quarterly

5 Year Performance

Fiscal Year Ending 10/31	1992	1991	1990	1989	1988
Net Assets ($mil):	85.20	83.20	91.80	100.80	98.40
Net Income Dist ($):	0.01	0.01	0.50	0.01	0.08
Cap Gains Dist ($):	0.00	0.00	0.00	0.00	0.00
Total Dist ($)	0.01	0.01	0.50	0.01	0.08
Yield from Dist (%)	0.26	0.23	10.40	0.20	1.45
Expense Ratio (%)	0.80	1.00	1.00	1.24	0.98
Portfolio Turnover (%)	N/A	N/A	N/A	N/A	N/A
NAV per share ($)	4.08	4.41	4.67	5.10	5.84
Market Price per share	3.88	3.88	4.44	4.81	5.00
Premium (Discount) (%)	(4.90)	(12.24)	(4.93)	(5.69)	(14.38)
Total Return, Stk Price (%)	0.26	(12.39)	2.70	(3.60)	(7.64)

Central Securities Corporation

375 Park Ave.
New York, NY 10152
(212) 688-3011

AMEX : CET
Transfer Agent
First Chicago Trust Co. of New York
30 W. Broadway
New York, NY 10015
(212) 791-6422

Growth & Income

12 Months Ending 12/31/92 Results

	Period End	Period Begin	Distributions	Yield Dist (%)	Total Return (%)
Share Price ($)	11.63	9.25	0.86	9.30	35.03
NAV per share ($)	14.33	11.87		7.25	27.97

Background: Formed in 1929 as Central Illinois Securities Corp. Adopted current name in 1959.

Objective: Seeks long-term capital appreciation. Income is secondary. Invests primarily in relatively few situations. Balance invested in a broad general market portfolio. Will use borrowings when deemed advisable.

Portfolio: (12/31/92) Common Stock 91.3%, Notes & Debentures 3.4%, Short-Term Debt Investments 5.1%. Sector Weightings: Electronics 15.5%, Communications 13%, Business Services 11.8%, Insurance 8.9%, Energy 8.6%. Largest Holdings: Reynolds & Reynolds, Analog Devices, Fleet Call, Inc., Plymouth Rock.

Capitalization: (12/31/92) Common stock outstanding 11,482,836. Convertible preferred shares outstanding 400,760. No long-term debt.

Beta: 0.59
Fund Manager: Internally Managed
Income Dist: Semi-Annually
Reinvestment Plan: No

Fee: 0.40%
Capital Gains Dist: Annually
Shareholder Reports: Quarterly

5 Year Performance

Fiscal Year Ending 12/31	1992	1991	1990	1989	1988
Net Assets ($mil):	165.60	131.70	111.20	129.40	118.90
Net Income Dist ($):	0.20	0.14	0.20	0.35	0.16
Cap Gains Dist ($):	0.66	0.45	0.03	0.09	0.92
Total Dist ($)	0.86	0.59	0.23	0.44	1.08
Yield from Dist (%)	9.30	7.61	2.39	4.82	13.71
Expense Ratio (%)	0.88	0.96	0.98	0.92	0.89
Portfolio Turnover (%)	18.56	16.69	7.25	14.33	9.25
NAV per share ($)	14.33	11.87	10.00	12.24	11.77
Market Price per share	11.63	9.25	7.75	9.63	9.13
Premium (Discount) (%)	(18.91)	(22.07)	(22.50)	(21.41)	(22.51)
Total Return, Stk Price (%)	35.03	26.97	(17.13)	10.30	29.57

Charles Allmon Trust, Inc.

4405 East-West Highway
Bethesda, MD 20814
(301) 986-5866

Growth

NYSE : GSO
Transfer Agent
PNC Bank, N.A.
Provident Financial Corp.
P.O. Box 8950
Wilmington, DE 19899
(800) 852-4750

12 Months Ending 12/31/92 Results

	Period End	Period Begin	Distributions	Yield Dist (%)	Total Return (%)
Share Price ($)	10.00	10.00	0.44	4.40	4.40
NAV per share ($)	10.28	10.40		4.23	3.08

Background: Initial public offering March 6, 1986 of 2,500,000 shares at $10 per share. Initial NAV was $9.35 per share. Prior to May 31, 1991, the fund was called Growth Stock Outlook Trust, Inc.

Objective: Seeks long-term capital appreciation. Income is a secondary objective. Fund portfolio favors small capitalized, lesser-known companies. The fund may invest up to 25% of its assets in foreign securities.

Portfolio: (12/31/92) U.S. Government Obligations 73.4%. Sector Weightings: Common Stock 25.4%, Insurance 3.4%, Utilities 3.4%, Banking 2.9%, Drugs/Toiletries 2.7%.

Capitalization: (12/31/92) Common stock outstanding 11,956,096. No long-term debt.

Beta: 0.22
Fund Manager: Growth Stock Outlook, Inc. **Fee:** 1.00%
Income Dist: Feb. & Dec. **Capital Gains Dist:** Annually
Reinvestment Plan: Yes **Shareholder Reports:** Quarterly

5 Year Performance

Fiscal Year Ending 12/31	1992	1991	1990	1989	1988
Net Assets ($mil):	122.90	125.30	120.90	124.30	127.80
Net Income Dist ($):	0.30	0.44	0.54	0.57	0.41
Cap Gains Dist ($):	0.14	0.21	0.08	0.07	0.00
Total Dist ($)	0.44	0.65	0.62	0.64	0.41
Yield from Dist (%)	4.40	6.34	6.20	6.82	4.43
Expense Ratio (%)	1.33	1.31	1.48	1.43	1.46
Portfolio Turnover (%)	19.00	25.00	41.00	25.00	24.00
NAV per share ($)	10.28	10.40	9.90	10.10	9.59
Market Price per share	10.00	10.00	10.25	10.00	9.38
Premium (Discount) (%)	(2.72)	(3.85)	3.54	(0.99)	(2.29)
Total Return, Stk Price (%)	4.40	3.90	8.70	13.43	5.84

Counsellors Tandem Securities Fund, Inc.

466 Lexington Ave.
New York, NY 10017-3147
(800) 888-6878

Growth

NYSE : CTF
Transfer Agent
Provident National Bank
c/o Provident Financial Processing Corp.
P.O. Box 8950
Wilmington, DE 19899
(800) 553-8080

12 Months Ending 12/31/92 Results

	Period End	Period Begin	Distributions	Yield Dist (%)	Total Return (%)
Share Price ($)	14.13	14.13	0.00	0.00	0.00
NAV per share ($)	16.54	16.88		0.00	(2.01)

Background: Initial public offering October 30, 1986 of 8,800,000 shares at $10 per share. Simultaneously 800,000 preferred shares were sold at $50 per share. Initial NAV was $9.30 per share. In 1990 the fund repurchased 303,042 preferred and 2,000,049 common through tender.

Objective: Seeks long-term appreciation consistent with the preservation of capital. Strives for stability and dependability of income. Normally invests at least 65% in dividend-paying stocks of utility companies.

Portfolio: (12/31/92) Common Stock 93.8%, U.S. Treasuries 0.4%, Short Term 5.8%. Sector Weightings: Utilities-Electric 33.9%, Telecommunications 11.7%, Gas 4.7%, Other 43.5%. Largest Holdings: Central & Southwest Corp., Philadelphia Electric, Southwestern Bell Corp., General Electric, Minnesota Power & Light.

Capitalization: (12/31/92) Common stock outstanding 2,803,462. Leveraged with 576,958 shares preferred stock, stated value $50 per share.

Beta: 0.32

Fund Manager: Warburg Pincus Counsellors, Inc.   **Fee:** 0.75%
Income Dist: Semi-Annually   **Capital Gains Dist:** Annually
Reinvestment Plan: Yes   **Shareholder Reports:** Quarterly

5 Year Performance

Fiscal Year Ending 12/31	1992	1991	1990	1989	1988
Net Assets ($mil):	75.20	76.90	65.00	108.50	84.90
Net Income Dist ($):	0.00	0.12	0.12	0.20	0.00
Cap Gains Dist ($):	0.00	0.00	0.00	0.00	0.00
Total Dist ($)	0.00	0.12	0.12	0.20	0.00
Yield from Dist (%)	0.00	1.16	1.04	3.20	0.00
Expense Ratio (%)	1.27	1.35	2.33	1.08	1.34
Portfolio Turnover (%)	27.00	26.00	41.00	67.00	51.00
NAV per share ($)	16.54	16.88	12.67	13.29	8.43
Market Price per share	14.13	14.13	10.38	11.50	6.25
Premium (Discount) (%)	(14.57)	(16.35)	(18.15)	(13.47)	(25.86)
Total Return, Stk Price (%)	0.00	37.28	(8.70)	87.20	51.33

Dover Regional Financial
1521 Locust St., Suite 500
Philadelphia, PA 19102
(215) 735-5001

OTC : DVRFS
Transfer Agent
Mellon Securities Trust Co.
85 Challenger Road
Overpeck Center
Ridgefield Park, NJ 07660
(800) 526-0801

Growth

12 Months Ending 12/31/92 Results

	Period End	Period Begin	Distributions	Yield Dist (%)	Total Return (%)
Share Price ($)	6.00	3.88	0.05	1.29	55.93
NAV per share ($)	7.39	5.54		0.90	34.30

Background: Initial public offering September 29, 1986.

Objective: Seeks long-term capital appreciation. Under normal conditions, the fund will invest at least 60% of its assets in equity securities of commercial banks and savings and loans.

Portfolio: (9/30/92) Common Stock 62.4%, Preferred Stock 0.8%, Shor Term 10.8%. Sector Weightings: Commercial Banks 58.6%, Thrifts 3.8%, Treasury Bills 4.4%, CDs 6.4%. Largest Holdings Provident Bankshares Corp., First Fidelity Bancorp, Commerce Bancorp, UJB Financial Corp, Baltimore Bancorp.

Capitalization: (12/31/92) Common stock outstanding 747,000 shares. No long-term debt.

Beta: 0.44
Fund Manager: Dover Financial Management Corp.
Income Dist: Quarterly
Reinvestment Plan: Yes

Fee: 0.10%
Capital Gains Dist: Annually
Shareholder Reports: Quarterly

5 Year Performance

Fiscal Year Ending 12/31	1992	1991	1990	1989	1988
Net Assets ($mil):	5.50	4.10	3.50	6.30	6.20
Net Income Dist ($):	0.05	0.10	0.29	0.14	0.19
Cap Gains Dist ($):	0.00	0.00	0.00	0.00	0.06
Total Dist ($)	0.05	0.10	0.29	0.14	0.25
Yield from Dist (%)	1.29	2.75	4.83	2.15	—
Expense Ratio (%)	2.35	2.50	2.02	1.96	1.99
Portfolio Turnover (%)	0.00	0.00	0.00	3.37	6.80
NAV per share ($)	7.39	5.54	4.67	8.42	8.29
Market Price per share	6.00	3.88	3.63	6.00	6.50
Premium (Discount) (%)	(18.81)	(29.96)	(22.27)	(28.74)	(21.59)
Total Return, Stk Price (%)	55.93	9.64	(34.67)	(5.54)	—

Engex, Inc.

44 Wall St.
New York, NY 10005
(212) 495-4200

AMEX : EGX
Transfer Agent
Continental Stock Transfer & Trust Co.
Two Broadway
New York, NY 10017
(212) 509-4000

Growth

12 Months Ending 12/31/92 Results

	Period End	Period Begin	Distributions	Yield Dist (%)	Total Return (%)
Share Price ($)	9.13	8.75	0.00	0.00	4.34
NAV per share ($)	11.83	11.23		0.00	5.34

Background: First organized on November 20, 1968 as the Emerging Securities Fund, an open-end, no-load fund that originally sold for $3.91 per share. Converted to a non-diversified, closed-end investment company in 1975 as Engex, Inc.

Objective: Seeks capital appreciation through investments in situations perceived to be undervalued with strong growth potential.

Portfolio: (9/30/92) Common Stock 68.52%, Units 4.19%, Limited Partnership 4.96%. Sector Weightings: Biotechnology 15.63%, Medical Technology 14.61%, Communications 8.89%, Health Care 7.1%, Environmental 6.17%.

Capitalization: (9/30/92) Common stock outstanding 977,223. No long-term debt.

Beta: 0.28

Fund Manager: American Investors Advisors Corp.   **Fee:** 1.00%
Income Dist: Annually   **Capital Gains Dist:** Annually
Reinvestment Plan: No   **Shareholder Reports:** Semi-Annually

5 Year Performance

Fiscal Year Ending 9/30	1992	1991	1990	1989	1988
Net Assets ($mil):	10.00	9.20	9.40	14.50	12.70
Net Income Dist ($):	0.00	0.00	1.36	0.00	0.00
Cap Gains Dist ($):	0.00	0.00	0.00	0.00	0.00
Total Dist ($)	0.00	0.00	1.36	0.00	0.00
Yield from Dist (%)	0.00	0.00	13.27	0.00	0.00
Expense Ratio (%)	2.11	2.66	2.34	2.25	2.31
Portfolio Turnover (%)	65.47	103.91	34.52	67.53	10.65
NAV per share ($)	10.20	9.42	9.59	14.82	12.98
Market Price per share	8.00	6.75	7.00	10.25	9.75
Premium (Discount) (%)	(21.57)	(28.34)	(27.01)	(30.84)	(24.88)
Total Return, Stk Price (%)	18.52	(3.57)	(18.44)	5.13	151.29

Gabelli Equity Trust, Inc. (The)

One Corporate Center
Rye, NY 10580-1434
(914) 921-5070

NYSE : GAB
Transfer Agent
State Street Bank & Trust Co.
P.O. Box 8200
Boston, MA 02266
(800) 465-5523

Growth

12 Months Ending 12/31/92 Results

	Period End	Period Begin	Distributions	Yield Dist (%)	Total Return (%)
Share Price ($)	10.25	10.13	1.06	10.46	11.65
NAV per share ($)	10.58	10.61		9.99	9.71

Background: Initial public offering August 14, 1986 of 40,000,000 shares at $10 per share. Initial NAV was $9.35 per share.

Objective: Seeks long-term growth of capital. Income is secondary. Invests in underpriced issues. Other factors influencing stock selection include favorable price/earnings and debt/equity ratios, as well as strong management. The fund has a target distribution of 10% per annum, distributed quarterly.

Portfolio: (12/31/92) Common Stocks 74.8%, Preferred Stocks 6.5%, Corporate Bonds 3.3%, Repurchase Agreements 9.9%. Sector Weightings: Telecommunications 10.8%, Broadcasting 7.7%, Cable 8.0%, Industrial Equipment & Supplies 7.4%, Publishing 8.0%.

Capitalization: (12/31/92) Common stock outstanding 68,537,691. No long-term debt.

Beta: 0.90
Fund Manager: Gabelli Funds, Inc. **Fee:** 0.75%
Income Dist: Quarterly **Capital Gains Dist:** Annually
Reinvestment Plan: Yes **Shareholder Reports:** Quarterly

5 Year Performance

Fiscal Year Ending 12/31	1992	1991	1990	1989	1988
Net Assets ($mil):	725.30	595.20	479.90	590.00	484.80
Net Income Dist ($):	0.19	0.27	0.53	0.29	0.21
Cap Gains Dist ($):	0.87	0.14	0.23	1.02	0.78
Total Dist ($)	1.06	0.41	0.76	1.31	0.99
Yield from Dist (%)	10.46	3.90	5.43	13.26	12.98
Expense Ratio (%)	1.22	1.24	1.18	1.18	1.25
Portfolio Turnover (%)	12.50	11.20	15.50	28.10	51.50
NAV per share ($)	10.58	10.61	10.49	13.34	11.22
Market Price per share	10.25	10.13	10.50	14.00	9.88
Premium (Discount) (%)	(3.12)	(4.62)	0.10	4.95	(12.03)
Total Return, Stk Price (%)	11.65	0.38	(19.57)	54.96	42.46

General American Investors Co., Inc.

450 Lexington Ave.
New York, NY 10017
(212) 916-8400 / (800) 436-8401

NYSE : GAM

Transfer Agent
Mellon Securities Trust Co.
P.O. Box 444
Pittsburgh, PA 15230
(412) 236-8000

Growth

12 Months Ending 12/31/92 Results

	Period End	Period Begin	Distributions	Yield Dist (%)	Total Return (%)
Share Price ($)	30.00	29.00	3.09	10.66	14.10
NAV per share ($)	28.56	30.60		10.10	3.43

Background: One of the nation's oldest publicly traded investment funds, it was established in 1927 by partners of Lazard Freres and Lehman Brothers.

Objective: Seeks long-term capital appreciation. Income is secondary. Normally remains fully invested in diversified equities.

Portfolio: (12/31/92) Stocks & Convertibles 96.3%, Short Term 3.7%. Sector Weightings: Health Care & Pharmaceuticals 30.5%, Consumer Products & Services 14.8%, Finance & Insurance 11.5%. Largest Holdings: Home Depot, Wal-Mart, Glaxo Holdings PLC-ADR, American International Group, Inc.

Capitalization: (12/31/92) Common stock outstanding 20,534,013. No long-term debt.

Beta: 0.49
Fund Manager: Internally Managed
Income Dist: Annually
Reinvestment Plan: Yes

Fee: 0.50%
Capital Gains Dist: Annually
Shareholder Reports: Quarterly

5 Year Performance

Fiscal Year Ending 12/31	1992	1991	1990	1989	1988
Net Assets ($mil):	586.50	587.20	382.20	381.90	301.80
Net Income Dist ($):	0.03	0.10	0.21	0.25	0.25
Cap Gains Dist ($):	3.06	2.04	1.70	1.48	1.90
Total Dist ($)	3.09	2.14	1.91	1.73	2.15
Yield from Dist (%)	10.66	12.59	10.54	12.93	16.86
Expense Ratio (%)	1.16	1.02	1.07	1.04	1.14
Portfolio Turnover (%)	14.42	21.30	18.77	26.91	19.37
NAV per share ($)	28.56	30.60	20.60	21.41	17.03
Market Price per share	30.00	29.00	17.00	18.13	13.38
Premium (Discount) (%)	5.04	(5.23)	(17.48)	(15.37)	(21.49)
Total Return, Stk Price (%)	14.10	83.18	4.30	48.43	21.80

Inefficient Market Fund (The)

NYSE : IMF

1345 Avenue of the Americas
New York, NY 10105
(800) 354-6565

Transfer Agent
U.S. Trust Co. of New York
770 Broadway
New York, NY 10003
(800) 354-6565

Growth

12 Months Ending 12/31/92 Results

	Period End	Period Begin	Distributions	Yield Dist (%)	Total Return (%)
Share Price ($)	9.88	8.88	0.05	0.56	11.82
NAV per share ($)	11.49	10.34		0.48	11.61

Background: Initial public offering January 23, 1990 of 4,000,000 shares at $12 per share.

Objective: Seeks long-term capital appreciation with emphasis on value investing. The fund will invest in companies with relatively small capitalization. Invests at least 50% in companies with less than $500 million capitalization. 10% of assets may be invested overseas. The fund began a 10% per annum payout policy in 1991.

Portfolio: (12/31/92) Common & Preferred Stocks 86.3%, Short Term 13.7%.

Capitalization: (12/31/92) Common stock outstanding 4,384,000. No long-term debt.

Beta: 0.28
Fund Manager: Smith Barney Harris Upham, Inc.
Fee: 0.75%
Income Dist: Annually
Capital Gains Dist: Annually
Reinvestment Plan: Yes
Shareholder Reports: Semi-Annually

5 Year Performance

Fiscal Year Ending 12/31	1992	1991	1990 (11 mos.)	1989	1988
Net Assets ($mil):	50.40	45.30	40.80	—	—
Net Income Dist ($):	0.05	0.14	0.37	—	—
Cap Gains Dist ($):	0.00	0.79	0.00	—	—
Total Dist ($)	0.05	0.93	0.37	—	—
Yield from Dist (%)	0.56	11.10	—	—	—
Expense Ratio (%)	1.36	1.28	1.32	—	—
Portfolio Turnover (%)	45.67	46.77	26.82	—	—
NAV per share ($)	11.49	10.34	9.32	—	—
Market Price per share	9.88	8.88	8.38	—	—
Premium (Discount) (%)	(14.01)	(14.22)	(10.19)	—	—
Total Return, Stk Price (%)	11.82	17.06	—	—	—

Jundt Growth Fund

1550 Utica Ave. S., Suite 950
Minneapolis, MN 55416
(800) 543-6217

NYSE : JF
Transfer Agent
Norwest Bank of Minnesota, N.A.
Sixth & Marquette
Minneapolis, MN 55479
(800) 468-9716

Growth

12 Months Ending 12/31/92 Results

	Period End	Period Begin	Distributions	Yield Dist (%)	Total Return (%)
Share Price ($)	14.88	16.00	0.00	0.00	(7.00)
NAV per share ($)	15.33	15.46		0.00	(0.84)

Background: Initial public offering November 27, 1991 of 29,000,000 shares at $15 per share. Initial NAV was $14.10 per share. An additional 1,445,511 shares were issued in a rights offering in March, 1992.

Objective: Seeks long-term capital appreciation by investing primarily in equities, including convertibles of companies believed by the adviser to have significant potential for long-term growth. Income is not a consideration. At least 65% of assets will be in equity securities. In the third quarter of every year the board will consider making a tender offer for shares at NAV.

Portfolio: (12/31/92) Security Type: Equities 100%. Sector Weightings: Retail 21.6%, Computer Software 17.1%, Communications 13.9%, Medical Devices 9.0%, Drugs 8.2%.

Capitalization: (6/30/92) Common stock outstanding 33,745,783. No long term debt.

Beta: 1.46
Fund Manager: Jundt Associates, Inc.
Income Dist: Annually
Reinvestment Plan: Yes

Fee: 1.00%
Capital Gains Dist: Annually
Shareholder Reports: Semi-Annually

5 Year Performance

Fiscal Year Ending 6/30	1992 (7 mos.)	1991	1990	1989	1988
Net Assets ($mil):	465.10	—	—	—	—
Net Income Dist ($):	0.12	—	—	—	—
Cap Gains Dist ($):	0.00	—	—	—	—
Total Dist ($)	0.12	—	—	—	—
Yield from Dist (%)	—	—	—	—	—
Expense Ratio (%)	1.37	—	—	—	—
Portfolio Turnover (%)	20.00	—	—	—	—
NAV per share ($)	13.78	—	—	—	—
Market Price per share	13.13	—	—	—	—
Premium (Discount) (%)	(4.79)	—	—	—	—
Total Return, Stk Price (%)	—	—	—	—	—

Liberty All-Star Equity Fund

Federal Reserve Plaza
Boston, MA 02210-2214
(800) 542- 3863 / (617) 722-6000

NYSE : USA
Transfer Agent
State Street Bank & Trust Co.
P.O. Box 366
Boston, MA 02101
(800) 451-6788

Growth

12 Months Ending 12/31/92 Results

	Period End	Period Begin	Distributions	Yield Dist (%)	Total Return (%)
Share Price ($)	11.13	10.75	1.07*	7.81	13.49
NAV per share ($)	10.78	11.20		7.50	5.80

Background: Initial public offering October 24, 1986. Initial NAV was $10 per share.

Objective: Seeks long-term capital appreciation and current income. Normally the fund will invest at least 65% of total assets in equity securities. Assets are allocated equally among multiple managers. Five separate portfolios managed by Columbus Circle Investors, Oppenheimer Capital, Provident Investment Counsel, Inc., Cooke & Bieler, and Newbold's Asset Management. The fund has a target distribution rate of 10% per annum, distributed quarterly.

Portfolio: (12/31/92) Common Stocks 94.4%, Short Term & Other 5.6%. Sector Weightings: Drugs/Health Care 15.5%, Retail 9.7%, Insurance 8.0%, Computers/Business Equipment 6.8%, Oil & Gas 6.1%.

Capitalization: (12/31/92) Shares of beneficial interest outstanding 53,679,000. No long-term debt.

Beta: 0.92
Fund Manager: Liberty Asset Management Co.   **Fee:** 0.80%
Income Dist: Quarterly   **Capital Gains Dist:** Annually
Reinvestment Plan: Yes   **Shareholder Reports:** Quarterly

5 Year Performance

Fiscal Year Ending 12/31	1992	1991	1990	1989	1988
Net Assets ($mil):	664.70	601.20	478.70	514.20	—
Net Income Dist ($):	0.18	0.15	0.20	0.20	0.16
Cap Gains Dist ($):	0.66	0.87	0.47	0.31	0.00
Total Dist ($)	1.07*	1.02	0.67	0.51	0.16
Yield from Dist (%)	7.81	13.16	8.12	7.03	2.67
Expense Ratio (%)	1.08	1.16	1.23	1.25	1.33
Portfolio Turnover (%)	57.00	72.12	67.57	69.89	72.58
NAV per share ($)	10.78	11.20	8.92	9.58	8.29
Market Price per share	11.13	10.75	7.75	8.25	7.25
Premium (Discount) (%)	3.25	(4.02)	(13.12)	(13.88)	(12.55)
Total Return, Stk Price (%)	13.49	51.87	2.06	20.83	23.50

* Includes $0.23 from paid-in capital.

Morgan Grenfell SMALLCap Fund, Inc.

885 Third Ave., 32 Floor
New York, NY 10022
(212) 230-2600

Transfer Agent
The Bank of New York
101 Barclay St.
New York, NY 10286
(800) 524-4458

Growth

12 Months Ending 12/31/92 Results

	Period End	Period Begin	Distributions	Yield Dist (%)	Total Return (%)
Share Price ($)	12.25	12.88	0.82	6.37	1.48
NAV per share ($)	11.97	12.30		6.67	3.98

Background: Diversified, team-managed fund. Initial public offering May 7, 1987 of 5,000,000 shares at $10 per share. Initial NAV was $9.27 per share. Fund manager is a subsidiary of London-based Morgan Grenfell Group PLC, a unit of Deutsche Bank AG.

Objective: Seeks long-term capital appreciation. Invests primarily in U.S. companies with capitalizations of $50 million to $500 million. Current income is secondary. Leverage may be employed up to 15% of assets.

Portfolio: (12/31/92) Common Stocks 92.6%, Commercial Paper 7.4%. Sector Weightings: Consumer 32.0%, Health Care 17.1%, Technology 14.3%, Credit-Sensitive 9.6%, Service Companies 8.0%.

Capitalization: (12/31/92) Common stock outstanding 5,682,063. No long-term debt.

Beta: 1.54
Fund Manager: Morgan Grenfell Capital Management   **Fee:** 1.00%
Income Dist: Quarterly   **Capital Gains Dist:** Annually
Reinvestment Plan: Yes   **Shareholder Reports:** Quarterly

5 Year Performance

Fiscal Year Ending 12/31	1992	1991	1990	1989	1988
Net Assets ($mil):	68.00	64.50	45.60	54.10	44.50
Net Income Dist ($):	0.00	0.00	0.00	0.00	0.00
Cap Gains Dist ($):	0.82	0.97	0.65	0.25	0.00
Total Dist ($)	0.82	0.97	0.65	0.25	0.00
Yield from Dist (%)	6.37	11.09	6.75	3.39	0.00
Expense Ratio (%)	1.44	1.79	2.01	2.13	2.56
Portfolio Turnover (%)	89.00	70.00	75.00	80.00	83.00
NAV per share ($)	11.97	12.30	8.70	10.80	8.87
Market Price per share	12.25	12.88	8.75	9.63	7.38
Premium (Discount) (%)	2.34	4.63	0.57	(10.93)	(16.91)
Total Return, Stk Price (%)	1.48	58.29	(2.39)	33.88	23.00

NAIC Growth

1515 E. Eleven Mile Rd.
Royal Oak, MI 48067
(313) 543-0612

OTC : GROW
Transfer Agent
NBD Bank, N.A.
P.O. Box 8204
Boston, MA 02266
(800) 257-1770

Growth

12 Months Ending 12/31/92 Results

	Period End	Period Begin	Distributions	Yield Dist (%)	Total Return (%)
Share Price ($)	9.50	10.75	0.18	1.67	(9.95)
NAV per share ($)	10.83	10.06		1.79	9.44

Background: Initial public offering July 2, 1990.

Objective: Seeks long-term growth. Minimum of 75% invested in equity securities, which may include preferred and convertible securities. The balance (25%) may be invested in government obligations, commercial paper or certificates of deposit. All debt securities must be rated AA or higher by S&P.

Portfolio: (12/31/92) Common Stock 79.0%, Bonds 2.0%, Short Term & Other 19.0%. Sector Weightings: Natural Resources 13.2%, Industrial Products 17.7%, Non-Durables 24.5%, Services 12.4%, Finance 8.1%. Largest Holdings: Archer-Daniels-Midland, Reuters Holdings, Mead, Cooper Industries, Philip Morris.

Capitalization: (12/31/92) Common shares outstanding 685,985. No long-term debt.

Beta: N/A
Fund Manager: National Association of Investors Corporation   **Fee:** 0.75%
Income Dist: Semi-Annually   **Capital Gains Dist:** Annually
Reinvestment Plan: Yes   **Shareholder Reports:** Semi-Annually

5 Year Performance

Fiscal Year Ending 12/31	1992	1991	1990 (5 mos.)	1989	1988
Net Assets ($mil):	7.43	6.20	4.90	—	—
Net Income Dist ($):	0.09	0.19	0.22	—	—
Cap Gains Dist ($):	0.09	0.08	0.00	—	—
Total Dist ($)	0.18	0.27	0.22	—	—
Yield from Dist (%)	1.67	2.29	—	—	—
Expense Ratio (%)	2.00	2.00	2.00	—	—
Portfolio Turnover (%)	3.50	1.46	0.00	—	—
NAV per share ($)	10.83	10.06	8.72	—	—
Market Price per share	9.50	10.75	11.81	—	—
Premium (Discount) (%)	(12.28)	6.86	35.44	—	—
Total Return, Stk Price (%)	(9.95)	(6.69)	—	—	—

Patriot Premium Dividend Fund I

101 Huntington Ave.
Boston, MA 02199-7603
(800) 843-0090

NYSE : PDF
Transfer Agent
State Street Bank & Trust Co.
225 Franklin St.
Boston, MA 02110
(800) 426-5523

Income

12 Months Ending 12/31/92 Results

	Period End	Period Begin	Distributions	Yield Dist (%)	Total Return (%)
Share Price ($)	10.38	9.38	0.80	8.53	19.19
NAV per share ($)	10.46	10.14		7.89	11.05

Background: Initial public offering October 28, 1988 of 12,500,000 shares at $10 per share. Initial NAV was $9.17 per share.

Objective: Seeks high current income from a portfolio of diversified dividend-paying preferred and common stocks.

Portfolio: (11/30/92) Security type: Common Stock 49.78, Preferred Stock 15.19%, U.S. Treasuries 29.34%, Cash & Equivalents 5.35%. Sector Weightings: Utilities 62.47%, Financial Services 2.5%. Largest Holdings: U.S. Treasuries, Pacific G&E, Southern Co., N.E. Electrical Systems, DPL Inc.

Capitalization: (9/30/92) Common stock outstanding 14,466,105. Leveraged with $68,500,000 in auction-rate preferred stock. No long-term debt.

Beta: 0.61
Fund Manager: John Hancock Advisors, Inc.
Income Dist: Monthly
Reinvestment Plan: Yes

Fee: 0.50%
Capital Gains Dist: Annually
Shareholder Reports: Semi-Annual

5 Year Performance

Fiscal Year Ending 9/30	1992	1991	1990	1989 (11 mos.)	1988
Net Assets ($mil):	219.90	205.80	179.90	206.00	—
Net Income Dist ($):	0.54	0.65	0.82	1.05	—
Cap Gains Dist ($):	0.26	0.19	0.22	0.10	—
Total Dist ($)	0.80	0.84	1.04	1.15	—
Yield from Dist (%)	8.89	9.20	10.40	—	—
Expense Ratio (%)	1.37	1.48	1.34	1.39	—
Portfolio Turnover (%)	99.83	100.82	123.84	196.88	—
NAV per share ($)	10.47	9.54	7.77	9.74	—
Market Price per share	10.50	9.00	9.13	10.00	—
Premium (Discount) (%)	0.29	(5.66)	17.37	2.67	—
Total Return, Stk Price (%)	25.56	7.78	1.70	—	—

Patriot Premium Dividend Fund II

101 Huntington Ave.
Boston, MA 02199-7603
(800) 843-0090

NYSE : PDT
Transfer Agent
State Street Bank & Trust Co.
225 Franklin St.
Boston, MA 02110
(800) 426-5523

Income

12 Months Ending 12/31/92 Results

	Period End	Period Begin	Distributions	Yield Dist (%)	Total Return (%)
Share Price ($)	11.75	11.63	0.90	7.74	8.77
NAV per share ($)	12.56	12.47		7.22	7.94

Background: Initial public offering December 21, 1989 of 14,950,000 shares at $12 per share. Initial NAV was $10.98 per share.

Objective: Seeks high current income consistent with modest growth of capital. The fund will pursue its objective by investing in a diversified portfolio of dividend-paying preferred and common equity securities.

Portfolio: (11/30/92) Common Stocks 52.09%, Preferred Stocks 15.6%, U.S. Treasuries 27.5%, Cash & Equivalents 4.44%. Sector Weightings: Utilities 67%, U.S. Treasuries 27.52%, Financial Services 0.73%. Largest Holdings: U.S. Treasuries, Pacific Gas & Electric, Southern Co., Consolidated Ed, Texas Utilities.

Capitalization: (11/30/92) Common stock outstanding 15,002,724. Leveraged with $100,000,000 in auction-rate preferred stock. No long-term debt.

Beta: 0.61
Fund Manager: John Hancock Advisors, Inc.
Income Dist: Monthly
Reinvestment Plan: Yes

Fee: 1.00%
Capital Gains Dist: Annually
Shareholder Reports: Semi-Annually

5 Year Performance

Fiscal Year Ending 10/31	1992	1991	1990 (10 mos.)	1989	1988
Net Assets ($mil):	284.20	270.70	245.40	—	—
Net Income Dist ($):	0.90	0.90	0.89	—	—
Cap Gains Dist ($):	0.00	0.00	0.00	—	—
Total Dist ($)	0.90	0.90	0.89	—	—
Yield from Dist (%)	8.57	8.78	—	—	—
Expense Ratio (%)	1.33	1.38	1.39	—	—
Portfolio Turnover (%)	99.24	157.38	288.46	—	—
NAV per share ($)	12.28	11.38	9.69	—	—
Market Price per share	11.38	10.50	10.25	—	—
Premium (Discount) (%)	(7.41)	(7.73)	5.78	—	—
Total Return, Stk Price (%)	16.95	11.22	—	—	—

Patriot Select Dividend Trust

101 Huntington Ave.
Boston, MA 02199-7603
(800) 843-0090

Transfer Agent
State Street Bank & Trust Co.
225 Franklin St.
Boston, MA 02110
(800) 426-5523

Income

12 Months Ending 12/31/92 Results

	Period End	Period Begin	Distributions	Yield Dist (%)	Total Return (%)
Share Price ($)	17.75	16.75	1.65	9.85	15.82
NAV per share ($)	16.22	16.57		9.96	7.85

Background: Initial public offering July 24, 1990 of 8,500,000 shares at $15 per share. Initial NAV was $13.86 per share.

Objective: Seeks high current income from a leveraged portfolio of high-grade common and preferred stocks. Under normal conditions, at least 65% of the trust's assets will be in dividend-paying securities.

Portfolio: (11/30/92) Common Stock 44.24%, U.S. Treasuries 30.45%, Preferred Stocks 19.53%, Cash & Equivalents 5.05%. Sector Weightings: Utility 61.85%, U.S. Treasuries 30.45%, Financial Services 1.95%. Largest Holdings: U.S. Treasuries, PDL, Inc., Southern Co., Consolidated Ed, Pacific G&E.

Capitalization: (6/30/92) Common stock outstanding 9,711,108. Leveraged with $70,000,000 auction-rate preferred stock. No long-term debt.

Beta: 0.42
Fund Manager: John Hancock Advisors, Inc.
Income Dist: Monthly
Reinvestment Plan: Yes

Fee: 0.80%
Capital Gains Dist: Annually
Shareholder Reports: Semi-Annually

5 Year Performance

Fiscal Year Ending 6/30	1992	1991 (11 mos.)	1990	1989	1988
Net Assets ($mil):	223.30	205.80	—	—	—
Net Income Dist ($):	1.09	0.85	—	—	—
Cap Gains Dist ($):	0.56	0.39	—	—	—
Total Dist ($)	1.65	1.24	—	—	—
Yield from Dist (%)	9.85	—	—	—	—
Expense Ratio (%)	1.42	1.39	—	—	—
Portfolio Turnover (%)	85.21	208.80	—	—	—
NAV per share ($)	15.78	14.08	—	—	—
Market Price per share	16.88	16.75	—	—	—
Premium (Discount) (%)	6.91	18.96	—	—	—
Total Return, Stk Price (%)	10.63	—	—	—	—

Preferred Income Fund

301 E. Colorado Blvd.
Pasadena, CA 91101
(818) 795-7300

NYSE : PFD
Transfer Agent
The Shareholder Services Group, Inc.
P.O. Box 1376
Boston, MA 02104
(800) 331-1710

Income

12 Months Ending 12/31/92 Results

	Period End	Period Begin	Distributions	Yield Dist (%)	Total Return (%)
Share Price ($)	18.38	18.00	2.94	16.33	18.44
NAV per share ($)	17.11	16.15		18.20	24.15

Background: Initial public offering January 31, 1991 of 7,600,000 shares at $15 per share. Initial NAV was $13.95 per share.

Objective: Seeks high current income consistent with preservation of capital. Under normal conditions, the fund invests at least 25% of its assets in securities issued by utilities, and at least 25% in securities issued by companies in the banking industry.

Portfolio: (11/30/92) Adjustable-Rate Preferred Stock 52.5%, Fixed-Rate Preferred Stock 44.0%, Repurchase Agreements 1.9%. Sector Weightings: Banking 37.5%, Utilities 34.4%, Insurance 2.8%.

Capitalization: (11/30/92) Common stock outstanding 8,448,969. Leveraged with 575 shares of money market cumulative preferred stock with a redemption price of $100,000. No long-term debt.

Beta: 0.36
Fund Manager: Flaherty & Crumrine, Inc.   **Fee:** 0.63%
Income Dist: Monthly   **Capital Gains Dist:** Annually
Reinvestment Plan: Yes   **Shareholder Reports:** Quarterly

5 Year Performance

Fiscal Year Ending 11/30	1992	1991 (10 mos.)	1990	1989	1988
Net Assets ($mil):	214.60	187.90	—	—	—
Net Income Dist ($):	1.72	0.99	—	—	—
Cap Gains Dist ($):	0.59	0.00	—	—	—
Total Dist ($)	2.31	0.99	—	—	—
Yield from Dist (%)	12.92	—	—	—	—
Expense Ratio (%)	1.63	1.67	—	—	—
Portfolio Turnover (%)	86.00	90.00	—	—	—
NAV per share ($)	18.59	16.56	—	—	—
Market Price per share	19.88	17.88	—	—	—
Premium (Discount) (%)	6.89	7.97	—	—	—
Total Return, Stk Price (%)	24.11	—	—	—	—

Putnam Dividend Income Fund
One Post Office Square
Boston, MA 02109
(800) 225-1581 / (617) 292-1000

NYSE : PDI
Transfer Agent
Putnam Investor Services
P.O. Box 2701
Boston, MA 02208
(800) 634-1587

Income

12 Months Ending 12/31/92 Results

	Period End	Period Begin	Distributions	Yield Dist (%)	Total Return (%)
Share Price ($)	12.25	10.88	1.16	10.66	23.25
NAV per share ($)	11.53	11.35		10.22	11.81

Background: Initial public offering September 28, 1989 of 8,800,000 shares at $12.50 per share. Initial NAV was $11.51 per share. A second offering of 1,320,000 shares was completed October 24, 1989.

Objective: Seeks current income. Invests in common and preferred stocks qualifying for the 70% dividend exclusions for corporations.

Portfolio: (11/30/92) Preferred Stocks 35.0%, ARPs 20%, Common Stocks 18%, Preferred Sinkers 19%, Convertibles 5%.

Capitalization: (6/30/92) Common stock outstanding 10,675,998. No long-term debt. Leveraged with $74,000,000 of remarketable preferred shares.

Beta: 0.50
Fund Manager: Putnam Management Company, Inc.　　　　　　　　　　**Fee:** 0.75%
Income Dist: Monthly　　　　　　　　　　　　　　**Capital Gains Dist:** Annually
Reinvestment Plan: Yes　　　　　　　　**Shareholder Reports:** Semi-Annually

5 Year Performance

Fiscal Year Ending 6/30	1992	1991	1990 (9 mos.)	1989	1988
Net Assets ($mil):	195.70	182.00	180.30	—	—
Net Income Dist ($):	1.19	1.25	0.92	—	—
Cap Gains Dist ($):	0.00	0.00	0.00	—	—
Total Dist ($)	1.19	1.25	0.92	—	—
Yield from Dist (%)	11.46	11.49	—	—	—
Expense Ratio (%)	1.64	2.02	1.48	—	—
Portfolio Turnover (%)	160.44	197.67	201.55	—	—
NAV per share ($)	11.38	10.21	10.26	—	—
Market Price per share	12.00	10.38	10.88	—	—
Premium (Discount) (%)	5.45	1.67	6.04	—	—
Total Return, Stk Price (%)	27.07	6.89	—	—	—

Royce Value Trust, Inc.

1414 Avenue of the Americas, 9th Floor
New York, NY 10019
(800) 221-4268

NYSE : RVT

Transfer Agent
State Street Bank & Trust Co.
P.O. Box 8200
Boston, MA 02266
(800) 426-5523

Growth

12 Months Ending 12/31/92 Results

	Period End	Period Begin	Distributions	Yield Dist (%)	Total Return (%)
Share Price ($)	12.25	10.38	0.90	8.67	26.69
NAV per share ($)	12.50	11.23		8.01	19.32

Background: Initial public offering November 19, 1986 of 10,000,000 shares at $10.00 per share. Initial NAV was $9.30 per share.

Objective: Seeks long-term capital appreciation. Invests in common stocks and other equity securities of small- and medium-sized companies (market capitalization of $15 million to $300 million), the selection of which emphasizes value investing.

Portfolio: (12/31/92) Common Stock 98.68%, Corporate Bonds 2.6%, Preferred Stocks 0.8%, Repurchase Agreements 5.1%, Liabilities & Other (7.3%). Sector Weightings: Business & Industrial Products 30.0%, Services 17.2%, Consumer Products 8.2%, Consumer Services 6.9%, Financial Services 21.2%.

Capitalization: (12/31/92) Common stock outstanding 16,197,304. No long-term debt.

Beta: 0.80
Fund Manager: Quest Advisory Corp.
Income Dist: Annually
Reinvestment Plan: Yes

Fee: 1.00%
Capital Gains Dist: Annually
Shareholder Reports: Quarterly

5 Year Performance

Fiscal Year Ending 12/31	1992	1991	1990	1989	1988
Net Assets ($mil):	202.50	166.50	118.30	130.50	107.30
Net Income Dist ($):	0.15	0.17	0.17	0.17	0.06
Cap Gains Dist ($):	0.75	0.44	0.15	0.35	0.45
Total Dist ($)	0.90	0.61	0.32	0.52	0.51
Yield from Dist (%)	8.67	7.50	3.37	6.40	7.56
Expense Ratio (%)	0.81	0.79	0.94	0.95	1.09
Portfolio Turnover (%)	40.40	34.01	28.16	36.06	29.26
NAV per share ($)	12.50	11.23	8.58	10.35	9.25
Market Price per share	12.25	10.38	8.13	9.50	8.13
Premium (Discount) (%)	(2.00)	(7.66)	(5.24)	(8.21)	(12.22)
Total Return, Stk Price (%)	26.69	35.18	(11.05)	23.25	28.00

Salomon Brothers Fund

7 World Trade Center
New York, NY 10048
(800) 725-6666 / (212) 783-1301

Transfer Agent
The Bank of New York
101 Barclay St.
New York, NY 10286
(800) 524-4458

Growth & Income

12 Months Ending 12/31/92 Results

	Period End	Period Begin	Distributions	Yield Dist (%)	Total Return (%)
Share Price ($)	13.75	13.88	1.00	7.20	6.27
NAV per share ($)	15.16	15.66		6.39	3.19

Background: Originally founded in 1929 by Lehman Brothers. The fund, formerly known as Lehman Corporation, was acquired by Salomon Brothers Asset Management on May 1, 1990. One of the largest traded public investment companies, with net assets of $1.1 billion as of December 31, 1991.

Objective: Seeks long-term capital growth through a portfolio of large capitalized blue-chip stocks. Generally will be fully invested. No more than 25% of assets will be in a single industry.

Portfolio: (12/31/92) Common Stocks 95.8%, Corporate Bonds 1.1%, Repurchase Agreement 2.8%. Sector Weightings: Consumer Products & Services 12.4%, Basic Industries 18.3%, Telecommunications & Utilities 10.4%, Financial Services 13.8%, Energy 9.7%, Health Care 12.2%. Largest Holdings: FNMA, American Home Products, Hewlett Packard, JP Morgan, Telefonos de Mexico S.A. de C.V.

Capitalization: (12/31/92) Common stock outstanding 73,161,000. No long-term debt.

Beta: 0.86
Fund Manager: Salomon Brothers Asset Management, Inc.   **Fee:** 0.50%
Income Dist: Quarterly   **Capital Gains Dist:** Annually
Reinvestment Plan: Yes   **Shareholder Reports:** Quarterly

5 Year Performance

Fiscal Year Ending 12/31	1992	1991	1990	1989	1988
Net Assets ($mil):	1,109.40	1,115.20	906.00	1,027.10	885.00
Net Income Dist ($):	0.40	0.47	0.49	0.59	0.51
Cap Gains Dist ($):	0.60	1.14	0.71	1.52	0.49
Total Dist ($)	1.00	1.61	1.20	2.11	1.00
Yield from Dist (%)	7.20	14.80	9.23	18.14	9.09
Expense Ratio (%)	0.43	0.43	0.46	0.44	0.47
Portfolio Turnover (%)	42.00	14.00	15.00	30.00	49.00
NAV per share ($)	15.16	15.66	13.33	15.58	14.37
Market Price per share	13.75	13.88	10.88	13.00	11.63
Premium (Discount) (%)	(9.30)	(11.43)	(18.45)	(16.56)	(19.14)
Total Return, Stk Price (%)	6.27	42.37	(7.08)	29.92	14.82

Source Capital, Inc.
11400 W. Olympic Blvd., Suite 1200
Los Angeles, CA 90064
(800) 982-4372 / (310) 473-0225

Growth & Income

NYSE : SOR
Transfer Agent
Chemical Bank
P.O. Box 24935
Church Street Station
New York, NY 10249
(212) 613-7147

12 Months Ending 12/31/92 Results

	Period End	Period Begin	Distributions	Yield Dist (%)	Total Return (%)
Share Price ($)	47.75	44.25	3.60	8.14	16.05
NAV per share ($)	42.87	41.23		8.73	12.71

Background: Initial public offering October 24, 1968 at $17.50 per share, with net assets of approximately $238 million. Known as SMC Investment Corporation until 1972 when the company recapitalized.

Objective: Common shareholders: Maximum growth and income consistent with preservation of capital. Preferred shareholders: Steady income. The fund has a 10% distribution target per annum, paid quarterly.

Portfolio: (12/31/92) Common Stock 62.85%, Convertibles 14.04%, Non-Convertible Securities 23.11%.

Capitalization: (12/31/92) Common stock outstanding 6,493,936. Preferred stock outstanding 1,969,212. Par value $3.00. No long-term debt.

Beta: 0.68
Fund Manager: First Pacific Advisors, Inc.
Income Dist: Quarterly
Reinvestment Plan: Yes

Fee: 0.73%
Capital Gains Dist: Annually
Shareholder Reports: Quarterly

5 Year Performance

Fiscal Year Ending 12/31	1992	1991	1990	1989	1988
Net Assets ($mil):	332.60	317.70	286.50	313.70	284.60
Net Income Dist ($):	1.02	1.21	1.69	1.63	1.70
Cap Gains Dist ($):	2.58	2.39	1.91	1.95	1.69
Total Dist ($)	3.60	3.60	3.60	3.58	3.39
Yield from Dist (%)	8.14	9.86	8.47	9.68	10.39
Expense Ratio (%)	0.94	0.97	0.97	0.96	1.00
Portfolio Turnover (%)	69.01	41.48	42.87	36.17	42.52
NAV per share ($)	42.87	41.23	36.94	41.95	37.38
Market Price per share	47.75	44.25	36.50	42.50	37.00
Premium (Discount) (%)	11.38	7.32	(1.19)	1.31	(1.02)
Total Return, Stk Price (%)	16.05	31.10	(5.65)	24.54	23.82

Tri-Continental Corporation

130 Liberty St., 24th Floor
New York, NY 10006
(800) 221-2450 / (212) 432-4100

NYSE : TY
Transfer Agent
Union Data Services Center, Inc.
130 Liberty St.
New York, NY 10006
(212) 432-4100

Growth & Income

12 Months Ending 12/31/92 Results

	Period End	Period Begin	Distributions	Yield Dist (%)	Total Return (%)
Share Price ($)	25.50	27.75	1.48	5.33	(2.77)
NAV per share ($)	28.03	28.57		5.18	3.29

Background: Organized in 1929, it is now the nation's largest diversified, closed-end investment company with a capital structure consisting of three different types of securities: preferred stock, common stock, and warrants.

Objective: Seeks growth and income through a highly diversified portfolio of larger capitalized growth companies with emphasis on the medical and drug industries.

Portfolio: (12/31/92) Common Stock 78.9%, U.S. Government 9.6%, Convertibles 7.2%, Short Term 2.7%, Corporate 1.6%. Sector Weightings: Consumer Goods & Services 12%, Finance & Insurance 11.3%, Government Securities 9.1%, Drugs & Health Care 7.1%, Energy 6.3%, Communications 6.1%.

Capitalization: (12/31/92) Common stock outstanding 74,500,725. Warrants outstanding 21,000. Preferred shares outstanding 752,740.

Beta: 0.83
Fund Manager: J. & W. Seligman & Co., Inc.   **Fee:** 0.45%
Income Dist: Quarterly   **Capital Gains Dist:** Annually
Reinvestment Plan: Yes   **Shareholder Reports:** Quarterly

5 Year Performance

Fiscal Year Ending 12/31	1992	1991	1990	1989	1988
Net Assets ($mil):	2,125.70	1,871.30	1,500.30	1,632.10	1,301.50
Net Income Dist ($):	0.78	0.78	0.86	0.84	0.81
Cap Gains Dist ($):	0.70	1.80	1.60	2.55	1.25
Total Dist ($)	1.48	2.58	2.46	3.39	2.06
Yield from Dist (%)	5.33	12.07	10.70	17.61	9.99
Expense Ratio (%)	0.67	0.67	0.56	0.55	0.57
Portfolio Turnover (%)	44.35	49.02	41.23	59.87	67.39
NAV per share ($)	28.03	28.57	24.60	27.44	23.55
Market Price per share	25.50	27.75	21.38	23.00	19.25
Premium (Discount) (%)	(9.03)	(2.87)	(13.13)	(16.18)	(18.26)
Total Return, Stk Price (%)	(2.77)	41.86	3.65	37.09	3.30

Zweig Fund (The)

900 Third Ave.
New York, NY 10022
(212) 755-9860

Transfer Agent
The Bank of New York
48 Wall St.
New York, NY 10015
(800) 524-4458

Growth

12 Months Ending 12/31/92 Results

	Period End	Period Begin	Distributions	Yield Dist (%)	Total Return (%)
Share Price ($)	13.00	13.75	1.14	8.29	2.84
NAV per share ($)	11.36	12.40		9.19	0.81

Background: Initial public offering October 2, 1986 of 34,000,000 shares at $10 per share. Initial NAV was $9.35 per share.

Objective: Seeks capital appreciation primarily through investments in equity securities and debt securities that represent opportunities for capital appreciation. Dividends and current income are incidental. During defensive periods the fund may be 100% in short-term securities. The fund invests based on a model largely influenced by the Fed Reserve Board's monetary policy. The fund has a 10% per annum distribution target, distributed quarterly.

Portfolio: (12/31/92) Common Stock 52.1%, U.S. Government Bonds 16.06%, Short Term 29.02%. Sector Weightings: Retail 6.3%, Media & Entertainment 4.6%, Banks 4.5%, Gas & Electric 3.4%, Oil & Oil Service Companies 2.9%. Largest Holdings: Medco Containment, Hasbro Inc., FNMA, Tele-Communications Inc., Bank of Boston.

Capitalization: (12/31/92) Common stock outstanding 44,005,118. No long-term debt.

Beta: 0.69
Fund Manager: Zweig Advisors, Inc. **Fee:** 0.85%
Income Dist: Quarterly **Capital Gains Dist:** Annually
Reinvestment Plan: Yes **Shareholder Reports:** Quarterly

5 Year Performance

Fiscal Year Ending 12/31	1992	1991	1990	1989	1988
Net Assets ($mil):	500.10	526.30	389.80	408.80	356.80
Net Income Dist ($):	0.10	0.30	0.49	0.52	0.25
Cap Gains Dist ($):	1.04	0.82	0.69	0.60	0.79
Total Dist ($)	1.14	1.12	1.18	1.12	1.04
Yield from Dist (%)	8.29	10.06	9.53	10.79	11.56
Expense Ratio (%)	1.26	1.28	1.27	1.31	1.39
Portfolio Turnover (%)	172.50	144.30	201.80	183.60	205.70
NAV per share ($)	11.36	12.40	10.48	11.43	10.35
Market Price per share	13.00	13.75	11.13	12.38	10.38
Premium (Discount) (%)	14.44	10.89	6.20	8.22	0.19
Total Return, Stk Price (%)	2.84	33.60	(0.57)	30.06	26.89

Domestic Equity Funds—Non Diversified

ASA Limited
P.O. Box 269
Florham Park, NJ 07932
(201) 377-3535

NYSE : ASA
Transfer Agent
First Chicago Trust Co. of New York
30 W. Broadway
New York, NY 10007-2192
(212) 791-6422

Business Man's Risk

12 Months Ending 12/31/92 Results

	Period End	Period Begin	Distributions	Yield Dist (%)	Total Return (%)
Share Price ($)	31.88	46.88	2.00	4.27	(27.73)
NAV per share ($)	29.04	42.12		4.75	(26.31)

Background: Incorporated in South Africa in June 1958. Initial public offering price was $28 per share.

Objective: Seeks income and capital appreciation. Assets to be invested primarily in South African gold and other mining industries with a minimum of 50% in gold mining companies. 20% may be invested in mining-related industries outside of South Africa.

Portfolio: (11/30/92) South African Gold Mining Shares 66.2%, Other Company Shares 29.2%, Cash & Other 4.6%.

Capitalization: (11/30/92) Common stock outstanding 9,600,000. No long-term debt.

Beta: 0.82
Fund Manager: ASA Limited
Income Dist: Quarterly
Reinvestment Plan: Yes

Fee: 0.13%
Capital Gains Dist: Annually
Shareholder Reports: Quarterly

5 Year Performance

Fiscal Year Ending 11/30	1992	1991	1990	1989	1988
Net Assets ($mil):	292.90	429.20	466.00	672.10	522.60
Net Income Dist ($):	1.10	1.97	2.08	2.60	3.00
Cap Gains Dist ($):	0.90	1.03	2.45	0.90	0.50
Total Dist ($)	2.00	3.00	4.53	3.50	3.50
Yield from Dist (%)	3.98	7.23	8.05	8.95	6.78
Expense Ratio (%)	0.70	0.66	0.43	0.51	0.52
Portfolio Turnover (%)	0.46	0.36	4.97	3.21	0.08
NAV per share ($)	30.51	44.71	48.54	70.01	54.44
Market Price per share	32.38	50.25	41.50	56.25	39.13
Premium (Discount) (%)	6.13	12.39	(14.50)	(19.65)	(28.14)
Total Return, Stk Price (%)	(31.58)	28.31	(18.17)	52.74	(17.44)

BGR Precious Metals, Inc.

6 Adelaide St. E.
Toronto, Ontario
Canada M5C 1H6
(416) 365-5129

Business Man's Risk

OTC : BPTT

Transfer Agent
The Montreal Trust Co. of Canada
151 Front St. W., 8th Floor
Toronto, Ontario
Canada M5J 2N1
(416) 860-5555

12 Months Ending 12/31/92 Results

	Period End	Period Begin	Distributions	Yield Dist (%)	Total Return (%)
Share Price ($)	6.25	7.63	2.25	29.49	11.40
NAV per share ($)	7.99	8.32		27.04	23.08

Background: Initial public offering October 1983 of $150 million at $10 for one share and one warrant. Initial NAV was $9.42 per share.

Objective: Seeks capital appreciation and inflation hedge by investments directly in precious metals and gold and silver equity shares in Canada, Australia and South Africa. May make use of options and futures contracts but will not make uncovered sales or deal in put options.

Portfolio: (4/1/93) Gold Bullion 9.0%, Gold Related Equities: Canada 51.0%, South Africa 12.0%, Australia 13.0%, U.S. 5.0%, Cash & Other Assets 10.0%.

Capitalization: (10/31/92) Common stock outstanding 5,835,338. No long-term debt.

Beta: 0.56
Fund Manager: BGR Management Ltd. **Fee:** 0.50%
Income Dist: Quarterly **Capital Gains Dist:** Annually
Reinvestment Plan: Yes **Shareholder Reports:** Quarterly

5 Year Performance

Fiscal Year Ending 1/31	1992	1991	1990	1989	1988
Net Assets ($mil):	49.10	50.20	73.60	70.60	84.90
Net Income Dist ($):	1.00	1.00	1.00	1.00	1.00
Cap Gains Dist ($):	0.00	0.00	0.00	0.00	0.00
Total Dist ($)	1.00	1.00	1.00	1.00	1.00
Yield from Dist (%)	13.11	12.30	9.76	10.53	9.76
Expense Ratio (%)	1.19	1.44	1.46	1.32	1.22
Portfolio Turnover (%)	0.00	0.00	0.00	0.00	0.00
NAV per share ($)	8.25	8.42	12.36	11.85	13.87
Market Price per share	7.63	7.63	8.13	10.25	9.50
Premium (Discount) (%)	(7.64)	(9.38)	(34.22)	(13.50)	(31.51)
Total Return, Stk Price (%)	13.11	6.15	(10.93)	18.42	2.44

Duff & Phelps Utilities Income Inc.

55 E. Monroe St., Suite 3600
Chicago, IL 60603
(312) 368-5510

Growth & Income

NYSE : DNP

Transfer Agent
The Bank of New York
Church Street Station
P.O. Box 11258
New York, NY 10286-1258
(800) 524-4458

12 Months Ending 12/31/92 Results

	Period End	Period Begin	Distributions	Yield Dist (%)	Total Return (%)
Share Price ($)	10.50	10.00	0.78	7.80	12.80
NAV per share ($)	9.67	9.55		8.17	9.42

Background: Initial public offering January 16, 1987 of 120,000,000 shares at $10 per share. Initial NAV was $9.30 per share.

Objective: Seeks current and long-term growth of income by investing in a portfolio of equity and fixed-income securities of public utilities companies.

Portfolio: (12/31/92) Common Stocks 55.0%, Bonds 42.7%. Sector Weightings: Electric 73.5%, Telecommunications 18.6%.

Capitalization: (12/31/92) Common stock outstanding 154,851,265. Leveraged with 5,000 preferred shares, stated value $100,000 per share. $18,230,130 senior note 8.75% to be paid by January 1994.

Beta: 0.70
Fund Manager: Duff & Phelps Investment Management Co. **Fee:** 0.60%
Income Dist: Monthly **Capital Gains Dist:** Annually
Reinvestment Plan: Yes **Shareholder Reports:** Quarterly

5 Year Performance

Fiscal Year Ending 12/31	1992	1991	1990	1989	1988
Net Assets ($mil):	1,998.00	1,863.40	1,663.30	1,728.40	1,548.70
Net Income Dist ($):	0.78	0.77	0.76	0.76	0.75
Cap Gains Dist ($):	0.00	0.00	0.00	0.00	0.00
Total Dist ($)	0.78	0.77	0.76	0.76	0.75
Yield from Dist (%)	7.80	8.80	8.81	9.64	9.52
Expense Ratio (%)	1.04	1.17	1.27	1.33	1.59
Portfolio Turnover (%)	43.30	41.09	58.99	92.25	65.68
NAV per share ($)	9.67	9.55	8.29	8.86	7.69
Market Price per share	10.50	10.00	8.75	8.63	7.88
Premium (Discount) (%)	8.58	4.71	5.55	(2.71)	2.34
Total Return, Stk Price (%)	12.80	23.09	10.20	19.16	9.52

First Financial Fund, Inc.

One Seaport Plaza
New York, NY 10292
(800) 451-6788 / (212) 214-3332

NYSE : FF

Transfer Agent
State Street Bank & Trust Co.
One Heritage Dr.
North Quincy, MA 02171
(800) 426-5523

Growth

12 Months Ending 12/31/92 Results

	Period End	Period Begin	Distributions	Yield Dist (%)	Total Return (%)
Share Price ($)	12.75	8.13	2.07	25.46	82.29
NAV per share ($)	13.29	9.23		22.43	66.41

Background: Initial public offering May 8, 1986 of 9,200,000 shares at $10 per share. Initial NAV was $9.25 per share.

Objective: Seeks long-term capital appreciation. Current income is secondary. Under normal conditions, at least 65% of the fund's assets will be held in small- to medium-sized financial institutions.

Portfolio: (12/31/92) Common Stock 90.6%, Convertible Bonds 0.7%, Non-Convertible Bonds 0.1%, Short-Term Investments 11.0%. Largest Holdings: Bankers Corp., North American Mortgage Co., American Residential Holding Co., Calumet Bancorp, Southwest Bancshares.

Capitalization: (12/31/92) Common stock outstanding 9,610,823. No long-term debt.

Beta: 0.76
Fund Manager: Wellington Management Co.
Income Dist: Quarterly
Reinvestment Plan: Yes

Fee: 0.75%
Capital Gains Dist: Annually
Shareholder Reports: Quarterly

5 Year Performance

Fiscal Year Ending 3/31	1992	1991	1990	1989	1988
Net Assets ($mil):	99.10	60.00	66.90	83.20	76.70
Net Income Dist ($):	0.11	0.18	0.26	0.19	0.18
Cap Gains Dist ($):	0.00	0.00	0.86	0.00	0.31
Total Dist ($)	0.11	0.18	1.12	0.19	0.49
Yield from Dist (%)	1.76	2.67	13.78	2.81	5.76
Expense Ratio (%)	1.65	2.14	1.59	1.45	1.46
Portfolio Turnover (%)	89.00	42.00	58.00	41.00	69.00
NAV per share ($)	10.50	6.35	7.09	9.32	8.58
Market Price per share	10.00	6.25	6.75	8.13	6.75
Premium (Discount) (%)	(4.76)	(1.57)	(4.80)	(12.88)	(21.33)
Total Return, Stk Price (%)	61.76	(4.74)	(3.20)	23.26	(14.82)

H&Q Healthcare Investors

50 Rowes Wharf, 4th Floor
Boston, MA 02110-3328
(800) 327-6679 / (617) 574-0567

NYSE : HQH
Transfer Agent
State Street Bank & Trust Co.
225 Franklin St.
Boston, MA 02110
(800) 426-5523

Growth

12 Months Ending 12/31/92 Results

	Period End	Period Begin	Distributions	Yield Dist (%)	Total Return (%)
Share Price ($)	19.00	25.75	0.00	0.00	(26.21)
NAV per share ($)	20.37	22.93		0.00	(11.16)

Background: Initial public offering April 23, 1987 of 5,500,000 shares at $10 per share. Initial NAV was $9.25 per share.

Objective: Seeks long-term capital appreciation through investments in health care and medical technology companies. May invest up to 25% in venture capital and restricted securities.

Portfolio: (9/30/92) Common Stocks 82.5%, Convertible Securities 17.3%, Short Term 3.1%. Sector Weightings: Biotechnology 30.7%, Managed Care 13.1%, Medical Supplies 10.8%, Medical Specialty 7.5%, Health Services 6.2%. Largest Holdings: U.S. Health Care, Martek, Medco Containment Services, Ribi ImmunoChem Research, ALZA.

Capitalization: (9/30/92) Shares of beneficial interest outstanding 5,549,198. No long-term debt.

Beta: 1.35
Fund Manager: Hambrecht & Quist Capital Management, Inc.   **Fee:** 1.00%
Income Dist: Annually   **Capital Gains Dist:** Annually
Reinvestment Plan: Yes   **Shareholder Reports:** Quarterly

5 Year Performance

Fiscal Year Ending 9/30	1992	1991	1990	1989	1988
Net Assets ($mil):	96.20	106.40	62.70	59.00	44.50
Net Income Dist ($):	0.04	0.06	0.00	0.00	0.00
Cap Gains Dist ($):	0.92	0.78	0.00	0.00	0.02
Total Dist ($)	0.96	0.84	0.00	0.00	0.02
Yield from Dist (%)	5.22	8.50	0.00	0.00	0.25
Expense Ratio (%)	1.72	1.73	1.74	1.89	1.98
Portfolio Turnover (%)	35.45	23.04	47.02	46.90	57.42
NAV per share ($)	17.34	19.21	11.31	10.65	8.04
Market Price per share	19.38	18.38	9.88	9.13	6.50
Premium (Discount) (%)	11.78	(4.31)	(12.76)	(14.34)	(19.11)
Total Return, Stk Price (%)	10.66	94.53	8.21	40.46	(19.80)

Hampton Utilities Trust

777 Mariners Island Blvd.
San Mateo, CA 94403-7777
(800) 342-5236 / (415) 378-2000

AMEX : HU

Transfer Agent
Provident National Bank
P.O. Box 8950
Wilmington, DE 19899
(800) 852-4750

Growth & Income

12 Months Ending 12/31/92 Results

	Period End	Period Begin	Distributions	Yield Dist (%)	Total Return (%)
Share Price ($)	14.25	13.38	0.35	2.62	9.12
NAV per share ($)	15.77	15.02		2.33	7.32

Background: Initial public offering March 7, 1988 of 1,022,500 capital shares at $10 per share (Initial NAV $9.35) and 200,000 cumulative preferred shares at $50 per share.

Objective: Seeks long-term capital appreciation and current income. Invests at least 65% in dividend-paying public utilities. Invests at least 75% in securities rated A.

Portfolio: (12/31/92) Common Stocks 94.0%, Government Securities 3.2%, Other 2.8%.

Capitalization: (12/31/92) Common stock outstanding 1,032,684. Leveraged with 200,100 shares preferred stock.

Beta: 0.59
Fund Manager: Franklin Advisers, Inc.
Income Dist: Quarterly
Reinvestment Plan: Yes

Fee: 0.80%
Capital Gains Dist: Annually
Shareholder Reports: Quarterly

5 Year Performance

Fiscal Year Ending 12/31	1992	1991	1990	1989	1988 (10 mos.)
Net Assets ($mil):	26.20	25.40	22.20	22.80	19.80
Net Income Dist ($):	0.27	0.28	0.36	0.38	0.28
Cap Gains Dist ($):	0.08	0.10	0.00	0.00	0.02
Total Dist ($)	0.35	0.38	0.36	0.38	0.29
Yield from Dist (%)	2.62	3.85	3.23	4.28	—
Expense Ratio (%)	1.17	1.33	1.25	1.45	1.14
Portfolio Turnover (%)	3.44	18.82	5.44	18.30	8.66
NAV per share ($)	15.77	15.02	12.02	12.71	9.80
Market Price per share	14.25	13.38	9.88	11.13	8.88
Premium (Discount) (%)	(9.64)	(10.99)	(17.80)	(12.51)	(9.49)
Total Return, Stk Price (%)	9.12	39.27	(8.00)	29.62	—

Petroleum & Resources Corporation

Seven St. Paul St., Suite 1140
Baltimore, MD 21202
(800) 638-2479 / (410) 752-5900

NYSE : PEO
Transfer Agent
The Bank of New York
101 Barclay St.
New York, NY 10007
(800) 524-4458

Growth

12 Months Ending 12/31/92 Results

	Period End	Period Begin	Distributions	Yield Dist (%)	Total Return (%)
Share Price ($)	25.25	26.00	2.00	7.69	4.81
NAV per share ($)	27.66	28.07		7.13	5.66

Background: Founded in 1929 as the Petroleum Corp. of America. Name was changed to Petroleum & Resources Corporation in April 1977.

Objective: Seeks capital appreciation consistent with preservation of principal. Portfolio is made up primarily of energy and natural resources stocks that pay regular dividends.

Portfolio: (9/30/92) Stocks & Convertible Securities 88.6%, Short Term 11.1%. Sector Weightings: International Oils 26.5%, Domestic Oils 14.5%, Energy Distributors 13.9%, Energy Producers 12.3%, Basic Industry 9.2%. Largest Holdings: Royal Dutch Petroleum , Atlantic Richfield, Exxon, Mobil, Texaco.

Capitalization: (12/31/92) Common stock outstanding 11,579,503. Of the common stock outstanding, 9.5% owned by Adams Express Co. No long-term debt.

Beta: 0.55
Fund Manager: Petroleum & Resources Corporation
Income Dist: Quarterly
Reinvestment Plan: Yes

Fee: 0.20%
Capital Gains Dist: Annually
Shareholder Reports: Quarterly

5 Year Performance

Fiscal Year Ending 12/31	1992	1991	1990	1989	1988
Net Assets ($mil):	350.10	343.90	308.60	352.80	248.40
Net Income Dist ($):	0.77	0.92	1.10	1.20	0.92
Cap Gains Dist ($):	1.23	1.23	1.25	1.20	1.20
Total Dist ($)	2.00	2.15	2.35	2.40	2.12
Yield from Dist (%)	7.69	8.56	8.70	11.43	10.22
Expense Ratio (%)	52.00	59.00	57.00	66.00	68.00
Portfolio Turnover (%)	15.06	11.41	18.41	18.68	14.35
NAV per share ($)	27.66	28.07	28.59	31.09	24.84
Market Price per share	25.25	26.00	25.13	27.00	21.00
Premium (Discount) (%)	(8.71)	(7.37)	(12.10)	(13.16)	(15.46)
Total Return, Stk Price (%)	4.81	12.02	1.78	40.00	11.42

Pilgrim Regional BankShares
10100 Santa Monica Blvd., 21st Floor
Los Angeles, CA 90067
(800) 334-3444 / (213) 551-0833

NYSE : PBS
Transfer Agent
Investors Fiduciary Trust Co.
P.O. Box 419338
Kansas City, MO 64141-6338
(816) 474-8786

Growth

12 Months Ending 12/31/92 Results

	Period End	Period Begin	Distributions	Yield Dist (%)	Total Return (%)
Share Price ($)	11.63	9.50	0.81*	7.26	30.95
NAV per share ($)	12.46	10.12		6.82	31.13

Background: Initial public offering January 24, 1986 of 10,000,000 shares at $10.00 per share. Original NAV was $9.30 per share.

Objective: Seeks long-term capital appreciation. Income is secondary. Invests at least 65% of assets in equity securities of regional banks and bank holding companies with consolidated assets of $1 billion or more. Balance may be invested in equity securities of money center banks, other financial services companies, and other issuers and debt securities. To minimize its discount to NAV, the fund has a policy of distributing 1.75% of its net asset value to shareholders quarterly.

Portfolio: (12/31/92) Common Stock 98.9%, Commercial Paper 2.0%, Agency Discount Notes 1.5%. Sector Weightings: Regional Banks 78.0%, Community Banks 13.6%, Thrifts 7.3%.

Capitalization: (12/31/92) Common stock outstanding 11,271,505. No long-term debt.

Beta: 0.80
Fund Manager: Pilgrim Management Corp.
Income Dist: Quarterly
Reinvestment Plan: Yes

Fee: 1.00%
Capital Gains Dist: Annually
Shareholder Reports: Quarterly

5 Year Performance

Fiscal Year Ending 12/31	1992	1991	1990	1989	1988
Net Assets ($mil):	140.60	101.10	74.90	102.60	95.70
Net Income Dist ($):	0.22	0.24	0.31	0.31	0.37
Cap Gains Dist ($):	0.47	0.00	0.00	0.44	0.00
Total Dist ($)	0.81*	0.24	0.31	0.75	0.37
Yield from Dist (%)	7.26	3.37	3.40	9.68	5.92
Expense Ratio (%)	1.24	1.31	1.29	1.26	1.18
Portfolio Turnover (%)	20.00	31.00	46.00	63.00	43.00
NAV per share ($)	12.46	10.12	7.49	10.26	9.54
Market Price per share	11.63	9.50	7.13	9.13	7.75
Premium (Discount) (%)	(6.66)	(6.13)	(4.94)	(11.11)	(18.76)
Total Return, Stk Price (%)	30.95	36.61	(19.51)	27.48	29.92

* Includes $0.12 return of capital.

Real Estate Securities Income Fund, Inc.

757 Third Ave.
New York, NY 10017
(212) 832-3232

AMEX : RIF
Transfer Agent
Mutual Funds Service Co.
126 High St.
Boston, MA 02110
(800) 437-9912

Income

12 Months Ending 12/31/92 Results

	Period End	Period Begin	Distributions	Yield Dist (%)	Total Return (%)
Share Price ($)	8.00	7.13	0.68*	9.12	21.74
NAV per share ($)	7.63	7.35		8.84	13.06

Background: Initial public offering August 23, 1988 of 2,400,000 shares at $10 per share. Initial NAV was $9.15 per share.

Objective: Seeks high current income. Capital appreciation is secondary. Invests at least 65% in shares of REITs, units of master limited partnerships, common and preferred stocks and convertible debt securities of real estate companies having attractive equity characteristics.

Portfolio: (12/31/92) Equities 84.6%, Fixed Income 21.0%, Short Term Liabilities (5.5%). Sector Weightings: Health Care 35.2%, Shopping Centers 34.0%, Office/Industrial 10.0%, Diversified 5.3%.

Capitalization: (12/31/92) Common stock outstanding 2,793,789. No long-term debt.

Beta: 0.54
Fund Manager: Cohen & Steers Capital Management, Inc.   **Fee:** 0.65%
Income Dist: Quarterly   **Capital Gains Dist:** Annually
Reinvestment Plan: Yes   **Shareholder Reports:** Quarterly

5 Year Performance

Fiscal Year Ending 12/31	1992	1991	1990	1989	1988 (4 mos.)
Net Assets ($mil):	21.30	20.40	14.80	20.70	23.90
Net Income Dist ($):	0.65	0.64	0.72	1.00	0.33
Cap Gains Dist ($):	0.00	0.00	0.00	0.00	0.00
Total Dist ($)	0.68*	0.64	0.72	1.00	0.33
Yield from Dist (%)	9.12	13.82	11.29	11.59	—
Expense Ratio (%)	1.63	1.66	1.88	1.29	2.90
Portfolio Turnover (%)	79.51	77.62	103.11	163.40	79.35
NAV per share ($)	7.63	7.35	5.33	7.46	8.75
Market Price per share	8.00	7.13	4.63	6.38	8.63
Premium (Discount) (%)	4.85	(3.13)	(13.13)	(14.61)	(1.49)
Total Return, Stk Price (%)	21.74	67.82	(16.14)	(14.48)	—

* Includes $0.03 return of capital.

Southeastern Thrift & Bank Fund, Inc.

101 Huntington Ave.
Boston, MA 02199
(617) 725-2192

OTC : STBF

Transfer Agent
Ameritrust Co. NA
900 Euclid Ave.
Cleveland, OH 4415
(800) 225-6258

Growth

12 Months Ending 12/31/92 Results

	Period End	Period Begin	Distributions	Yield Dist (%)	Total Return (%)
Share Price ($)	13.25	7.25	0.04	0.55	83.31
NAV per share ($)	15.53	8.84		0.45	76.13

Background: Initial public offering August 23, 1989 of 2,110,000 shares at $12 per share. Initial NAV was $11.16 per share.

Objective: Seeks capital appreciation through investments in savings and loan institutions and commercial banks.

Portfolio: (11/30/92) Common Stocks 96.85%, Convertible Bonds 0.28%,. Cash & Equivalents 2.87%. Largest Holdings: SoCarolina Fed, DF Southeastern, United Financial Corp SC, Gwinnett Bancshares, Fortune Bancorp.

Capitalization: (11/30/92) Common stock outstanding 1,992,483. No long-term debt.

Beta: 0.55
Fund Manager: John Hancock Advisors, Inc.   **Fee:** 0.65%
Income Dist: Quarterly   **Capital Gains Dist:** Annually
Reinvestment Plan: Yes   **Shareholder Reports:** Semi-Annually

5 Year Performance

Fiscal Year Ending 6/30	1992	1991	1990 (10 mos.)	1989	1988
Net Assets ($mil):	25.60	15.40	15.60	—	—
Net Income Dist ($):	0.10	0.17	0.13	—	—
Cap Gains Dist ($):	0.00	0.00	0.00	—	—
Total Dist ($)	0.10	0.17	0.13	—	—
Yield from Dist (%)	1.60	3.48	—	—	—
Expense Ratio (%)	2.17	2.76	1.73	—	—
Portfolio Turnover (%)	41.98	18.48	16.33	—	—
NAV per share ($)	12.86	7.71	7.73	—	—
Market Price per share	10.75	6.25	4.88	—	—
Premium (Discount) (%)	(16.41)	(18.94)	(37.00)	—	—
Total Return, Stk Price (%)	73.60	31.56	—	—	—

Dual Purpose Equity Funds

Convertible Holdings, Inc.—*Capital Shares*
P.O. Box 9011
Princeton, NJ 08543-9011
(609) 282-2800

NYSE : CNV
Transfer Agent
State Street Bank & Trust Co.
225 Franklin St.
Boston, MA 02110
(617) 328-5000

Growth

12 Months Ending 12/31/92 Results

	Period End	Period Begin	Distributions	Yield Dist (%)	Total Return (%)
Share Price ($)	9.25	6.88	0.12	1.74	36.19
NAV per share ($)	12.87	10.91		1.10	19.07

Background: Initial public offering August 2, 1985 of 13,605,400 capital shares at $8.50 per share and 13,605,400 income shares at $11.50 per share. Formerly known as Merrill Lynch Convertible Securities.

Objective: Capital Shareholders: Long term capital appreciation. Income Shareholders: Current long term growth. Minimum cumulative dividend on the income shares is $1 per share per year and redeemable on July 31, 1997 for $9.30 per share plus accumulated dividends. Capital shareholders will receive remaining assets.

Portfolio: (12/31/92) Convertible Debentures 61.9%, Common Stocks 20.1%, Convertible Preferred Stocks 12.0%, Short Term 6.7%. Sector Weightings: Banking & Finance 17.2%, Retail 6.4%, Manufactured Housing 4.8%, Oil & Gas Producers 4.3%, Drugs 4.0%.

Capitalization: (12/31/92) Common stock outstanding 13,051,000.

Beta: 0.86
Fund Manager: Merrill Lynch Asset Management
Income Dist: Annually
Reinvestment Plan: No

Fee: 0.60%
Capital Gains Dist: Annually
Shareholder Reports: Quarterly

5 Year Performance

Fiscal Year Ending 12/31	1992	1991	1990	1989	1988
Net Assets ($mil):	289.40	275.00	230.80	264.30	245.00
Net Income Dist ($):	0.00	0.00	0.00	0.00	0.00
Cap Gains Dist ($):	0.12	0.00	0.00	0.00	0.00
Total Dist ($)	0.12	0.00	0.00	0.00	0.00
Yield from Dist (%)	1.74	0.00	0.00	0.00	0.00
Expense Ratio (%)	0.80	0.83	0.86	0.80	0.79
Portfolio Turnover (%)	76.54	54.90	40.28	50.47	48.72
NAV per share ($)	12.87	10.91	7.67	10.12	8.69
Market Price per share	9.25	6.88	4.13	5.50	4.25
Premium (Discount) (%)	(28.13)	(37.03)	(46.15)	(45.65)	(51.09)
Total Return, Stk Price (%)	36.19	66.59	(24.91)	29.41	9.54

Convertible Holdings, Inc.—*Income Shares*

P.O. Box 9011
Princeton, NJ 08543-9011
(609) 282-2800

NYSE : CNV+
Transfer Agent
State Street Bank & Trust Co.
225 Franklin St.
Boston, MA 02110
(617) 328-5000

Income

12 Months Ending 12/31/92 Results

	Period End	Period Begin	Distributions	Yield Dist (%)	Total Return (%)
Share Price ($)	11.25	12.63	1.36	10.77	(0.16)
NAV per share ($)	9.30	9.31		14.61	14.50

Background: Initial public offering August 2, 1985 of 13,605,400 capital shares at $8.50 per share and 13,605,400 income shares at $11.50 per share. Formerly known as Merrill Lynch Convertible Securities.

Objective: Capital Shareholders: Long term capital appreciation. Income Shareholders: Current long term growth. Minimum cumulative dividend on the income shares is $1 per share per year and redeemable on July 31, 1997 for $9.30 per share plus accumulated dividends. Capital shareholders will receive remaining assets.

Portfolio: (12/31/92) Convertible Debentures 61.9%, Common Stocks 20.1%, Convertible Preferred Stocks 12.0%, Short Term 6.7%. Sector Weightings: Banking & Finance 17.2%, Retail 6.4%, Manufactured Housing 4.8%, Oil & Gas Producers 4.3%, Drugs 4.0%.

Capitalization: (12/31/92) Common stock outstanding 13,051,000.

Beta: (0.02)
Fund Manager: Merrill Lynch Asset Management **Fee:** 0.60%
Income Dist: Annually **Capital Gains Dist:** Annually
Reinvestment Plan: No **Shareholder Reports:** Quarterly

5 Year Performance

Fiscal Year Ending 12/31	1992	1991	1990	1989	1988
Net Assets ($mil):	289.40	275.00	230.80	264.30	245.00
Net Income Dist ($):	1.36	1.40	1.38	1.41	1.47
Cap Gains Dist ($):	0.00	0.00	0.00	0.00	0.00
Total Dist ($)	1.36	1.40	1.38	1.41	1.47
Yield from Dist (%)	10.77	12.87	12.00	12.26	14.00
Expense Ratio (%)	0.80	0.83	0.86	0.80	0.79
Portfolio Turnover (%)	76.54	54.90	40.28	50.47	48.72
NAV per share ($)	9.30	9.31	9.30	9.30	9.32
Market Price per share	11.25	12.63	10.88	11.50	11.50
Premium (Discount) (%)	20.97	35.55	16.88	23.66	23.39
Total Return, Stk Price (%)	(0.16)	28.95	6.61	12.26	23.52

Gemini II Inc.—*Capital Shares*   **NYSE : GMI**

P.O. Box 823   *Transfer Agent*
Valley Forge, PA 19482   First National Bank of Boston
(800) 662-7447 / (215) 647-6000   P.O. Box 644
                                                                                Boston, MA 02102
                                                                (800) 662-2739 / (617) 575-2900

Growth

12 Months Ending 12/31/92 Results

	Period End	Period Begin	Distributions	Yield Dist (%)	Total Return (%)
Share Price ($)	14.88	13.25	0.08	0.60	12.91
NAV per share ($)	18.71	16.28		0.49	15.42

Background: Initial public offering February 15, 1985. $200,000,000 underwriting with initial NAV of $9.30 per share.

Objective: Capital Shareholders: Long term capital growth. Income Shareholders: Current income and growth. Invests at least 80% of assets in common stock with low price/earnings ratios, and above average yields. Income shares are redeemable January 31, 1997 at $9.30 per share plus accumulated dividends.

Portfolio: (12/31/92) Common Stocks 60.1%, Convertible Preferred Stocks 16.4%, Bonds 13.6%, U.S. Government Obligations 8.9%, Cash & Other 1.0%.

Capitalization: (12/31/92) Common stock outstanding 10,920,550 shares of each class.

Beta: 0.65
Fund Manager: Wellington Management   **Fee:** 0.35%
Income Dist: Quarterly   **Capital Gains Dist:** Annually
Reinvestment Plan: No   **Shareholder Reports:** Semi-Annually

5 Year Performance

Fiscal Year Ending 12/31	1992	1991	1990	1989	1988
Net Assets ($mil):	306.20	279.90	227.70	—	—
Net Income Dist ($):	0.00	0.00	0.00	0.00	0.00
Cap Gains Dist ($):	0.08	0.22	0.11	0.19	0.22
Total Dist ($)	0.08	0.22	0.11	0.19	0.22
Yield from Dist (%)	0.60	2.35	0.70	1.48	2.07
Expense Ratio (%)	0.00	0.00	0.00	0.00	0.00
Portfolio Turnover (%)	0.00	0.00	0.00	0.00	0.00
NAV per share ($)	18.71	16.28	11.51	17.44	16.56
Market Price per share	14.88	13.25	9.38	15.63	12.88
Premium (Discount) (%)	(20.52)	(18.61)	(18.59)	(10.44)	(22.28)
Total Return, Stk Price (%)	12.91	43.60	(39.28)	22.83	23.24

Gemini II Inc.—*Income Shares*

P.O. Box 823
Valley Forge, PA 19482
(800) 662-7447 / (215) 669-1000

Transfer Agent
First National Bank of Boston
P.O. Box 644
Boston, MA 02102
(800) 662-2739 / (617) 575-2900

Income

12 Months Ending 12/31/92 Results

	Period End	Period Begin	Distributions	Yield Dist (%)	Total Return (%)
Share Price ($)	12.00	13.38	1.67	12.48	2.17
NAV per share ($)	9.33	9.34		17.88	17.77

Background: Initial public offering February 15, 1985. $200,000,000 underwriting with initial NAV of $9.30 per share.

Objective: Capital Shareholders: Long term capital growth. Income Shareholders: Current income and growth. Invests at least 80% of assets in common stock with low price/earnings ratios, and above average yields. Income shares are redeemable on January 31, 1997 at $9.30 per share plus accumulated dividends.

Portfolio: (12/31/92) Common Stocks 60.1%, Convertible Preferred Stocks 16.4%, Bonds 13.6%, U.S. Government Obligations 8.9%, Cash & Other 1.0%.

Capitalization: (12/31/92) Common stock outstanding 10,920,550 shares of each class.

Beta: 0.18
Fund Manager: Wellington Management Co. **Fee:** 0.35%
Income Dist: Quarterly **Capital Gains Dist:** Annually
Reinvestment Plan: No **Shareholder Reports:** Semi-Annually

5 Year Performance

Fiscal Year Ending 12/31	1992	1991	1990	1989	1988
Net Assets ($mil):	306.20	279.90	227.70	—	—
Net Income Dist ($):	1.67	1.65	1.66	1.59	1.42
Cap Gains Dist ($):	0.00	0.00	0.00	0.00	0.00
Total Dist ($)	1.67	1.65	1.66	1.59	1.42
Yield from Dist (%)	12.48	14.67	12.77	12.72	11.95
Expense Ratio (%)	0.00	0.00	0.00	0.00	0.00
Portfolio Turnover (%)	0.00	0.00	0.00	0.00	0.00
NAV per share ($)	9.33	9.34	9.34	9.37	9.38
Market Price per share	12.00	13.38	11.25	13.00	12.50
Premium (Discount) (%)	28.62	43.15	20.45	38.74	33.26
Total Return, Stk Price (%)	2.17	33.60	(0.69)	16.72	17.17

294   *Closed-End Funds*

Quest for Value Dual Purpose Fund, Inc.—*Capital Shares*

One World Financial Center, 37th Fl.
New York, NY 10281
(800) 525-1103 / (212) 667-7561

NYSE : KFV

Transfer Agent
State Street Bank & Trust Co.
P.O. Box 366
Boston, MA 02101
(800) 232-3863

Growth

12 Months Ending 12/31/92 Results

	Period End	Period Begin	Distributions	Yield Dist (%)	Total Return (%)
Share Price ($)	23.00	17.63	1.29	7.32	37.78
NAV per share ($)	26.29	22.59		5.71	22.09

Background: Initial public offering February 3, 1987. 18,000,000 capital shares and 18,000,000 income shares sold at $12.50 per share. Initial NAV for both classes of stock was $11.60 or $417.6 million in total assets.

Objective: Capital Shareholders: Long term capital appreciation and preservation of capital. Income Shareholders: Current income and long term growth. May invest no more than 25% in securities of issuers in any single foreign country. The fund will liquidate or convert to an open-end fund in January 1997, at which time the Capital shares will be redeemable at their NAV.

Portfolio: (12/31/92) Common Stocks 74.7%, Convertible Preferred Stocks 13.5%, Convertible Bonds 4.3%, Corporate Bonds & Notes 9.4%.

Capitalization: (6/30/92) Common stock outstanding 22,450,639.

Beta: 0.63
Fund Manager: Quest for Value Advisors, Inc.
Income Dist: Annually
Reinvestment Plan: No

Fee: 0.75%
Capital Gains Dist: Annually
Shareholder Reports: Quarterly

5 Year Performance

Fiscal Year Ending 12/31	1992	1991	1990	1989	1988
Net Assets ($mil):	682.40	615.70	504.70	534.00	425.40
Net Income Dist ($):	0.00	0.00	0.00	0.00	0.00
Cap Gains Dist ($):	1.29	0.01	0.20	0.00	0.00
Total Dist ($)	1.29	0.01	0.20	0.00	0.00
Yield from Dist (%)	7.32	0.08	1.42	0.00	0.00
Expense Ratio (%)	0.74	0.77	0.81	0.83	0.86
Portfolio Turnover (%)	45.00	62.00	78.00	76.00	155.00
NAV per share ($)	26.29	22.59	16.43	18.05	11.93
Market Price per share	23.00	17.63	12.00	14.13	8.63
Premium (Discount) (%)	(12.51)	(21.96)	(26.96)	(21.77)	(27.75)
Total Return, Stk Price (%)	37.78	47.00	(13.66)	63.73	35.27

Quest for Value Dual Purpose Fund, Inc.—*Income Shares*

One World Financial Center, 37th Fl.
New York, NY 10281
(800) 525-1103 / (212) 667-7500

NYSE : KFV+
Transfer Agent
State Street Bank & Trust Co.
P.O. Box 366
Boston, MA 02101
(800) 232-3863

Income

12 Months Ending 12/31/92 Results

	Period End	Period Begin	Distributions	Yield Dist (%)	Total Return (%)
Share Price ($)	13.00	13.38	1.34	10.01	7.17
NAV per share ($)	11.61	11.60		11.55	11.64

Background: Initial public offering on February 3, 1987. 18,000,000 capital shares and 18,000,000 income shares sold at $12.50 per share. Initial NAV for both classes of stock was $11.60 or $417.6 million in total assets.

Objective: Capital Shareholders: Long term capital appreciation and preservation of capital. Income Shareholders: Current income and long term growth. May invest no more than 25% in securities of issuers in any single foreign country. The income shares are scheduled to be redeemed in January of 1997 at $11.60 per share plus all accumulated and unpaid dividends.

Portfolio: (12/31/92) Common Stocks 74.7%, Convertible Preferred Stocks 13.5%, Convertible Bonds 4.3%, Corporate Bonds & Notes 9.4%.

Capitalization: (6/30/92) Common stock outstanding 22,450,639.

Beta: 0.02
Fund Manager: Quest for Value Advisors, Inc.   **Fee:** 0.75%
Income Dist: Quarterly   **Capital Gains Dist:** Annually
Reinvestment Plan: Yes   **Shareholder Reports:** Quarterly

5 Year Performance

Fiscal Year Ending 12/31	1992	1991	1990	1989	1988
Net Assets ($mil):	682.40	615.70	504.70	534.00	425.40
Net Income Dist ($):	1.34	1.37	1.58	1.49	1.05
Cap Gains Dist ($):	0.00	0.00	0.00	0.00	0.00
Total Dist ($)	1.34	1.37	1.58	1.49	1.05
Yield from Dist (%)	10.01	10.64	12.15	14.19	12.00
Expense Ratio (%)	0.74	0.77	0.81	0.83	0.86
Portfolio Turnover (%)	45.00	62.00	78.00	76.00	155.00
NAV per share ($)	11.61	11.60	11.60	11.61	11.69
Market Price per share	13.00	13.38	12.88	13.00	10.50
Premium (Discount) (%)	11.97	15.26	11.03	11.97	(10.18)
Total Return, Stk Price (%)	7.17	14.52	11.23	38.00	32.00

Multi Country (Regional) Equity Funds

Alliance Global Environment Fund

1345 Avenue of the Americas
New York, NY 10105
(800) 247-4154 / (212) 969-1000

NYSE : AEF
Transfer Agent
State Street Bank & Trust Co.
225 Franklin St.
Boston, MA 02110
(800) 426-5523

Growth

12 Months Ending 12/31/92 Results

	Period End	Period Begin	Distributions	Yield Dist (%)	Total Return (%)
Share Price ($)	9.63	11.63	0.18	1.55	(15.65)
NAV per share ($)	11.38	13.35		1.35	(13.41)

Background: Initial public offering June 1, 1990 of 6,000,000 shares at $15 per share. Initial NAV was $13.95 per share.

Objective: Seeks long-term capital appreciation. Invests in companies expected to benefit from increased global awareness for a cleaner environment.

Portfolio: (10/31/92) Common & Preferred Stock 90.3%, Short Term 9.0%, Convertible Bonds 0.5%. Country Exposure: U.S. 50.2%, U.K. 15.9%, France 9.7%, Japan 4.7%, Germany 3.2%.

Capitalization: (10/31/92) Common stock outstanding 6,907,000. No long-term debt.

Beta: 0.22
Fund Manager: Alliance Capital Management L.P.
Income Dist: Annually
Reinvestment Plan: Yes

Fee: 0.10%
Capital Gains Dist: Annually
Shareholder Reports: Semi-Annually

5 Year Performance

Fiscal Year Ending 10/31	1992	1991	1990 (5 mos.)	1989	1988
Net Assets ($mil):	74.40	90.60	86.00	—	—
Net Income Dist ($):	0.10	0.25	0.00	—	—
Cap Gains Dist ($):	0.08	0.09	0.00	—	—
Total Dist ($)	0.18	0.34	0.00	—	—
Yield from Dist (%)	1.58	3.36	—	—	—
Expense Ratio (%)	1.63	1.49	1.72	—	—
Portfolio Turnover (%)	41.00	32.00	4.00	—	—
NAV per share ($)	10.78	13.12	12.46	—	—
Market Price per share	9.50	11.38	10.13	—	—
Premium (Discount) (%)	(11.87)	(13.26)	(18.78)	—	—
Total Return, Stk Price (%)	(14.94)	15.70	—	—	—

America's All Season Fund

201 W. Canton Ave., Suite 100
Winter Park, FL 32789
(800) 432-0000 / (407) 629-1400

OTC : FUND

Transfer Agent
State Street Bank & Trust Co.
225 Franklin St.
Boston, MA 02110
(800) 333-4222

Growth

12 Months Ending 12/31/92 Results

	Period End	Period Begin	Distributions	Yield Dist (%)	Total Return (%)
Share Price ($)	4.00	4.50	0.42*	3.51	(1.78)
NAV per share ($)	5.11	6.01		2.16	(7.99)

Background: Initial public offering March 2, 1988 of 5,000,000 shares at $6.00 per share. Initial NAV was $5.51 per share.

Objective: Seeks to achieve long-term capital appreciation without undue risk and with preservation of capital. Any current income achieved by the fund is incidental. The fund may invest up to 25% in gold or silver bullion, or in certificates for gold or silver.

Portfolio: (12/31/92) Common Stocks 71.5%, Foreign Government Obligations 20.22%, Foreign Bank Obligations 26.37%. Country Exposure: U.S. 39.9%, Switzerland 10.3%, U.K. 6.2%, Australia 3.6%, Singapore 3.4%. Largest Holdings: Merck & Co., Procter & Gamble Co., Swiss Bank Corp., Hauser Research, Cadbury Schweppes.

Capitalization: (12/31/92) Common stock outstanding 8,742,557. No long-term debt.

Beta: 0.44
Fund Manager: Veitia & Associates, Inc.
Income Dist: Quarterly
Reinvestment Plan: Yes

Fee: 1.00%
Capital Gains Dist: Annually
Shareholder Reports: Semi-Annually

5 Year Performance

Fiscal Year Ending 12/31	1992	1991	1990	1989	1988 (9 mos.)
Net Assets ($mil):	43.60	52.50	48.80	51.70	—
Net Income Dist ($):	0.13	0.17	0.24	0.23	0.25
Cap Gains Dist ($):	0.00	0.11	0.05	0.03	0.00
Total Dist ($)	0.42*	0.28	0.29	0.26	0.25
Yield from Dist (%)	2.89	5.33	5.80	4.00	—
Expense Ratio (%)	2.21	2.36	2.45	1.99	2.17
Portfolio Turnover (%)	267.00	269.00	312.00	244.00	30.00
NAV per share ($)	4.99	6.01	5.59	5.91	5.52
Market Price per share	4.00	4.50	5.25	5.00	6.50
Premium (Discount) (%)	(19.84)	(25.12)	(6.08)	(15.40)	17.75
Total Return, Stk Price (%)	(1.78)	(8.95)	10.80	(19.08)	—

Includes $0.29 from "other sources".

Asia Pacific Fund, Inc. (The)

One Seaport Plaza
New York, NY 10292
(800) 451-6788 / (212) 214-3334

NYSE : APB

Transfer Agent
State Street Bank & Trust Co.
1 Heritage Dr
North Quincy, MA 02171
(800) 426-5523

Growth

12 Months Ending 12/31/92 Results

	Period End	Period Begin	Distributions	Yield Dist (%)	Total Return (%)
Share Price ($)	15.00	12.75	1.74	13.65	31.29
NAV per share ($)	12.46	12.24		14.22	16.01

Background: Initial public offering April 24, 1987 of 8,650,000 shares at $10 per share. Initial NAV was $9.30 per share.

Objective: Seeks long-term capital appreciation by participating in the economies of Asian Pacific countries through a diversified portfolio of equity securities.

Portfolio: (9/30/92) Equities & Equity Equivalents 104.8%, Repurchase Agreements 12.9%, Liabilities in excess of other Net Assets (17.7%). Country Exposure: Hong Kong 55.9%, Malaysia 18.2%, Singapore 10.6%, Thailand 12.9%, Philippines 2.4%, Korea 2.3%, Indonesia 1.9%, Pakistan 0.6%.

Capitalization: (3/31/92) Common stock outstanding 8,833,915. Leveraged 15.6%.

Beta: 0.93
Fund Manager: Baring International Investment Ltd.
Income Dist: Annually
Reinvestment Plan: Yes

Fee: 1.10%
Capital Gains Dist: Annually
Shareholder Reports: Quarterly

5 Year Performance

Fiscal Year Ending 3/31	1992	1991	1990	1989	1988 (11 mos.)
Net Assets ($mil):	116.80	124.90	136.10	94.70	67.50
Net Income Dist ($):	0.13	0.04	0.01	0.06	0.00
Cap Gains Dist ($):	2.34	1.24	0.14	0.01	0.00
Total Dist ($)	2.47	1.28	0.15	0.07	0.00
Yield from Dist (%)	17.80	9.22	1.67	1.12	—
Expense Ratio (%)	1.92	1.85	1.72	2.02	1.99
Portfolio Turnover (%)	63.00	37.00	46.00	39.00	45.00
NAV per share ($)	13.23	14.20	15.71	10.93	7.79
Market Price per share	15.50	13.88	13.88	9.00	6.25
Premium (Discount) (%)	17.16	(2.32)	(11.71)	(17.66)	(19.77)
Total Return, Stk Price (%)	29.47	9.22	55.89	45.12	—

Clemente Global Growth Fund, Inc.

152 W. 57th St.
New York, NY 10019
(212) 765-0700

NYSE : CLM
Transfer Agent
The Bank of New York
101 Barclay St.
New York, NY 10007
(800) 524-4458

Growth

12 Months Ending 12/31/92 Results

	Period End	Period Begin	Distributions	Yield Dist (%)	Total Return (%)
Share Price ($)	7.75	9.13	1.05	11.50	(3.61)
NAV per share ($)	9.43	10.82		9.70	(3.14)

Background: Initial public offering on June 23, 1987 had 6,000,000 common shares at $10 per share. Initial NAV was $9.23 per share.

Objective: Seeks long-term capital appreciation. Invests in equity securities of small- and medium-sized companies throughout the world. Will invest between 50% and 75% in securities traded outside the United States.

Portfolio: (12/31/92) Common Stock 95.0%, Short Term 16.2%, Other Assets, Less Liabilities (11.2%). Country Exposure: U.S. 29.7%, Japan 13.9%, Hong Kong 12.2%, Mexico 10.8%, Korea 7.4%, Philippines 5.7%.

Capitalization: (12/31/92) Common stock outstanding 5,892,400. No long-term debt.

Beta: 0.52
Fund Manager: Clemente Capital, Inc.　　　　　　　　　　**Fee:** 1.00%
Income Dist: Annually　　　　　　　　　　**Capital Gains Dist:** Annually
Reinvestment Plan: Yes　　　　　　　　　　**Shareholder Reports:** Quarterly

5 Year Performance

Fiscal Year Ending 12/31	1992	1991	1990	1989	1988
Net Assets ($mil):	55.50	63.80	57.70	69.00	51.40
Net Income Dist ($):	0.02	0.00	0.00	0.00	0.02
Cap Gains Dist ($):	1.03	0.35	0.16	0.16	0.04
Total Dist ($)	1.05	0.35	0.16	0.16	0.06
Yield from Dist (%)	11.50	4.12	1.58	2.17	1.04
Expense Ratio (%)	2.23	2.64	2.76	2.70	2.38
Portfolio Turnover (%)	82.49	66.11	28.69	67.35	97.64
NAV per share ($)	9.43	10.82	9.79	11.71	8.72
Market Price per share	7.75	9.13	8.50	10.13	7.38
Premium (Discount) (%)	(17.82)	(15.71)	(13.18)	(13.58)	(15.48)
Total Return, Stk Price (%)	(3.61)	11.53	(14.51)	39.43	29.39

Europe Fund, Inc. (The)

780 Third Ave.
New York, NY 10017
(800) 543-6217

NYSE : EF
Transfer Agent
The Bank of New York
101 Barclay St.
New York, NY 10286
(800) 524-4458

Growth

12 Months Ending 12/31/92 Results

	Period End	Period Begin	Distributions	Yield Dist (%)	Total Return (%)
Share Price ($)	9.88	11.50	0.88*	2.17	(6.43)
NAV per share ($)	10.74	12.59		1.98	(7.70)

Background: Initial public offering May 3, 1990 of 8,337,500 shares at $15 per share. Initial NAV was $13.90.

Objective: Seeks capital appreciation through investments in European securities. May invest in Eastern Europe when opportunities are available. The fund has a mandatory requirement to make minimum annual distributions of 7% of its NAV per share.

Portfolio: (12/31/92) Common Stocks & Warrants 94.1%, Preferred Stocks 3.9%, Convertible Bonds 0.8%. Country Exposure: U.K. 44.1%, Germany 13.6%, Switzerland 11.7%, France 11.7%, The Netherlands 4.9%.

Capitalization: (12/31/92) Common stock outstanding 8,344,592. No long-term debt.

Beta: 0.64

Fund Manager: Warburg Investment Management, Inc.
Income Dist: Annually
Reinvestment Plan: Yes

Fee: 0.75%
Capital Gains Dist: Annually
Shareholder Reports: Quarterly

5 Year Performance

Fiscal Year Ending 12/31	1992	1991	1990 (6 mos.)	1989	1988
Net Assets ($mil):	89.60	105.10	114.60	—	—
Net Income Dist ($):	0.25	1.06	0.00	—	—
Cap Gains Dist ($):	0.00	0.55	0.00	—	—
Total Dist ($)	0.88*	1.61	0.00	—	—
Yield from Dist (%)	2.17	14.15	—	—	—
Expense Ratio (%)	1.47	1.56	1.00	—	—
Portfolio Turnover (%)	83.15	94.63	25.25	—	—
NAV per share ($)	10.74	12.59	13.73	—	—
Market Price per share	9.88	11.50	11.38	—	—
Premium (Discount) (%)	(8.01)	(8.66)	(17.12)	—	—
Total Return, Stk Price (%)	(6.43)	15.20	—	—	—

* Includes $0.63 return of capital.

European Warrant Fund, Inc. (The)

330 Madison Ave.
New York, NY 10017
(212) 297-3800

NYSE : EWF
Transfer Agent
The Shareholder Services Group
Exchange Place
Boston, MA 02109
(800) 331-1740

Growth

12 Months Ending 12/31/92 Results

	Period End	Period Begin	Distributions	Yield Dist (%)	Total Return (%)
Share Price ($)	7.38	5.75	0.16	2.78	31.13
NAV per share ($)	7.43	6.71		2.38	13.11

Background: Initial public offering July 17, 1990 of 6,000,000 shares at $12 per share. Initial NAV was $11.16 per share.

Objective: Seeks capital appreciation from a portfolio of European warrants and common stock. The fund may engage in hedging strategies involving futures and options.

Portfolio: (3/31/92) Warrants 59.3%, Common Stocks 6.7%, Treasuries 7.8%, Government Bonds 4.0%. Country Exposure: Germany 27.6%, Switzerland 12.5%, France 10.7%, Italy 3.0%, U.K. 3.0%.

Capitalization: (3/31/92) Common stock outstanding 6,040,828. No long-term debt.

Beta: 0.58

Fund Manager: Julius Baer Securities, Inc.
Income Dist: Annually
Reinvestment Plan: Yes

Fee: 1.25%
Capital Gains Dist: Annually
Shareholder Reports: Semi-Annually

5 Year Performance

Fiscal Year Ending 3/31	1992	1991 (9 mos.)	1990	1989	1988
Net Assets ($mil):	45.70	59.40	—	—	—
Net Income Dist ($):	0.02	0.00	—	—	—
Cap Gains Dist ($):	0.42	0.00	—	—	—
Total Dist ($)	0.44	0.00	—	—	—
Yield from Dist (%)	5.77	—	—	—	—
Expense Ratio (%)	2.44	2.36	—	—	—
Portfolio Turnover (%)	100.00	248.00	—	—	—
NAV per share ($)	7.57	9.88	—	—	—
Market Price per share	6.38	7.63	—	—	—
Premium (Discount) (%)	(15.85)	(22.77)	—	—	—
Total Return, Stk Price (%)	(10.62)	—	—	—	—

G.T. Greater Europe Fund

50 California St., 27th Fl.
San Francisco, CA 94111
(800) 824-1580 / (415) 392-6181

NYSE : GTF
Transfer Agent
Boston Financial Data Services
P.O. Box 8200
Boston, MA 02266
(800) 426-5523

Growth

12 Months Ending 12/31/92 Results

	Period End	Period Begin	Distributions	Yield Dist (%)	Total Return (%)
Share Price ($)	9.00	9.50	0.00	0.00	(5.26)
NAV per share ($)	10.57	11.32		0.00	(6.63)

Background: Initial public offering March 29, 1990 of 16,000,000 shares at $15 per share. Initial NAV was $14.10 per share.

Objective: Seeks long-term capital appreciation. The fund will invest at least 65% of assets in European equity securities, both in established and emerging markets. The remainder may be in countries outside of Europe, as long as such companies have connections with European companies.

Portfolio: (10/31/92) Equity Instruments 85.6%, Warrants 0.6%, Fixed-Income 14.3%, Short Term 0.5%. Country Exposure: U.K. 26.5%, Germany 17.0%, Netherlands 15.6%, Switzerland 13.5%, France 12.5%. Largest Holdings: Barclays Bank, Westminster Bank, Elsevier N.V., SMH, Grolsche Bierbrouw.

Capitalization: (10/31/92) Common stock outstanding 16,007,100. No long-term debt.

Beta: 0.48
Fund Manager: G.T. Capital Management, Inc.   **Fee:** 1.25%
Income Dist: Annually   **Capital Gains Dist:** Annually
Reinvestment Plan: No   **Shareholder Reports:** Semi-Annually

5 Year Performance

Fiscal Year Ending 10/31	1992	1991	1990 (7 mos.)	1989	1988
Net Assets ($mil):	166.00	175.10	191.10	—	—
Net Income Dist ($):	0.02	0.15	0.00	—	—
Cap Gains Dist ($):	0.09	0.01	0.00	—	—
Total Dist ($)	0.11	0.16	0.00	—	—
Yield from Dist (%)	1.14	1.64	—	—	—
Expense Ratio (%)	1.92	1.87	1.78	—	—
Portfolio Turnover (%)	109.00	47.00	41.00	—	—
NAV per share ($)	10.37	10.94	11.94	—	—
Market Price per share	9.38	9.63	9.75	—	—
Premium (Discount) (%)	(9.64)	(11.97)	(18.34)	—	—
Total Return, Stk Price (%)	(1.45)	0.41	—	—	—

Latin America Equity Fund, Inc. (The)
153 E. 53rd St., 58th Fl.
New York, NY 10022
(212) 832-2626

NYSE : LAQ
Transfer Agent
Provident Financial Processing Corp.
P.O. Box 8950
Wilmington, DE 19899
(800) 852-4750

Growth

12 Months Ending 12/31/92 Results

	Period End	Period Begin	Distributions	Yield Dist (%)	Total Return (%)
Share Price ($)	14.00	13.50	1.71*	11.33	16.37
NAV per share ($)	14.37	15.44		19.91	4.15

Background: Initial public offering October 26,1991 of 6,000,000 shares at $15 per share. Initial NAV was $13.85 per share.

Objective: Seeks long-term capital appreciation by investing in Latin American equity securities. The fund's policy is to invest at least 80% of its total assets in Latin American equity securities. Up to 20% may be invested in corporate debt securities of Latin American issuers. May hold small portion in U.S. Government securites during defensive periods.

Portfolio: (12/31/92) Common & Preferred Stock 90.84%, Bonds 1.60%, Cash & Equivalents 5.31%. Country Exposure: Argentina 14.59%, Brazil 12.85%, Chile 17.85%, Mexico 40.52%, Venezuela 2.76%, U.S. 4.65%.

Capitalization: (12/31/92) Common stock outstanding 6,008,348. No long-term debt.

Beta: 0.78
Fund Manager: BEA Associates
Income Dist: Annually
Reinvestment Plan: Yes

Fee: 1.25%
Capital Gains Dist: Annually
Shareholder Reports: Semi-Annually

5 Year Performance

Fiscal Year Ending 12/31	1992	1991 (2 mos.)	1990	1989	1988
Net Assets ($mil):	86.40	92.80	—	—	—
Net Income Dist ($):	0.21	0.06	—	—	—
Cap Gains Dist ($):	1.32	0.01	—	—	—
Total Dist ($)	1.71*	0.70	—	—	—
Yield from Dist (%)	11.33	—	—	—	—
Expense Ratio (%)	2.20	2.35	—	—	—
Portfolio Turnover (%)	68.70	69.50	—	—	—
NAV per share ($)	14.37	15.44	—	—	—
Market Price per share	14.00	13.50	—	—	—
Premium (Discount) (%)	(2.57)	(12.56)	—	—	—
Total Return, Stk Price (%)	16.37	—	—	—	—

Includes $0.18 return of capital.

Latin America Investment Fund, Inc. (The)
153 E. 53rd St., 58th Fl.
New York, NY 10022
(212) 832-2626

Transfer Agent
Provident Financial Processing Corp.
P.O. Box 8950
Wilmington, DE 19899
(800) 852-4750

Growth

12 Months Ending 12/31/92 Results

	Period End	Period Begin	Distributions	Yield Dist (%)	Total Return (%)
Share Price ($)	24.38	26.50	8.52*	32.15	24.15
NAV per share ($)	25.36	26.05		32.71	30.06

Background: Initial public offering July 1, 1990 of 4,00,000 shares at $15 per share. Initial NAV was $13.95 per share.

Objective: Seeks long-term capital appreciation. Under normal conditions, the fund will invest at least 65% of its assets in Brazilian, Chilean, and Mexican securities. Up to 10% may be invested in each of the following: Argentina, Bolivia, Columbia, Costa Rica, Cuba, Dominican Republic, Ecuador, El Salvador, Guatemala, Honduras, Nicaragua, Panama, Paraguay, Peru, Uraguay, and Venezuela.

Portfolio: (12/31/92) Common & Preferred Stock 85.44%. Country Exposure: Mexico 38.12%, Chile 15.58%, Brazil 12.82%, Argentina 11.4%, Colombia 3.50%, Venezuela 2.72%.

Capitalization: (12/31/92) Common stock outstanding 4,032,562. No long-term debt.

Beta: 1.20
Fund Manager: BEA Associates
Income Dist: Annually
Reinvestment Plan: Yes

Fee: 1.06%
Capital Gains Dist: Annually
Shareholder Reports: Semi-Annually

5 Year Performance

Fiscal Year Ending 12/31	1992	1991	1990 (5 mos.)	1989	1988
Net Assets ($mil):	102.30	104.40	57.10	—	—
Net Income Dist ($):	0.00	0.63	0.27	—	—
Cap Gains Dist ($):	2.44	2.83	0.00	—	—
Total Dist ($)	8.52*	3.46	0.27	—	—
Yield from Dist (%)	32.15	31.09	—	—	—
Expense Ratio (%)	2.31	2.30	3.27	—	—
Portfolio Turnover (%)	55.40	82.39	125.97	—	—
NAV per share ($)	25.36	26.05	14.24	—	—
Market Price per share	24.38	26.50	11.13	—	—
Premium (Discount) (%)	(3.86)	1.73	(21.84)	—	—
Total Return, Stk Price (%)	24.15	169.18	—	—	—

* Includes $6.065 declared 12/28/92, payable 1/25/93.

Multi Country (Regional) Equity Funds 305

Morgan Stanley Emerging Markets Fund

1221 Avenue of the Americas
New York, NY 10020
(212) 296-7100

NYSE : MSF
Transfer Agent
First National Bank of Boston
One Exchange Plaza, 55 Broadway
New York, NY 10006
(800) 662-2739 / (617) 575-2900

Growth

12 Months Ending 12/31/92 Results

	Period End	Period Begin	Distributions	Yield Dist (%)	Total Return (%)
Share Price ($)	18.13	14.50	0.02	0.14	25.17
NAV per share ($)	16.74	14.71		0.14	13.94

Background: Initial public offering October 24, 1991 of 4,600,000 shares at $15 per share. Initial NAV was $14.10 per share.

Objective: Seeks long-term capital appreciation. At least 65% of assets will be invested in the equity securities of emerging countries. Up to 25% of assets may be in unlisted securities. Options and futures transactions may be used for hedging purposes.

Portfolio: (9/30/92) Common Stocks 96.0%, Repurchase Agreements 2.5%, Foreign Currencies 1.2%, Government Bond 0.3%. Country Exposure: Indonesia 15.3%, Brazil 13.9%, Thailand 10.4%, Hong Kong 9.6%, Malaysia 8.5%.

Capitalization: (9/30/92) Common stock outstanding 10,567,191. No long-term debt.

Beta: 0.61
Fund Manager: Morgan Stanley Asset Management, Inc.   **Fee:** 1.25%
Income Dist: Annually   **Capital Gains Dist:** Annually
Reinvestment Plan: Yes   **Shareholder Reports:** Semi-Annually

5 Year Performance

Fiscal Year Ending 12/31	1992	1991 (2 mos.)	1990	1989	1988
Net Assets ($mil):	176.90	155.30	—	—	—
Net Income Dist ($):	0.01	0.04	—	—	—
Cap Gains Dist ($):	0.01	0.00	—	—	—
Total Dist ($)	0.02	0.04	—	—	—
Yield from Dist (%)	0.14	—	—	—	—
Expense Ratio (%)	2.02	2.25	—	—	—
Portfolio Turnover (%)	60.00	2.00	—	—	—
NAV per share ($)	16.74	14.71	—	—	—
Market Price per share	18.13	14.50	—	—	—
Premium (Discount) (%)	8.30	(1.43)	—	—	—
Total Return, Stk Price (%)	25.17	—	—	—	—

Scudder New Asia Fund, Inc.

345 Park Ave.
New York, NY 10154
(617) 330-5602

NYSE : SAF
Transfer Agent
State Street Bank & Trust Co.
P.O. Box 8200
Boston, MA 02266-8200
(617) 328-5000

Growth

12 Months Ending 12/31/92 Results

	Period End	Period Begin	Distributions	Yield Dist (%)	Total Return (%)
Share Price ($)	14.25	15.13	0.51	3.37	(2.45)
NAV per share ($)	14.73	14.94		3.41	2.01

Background: Initial public offering June 18, 1987 of 7,000,000 shares at $12 per share. Initial NAV was $11.16 per share.

Objective: Seeks long-term capital appreciation. Invests in equity securities (including ADRs) of Asian companies traded in a market permitting foreign investor participation. Will invest at least 50% in equities of smaller Japanese companies. May utilize enhancements and buy non-publicly traded securities.

Portfolio: (6/31/92) Common Stocks 85.1%, Convertible Bonds 5.0%, Limited Partnership 0.7%, Preferred Stock 0.1%. Country Exposure: Japan 19.3%, Hong Kong 13.9%, Thailand 14.6%, Malaysia 9.8%, Korea 8.0%. Sector Weightings: Financial 17.9%, Consumer Discretionary 12.6%, Communications 11.4%, Manufacturing 11.3%, Consumer Staples 8.7%.

Capitalization: (12/31/92) Common stock outstanding 7,076,615. No long-term debt.

Beta: 0.67

Fund Manager: Scudder, Stevens & Clark, Inc.   **Fee:** 1.15%
Income Dist: Annually   **Capital Gains Dist:** Annually
Reinvestment Plan: Yes   **Shareholder Reports:** Quarterly

5 Year Performance

Fiscal Year Ending 12/31	1992	1991	1990	1989	1988
Net Assets ($mil):	104.20	105.50	94.80	114.70	84.40
Net Income Dist ($):	0.08	0.08	0.08	0.00	0.05
Cap Gains Dist ($):	0.43	0.11	2.11	1.38	0.00
Total Dist ($)	0.51	0.19	2.19	1.38	0.05
Yield from Dist (%)	3.37	1.58	13.79	15.54	0.75
Expense Ratio (%)	1.76	1.79	1.77	1.88	1.90
Portfolio Turnover (%)	13.70	12.30	24.10	61.10	37.20
NAV per share ($)	14.73	14.94	13.44	16.36	12.04
Market Price per share	14.25	15.13	12.00	15.88	8.88
Premium (Discount) (%)	(3.26)	1.20	(10.71)	(2.93)	(26.33)
Total Return, Stk Price (%)	(2.45)	27.67	(10.64)	94.37	34.69

Scudder New Europe Fund, Inc.
345 Park Ave.
New York, NY 10154
(617) 330-5602

NYSE : NEF
Transfer Agent
The First National Bank of Boston
P.O. Box 644
Boston, MA 0102
(617) 575-2900

Growth

12 Months Ending 12/31/92 Results

	Period End	Period Begin	Distributions	Yield Dist (%)	Total Return (%)
Share Price ($)	7.63	8.50	0.20	2.35	(7.88)
NAV per share ($)	8.82	10.07		1.99	(10.43)

Background: Initial public offering February 16, 1990 of 16,000,000 shares at $12.50 per share. Initial NAV was $11.55 per share.

Objective: Seeks long-term capital appreciation through investment in equity securities. 65% of total assets will be invested in companies traded on smaller or emerging European markets and companies that are viewed as likely to benefit from changes and developments throughout Europe.

Portfolio: (10/31/92) Common Stocks 86.1%, Repurchase Agreements 5.0%, Preferred Stocks 8.6%. Country Exposure: Germany 18.6%, France 17.4%, Netherlands 9.6%, U.K. 12.3%, Switzerland 11.7%. Sector Weightings: Basic 19.1%, Financial 12.8%, Durables 12%.

Capitalization: (12/31/92) Common stock outstanding 16,030,000. No long-term debt.

Beta: 0.66
Fund Manager: Scudder, Stevens & Clark, Inc.   **Fee:** 1.25%
Income Dist: Annually   **Capital Gains Dist:** Annually
Reinvestment Plan: Yes   **Shareholder Reports:** Quarterly

5 Year Performance

Fiscal Year Ending 10/31	1992	1991	1990 (8 mos.)	1989	1988
Net Assets ($mil):	146.20	162.10	176.30	—	—
Net Income Dist ($):	0.15	0.47	0.00	—	—
Cap Gains Dist ($):	0.13	0.20	0.00	—	—
Total Dist ($)	0.28	0.67	0.00	—	—
Yield from Dist (%)	3.11	7.76	—	—	—
Expense Ratio (%)	1.76	1.85	1.84	—	—
Portfolio Turnover (%)	25.70	31.70	104.50	—	—
NAV per share ($)	9.12	10.12	11.01	—	—
Market Price per share	8.25	9.00	8.63	—	—
Premium (Discount) (%)	(9.54)	(11.07)	(21.71)	—	—
Total Return, Stk Price (%)	(5.22)	12.05	—	—	—

Templeton Emerging Markets Fund, Inc.

700 Central Ave.
St. Petersburg, FL 33701
(800) 237-0738 / (813) 823-8712

Growth

NYSE : EMF
Transfer Agent
Mellon Financial Services
85 Challenger Road
Overpark Center
Ridgefield Park, NJ 07660
(800) 526-0801

12 Months Ending 12/31/92 Results

	Period End	Period Begin	Distributions	Yield Dist (%)	Total Return (%)
Share Price ($)	14.50	22.25	6.02	27.06	(7.78)
NAV per share ($)	12.32	16.94		35.54	8.26

Background: Initial public offering February 26, 1987, of 11,500,000 shares at $10 per share. Initial NAV was $9.25 per share.

Objective: Seeks long-term capital appreciation. Invests at least 75% of total assets in equity securities of emerging countries (low or middle income as determined by the World Bank). The fund may use various hedging strategies.

Portfolio: (11/30/92) Common Stocks 72.4%, Preferred Stocks 9.9%, Bonds 1.6%, Cash & Other 15.9%. Country Exposure: Brazil 11.1%, Philippines 10.7%, Turkey 9.8%, Malaysia 8.7%, Thailand 7.7%.

Capitalization: (8/31/92) Common stock outstanding 12,977,871.

Beta: 1.04
Fund Manager: Templeton, Galbraith & Hansberger, Ltd.　　　　　　　**Fee:** 1.25%
Income Dist: Monthly　　　　　　　　　　　　**Capital Gains Dist:** Annually
Reinvestment Plan: Yes　　　　　　　　　　**Shareholder Reports:** Quarterly

5 Year Performance

Fiscal Year Ending 8/31	1992	1991	1990	1989	1988
Net Assets ($mil):	243.30	210.60	177.40	143.20	104.60
Net Income Dist ($):	0.08	0.24	0.16	0.14	0.20
Cap Gains Dist ($):	3.96	1.64	0.17	0.18	0.10
Total Dist ($)	4.04	1.88	0.33	0.32	0.30
Yield from Dist (%)	20.72	13.70	2.72	4.13	2.67
Expense Ratio (%)	1.91	1.91	1.89	2.03	2.07
Portfolio Turnover (%)	53.45	33.53	23.53	13.15	12.31
NAV per share ($)	18.74	18.16	15.40	12.44	9.08
Market Price per share	21.88	19.50	14.38	12.13	7.75
Premium (Discount) (%)	16.76	7.38	(6.69)	(2.57)	(14.65)
Total Return, Stk Price (%)	32.92	48.68	21.27	60.65	(28.44)

Templeton Global Utilities, Inc.
700 Central Ave.
St. Petersburg, FL 33701
(800) 237-0738 / (813) 823-8712

NYSE : TGU
Transfer Agent
Mellon Financial Services
85 Challenger Road
Overpark Center
Ridgefield Park, NJ 07660
(800) 526-0801

Growth & Income

12 Months Ending 12/31/92 Results

	Period End	Period Begin	Distributions	Yield Dist (%)	Total Return (%)
Share Price ($)	13.63	12.13	0.87	7.17	19.54
NAV per share ($)	13.09	12.89		6.75	8.30

Background: Initial public offering May 23, 1990 of 3,000,000 shares at $12 per share. Initial NAV was $11.03 per share.

Objective: Seeks high level of total return. The fund invests at least 65% of its assets in equity and debt securities issued by domestic and foreign utilities. Assets will be in a minimum of three countries, one of which is the U.S. The balance of the fund's assets may be invested in domestic and foreign non-utility securities.

Portfolio: (8/31/92) Common Stocks 58.1%, Bonds 31.7%, Short Term 6.0%. Country Exposure: U.S. 63.9%, U.K. 9.6%, Spain 6.7%, Hong Kong 4.3%, France 3.7%.

Capitalization: (8/31/92) Common stock outstanding 3,041,628. No long-term debt.

Beta: 0.98
Fund Manager: Templeton, Galbraith & Hansberger Ltd.   **Fee:** 0.60%
Income Dist: Monthly   **Capital Gains Dist:** Annually
Reinvestment Plan: Yes   **Shareholder Reports:** Quarterly

5 Year Performance

Fiscal Year Ending 8/31	1992	1991	1990 (7 mos.)	1989	1988
Net Assets ($mil):	40.70	35.90	31.90	—	—
Net Income Dist ($):	0.61	0.68	0.06	—	—
Cap Gains Dist ($):	0.00	0.00	0.00	—	—
Total Dist ($)	0.61	0.68	0.06	—	—
Yield from Dist (%)	5.42	6.48	—	—	—
Expense Ratio (%)	1.44	1.55	1.29	—	—
Portfolio Turnover (%)	15.21	19.85	0.47	—	—
NAV per share ($)	13.38	11.85	10.60	—	—
Market Price per share	13.50	11.25	10.50	—	—
Premium (Discount) (%)	0.90	(5.06)	(0.94)	—	—
Total Return, Stk Price (%)	25.42	13.62	—	—	—

Worldwide Value Fund, Inc.

P.O. Box 1476
111 S. Calvert St., Suite 1560
Baltimore, MD 21203-1476
(410) 539-3400

NYSE : VLU
Transfer Agent
State Street Bank & Trust Co.
P.O. Box 1790
Boston, MA 02105
(800) 426-5523

Growth

12 Months Ending 12/31/92 Results

	Period End	Period Begin	Distributions	Yield Dist (%)	Total Return (%)
Share Price ($)	12.00	12.50	0.04	0.32	(3.68)
NAV per share ($)	14.29	15.44		0.26	(7.19)

Background: Initial public offering August, 1986 of 3,000,000 shares at $20 per share. Initial NAV was $18.50.

Objective: Seeks long-term capital appreciation. At least 65% of assets will be invested in equity securities throughout the world. Up to 35% may be in debt securities. During temporary defensive periods, the fund may be 100% in debt securities.

Portfolio: (12/31/92) Common Stocks & Units 94.9%, Preferred Stocks 1.0%, Short Term & Other 4.1%. Country Exposure: U.K. 37.0%, France 15.0%, Germany 12.0%, Switzerland 8.0%, Netherlands 7.0%.

Capitalization: (12/31/92) Common stock outstanding 3,005,000. No long-term debt.

Beta: 0.77
Fund Manager: Lombard Odier International
Income Dist: Annually
Reinvestment Plan: Yes

Fee: 1.00%
Capital Gains Dist: Annually
Shareholder Reports: Quarterly

5 Year Performance

Fiscal Year Ending 12/31	1992	1991	1990	1989	1988
Net Assets ($mil):	42.90	46.40	44.00	60.50	58.70
Net Income Dist ($):	0.04	0.21	0.08	0.19	0.00
Cap Gains Dist ($):	0.00	0.00	0.85	1.42	1.00
Total Dist ($)	0.04	0.21	0.93	1.61	1.00
Yield from Dist (%)	0.32	1.73	4.89	9.98	8.33
Expense Ratio (%)	2.20	2.30	2.40	2.20	2.20
Portfolio Turnover (%)	148.40	91.90	84.30	121.50	95.60
NAV per share ($)	14.29	15.44	14.65	20.14	19.53
Market Price per share	12.00	12.50	12.13	19.00	16.13
Premium (Discount) (%)	(16.03)	(19.04)	(17.27)	(5.66)	(17.46)
Total Return, Stk Price (%)	(3.68)	4.78	(31.26)	27.77	42.75

Z-Seven Fund, Inc.

2651 W. Guadalupe, Suite B-233
Mesa, AZ 85202
(602) 897-6214

OTC : ZSEV
Transfer Agent
Mellon Securities Trust Co.
One New York Plaza, 14th Fl.
New York, NY 10081
(212) 676-6000

Growth

12 Months Ending 12/31/92 Results

	Period End	Period Begin	Distributions	Yield Dist (%)	Total Return (%)
Share Price ($)	17.00	21.50	0.00	0.00	(20.93)
NAV per share ($)	15.12	17.65		0.00	(14.33)

Background: Initial public offering on December 29, 1983, at $15 per share. Initial NAV was $13.80 per share

Objective: Seeks long-term capital appreciation. The manager utilizes a proprietary screen of seven criteria, including analyses of accounting procedures, balance sheets, and earnings. The most rigid criteria is the refusal to purchase a stock selling at more than 9 times earnings.

Portfolio: (12/31/92) Common Stock 101.44%, Liabilities in Excess of Other Assets (1.44%). Country Exposure: U.K. 63.84%, U.S. 20.39%, Western Europe 15.77%.

Capitalization: (12/31/92) Common stock outstanding 1,634,429. No long-term debt.

Beta: 0.33
Fund Manager: Top Fund Management, Inc.
Income Dist: Annually
Reinvestment Plan: No

Fee: 1.25%
Capital Gains Dist: Annually
Shareholder Reports: Quarterly

5 Year Performance

Fiscal Year Ending 12/31	1992	1991	1990	1989	1988
Net Assets ($mil):	24.70	22.70	15.80	18.20	21.10
Net Income Dist ($):	0.00	0.00	0.13	0.45	0.00
Cap Gains Dist ($):	0.00	0.00	0.00	0.00	0.00
Total Dist ($)	0.00	0.00	0.13	0.45	0.00
Yield from Dist (%)	0.00	0.00	1.00	2.71	0.00
Expense Ratio (%)	2.35	4.33	2.63	1.16	2.73
Portfolio Turnover (%)	17.94	44.12	42.82	87.29	4.73
NAV per share ($)	15.12	17.65	12.16	13.25	14.33
Market Price per share	17.00	21.50	12.75	13.00	16.63
Premium (Discount) (%)	12.43	21.81	4.85	(1.89)	15.98
Total Return, Stk Price (%)	(20.93)	68.63	(0.92)	(19.12)	9.05

Single Country Equity Funds

Argentina Fund   **NYSE : AF**
345 Park Ave.   *Transfer Agent*
New York, NY 10154-0004   State Street Bank & Trust Co.
(212) 326-6230   P.O. Box 8300
                                                     Boston, MA 02266-8300
                                                          (800) 426-5523

Growth

12 Months Ending 12/31/92 Results

	Period End	Period Begin	Distributions	Yield Dist (%)	Total Return (%)
Share Price ($)	12.25	14.25	0.14	0.98	(13.05)
NAV per share ($)	9.68	11.15		1.26	(11.93)

Background: Initial public offering October, 1991 of 5,000,000 shares at $12 per share. Initial NAV was $10.98.

Objective: Seeks long-term capital appreciation by investing at least 65% of its assets in equity securities of Argentine issuers. Up to 30% may also be invested in Argentine government and corporate debt securities. Up to 5% may be invested in securities with ratings comparable to S&P's rating of C or below.

Portfolio: (10/31/92) Equity Securities 65.5%, Debt Securities 17.9%, Repurchase Agreements 3.7%, Commercial Paper 11.1%. Sector Weightings: Food & Beverage 22.8%, Telecommunications 17.2%, Conglomerates 6.9%, Petroleum 5.1%, Banking 4.1%.

Capitalization: (10/31/92) Common stock outstanding 5,770,263. No long-term debt.

Beta: 1.09
Fund Manager: Scudder, Stevens & Clark, Inc.   **Fee:** 1.30%
Income Dist: Annually   **Capital Gains Dist:** Annually
Reinvestment Plan: Yes   **Shareholder Reports:** Quarterly

5 Year Performance

Fiscal Year Ending 10/31	1992	1991 (9 days)	1990	1989	1988
Net Assets ($mil):	53.90	63.30	—	—	—
Net Income Dist ($):	0.06	0.00	—	—	—
Cap Gains Dist ($):	0.00	0.00	—	—	—
Total Dist ($)	0.06	0.00	—	—	—
Yield from Dist (%)	0.41	—	—	—	—
Expense Ratio (%)	2.24	2.55	—	—	—
Portfolio Turnover (%)	26.50	—	—	—	—
NAV per share ($)	9.35	10.99	—	—	—
Market Price per share	9.63	14.63	—	—	—
Premium (Discount) (%)	2.99	33.12	—	—	—
Total Return, Stk Price (%)	(33.77)	—	—	—	—

Austria Fund (The)
1345 Avenue of the Americas
New York, NY 10105
(800) 247-4154 / (212) 969-1000

NYSE : OST
Transfer Agent
State Street Bank & Trust Co.
225 Franklin St.
Boston, MA 02110
(800) 426-5523

Growth

12 Months Ending 12/31/92 Results

	Period End	Period Begin	Distributions	Yield Dist (%)	Total Return (%)
Share Price ($)	6.88	8.88	0.16	1.80	(20.72)
NAV per share ($)	7.47	9.57		1.67	(20.27)

Background: Initial public offering September 28, 1989, of 5,750,000 shares at $12 per share. Initial NAV was $11.16 per share. A second offering was made February 1990 of 2,500,000 additional shares. Net proceeds were $16 per share.

Objective: Seeks long-term capital appreciation from a portfolio primarily of Austrian securities.

Portfolio: (11/30/92) Equities 89.6%, Unlisted Securities 6.8%, Cash & Short Term 3.0%, Fixed Income 0.6%. Sector Weightings: Basic Industries 21.9%, Financial Services 19.9%, Consumer Products & Services 18.8%, Capital Goods 14.5%, Utilities 12.8%. Largest Holdings: OEMV AG (Energy), Creditanstalt Bankverein (Banking), EVN (Utilities), Oesterreichische Elektrizitaetswirtschafts CIA (Utilities), Immuno International (Healthcare).

Capitalization: (8/31/92) Common stock outstanding 8,259,015. No long-term debt.

Beta: 0.84
Fund Manager: Alliance Capital Management L.P.   **Fee:** 1.00%
Income Dist: Annually   **Capital Gains Dist:** Annually
Reinvestment Plan: Yes   **Shareholder Reports:** Quarterly

5 Year Performance

Fiscal Year Ending 8/31	1992	1991	1990 (11 mos)	1989	1988
Net Assets ($mil):	73.40	89.90	120.10	—	—
Net Income Dist ($):	0.00	0.06	0.06	—	—
Cap Gains Dist ($):	0.14	0.36	0.01	—	—
Total Dist ($)	0.14	0.42	0.07	—	—
Yield from Dist (%)	1.47	3.73	—	—	—
Expense Ratio (%)	1.92	1.78	1.82	—	—
Portfolio Turnover (%)	56.00	34.00	24.00	—	—
NAV per share ($)	8.89	10.89	14.54	—	—
Market Price per share	7.75	9.50	11.25	—	—
Premium (Discount) (%)	(12.82)	(12.76)	(22.63)	—	—
Total Return, Stk Price (%)	(16.95)	(11.82)	—	—	—

Brazil Fund, Inc. (The)

345 Park Ave.
New York, NY 10154
(212) 326-6200

Growth

NYSE : BZF

Transfer Agent
First National Bank of Boston
P.O. Box 644
Boston, MA 02102-0644
(617) 575-2900

12 Months Ending 12/31/92 Results

	Period End	Period Begin	Distributions	Yield Dist (%)	Total Return (%)
Share Price ($)	13.63	14.75	0.66	4.47	(3.12)
NAV per share ($)	14.12	13.80		4.78	7.10

Background: Initial public offering March 31, 1988 of 12,000,000 shares at $12.50 per share. Initial NAV was $11.63 per share.

Objective: Seeks long-term capital appreciation through investments primarily in equity securities of Brazilian companies.

Portfolio: (12/31/92) Equity Securities 97.3%, Commercial Paper 4.3%, Short Term Investments 1.3%. Sector Weightings: Food & Beverage 15.9%, Telecommunications 12.7%, Forest Products 10.6%, Mining 9.7%. Largest Holdings: Telecomunicacoes Brasileiras, Companhia Souza Cruz Industria e Comercio, Banco Itau, Companhia Vale do Rio Doce, Companhia Cervejaria Brahma.

Capitalization: Common stock outstanding 12,081,227. No long-term debt.

Beta: 1.39
Fund Manager: Scudder, Stevens & Clark, Inc.
Income Dist: Annually
Reinvestment Plan: Yes

Fee: 1.25%
Capital Gains Dist: Annually
Shareholder Reports: Quarterly

5 Year Performance

Fiscal Year Ending 12/31	1992	1991	1990	1989	1988 (8 mos.)
Net Assets ($mil):	170.60	166.60	72.00	226.90	154.90
Net Income Dist ($):	0.00	0.00	0.12	0.89	0.41
Cap Gains Dist ($):	0.66	0.00	0.00	1.36	0.28
Total Dist ($)	0.66	0.00	0.12	2.25	0.69
Yield from Dist (%)	4.47	0.00	0.93	28.55	—
Expense Ratio (%)	2.22	2.15	2.25	2.01	1.90
Portfolio Turnover (%)	7.94	12.69	4.31	14.02	0.74
NAV per share ($)	14.12	13.80	5.97	18.85	12.90
Market Price per share	13.63	14.75	6.63	12.88	7.88
Premium (Discount) (%)	(3.47)	6.88	11.06	(31.67)	(38.91)
Total Return, Stk Price (%)	(3.12)	122.47	(47.59)	92.01	—

Chile Fund, Inc. (The)

153 E. 53rd St., 58th Fl.
New York, NY 10022
(212) 832-2626

NYSE : CH

Transfer Agent
Provident Financial Processing Corp.
P.O. Box 8950
Wilmington, DE 19899
(800) 553-8080

Growth

12 Months Ending 12/31/92 Results

	Period End	Period Begin	Distributions	Yield Dist (%)	Total Return (%)
Share Price ($)	33.13	23.88	3.22	13.48	52.18
NAV per share ($)	31.10	29.68		10.85	15.63

Background: Initial public offering October 3, 1989 of 5,300,000 shares at $15 per share. Initial NAV was $13.75 per share.

Objective: Seeks capital appreciation and dividend income through a portfolio of Chilean equities and bonds.

Portfolio: (12/31/92) Chilean Common Stock 97.2%, United Kingdom Common Stock 1.8%, Canada 0.02%, Other 0.8%. Sector Weightings: Electrical Distribution 19.6%, Telecommunications 17.5%. Electrical Generators 15.6%, Beverage/Liquor/Tobacco 7.1%, Paper 6.9%.

Capitalization: (12/31/92) Common stock outstanding 5,420,610. No long-term debt.

Beta: 0.77

Fund Manager: BEA Associates

Income Dist: Annually

Reinvestment Plan: Yes

Fee: 1.20%

Capital Gains Dist: Annually

Shareholder Reports: Semi-Annually

5 Year Performance

Fiscal Year Ending 12/31	1992	1991	1990	1989 (3 mos.)	1988
Net Assets ($mil):	168.60	160.40	93.70	79.50	—
Net Income Dist ($):	0.77	0.98	1.25	0.05	—
Cap Gains Dist ($):	2.45	2.18	0.00	0.00	—
Total Dist ($)	3.22	3.16	1.25	0.05	—
Yield from Dist (%)	13.48	20.39	8.00	—	—
Expense Ratio (%)	1.71	1.75	2.04	1.98	—
Portfolio Turnover (%)	6.29	19.32	12.63	9.52	—
NAV per share ($)	31.10	29.68	17.44	14.79	—
Market Price per share	33.13	23.88	15.50	15.63	—
Premium (Discount) (%)	6.50	(19.58)	(11.12)	5.68	—
Total Return, Stk Price (%)	52.18	74.45	7.17	—	—

Emerging Germany Fund, Inc.

One Battery Park Plaza
New York, NY 10004
(800) 356-6122

Transfer Agent
State Street Bank & Trust Co.
P. O. Box 8200
Boston, MA 02266
(800) 426-5523

Growth

12 Months Ending 12/31/92 Results

	Period End	Period Begin	Distributions	Yield Dist (%)	Total Return (%)
Share Price ($)	6.38	7.75	0.11	1.42	(16.26)
NAV per share ($)	7.45	8.86		1.24	(14.67)

Background: Initial public offering April 5, 1990 of 14,000,000 shares at $12 per share. Initial NAV was $11.16 per share.

Objective: Seeks long-term capital appreciation. Invests in small- to medium-sized German companies. The fund may invest up to 20% of its assets in former East German companies and up to 10% in other Eastern European companies.

Portfolio: (12/31/92) German Equity Securities 93.3%, Swiss Equity Securities 1.07%, Short Term 3.0%. Sector Weightings: Banking 19.4%, Insurance 9.9%, Automobiles 8.4%, Chemicals 8.2%, Machinery & Engineering 7.42%. Largest Holdings: Siemens AG, Deutsche Bank AG, Allianz Holding AG, AMB Holding AG, Mercedes Automobil Holding AG.

Capitalization: (12/31/92) Common stock outstanding 14,008,000. No long-term debt.

Beta: 0.68
Fund Manager: Asset Management Advisors
Income Dist: Annually
Reinvestment Plan: Yes

Fee: 0.70%
Capital Gains Dist: Annually
Shareholder Reports: Quarterly

5 Year Performance

Fiscal Year Ending 12/31	1992	1991	1990 (6 mos.)	1989	1988
Net Assets ($mil):	104.40	124.10	131.70	—	—
Net Income Dist ($):	0.07	0.07	0.16	—	—
Cap Gains Dist ($):	0.04	0.16	0.04	—	—
Total Dist ($)	0.11	0.23	0.20	—	—
Yield from Dist (%)	1.42	3.01	—	—	—
Expense Ratio (%)	1.49	1.70	1.51	—	—
Portfolio Turnover (%)	54.00	52.00	13.00	—	—
NAV per share ($)	7.45	8.86	9.40	—	—
Market Price per share	6.38	7.75	7.63	—	—
Premium (Discount) (%)	(14.36)	(12.53)	(18.94)	—	—
Total Return, Stk Price (%)	(16.26)	4.59	—	—	—

Emerging Mexico Fund

NYSE : MEF

1285 Avenue of the Americas
New York, NY 10019
(800) 852-4750

Transfer Agent
Provident Financial Processing Corp.
P.O. Box 8950
Wilmington, DE 19899
(800) 553-8080

Growth

12 Months Ending 12/31/92 Results

	Period End	Period Begin	Distributions	Yield Dist (%)	Total Return (%)
Share Price ($)	17.25	18.00	4.90	27.22	23.06
NAV per share ($)	17.16	18.39		26.64	19.96

Background: Initial public offering October 2, 1990 of 5,000,000 shares at $12 per share. Initial NAV was $11.16 per share.

Objective: Seeks long-term capital appreciation through investment primarily in Mexican equity securities. The fund invests at least 65% in Mexican equities. Up to 25% of assets may be invested in unlisted securities, private placements, joint ventures, and partnerships. The fund may engage in options and futures transactions for hedging purposes.

Portfolio: (12/31/92) Common Stocks 105.0%, Mexican Government Obligations 23.53%, Liabilities (28.58%). Sector Weightings: Retail 24.2%, Financial Services 18.6%, Construction 18.2%, Communications 15.6%, Food/Beverage/Tobacco 11.6%. Largest Holdings: Cifra, Grupo Financiero Banamex, Grupo Carso, Telefonos de Mexico, Empresa Tolteca de Mexico.

Capitalization: (12/31/92) Common stock outstanding 5,009,000. No long-term debt.

Beta: 1.25

Fund Manager: Santander Mangement, Inc.
Income Dist: Annually
Reinvestment Plan: Yes

Fee: 0.90%
Capital Gains Dist: Annually
Shareholder Reports: Semi-Annually

5 Year Performance

Fiscal Year Ending 6/30	1992	1991 (8 mos.)	1990	1989	1988
Net Assets ($mil):	99.90	86.30	—	—	—
Net Income Dist ($):	0.32	0.30	—	—	—
Cap Gains Dist ($):	2.40	0.01	—	—	—
Total Dist ($)	2.72	0.31	—	—	—
Yield from Dist (%)	18.59	—	—	—	—
Expense Ratio (%)	1.72	2.22	—	—	—
Portfolio Turnover (%)	65.00	87.00	—	—	—
NAV per share ($)	19.94	17.23	—	—	—
Market Price per share	17.63	14.63	—	—	—
Premium (Discount) (%)	(11.58)	(15.15)	—	—	—
Total Return, Stk Price (%)	39.10	—	—	—	—

First Australia Fund

One Seaport Plaza
New York, NY 10292
(800) 451-6788 / (212) 214-3334

AMEX : IAF

Transfer Agent
State Street Bank & Trust Co.
One Heritage Drive
North Quincy, MA 02171
(800) 451-6788

Growth

12 Months Ending 12/31/92 Results

	Period End	Period Begin	Distributions	Yield Dist (%)	Total Return (%)
Share Price ($)	7.75	9.13	0.18	1.97	(13.14)
NAV per share ($)	8.66	10.57		1.70	(16.37)

Background: Initial public offering December 15, 1985 of 5,800,000 shares at $10 per share. Initial NAV was $9.25 per share.

Objective: Seeks long-term capital appreciation through equity investments in Australian securities and bonds. Current income is secondary. May engage in options strategies.

Portfolio: (10/31/92) Stocks & Convertibles 92.4%, Corporate Bonds 2.9%, Short Term & Other 4.7%. Sector Weightings: Natural Resources 34.8%, Diversified Industrials 22.3%, Services 29.0%. Largest Holdings: Broken Hill Proprietary Co., National Australia Bank, TNT Limited.

Capitalization: (10/31/92) Common stock outstanding 6,319,200. No long-term debt.

Beta: 0.96
Fund Manager: EquitiLink Australia Limited
Income Dist: Semi-Annually
Reinvestment Plan: Yes

Fee: 1.10%
Capital Gains Dist: Annually
Shareholder Reports: Quarterly

5 Year Performance

Fiscal Year Ending 10/31	1992	1991	1990	1989	1988
Net Assets ($mil):	50.90	66.40	55.00	63.40	—
Net Income Dist ($):	0.26	0.42	0.59	0.26	0.28
Cap Gains Dist ($):	0.00	0.01	0.03	0.05	0.82
Total Dist ($)	0.26	0.43	0.62	0.31	1.10
Yield from Dist (%)	2.67	5.83	7.18	3.44	12.39
Expense Ratio (%)	1.90	2.25	2.14	2.18	2.30
Portfolio Turnover (%)	39.00	82.00	68.00	56.00	31.00
NAV per share ($)	8.46	11.03	9.14	10.56	10.98
Market Price per share	7.75	9.75	7.38	8.63	9.00
Premium (Discount) (%)	(8.39)	(11.60)	(19.37)	(18.37)	(18.03)
Total Return, Stk Price (%)	(17.85)	37.94	(7.30)	(0.67)	13.74

First Iberian Fund, Inc.

345 Park Ave.
New York, NY 10154
(617) 330-5602

AMEX : IBF
Transfer Agent
State Street Bank & Trust Co.
P.O. Box 8200
Boston, MA 02266-8200
(617) 328-5000

Growth

12 Months Ending 12/31/92 Results

	Period End	Period Begin	Distributions	Yield Dist (%)	Total Return (%)
Share Price ($)	5.88	7.75	0.40	5.16	(18.97)
NAV per share ($)	6.88	9.18		4.36	(20.70)

Background: Initial public offering April 13, 1988 of 6,500,000 shares at $10 per share. Initial NAV was $9.16 per share.

Objective: Seeks capital appreciation through investments primarily in equity securities of Spanish and Portuguese companies.

Portfolio: (9/30/92) Common Stocks 90.3%, Bonds 8.2%, Convertible Bonds 1.5%. Country Exposure: Spain 94.1%, Portugal 5.9%. Sector Weightings: Utilities 23.4%, Banking 22.8%, Transportation 16.6%, Telecommunications 6.5%, Food Wholesalers 4.2%.

Capitalization: (9/30/92) Common stock outstanding 6,511,154. No long-term debt.

Beta: 0.88
Fund Manager: Scudder, Stevens & Clark, Inc.   **Fee:** 1.00%
Income Dist: Semi-Annually   **Capital Gains Dist:** Annually
Reinvestment Plan: Yes   **Shareholder Reports:** Semi-Annually

5 Year Performance

Fiscal Year Ending 9/30	1992	1991	1990	1989	1988 (5 mos.)
Net Assets ($mil):	47.30	60.60	57.30	70.20	57.00
Net Income Dist ($):	0.15	0.20	0.12	0.25	0.00
Cap Gains Dist ($):	0.00	0.82	0.13	0.00	0.00
Total Dist ($)	0.15	1.02	0.25	0.25	0.00
Yield from Dist (%)	1.90	13.82	1.67	2.98	—
Expense Ratio (%)	2.45	2.30	2.18	2.08	2.72
Portfolio Turnover (%)	32.00	23.00	22.00	26.00	0.00
NAV per share ($)	7.27	9.31	8.80	10.78	8.75
Market Price per share	6.25	7.88	7.38	15.00	8.38
Premium (Discount) (%)	(14.03)	(15.36)	(16.25)	39.15	(4.34)
Total Return, Stk Price (%)	(18.78)	20.60	(49.13)	81.98	—

First Philippine Fund, Inc.
152 W. 57th St.
New York, NY 10019
(212) 765-0700

NYSE : FPF
Transfer Agent
The Bank of New York
101 Barclay St.
New York, NY 10286
(800) 524-4458

Growth

12 Months Ending 12/31/92 Results

	Period End	Period Begin	Distributions	Yield Dist (%)	Total Return (%)
Share Price ($)	10.25	8.63	0.57	6.60	25.38
NAV per share ($)	13.12	11.27		5.06	21.47

Background: Initial public offering November 15, 1989 of 7,800,000 shares at $12 per share. Initial NAV was $11.16 per share.

Objective: Seeks long-term capital appreciation. Invests at least 80% of assets in equity securities of Philippine companies.

Portfolio: (6/30/92) Common Stocks 83.1%, Philippine Treasury Bills 2.2%, U.S. Securities 14.5%. Sector Weightings: Telecommunications 22.8%, Food & Beverage 17.4%, Conglomerates 8.6%, Electric Utilities 7.0%, Banking 7.0%. Largest Holdings: Philippine Long Distance Holdings, San Miguel Corp., Ayala Corp., Manila Electric, Ayala Land, Inc.

Capitalization: (6/30/92) Common stock outstanding 8,980,000. No long-term debt.

Beta: 0.48
Fund Manager: Clemente Capital, Inc.   **Fee:** 1.00%
Income Dist: Annually   **Capital Gains Dist:** Annually
Reinvestment Plan: Yes   **Shareholder Reports:** Quarterly

5 Year Performance

Fiscal Year Ending 6/30	1992	1991	1990 (7 mos.)	1989	1988
Net Assets ($mil):	130.90	92.90	98.50	—	—
Net Income Dist ($):	0.19	0.59	0.08	—	—
Cap Gains Dist ($):	0.00	0.00	0.00	—	—
Total Dist ($)	0.19	0.59	0.08	—	—
Yield from Dist (%)	2.53	6.29	—	—	—
Expense Ratio (%)	1.79	1.90	2.00	—	—
Portfolio Turnover (%)	21.61	1.03	0.00	—	—
NAV per share ($)	14.58	10.35	10.97	—	—
Market Price per share	11.50	7.50	9.38	—	—
Premium (Discount) (%)	(21.12)	(27.54)	(14.59)	—	—
Total Return, Stk Price (%)	55.87	(13.75)	—	—	—

France Growth Fund, Inc. (The)
1285 Avenue of the Americas
New York, NY 10019
(212) 713-2000

NYSE : FRF
Transfer Agent
Provident National Bank
103 Bellevue Parkway
Wilmington, DE 19809
(800) 852-4750

Growth

12 Months Ending 12/31/92 Results

	Period End	Period Begin	Distributions	Yield Dist (%)	Total Return (%)
Share Price ($)	9.25	8.88	0.04	0.45	4.62
NAV per share ($)	10.53	10.75		0.37	(1.67)

Background: Initial public offering May 1990 of 10,000,000 shares at $12 per share. Initial NAV was $11.16 per share.

Objective: Seeks long-term capital appreciation through equity investments primarily in French companies. The fund may engage in hedging activities using futures and options.

Portfolio: (12/31/92) Common Stocks 97.8%, Short Term & Other 2.2%. Sector Weightings: Food & Beverage 12.9%, Financial Services 11.1%, Electrical & Electronics 9.53%, Oil & Gas 8.0%, Distribution Services 5.7%. Largest Holdings: Alcatel Alsthom, Alf Equitaine, L'Oreal, Societe Generale, BSN.

Capitalization: (12/31/92) Common stock outstanding 11,509,000. No long-term debt.

Beta: 0.67
Fund Manager: Indosuez International Investment Services   **Fee:** 0.90%
Income Dist: Annually   **Capital Gains Dist:** Annually
Reinvestment Plan: Yes   **Shareholder Reports:** Semi-Annually

5 Year Performance

Fiscal Year Ending 12/31	1992	1991	1990 (8 mos.)	1989	1988
Net Assets ($mil):	121.20	123.80	118.80	—	—
Net Income Dist ($):	0.02	0.14	0.35	—	—
Cap Gains Dist ($):	0.02	0.10	0.17	—	—
Total Dist ($)	0.04	0.24	0.52	—	—
Yield from Dist (%)	0.45	2.78	—	—	—
Expense Ratio (%)	1.76	2.14	2.18	—	—
Portfolio Turnover (%)	40.00	75.00	16.00	—	—
NAV per share ($)	10.53	10.75	10.33	—	—
Market Price per share	9.25	8.88	8.63	—	—
Premium (Discount) (%)	(12.16)	(17.49)	(16.46)	—	—
Total Return, Stk Price (%)	4.62	5.68	—	—	—

Future Germany Fund, Inc. (The)

31 W. 52nd St
New York, NY 10019
(800) 437-6269 / (212) 474-7000

NYSE : FGF

Transfer Agent
Investors Bank & Trust Co.
P.O. Box 1537
Boston, MA 02205
(800) 437-6269

Growth

12 Months Ending 12/31/92 Results

	Period End	Period Begin	Distributions	Yield Dist (%)	Total Return (%)
Share Price ($)	11.50	12.75	0.30	2.35	(7.45)
NAV per share ($)	12.98	14.58		2.06	(8.92)

Background: Initial public offering March 6, 1990 of 13,500,000 shares at $18 per share. Initial NAV was $16.70 per share.

Objective: Seeks long-term capital appreciation through investments in German securities, especially those that may benefit from reunification. Up to 20% of assets may be invested outside the country, limited to 10% in any single country. For hedging purposes, the fund may invest in put and call options and futures transactions.

Portfolio: (10/31/92) Common Stocks 78.8%, Preferred Stocks 5.9%, Warrants 8.3%, Time Deposits 2.7%, Repurchase Agreements 8.3%, Liabilities (4.0%). Sector Weightings: Banking 17.0%, Electrical 15.2%, Chemical 12.8%, Utilities 11.4%, Insurance 10.1%. Largest Holdings: Siemens, Dresdner Bank, Allianz Holding, VEBA.

Capitalization: (10/31/92) Common stock outstanding 12,064,306. No long-term debt.

Beta: 1.20
Fund Manager: Deutsche Asset Management Corp. **Fee:** 0.35%
Income Dist: Annually **Capital Gains Dist:** Annually
Reinvestment Plan: Yes **Shareholder Reports:** Semi-Annually

5 Year Performance

Fiscal Year Ending 10/31	1992	1991	1990 (8 mos.)	1989	1988
Net Assets ($mil):	163.60	166.60	185.50	—	—
Net Income Dist ($):	0.00	0.22	0.00	—	—
Cap Gains Dist ($):	0.00	0.06	0.00	—	—
Total Dist ($)	0.00	0.28	0.00	—	—
Yield from Dist (%)	0.00	2.24	—	—	—
Expense Ratio (%)	1.47	1.29	1.46	—	—
Portfolio Turnover (%)	38.55	42.84	8.85	—	—
NAV per share ($)	13.56	13.60	14.68	—	—
Market Price per share	12.25	12.38	12.50	—	—
Premium (Discount) (%)	(9.66)	(9.04)	(14.85)	—	—
Total Return, Stk Price (%)	(1.05)	1.28	—	—	—

Germany Fund

31 W. 52nd St., 2nd Floor
New York, NY 10019
(800) 437-6269 / (212) 474-7000

NYSE : GER

Transfer Agent
Investors Bank & Trust Co.
89 South St.
Boston, MA 02111
(800) 642-0144

Growth

12 Months Ending 12/31/92 Results

	Period End	Period Begin	Distributions	Yield Dist (%)	Total Return (%)
Share Price ($)	10.13	12.13	0.38	3.13	(13.36)
NAV per share ($)	9.78	10.95		3.47	(7.21)

Background: Initial public offering July 18, 1986 of 7,500,000 shares at $10 per share. Initial NAV was $9.30 per share.

Objective: Seeks capital appreciation through investments in German equity securities.

Portfolio: (12/31/92) Common Stocks 85.4%, Preferred Stocks 6.1%, Repurchase Agreement 17.7%. Sector Weightings: Banking 15.7%, Electrical 15.0%, Chemical 12.0%, Utilities 11.3%, Automotive 10.1%. Largest Holdings: Siemens, Allianz Holding, Bayer, Dresdner Bank, Bayerische Hypotheken-und Wechsel-Bank.

Capitalization: (12/31/92) Common stock outstanding 13,139,596. No long-term debt.

Beta: 0.78
Fund Manager: Deutsche Asset Management GmbH
Income Dist: Annually
Reinvestment Plan: Yes

Fee: 0.35%
Capital Gains Dist: Annually
Shareholder Reports: Quarterly

5 Year Performance

Fiscal Year Ending 12/31	1992	1991	1990	1989	1988
Net Assets ($mil):	128.60	144.20	144.50	158.50	65.70
Net Income Dist ($):	0.12	0.00	0.11	11.00	0.02
Cap Gains Dist ($):	0.26	0.19	0.14	0.19	0.01
Total Dist ($)	0.38	0.19	0.25	11.19	0.03
Yield from Dist (%)	3.13	1.73	1.30	149.20	0.41
Expense Ratio (%)	1.61	25.00	1.58	1.77	2.01
Portfolio Turnover (%)	49.00	37.00	34.00	36.00	26.00
NAV per share ($)	9.78	10.95	11.05	12.15	8.23
Market Price per share	10.13	12.13	11.00	19.25	7.50
Premium (Discount) (%)	3.58	10.68	(0.45)	58.44	(8.87)
Total Return, Stk Price (%)	(13.36)	12.00	(41.56)	305.87	2.03

NYSE : GSP
Transfer Agent
Investors Fiduciary Trust Co.
127 W. 10th St.
Kansas City, MO 64105
(816) 474-8786

Growth

12 Months Ending 12/31/92 Results

	Period End	Period Begin	Distributions	Yield Dist (%)	Total Return (%)
Share Price ($)	7.63	9.38	0.00	0.00	(18.66)
NAV per share ($)	8.96	11.71		0.00	(23.48)

Background: Initial public offering February 14, 1990 of 17,431,000 shares at $12 per share. Initial NAV was $11.16 per share.

Objective: Seeks long-term capital appreciation by investing primarily in Spanish equities.

Portfolio: (11/30/92) Common Stocks 67.3%, Convertible Corporate Obligations 6.9%, Government Bonds 19.6%, Cash Equivalents 4.1%. Sector Weightings: Electrical/Utilities 19.0%, Telecommunications & Motorways 11.2%, Banking 13.3%, Food & Tobacco 4.8%, Construction & Development 3.2%. Largest Holdings: Banco Popular Espanol, Banco Bilbao-Vizcaya, Iberdrola I.S.A., Compania Telefonica Nacional de Espana, Empresa Nacional de Electricidad.

Capitalization: (11/30/92) Common stock outstanding 17,370,000. No long-term debt.

Beta: 0.83
Fund Manager: Kemper Financial Services, Inc.   **Fee:** 0.35%
Income Dist: Annually   **Capital Gains Dist:** Annually
Reinvestment Plan: Yes   **Shareholder Reports:** Semi-Annually

5 Year Performance

Fiscal Year Ending 11/30	1992	1991	1990 (9 mos.)	1989	1988
Net Assets ($mil):	156.20	192.90	186.60	—	—
Net Income Dist ($):	0.15	0.36	0.00	—	—
Cap Gains Dist ($):	0.00	0.00	0.00	—	—
Total Dist ($)	0.15	0.36	0.00	—	—
Yield from Dist (%)	1.52	4.24	—	—	—
Expense Ratio (%)	1.22	1.23	1.26	—	—
Portfolio Turnover (%)	72.00	104.00	19.00	—	—
NAV per share ($)	8.99	11.08	10.71	—	—
Market Price per share	7.63	9.88	8.50	—	—
Premium (Discount) (%)	(15.13)	(10.92)	(20.63)	—	—
Total Return, Stk Price (%)	(21.26)	20.47	—	—	—

India Growth Fund, Inc.

1285 Avenue of the Americas
New York, NY 10019
(212) 713-2000

NYSE : IGF
Transfer Agent
Provident Financial Processing Corp.
P.O. Box 8950
Wilmington, DE 19899
(800) 852-4750

Growth

12 Months Ending 12/31/92 Results

	Period End	Period Begin	Distributions	Yield Dist (%)	Total Return (%)
Share Price ($)	15.38	14.12	0.00	0.00	8.92
NAV per share ($)	15.88	16.60		0.00	(4.34)

Background: Initial public offering August 12, 1988 of 5,000,000 shares at $12 per share. Initial NAV was $11.16 per share.

Objective: Seeks long-term capital appreciation through investment in the Indian equity market.

Portfolio: (12/31/92): Common Stocks 96.3%, Convertible Bonds 4.2%, Short Term & Other Assets Less Liabilities (0.5%). Sector Weightings: Consumer Products 15.1%, Textiles 13.2%, Automobile-Related 7.9%, Chemicals & Dyes 5.5%, Fertilizers/Pesticides 5.2%. Largest Holdings: Colgate-Palmolive of India, ITC Ltd., Century Textiles, Grasim Industries, TISCO.

Capitalization: (12/31/92) Common stock outstanding 5,024,584. No long-term debt.

Beta: 1.18
Fund Manager: Unit Trust of India Advisory
Income Dist: Annually
Reinvestment Plan: Yes

Fee: 0.75%
Capital Gains Dist: Annually
Shareholder Reports: Quarterly

5 Year Performance

Fiscal Year Ending 6/30	1992	1991	1990	1989 (10 mos.)	1988
Net Assets ($mil):	93.30	70.80	64.50	—	—
Net Income Dist ($):	0.00	0.00	0.37	0.15	—
Cap Gains Dist ($):	0.93	0.16	0.73	0.15	—
Total Dist ($)	0.93	0.16	1.10	0.30	—
Yield from Dist (%)	7.91	1.00	9.36	—	—
Expense Ratio (%)	2.00	3.00	3.27	2.32	—
Portfolio Turnover (%)	27.00	13.50	19.20	38.80	—
NAV per share ($)	18.57	14.12	12.86	14.23	—
Market Price per share	16.00	11.75	16.00	11.75	—
Premium (Discount) (%)	(13.84)	(16.78)	24.42	(17.43)	—
Total Return, Stk Price (%)	44.09	(25.56)	45.53	—	—

Indonesia Fund, Inc. (The)   **NYSE : IF**
153 E. 53rd St., 58th Floor   *Transfer Agent*
New York, NY 10022   Provident Financial Processing Corp.
(212) 832-2626   103 Bellevue Parkway
                                                                  Wilmington, DE 19808
                                                                       (800) 852-4750

Growth

12 Months Ending 12/31/92 Results

	Period End	Period Begin	Distributions	Yield Dist (%)	Total Return (%)
Share Price ($)	9.00	8.38	0.00	0.00	7.40
NAV per share ($)	7.63	7.72		0.00	(1.17)

Background: Initial public offering March, 1990 of 4,607,169 shares at $15 per share. Initial NAV was $13.78.

Objective: Seeks long-term capital appreciation. Invests in Indonesian securities.

Portfolio: (12/31/92) Common Stock 90.1%, Short Term 9.9%. Sector Weightings: Textiles 13.1%, Food Products 6.8%, Hotels 6.3%, Real Estate 5.86%, Construction 4.5%. Largest Holdings: Astra International, Indorama Synthetics, Duta Angadda Realty, Jakarta International Hotel, Semen Cieinong

Capitalization: (12/31/92) Common stock outstanding 4,608,989. No long-term debt.

Beta: 0.99
Fund Manager: BEA Associates   **Fee:** 1.00%
Income Dist: Annually   **Capital Gains Dist:** Annually
Reinvestment Plan: Yes   **Shareholder Reports:** Quarterly

5 Year Performance

Fiscal Year Ending 12/31	1992	1991	1990 (10 mos.)	1989	1988
Net Assets ($mil):	35.20	35.60	47.80	—	—
Net Income Dist ($):	0.00	0.05	0.19	—	—
Cap Gains Dist ($):	0.00	0.00	0.53	—	—
Total Dist ($)	0.00	0.05	0.72	—	—
Yield from Dist (%)	0.00	0.51	—	—	—
Expense Ratio (%)	2.04	2.00	2.15	—	—
Portfolio Turnover (%)	22.39	32.27	21.73	—	—
NAV per share ($)	7.63	7.72	10.38	—	—
Market Price per share	9.00	8.38	9.88	—	—
Premium (Discount) (%)	17.96	8.42	(4.82)	—	—
Total Return, Stk Price (%)	7.40	(14.68)	—	—	—

Irish Investment Fund, Inc. (The)
1 Exchange Place
Boston, MA 02109
(800) 468-6475

Transfer Agent
American Stock Transfer & Trust Co.
40 Wall St.
New York, NY 10005
(800) 468-6475

Growth

12 Months Ending 12/31/92 Results

	Period End	Period Begin	Distributions	Yield Dist (%)	Total Return (%)
Share Price ($)	6.63	7.63	0.42	5.50	(7.60)
NAV per share ($)	7.84	9.74		4.31	(15.20)

Background: Initial public offering March 30, 1990 of 5,000,000 shares at $12 per share. Initial NAV was $11.16 per share.

Objective: Seeks long-term capital appreciation. At least 65% of assets will be invested in Irish equity securities. Up to 35% may be invested in fixed-income securities or equity securities outside of Ireland related to the Irish economy.

Portfolio: (10/31/92) Irish Common Stocks 77.6%, Irish Convertible Preferred Stock 4.9%, United Kingdom Common Stocks 8.2%, Short Term & Other 9.3%. Largest Holdings: AIB, Smurfit (Jefferson) Group, CRH, Independent Newspapers, Kerry Group.

Capitalization: (10/31/92) Common stock outstanding 5,009,000. No long-term debt.

Beta: 0.55
Fund Manager: Bank of Ireland Asset Management Ltd.   **Fee:** 0.75%
Income Dist: Annually   **Capital Gains Dist:** Annually
Reinvestment Plan: Yes   **Shareholder Reports:** Quarterly

5 Year Performance

Fiscal Year Ending 10/31	1992	1991	1990 (9 mos.)	1989	1988
Net Assets ($mil):	40.00	48.80	50.30	—	—
Net Income Dist ($):	0.23	0.33	0.00	—	—
Cap Gains Dist ($):	0.00	0.00	0.00	—	—
Total Dist ($)	0.23	0.33	0.00	—	—
Yield from Dist (%)	3.29	4.55	—	—	—
Expense Ratio (%)	1.80	2.03	1.70	—	—
Portfolio Turnover (%)	7.00	28.00	6.00	—	—
NAV per share ($)	7.99	9.75	10.04	—	—
Market Price per share	7.88	7.00	7.25	—	—
Premium (Discount) (%)	(1.38)	(28.21)	(27.79)	—	—
Total Return, Stk Price (%)	15.86	1.10	—	—	—

Italy Fund, Inc. (The)   NYSE : ITA
2 World Trade Center   *Transfer Agent*
New York, NY 10048   Shareholders Services Group, Inc.
(212) 298-6236   P.O. Box 1376
                                                            Boston, MA 02104
                                                              (800) 331-1710

Growth

12 Months Ending 12/31/92 Results

	Period End	Period Begin	Distributions	Yield Dist (%)	Total Return (%)
Share Price ($)	7.50	8.88	0.00	0.00	(15.54)
NAV per share ($)	7.82	10.99		0.00	(28.84)

Background: Initial public offering February 28, 1986 of 6,333,961 shares at $12 per share. Initial NAV was $11.16 per share.

Objective: Seeks total return with at least 65% of assets invested in Italian equity and debt securities. May invest in non-Italian companies that have operations or sales in Italy. May invest up to 25% in unlisted securities.

Portfolio: (7/31/92) Stocks 85.8%, Warrants 0.9%, Fixed-Income Investments 11.3%, Time Deposits 1.4%. Sector Weightings: Insurance 20.5%, Communications 14.9%, Financial 14.1% Banking 12.6%. Largest Holdings: Sirti S.P.A., Alleanza, Parlamat Finanziaria, Instituto Bancario San Paolo Torino, Finanziaria Agro-Industriale.

Capitalization: (1/31/92) Common stock outstanding 6,334,901. No long-term debt.

Beta: 0.98
Fund Manager: ShearsonLehman Global Asset Management, Ltd.   **Fee:** 0.75%
Income Dist: Annually   **Capital Gains Dist:** Annually
Reinvestment Plan: Yes   **Shareholder Reports:** Quarterly

5 Year Performance

Fiscal Year Ending 1/31	1992	1991	1990	1989	1988
Net Assets ($mil):	70.20	72.10	83.90	62.70	57.40
Net Income Dist ($):	0.25	0.34	0.15	0.19	0.36
Cap Gains Dist ($):	0.24	0.58	0.00	0.00	1.37
Total Dist ($)	0.49	0.92	0.15	0.19	1.73
Yield from Dist (%)	4.90	5.26	1.88	2.71	14.26
Expense Ratio (%)	1.53	1.80	1.90	1.99	1.92
Portfolio Turnover (%)	24.00	24.00	15.00	15.00	19.00
NAV per share ($)	11.08	11.37	13.24	9.91	9.07
Market Price per share	9.50	10.00	17.50	8.00	7.00
Premium (Discount) (%)	(14.26)	(12.05)	32.18	(19.27)	(22.82)
Total Return, Stk Price (%)	(0.10)	(37.60)	120.63	17.00	(28.03)

Jakarta Growth Fund, Inc.

180 Maiden Ln.
New York, NY 10038
(800) 833-0018 / (212) 509-8181

Transfer Agent
State Street Bank & Trust Co.
P.O. Box 8200
Boston, MA 021105
(800) 426-5523

Growth

12 Months Ending 12/31/92 Results

	Period End	Period Begin	Distributions	Yield Dist (%)	Total Return (%)
Share Price ($)	7.13	5.75	0.08	1.39	25.39
NAV per share ($)	6.28	6.19		1.29	2.75

Background: Initial public offering April 11, 1990 of 5,000,000 shares at $12 per share. Initial NAV was $11.16 per share.

Objective: Seeks long-term capital appreciation through investments primarily in Indonesian equities. Invests 65% of assets in companies listed on the Jakarta stock exchange. The balance will be invested in unlisted or U.S. dollar-denominated fixed-income securities.

Portfolio: (9/30/92) Stocks 87.0%, Short Term 13.0%. Sector Weightings: Nondurables 44.1%, Industrial Products 15.8%, Natural Resources 15.4%, Services 12.0%, Finance 6.4%. Largest Holdings: Kalbe Farma, Indorama Synthetics, Metro Data Electronics, HM Sampoerna, Dynaplast.

Capitalization: (9/30/92) Common stock outstanding 5,009,000. No long-term debt.

Beta: 0.81
Fund Manager: Nomura Capital Management
Income Dist: Annually
Reinvestment Plan: Yes

Fee: 1.10%
Capital Gains Dist: Annually
Shareholder Reports: Semi-Annually

5 Year Performance

Fiscal Year Ending 3/31	1992	1991 (11 mos.)	1990	1989	1988
Net Assets ($mil):	32.50	42.60	—	—	—
Net Income Dist ($):	0.12	0.14	—	—	—
Cap Gains Dist ($):	0.06	0.00	—	—	—
Total Dist ($)	0.18	0.14	—	—	—
Yield from Dist (%)	2.32	—	—	—	—
Expense Ratio (%)	2.15	1.83	—	—	—
Portfolio Turnover (%)	24.20	7.00	—	—	—
NAV per share ($)	6.49	8.51	—	—	—
Market Price per share	7.13	7.75	—	—	—
Premium (Discount) (%)	9.86	(8.93)	—	—	—
Total Return, Stk Price (%)	(5.68)	—	—	—	—

Japan OTC Equity Fund, Inc.

180 Maiden Ln.
New York, NY 10038
(800) 833-0018 / (212) 509-8181

Transfer Agent
State Street Bank & Trust Co.
P.O. Box 1713
Boston, MA 02105
(800) 426-5523

Growth

12 Months Ending 12/31/92 Results

	Period End	Period Begin	Distributions	Yield Dist (%)	Total Return (%)
Share Price ($)	7.63	10.38	0.00	0.00	(26.49)
NAV per share ($)	6.92	10.14		0.00	(31.76)

Background: Initial public offering March 19, 1990 of 8,500,000 shares at $12 per share. Initial NAV was $11.08 per share.

Objective: Seeks long-term capital appreciation from a portfolio of Japanese equities traded in the Japanese Over-The-Counter Market.

Portfolio: (8/31/92) Japanese Equity Securities 88.4%, Short Term 12.8%. Sector Weightings: Machinery/ Machine Tools 12.4%, Construction/Housing 11.5%, Retail/Wholesale 11.5%, Miscellaneous Manufacturing 8.7%. Largest Holdings: Levi Strauss Japan, Ishiguro Homa Corp., Nippon Kanzai Co., Aiya & Co., Nakayama Kiko Co.

Capitalization: (9/30/92) Common stock outstanding 8,509,000. No long-term debt.

Beta: 0.92
Fund Manager: Nomura Capital Management, Inc.   **Fee:** 1.10%
Income Dist: Annually   **Capital Gains Dist:** Annually
Reinvestment Plan: Yes   **Shareholder Reports:** Semi-Annually

5 Year Performance

Fiscal Year Ending 2/28	1992	1991 (11 mos.)	1990	1989	1988
Net Assets ($mil):	82.20	85.00	—	—	—
Net Income Dist ($):	0.19	0.24	—	—	—
Cap Gains Dist ($):	0.00	0.46	—	—	—
Total Dist ($)	0.19	0.70	—	—	—
Yield from Dist (%)	1.50	—	—	—	—
Expense Ratio (%)	1.51	1.43	—	—	—
Portfolio Turnover (%)	36.00	32.00	—	—	—
NAV per share ($)	9.66	9.99	—	—	—
Market Price per share	10.13	12.63	—	—	—
Premium (Discount) (%)	4.87	26.43	—	—	—
Total Return, Stk Price (%)	(18.29)	—	—	—	—

Korea Fund, Inc.

345 Park Ave.
New York, NY 10154
(800) 426-5523

NYSE : KF
Transfer Agent
State Street Bank & Trust Co.
P.O. Box 8200
Boston, MA 02266
(617) 328-5000

Growth

12 Months Ending 12/31/92 Results

	Period End	Period Begin	Distributions	Yield Dist (%)	Total Return (%)
Share Price ($)	14.00	15.63	0.24	1.54	(8.89)
NAV per share ($)	10.62	10.55		2.27	2.94

Background: Initial public offering August 22, 1984 of 5,000,000 shares at $12 per share. Initial NAV was $11.16 per share.

Objective: Seeks long-term capital appreciation. Invests at least 80% of assets in stocks listed on the Korea stock exchange. The balance may be invested in OTC securities.

Portfolio: (9/30/92) Common Stocks 97.0%, Preferred Stock 2.9%, Repurchase Agreements 0.1%. Sector Weightings: Basic Industry 20.3%, Consumer Cyclical 16.6%, Financials 15.9%, Consumer Nondurable 13.9%, Technology 13.4%. Largest Holdings: Samsung Electronics, Cheil Food and Chemical Co., Hankook Tire Mfg., Hyundai Motor Services Co., Keum Kang Co.

Capitalization: (12/31/92) Common stock outstanding 22,450,639. No long-term debt.

Beta: 0.81
Fund Manager: Scudder, Stevens & Clark
Income Dist: Annually
Reinvestment Plan: Yes

Fee: 1.15%
Capital Gains Dist: Annually
Shareholder Reports: Quarterly

5 Year Performance

Fiscal Year Ending 6/30	1992	1991	1990	1989	1988
Net Assets ($mil):	241.50	228.40	303.00	322.80	271.40
Net Income Dist ($):	0.06	0.00	0.08	0.11	0.29
Cap Gains Dist ($):	0.34	2.20	1.88	1.74	0.68
Total Dist ($)	0.40	2.20	1.96	1.85	0.97
Yield from Dist (%)	2.83	9.94	6.20	2.63	4.15
Expense Ratio (%)	1.52	1.47	1.44	1.54	1.53
Portfolio Turnover (%)	18.20	19.20	17.90	15.10	19.70
NAV per share ($)	10.75	10.27	14.45	16.84	13.97
Market Price per share	11.38	14.13	22.13	31.63	70.25
Premium (Discount) (%)	5.86	37.49	53.15	87.77	402.86
Total Return, Stk Price (%)	(16.63)	(26.21)	(23.84)	(52.34)	204.62

Malaysia Fund, Inc. (The)

1221 Avenues of the Americas
New York, NY 10020
(212) 296-7100

NYSE : MF

Transfer Agent
The First National Bank of Boston
P.O. Box 644
Boston, MA 02102
(617) 575-2900

Growth

12 Months Ending 12/31/92 Results

	Period End	Period Begin	Distributions	Yield Dist (%)	Total Return (%)
Share Price ($)	16.25	11.75	0.00	0.00	38.30
NAV per share ($)	16.28	13.55		0.00	20.15

Background: Initial public offering May 2, 1987 of 7,000,000 common shares at $12 per share. Initial NAV was $11.16 per share. This fund is the first vehicle available for investment primarily in the Malaysian economy.

Objective: Seeks long-term capital appreciation. Invests at least 80% in Malaysian equities with the balance in Malaysian debt securities. Distributions to foreign investors are exempt from Malaysian income tax.

Portfolio: (12/31/92) Malaysia Common Stocks 90.0%, Short Term & Other 10.0% Sector Weightings: Industrial 17.5%, Entertainment 14.6%, Telecommunications 11.7%, Raw/Intermediate Materials 7.5%, Transportation 6.4%, Construction 5.2%. Largest Holdings: Telekom Malaysia, Genting Bhd, Resorts World Bhd, Malaysian International Shipping, Malayan Banking Bhd.

Capitalization: (12/31/92) Common stock outstanding 7,259,336. No long-term debt.

Beta: 1.00
Fund Manager: Morgan Stanley Asset Management Inc.   **Fee:** 0.90%
Income Dist: Annually   **Capital Gains Dist:** Annually
Reinvestment Plan: Yes   **Shareholder Reports:** Quarterly

5 Year Performance

Fiscal Year Ending 12/31	1992	1991	1990	1989	1988
Net Assets ($mil):	118.20	98.30	90.10	99.90	65.20
Net Income Dist ($):	0.00	0.07	0.21	0.11	0.17
Cap Gains Dist ($):	0.00	0.00	0.00	0.00	0.00
Total Dist ($)	0.00	0.07	0.21	0.11	0.17
Yield from Dist (%)	0.00	0.62	1.12	1.47	2.83
Expense Ratio (%)	1.72	1.70	1.93	1.95	2.29
Portfolio Turnover (%)	37.90	14.90	17.80	30.20	13.70
NAV per share ($)	16.28	13.55	12.41	13.77	8.98
Market Price per share	16.25	11.75	11.38	18.75	7.50
Premium (Discount) (%)	(0.18)	(13.28)	(8.30)	36.17	(16.48)
Total Return, Stk Price (%)	38.30	3.87	(38.19)	151.47	27.83

Mexico Equity and Income Fund, Inc.

World Financial Center
200 Liberty St.
New York, NY 10281
(212) 667-5000

NYSE : MXE
Transfer Agent
Provident National Bank
c/o Provident Financial Processing
Wilmington, DE 19899
(800) 553-8080

Growth

12 Months Ending 12/31/92 Results

	Period End	Period Begin	Distributions	Yield Dist (%)	Total Return (%)
Share Price ($)	15.00	12.88	1.53	11.88	28.34
NAV per share ($)	16.65	15.27		10.02	19.06

Background: Initial public offering August 21, 1990 of 6,000,000 shares at $12 per share. Initial NAV was $11.40 per share.

Objective: Seeks total return from income and growth by investing 50% in convertible debt securities and the remainder in Mexican equities to seek a total return from income and growth.

Portfolio: (7/31/92) Mexican Common Stock 68.2%, Government Bonds 12.5%, Convertible Debt Securities 10.9%, Short Term 6.9%. Sector Weightings: Retailing 15.5%, Telecommunications 11.8%, Conglomerates 9.5%, Paper 8.4%. Largest Holdings: Telmex, Cemex, Banamex, Kimberly Clark de Mexico, Cifra.

Capitalization: (7/31/92) Common stocks outstanding 6,311,792. No long-term debt.

Beta: 0.79
Fund Manager: Advantage Advisors, Inc. **Fee:** 0.40%
Income Dist: Annually **Capital Gains Dist:** Annually
Reinvestment Plan: Yes **Shareholder Reports:** Semi-Annually

5 Year Performance

Fiscal Year Ending 7/31	1992	1991 (11 mos.)	1990	1989	1988
Net Assets ($mil):	101.20	94.70	—	—	—
Net Income Dist ($):	0.96	0.58	—	—	—
Cap Gains Dist ($):	0.01	0.00	—	—	—
Total Dist ($)	0.97	0.58	—	—	—
Yield from Dist (%)	7.46	—	—	—	—
Expense Ratio (%)	1.62	1.98	—	—	—
Portfolio Turnover (%)	15.08	8.18	—	—	—
NAV per share ($)	16.03	15.08	—	—	—
Market Price per share	14.75	13.00	—	—	—
Premium (Discount) (%)	(7.99)	(13.79)	—	—	—
Total Return, Stk Price (%)	20.92	—	—	—	—

Mexico Fund, Inc.

399 Park Ave., 37th Fl.
New York, NY 10022
(212) 750-4200

NYSE : MXF

Transfer Agent
American Stock Transfer & Trust Co.
40 Wall St.
New York, NY 10004
(212) 936-5100

Growth

12 Months Ending 12/31/92 Results

	Period End	Period Begin	Distributions	Yield Dist (%)	Total Return (%)
Share Price ($)	23.25	22.25	2.96	13.30	17.80
NAV per share ($)	25.31	25.32		11.69	11.65

Background: Initial public offering June 11, 1981. Beginning net assets equaled $104.7 million. On March 20, 1992, a rights offering of 6,573,735 shares raised an additional $125,830,536.

Objective: Seeks capital appreciation. Invests in securities and bonds traded on the Mexican stock exchange.

Portfolio: (10/31/92) Common Stocks 92.82%, Time Deposits 7.79%. Sector Weightings: Retail Trade 19.4%, Holdings 18.32%, Financial Groups 11.54%, Time Deposits 7.79%, Commercial Paper 6.0%. Largest Holdings: Cifra S.A. de C.V., Cemex S.A., Telefonos de Mexico S.A. de C.V., Grupo Carso S.A. de C.V., Grupo Financiero Banamex Accival S.A. de C.V.

Capitalization: (10/31/93) Common stock outstanding 26,292,000. No long-term debt.

Beta: 0.71

Fund Manager: Impulsora del Fondo Mexico, S.A. de C.V.	**Fee:** 0.85%
Income Dist: Annually	**Capital Gains Dist:** Annually
Reinvestment Plan: No	**Shareholder Reports:** Quarterly

5 Year Performance

Fiscal Year Ending 10/31*	1992	1991	1990	1989	1988
Net Assets ($mil):	654.90	474.70	303.30	202.40	145.30
Net Income Dist ($):	0.48	0.36	0.56	0.45	0.15
Cap Gains Dist ($):	1.03	0.00	0.00	0.00	0.00
Total Dist ($)	1.51	0.36	0.56	0.45	0.15
Yield from Dist (%)	6.60	2.44	6.40	7.83	2.44
Expense Ratio (%)	1.06	1.37	1.60	1.77	1.74
Portfolio Turnover (%)	15.59	12.53	8.88	10.54	19.58
NAV per share ($)................................	24.91	24.07	15.38	10.26	7.37
Market Price per share	23.25	22.88	14.75	8.75	5.75
Premium (Discount) (%)	(6.66)	(4.94)	(4.10)	(14.72)	(21.98)
Total Return, Stk Price (%)	8.22	57.56	74.97	60.00	(3.91)

* Prior to 1992, the fund's fiscal year ended 5/31.

New Germany Fund, Inc. (The)
31 W. 52nd St.
New York, NY 10019
(800) 437-6269 / (212) 474-7000

Transfer Agent
Investors Bank & Trust Co.
89 South St.
Boston, MA 02111
(800) 437-6269

Growth

12 Months Ending 12/31/92 Results

	Period End	Period Begin	Distributions	Yield Dist (%)	Total Return (%)
Share Price ($)	9.38	10.75	0.18	1.67	(11.07)
NAV per share ($)	11.00	12.63		1.43	(11.48)

Background: Initial public offering January 30, 1990 of 28,750,000 shares at $15 per share. Initial NAV was $13.95 per share.

Objective: Seeks long-term capital appreciation primarily through investment in equity securities of German companies with small to medium capitalization. Up to 20% may be invested outside of Germany, restricted to 10% in any one country.

Portfolio: (12/31/92) German Common & Preferred Stocks & Warrants 82.4%, French Common Stocks 4.8%, Norwegian Common Stocks 2.3%, Swiss Common Stocks 4.1%, Repurchase Agreements 7.6%. Sector Weightings: Electrical 16.7%, Banking 13.5%, Construction 12.4%, Engineering 7.4%, Steel/Metals 7.1%. Largest Holdings: Siemens, Weru AG, Deutsche Pfandbrief-und Hypothekenbank AG, Bilfinger und Berger AG.

Capitalization: (12/31/92) Common stock outstanding 27,272,000. No long-term debt.

Beta: 1.27
Fund Manager: Deutsche Asset Management GmbH
Income Dist: Annually
Reinvestment Plan: Yes

Fee: 0.35%
Capital Gains Dist: Annually
Shareholder Reports: Quarterly

5 Year Performance

Fiscal Year Ending 12/31	1992	1991	1990 (11 mos.)	1989	1988
Net Assets ($mil):	298.10	344.60	358.40	—	—
Net Income Dist ($):	0.14	0.00	0.21	—	—
Cap Gains Dist ($):	0.04	0.07	0.05	—	—
Total Dist ($)	0.18	0.07	0.26	—	—
Yield from Dist (%)	1.67	0.62	—	—	—
Expense Ratio (%)	1.28	1.13	1.21	—	—
Portfolio Turnover (%)	42.00	48.97	36.02	—	—
NAV per share ($)	11.00	12.63	12.76	—	—
Market Price per share	9.38	10.75	11.25	—	—
Premium (Discount) (%)	(14.73)	(14.89)	(11.83)	—	—
Total Return, Stk Price (%)	(11.07)	(3.82)	—	—	—

Portugal Fund, Inc.
One Citicorp Plaza
153 E. 53rd St.
New York, NY 10022
(212) 832-2626

NYSE : PGF
Transfer Agent
Provident National Bank
P.O. Box 8950
Wilmington, DE 19899
(800) 553-8080

Growth

12 Months Ending 12/31/92 Results

	Period End	Period Begin	Distributions	Yield Dist (%)	Total Return (%)
Share Price ($)	8.00	9.75	0.06	0.62	(17.33)
NAV per share ($)	8.90	10.77		0.56	(16.81)

Background: Initial public offering November 1, 1989 of approximately 4,600,000 shares at $15 per share. Initial NAV was $13.95 per share.

Objective: Seeks total return including income and capital appreciation. The fund will invest at least 75% in Portuguese equity and debt securities. Up to 25% may be invested in non-Portuguese equity and debt securities. The fund may engage in hedging transactions.

Portfolio: (12/31/92) Common Stocks 77.9%, Convertible Bonds 1.18%, U.S. Treasuries 20.9%. Sector Weightings: Banks 15.37%, Construction/Public Works 13.55%, Retail Trade 11.9%, Metal Product/Machine 9.3%, Holding Cos. 6.2%. Largest Holdings: Continente SA, Modelo Hipermercados, Jeronimo Martins, Engil-Sociedade Construcao Civil, Banco Portuguese de Investimento, Filmes Lusomundo.

Capitalization: (12/31/92) Common stock outstanding 5,298,058. No long-term debt.

Beta: 0.79
Fund Manager: BEA Associates
Income Dist: Annually
Reinvestment Plan: Yes

Fee: 1.20%
Capital Gains Dist: Annually
Shareholder Reports: Semi-Annually

5 Year Performance

Fiscal Year Ending 12/31	1992	1991	1990	1989 (2 mos.)	1988
Net Assets ($mil):	47.10	57.00	58.10	73.00	—
Net Income Dist ($):	0.06	0.11	0.12	0.04	—
Cap Gains Dist ($):	0.00	0.00	0.00	0.04	—
Total Dist ($)	0.06	0.11	0.12	0.08	—
Yield from Dist (%)	0.62	1.19	0.71	—	—
Expense Ratio (%)	1.92	1.96	2.04	2.26	—
Portfolio Turnover (%)	39.07	13.31	10.09	0.00	—
NAV per share ($)	8.90	10.77	10.96	13.79	—
Market Price per share	8.00	9.75	9.25	17.00	—
Premium (Discount) (%)	(10.11)	(9.47)	(15.60)	23.28	—
Total Return, Stk Price (%)	(17.33)	6.59	(44.88)	—	—

ROC Taiwan Fund, Inc.

100 E. Pratt St.
Baltimore, MD 21202
(800) 343-9567

NYSE : ROC

Transfer Agent
State Street Bank & Trust Co.
225 Franklin St.
Boston, MA 02110
(800) 426-5523

Growth

12 Months Ending 12/31/92 Results

	Period End	Period Begin	Distributions	Yield Dist (%)	Total Return (%)
Share Price ($)	8.75	10.25	0.02	0.20	(14.44)
NAV per share ($)	8.51	9.53		0.21	(10.49)

Background: Commenced operations on October 27, 1983 as an open-end fund. Converted to a closed-end fund May 9, 1989. On date of reorganization, NAV was $13.50 per share.

Objective: Seeks long-term capital appreciation through investments in securities, primarily equities, traded on the Republic of China (ROC) Taiwan Exchange.

Portfolio: (12/31/92) Common & Preferred Stock 61.4%, Bonds 2.8%, Short Term 35.4%. Sector Weightings: Electric/Electronic 11.7%, Steel/Metals 7.7%, Textiles 7.4%, Cement 7.0%, Plastics 6.6%. Largest Holdings: President Enterprise Corp., Teco Electric and Machinery, Asia Cement Corp.,Tung Ho Steel, Nan Ya Plastics.

Capitalization: (12/31/92) Common stock outstanding 27,871,000. No long-term debt.

Beta: 0.77
Fund Manager: International Investment Trust **Fee:** 1.45%
Income Dist: Annually **Capital Gains Dist:** Annually
Reinvestment Plan: Yes **Shareholder Reports:** Quarterly

5 Year Performance

Fiscal Year Ending 12/31	1992	1991	1990	1989	1988
Net Assets ($mil):	237.20	244.10	235.70	370.70	185.90
Net Income Dist ($):	0.02	0.75	0.22	0.43	0.01
Cap Gains Dist ($):	0.00	0.00	0.00	0.00	0.00
Total Dist ($)	0.02	0.75	0.22	0.43	0.01
Yield from Dist (%)	0.20	9.68	1.68	—	—
Expense Ratio (%)	2.47	2.11	2.03	1.93	1.77
Portfolio Turnover (%)	45.00	35.00	27.00	30.00	38.00
NAV per share ($)	8.51	9.53	9.15	14.38	8.58
Market Price per share	8.75	10.25	7.75	13.13	—
Premium (Discount) (%)	2.82	7.56	(15.30)	(8.76)	(100.00)
Total Return, Stk Price (%)	(14.44)	41.94	(39.30)	—	—

Singapore Fund, Inc.

c/o Daiwa Securities Trust Co.
One Evertrust Plaza, 9th Floor
Jersey City, NJ 07302
(800) 933-3440 / (201) 915-3020

NYSE : SGF
Transfer Agent
State Street Bank & Trust Co.
225 Franklin St.
Boston, MA 02110
(800) 426-5523

Growth

12 Months Ending 12/31/92 Results

	Period End	Period Begin	Distributions	Yield Dist (%)	Total Return (%)
Share Price ($)	9.75	10.25	0.33	3.22	(1.66)
NAV per share ($)	11.04	12.10		2.73	(6.03)

Background: Initial public offering July 31, 1990 of 5,000,000 shares at $12 per share. Initial NAV was $10.95 per share.

Objective: Seeks long-term capital appreciation. The fund intends to hold at least 65% of its total assets in equity securities of Singapore companies.

Portfolio: (10/31/92) Common Stock & Warrants 84.8%, Time Deposits 12.14%, Convertible Bonds 2.8%. Sector Weightings: Banks 14.6%, Commercial & Industrial 11.5%, Shipyards 10.8%, Marine Transportation 6.6%, Air Transportation 6.5%. Largest Holdings: Overseas Chinese Banking Corp. Ltd., Singapore Airlines Ltd., Singapore Press Holdings Ltd., Overseas Union Bank Ltd., Keppell Corp. Ltd.

Capitalization: (10/31/92) Common stock outstanding 5,089,084. No long-term debt.

Beta: 0.83
Fund Manager: Daiwa International Capital Management, Ltd.   **Fee:** 0.80%
Income Dist: Annually   **Capital Gains Dist:** Annually
Reinvestment Plan: Yes   **Shareholder Reports:** Semi-Annually

5 Year Performance

Fiscal Year Ending 10/31	1992	1991	1990 (3 mos.)	1989	1988
Net Assets ($mil):	52.80	59.40	55.70	—	—
Net Income Dist ($):	0.08	0.20	0.00	—	—
Cap Gains Dist ($):	0.52	0.01	0.00	—	—
Total Dist ($)	0.60	0.21	0.00	—	—
Yield from Dist (%)	6.07	2.33	—	—	—
Expense Ratio (%)	2.63	2.56	2.83	—	—
Portfolio Turnover (%)	23.66	29.53	0.00	—	—
NAV per share ($)	10.38	11.72	11.12	—	—
Market Price per share	10.25	9.88	9.00	—	—
Premium (Discount) (%)	(1.25)	(15.78)	(19.06)	—	—
Total Return, Stk Price (%)	9.82	12.11	—	—	—

Spain Fund, Inc.

1345 Avenue of the Americas
New York, NY 10105
(800) 247-4154

NYSE : SNF

Transfer Agent
State Street Bank & Trust Co.
225 Franklin St.
Boston, MA 02110
(800) 426-5523

Growth

12 Months Ending 12/31/92 Results

	Period End	Period Begin	Distributions	Yield Dist (%)	Total Return (%)
Share Price ($)	8.25	13.00	0.18	1.38	(35.15)
NAV per share ($)	8.18	11.96		1.51	(30.10)

Background: Initial public offering June 21, 1988 of 10,000,000 shares at $12 per share. Initial NAV was $11.10 per share.

Objective: Seeks long-term capital appreciation. Under normal conditions the fund will invest at least 65% of its assets in Spanish equity securities and up to 35% in AA corporate debt securities and Spanish government bonds.

Portfolio: (11/30/92) Common Stock 90.3%, Convertible Bonds 1.9%, Cash & Commercial Paper 2.5%. Sector Weightings: Financial Services 24.5%, Utilities 18.5%, Food & Tobacco 16.0%, Oil & Chemical 8.2%, Telecommunications 6.0%. Largest Holdings: Repsol S.A. (Petroleum), Banco Intercontinental (Banking), Banco De Santander (Banking), Tabacalera S.A. Series A (Tobacco), Iberdrola S.A. (Utilities).

Capitalization: (11/30/92) Common stock outstanding 10,019,066. No long-term debt.

Beta: 0.62
Fund Manager: Alliance Capital Management L.P.
Income Dist: Annually
Reinvestment Plan: Yes

Fee: 1.10%
Capital Gains Dist: Annually
Shareholder Reports: Quarterly

5 Year Performance

Fiscal Year Ending 11/30	1992	1991	1990	1989	1988 (5 mos.)
Net Assets ($mil):	82.90	116.70	122.70	144.10	117.20
Net Income Dist ($):	0.15	0.14	0.13	0.14	0.00
Cap Gains Dist ($):	0.22	1.15	0.85	0.02	0.00
Total Dist ($)	0.37	1.29	0.98	0.16	0.00
Yield from Dist (%)	2.79	10.21	3.48	1.54	—
Expense Ratio (%)	2.34	1.98	2.22	1.93	1.90
Portfolio Turnover (%)	43.00	35.00	41.00	32.00	3.00
NAV per share ($)	8.28	11.65	12.26	14.40	11.71
Market Price per share	8.38	13.25	12.63	28.13	10.38
Premium (Discount) (%)	1.21	13.73	2.94	95.35	(11.44)
Total Return, Stk Price (%)	(33.96)	15.12	(51.62)	172.54	—

Swiss Helvetia Fund, Inc.

521 Fifth Ave.
New York, NY 10175
(212) 867-7660

Growth

NYSE : SWZ
Transfer Agent
Provident Financial Process Corp.
Provident National Bank
P.O. Box 8950
Wilmington, DE 19899
(800) 553-8080

12 Months Ending 12/31/92 Results

	Period End	Period Begin	Distributions	Yield Dist (%)	Total Return (%)
Share Price ($)	13.88	13.25	0.03	0.23	4.98
NAV per share ($)	14.62	13.80		0.22	6.16

Background: Initial public offering August 27, 1987 of 8,000,000 shares at $15 per share. Initial NAV was $13.95 per share.

Objective: Seeks long-term capital appreciation through investment in equities and equity-linked Swiss securities. Does not intend to trade for short-term profits. May purchase private placements.

Portfolio: (12/31/92) Common Stocks & Warrants 99.1%, Short Term 0.9%. Sector Weightings: Pharmaceuticals 23.3%, Banks 20.02%, Food, Beverages 18.5%, Insurance 10.3%, Machinery, Metals 8.7%. Largest Holdings: Nestle, Roche, Union Bank of Switzerland, Sandoz, Zurich Ins.

Capitalization: (12/31/92) Common stock outstanding 8,808,645. No long-term debt.

Beta: 0.58
Fund Manager: Helvetia Capital Corporation | **Fee:** 1.00%
Income Dist: Annually | **Capital Gains Dist:** Annually
Reinvestment Plan: Yes | **Shareholder Reports:** Quarterly

5 Year Performance

Fiscal Year Ending 12/31	1992	1991	1990	1989	1988
Net Assets ($mil):	128.80	110.50	105.40	104.40	88.00
Net Income Dist ($):	0.03	0.03	0.05	0.00	0.02
Cap Gains Dist ($):	0.00	0.00	0.00	0.00	0.00
Total Dist ($)	0.03	0.03	0.05	0.00	0.02
Yield from Dist (%)	0.23	0.25	0.33	0.00	0.21
Expense Ratio (%)	1.69	1.85	1.77	1.80	1.83
Portfolio Turnover (%)	13.09	41.08	43.83	30.46	63.46
NAV per share ($)	14.62	13.80	13.17	13.04	10.99
Market Price per share	13.88	13.25	11.88	15.13	9.63
Premium (Discount) (%)	(5.06)	(3.99)	(9.87)	15.95	(12.47)
Total Return, Stk Price (%)	4.98	11.78	(21.15)	57.11	1.58

Taiwan Fund, Inc.
82 Devonshire St.
Boston, MA 02109
(800) 544-6666

NYSE : TWN
Transfer Agent
State Street Bank & Trust Co.
225 Franklin St.
Boston, MA 02110
(800) 451-6788

Growth

12 Months Ending 12/31/92 Results

	Period End	Period Begin	Distributions	Yield Dist (%)	Total Return (%)
Share Price ($)	18.75	24.63	0.12	0.49	(23.39)
NAV per share ($)	19.03	20.89		0.57	(8.33)

Background: Initial public offering December 1986 of 2,030,000 shares of common stock at $12.00 per share. Initial NAV was $11.16 per share.

Objective: Seeks long-term capital appreciation. The fund will invest at least 75% of its assets in stocks listed on the Taiwanese stock exchange.

Portfolio: (8/31/92) Common Stocks 38.3%, Government Securities 15.1%, Short Term 46.6%. Sector Weightings: Building Materials 7.2%, Paper & Forest Products 5.4%, Textiles & Apparel 4.6%, Autos, Tires & Accessories 4.6%, Chemicals & Plastics 3.2%. Largest Holdings: Kuo Chan Development & Construction, Chung Hwa Pulp Corp., Yuen Foong Yu Paper Manufacturing, Teco Electric & Machinery Co., China Motor Co.

Capitalization: (8/31/92) Common stock outstanding 8,037,350. No long-term debt.

Beta: 0.64
Fund Manager: China Securities Investment Trust Corp.   **Fee:** 1.50%
Income Dist: Annually   **Capital Gains Dist:** Annually
Reinvestment Plan: Yes   **Shareholder Reports:** Quarterly

5 Year Performance

Fiscal Year Ending 8/31	1992	1991	1990	1989	1988
Net Assets ($mil):	158.20	125.00	69.60	66.90	66.00
Net Income Dist ($):	0.00	0.00	0.53	0.00	0.00
Cap Gains Dist ($):	0.00	0.00	1.16	14.75	10.35
Total Dist ($)	0.00	0.00	1.69	14.75	10.35
Yield from Dist (%)	0.00	0.00	4.60	44.19	32.98
Expense Ratio (%)	2.94	3.47	2.34	2.11	2.50
Portfolio Turnover (%)	129.00	298.00	226.00	169.00	141.06
NAV per share ($)	19.68	19.67	16.51	22.35	22.23
Market Price per share	17.87	24.13	22.50	36.75	33.38
Premium (Discount) (%)	(9.20)	22.62	36.28	64.47	50.11
Total Return, Stk Price (%)	(25.94)	7.24	(34.18)	54.28	39.36

Thai Capital Fund

One Evertrust Plaza, 9th Fl.
Jersey City, NJ 07302
(800) 933-3440 / (201) 915-3020

NYSE : TC

Transfer Agent
State Street Bank & Trust Co.
P.O. Box 366
Boston, MA 02266
(800) 426-5523

Growth

12 Months Ending 12/31/92 Results

	Period End	Period Begin	Distributions	Yield Dist (%)	Total Return (%)
Share Price ($)	11.13	9.13	0.25	2.74	24.64
NAV per share ($)	12.02	9.09		2.75	34.98

Background: Initial public offering May 22, 1990 of 6,000,000 shares at $12 per share. Initial NAV was $11.16 per share.

Objective: Seeks long-term capital appreciation. The fund will invest primarily in Thai equity securities through an investment plan that is regulated by the Thai Government.

Portfolio: (12/31/92) Thai Common Stocks 93.70%, Thai Short Term 6.64%, U.S. Government Short Term 2.70%. Sector Weightings: Banks 24.20%, Building 6.63%, Finance & Securities 20.01%. Largest Holdings: Bangkok Bank 7.88%, The Siam Cement Co. 4.16%, The Siam Commercial Bank 4.01%.

Capitalization: (12/31/92) Common stock outstanding 6,162,969. No long-term debt.

Beta: 2.49
Fund Manager: Daiwa Securities Trust Company   **Fee:** 0.60%
Income Dist: Annually   **Capital Gains Dist:** Annually
Reinvestment Plan: Yes   **Shareholder Reports:** Semi-Annually

5 Year Performance

Fiscal Year Ending 12/31	1992	1991	1990 (7 mos.)	1989	1988
Net Assets ($mil):	74.10	56.00	50.20	—	—
Net Income Dist ($):	0.13	0.21	0.00	—	—
Cap Gains Dist ($):	0.12	0.07	0.00	—	—
Total Dist ($)	0.25	0.28	0.00	—	—
Yield from Dist (%)	2.74	4.15	—	—	—
Expense Ratio (%)	2.58	2.97	243.00	—	—
Portfolio Turnover (%)	87.95	78.83	10.19	—	—
NAV per share ($)	12.02	9.09	8.16	—	—
Market Price per share	11.13	9.13	6.75	—	—
Premium (Discount) (%)	(7.40)	0.33	(17.28)	—	—
Total Return, Stk Price (%)	24.64	39.41	—	—	—

Thai Fund, Inc. (The)

NYSE : TTF

1221 Avenue of the Americas
New York, NY 10020
(617) 728-1158

Transfer Agent
The First National Bank of Boston
150 Royall St.
Canton, MA 02021
(617) 575-2900

Growth

12 Months Ending 12/31/92 Results

	Period End	Period Begin	Distributions	Yield Dist (%)	Total Return (%)
Share Price ($)	18.75	15.25	0.87	5.70	28.66
NAV per share ($)	20.72	15.41		5.65	40.10

Background: Initial public offering of 8,333,333 common shares at $12 per share on February 17, 1988. Initial NAV was $11.16 per share.

Objective: Seeks long-term capital appreciation. Invests 80% of its assets in equity securities of Thai companies. The remainder may be invested in baht-denominated debt and money market instruments. No more than 20% may be invested in non-baht-denominated investments. Invests in Thailand through an investment plan regulated by the Thai Government.

Portfolio: (11/30/92) Common Stocks 96.0%. Cash & Equivalents 4.5%. Sector Weightings: Finance 56.2%, Industrial Products 12.6%, Nondurables 12.4%, Consumer Services 7.4%. Largest Holdings: Bangkok Bank, Thai Farmers Bank, Siam Cement Co., Siam Commercial Bank..

Capitalization: (11/30/92) Common stock outstanding 9,592,000. Fund is leveraged.

Beta: 1.01

Fund Manager: Morgan Stanley Asset Management

Fee: 0.69%

Income Dist: Annually

Capital Gains Dist: Annually

Reinvestment Plan: Yes

Shareholder Reports: Quarterly

5 Year Performance

Fiscal Year Ending 12/31	1992	1991	1990	1989	1988 (10 mos.)
Net Assets ($mil):	209.40	154.30	128.70	181.20	98.20
Net Income Dist ($):	0.36	0.21	0.21	0.36	0.29
Cap Gains Dist ($):	0.51	0.47	1.68	2.09	0.00
Total Dist ($)	0.87	0.68	1.89	2.45	0.29
Yield from Dist (%)	5.70	4.42	5.86	20.85	—
Expense Ratio (%)	1.69	1.44	1.35	1.51	1.50
Portfolio Turnover (%)	23.60	9.60	17.60	51.10	0.90
NAV per share ($)	20.72	15.41	13.08	18.88	10.24
Market Price per share	18.75	15.25	15.38	32.25	11.75
Premium (Discount) (%)	(9.51)	(1.04)	17.51	70.82	14.75
Total Return, Stk Price (%)	28.66	3.58	(46.45)	195.32	—

Turkish Investment Fund, Inc. (The)

Vanguard Financial Center
P.O. Box 1102
Valley Forge, PA 19482
(800) 548-7786

Growth

NYSE : TKF

Transfer Agent
Investor's Bank & Trust Co.
1 Lincoln Plaza, 89 South St.
Boston, MA 02111
(800) 342-8756

12 Months Ending 12/31/92 Results

	Period End	Period Begin	Distributions	Yield Dist (%)	Total Return (%)
Share Price ($)	5.25	7.63	0.04	0.52	(30.67)
NAV per share ($)	4.60	7.50		0.53	(38.13)

Background: Initial public offering on December 4, 1989 of 7,000,000 shares at $12 per share. Initial NAV was $11.16 per share.

Objective: Seeks long-term capital appreciation. Under normal conditions at least 80% of the fund's assets will be invested in equity securities of Turkish companies. The balance may be invested in dollar and lira denominated debt securities.

Portfolio: (10/31/92) Common Stocks 94.1%, Short Term 5.9%. Sector Weightings: Nondurables 34.2%, Industrial Products 28.5%, Utilities 11.6%, Natural Resources 8.6%, Services 2.8%. Largest Holdings: Ege Biracilik, Gundy Biracilik, Arcelik, Maret, Sabah.

Capitalization: (10/31/92) Common stock outstanding 7,032,370. No long-term debt.

Beta: 1.02
Fund Manager: Morgan Stanley Asset Management Inc.   **Fee:** 0.91%
Income Dist: Annually   **Capital Gains Dist:** Annually
Reinvestment Plan: Yes   **Shareholder Reports:** Quarterly

5 Year Performance

Fiscal Year Ending 10/31	1992	1991	1990 (10 mos.)	1989	1988
Net Assets ($mil):	33.00	36.30	89.80	—	—
Net Income Dist ($):	0.07	0.00	0.03	—	—
Cap Gains Dist ($):	0.17	0.07	0.00	—	—
Total Dist ($)	0.24	0.07	0.03	—	—
Yield from Dist (%)	3.25	0.78	—	—	—
Expense Ratio (%)	2.55	2.42	1.65	—	—
Portfolio Turnover (%)	28.00	45.00	1.00	—	—
NAV per share ($)	4.69	5.16	12.78	—	—
Market Price per share	6.00	7.38	9.00	—	—
Premium (Discount) (%)	27.93	42.83	(29.58)	—	—
Total Return, Stk Price (%)	(15.45)	(17.22)	—	—	—

United Kingdom Fund, Inc.

55 Water St.
New York, NY 10041
(212) 272-6404

NYSE : UKM

Transfer Agent
The Bank of New York
101 Barclay St.
New York, NY 10286
(800) 524-4458 / (212) 815 2315

Growth

12 Months Ending 12/31/92 Results

	Period End	Period Begin	Distributions	Yield Dist (%)	Total Return (%)
Share Price ($)	9.25	9.13	0.55	6.02	7.34
NAV per share ($)	10.24	10.55		5.21	2.27

Background: Initial public offering August 6, 1987 of 4,000,000 shares at $12.50 per share. Initial NAV was $11.63 per share.

Objective: Seeks long-term capital appreciation. Under normal conditions at least 65% of the fund's assets will be invested in United Kingdom equity securities. The remainder will be in debt securities, private placements, or securities traded on the OTC market.

Portfolio: (12/31/92) Common Stocks 99.5%, Short Term 2.3%, Other (1.7%). Sector Weightings: Food Manufacturing 12.5%, Oil & Gas 11.5%, Stores 11.0%, Electricity 8.2%, Electronics 5.9%. Largest Holdings: BAT Industries, Great Universal Stores, General Electric Co., East Midlands Electricity, Shell Transport & Trading.

Capitalization: (9/30/92) Common stock outstanding 4,008,602. No long-term debt.

Beta: 0.67
Fund Manager: Warburg Investment Management International Ltd.　　**Fee:** 0.75%
Income Dist: Annually　　　　　　　　　　**Capital Gains Dist:** Annually
Reinvestment Plan: Yes　　　　　　　　　　**Shareholder Reports:** Quarterly

5 Year Performance

Fiscal Year Ending 3/31	1992	1991	1990	1989	1988 (8 mos.)
Net Assets ($mil):	39.80	46.80	41.60	48.70	43.90
Net Income Dist ($):	0.45	0.00	0.35	0.22	0.13
Cap Gains Dist ($):	0.38	0.73	0.25	0.43	0.22
Total Dist ($)	0.83	0.73	0.60	0.65	0.35
Yield from Dist (%)	8.10	8.34	6.00	7.32	—
Expense Ratio (%)	1.74	2.19	1.92	1.89	1.99
Portfolio Turnover (%)	47.30	36.37	22.07	40.91	22.15
NAV per share ($)	9.93	11.67	10.38	12.15	10.94
Market Price per share	8.88	10.25	8.75	10.00	8.88
Premium (Discount) (%)	(10.57)	(12.17)	(15.70)	(17.70)	(18.92)
Total Return, Stk Price (%)	(5.27)	25.49	(6.50)	19.93	—

10
New Funds—1992

New Bond Funds—1992

2002 Target Term Trust

1285 Avenue of the Americas
New York, NY 10019
(212) 713-2000

NYSE : TTR

Transfer Agent
State Street Bank & Trust Co.
1776 Heritage Dr.
North Quincy, MA 02171
(800) 426-5523

Income

Background: Initial public offering December 24, 1992 at $15 per share. Initial NAV was $14.10 per share.

Objective: Seeks high monthly income and to return $15 per share to shareholders on or about November 30, 2002.

Portfolio: Not available.

Capitalization: (12/31/92) Common stock outstanding 9,506,667. No long-term debt.

Fund Manager: Mitchell Hutchins Asset Management	**Fee:** 0.50%
Income Dist: Monthly	**Capital Gains Dist:** Monthly
Reinvestment Plan: Yes	**Shareholder Reports:** N/A

Alliance World Dollar Government Fund, Inc.

1345 Avenue of the Americas
New York, NY 10105
(800) 247-4154 / (212) 969-1000

NYSE : AWG

Transfer Agent
Shareholder Services Group
Exchange Place
Boston, MA 02109
(800) 331-3120

Income

Background: Initial public offering October 30, 1992 of 4,000,000 shares at $15 per share. Initial NAV was $13.95 per share.

Objective: Seeks high current income from a portfolio of investments in U.S. dollar-denominated fixed-income securities issued by foreign governments.

Portfolio: (12/31/92) U.S. Government Securities 26.9%, Foreign 71.6%, Cash & Equivalents 1.5%. Country Exposure: Philippines 13.7%, Mexico 12.8%, Argentina 10.9%, Venezuela 10.4%, Brazil 6.4%.

Capitalization: (12/31/92) Common stock outstanding 7,257,200. No long-term debt.

Fund Manager: Alliance Capital Management L.P.	**Fee:** 0.65%
Income Dist: Monthly	**Capital Gains Dist:** Annually
Reinvestment Plan: Yes	**Shareholder Reports:** Semi-Annually

American Adjustable Rate Term Trust, Inc.—1999

Piper Jaffray Tower
222 S. Ninth St.
Minneapolis, MN 55402-3804
(800) 333-6000 / (612) 342-6426

NYSE : EDJ
Transfer Agent
Investors Fiduciary Trust Co.
127 W. 10th St.
Kansas City, MO 64105
(816) 474-8786

Income

Background: Initial Public Offering September 17, 1992 of 16,500,000 shares at $10 per share. Initial NAV was $9.60 per share.

Objective: Seeks a high level of current income and to return $10 per share to investors on March 31, 1999. The fund will invest primarily in mortgage-backed securities that have adjustable interest rates.

Portfolio: (12/31/92) U.S. Government Agency ARMs 53.3%, Private ARMs 11.1%, Other Agencies 15.2%, Tax-Exempt Zeros 6.5%, Short Term 9.8%, Canadian Government 3.7%, Other 0.4%.

Capitalization: (12/31/92) Common stock outstanding 16,510,000. No long-term debt.

Fund Manager: Piper Capital Management, Inc.	**Fee:** 0.35%
Income Dist: Monthly	**Capital Gains Dist:** Monthly
Reinvestment Plan: Yes	**Shareholder Reports:** N/A

American Adjustable Rate Term Trust, Inc.—1998

Piper Jaffray Tower
222 S. Ninth St.
Minneapolis, MN 55402-3804
(800) 333-6000 / 612) 342-6426

NYSE : DDJ
Transfer Agent
Investors Fiduciary Trust Co.
127 W. 10th St.
Kansas City, MO 64105
(816) 474-8786

Income

Background: Initial public offering January 17, 1992 of 34,000,000 shares at $10 per share. Initial NAV was $9.60 per share.

Objective: Seeks high current income and to return $10 per share to common shareholders on or about March 31, 1998. The fund will invest primarily in adjustable-rate mortgage-backed securities.

Portfolio: (12/22/92) Private ARMs 39.5%, Agency ARMs 30.5%, Other Agencies 16.7%, Tax-Exempt Zero-Coupon Bonds 7.4%, Short Term 2.9%, Canadian Government 2.9%, Other 0.1%.

Capitalization: (8/31/92) Common Stock Outstanding 57,024,936. No long-term debt.

Fund Manager: Piper Capital Management, Inc.	**Fee:** 0.35%
Income Dist: Monthly	**Capital Gains Dist:** Annually
Reinvestment Plan: Yes	**Shareholder Reports:** Semi-Annually

American Municipal Term Trust III

NYSE : CXT

Piper Jaffray Tower
222 S. Ninth St.
Minneapolis, MN 55402-3804
(800) 333-6000 / (612) 342-6426

Transfer Agent
Investors Fiduciary Trust Co.
127 W. 10th St.
Kansas City, MO 64105
(800) 543-1627

Income

Background: Initial public offering November 19, 1992 of 4,600,000 shares at $10 per share. Initial NAV was $9.50 per share.

Objective: To provide high current income exempt from regular Federal income tax and to return $10 per share to investors on or shortly before April 15, 2003. The fund will invest in a diversified portfolio of high-quality municipal obligations, including municipal Zero-Coupon securities.

Portfolio: (12/31/92) Municipal Bonds 135.9%, Liabilities & Other (35.8%). Portfolio Ratings: AAA 58.0%, AA 16.0%, A 15.0%, BBB 7.0%, Non-Rated 4.0%.

Capitalization: Common stock outstanding 4,610,000. Leveraged with 2,000 shares preferred stock.

Fund Manager: Piper Capital Management, Inc.	**Fee:** 0.25%
Income Dist: Monthly	**Capital Gains Dist:** Monthly
Reinvestment Plan: Yes	**Shareholder Reports:** N/A

American Strategic Income Portfolio II

NYSE : BSP

Piper Jaffray Tower
222 S. Ninth Street
Minneapolis, MN 55402-3804
(800) 333-6000 / (612) 342-6426

Transfer Agent
Investors Fiduciary Trust Co.
127 W. 10th St.
Kansas City, MO 64105
(800) 543-1627

Income

Background: Initial public offering July 30, 1992, of 18,000,000 shares at $15 per share. Initial NAV was $14.07 per share.

Objective: Seeks high current income. Capital appreciation is secondary.

Portfolio: (11/30/92) Agency-Backed CMOs 28.6%, U.S. Agency Mortgage Securities 19.2%, U.S. Governments 25.9%, Whole Loan and Participation Mortgages 11.5%, Short Term 4.5%, Non-Agency CMOs 10.3%, Other 0.4%.

Capitalization: (11/30/92) Common stock outstanding 20,046,496. No long-term debt.

Fund Manager: Piper Capital Management, Inc.	**Fee:** 0.20%
Income Dist: Monthly	**Capital Gains Dist:** Annually
Reinvestment Plan: Yes	**Shareholder Reports:** Semi-Annually

BlackRock 1999 Term Trust
1285 Avenue of the Americas
New York, NY 10019
(800) 227-7236 / (212) 713-2848

NYSE : BNN
Transfer Agent
State Street Bank & Trust Co.
1776 Heritage Dr.
North Quincy, MA 02171
(800) 426-5523

Income

Background: Initial public offering December 18, 1992. Offer price was $10 per share. Initial NAV was $9.45 per share.

Objective: Seeks high monthly income and to return $10 per share to shareholders on or about December 31, 1999.

Portfolio: Not available.

Capitalization: (12/31/92) Common stock outstanding 19,010,583.

Fund Manager: BlackRock Financial Management L.P.　　　　**Fee:** 0.40%
Income Dist: Monthly　　　　**Capital Gains Dist:** Monthly
Reinvestment Plan: Yes　　　　**Shareholder Reports:** N/A

BlackRock 2001 Term Trust, Inc.
1285 Avenue of the Americas
New York, NY 10019
(800) 227-7236 / (212) 214-3334

NYSE : BLK
Transfer Agent
State Street Bank & Trust Co.
One Heritage Dr.
North Quincy, MA 02171
(800) 451-6788

Income

Background: Initial public offering August 21, 1992 at $10 per share. Initial NAV was $9.44 per share.

Objective: Seeks high monthly income and to return $10 per share to investors on June 30, 2001. The fund may borrow for leveraging purposes.

Portfolio: (1/29/93) Mortgage-Backed Securities 68.0%, Zero-Coupon Bonds 25.0%, Municipal Bonds 7.0%. Average Quality AAA.

Capitalization: (12/31/92) Common stock outstanding 142,010,583. No long-term debt.

Fund Manager: BlackRock Financial Management L.P.　　　　**Fee:** 0.40%
Income Dist: Monthly　　　　**Capital Gains Dist:** Monthly
Reinvestment Plan: Yes　　　　**Shareholder Reports:** N/A

BlackRock California Insured Municipal 2008

NYSE : BFC

800 Scudders Mill Rd.
Plainsboro, NJ 08536
(800) 227-7236 / (212) 214-3334

Transfer Agent
State Street Bank & Trust Co.
One Heritage Dr.
North Quincy, MA 02171
(800) 451-6788

Tax-Free Income

Background: Initial public offering September 1992 at $15 per share. Initial NAV was $14.06.

Objective: Seeks income exempt from Federal and California State income taxes. At least 80% of assets will be invested in insured California Municipal Bonds rated AAA.

Portfolio: (12/31/92) Long Term Municipal Bonds 131.6%, Short Term 25.1%.

Capitalization: (12/31/92) Common Stock outstanding 10,407,093. No long-term debt.

Fund Manager: BlackRock Financial Management L.P.	**Fee:** 0.35%
Income Dist: Monthly	**Capital Gains Dist:** Annually
Reinvestment Plan: Yes	**Shareholder Reports:** Semi-Annually

---

BlackRock Florida Insured Municipals 2008

NYSE : BRF

800 Scudders Mill Rd.
Plainsboro, NJ 08536
(800) 227-7236 / (212) 214-3334

Transfer Agent
State Street Bank & Trust Co.
One Heritage Dr.
North Quincy, MA 02171
(800) 451-6788

Tax-Free Income

Background: Initial public offering September 1992 at $15 per share. Initial NAV was $14.10 per share.

Objective: Seeks income exempt from Federal and Florida State income taxes. At least 80% of assets will be invested in insured Florida municipal bonds rated AAA.

Portfolio: (12/31/92) Municipal Bonds 100%.

Capitalization: (12/31/92) Common stock outstanding 8,707,093. No long-term debt.

Fund Manager: BlackRock Financial Management L.P.	**Fee:** 0.35%
Income Dist: Monthly	**Capital Gains Dist:** Annually
Reinvestment Plan: Yes	**Shareholder Reports:** Semi-Annually

BlackRock Insured Municipal 2008 Trust

800 Scudders Mill Rd.
Plainsboro, NJ 08536
(800) 688-0928 / (609) 282-0928

NYSE : BRM
Transfer Agent
State Street Bank & Trust Co.
One Heritage Dr.
North Quincy, MA 02171
(800) 451-6788

Tax-Free Income

Background: Initial public offering September 18, 1992 of 25,000,000 shares at $15 per share. Initial NAV was $14.07 per share.

Objective: Seeks current income exempt from Federal income taxes and to return $15 per share to common shareholders on or about December 31, 2002.

Portfolio: (12/31/92) Municipal Bonds 141.6%, Short Term 26.8%, Liabilities in excess of other assets (15.5%). Average Quality AAA.

Capitalization: (12/31/92) Common stock outstanding 27,207,093. Leveraged with 4,120 shares preferred stock, stated value $50,000 per share.

Fund Manager: BlackRock Financial Management L.P.	**Fee:** 0.35%
Income Dist: Monthly	**Capital Gains Dist:** Annually
Reinvestment Plan: Yes	**Shareholder Reports:** Quarterly

BlackRock Insured Municipal Term Trust, Inc.

1285 Avenue of the Americas
New York, NY 10019
(800) 227-7236 / (212) 713-2848

NYSE : BMT
Transfer Agent
State Street Bank & Trust Co.
One Heritage Dr.
North Quincy, MA 02171
(800) 451-6788

Tax-Free Income

Background: Initial public offering on February 21, 1992 of 22,500,000 shares at $10 per share. Initial NAV was $9.40 per share.

Objective: Seeks current income exempt from Federal income tax and to return $10 per common share to investors on or about December 31, 2010. Will invest in a portfolio of high credit quality municipal securities. At least 80% must be municipal obligations that are insured as to the timely payment of both principal and interest.

Portfolio: (12/31/92) Municipal Bonds 146.3%, Short Term 3.0%, Liabilities & Other 1.3%. Average Quality AAA.

Capitalization: (12/31/92) Common stock outstanding 25,885,639. Leveraged with 3,000 shares preferred stock, stated value $50,000 per share.

Fund Manager: BlackRock Financial Management L.P.	**Fee:** 0.35%
Income Dist: Monthly	**Capital Gains Dist:** Annually
Reinvestment Plan: Yes	**Shareholder Reports:** Semi-Annually

BlackRock Investment Quality Term Trust

One Seaport Plaza
New York, NY 10292
(800) 227-7236 / (212) 214-3334

NYSE : BQT
Transfer Agent
State Street Bank & Trust Co.
225 Franklin St.
Boston, MA 02110
(800) 426-5523

Income

Background: Initial public offering April 20, 1992 at $10 per share. Initial NAV was $9.38 per share.

Objective: Seeks high monthly income from a portfolio of fixed-income securities. The fund expects to return $10 per share to investors on or about December 31, 2004.

Portfolio: (12/31/92) Mortgage Backed Securities 46.0%, Corporate Bonds 37.0%, U.S. Government Securities 11.0%, Asset Backed 2.0%, Municipal Zero-Coupon Bonds 4.0%.

Capitalization: (12/31/92) Common stock outstanding 36,810,639. No long-term debt.

Fund Manager: BlackRock Financial Management L.P.	**Fee:** 0.60%
Income Dist: Monthly	**Capital Gains Dist:** Annually
Reinvestment Plan: Yes	**Shareholder Reports:** Semi-Annually

---

BlackRock New York Insured Municipals 2008

800 Scudders Mill Rd.
Plainsboro, NJ 08536
(800) 227-7236 / (212) 214-3334

NYSE : BLN
Transfer Agent
State Street Bank & Trust Co.
One Heritage Dr.
North Quincy, MA 02171

Tax-Free Income

(800) 451-6788

Background: Initial public offering September 1992 at $15 per share. Initial NAV was $14.06 per share.

Objective: Seeks income exempt from Federal, New York State and City income taxes.

Portfolio: (12/31/92) Municipal Bonds & Notes 133.7%. Sector Weightings: Transportation 27%, City, State & County 16%, Water & Sewer 15%, Hospital 8%.

Capitalization: (12/31/92) Common shares outstanding 11,257,093. No long-term debt.

Fund Manager: BlackRock Financial Management L.P.	**Fee:** 0.35%
Income Dist: Monthly	**Capital Gains Dist:** Annually
Reinvestment Plan: Yes	**Shareholder Reports:** Semi-Annually

First Commonwealth Fund, Inc. (The)

800 Scudders Mill Rd.
Plainsboro, NJ 08536
(609) 282-4600

NYSE : FCO
Transfer Agent
State Street Bank & Trust Co.
P.O. Box 8200
Boston, MA 02266
(800) 543-6217

Income

Background: Initial public offering February 20, 1992 of 7,850,000 shares at $15 per share. Initial NAV was $14.05 per share.

Objective: Seeks high current income. Capital appreciation is secondary. Will invest in securities denominated in Australian, Canadian, and New Zealand Dollars, and the U.K. Pound Sterling. No more than 50% of assets will be in securities of any one currency denomination.

Portfolio: (10/31/92) Government, Semi-Government, and Provinicial Bonds 67.0%, Corporate & Eurobonds 30.4%, Short Term 2.5%. Country Exposure: Australia 48.6%, Canada 27.3%, U.K. 22.1%, New Zealand 1.4%, U.S. 0.6%. Portfolio Ratings: AAA 57.5%, AA 26.1%, A 16.4%.

Capitalization: (10/31/92) Common stock outstanding 9,176,000. Leveraged with 600 preferred shares, stated value $50,000 per share.

Fund Manager: EquitiLink Australia Limited
Income Dist: Monthly
Reinvestment Plan: Yes

Fee: 0.65%
Capital Gains Dist: Annually
Shareholder Reports: Quarterly

Hyperion 1997 Term Trust

520 Madison Ave.
New York, NY 10022
(212) 980-8400

NYSE : HTA
Transfer Agent
State Street Bank & Trust Co.
1776 Heritage Dr.
North Quincy, MA 02171
(800) 426-5523

Income

Background: Initial public offering October 23, 1992 at $10 per share. Initial NAV was $9.40 per share.

Objective: Seeks high current income and to return $10 per share to shareholders on or about November 30, 1997.

Portfolio: Not available.

Capitalization: (12/31/92) Common stock outstanding 60,610,527. No long-term debt.

Fund Manager: Hyperion Capital Management , Inc.
Income Dist: Monthly
Reinvestment Plan: Yes

Fee: 0.50%
Capital Gains Dist: Monthly
Shareholder Reports: N/A

Hyperion 1999 Term Trust, Inc.

520 Madison Ave.
New York, NY 10022
(212) 980-8400

NYSE : HTT

Transfer Agent
State Street Bank & Trust Co.
1776 Heritage Dr.
North Quincy, MA 02171
(800) 426-5523

Income

Background: Initial public offering June 18, 1992 of 6,000,000 shares at $10 per share. Initial NAV was $9.40 per share.

Objective: Seeks high current income and to return $10 per share to shareholders on or about November 30, 1999.

Portfolio: (6/30/92) Mortgage-Backed 86%, Municipal Bonds 14%.

Capitalization: (12/31/92) Common stock outstanding 66,610,527. No long-term debt.

Fund Manager: Hyperion Capital Management, Inc.
Income Dist: Monthly
Reinvestment Plan: Yes

Fee: 0.50%
Capital Gains Dist: Monthly
Shareholder Reports: N/A

Hyperion 2002 Term Trust

620 Madison Ave.
New York, NY 10022
(212) 980-8400

NYSE : HTB

Transfer Agent
State Street Bank & Trust Co.
1776 Heritage Dr.
North Quincy, MA 02171
(800) 426-5523

Income

Background: Initial public offering June 18, 1992. Offer price was $10 per share. Initial NAV was $9.40 per share.

Objective: Seeks high current income and to return $10 per share to shareholders on or about November 30, 1999.

Portfolio: (12/31/92) Corporate Bonds 88.8%, Short Term & Other 11.2%.

Capitalization: (12/31/92) Common stock outstanding 63,260,639. No long-term debt.

Fund Manager: Hyperion Capital Management, Inc.
Income Dist: Monthly
Reinvestment Plan: Yes

Fee: 0.50%
Capital Gains Dist: Monthly
Shareholder Reports: N/A

Income Opportunities 1999

P.O. Box 9011
Princeton, NJ 08543
(800) 426-5523 / (609) 282-2800

NYSE : IOF
Transfer Agent
The Bank of New York
101 Barclay St.
New York, NY 10286
(800) 524-4458

Income

Background: Initial public offering September 21, 1992 at $10 per share. Initial NAV was $9.50 per share.

Objective: Seeks high current income and to return $10 per share to common shareholders on or about December 31, 1999.

Portfolio: (10/31/92) Mortgage-Backed 70%, Corporate Bonds & Notes 10%, Municipal Bonds 10%, Treasuries 10%.

Capitalization: (12/31/92) Common stock outstanding 55,510,527. No long-term debt.

Fund Manager: Fund Asset Management	**Fee:** 0.75%
Income Dist: Monthly	**Capital Gains Dist:** Monthly
Reinvestment Plan: Yes	**Shareholder Reports:** N/A

Income Opportunities 2000

P.O. Box 9011
Princeton, NJ 08543-9011
(800) 426-5523 / (609) 282-2800

NYSE : IFT
Transfer Agent
The Bank of New York
101 Barclay St.
New York, NY 10286
(800) 524-4458

Income

Background: Initial public offering December 21, 1992 at $10 per share. Initial NAV was $9.50 per share.

Objective: Seeks high monthly income and to return $10 per share to shareholders on or about December 31, 2000.

Portfolio: Not available.

Capitalization: (12/31/92) Common stock outstanding 13,510,527. No long-term debt.

Fund Manager: Fund Asset Management	**Fee:** 0.75%
Income Dist: Monthly	**Capital Gains Dist:** Monthly
Reinvestment Plan: Yes	**Shareholder Reports:** N/A

InterCapital Insured Municipal Trust

InterCapital Division
Two World Trade Center
New York, NY 10048
(800) 869-3863 / (212) 392-2550

NYSE : IMT
Transfer Agent
Dean Witter Trust Co.
Two Montgomery St.
Jersey City, NJ 07302
(800) 526-3143

Tax-Free Income

Background: Initial public offering February 28, 1992 of 23,000,000 shares at $15 per share. Initial NAV was $14.06.

Objective: A diversified investment trust organized in 1991 to provide current income exempt from Federal income taxes. The trust invests in tax-exempt municipal obligations which are covered by insurance which guarantees payment of principal and interest.

Portfolio: (10/31/92) Municipal Bonds 97.5%, Short Term Municipal Obligations 0.6%. Sector Weightings: Hospitals 18.1, Water & Sewer 17.4%, General Obligation 12.9%, Industrial Development/Pollution Control 12.5%, Electric 10.2%. Portfolio Ratings: AAA 100%.

Capitalization: (10/31/92) Common shares of beneficial interest outstanding 23,507,113. $180,000,000 in auction rate preferred stock. No long-term debt.

Fund Manager: Dean Witter Reynolds InterCapital Division	**Fee:** 0.35%
Income Dist: Monthly	**Capital Gains Dist:** Annually
Reinvestment Plan: Yes	**Shareholder Reports:** Semi-Annually

---

InterCapital Quality Municipal Income Trust

InterCapital Division
Two World Trade Center
New York, NY 10048
(800) 869-3863 / (212) 392-2550

NYSE : IQI
Transfer Agent
Dean Witter Trust Co.
2 Montgomery St.
Jersey City, NJ 07302
(800) 526-3143

Income

Background: Initial public offering September 22, 1992 at $15 per share. Initial NAV was $14.06 per share.

Objective: Seeks current income exempt from regular Federal income taxes.

Portfolio: (12/31/92) Municipal Bonds 100.0%. Portfolio Ratings: Non-Rated 100.0%.

Capitalization: (12/31/92) Common stock outstanding 59,412,271. No long-term debt.

Fund Manager: Dean Witter Reynolds InterCapital Division	**Fee:** 0.35%
Income Dist: Monthly	**Capital Gains Dist:** Monthly
Reinvestment Plan: Yes	**Shareholder Reports:** N/A

Latin America Dollar Income Fund, Inc. (The)
345 Park Ave.
New York, NY 10154
(617) 330-5602

NYSE : LBF
Transfer Agent
State Street Bank & Trust Co.
P.O. Box 8200
Boston, MA 02266-8200
(800) 426-5523

Income

Background: Initial public offering July 24, 1992 of 4,000,000 shares at $15 per share. Initial NAV was $14.03 per share.

Objective: Seeks high current income. Capital appreciation is secondary. Under normal conditions, at least 80% of the Fund's total assets will be invested in dollar-denominated Latin American Debt Instruments, and at least 65% of the Fund's income will be derived from dollar-denominated Latin American Debt Instruments. The fund may borrow for leveraging purposes.

Portfolio: (10/31/92) U.S. Dollar-Denominated Debt 81.5%, Mexican Peso-Denominated Debt 9.6%, Short Term 8.9%. Country Exposure: Venezuela 21.3%, Argentina 20.4%, Mexico 17.1%, Brazil 16.8%, Jamaica 2.6%.

Capitalization: (10/31/92) Common stock outstanding 5,761,251. No long-term debt.

Fund Manager: Scudder, Stevens & Clark	**Fee:** 1.20%
Income Dist: Quarterly	**Capital Gains Dist:** Annually
Reinvestment Plan: Yes	**Shareholder Reports:** Semi-Annually

Liberty Term Trust 1999
Federated Investors Tower
Pittsburgh, PA 15222-3779
(412) 288-1900

NYSE : LTT
Transfer Agent
State Street Bank & Trust Co.
1776 Heritage Dr.
North Quincy, MA 02171
(800) 426-5523

Income

Background: Initial public offering April 2, 1992 at $10 per share. Initial NAV was $9.50 per share.

Objective: Seeks high monthly income and to return $10 per share to common shareholders on or about December 31, 1999.

Portfolio: (12/31/92) Mortgage-Related Securities 63.0%, U.S. Treasury Notes 5.0%, Other 31.0%.

Capitalization: (12/31/92) Common stock outstanding 5,625,018. No long-term debt.

Fund Manager: Federated Advisors	**Fee:** 0.50%
Income Dist: Monthly	**Capital Gains Dist:** Monthly
Reinvestment Plan: Yes	**Shareholder Reports:** N/A

Managed Municipals Portfolio

NYSE : MMU

Two World Trade Center
New York, NY 10048
(212) 298-7350

Transfer Agent
Shareholder Services Group
P.O. Box 1376
Boston, MA 02105
(800) 331-3120

Tax-Free Income

Background: Initial public offering June 18, 1992 at $10 per share. Initial NAV was $9.50 per share.

Objective: Seeks a high level of current income exempt from regular Federal income tax, consistent with preservation of capital.

Portfolio: (9/30/92) Municipal Bonds 79.6%, Cash & Other 20.4%. Portfolio Ratings: AAA 19.0%, AA 40.0%, A 20.0%, BBB 10.0%, Non-Rated 10.0%.

Capitalization: (9/30/92) Common stock outstanding 34,152,990. No long-term debt.

Fund Manager: Shearson Lehman Advisors	**Fee:** 0.70%
Income Dist: Monthly	**Capital Gains Dist:** Annually
Reinvestment Plan: Yes	**Shareholder Reports:** N/A

Managed Municipals Portfolio II

NYSE : MTU

Two World Trade Center
New York, NY 10048
(212) 298-7350

Transfer Agent
Shareholder Services Group
P.O. Box 1376
Boston, MA 02105
(800) 331-3120

Tax-Free Income

Background: Initial public offering October 15, 1992 at $12 per share. There were no commission charges—the fund was sold at NAV.

Objective: Seeks high current income exempt from regular Federal income taxes, consistent with preservation of capital.

Portfolio: (12/31/92) Municipal Bonds 102.0%, Other Assets, Liabilities (2.0%). Portfolio Ratings: AAA 12.0%, AA 30.0%, A 28.0%, BBB 17.0%, Non-Rated 13.0%.

Capitalization: (12/31/92) Common stock outstanding 11,216,558. No long-term debt.

Fund Manager: Shearson Lehman Advisors	**Fee:** 0.70%
Income Dist: Monthly	**Capital Gains Dist:** Monthly
Reinvestment Plan: Yes	**Shareholder Reports:** N/A

Minnesota Municipal Term Trust II

Piper Jaffray Tower
222 S. Ninth St.
Minneapolis, MN 55402
(800) 333-6000 / (612) 342-6426

AMEX : MNB

Transfer Agent
Invested Fiduciary Trust Co.
127 W. 10th St.
Kansas City, MO 64105
(816) 474-8786

Tax-Free Income

Background: Initial public offering April 30, 1992 at $10 per share. Initial NAV was $9.45.

Objective: Seeks current income exempt from Federal and Minnesota State income taxes.

Portfolio: (12/31/92) Minnesota Municipal Coupons 93.06%, Minnesota Municipal Zeros 6.94%. Portfolio Ratings: AAA 53.0%, AA 21.0%, A 16.0%, BBB 10.0%.

Capitalization: (12/31/92) Common stock outstanding 3,460,000. Leveraged with 347 shares preferred stock with $50,000 per share liquidation preference. No long-term debt.

Fund Manager: Piper Capital Management, Inc.	**Fee:** 0.25%
Income Dist: Monthly	**Capital Gains Dist:** Annually
Reinvestment Plan: Yes	**Shareholder Reports:** Semi-Annually

---

MuniYield California

P.O. Box 9011
Princeton, NJ 08543
(800) 426-5523 / (609) 282-2800

NYSE : MYC

Transfer Agent
The Bank of New York
110 Washington St.
New York, NY 10286
(800) 524-4458

Tax-Free Income

Background: Initial public offering February 21, 1991 of 14,750,000 shares at $15 per share. Initial NAV was $14.75 per share.

Objective: Seeks income exempt from Federal and California State income taxes.

Portfolio: (10/31/92) Municipal Bonds 99.3%. State Weightings: California 95.7%, Puerto Rico 3.6%.

Capitalization: (10/31/92) Common stock outstanding 16,637,188 shares. Fund is leveraged with 2,400 shares auction rate preferred stock with a $50,000 per share liquidation preference. No long-term debt.

Fund Manager: Fund Asset Management, Inc.	**Fee:** 0.50%
Income Dist: Monthly	**Capital Gains Dist:** Annually
Reinvestment Plan: Yes	**Shareholder Reports:** Quarterly

MuniYield California Insured

P.O. Box 9011
Princeton, NJ 08543-9011
(800) 426-5523 / (609) 282-2800

NYSE : MIC
Transfer Agent
State Street Bank & Trust Co.
225 Franklin St.
Boston, MA 02110
(617) 328-5000

Tax-Free Income

Background: Initial public offering June 26, 1992 of 15,000,000 shares at $15 per share. Initial NAV was $14.18 per share.

Objective: Seeks a high level of current income exempt from regular Federal and California State income taxes.

Portfolio: (10/31/92) Municipal Bonds 99.8%, Other 0.2%. State Weightings: California 96.1%, Puerto Rico 3.7%. Portfolio Ratings: AAA 82.1%, AA 1.2%, A 7.9%, BBB 6.5%, Non-Rated 2.3%.

Capitalization: (10/31/92) Common stock outstanding 15,989,091. Leveraged with 2,000 preferred shares, stated value $50,000 per share. No long-term debt.

Fund Manager: Fund Asset Management, Inc.	**Fee:** 0.50%
Income Dist: Monthly	**Capital Gains Dist:** Annually
Reinvestment Plan: Yes	**Shareholder Reports:** Quarterly

MuniYield California Insured II

P.O. Box 9011
Princeton, NJ 08543
(800) 426-5523 / (609) 282-2800

NYSE : MCA
Transfer Agent
State Street Bank & Trust Co.
225 Franklin St.
Boston, MA 02110
(617) 328-5000

Tax-Free Income

Background: Initial Public Offering October 30, 1992 of 12,000,000 shares at $15 per share. Initial NAV was $14 per share.

Objective: Seeks high current income exempt from regular Federal and California State income taxes, consistent with prudent investment management. At least 80% of assets will be invested in insured municipal obligations.

Portfolio: (10/31/92) Municipal Bonds 39.2%, Cash & Equivalents 60.8%. State Weightings: California 37.7%, Puerto Rico 1.7%. Portfolio Ratings: Investment Grade 100%.

Capitalization: (10/31/92) Common stock outstanding 12,617,845. No long term debt.

Fund Manager: Fund Asset Management, Inc.	**Fee:** 0.50%
Income Dist: Monthly	**Capital Gains Dist:** Annually
Reinvestment Plan: Yes	**Shareholder Reports:** Quarterly

MuniYield Florida

P.O. Box 9011
Princeton, NJ 08543
(800) 426-5523 / (609) 282-2800

NYSE : MYF

Transfer Agent
The Bank of New York
110 Washington St.
New York, NY 10286
(800) 524-4458

Tax-Free Income

Background: Initial public offering February 21, 1992 of 7,000,000 shares at $15 per share. initial NAV was 14.18 per share.

Objective: Seeks high current income exempt from regular Federal income tax, consistent with prudent investment management.

Portfolio: (10/31/92) Municipal Bonds 100.9%, Liabilities & Other (0.9%). State Weightings: Florida 100%. Portfolio Ratings: Investment Grade 100%.

Capitalization: (10/31/92) Shares of beneficial stock outstanding 7,679,339. Fund is leveraged with 1,210 shares auction rate preferred stock with a $50,000 per share liquidation preference. No long-term debt.

Fund Manager: Fund Asset Management, Inc. **Fee:** 0.50%
Income Dist: Monthly **Capital Gains Dist:** Annually
Reinvestment Plan: Yes **Shareholder Reports:** Quarterly

MuniYield Florida Insured

P.O. Box 9011
Princeton, NJ 08543
(800) 426-5523 / (609) 282-2800

NYSE : MFT

Transfer Agent
The Bank of New York
110 Washington St.
New York, NY 10286
(800) 524-4458

Tax-Free Income

Background: Initial public offering October 30, 1992 of 8,209,011 shares of beneficial interest at $15 per share. Initial NAV was $14.18 per share.

Objective: Seeks high current income exempt from regular Federal and Florida State income taxes, consistent with prudent investing. Under normal conditions, at least 80% of assets will be invested in insured municipal obligations.

Portfolio: (10/31/92) Municipal Bonds 30.2%, Cash & Equivalents 69.8%. State Weightings: Florida 100%.

Capitalization: (10/31/92) Shares of beneficial interest outstanding 8,216,066. No long-term debt.

Fund Manager: Fund Asset Management, Inc. **Fee:** 0.50%
Income Dist: Monthly **Capital Gains Dist:** Annually
Reinvestment Plan: Yes **Shareholder Reports:** Quarterly

MuniYield Insured

P.O. Box 9011
Princeton, NJ 08543
(800) 426-5523 / (609) 282-2800

NYSE : MYI
Transfer Agent
State Street Bank & Trust Co.
225 Franklin St.
Boston, MA 02110
(617) 328-5000

Tax-Free Income

Background: Initial public offering was March, 1992 at $15 per share. Initial NAV was $14.18 per share.

Objective: Seeks high current income exempt from Federal income taxes.

Portfolio: (10/31/92) Municipal Bonds 99.7%. Portfolio Ratings: AAA 90%, A 10%.

Capitalization: (10/31/92) Common stock outstanding 44,734,742 shares. Fund is leveraged with 6,400 shares auction rate preferred stock with a $50,000 per share liquidation preference. No long-term debt.

Fund Manager: Fund Asset Management, Inc.	**Fee:** 0.50%
Income Dist: Monthly	**Capital Gains Dist:** Annually
Reinvestment Plan: Yes	**Shareholder Reports:** Quarterly

MuniYield Insured II

P.O. Box 9011
Princeton, NJ 08543-9011
(800) 426-5523 / (609) 282-2800

NYSE : MTI
Transfer Agent
State Street Bank & Trust Co.
225 Franklin St.
Boston, MA 02110
(617) 328-5000

Background: Initial public offering October 30, 1992 of 16,291,059 shares of beneficial interest at $15 per share. Initial NAV was $14.18 per share.

Objective: Seeks high current income exempt from regular Federal income taxes, consistent with prudent investment management.

Portfolio: (10/31/92) Municipal Bonds 86.3%, Short Term & Other 13.7%. Portfolio Ratings: AAA 85.8%, A 8.7%, BBB 4.1%, Non-Rated 1.4%.

Capitalization: (10/31/92) Common stock outstanding 16,298,114 shares. No long-term debt.

Fund Manager: Fund Asset Management, Inc.	**Fee:** 0.50%
Income Dist: Monthly	**Capital Gains Dist:** Annually
Reinvestment Plan: Yes	**Shareholder Reports:** Quarterly

MuniYield Michigan

P.O. Box 9011
Princeton, NJ 08543
(800) 426-5523 / (609) 282-2800

NYSE : MYM
Transfer Agent
The Bank of New York
110 Washington St.
New York, NY 10286
(800) 524-4458

Tax-Free Income

Background: Initial public offering February 21, 1992 of 6,750,000 shares at $15 per share. Initial NAV was $14.18.

Objective: Seeks current income exempt from Federal and Michigan State income taxes, consistent with prudent investment management.

Portfolio: (10/31/92) Municipal Bonds 99.3%. State Weightings: Michigan 99.3%. Portfolio Ratings: Investment Grade 100%.

Capitalization: (10/31/92) Common stock outstanding 7,519,130 shares. Fund is leveraged with 1,100 shares auction rate preferred stock with a $50,000 per share liquidation preference. No long-term debt.

Fund Manager: Fund Asset Management, Inc.	**Fee:** 0.50%
Income Dist: Monthly	**Capital Gains Dist:** Annually
Reinvestment Plan: Yes	**Shareholder Reports:** Quarterly

MuniYield Michigan Insured

P.O. Box 9011
Princeton, NJ 08543
(800) 426-5523 / (609) 282-2800

NYSE : MIY
Transfer Agent
The Bank of New York
110 Washington St.
New York, NY 10286
(800) 524-4458

Tax-Free Income

Background: Initial public offering October 30, 1992 of 7,188,022 shares at $15 per share. Initial NAV was $14.18 per share.

Objective: Seeks high income exempt from regular Federal and Michigan State taxes, consistent with prudent investment management. At least 80% of assets will be invested in insured municipal obligations.

Portfolio: (10/31/92) Municipal Bonds 37.2%, Cash & Equivalents 62.8%. State Weightings: Michigan 100%. Portfolio Ratings: Investment Grade 100%.

Capitalization: (10/31/92) Common stock outstanding 7,195,077 shares. No long-term debt.

Fund Manager: Fund Asset Management, Inc.	**Fee:** 0.50%
Income Dist: Monthly	**Capital Gains Dist:** Annually
Reinvestment Plan: Yes	**Shareholder Reports:** Quarterly

MuniYield New Jersey

P.O. Box 9011
Princeton, NJ 08543
(800) 426-5523 / (609) 282-2800

Transfer Agent
The Bank of New York
110 Washington St.
New York, NY 10286
(800) 524-4458

Tax-Free Income

Background: Initial public offering May 1, 1992 of 8,410,000 at $15 per share. Initial NAV was $14.18 per share.

Objective: Seeks high current income exempt from Federal and New Jersey State income taxes consistent with the preservation of capital. Invests in New Jersey municipal obligations.

Portfolio: (11/30/92) Municipal Bonds 98.0%, Other 2.0%. State Weightings: New Jersey 95.1%, Puerto Rico 2.9%.

Capitalization: (11/30/92) Common stock outstanding 8,599,629 shares. Leveraged with 1,200 shares auction market preferred stock, stated value $50,000 per share. No long-term debt.

Fund Manager: Fund Asset Management, Inc.	**Fee:** 0.50%
Income Dist: Monthly	**Capital Gains Dist:** Annually
Reinvestment Plan: No	**Shareholder Reports:** Quarterly

MuniYield New Jersey Insured

P.O. Box 9011
Princeton, NJ 08543
(800) 426-5523 / (609) 282-2800

NYSE : MJI

Transfer Agent
The Bank of New York
110 Washington St.
New York, NY 10286
(800) 524-4458

Tax-Free Income

Background: Initial public offering October 30, 1992 of 7,959,245 at $15 per share. Initial NAV was $14.18 per share.

Objective: Seeks high current income exempt from Federal and New Jersey State income taxes consistent with the preservation of capital. Invests in municipal obligations considered investment-grade or of comparable quality.

Portfolio: (10/31/92) Municipal Bonds 41.3%, Other 58.7%. Portfolio Ratings: AAA 100%.

Capitalization: (10/31/92) Common stock outstanding 7,966,300 shares. Leveraged with 1,120 shares of preferred stock, stated value $50,000 per share. No long-term debt.

Fund Manager: Fund Asset Management, Inc.	**Fee:** 0.50%
Income Dist: Monthly	**Capital Gains Dist:** Annually
Reinvestment Plan: No	**Shareholder Reports:** Quarterly

MuniYield New York Insured

NYSE : MYN

P.O. Box 9011
Princeton, NJ 08543
(800) 426-5523 / (609) 282-2800

Transfer Agent
The Bank of New York
110 Washington St.
New York, NY 10286
(800) 524-4458

Tax-Free Income

Background: Initial public offering March 16, 1992 at $15 per share. Initial NAV was $14.18 per share.

Objective: Seeks high current income exempt from regular Federal, New York State and City income taxes, consistent with prudent investment management.

Portfolio: (10/31/92) Municipal Bonds 97.9%, Short Term & Other 2.1%. Portfolio Ratings: AAA 83.0%, A 2.0%, BBB 15.0%.

Capitalization: (10/31/92) Common stock outstanding 11,878,078 shares. Fund is leveraged with 1,700 shares preferred stock, stated value $50,000 per share. No long-term debt.

Fund Manager: Fund Asset Management, Inc.	**Fee:** 0.50%
Income Dist: Monthly	**Capital Gains Dist:** Annually
Reinvestment Plan: Yes	**Shareholder Reports:** Quarterly

MuniYield New York Insured II

NYSE : MYT

P.O. Box 9011
Princeton, NJ 08543
(800) 426-5523 / (609) 282-2800

Transfer Agent
State Street Bank & Trust Co.
225 Franklin St.
Boston, MA 02110
(617) 328-5000

Tax-Free Income

Background: Initial public offering June 26, 1992 of 10,528,000 at $15 per share. Initial NAV was $14.18 per share.

Objective: Seeks a high level of current income exempt from Federal, New York State and City income taxes, consistent with investment policies. The fund may issue preferred shares for leveraging purposes.

Portfolio: (10/31/92) New York Municipal Obligations 99.3%, Other 0.7%. Portfolio Ratings: AAA 98%, A 1.3%, BBB 0.7%.

Capitalization: (10/31/92) Common stock outstanding 10,918,194 shares. Fund is leveraged with 1,400 shares preferred stock. No long-term debt.

Fund Manager: Fund Asset Management, Inc.	**Fee:** 0.50%
Income Dist: Monthly	**Capital Gains Dist:** Annually
Reinvestment Plan: No	**Shareholder Reports:** Quarterly

MuniYield New York Insured III

P.O. Box 9011
Princeton, NJ 08543
(800) 426-5523 / (609) 282-2800

NYSE : MYY
Transfer Agent
State Street Bank & Trust Co.
1776 Heritage Dr.
North Quincy, MA 02171
(800) 426-5523

Tax-Free Income

Background: Initial public offering June 19, 1992 at $15 per share. Initial NAV was $14.13 per share.

Objective: Seeks a high level of current income exempt from regular Federal and New York State and City income taxes. Invests primarily in long-term investment-grade New York municipal securities. The fund may leverage up to 35% using preferred stock.

Portfolio: (12/31/92) Municipal Bonds 71.3%, Short Term & Other 28.7%. Portfolio Ratings: AAA 75.0%, BBB 19.0%, Non-Rated 7.0%.

Capitalization: (12/31/92) Common stock outstanding 3,607,055. No long-term debt.

Fund Manager: Merrill Lynch Asset Management	**Fee:** 0.50%
Income Dist: Monthly	**Capital Gains Dist:** Monthly
Reinvestment Plan: Yes	**Shareholder Reports:** Quarterly

MuniYield Pennsylvania

P.O. Box 9011
Princeton, NJ 08543
(800) 426-5523 / (609) 282-2800

NYSE : MPA
Transfer Agent
State Street Bank & Trust Co.
225 Franklin St.
Boston, MA 02110
(617) 328-5000

Tax-Free Income

Background: Initial public offering October 30, 1992 of 5,533,932 shares at $15 per share. Initial NAV was $14.18 per share.

Objective: Seeks high current income exempt from regular Federal and Pennsylvania State income taxes, consistent with prudent investment management.

Portfolio: (10/31/92) Municipal Bonds 78.8%, Cash & Equivalents 21.2%. State Weightings: Pennsylvania 100%. Portfolio Ratings: Investment Grade 100%.

Capitalization: (10/31/92) Shares of beneficial interest outstanding 5,540,987. No long-term debt.

Fund Manager: Fund Asset Management, Inc.	**Fee:** 0.50%
Income Dist: Monthly	**Capital Gains Dist:** Annually
Reinvestment Plan: Yes	**Shareholder Reports:** Quarterly

MuniYield Quality Fund, Inc.

P.O. Box 9011
Princeton, NJ 08543-9011
(800) 426-5523 / (609) 282-2800

NYSE : MQY

Transfer Agent
State Street Bank & Trust Co.
225 Franklin St.
Boston, MA 02110
(617) 328-5000

Tax-Free Income

Background: Initial public offering June 26, 1992 of 30,000,000 shares at $15 per share. Initial NAV was $14.18 per share.

Objective: Seeks a high level of current income exempt from Federal income tax. The fund may issue preferred shares for leveraging purposes.

Portfolio: (10/31/92) Municipal Bonds 98.7%, Other 1.3%. Portfolio Ratings: A or better 74.0%, Lower 26.0%.

Capitalization: (10/31/92) Common stock outstanding 30,155,654. Leveraged with 4,000 shares preferred stock, stated value $50,000 per share. No long-term debt.

Fund Manager: Fund Asset Management, Inc.
Income Dist: Monthly
Reinvestment Plan: Yes

Fee: 0.50%
Capital Gains Dist: Annually
Shareholder Reports: Quarterly

MuniYield Quality II

P.O. Box 9011
Princeton, NJ 08543
(800) 426-5523 / (609) 282-2800

NYSE : MQT

Transfer Agent
The Bank of New York
110 Washington St.
New York, NY 10286
(800) 524-4458

Tax-Free Income

Background: Initial public offering September 21, 1992 at $15 per share. Initial NAV was $14.18 per share.

Objective: Seeks high current income exempt from regular Federal income taxes.

Portfolio: (10/31/92) Municipal Bonds 101.3%. Portfolio Ratings: AAA 13.2%, AA 10.8%, A 50.3%, BBB 20.3%, Non-Rated 4.3%.

Capitalization: (10/31/92) Common stock outstanding 21,907,055 shares. Fund is leveraged with 3,000 shares preferred stock, stated value $50,000 per share. No long-term debt.

Fund Manager: Fund Asset Management, Inc.
Income Dist: Monthly
Reinvestment Plan: Yes

Fee: 0.50%
Capital Gains Dist: Annually
Shareholder Reports: Quarterly

Nuveen Arizona Premium Income Municipal Fund

NYSE : NAZ

John Nuveen & Co., Inc. *Transfer Agent*
Investment Bankers U.S. Trust
333 W. Wacker Dr. Nuveen Exchange-Traded Fund Investment Services
Chicago, IL 60606 770 Broadway
(800) 252-4630 / (312) 917-7700 New York, NY 10003
(800) 257-8787

Income

Background: Initial public offering November 19, 1992 at $15 per share. Initial NAV was $14.05 per share.

Objective: Seeks current income exempt from regular Federal and Arizona State income taxes. Capital appreciation is secondary.

Portfolio: (12/31/92) Municipal Bonds 38.5%, Short Term & Other 61.5%. Portfolio Ratings: AAA 50.0%, AA 15.0%, A 34.0%, BBB 1.0%.

Capitalization: (12/31/92) Common stock outstanding 3,807,118. No long-term debt.

Fund Manager: Nuveen Advisory Corporation	**Fee:** 0.65%
Income Dist: Monthly	**Capital Gains Dist:** Monthly
Reinvestment Plan: Yes	**Shareholder Reports:** Semi-Annually

---

Nuveen Insured California Premium Income Municipal Fund

NYSE : NPC

John Nuveen & Co., Inc. *Transfer Agent*
Investment Bankers U.S. Trust
333 W. Wacker Dr. Nuveen Exchange-Traded Fund Investor Services
Chicago, IL 60606 770 Broadway
(800) 257-8787 / (312) 917-7810 New York, NY 10003
(800) 257-8787

Tax-Free Income

Background: Initial public offering November 19, 1992 at $15 per share. Initial NAV was $14.05 per share.

Objective: Seeks current income exempt from regular Federal and California State income taxes. Capital appreciation is secondary.

Portfolio: (12/31/92) Municipal Bonds 63.7%, Short Term & Other 36.3%. Portfolio Ratings: AAA 92.0%, A 8.0%.

Capitalization: (12/31/92) Common stock outstanding 5,807,118. No long-term debt.

Fund Manager: Nuveen Advisory Corporation	**Fee:** 0.65%
Income Dist: Monthly	**Capital Gains Dist:** Monthly
Reinvestment Plan: Yes	**Shareholder Reports:** Semi-Annually

Nuveen Insured California Select Tax-Free Income Portfolio

NYSE : NXC

John Nuveen & Co., Inc.
Investment Bankers
333 W. Wacker Dr.
Chicago, IL 60606
(800) 252-4630 / (312) 917-7700

Transfer Agent
U.S. Trust
Nuveen Exchange-Traded Fund Investor Services
770 Broadway
New York, NY 10003
(800) 257-8787

Tax-Free Income

Background: Initial public offering June 19, 1992 at $15 per share. Initial NAV was $14.15 per share.

Objective: Seeks income exempt from Federal and California State income taxes. The Trust intends to liquidate all assets 20-25 years after the initial public offering and make a single liquidating distribution to shareholders.

Portfolio: (12/1/92) Sector Weightings: Public Power 16.0%, Water & Sewer 14.9%, Health Care 11.3%. All Bonds are insured or backed by escrow account.

Capitalization: (9/30/92) Shares of beneficial interest outstanding 6,257,068. No long-term debt.

Fund Manager: Nuveen Advisory Corporation
Income Dist: Monthly
Reinvestment Plan: Yes
Fee: 0.30%
Capital Gains Dist: Annually
Shareholder Reports: Semi-Annually

Nuveen Insured Florida Premium Income Municipal Fund

NYSE : NFL

John Nuveen & Co., Inc.
Investment Bankers
333 W. Wacker Dr.
Chicago, IL 60606
(800) 252-4630 / (312) 917-7700

Transfer Agent
U.S. Trust
Nuveen Exchange-Traded Fund Investor Services
770 Broadway
New York, NY 10003
(800) 257-8787

Tax-Free Income

Background: Initial public offering December 18, 1992 at $15 per share. Initial NAV was $14.05 per share.

Objective: Seeks current income exempt from regular Federal and Florida intangible income taxes. Capital appreciation is secondary.

Portfolio: (12/31/92) Municipal Bonds 24.6%, Short Term & Other 75.4%. Portfolio Ratings: AAA 100%.

Capitalization: (12/31/92) Common stock outstanding 8,669,618. No long-term debt.

Fund Manager: Nuveen Advisory Corporation
Income Dist: Monthly
Reinvestment Plan: Yes
Fee: 0.65%
Capital Gains Dist: Monthly
Shareholder Reports: Semi-Annually

Nuveen Insured New York Premium Income Municipal Fund

NYSE : NNF

John Nuveen & Co., Inc.
Investment Bankers
333 W. Wacker Dr.
Chicago, IL 60606
(800) 252-4630 / (312) 917-7700

Transfer Agent
U.S. Trust
Nuveen Exchange-Traded Fund Investor Services
770 Broadway
New York, NY 10003
(800) 257-8787

Tax-Free Income

Background: Initial public offering December 18, 1992 at $15 per share. Initial NAV was $14.05 per share.

Objective: Seeks current income exempt from regular Federal and New York State and City income taxes. Capital appreciation is secondary.

Portfolio: (12/31/92) Municipal Bonds 33.3%, Short Term & Other 66.7%. Portfolio Ratings: AAA 86.0%, Non-Rated 14.0%.

Capitalization: (12/31/92) Common stock outstanding 3,997,118. No long-term debt.

Fund Manager: Nuveen Advisory Corporation	**Fee:** 0.65%
Income Dist: Monthly	**Capital Gains Dist:** Monthly
Reinvestment Plan: Yes	**Shareholder Reports:** Semi-Annually

---

Nuveen Insured New York Select Tax-Free Income Portfolio

NYSE : NXN

John Nuveen & Co., Inc.
Investment Bankers
333 W. Wacker Dr.
Chicago, IL 60606
(800) 252-4630 / (312) 917-7700

Transfer Agent
U.S. Trust
Nuveen Exchange-Traded Fund Investor Services
770 Broadway
New York, NY 10003
(800) 257-8787

Tax-Free Income

Background: Initial public offering June 19, 1992 of 3,500,000 shares at $15 per share. Initial NAV was $ 14.15.

Objective: Seeks income exempt from Federal and New York State and City income taxes.

Portfolio: (12/1/92) Sector Weightings: Education 23.6%, Housing 14.4%, Water & Sewer 12.9%. All bonds are insured or backed by escrow accounts.

Capitalization: (9/30/92) Shares of beneficial interest outstanding 3,907,068. No long-term debt.

Fund Manager: Nuveen Advisory Corporation	**Fee:** 0.30%
Income Dist: Monthly	**Capital Gains Dist:** Annually
Reinvestment Plan: Yes	**Shareholder Reports:** Semi-Annually

Nuveen Insured Premium Income Municipal Fund   NYSE : NPE

John Nuveen & Co., Inc.   *Transfer Agent*
Investment Bankers   U.S. Trust
333 W. Wacker Dr.   Nuveen Exchange-Traded Fund Investor Services
Chicago, IL 60606   770 Broadway
(800) 252-4630 / (312) 917-7700   New York, NY 10003
                                         (800) 257-8787

Tax-Free Income

Background: Initial public offering December 18, 1992 at $15 per share. Initial NAV was $14.05 per share.

Objective: Seeks current income exempt from regular Federal income taxes. Capital appreciation is secondary.

Portfolio: (12/31/92) Municipal Bonds 52.4%, Short Term & Other 47.6%. Portfolio Ratings: AAA 94.0%, A 6.0%.

Capitalization: (12/31/92) Common stock outstanding 14,392,118. No long-term debt.

Fund Manager: Nuveen Advisory Corporation	**Fee:** 0.65%
Income Dist: Monthly	**Capital Gains Dist:** Monthly
Reinvestment Plan: Yes	**Shareholder Reports:** Semi-Annually

---

Nuveen Michigan Premium Income Municipal Fund   NYSE : NMP

John Nuveen & Co., Inc.   *Transfer Agent*
Investment Bankers   U.S. Trust
333 W. Wacker Dr.   Nuveen Exchange-Traded Fund Investor Services
Chicago, IL 60606   770 Broadway
(800) 252-4630 / (312) 917-7700   New York, NY 10003
                                         (800) 257-8787

Tax-Free Income

Background: Initial public offering December 18, 1992 at $15 per share. Initial NAV was $14.05 per share.

Objective: Seeks current income exempt from regular Federal and Michigan State income taxes. Capital appreciation is secondary.

Portfolio: (12/31/92) Municipal Bonds 11.0%, Short Term & Other 89.0%. Portfolio Ratings: AAA 84.0%, A 16.0%.

Capitalization: (12/31/92) Common stock outstanding 4,627,118. No long-term debt.

Fund Manager: Nuveen Advisory Corporation	**Fee:** 0.65%
Income Dist: Monthly	**Capital Gains Dist:** Monthly
Reinvestment Plan: Yes	**Shareholder Reports:** Semi-Annually

Nuveen New Jersey Premium Income Municipal Fund

NYSE : NNJ

John Nuveen & Co., Inc.
Investment Bankers
333 W. Wacker Dr.
Chicago, IL 60606
(800) 252-4630 / (312) 917-7700

Transfer Agent
U.S. Trust Co. of New York
Nuveen Exchange-Traded Fund Investor Services
770 Broadway
New York, NY 10003
(800) 257-8787

Tax-Free Income

Background: Initial public offering December 18, 1992 at $15 per share. Initial NAV was $14.05 per share.

Objective: Seeks current income exempt from regular Federal and New Jersey State income taxes. Capital appreciation is secondary.

Portfolio: (12/31/92) Municipal Bonds 41.7%, Short Term & Other 58.3%. Portfolio Ratings: AAA 23.0%, AA 47.0%, A 30.0%.

Capitalization: (12/31/92) Common stock outstanding 5,152,118. No long-term debt.

Fund Manager: Nuveen Advisory Corporation	**Fee:** 0.65%
Income Dist: Monthly	**Capital Gains Dist:** Monthly
Reinvestment Plan: Yes	**Shareholder Reports:** Semi-Annually

Nuveen Ohio Premium Income

AMEX : NOH

John Nuveen & Co., Inc.
Investment Bankers
333 W. Wacker Dr.
Chicago, IL 60606
(800) 257-8787 / (312) 917-7700

Transfer Agent
U.S. Trust
Nuveen Exchange-Traded Fund Investor Services
770 Broadway
New York, NY 10003
(800) 257-8787

Tax-Free Income

Background: Initial public offering December 18, 1992 at $15 per share. Initial NAV was $14.05 per share.

Objective: Seeks current income exempt from regular Federal and Ohio State income taxes. Capital appreciation is secondary.

Portfolio: (12/31/92) Municipal Bonds 12.9%, Short Term & Other 87.1%. Portfolio Ratings: AAA 25.0%, A 75.0%.

Capitalization: (12/31/92) Common stock outstanding 3,157,118. No long-term debt.

Fund Manager: Nuveen Advisory Corporation	**Fee:** 0.65%
Income Dist: Monthly	**Capital Gains Dist:** Monthly
Reinvestment Plan: Yes	**Shareholder Reports:** Semi-Annually

Nuveen Pennsylvania Premium Income Municipal Fund

NYSE : NPA

John Nuveen & Co., Inc.
Investment Bankers
333 W. Wacker Dr.
Chicago, IL 60606
(800) 252-4630 / (312) 917-7700

Transfer Agent
U.S. Trust
Nuveen Exchange-Traded Fund Investor Services
770 Broadway
New York, NY 10003
(800) 257-8787

Tax-Free Income

Background: Initial public offering December 21, 1992 at $15 per share. Initial NAV was $14.05 per share.

Objective: Seeks current income exempt from regular Federal and Pennsylvania State income taxes. Capital appreciation is secondary.

Portfolio: (12/31/92) Municipal Bonds 12.4%, Short Term & Other 87.6%. Portfolio Ratings: AAA 34.0%, BBB 45.0%, Non-Rated 21.0%.

Capitalization: (12/31/92) Common stock outstanding 5,467,118. No long-term debt.

Fund Manager: Nuveen Advisory Corporation
Income Dist: Monthly
Reinvestment Plan: Yes

Fee: 0.65%
Capital Gains Dist: Monthly
Shareholder Reports: Semi-Annually

Nuveen Premium Income Municipal Fund II

NYSE : NPM

John Nuveen & Co., Inc.
Investment Bankers
333 W. Wacker Dr.
Chicago, IL 60606
(800) 252-4630 / (312) 917-7700

Transfer Agent
U.S. Trust
Nuveen Exchange-Traded Investor Services
770 Broadway
New York, NY 10003
(800) 257- 8787

Tax-Free Income

Background: Initial public offering July 23, 1992 of 40,700,000 shares at $15 per share. Initial NAV was $14.05 per share.

Objective: Seeks high current tax-free income from a diversified portfolio of investment-grade, tax-exempt municipal obligations rated BBB or better. Not more than 20% of assets may be invested in non-rated securities the advisor deems to be of investment-grade quality. During temporary defensive periods, may invest up to 100% in taxable securities.

Portfolio: (1/1/93) Municipal Bonds 97.8%, Other 2.2%. Sector Weightings: General Obligations 14.9%, Housing 11.4%, Health Care 11.2%. Portfolio Ratings: AAA 29.0%, AA 13.0%, A 33.0%, BBB 23.0%, Non-Rated 2.0%.

Capitalization: (10/31/92) Common Stocks outstanding 40,707,000. No long-term debt.

Fund Manager: Nuveen Advisory Corporation
Income Dist: Monthly
Reinvestment Plan: Yes

Fee: 0.65%
Capital Gains Dist: Annually
Shareholder Reports: Semi-Annually

Nuveen Premium Income Municipal Fund III

John Nuveen & Co., Inc.
Investment Bankers
333 W. Wacker Dr.
Chicago, IL 60606
(800) 252-4630 / (312) 917-7700

NYSE : NPN

Transfer Agent
U.S. Trust
Nuveen Exchange-Traded Fund Investor Services
770 Broadway
New York, NY 10003
(800) 257-8787

Tax-Free Income

Background: Initial public offering October 23, 1992 of 6,750,000 shares at $15 per share. Initial NAV was $14.05 per share.

Objective: Seeks high current tax-free income from a diversified portfolio of investment-grade, tax-exempt municipal obligations rated BBB or better. Not more than 20% of assets may be invested in non-rated securities the advisor deems to be of investment-grade quality. During the temporary defensive periods, may invest up to 100% in taxable securities.

Portfolio: (10/31/92) Municipal Bonds 97.8%, Short Term & Other 1.2%. Portfolio Ratings: AAA 29.0%, AA 13.0%, A 33.0%, BBB 23.0%, Non-Rated 2.0%.

Capitalization: (10/31/92) Common stock outstanding 6,757,000. No long-term debt.

Fund Manager: Nuveen Advisory Corporation   **Fee:** 0.65%
Income Dist: Monthly   **Capital Gains Dist:** Annually
Reinvestment Plan: Yes   **Shareholder Reports:** Semi-Annually

---

Nuveen Select Maturities Municipal II

John Nuveen & Co., Inc.
Investment Bankers
333 W. Wacker Dr.
Chicago, IL 60606
(800) 252-4630 / (312) 917-7700

NYSE : NIR

Transfer Agent
U.S. Trust
Nuveen Exchange-Traded Fund Investor Services
770 Broadway
New York, NY 10003
(800) 257-8787

Tax-Free Income

Background: Initial public offering October 23, 1992 at $12 per share. Initial NAV was $11.30 per share.

Objective: Seeks current income exempt from regular Federal income taxes. At least 80% of assets will be invested in investment-grade municipal obligations.

Portfolio: (12/31/92) Municipal Bonds 98.9%, Cash & Equivalents 1.1%. Portfolio Ratings: AAA 16%, AA 35%, A 39%, BBB 5%, Lower or Non-Rated 6%.

Capitalization: (12/31/92) Common stock outstanding 4,480,295. No long-term debt.

Fund Manager: Nuveen Advisory Corporation   **Fee:** 0.50%
Income Dist: Monthly   **Capital Gains Dist:** Annually
Reinvestment Plan: Yes   **Shareholder Reports:** Semi-Annually

Nuveen Select Maturity Municipal Fund

John Nuveen & Co., Inc.
Investment Bankers
333 W. Wacker Dr.
Chicago, IL 60606
(800) 252-4630 / (312) 917-7700

NYSE : NIM

Transfer Agent
U.S. Trust
Nuveen Exchange-Traded Fund Investor Services
770 Broadway
New York, NY 10003
(800) 257-8787

Tax-Free Income

Background: Initial public offering September 18, 1992 at $12 per share. Initial NAV was $11.30 per share.

Objective: Seeks income exempt from Federal income tax. At least 80% of assets will be invested in investment-grade municipal obligations.

Portfolio: (12/31/92) Municipal Bonds 98.8%, Short Term & Other 1.2%. Portfolio Ratings: AAA 21.0%, AA 33.0%, A 35.0%, BBB 6.0%, Non-Rated 5.0%.

Capitalization: (12/31/92) Common stock outstanding 7,808,850. No long-term debt.

Fund Manager: Nuveen Advisory Corporation
Income Dist: Monthly
Reinvestment Plan: Yes

Fee: 0.50%
Capital Gains Dist: Annually
Shareholder Reports: Semi-Annually

Nuveen Select Quality Municipal Fund

John Nuveeen & Co., Inc.
Investment Bankers
333 W. Wacker Dr.
Chicago, IL 60606
(800) 252-4630 / (312) 917-7700

NYSE : NQS

Transfer Agent
U.S. Trust
Nuveen Exchange-Traded Fund Investor Services
770 Broadway
New York, NY 10003
(800) 257-8787

Tax-Free Income

Background: Initial public offering March 21, 1992 of 32,250,000 shares at $15 per share. Initial NAV was $14.05 per share.

Objective: Seeks current income exempt from regular Federal income taxes. Capital appreciation is secondary. The fund will invest substantially all of its assets in long-term investment-grade municipal bonds. 80% of the portfolio will be rated BBB or better. Up to 20% may be in unrated securities the fund adviser deems to be of investment-grade quality.

Portfolio: (10/31/92) Municipal Bonds 97.6%, Short Term & Other 2.4%. State Weightings: Texas 9.6%, New York 7.5%, Massachusetts 7.3%, Utah 5.8%, Washington 5.2%. Portfolio Ratings: AAA 25.0%, AA 25.0%, A 30.0%, BBB 16.0%, Non-Rated 4.0%.

Capitalization: (10/31/92) Commmon stock outstanding 32,691,000. Leveraged with 4,800 auction-rate preferreds, stated value $50,000 per share. No long-term debt.

Fund Manager: Nuveen Advisory Corporation
Income Dist: Monthly
Reinvestment Plan: Yes

Fee: 0.65%
Capital Gains Dist: Annually
Shareholder Reports: Semi-Annually

Nuveen Select Tax Free Income Portfolio

NYSE : NXP

John Nuveen & Co., Inc.
Investment Bankers
333 W. Wacker Dr.
Chicago, IL 60606
(800) 252-4630 / (312) 917-7700

Transfer Agent
U.S. Trust
Nuveen Exchange-Traded Fund Investor Services
770 Broadway
New York, NY 10003
(800) 257-8787

Tax-Free Income

Background: Initial public offering March 19, 1992 of 15,250,000 shares at $15 per share. Initial NAV was $14.23 per share.

Objective: Seeks current income exempt from regular Federal income tax.

Portfolio: (12/31/92) Municipal Bonds 100%. Sector Weightings: Transportation 47%, Housing 15%, Electric Utilities 13%. State Weightings: New York 7.7%, Washington 5.5%, Colorado 4.8%, Oklahoma 4.7%, Illinois 2.1%. Portfolio Ratings: AAA 15.4%, AA 24.2%, A 33.0%, BBB 23.6%, Non-Rated 0.7%.

Capitalization: (3/31/92) Shares of beneficial interest outstanding 15,257,028. No long-term debt.

Fund Manager: Nuveen Advisory Corporation
Income Dist: Monthly
Reinvestment Plan: Yes

Fee: 0.25%
Capital Gains Dist: Annually
Shareholder Reports: Semi-Annually

Nuveen Select Tax-Free Income Portfolio II

NYSE : NXQ

John Nuveen & Co., Inc.
Investment Bankers
333 W. Wacker Dr.
Chicago, IL 60606
(800) 252-4630 / (312) 917-7700

Transfer Agent
U.S. Trust
Nuveen Exchange-Traded Fund Investor Services
770 Broadway
New York, NY 10003
(800) 257-8787

Tax-Free Income

Background: Initial public offering May 21, 1992 of 16,500,000 shares at $15 per share. Initial NAV was $14.15 per share.

Objective: Seeks income exempt from Federal income tax. Trust intends to liquidate the portfolio on or about June 2017 and make a liquidating distribution to shareholders.

Portfolio: (12/1/92) Municipal Bonds 100%. Portfolio Ratings: AAA 25.3%, AA 19.1%, A 36.9%, BBB 18.5%.

Capitalization: (12/31/92) Common stock outstanding 17,607,068. No long-term debt.

Fund Manager: Nuveen Advisory Corporation
Income Dist: Monthly
Reinvestment Plan: Yes

Fee: 0.30%
Capital Gains Dist: Annually
Shareholder Reports: Semi-Annually

Nuveen Select Tax-Free Income Portfolio III

NYSE : NXR

John Nuveen & Co., Inc.
Investment Bankers
333 W. Wacker Dr.
Chicago, IL 60606
(800) 252-4630 / (312) 917-7700

Transfer Agent
U.S. Trust
Nuveen Exchange-Traded Fund Investor Services
770 Broadway
New York, NY 10003
(800) 257-8787

Tax-Free Income

Background: Initial public offering July 24, 1992 at $15 per share. Initial NAV was $14.15 per share.

Objective: Seeks stable dividends exempt from Federal income tax consistent with the preservation of capital.

Portfolio: (12/1/92) Municipal Bonds 100%. Portfolio Ratings: AAA 16.5%, AA 17.2%, A 38.5%, BBB 22.9%, Non-Rated 4.7%.

Capitalization: (12/31/92) Common stock outstanding 6,507,068. No long-term debt.

Fund Manager: Nuveen Advisory Corporation	**Fee:** 0.30%
Income Dist: Monthly	**Capital Gains Dist:** Monthly
Reinvestment Plan: Yes	**Shareholder Reports:** Semi-Annually

Nuveen Select Tax-Free Income Portfolio IV

NYSE : NXS

John Nuveen & Co., Inc.
Investment Bankers
333 W. Wacker Dr.
Chicago, IL 60606
(800) 252-4630 / (312) 917-7700

Transfer Agent
U.S. Trust
Nuveen Exchange-Traded Fund Investor Services
770 Broadway
New York, NY 10003
(800) 257-8787

Tax-Free Income

Background: Initial public offering September 18, 1992 at $15 per share. Initial NAV was $14.15 per share.

Objective: Seeks to provide stable dividends exempt from regular Federal income taxes, consistent with the preservation of capital.

Portfolio: (12/1/92) Municipal Bonds 100%. Portfolio Ratings: AAA 21.4%, AA 24.8%, A 39.7%, BBB 14.0%.

Capitalization: (12/31/92) Common stock outstanding 6,353,141. No long-term debt.

Fund Manager: Nuveen Advisory Corporation	**Fee:** 0.30%
Income Dist: Monthly	**Capital Gains Dist:** Annually
Reinvestment Plan: Yes	**Shareholder Reports:** Semi-Annually

Nuveen Texas Premium Income Municipal Fund

AMEX : NTE

John Nuveen & Co., Inc.
Investment Bankers
333 W. Wacker Dr.
Chicago, IL 60606
(800) 252-4630 / (312) 917-7700

Transfer Agent
U.S. Trust
Nuveen Exchange-Traded Fund Investor Services
770 Broadway
New York, NY 10003
(800) 257-8787

Tax-Free Income

Background: Initial public offering December 21, 1992 at $15 per share. Initial NAV was $14.05 per share.

Objective: Seeks current income exempt from regular Federal income tax. Capital appreciation is secondary.

Portfolio: (12/31/92) Municipal Bonds 37.5%, Short Term & Other 62.5%. Portfolio Ratings: AAA 24.0%, AA 9.0%, A 67.0%.

Capitalization: (12/31/92) Common stock outstanding 2,343,368. No long-term debt.

Fund Manager: Nuveen Advisory Corporation	**Fee:** 0.65%
Income Dist: Monthly	**Capital Gains Dist:** Monthly
Reinvestment Plan: Yes	**Shareholder Reports:** Semi-Annually

PaineWebber Premier Tax-Free Income Fund

NYSE : PPM

1285 Avenue of the Americas
New York, NY 10019
(212) 713-2000

Transfer Agent
Provident National Bank
P.O. Box 8950
Wilmington, DE 19899
(800) 852-4750

Tax-Free Income

Background: Initial public offering October 29, 1992 at $15 per share. PaineWebber, Inc. (the underwriter) will be reimbursed for organizational expenses (estimated at $235,000) over a five-year period, amortized against income. Initial NAV was $15 per share.

Objective: Seeks high current income exempt from regular Federal income tax, consistent with the preservation of capital.

Portfolio: Not available.

Capitalization: (12/31/92) Common stock outstanding 10,356,667. No long-term debt.

Fund Manager: Mitchell Hutchins Asset Management	**Fee:** 0.90%
Income Dist: Monthly	**Capital Gains Dist:** Monthly
Reinvestment Plan: Yes	**Shareholder Reports:** N/A

Pilgrim Prime Rate Trust

10100 Santa Monica Blvd.
Los Angeles, CA 90067
(800) 331-1080

NYSE : PPR

Transfer Agent
Investors Fiduciary Trust Co.
c/o DST Systems Inc.
P.O. Box 419368
Kansas City, MO 64141
(816) 474-8786

Income

Background: Commenced operations May 12, 1988. Prior to PPR's listing on the NYSE on March 9, 1992 its shares were continuously offered through broker-dealers at net asset value plus a sales charge of up to 3% of the offering price.

Objective: Seeks high current income consistent with preservation of capital.

Portfolio: (11/30/92) Senior Collateralized Loan Participations 90.2%, Short Term 8.6%, Common Stock, Preferred Stock & Other 0.9%. Sector Weightings: Transportation Products & Services 11.6%, Electronic Equipment 8.0%, Paper Products 6.6%, Food Stores 8.9%, Health Care Products & Services 6.68%.

Capitalization: (12/24/92) Common stock outstanding 80,283,000. No long-term debt.

Fund Manager: Pilgrim Management Corp.
Income Dist: Monthly
Reinvestment Plan: Yes

Fee: 0.85%
Capital Gains Dist: Annually
Shareholder Reports: Quarterly

Putnam California Investment Grade Municipal Trust

One Post Office Square
Boston, MA 02109
(800) 634-1587

NYSE : PCA

Transfer Agent
Putnam Investor Services
One Post Office Square
Boston, MA 02109
(800) 634-1587

Tax-Free Income

Background: Initial public offering November 19, 1992 of 4,000,000 shares at $15 per share. Initial NAV was $14.10 per share.

Objective: Seeks income exempt from regular Federal and California State income taxes. Invests solely in investment-grade California tax-exempt securities. May use leverage.

Portfolio: (12/31/92) Municipal Bonds 98.0%, Short Term & Other 2.0%. Portfolio Ratings: AAA 31.0%, AA 35.0%, A 30.0%, BBB 4.0%.

Capitalization: (12/31/92) Common stock outstanding 2,607,092. No long-term debt.

Fund Manager: Putnam Management Company, Inc.
Income Dist: Monthly
Reinvestment Plan: Yes

Fee: 0.70%
Capital Gains Dist: Monthly
Shareholder Reports: N/A

Putnam Investment Grade Municipal Trust II
One Post Office Square
Boston, MA 02109
(800) 225-1581 / (617) 292-1000

NYSE : PMG
Transfer Agent
Putnam Fiduciary Trust Co.
Putnam Investor Services
P.O. Box 41203
Providence, RI 02940-1203

Tax-Free Income

(800) 225-1581

Background: Initial public offering November 19, 1992 of 11,700,000 shares at $15 per share. Initial NAV was $14.10 per share.

Objective: Seeks a high level of current income exempt from Federal income tax, consistent with preservation of capital. The fund will invest in a diversified portfolio of "investment-grade" tax-exempt securities which Putnam believes do not involve undue risk to income or principal. The fund may invest 20% of its assets in tax-exempt securities subject to the Federal alternative minimum tax. The fund may engage in interest-rate and other hedging transactions.

Portfolio: (12/31/92) Municipal Bonds 98.5%, Short Term & Other 1.5%. Portfolio Ratings AAA 28.0%, AA 31.0%, A 13.0%, BBB 25.0%, Non-Rated 3.0%.

Capitalization: (12/31/92) Common stock outstanding 11,707,092. No long-term debt.

Fund Manager: Putnam Management Company, Inc.	**Fee:** 0.70%
Income Dist: Monthly	**Capital Gains Dist:** Annually
Reinvestment Plan: Yes	**Shareholder Reports:** N/A

Putnam New York Investment Grade Municipal Trust
One Post Office Square
Boston, MA 02109
(800) 634-1587 / (617) 292-1000

NYSE : PMN
Transfer Agent
Putnam Investor Services
P.O. Box 2701
Boston, MA 02208
(800) 634-1587

Income

Background: Initial public offering November 20, 1992 of 2,600,000 shares at $15 per share. Initial NAV was $14.10 per share.

Objective: Seeks high current income exempt from regular Federal and New York State and City income taxes, consistent with preservation of capital.

Portfolio: (12/31/92) Municipal Bonds 94.8%, Short Term & Other 5.2%. Portfolio Ratings: AAA 16.0%, AA 16.0%, A 23.0%, BBB 46.0%.

Capitalization: (12/31/92) Common stock outstanding 4,007,092. No long-term debt.

Fund Manager: Putnam Management Company, Inc.	**Fee:** 0.70%
Income Dist: Monthly	**Capital Gains Dist:** Monthly
Reinvestment Plan: Yes	**Shareholder Reports:** N/A

Putnam Tax-Free Health Care Fund

One Post Office Square
Boston, MA 02109
(800) 225-1581

NYSE : PMH
Transfer Agent
Putnam Investor Services
P.O. Box 41203
Providence, RI 02940
(800) 634-1587

Tax-Free Income

Background: Initial public offering June, 1992 at $15 per share. Initial NAV was $13.90.

Objective: Seeks a high level of current income exempt from Federal income tax, consistent with the preservation of capital. Will invest primarily in a portfolio of tax-exempt securities in the health care sector.

Portfolio: (10/31/92) Municipal Bonds 100%. Portfolio Rating: Average Rating BBB.

Capitalization: (11/30/92) Common stock outstanding 13,807,168. No long-term debt.

Fund Manager: Putnam Management Company, Inc.	**Fee:** 0.70%
Income Dist: Monthly	**Capital Gains Dist:** Annually
Reinvestment Plan: Yes	**Shareholder Reports:** Semi-Annually

---

Smith Barney Intermediate Municipal Fund, Inc.

1345 Avenue of the Americas
New York, NY 10105
(212) 698-5349

NYSE : SBI
Transfer Agent
Provident National Bank
P.O. Box 8950
Wilmington, DE 19899
(800) 852-4750

Tax-Free Income

Background: Initial public offering February 5, 1992 at $10 per share. Initial NAV was $10 per share. Offering expenses will be reimbursed from management fees.

Objective: Seeks high current income exempt from regular Federal income taxes, consistent with prudent investment management.

Portfolio: (12/31/92) Municipal Bonds 100.0%. Portfolio Ratings: AAA 35.0%, AA 15.0%, A 35.0%, BBB 14.0%, Non-Rated 1.0%.

Capitalization: (12/31/92) Common stock outstanding 8,057,595. No long-term debt.

Fund Manager: Mutual Management Corp.	**Fee:** 0.60%
Income Dist: Monthly	**Capital Gains Dist:** Monthly
Reinvestment Plan: Yes	**Shareholder Reports:** N/A

Smith Barney Municipal Fund

AMEX : SBT

1345 Avenue of the Americas
New York, NY 10105
(212) 698-5349

Transfer Agent
Provident National Bank
P.O. Box 8950
Wilmington, DE 19899
(800) 852-4750

Tax-Free Income

Background: Initial public offering July 31, 1992 at $15 per share. Initial NAV was $15 per share. Offering expenses will be reimbursed from management fees.

Objective: Seeks high current income exempt from regular Federal income taxes. The fund will invest mainly in municipal securities with maturities of less than 15 years and may borrow or issue preferred shares for leverage.

Portfolio: (12/31/92) Municipal Bonds 100.0%. Portfolio Ratings: AAA 27.0%, AA 12.0%, A 46.0%, BBB 16.0%.

Capitalization: (12/31/92) Common stock outstanding 4,021,161. No long-term debt.

Fund Manager: Mutual Management Co.   **Fee:** 0.70%
Income Dist: Monthly   **Capital Gains Dist:** Monthly
Reinvestment Plan: Yes   **Shareholder Reports:** N/A

Strategic Global Income Fund, Inc.

NYSE : SGL

1285 Avenue of the Americas
New York, NY 10019
(212) 713-2000

Transfer Agent
Provident National Bank
c/o Provident Financial Processing
Wilmington, DE 19899
(800) 553-8080

Income

Background: Initial public offering January 24, 1992 of 19,000,000 shares at $15 per share. Initial NAV was $14.03 per share.

Objective: Seeks high current income. Capital appreciation is secondary. Under normal market conditions, the fund will invest at least 65% of assets in U.S. Government debt securities, Foreign Government debt securities, Corporate Obligations, or Preferred Stock rated no lower than BBB.

Portfolio: (12/31/92) Bonds 75.3%, Short Term & Other 24.8%. Country Exposure: U.S. 30.0%, Mexico 16.0%, Australia 12.0%, Canada 8.0%, Germany 6.0%.

Capitalization: (12/31/92) Common stock outstanding 21,407,128. No long-tern debt.

Fund Manager: Mitchell Hutchins Asset Management   **Fee:** 1.00%
Income Dist: Quarterly   **Capital Gains Dist:** Annually
Reinvestment Plan: Yes   **Shareholder Reports:** Semi-Annually

TCW/ Dean Witter Term Trust 2002
Two World Trade Center
New York, NY 10048
(800) 869-3863 / (212) 392-2550

NYSE : TRM
Transfer Agent
Dean Witter Trust Co.
2 Montgomery St.
Jersey City, NJ 07302
(800) 526-3143

Income

Background: Initial public offering November 20, 1992 at $10 per share. Initial NAV was $9.40 per share.

Objective: Seeks high current income and to return $10 per share to common shareholders on or about December 31, 2002.

Portfolio: Not available.

Capitalization: Not available.

Fund Manager: TCW Funds Management	**Fee:** 0.39%
Income Dist: Monthly	**Capital Gains Dist:** Monthly
Reinvestment Plan: Yes	**Shareholder Reports:** N/A

Van Kampen Merritt Advantage Municipal Trust
One Parkview Plaza
Oakbrook Terrace, IL 60181
(800) 225-2222

NYSE : VKA
Transfer Agent
State Street Bank & Trust Co.
225 Franklin St.
Boston, MA 02101
(800) 341-2929

Tax-Free Income

Background: Initial public offering September 25, 1992 of 19,100,085 shares at $15 per share. Initial NAV was $14.84.

Objective: Seeks high current income exempt from regular Federal income taxes. The fund's capital structure is leveraged, enabling it to increase yield by taking advantage of the spread between short- and long-term rates.

Portfolio: (10/31/92) Municipal Bonds 93.0%, Short Term 33.1%, Liabilities (26.1%). Portfolio Ratings: AAA 12.2%, AA 19.9%, A 43.3%, BBB 24.6%.

Capitalization: (10/31/92) Common stock outstanding 19,106,785. Leveraged with 3,800 shares preferred stock, stated value $50,000 per share. No long-term debt.

Fund Manager: Van Kampen Merritt Investment Advisory Corp.	**Fee:** 0.65%
Income Dist: Monthly	**Capital Gains Dist:** Annually
Reinvestment Plan: No	**Shareholder Reports:** Semi-Annually

Van Kampen Merritt Advantage Pennsylvania

One Parkview Plaza
Oakbrook Terrace, IL 60181
(800) 225-2222

NYSE : VAP
Transfer Agent
State Street Bank & Trust Co.
225 Franklin St.
Boston, MA 02101
(800) 341-2929

Tax-Free Income

Background: Initial public offering September 25, 1992 of 4,400,000 shares at $15 per share. Initial NAV was $14.72 per share.

Objective: Seeks a high level of current income exempt from Federal and Pennsylvania State income taxes as well as some local income and personal property taxes.

Portfolio: (10/31/92) Municipal Bonds 61.4%, Short Term 38.6%. Portfolio Ratings: AAA 73.1%, AA 9.1%, A 17.8%.

Capitalization: (10/31/92) Common shares outstanding 4,361,902. Leveraged with 800 shares preferred stock, stated value $50,000 per share. No long-term debt.

Fund Manager: Van Kampen Merritt Investment Advisory Corp.   **Fee:** 0.65%
Income Dist: Monthly   **Capital Gains Dist:** Annually
Reinvestment Plan: Yes   **Shareholder Reports:** Semi-Annually

Van Kampen Merritt Municipal Opportunity Trust

One Parkview Plaza
Oakbrook Terrace, IL 60181
(800) 225-2222

NYSE : VMO
Transfer Agent
State Street Bank & Trust Co.
225 Franklin St.
Boston, MA 02101
(800) 341-2929

Income

Background: Initial public offering April, 1992 at $15 per share. Initial NAV was $15 per share.

Objective: Seeks a high level of current income exempt from Federal income tax, consistent with preservation of capital. The fund will invest primarily in a diversified portfolio of municipal securities which the Fund's investment advisor believes do not involve undue risk to income or principal. Under normal market conditions, the Fund will invest substantially all of its assets in municipal securities rated investment-grade at the time of investment.

Portfolio: (10/31/92) Municipal Bonds 97.8%, Other Assets 5.3%. State Weightings: Illinois 15.3%, New York 12.0%, Colorado 7.0%, New Jersey 5.3%, Texas 5.2%.

Capitalization: (10/31/92) Common stock outstanding 15,352,891. No long-term debt.

Fund Manager: Van Kampen Merritt Investment Advisory Corp.   **Fee:** 0.65%
Income Dist: Monthly   **Capital Gains Dist:** Annually
Reinvestment Plan: Yes   **Shareholder Reports:** Quarterly

Van Kampen Merritt Trust for Insured Municipals

One Parkview Plaza
Oakbrook Terrace, IL 60181
(800) 225-2222

Transfer Agent
State Street Bank & Trust Co.
225 Franklin St.
Boston, MA 02101
(800) 341-2929

Tax-Free Income

Background: Initial public offering January 24, 1992 of 9,612,586 shares at $15 per share. Initial NAV was $14.74 per share.

Objective: Seeks income exempt from Federal income tax, consistent with preservation of capital. The fund will invest primarily in insured municipal issues.

Portfolio: (9/30/92) Municipal Bonds 97.8%, Cash & Other 2.2%. Portfolio Ratings: AAA 100%.

Capitalization: (10/31/92) Common shares outstanding 9,619,286. Leveraged with 1,800 shares preferred stock, stated value $50,000 per share. No long-term debt.

Fund Manager: Van Kampen Merritt Investment Advisory Corp. **Fee:** 0.60%
Income Dist: Monthly **Capital Gains Dist:** Annually
Reinvestment Plan: No **Shareholder Reports:** Semi-Annually

Van Kampen Merritt Trust for Investment Grade California Municipals   NYSE : VIC

One Parkview Plaza
Oakbrook Terrace, IL 60181
(800) 225-2222

Transfer Agent
State Street Bank & Trust Co.
225 Franklin St.
Boston, MA 02101
(800) 426-5523

Tax-Free Income

Background: Initial public offering March 27, 1992 of 4,612,542 shares at $15 per share. Initial NAV was $14.70 per share.

Objective: Seeks current income exempt from regular Federal and California State income taxes, consistent with the preservation of capital. Under normal market conditions, substantially all of the fund's assets will be invested in California municipal securities rated investment-grade at the time of purchase.

Portfolio: (10/31/92) Municipal Bonds 94.1%, Cash & Other 5.9%. State Weightings: California 90.0%, Guam 4.3%, Puerto Rico 4.4%. Portfolio Ratings: AAA 30.1%, AA 30.5%, A 34.3%, BBB 5.1%.

Capitalization: (10/31/92) Common shares outstanding 4,619,242. Leveraged with 900 preferred shares, stated value $50,000 per share. No long-term debt.

Fund Manager: Van Kampen Merritt Investment Advisory Corp. **Fee:** 0.65%
Income Dist: Monthly **Capital Gains Dist:** Annually
Reinvestment Plan: Yes **Shareholder Reports:** Semi-Annually

Van Kampen Merritt Trust for Investment Grade Florida Municipals   **NYSE : VTF**

One Parkview Plaza
Oakbrook Terrace, IL 60181
(800) 225-2222

Transfer Agent
State Street Bank & Trust Co.
225 Franklin St.
Boston, MA 02101
(800) 426-5523

Tax-Free Income

Background: Initial public offering March 19, 1992 of 4,129,102 shares at $15 per share. Initial NAV was $14.70 per share.

Objective: Seeks a high level of current income exempt from Federal income tax, consistent with the preservation of capital. The fund also seeks to offer its shareholders securities exempt from Florida intangible property taxes.

Portfolio: (10/31/92) Municipal Bonds 97.4%, Cash & Other 2.6%. State Weightings: Florida 94.4%, Puerto Rico 3.0%. Portfolio Ratings: AAA 72%, AA 11.7%, A 13.2%, BBB 3.1%.

Capitalization: (10/31/92) Common stock outstanding 4,137,307. Leveraged with 800 shares preferred stock, stated value $50,000 per share. No long-term debt.

Fund Manager: Van Kampen Merritt Investment Advisory Corp.   **Fee:** 0.65%
Income Dist: Monthly   **Capital Gains Dist:** Annually
Reinvestment Plan: Yes   **Shareholder Reports:** Semi-Annually

---

Van Kampen Merritt Trust for Investment Grade Municipals   **NYSE : VGM**

One Parkview Plaza
Oakbrook Terrace, IL 60181
(800) 225-2222

Transfer Agent
State Street Bank & Trust Co.
225 Franklin St.
Boston, MA 02101
(800) 341-2929

Tax-Free Income

Background: Initial public offering January, 1992 of 27,006,449 shares at $15 per share. Initial NAV was $14.79 per share.

Objective: Seeks high current income exempt from Federal income tax, consistent with the preservation of capital.

Portfolio: (10/31/92) Municipal Bonds 98.8%, Short Term & Other 1.2%. State Weightings: New York 17.8%, Illinois 12.5%, New Jersey 9.7%, Colorado 6.9%, Massachusetts 4.2%. Portfolio Ratings: AAA 13.8%, AA 14.8%, A 32.2%, BBB 39.2%.

Capitalization: (10/31/92) Common stock outstanding 27,013,149. Leveraged with 5,300 shares preferred stock, stated value $50,000 per share. No long-term debt.

Fund Manager: Van Kampen Merritt Investment Advisory Corp.   **Fee:** 0.65%
Income Dist: Monthly   **Capital Gains Dist:** Annually
Reinvestment Plan: Yes   **Shareholder Reports:** Semi-Annually

Van Kampen Merritt Trust for Investment Grade New Jersey Municipals

NYSE : VTJ
Transfer Agent
State Street Bank & Trust Co.
225 Franklin St.
Boston, MA 02101
(800) 341-2929

One Parkview Plaza
Oakbrook Terrace, IL 60181
(800) 225-2222

Tax-Free Income

Background: Initial public offering March 27, 1992 of 3,915,564 at $15 per share. Initial NAV was $14.68 per share.

Objective: Seeks current income exempt from Federal and New Jersey State income taxes, consistent with the preservation of capital. Invests primarily in investment-grade municipal obligations.

Portfolio: (10/31/92) Municipal Bonds 87.3%, Cash & Other 12.7%. Sector Weightings: Waste Disposal 13.7%, Water & Sewer 13.2%, Industrial Revenue 11.9%, Health Care 11.1%, Transportation 10%. Portfolio Ratings: AAA 48.9%, AA 20.1%, A 23.5%, BBB 7.5%.

Capitalization: (10/31/92) Common shares outstanding 3,925,373. Leveraged with 800 preferred stock, stated value $50,000 per share. No long-term debt.

Fund Manager: Van Kampen Merritt Investment Advisory Corp.   **Fee:** 0.65%
Income Dist: Monthly   **Capital Gains Dist:** Annually
Reinvestment Plan: Yes   **Shareholder Reports:** Quarterly

Van Kampen Merritt Trust for Investment Grade Pennsylvania Municipals

NYSE : VTP
Transfer Agent
State Street Bank & Trust Co.
225 Franklin St.
Boston, MA 02101
(800) 341-2929

One Parkview Plaza
Oakbrook, IL 60181
(800) 225-2222

Tax-Free Income

Background: Initial public offering March 27, 1992 of 7,393,060 shares at $15 per share. Initial NAV was $14.91 per share.

Objective: Seeks high current income exempt from regular Federal and Pennsylvania State income taxes, consistent with the preservation of capital.

Portfolio: (10/31/92) Municipal Bonds 98.1%, Cash & Other 1.9%. Portfolio Ratings: AAA 73.7%, AA 8.7%, A 12.6%, BBB 5.0%.

Capitalization: (10/31/92) Common shares outstanding 7,415,049. Leveraged with $70,000,000 in preferred stock. No long-term debt.

Fund Manager: Van Kampen Merritt Investment Advisory Corp.   **Fee:** 0.65%
Income Dist: Monthly   **Capital Gains Dist:** Annually
Reinvestment Plan: No   **Shareholder Reports:** Semi-Annually

Van Kampen Trust for Investment Grade New York Municipals

One Parkview Plaza
Oakbrook Terrace, IL 60181
(800) 225-2222

NYSE : VTN
Transfer Agent
State Street Bank & Trust Co.
225 Franklin St.
Boston, MA 02101
(800) 341-2929

Tax-Free Income

Background: Initial public offering March 27, 1992 of 6,186,514 shares at $15 per share. Initial NAV was $14.74 per share.

Objective: Seeks a high level of current income exempt from regular Federal and New York State income taxes, consistent with the preservation of capital.

Portfolio: (10/31/92) Municipal Bonds 98.6%, Cash & Other Assets 1.4%. Portfolio Ratings: AAA 30.9%, AA 29.2%, A 24.8%, BBB 15.1%.

Capitalization: (10/31/92) Common shares outstanding 6,200,987. Leveraged with 1,200 preferred shares, stated value $50,000 per share. No long-term debt.

Fund Manager: Van Kampen Merritt Investment Advisory Corp.   **Fee:** 0.65%
Income Dist: Monthly   **Capital Gains Dist:** Annually
Reinvestment Plan: No   **Shareholder Reports:** Semi-Annually

---

Voyageur Minnesota Municipal Income Fund, Inc.

100 S. Fifth St., Suite 2200
Minneapolis, MN 55402
(612) 376-7000

AMEX : VMN
Transfer Agent
Norwest Bank of Minnesota
P.O. Box 738
St. Paul, MN 55075
(800) 468-9716

Tax-Free Income

Background: Initial public offering April 28, 1992 of 2,250,000 shares at $15 per share. Initial NAV was $13.95 per share.

Objective: Seeks current income exempt from regular Federal and Minnesota State income taxes, consistent with preservation of capital.

Portfolio: (12/31/92) Municipal Bonds 99.6%, Short Term & Other 0.4%. Portfolio Ratings: AAA 51.0%, AA 17.0%, A 28.0%, Non-Rated 5.0%.

Capitalization: (12/31/92) Common stock outstanding 2,594,700. No long-term debt.

Fund Manager: Voyageur Fund Management   **Fee:** 0.40%
Income Dist: Monthly   **Capital Gains Dist:** Monthly
Reinvestment Plan: Yes   **Shareholder Reports:** N/A

New Equity Funds—1992

Brazilian Equity Fund

One Citicorp Center, 58th Fl.
New York, NY 10022
(212) 832-2626

NYSE : BZL

Transfer Agent
Provident National Bank
P.O. Box 8950
Wilmington, DE 19899
(800) 852-4750

Growth

Background: Initial public offering April 3, 1992 at $15 per share. Initial NAV was $13.95 per share.

Objective: Seeks long-term capital appreciation through investments primarily in Brazilian equity securities.

Portfolio: (12/31/92) Common Stocks 89.9%, Corporate Bonds 1.0%, Short Term & Other 9.2%. Sector Weightings: Natural Resources 27.5%, Utilities 29.8%, Nondurables 16.5%, Industrial Products 6.8%, Retail 6.6%. Largest Holdings: Telebras, Vale do Rio Doce, Souza Cruz Industria, Bradesco, Sadia Concordia Industrial.

Capitalization: (12/31/92) Common stock outstanding 4,607,169. No long-term debt.

Fund Manager: BEA Associates	**Fee:** 1.35%
Income Dist: Annually	**Capital Gains Dist:** Annually
Reinvestment Plan: Yes	**Shareholder Reports:** N/A

China Fund, Inc. (The)

405 Lexington Ave.
New York, NY 10174
(212) 808-0500

NYSE : CHN

Transfer Agent
State Street Bank & Trust Co.
225 Franklin St.
Boston, MA 02110
(800) 426-5523

Growth

Background: Initial public offering July 10, 1992 of 7,250,000 shares at $15 per share. Initial NAV was $13.95 per share.

Objective: Seeks long-term capital appreciation by investing in equity securities of companies which derive substantial profits from assets or investments in China.

Portfolio: Not available.

Capitalization: (12/31/92) Common stock outstanding 8,007,168. No long-term debt.

Fund Manager: Wardley Investment Services	**Fee:** 1.50%
Income Dist: Annually	**Capital Gains Dist:** Annually
Reinvestment Plan: Yes	**Shareholder Reports:** Semi-Annually

Emerging Markets Income
7 World Trade Center
New York, NY 10048
(800) 848-4357

NYSE : EMD
Transfer Agent
American Stock & Transfer Trust
40 Wall St.
New York, NY 10004
(212) 936-5100

Income

Background: Initial public offering October 23, 1992 at $15 per share. Initial NAV was $13.95 per share..

Objective: Seeks high current income. Capital appreciation is secondary. The fund will invest at least 65% of assets in debt securities of government and governemnt-related issuers in emerging market countries, and of organizations that restructure such debt obligations.

Portfolio: (12/31/92) Bonds 99.0%. Country Exposure: Mexico 23.0%, Brazil 21.0%, Morocco 19.0%, Philippines 11.0%, Argentina 8.0%.

Capitalization: (12/31/92) Common stock outstanding 3,512,000.

Fund Manager: Advantage Advisers, Inc.	**Fee:** 0.70%
Income Dist: Quarterly	**Capital Gains Dist:** Quarterly
Reinvestment Plan: Yes	**Shareholder Reports:** N/A

Emerging Markets Telecommunications Fund, Inc. (The)
One Citicorp Center, 58th Fl.
New York, NY 10022
(212) 832-2626

NYSE : ETF
Transfer Agent
Provident National Bank
P.O. Box 8950
Wilmington, DE 19899
(800) 852-4750

Growth

Background: Initial public offering June, 1992 at $15 per share. Initial NAV was $13.85 per share.

Objective: Seeks long-term capital appreciation by investing primarily in telecommunication companies in emerging markets.

Portfolio: (11/30/92) Equities 91.4%, Short Term 7.61%, Cash & Other 0.99%. Sector Weightings: Local and/or Long Distance Phone Service 63.9%, Electric Utilities 13.2%, Telecommunications Equipment 6.4%. Geographic Breakdowns: Latin America 57.3%, Asia 16.7%, Middle East 10.8%.

Capitalization: (11/30/92) Common stock outstanding 8,344,669. No long-term debt.

Fund Manager: BEA Associates	**Fee:** 1.25%
Income Dist: Annually	**Capital Gains Dist:** Annually
Reinvestment Plan: Yes	**Shareholder Reports:** Semi-Annually

First Israel Fund

One Citicorp Center, 58th Fl.
153 E. 53rd St.
New York, NY 10022
(212) 832-2626

NYSE : ISL

Transfer Agent
State Street Bank & Trust Co.
225 Franklin St.
Boston, MA 02110
(800) 638-8540

Growth

Background: Initial public offering October 22, 1992 of 5,000,000 shares at $15 per share. Initial NAV was $13.95 per share. 4,000,000 shares were offered in the U.S. and Canada, and 1,000,000 shares were offered outside the U.S. and Canada but not in Israel.

Objective: Seeks long-term capital appreciation. At least 65% of assets will be invested in Israeli securities at all times. Up to 35% may be invested in securities of companies that are substantially involved in or with Israel.

Portfolio: (12/31/92) Equities 54.1%, Cash & Equivalents 45.9%. Sector Weightings: Industrial Products 43.8%, Utilities 26.0%, Finance 11.7%.

Capitalization: (12/31/92) Common stock outstanding 5,007,169. No long-term debt.

Fund Manager: BEA Associates	**Fee:** 1.40%
Income Dist: Annually	**Capital Gains Dist:** Annually
Reinvestment Plan: Yes	**Shareholder Reports:** Semi-Annually

---

Global Health Sciences

7800 E. Union Ave., Suite 800
P.O. Box 2920
Denver, CO 80201
(800) 528-8765

NYSE : GHS

Transfer Agent
State Street Bank & Trust Co.
225 Franklin St.
Boston, MA 02110
(800) 426-5523

Growth

Background: Initial public offering January, 1992 at $15 per share. Initial NAV was $13.95 per share.

Objective: Seeks capital appreciation by investing in health science companies worldwide.

Portfolio: (1/29/92) Domestic Common Stock 48.6%, Foreign Common Stock 17.6%, Private Placements 12.8%, Cash 21.0%. Sector Weightings: Pharmaceuticals 25.0%, Health Care Delivery 21.0%, Medical Devices and Supplies 15.0%, Biotechnology 14.0%, REITs 4.0%. Largest Holdings: Astra AB, Roche Holdings, Amgen, Inc., Synergen, Inc., SmithKline Beecham PLC.

Capitalization: (10/31/92) Common stock outstanding 20,507,200. No long-term debt.

Fund Manager: Invesco Trust Co.	**Fee:** 1.00%
Income Dist: Annually	**Capital Gains Dist:** Annually
Reinvestment Plan: Yes	**Shareholder Reports:** Semi-Annually

Greater China Fund (The)

NYSE : GCH

1285 Avenue of the Americas
New York, NY 10019
(212) 713-2000

Transfer Agent
Provident Financial Processing Corp.
103 Bellevue Parkway
Wilmington, DE 19809
(800) 852-4750

Growth

Background: Initial public offering July 23, 1992 of 6,750,000 shares at $15 per share. Initial NAV was $13.95 per share.

Objective: Seeks long-term capital appreciation through investments in Chinese companies listed on stock exchanges in China, Hong Kong, Korea, Singapore and Taiwan.

Portfolio: (12/31/92) Equity Securities: China 10.1%, Hong Kong 47.1%, Korea 0.9%, Short Term & Other 41.9%. Sector Weightings: Real Estate Development 10.8%, Civil Engineering 5.6%, General Trading 5.5%, Retailing 4.0%, Telecommunications 3.4%.

Capitalization: (12/31/92) Common stock outstanding 6,757,200. No long-term debt.

Fund Manager: Baring International Investment Ltd.	**Fee:** 1.25%
Income Dist: Annually	**Capital Gains Dist:** Annually
Reinvestment Plan: Yes	**Shareholder Reports:** Semi-Annually

---

H & Q Life Sciences Investors

NYSE : HQL

50 Rowes Wharf, 4th Fl.
Boston, MA 02110-3328
(800) 327-6679 / (617) 574-0567

Transfer Agent
State Street Bank & Trust Co.
P.O. Box 8200
Boston, MA 02266-8200
(800) 451-6788

Growth

Background: Initial public offering May 8, 1992 of 3,850,000 shares at $15 per share. Initial NAV was $13.95 per share.

Objective: Seeks long-term capital appreciation. Invests primarily in equity and related securities of U.S. and foreign companies principally engaged in the development, production or distribution of products or services related to scientific advances in health care, agriculture and environmental management.

Portfolio: (9/30/92) Common Stocks 77.1%, Convertibles 9.1%, REITs 4.0%, Liquid Assets 16.0%. Sector Weightings: Agricultureal/Environmental Technologies 6.3%, Biotechnology 33.9%, Medical Supplies 13.0%, Medical Specialty 9.8%, Pharmaceuticals 6.3%. Largest Holdings: Immunex 4.37%, LTC Prop 4.0%, St. Jude Medical 3.17%, Biogen 3.13%, Chiron 2.82%.

Capitalization: (9/30/92) Shares of beneficial interest outstanding 3,858,600. No long-term debt.

Fund Manager: Hambrecht & Quist Capital Management, Inc.	**Fee:** 1.00%
Income Dist: Annually	**Capital Gains Dist:** Annually
Reinvestment Plan: Yes	**Shareholder Reports:** Semi-Annually

Japan Equity

c/o Daiwa Securities Trust Co.
One Evertrust Plaza, 9th Fl.
Jersey City, NJ 07302
(800) 933-3440

NYSE : JEQ

Transfer Agent
Provident National Bank
P.O. Box 8950
Wilmington, DE 19899
(800) 852-4750

Growth

Background: Initial public offering July 24, 1992 of 6,000,000 shares at $10 per share. Initial NAV was $9.26 per share.

Objective: Seeks to outperform over the long term, on a total return basis, the non-financial services sectors of the Tokyo Stock Price Index (TOPIX), a composite market-capitalization weighted index of all common stocks listed on the First Section of the Tokyo Stock Exchange.

Portfolio: (10/31/92) Japanese Common Stocks 95.6%, Short Term 3.6%. Sector Weightings: Commerce 17.2%, Construction 13.5%, Transportation Equipment 10.0%, Electrical Machinery 9.9%, Chemicals 8.7%. Largest Holdings: Aisin Seiki Co., Mitsui Fudosan Co., Maeda Corp., Sekisui Chemical, Japan Synthetic Rubber.

Capitalization: (10/31/92) Common stock outstanding 6,011,000. No long-term debt.

Fund Manager: Daiwa Securities Trust Company	**Fee:** 0.60%
Income Dist: Annually	**Capital Gains Dist:** Annually
Reinvestment Plan: Yes	**Shareholder Reports:** Semi-Annually

---

Jardine Fleming China Region Fund, Inc.

100 E. Pratt St.
Baltimore, MD 21202
(800) 638-8540

NYSE : JFC

Transfer Agent
State Street Bank & Trust Co.
225 Franklin St.
Boston, MA 02110
(800) 638-8540

Growth

Background: Initial public offering July 16, 1992 of 4,000,000 shares at $15 per share. Initial NAV was $13.95 per share.

Objective: Seeks long-term capital appreciation. Invests in securities of companies in China, Hong Kong, Taiwan and Macau. Will invest at least 65% in common stock, preferred stock and equity-related securities (including convertible debt obligations, warrants and rights) issued by such companies. May also invest up to 25% in China Region unlisted equity securities.

Portfolio: (12/31/92) Common Stocks & Warrants: Hong Kong 64.3%, Korea 0.1%, U.S. Time Deposits 34.7%. Sector Weightings: Property 15.2%, Food 9.9%, Industrial 6.9%, Retailing 6.4%, Textiles 5.6%. Largest Holdings: Champion Tech Holdings, Television Broadcasts, Wo Kee Hong (Holdings) Dairy Farm International Holdings, Wharf Holdings.

Capitalization: (12/31/92) Common stock outstanding 6,807,169. No long-term debt.

Fund Manager: Jardine Fleming International Management	**Fee:** 1.50%
Income Dist: Annually	**Capital Gains Dist:** Annually
Reinvestment Plan: Yes	**Shareholder Reports:** Semi-Annually

New Equity Funds—1992 **395**

Korean Investment Fund (The)

1345 Avenue of the Americas
New York, NY 10105
(800) 247-4154 / (212) 969-1000

NYSE : KIF

Transfer Agent
State Street Bank & Trust Co.
1776 Heritage Dr.
North Quincy, MA 02171
(800) 426-5523

Growth

Background: Initial public offering February 13, 1992 of 4,200,000 at $12 per share. Initial NAV was $10.90 per share.

Objective: Seeks long-term capital appreciation from investments primarily in equity securities of Korean companies.

Portfolio: (12/31/92) Common Stock 96.0%, Cash & Equivalents 4.0%. Industry Weightings: Industrial Products 31.2%, Natural Resources 20.9%, Finance 17.3%, Non-Durables 14.8%, Transportation 4.7%. Largest Holdings: Hannong, Ki San, Hana Bank, Shin Han Investment/Finance, Hyundai Precision Industries.

Capitalization: (12/31/92) Common shares outstanding: 4,209,000.

Fund Manager: Alliance Capital Management L.P.	**Fee:** 1.05%
Income Dist: Annually	**Capital Gains Dist:** Annually
Reinvestment Plan: Yes	**Shareholder Reports:** Semi-Annually

---

Latin American Discovery Fund, Inc. (The)

1221 Avenue of the Americas
New York, NY 10029
(212) 296-7100

NYSE : LDF

Transfer Agent
First National Bank of Boston
P.O. Box 644
Boston , MA 02102
(617) 575-2900

Growth

Background: Initial public offering June 16, 1992 of 3,300,000 shares at $15 per share. Initial NAV was $14.10 per share.

Objective: Seeks long-term capital appreciation. Normally invests at least 80% in equity securities of Latin American issuers and, from time to time, in debt securities issued or guaranteed by a Latin American government or government entity. At least 55% will be invested in listed equity securities of Argentine, Brazilian, Chilean and Mexican issuers. Will also actively invest in markets in other Latin American countries.

Portfolio: (12/31/92) Common stock 99.0%. Country Weightings: Mexico 38.9%, Brazil 34.4%, Peru 9.5%, Argentina 7.5%, Chile 6.0%.

Capitalization: (12/31/92) Common stock outstanding 5,757,092. No long-term debt.

Fund Manager: Morgan Stanley Asset Management	**Fee:** 0.75%
Income Dist: Annually	**Capital Gains Dist:** Annually
Reinvestment Plan: Yes	**Shareholder Reports:** Quarterly

Patriot Global Dividend

101 Huntington Ave.
Boston, MA 02199
(800) 843-0090

NYSE : PGD

Transfer Agent
State Street Bank & Trust Co.
225 Franklin St.
Boston, MA 02110
(800) 426-5523

Growth & Income

Background: Initial public offering July 24, 1992 of 7,250,000 shares at $15 per share. Initial NAV was $13.95 per share.

Objective: Seeks high current income along with modest growth of capital. The fund may issue preferred shares for leveraging purposes. At least 80% will be invested in debt obligations rated "A" or higher by Moody's.

Portfolio: (11/30/92) Common Stock 37.61%, Preferred Stock 35.94%, U.S. Treasuries 11.21%, Cash & Equivalents 15.5%. Sector Weightings: Utilities 39.7%, Financial Services 12.01%, Cash & Equivalents 15.5%, Industrial 5.6%. Largest Holdings: U.S. Treasuries, Banco Banesto, Public Service Enterprise Group, Enterprise Oil, Houston Ind.

Capitalization: Common stock outstanding 8,344,700. Leveraged with $60,000,000 in Dutch Auction Rate Transferables (DARTS).

Fund Manager: John Hancock Advisors, Inc.	**Fee:** 0.80%
Income Dist: Monthly	**Capital Gains Dist:** Annually
Reinvestment Plan: Yes	**Shareholder Reports:** Semi-Annually

---

Preferred Income Opportunity Fund

301 E. Colorado Blvd.
Pasadena, CA 91101
(818) 795-7300

NYSE : PFO

Transfer Agent
The Shareholder Services Group, Inc.
P.O. Box 1376
Boston, MA 02104
(800) 331-1710

Income

Background: Initial public offering February 6, 1992 of 8,700,000 shares at $12.50 per share. Initial NAV was $11.625 per share.

Objective: Seeks income. Capital appreciation is secondary. Normally, will invest at least 25% in securities issued by utilities. May invest up to 25% in securities of companies in the banking industry. Up to 15% may be in common stocks.

Portfolio: (11/31/92) Preferred Stock 95.9%. Sector Weightings: Utilities 65.7%, Banking 23.0%, Insurance 3.5%, Other 2.8%.

Capitalization: (11/30/92) Common stock outstanding 10,266,419 shares. Leveraged with 700 Cumulative Preferred Shares, redemption value $100,000 per share.

Fund Manager: Flaherty & Crumrine, Inc.	**Fee:** 0.63%
Income Dist: Monthly	**Capital Gains Dist:** Annually
Reinvestment Plan: Yes	**Shareholder Reports:** Quarterly

Appendix
Sources of Additional Information

Essential to any investment decision is understanding the investment vehicle. The following reference list of financial publications, newsletters, books, and associations is provided to readily locate additional closed-end fund data.

The American Association of Individual Investors
625 North Michigan Avenue, Suite 1900
Chicago, IL 60611
(312) 280-0170 FAX (312) 280-9883

A 14-year-old association with over 100,000 members assists individuals in becoming effective managers of their own assets through programs of education, information, and research. A one-year membership includes the monthly AAII Journal, the comprehensive book, *The Individual Investor's Guide to No-Load Mutual Funds*, an annual year-end tax planning guide, membership in local chapter groups, and discounts on investment publications, software, and videocourses.

Source: The Complete Guide to Investment Information (How to Find It and How to Use It) by Jae K. Shim, Ph.D. and Joel G. Siegel, Ph.D.

International Publishing Corporation, Inc.
625 N. Michigan Ave., Suite 1920
Chicago, IL 60611
(312) 943-7354 / (800) 488-4149 / FAX (312) 642-0679

A comprehensive investment information handbook that shows where to find investment instrument information and gives advice on how to read and interpret the various data sources. Includes large numbers of illustra-tions and examples, handy formulas for investment decision making, an investment quick-reference matrix, a glossary of essential investment terms, and a meticulously compiled index for ease of use.

Closed-End Fund Digest
1224 Coast Village Circle, Suite 11
Santa Barbara, CA 93108
(800) 282-2335 / (805) 565-5651/ FAX (805) 565-3433

A 12-page monthly newsletter devoted exclusively to closed-end funds, featuring four model portfolios:balanced, global, income (tax-free), income (taxable); monthly performance data, including buy/sell recommendations, on all equity and bond closed-end funds (see Figure 1.1. of this *Guide*); editorial comments; Manager's Comments; and Global News. Subscribers to the newsletter receive a copy of this *Guide*.

The Investor's Guide to Closed-End Mutual Funds
Thomas Herzfeld
P.O. Box 161465 Miami, FL 31116
(305) 271-1900 / FAX (305) 270-1040

A monthly newsletter on closed-end funds features buy/sell recommendations, performance figures, and one model portfolio.

The Scott Letter: Closed-End Fund Report
Cole Publishing
318 William St.
Fredericksburg, VA 22401
(800) 356-3508 (804) 741-8707

A monthly newsletter featuring model portfolios, manager interviews, and commentary.

Morningstar Closed-End Funds
53 West Jackson Blvd.
Chicago, IL 60604
(800) 876-5005 / (312) 427-1985 / FAX (312) 427-9215

A comprehensive source of closed-end fund data updated every two weeks.

Mutual Fund Forecaster
The Institute of Econometric Research
3471 North Federal Highway
Fort Lauderdale, FL 33306
(800) 327-6720 / (305) 563-9000 / FAX (305) 563-9003

Mutual fund selection and market predictions. Covers some 60 closed-end funds.

Lipper Closed-End Bond and Closed-End Equity Funds Analysis
Lipper Analytical Services, Inc.
1380 Lawrence Street, Suite 950
Denver, CO 80204
(303) 534-3472 / FAX (303) 573-5702
Exhaustive data for the professional investor.

Investment Company Institute
1600 M Street NW, Suite 600
Washington, DC 20036
(202) 293-7700 / FAX (202) 955-6230

The trade association for the investment company industry.

Standard & Poor's Stock Reports
Standard & Poor's Corporation
25 Broadway
New York, NY 10004
(212) 208-8000 / FAX (212) 509-8994

400   Closed-End Funds

Reports include statistics on companies traded on NYSE, AMEX, and OTC markets. Each report is a succinct profile of the company's activities and financial position, supported by extensive statistics that facilitate quick year-to-year comparisons.

Value Line Investment Survey
Value Line, Inc.
711 Third Avenue
New York, NY 10017
(212) 687-3965 / (800) 634-3583 / FAX (212) 338-9623

Weekly publication with in-depth descriptions on a multitude of stocks and closed-end funds. Gives ratings and opinions.

CDA Wiesenberger Companies Service
1355 Piccard Dr.
Rockville, MA 20850
(800) 232-2285 / (301) 975-9600 / FAX (301) 590-1389

Publishes quarterly and annual reports which provide performance results on selected closed-end funds.

FINANCIAL PRESS

Barron's
Dow Jones & Company
 200 Liberty Street
New York, NY 10281
(212) 416-2700 / FAX (212) 416-2829

Publishes both equity and bond figures for closed-end funds. Has weekly feature on mutual funds and often contains articles concerning closed-end funds.

The New York Times
229 W. 43rd Street
New York, NY 10036
(212) 556-1234

Closed-end fund equity figures appear in the Saturday edition and bond figures appear in the Wednesday edition.

The Wall Street Journal
200 Liberty Street
New York, NY 10281
(212) 416-2000 / FAX (212) 416-2658

Closed-end equity fund figures for the preceding Friday (NAV, market price, discount/premium) are published in the Monday edition under the heading "Publicly Traded Funds".

BROKERAGE HOUSES

The following brokerage houses cover closed-end funds. Contact your local branch for the latest reports:

A.G. Edwards & Sons, Inc.
PaineWebber Securities
Prudential Bache Securities
Smith Barney Harris Upham & Co., Inc.
Shearson Lehman
Merrill Lynch
Kidder Peabody

Index of Funds

One-of-a-Kind Investment Information Guide

It took a seasoned financial planner a mere five minutes of leafing through this book's 400-plus pages to recognize its enormous potential value for both financial beginners and old pro's.

For her client, an admitted neophyte, *SOURCE: The Complete Guide to Investment Information, Where to Find It and How to Use It* provides a painless education in how to discover the most pertinent investment information and how to employ it — not to mention how to better understand what the financial planner and her stockbroker are talking about. For more experienced investors, it offers the one-stop convenience of up-to-date source information; as such it's a first-of-its kind tool.

SOURCE is an investment information handbook designed for students of finance and investments as well as for practical investors. *SOURCE* shows where to find information and advice on different types of investment instruments and how to read and interpret those sources. *SOURCE* breaks down the information into an overview, a look at how to choose the right type of security in each investment category, how to read related information given for each source. From the most common and accessible daily newspaper or radio report to the most sophisticated and often costly investment newsletter, no information source is overlooked.

Want to know about risk-adjusted yield, discount yield, dividend yield, current yield, beta, P/E ratio, 7-day compound yield, market indexes and averages, how to read ticker tape quotations, how to read financial statements, and how to interpret economic, industry, and company information? *SOURCE* provides the know-how. Liberally illustrated with artwork from representative information sources, *SOURCE* devotes whole chapters to key investment categories: common and preferred stocks; fixed-income securities; mutual funds; warrants, options, and futures; and tangibles such as real estate and collectibles and precious metals and coins.

SOURCE, by Jae K. Shim and Joel G. Siegel, who also co-authored the best-selling *The Vest-Pocket MBA*, is an invaluable one-of-a-kind investment decision making tool for both beginning and experienced investors.

Send me ____copies of SOURCE: The Complete Guide to Investment Information, Where to Find It and How to Use It by Jae K. Shim and Joel G. Siegel at $29.95 each (hardcover).

Name _____

Address_____

City/State/Zip_____

Please make checks payable to International Publishing Corporation. Add $2.00 for each book to cover shipping and handling. (Illinios residents add 8.75% sales tax.)

Payment $ _____ , or charge my VISA MasterCard # _____ Exp. _____

Signature_____

MAIL TO: International Publishing Corp, Inc., 625 N. Michigan Ave., Suite 1920, Chicago IL, 60611 or call 1-800-488-4149.
